EXPORT/IMPORT PROCEDURES and DOCUMENTATION

REVISED and UPDATED FOURTH EDITION

THOMAS E. JOHNSON
and
DONNA L. BADE

AMACOM

American Management Association

New York • Atlanta • Brussels • Chicago • Mexico City • San Francisco
Shanghai • Tokyo • Toronto • Washington, D.C.

Library of Congress Cataloging-in-Publication Data

Johnson, Thomas E., 1948-
Export/import procedures and documentation / Thomas E. Johnson and Donna L. Bade.
p. cm.
Includes index.
ISBN-13: 978-0-8144-1550-4
ISBN-10: 0-8144-1550-4
1. Export marketing—United States. 2. Exports—United States—Forms. 3. Imports—United States—Forms. 4. Foreign trade regulation. 5. International trade. I. Bade, Donna L. II. Title.
HF1416.5.J64 2010
658.8'4—dc22

2009040382

About AMA
American Management Association (www.amanet.org) is a world leader in talent development, advancing the skills of individuals to drive business success. Our mission is to support the goals of individuals and organizations through a complete range of products and services, including classroom and virtual seminars, webcasts, webinars, podcasts, conferences, corporate and government solutions, business books and research. AMA's approach to improving performance combines experiential learning—learning through doing—with opportunities for ongoing professional growth at every step of one's career journey.

Printing number

10 9 8 7 6 5 4 3

Contents

Foreword

Engaging in international trade is a never-ending challenge for a host of reasons: political turmoil in one or another country, market uncertainties, compliance requirements, payment problems, shipping delays, and a lot of changing procedures and documentation to contend with in every country, including our own. While there is a favorable trend toward global harmonization, we're not there yet.

And on top of all these issues, there is the global recession that started in late 2008, with plummeting consumer demand and shrinking trade finance. Only time will tell how long those conditions will persist. But make no mistake: Global trade with new and different opportunities will endure, as it always has. Most experienced exporters and importers confirm their belief that the overall rewards are still worth the risks and difficulties.

While the economic competition in world markets is greater than ever, so are the potential benefits. Practical knowledge, training, and persistence by America's business community are vital to our future success in the international arena. We need to maintain our efforts to produce high-quality products and services and to market them aggressively and competitively abroad.

At the same time, U.S. companies more than ever recognize that to be globally competitive in their exports, they must also look to other countries for needed raw materials, components, and final products and compare them with those that are produced in this country. That is what the global economy is all about—breaking down international barriers and encouraging the free flow of goods, services, technology, and capital.

It is essentially for these reasons that Tom Johnson originally decided to write this book and Donna Bade agreed to update it with this new edition. It has been my pleasure to have worked with Tom and Donna around the country over many years, conducting training seminars and counseling companies on international trade. We continue to be heartened by the ever-expanding interest we see expressed by companies in exporting and importing.

The special value of this book is that it takes a myriad of increasingly complex foreign trade rules, regulations, procedures, and practices and integrates them into a useful "how-to" volume explaining the export and import process in great detail.

While the book covers all the basic export/import procedures and documentation, experienced foreign traders also are likely to find many new nuggets of practical, cost-saving information and advice. The learning process never stops. Donna and I meet many exporters and importers each year who are motivated to attend seminars and workshops because of problems that suddenly surfaced in their trading operations due to currency fluctuations, cultural differences, or a penalty imposed because of incorrect documentation or security infractions.

To their chagrin, these exporters and importers quickly discovered that they were not as knowledgeable or as current as they had thought. Advance preparation and planning invariably would have prevented these problems.

Export/Import Procedures and Documentation serves as an invaluable guide to international trade operations and contains a sample of virtually every relevant document used in foreign trade. Equally important, the reasons for government-imposed documentary and procedural requirements are clearly explained.

As in most endeavors, the basic ingredients of enthusiasm, interest, and hard work are important to achieving success in exporting and importing, but they alone are not sufficient. The additional critical factors needed are technical knowledge and training, which will lead to success for those who carefully apply what they learn. This all-encompassing book makes that learning process orderly and understandable.

We hope you enjoy competing in today's global environment and achieving all the rewards it can offer you and your business.

Eugene J. Schreiber
Managing Director
World Trade Center of New Orleans

Preface

When Tom Johnson recommended to AMACOM that I update the 4th edition of *Export/Import Procedures and Documentation*, I was excited to be offered this opportunity. While much of the law surrounding international contracting has not changed over the last five years, many of the procedures, the rules of compliance and the associated documentation have definitely changed. To that end, I have included new information about the movement to the Internet-based documentation, including the Customs & Border Protection's Automated Commercial Environment (ACE) on the import side and the Internet filing of export licenses through the Department of State's and the Department of Commerce's proprietary websites. There is also new information buying and selling through the Internet, something critical to all commercial businesses. Over the past few years a number of new Free Trade Agreements were enacted, each with its own sets of rules, and these are highlighted in this edition as well as new security procedures that have moved Customs' data collection on imports offshore in advance of loading. High profile instances of melamine in animal food, high lead content in toys, illegal logging, and the infestation of the Asian Longhorn Beetle have brought increased scrutiny to the U.S. import controls exercised by other government agencies, so there are increased compliance measures under the Consumer Products Safety Commission, the Food and Drug Administration, and the USDA. These issues are all addressed in this new edition.

My career in international trade was never intentional, as I believe is the case with most people who end up in this field. It began in Detroit, Michigan, working for a customshouse broker (as the job was known then). I was straight out of college, in need of a job, and I had no idea what a customshouse broker did...build custom houses? However, I did well on a math test and was hired. I soon learned about the business from some excellent mentors and eventually took the customs brokers' exam. Although I moved several times and eventually attended law school, I never thought about changing careers. It is the constant evolution of international agreements, the revised focus of each new administration, and the broad spectrum of agencies that regulate the movement of goods in and out of the country that make this business an ongoing challenge.

I was introduced to Tom Johnson while serving at the President of the Chicago Customs Brokers and Freight Forwarders Association. I was speaking on a panel at the American Association of Exporters and Importers meeting in Chicago and he invited me to join him as a speaker for the American Management Association's Import/Export seminar along with Gene Schreiber of the World Trade Center in New Orleans. After I finished law school, Tom was instrumental in hiring me for my first position as a lawyer with Baker & McKenzie. Subsequently, we both moved to Sandler, Travis & Rosenberg, P.A., the leading boutique law firm dedicated to this field, where I continued to learn and grow with the other professionals in this fascinating field. Tom has now retired, but we still keep in touch and I am grateful for his counsel and advice over the years.

I am currently a member of Sandler, Travis & Rosenberg, P.A., and manage the firm's Chicago office. I have lectured on import and export trade regulations for many years and served as an adjunct professor teaching Import/Export Trade Law in the LLM program at The John Marshall Law School. I currently serve on the Board of Advisors for the LLM program there.

I wish to acknowledge and express my appreciation for the assistance provided by Mark Segrist for his research help and Gloria Barrientos in putting this edition together. Thanks as well to Nicole Kehoskie, Christie Padilla, and Lee Sandler at Sandler, Travis & Rosenberg, P.A., for their moral support; as well as Kathleen Goff, Coleen Clarke, and Bob Kielbas at Roanoke Insurance. I also wish to thank my editor Robert Nirkind for walking me through this process. Finally, my deepest appreciation goes to my family, Thomas, Lindsey, and Tom, for their patience.

The information contained herein is accurate as far as I am aware and is based on sources available to me. Nevertheless, it is not legal advice, and specific legal advice based upon the facts and circumstances of the reader's own situation should be sought in making export or import decisions.

Any comments or suggestions for the improvement of this book will be gratefully accepted.

Donna L. Bade
Sandler, Travis & Rosenberg, P.A.
Chicago, Illinois

Acknowledgements

The author gratefully acknowledges the courtesy of the following for inclusion of their forms in this book:

Apperson Business Forms – www.appersonprint.com

United States Council for International Business – www.uscib.org

Roanoke Trade Services, Inc. – www.roanoketrade.com

Unz & Co. – www.unzco.com

Tops Business Forms – www.tops-products.com

West Publishing Company – www.west.thomson.com

First National Bank of Chicago – www.nndb.com

Shipping Solutions, a division of Intermart, Inc. – www.shipsolutions.com

SGS North America – www.sgs.com

About the Authors

Thomas E. Johnson is a former partner in the law firms of Baker & McKenzie and Sandler, Travis & Rosenberg, P.A. He has been appointed five times by the U.S. secretary of commerce to the Illinois District Export Council, and is past president of the International Trade Club of Chicago.

Donna L. Bade is a partner in the international trade law firm of Sandler, Travis & Rosenberg, P.A., and manages the firm's Chicago office. Her practice is focused on import and export trade law, trade regulations and customs law, regulatory law, and transportation law.

Ms. Bade is a licensed customs broker, and has extensive experience advising companies in the areas of tariff classification, valuation, country of origin marking, and utilization of preference programs. She has represented clients before U.S. Customs and Border Protection on focused assessments and before other government agencies with responsibilities over import and export transactions. She also helps companies develop internal compliance programs. She worked as a customs broker and freight forwarder for many years in the ports of Detroit, St. Louis, and Chicago and brings that experience to her understanding of the supply chain and importing process.

In addition, Ms. Bade has extensive experience assisting clients with export control, licensing, commodity jurisdiction, and compliance issues. She has represented companies before the Bureau of Industry and Security, the Office of Foreign Assets Control, and the Department of State. She has also worked with companies to establish export management systems and has provided training to foreign branches and subsidiaries on U.S. export controls.

Ms. Bade also counsels customs brokers and freight forwarders regarding licensing and other issues before CBP and the Federal Maritime Commission.

Ms. Bade has lectured extensively on issues pertaining to import and export law and procedures on behalf of various organizations. She has taught import and export law as an adjunct professor and served on the board of advisors to the John Marshall Law School's LLM program in international business and trade.

Part 1

Organizing for Export and Import Operations

Chapter 1

Organizing for Export and Import Operations

Smooth, efficient, and compliance-oriented (and, therefore, profitable) exporting or importing requires that certain personnel must have specialized knowledge. The personnel involved and their organization vary from company to company, and sometimes the same personnel have roles in both exporting and importing. In small companies, one person may perform all of the relevant functions, while in large companies or companies with a large amount of exports or imports, the number of personnel may be large. In addition, as a company decides to perform in-house the work that it previously contracted with outside companies (such as customs brokers, freight forwarders, consultants, packing companies, and others) to perform, the export/import department may grow. As business increases, specialties may develop within the department, and the duties performed by any one person may become narrower.

A. Export Department

For many companies, the export department begins in the sales or marketing department. That department may develop leads or identify customers located in other countries. Inquiries or orders may come from potential customers through the company's web site where the destination is not identified. When such orders come in, the salespeople need to determine what steps are different from its domestic sales in order to fill those export orders. Often the exporter's first foreign sales are to Canada or Mexico. Because the export order may require special procedures in manufacturing, credit checking, insuring, packing, shipping, and collection, it is likely that a number of people within the company will have input on the appropriate way to fill the order. As export orders increase (for example, as a result of an overseas distributor having been appointed or through an expansion of Internet sales), the handling of such orders should become more routine and the assignment of the special procedures related to an export sale should be given to specific personnel. It will be necessary to interface with freight forwarders, couriers, banks, packing companies, steamship lines, airlines, translators, government agencies, domestic transportation companies, and attorneys. Because most manufacturers have personnel who must interface with domestic transportation companies (traffic or logistics department), often additional personnel will be assigned to that department to manage export shipments and interface with other outside services. Some of this interface, such as with packing companies and steamship lines, and possibly government agencies and banks, may be handled by a freight forwarder. The number of personnel needed and the assignment of responsibilities depend upon the size of the company and the volume of exports involved. A chart for a company with a large export department is shown in Figure 1–1. The way in which an export order is processed at the time of quotation, order entry, shipment, and collection is shown in Figures 1–2, 1–3, 1–4, and 1–5, respectively. Smaller companies will combine some of these functions into tasks for one or more persons.

B. Import Department

A manufacturer's import department often grows out of the purchasing department, whose personnel have been assigned the responsibility of procuring raw materials or components for the manufacturing process. For importers or trading companies that deal in finished goods, the import department may begin as the result of being appointed as the U.S. distributor for a foreign manufacturer or from purchasing a product produced by a foreign manufacturer that has U.S. sales potential. Because foreign manufacturers often sell their products ex-factory or FOB plant, a U.S. company that intends to import such products must familiarize itself with ocean shipping, insurance, U.S. Customs clearance, and other procedural matters. Increasingly, a number of U.S. manufacturers are moving their manufacturing operations overseas to cheaper labor regions and importing products they formerly manufactured in the United States. That activity will also put them in contact with foreign freight forwarders, U.S. customs brokers, banks, the U.S. Customs and Border Protection, marine insurance companies, and other service companies.

C. Combined Export and Import Departments

In many companies, some or all of the functions of the export and import departments are combined in some way. In smaller companies, where the volume of exports or imports does not justify more personnel, one or two persons may have responsibility for both export and import procedures and documentation. As companies grow larger or the volume of export/import business increases, these functions tend to be separated more into export departments and import departments. However, because both departments may end up being in contact with some of the same outside parties (such as banks, those freight forwarders that are also customs brokers, or domestic transportation companies), some of these activities may be consolidated in specific persons for both export and import, while other personnel will work exclusively on exports or on imports. A diagram of the interrelationships between the export and import personnel in the company and outside service providers is shown in Figure 1–6.

(*Text continues on page 8.*)

Figure 1–1. Export organization chart.

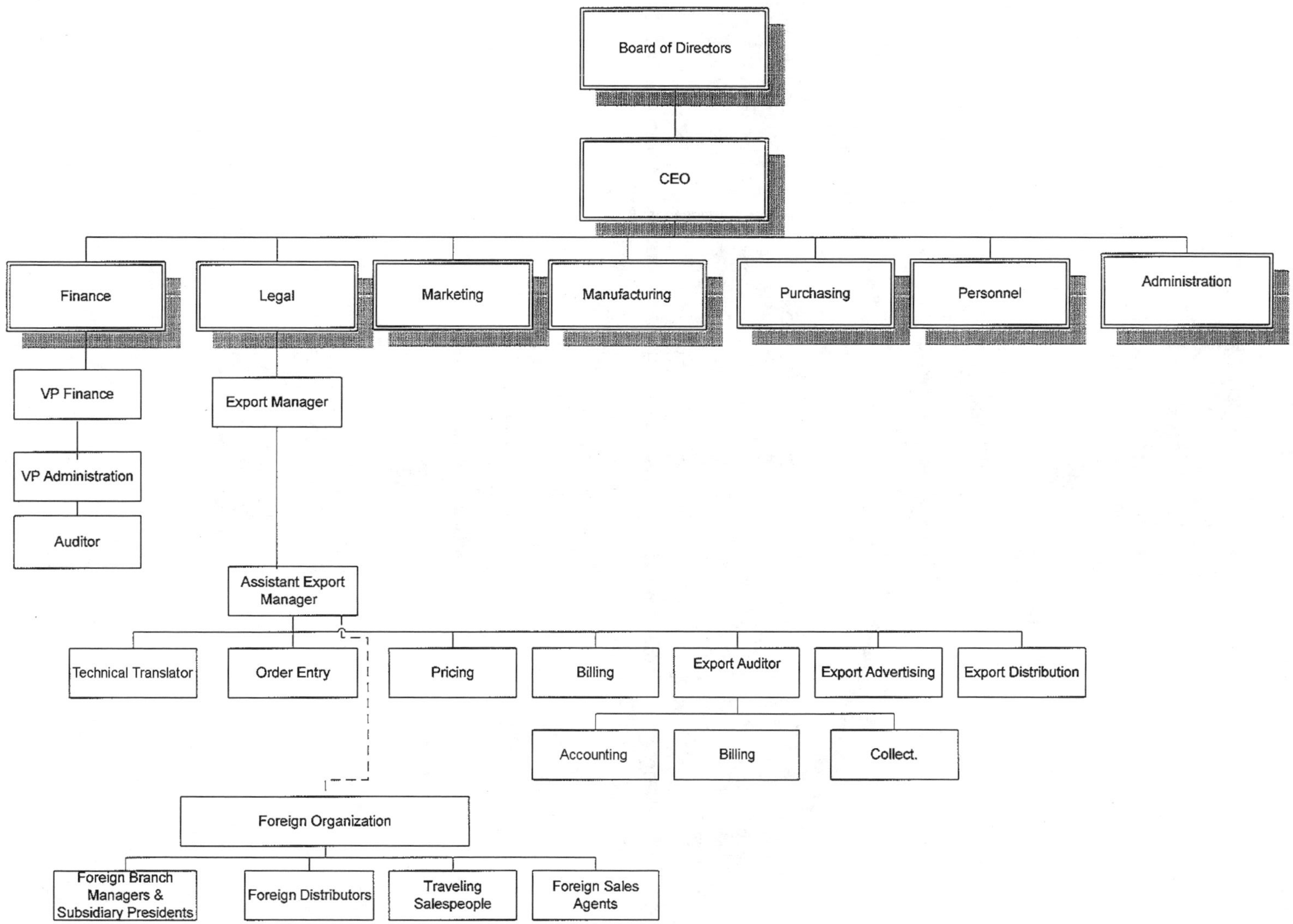

Figure 1–2. Export order processing—quotation.

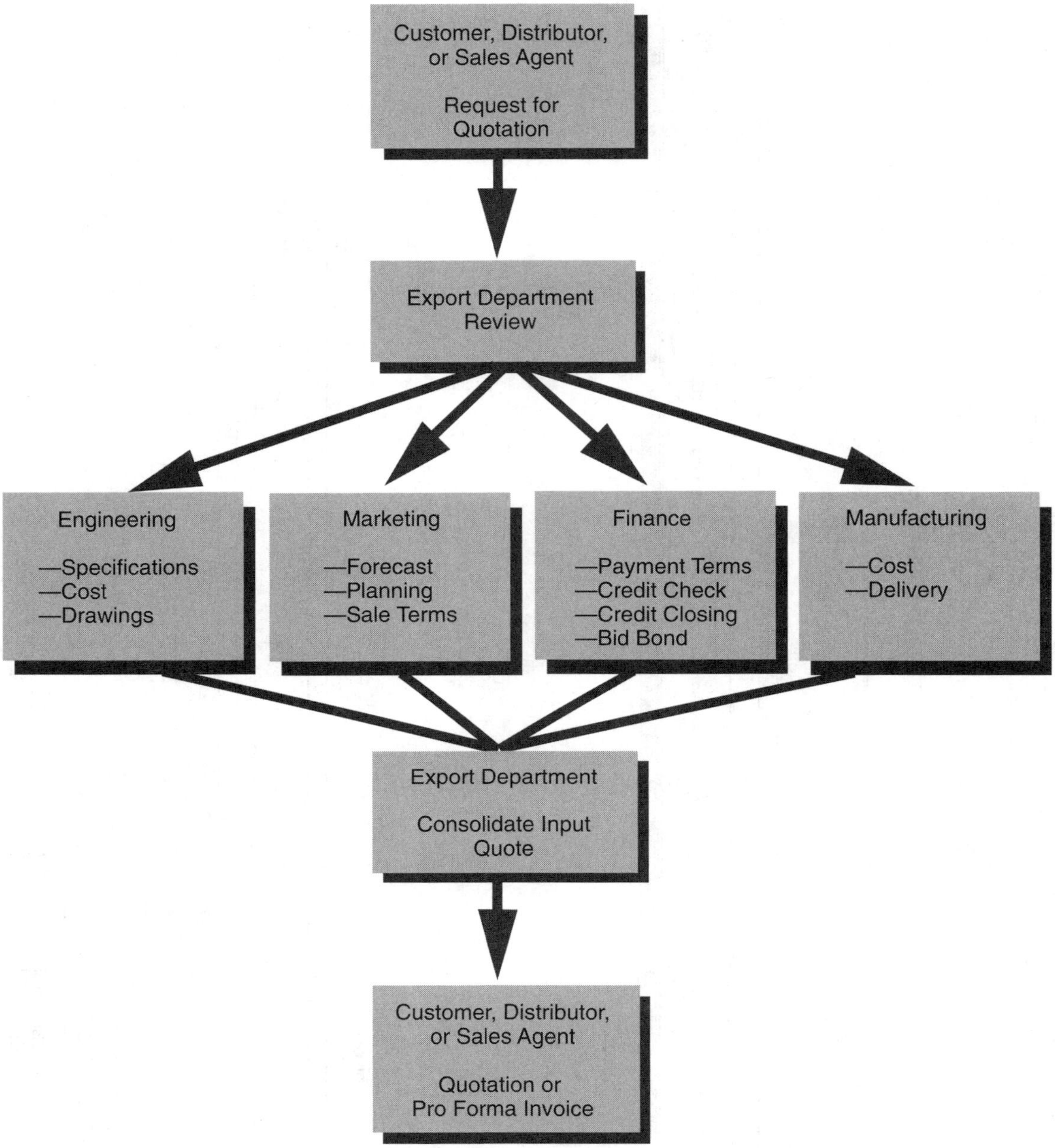

Figure 1–3. Export order processing—order entry.

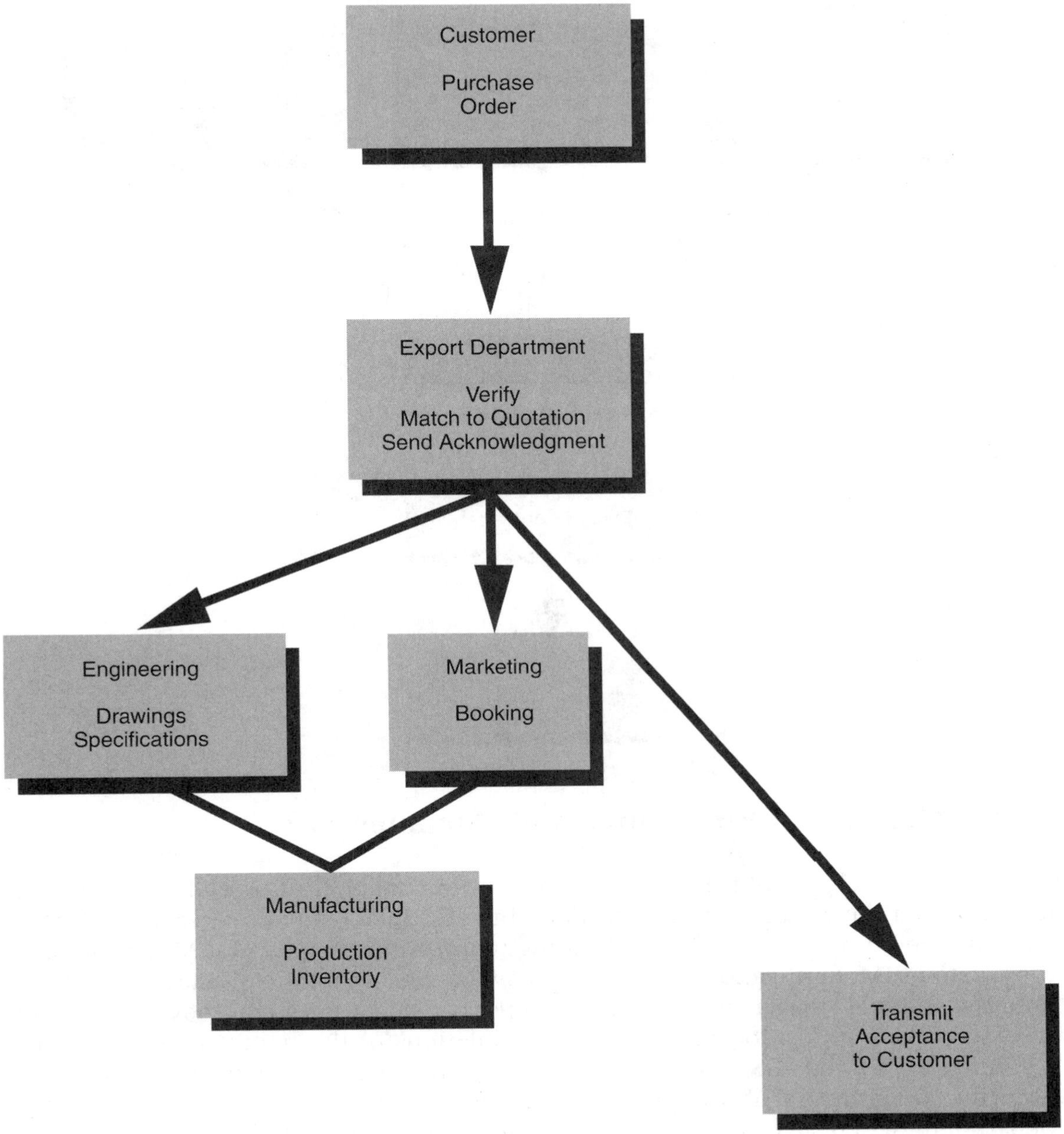

Figure 1–4. Export order processing—shipment.

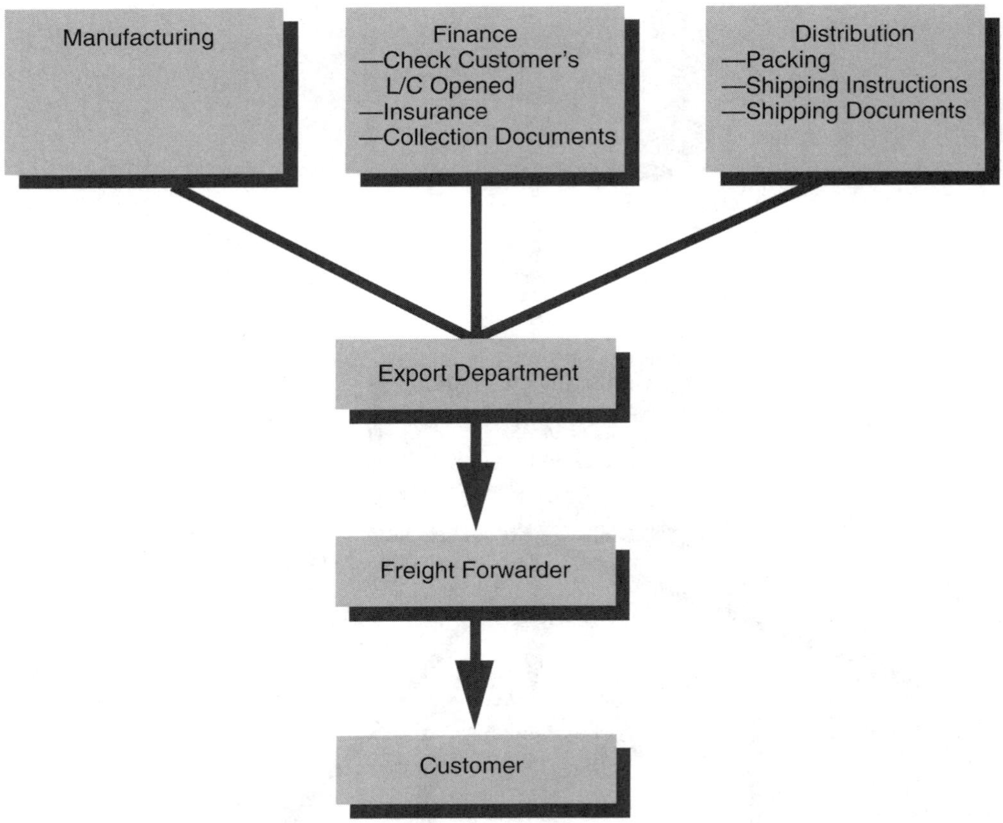

D. Manuals of Procedures and Documentation

It is often very helpful for companies to have a manual of procedures and documentation for their export and import departments. Such manuals serve as a reference tool for smooth operation and as a training tool for new employees. Moreover, since the Customs Modernization Act, such manuals *are required* to establish that the importer is using "reasonable care" in its importing operations, and they have become essential in the mitigation of penalties for violations of the import and export laws administered by the U.S. Customs and Border Protection; the Bureau of Industry & Security, Department of Commerce; and the Office of Foreign Assets Control, Department of Treasury. Such manuals should be customized to the particular company. They should describe the company's export and import processes. They should contain names, telephone numbers, and contact persons at the freight forwarders and customs brokers, steamship companies, packing companies, and other services that the company has chosen to utilize as well as government agencies required for the import or export of the company's commodities. They should contain copies of the forms that the company has developed or chosen to use in export sales and import purchases and transportation, identify the internal routing of forms and documentation

Figure 1–5. Export order processing—collection.

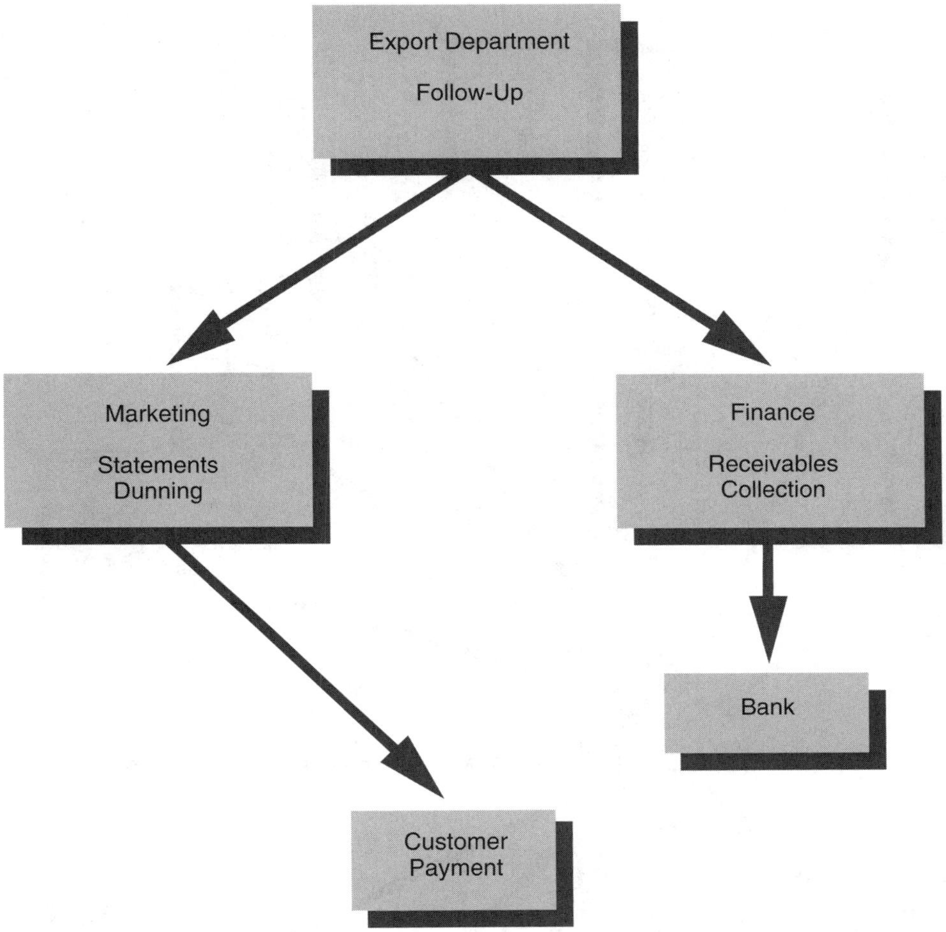

within the company for proper review and authorization, and contain job descriptions for the various personnel who are engaged in export/import operations. The manuals should be kept electronically and disseminated via hard copy or the company intranet to key personnel. The manuals must be updated as changes in policies, procedures, contact persons, telephone numbers, forms, or government regulations occur. Sample tables of contents for export and import manuals are shown in Figures 1–7 and 1–8, respectively.

E. Record-Keeping Compliance

Exporters and importers have always had an obligation to maintain records relating to their international trade transactions. Recently, however, these obligations have become mandatory due to changes in the law. As the volume of export and import

(*Text continues on page 12.*)

Figure 1–6. Interrelationships with outside service providers.

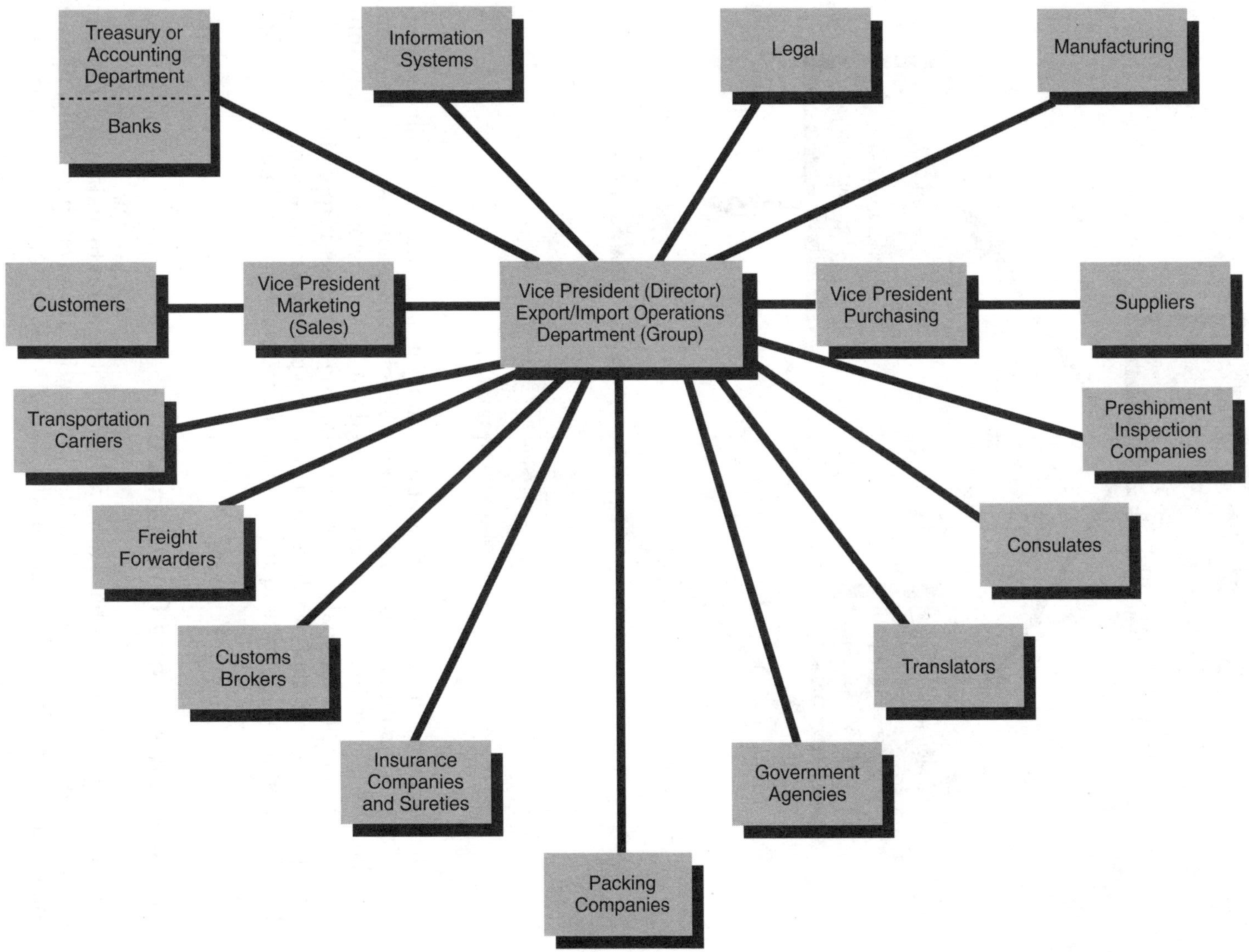

Figure 1–7. Export manual table of contents.

I. Statement of Manual's Purpose
- Company Policies Relating to Export

II. The Export Department
- Role
- Function/Operation Statement
- Organization Chart—Positions; Export Compliance Manager
- Job Descriptions and Responsibilities
- Initial and Periodic Training Requirements
- Procedures for Disseminating Current Regulatory Developments Information

III. Export Procedures
- Preliminary Considerations
- Formation of Sales Agreement
- List of Existing Agents and Distributors
- List of Freight Forwarders, Steamship Companies, Insurance Brokers, Packing Companies, Attorneys
- Collections and Banking Procedures (Drafts, Letters of Credit)
- Record-Keeping Compliance

IV. Export Documents (Samples of Company-Approved Standard Forms)
- Quotations, Costing Sheets
- Purchase Order Acknowledgments
- Purchase Order Acceptances
- Terms and Conditions
- Invoices (Commercial, Pro Forma, and Special Customs)
- Electronic Export Information (Shipper's Export Declaration) Automated Export System Records
- Powers of Attorney
- Shipper's Letter of Instructions
- Bills of Lading
- Packing Lists
- Inspection Certificates
- Insurance Certificates
- Dock and Warehouse Receipts
- Consulate Invoices
- Certificates of Origin
- Delivery Instructions
- Declarations for Dangerous Goods (if applicable)

V. Export Licenses
- Procedures for Determining Applicability of Regulations, Including Exemptions
- Procedures for Monitoring Changes in Products

(*continues*)

Figure 1–7. *(continued)*

- Procedures for Monitoring Changes to Denied Persons and Specially Designated Nationals
- Lists of Embargoed Countries and Areas of Concern
- Procedures for Applying for Export Licenses
- Procedures for Ensuring Shipment in Accordance with License Requirements
- Procedures for Reporting or Other Compliance in Accordance with License Provisos

commerce has increased, it has become necessary to automate such transactions. The use of electronic purchase orders, acceptances, and invoices, and the related need for the government agencies to reduce their own paperwork burden, has spurred the government initiatives. Under the Customs Modernization Act, the U.S. Customs and Border Protection agreed to allow electronic filing of customs entries, and under the Automated Export System, the Departments of Commerce and Customs have established a program for the electronic filing of export documentation. Under these scenarios, export and import trade is facilitated; however, the potential for exporters or importers to avoid their legal responsibilities, including filing fraudulent entries with improper values or classifications or evading their responsibilities to obtain export licenses, is substantially increased. As a result, in the Customs Modernization Act, new penalties were imposed upon importers who fail to keep proper documentation, which Customs intends to audit from time to time to verify that the electronic filings are accurate. Now, even if the electronic filing was accurate, if an importer or exporter fails to provide documents requested by Customs, it can be fined up to $100,000 (or 75 percent of the appraised value, whichever is less) if the failure to produce a document is intentional, or $10,000 (or 40 percent of the appraised value, whichever is less) if it is negligent or accidental.

Other laws, such as the Export Administration Act, the Foreign Trade Statistics Regulations, the North American Free Trade Agreement, and the various other free trade agreements, also impose record-keeping requirements on exporters. For companies that engage in both exporting and importing, it is important to establish a record-keeping compliance program that maintains the documents required by all the laws regulating international trade. In general, U.S. export and import laws require that the records be kept for a period of five years from the date of import or export (or three years from date of payment on drawback entries). However, other laws—for example, state income tax laws or foreign laws—may require longer periods.

U.S. Customs and Border Protection has issued a *Recordkeeping Compliance Handbook* describing in detail its interpretation of the proper record-keeping responsibilities for importers. This *Handbook* states that Customs expects each importer to designate a manager of record-keeping compliance who can act as the point of contact for all document requests from Customs and who is responsible for managing and administering the record-keeping compliance within the company. The manager, as well as all employees involved in importing (and exporting), is expected to receive regular training on compliance with the customs laws and on

Figure 1–8. Import manual table of contents.

I. Statement of Manual's Purpose
- Company Policies Relating to Import

II. The Import Department
- Role
- Function/Operation Statement
- Organization Chart—Positions; Import Compliance Manager
- Job Descriptions and Responsibilities
- Procedures for Disseminating Current Regulatory Developments Information

III. Import Procedures
- Preliminary Considerations
- Formation of Purchase Agreement
- List of Existing Suppliers
- List of Customs Brokers, Foreign Freight Forwarders, Steamship Companies, Airlines, Insurance Brokers, Inland Carriers, Attorneys
- Payment and Banking Procedures (Drafts, Letters of Credit)
- Record-Keeping Compliance

IV. Import Documents (Samples of Company-Approved Standard Forms, Customs Forms)
- Requests for Quotations
- Purchase Orders
- Terms and Conditions
- Invoices (Commercial, Pro Forma)
- Bills of Lading
- Packing Lists
- Inspection Certificates
- Customs Broker's Letter of Instructions
- Customs Entries (CF3461 Entry/Immediate Delivery and CF7501 Entry Summary)
- Certificates of Origin (NAFTA, other FTA)
- Other Government Agency Required Documentation
- Liquidation Information
- Notices of Redelivery, Request for Information, and Notices of Action and Responses
- Requests for Reliquidation
- Protests, Petitions, Post-Entry Amendments
- Reconciliation Entries
- Summons, Warrants, Subpoenas, Seizure Notices
- Prepenalty and Penalty Notices
- Liquidated Damages Notices
- ITC Questionnaires
- Surety Bond Information

documentation and record-keeping requirements. Each company is expected to maintain a procedures manual to ensure compliance with all customs laws and record-keeping requirements.

F. Software

Many companies offer software programs for managing the export process, including order taking, generation of export documentation, compliance with export control regulations, calculation of transportation charges and duties, and identification of trade leads. On the import side, a substantial number of companies offer "supply chain management" (SCM) software. A search on any Internet search engine will link the user to a number of these companies. The use of software enables companies to process import and export documentation more efficiently, but the legal burden of accuracy always remains with the importer or exporter.

G. Federal, State, International, and Foreign Law

The Constitution of the United States specifically provides that the U.S. Congress shall have power to regulate exports and imports (Art. 1, §8). This means that exporting or importing will be governed primarily by federal law rather than state law. On the other hand, the law of contracts, which governs the formation of international sales and purchase agreements and distributor and sales agent agreements, is almost exclusively governed by state law, which varies from state to state. As discussed in Chapter 3, Section B.2.m, and Chapter 7, Section B.2.l, a number of countries, including the United States, have entered into an international treaty that governs the sale of goods and will supersede the state law of contracts in certain circumstances. Finally, in many circumstances, the laws of the foreign country will govern at least as to that portion of the transaction occurring within its borders, and in certain situations, it may govern the international sales and purchase agreements as well. Most of the procedures and forms that are used in exporting and importing have been developed to fulfill specific legal requirements, so that an exporter or importer should disregard such procedures and forms only after confirming that doing so will not subject the company to legal risks or penalties.

Part II

Exporting: Procedures and Documentation

Chapter 2

Exporting: Preliminary Considerations

This chapter will discuss the preliminary considerations that anyone intending to export should consider. Before beginning to export and on each export sale thereafter, a number of considerations should be addressed to avoid costly mistakes and difficulties. Those companies that begin exporting or continue to export without having addressed the following issues will run into problems sooner or later.

A. Products

Initially, the exporter should think about certain considerations relating to the product it intends to export. For example, is the product normally utilized as a component in a customer's manufacturing process? Is it sold separately as a spare part? Is the product a raw material, commodity, or finished product? Is it sold singly or as part of a set or system? Does the product need to be modified—such as the size, weight, or color—to be salable in the foreign market? Is the product new or used? (If the product is used, some countries prohibit importation or require independent appraisals of value, which can delay the sale.) Often the appropriate methods of manufacturing and marketing, the appropriate documentation, the appropriate procedures for exportation, and the treatment under foreign law, including foreign customs laws, will depend upon these considerations.

Some products are subject to special export limitations and procedures. In addition to the general export procedures discussed in this part, exporters of munitions; narcotics and controlled substances; nuclear equipment, materials, and waste; watercraft; natural gas; electric power; hazardous substances; biological products; consumer products not conforming to applicable product safety standards; adulterated or misbranded food, drugs, medical devices, and cosmetics; endangered species; ozone-depleting chemicals; flammable fabrics; precursor chemicals; tobacco seeds and plants; fish and wildlife; crude oil; certain petroleum-based chemicals and products; and pharmaceuticals intended for human or animal use must give notices or apply for special licenses, permits, or approvals from the appropriate U.S. government agency before exporting such products.

B. Volume

What is the expected volume of export of the product? Will this be an isolated sale of a small quantity or an ongoing series of transactions amounting to substantial quantities? Small quantities may be exported under purchase orders and purchase order acceptances. Large quantities may require more formal international sales agreements; more secure methods of payment; special shipping, packing, and handling procedures; the appointment of sales agents and/or distributors in the foreign country; or after-sales service (see the discussion in Chapter 3).

C. Country Market and Product Competitiveness Research

On many occasions, a company's sole export sales business consists of responding to orders from customers located in foreign countries without any active sales efforts by the company. However, as a matter of successful exporting, it is imperative that the company adequately evaluate the various world markets where its product is likely to be marketable. This will include a review of macroeconomic factors such as the size of the population and the economic development level and buying power of the country, and more specific factors, such as the existence of competitive products in that country. The United Nations publishes its *International Trade Statistics Yearbook* (http://comtrade.un.org/), and the International Monetary Fund (IMF) publishes its *Direction of Trade Statistics Yearbook* (http://www.imf.org/external/) showing what countries are buying and importing all types of products. The U.S. Department of Commerce, Bureau of Census gathers and publishes data to assist those who are interested in evaluating various country markets, including its International Data Base and Export and Import Trade Data Base (http://www.census.gov/foreign-trade/statistics/country/index.html). It has also compiled detailed assessments of the international competitiveness of many U.S. products and information on foreign trade fairs to identify sales opportunities for such products. Another useful tool for evaluating the political and commercial risk of doing business in a particular country is the Country Limitation Schedule published periodically by the Export-Import Bank of the United States (http://www.exim.gov/tools/country/country_limits.cfm). An excerpt from the Department of Commerce's web site, Export.gov (http://www.export.gov/exportbasics/index.asp), which provides information about the basics of exporting, Frequently Asked Questions, and information on marketing, finance, and logistics, is included in Appendix A. See also Appendix K listing web sites for marketing information and trade leads. Of course, other private companies also publish data, such as those contained in the Dun & Bradstreet *Exporters Encyclopedia* or BNA's *Export Reference*

Manual. With limited personnel and resources, all companies must make strategic decisions about which countries they will target for export sales and how much profit they are likely to obtain by their efforts in various countries.

D. Identification of Customers: End Users, Distributors, and Sales Agents

Once a company has evaluated the countries with the best market potential and the international competitiveness of its products, the specific purchasers, such as end users of the products, sales agents who can solicit sales in that country for the products, or distributors who are willing to buy and resell the products in that country, must be identified. This is a highly important decision, and some of the worst experiences in exporting result from not having done adequate homework in selecting customers, sales agents, and distributors. It is far more efficient and profitable to spend significant amounts of time evaluating potential customers, sales agents, and distributors than to have to start over again because such customers, sales agents, or distributors turn out to be unable to pay, unable to perform, or difficult to work with. The U.S. Department of Commerce International Trade Administration offers a number of services and publications, such as overseas trade missions and fairs, "matchmaker" events, the National Trade Data Bank, Export Contact List Service, Customized Sales Survey, Trade Opportunities Program, the International Partner Search, Gold Key Service, International Company Profiles, *Commerce Business Daily*, and *Commercial News U.S.A.*, all designed to assist U.S. companies in identifying possible customers.

Once potential customers have been identified, if an ongoing relationship is contemplated, a personal visit to evaluate the customer is essential. One efficient way is to arrange a schedule of interviews at its foreign offices where representatives of the U.S. company could meet with numerous potential customers, sales agents, and distributors in that country in the course of a two- or three-day period. Based on such meetings, one or more distributors or sales agents can be selected, or the needs of a customer can be clearly understood.

In evaluating potential customers, sales agents, and distributors, it is important to obtain a credit report. Credit reports are available from Dun & Bradstreet, www.dnb.com; Graydon America, www.graydon.com; Teikoku Data Bank America, Inc. [Japan], http://www.tdb.co.jp/english/index.html; Owens Online, http://www.tdb.co.jp/english/index.html; and local offices of the U.S. Department of Commerce (International Company Profiles), http://www.export.gov/salesandmarketing/ism_market_research.asp.

E. Compliance With Foreign Law

Prior to exporting to a foreign country or even agreeing to sell to a customer in a foreign country, a U.S. company should be aware of any foreign laws that might affect the sale. Information about foreign law often can be obtained from the customer or distributor to which the U.S. company intends to sell. However, if the customer or distributor is incorrect in the information that it gives to the exporter, the exporter may pay dearly for having relied solely upon the advice of the customer. Incorrect information about foreign law may result in the prohibition of importation of the exporter's product, or it may mean that the customer cannot resell the product as profitably as expected. Unfortunately, customers often overlook those things that may be of the greatest concern to the exporter. As a result, it may be necessary for the U.S. exporter to confirm its customer's advice with third parties, including attorneys, banks, or government agencies, to feel confident that it properly understands the foreign law requirements. Some specific examples are as follows:

1. *Industry Standards*

Foreign manufacturers and trade associations often promulgate industry standards that are enacted into law or that require compliance in order to sell successfully there. It may be necessary to identify such standards even prior to manufacture of the product that the company intends to sell for export or to modify the product prior to shipment. Or, it may be necessary to arrange for the importing customer to make such modifications. Sometimes compliance with such standards is evidenced by certain marks on the product, such as "JIS" (Japan), "CSA" (Canada), and "UL" (Underwriters Laboratories—U.S.).

One type of foreign safety standard that is becoming important is the "CE" mark required for the importation of certain products into the European Community. The European Community has issued directives relating to safety standards for the following important products: toys, simple pressure vessels and telecommunications terminal equipment, machinery, gas appliances, electromagnetic compatibility, low-voltage products, and medical devices (see www.newapproach.org.). Products not conforming to these directives are subject to seizure and the assessment of fines. The manufacturer may conduct its own conformity assessment and self-declare compliance in most cases. For some products, however, the manufacturer is required (and in all cases may elect) to hire an authorized independent certifying service company to conduct the conformity assessment. The manufacturer must maintain a Technical Construction File to support the declaration and must have an authorized representative located within the European Community to respond to enforcement actions.

The ISO 9000 quality standards are becoming increasingly important for European sales. One helpful source of information in the United States is the National Center for Standards and Certification Information, a part of the Department of Commerce National Institute of Standards and Technology, www.nist.gov, which maintains collections of foreign government standards by product. The National Technical Information Service, www.ntis.gov, the Foreign Agricultural Service of the Department of Agriculture, www.fas.usda.gov, and the American National Standards Institute, www.ansi.org, which maintains over 100,000 worldwide product standards on its NSSN network, also collect such information. Canada has the

Standards Council, www.scc.ca, and Germany has the Deutsches Institut für Normung (DIN), http://www.din.de/cmd?level=tpl-home&languageid=en.

2. Foreign Customs Laws

The countries of export destination may have absolute quotas on the quantity of products that can be imported. Importation of products in excess of the quota will be prohibited. Similarly, it is important to identify the amount of customs duties that will be assessed on the product, which will involve determining the correct tariff classification for the product under foreign law in order to determine whether the tariff rate will be so high that it is unlikely that sales of the product will be successful in that country, and to evaluate whether a distributor will be able to make a reasonable profit if it resells at the current market price in that country. It is especially important to confirm that there are no antidumping, countervailing, or other special customs duties imposed on the products. These duties are often much higher than regular *ad valorem* duties, and may be applied to products imported to the country even if the seller was not subject to the original antidumping investigation.

Some countries, such as Ethiopia, Belarus, Cambodia, Yugoslavia, Kazakhstan, Lebanon, Liberia, Saudi Arabia, and Ukraine, do not fully adhere to the GATT Valuation Code and may assess duties on fair market value rather than invoice price.

Another problem is "assists." If the buyer will be furnishing items used in the production of merchandise, such as tools, dies, molds, raw materials, or engineering or development services, to the seller, the importer of record (whether that is the buyer or the seller through an agent) may be required to pay customs duties on such items, and the seller may be required to identify such items in its commercial invoices.

Many countries have severe penalties for import violations; for example, France assesses a penalty of two times the value of the merchandise, India assesses a penalty of five times the value of the merchandise, and China confiscates the merchandise. See Appendix K listing web sites for foreign customs agencies and tariff information.

In any case, where there is doubt as to the correct classification or valuation of the merchandise, duty rate, or existence of assists, the importer (whether buyer or seller) may wish to seek an administrative ruling from the foreign customs agency. This will usually take some period of time, and the seller and buyer may have to adjust their production and delivery plans accordingly. (A more thorough understanding of the types of considerations that the buyer may have to take into account under its customs laws can be gained by reviewing the similar considerations for a U.S. importer discussed in Chapter 6, Section F).

3. Government Contracting

Sales to foreign governments, government agencies, or partially government owned private businesses often involve specialized procedures and documentation. Public competitive bidding and compliance with invitations to bid and acquisition regulations, and providing bid bonds, performance bonds, guarantees, standby letters of credit, and numerous certifications may be required. Commissions may be prohibited, or the disclosure of commissions paid may be required. Government purchases may qualify for customs duty, quota, or import license exemptions. Barter or countertrade may be necessary.

4. *Buy American Equivalent Laws*

Foreign government agencies often promulgate regulations that are designed to give preferential treatment to products supplied by manufacturers in their own country. This may consist of an absolute preference, or it may be a certain price differential preference. Determining whether such laws or agency regulations exist for your company's products is mandatory if government sales are expected to be important.

5. *Exchange Controls and Import Licenses*

Unlike the United States, many nations of the world have exchange control systems designed to limit the amount of their currency that can be used to buy foreign products. These nations require that an import license from a central bank or the government be obtained in order for customers in that country to pay for imported products. For a U.S. exporter who wishes to get paid, it is extremely important to determine (1) whether an exchange control system exists and an import license is necessary in the foreign country, (2) what time periods are necessary to obtain such licenses, and (3) the conditions that must be fulfilled and documentation that must be provided in order for the importer to obtain such licenses. (See www.imf.org.)

6. *Value-Added Taxes*

Many countries impose a value-added tax on the stages of production and distribution. Such taxes usually apply to imported goods, so that the importer, in addition to paying customs duties, must pay a value-added tax based, usually, on the customs value plus duties. When the importer marks up and resells the goods, it will collect the tax from the purchaser, which it must remit to the tax authorities after taking a credit for the taxes due on importation. (Exporters are often exempt from the value-added tax.) The amount of value-added tax can be significant, as it is usually higher than traditional sales taxes, and, therefore, whether the product can be priced competitively in the foreign market is a matter of analysis.

7. *Specialized Laws*

Foreign countries often enact specialized laws prohibiting the importation of certain products except in compliance with such laws. In the United States, there are many special laws regulating the domestic sale and importation of a wide variety of products (see Chapter 6, Section A). Some U.S. laws regulate all products manufactured in the United States; others do not apply to products being manufactured for export. In any case, like the United States, foreign countries often have special laws affecting certain products or classes of products, and the existence of such regulation should be ascertained prior to manufacture, prior to entering into an agreement to sell, and even prior to quoting prices or delivery dates to a customer.

F. Export Controls and Licenses

This subject is treated in detail in Chapter 5. However, it is a very important preliminary consideration because if an export license from the U.S. Department of Commerce, Bureau of Industry and Security is required, and such license is not obtained by the exporter, U.S. Customs and Border Protection will detain the shipment, and the sale cannot be completed. Even if the exporter sells ex-factory and the buyer is technically responsible for U.S. inland transportation, export, and ocean shipment, the buyer may file a lawsuit if the exporter does not inform the customer that an export license is necessary and the shipment is detained. The method for determining whether an export license is required for a particular product is discussed in Chapter 5.

G. Patent, Trademark, and Copyright Registrations and Infringements

These rights are sometimes called intellectual or industrial property rights. This topic includes two common problems. First, a U.S. company that invents and manufactures a product may secure a patent, trademark, or copyright in the United States, but might not apply for any registration of its rights in a foreign country. In many countries, if the U.S. rights are not filed there within a specific period, such as one year after filing in the United States, they are forever lost and are part of the public domain in the foreign country. This means that without registering its rights in that country, an exporter cannot prevent copying, pirating, and the marketing of imitation products.

Second, without conducting a patent, trademark, or copyright search, a U.S. company cannot know whether the product that it is exporting will infringe a patent, trademark, or copyright that has been filed in a foreign country. Unfortunately, in many foreign countries, the first person to file a patent, trademark, or copyright will be the legal owner, even if the product was previously invented and used by someone in another country. Consequently, it is not uncommon for foreign competitors, distributors, or customers to register a U.S. company's patents, trademarks, or copyrights, so that if the U.S. company exports to the foreign country, this would result in an infringement of the intellectual property rights that the foreign entity now owns in that country. Thus, in order for the U.S. company to export its products to that country, it may have to negotiate to obtain a license and pay a royalty to the foreign company or to purchase back the intellectual property rights that have been registered there. In sales documentation commonly used in the United States, the U.S. manufacturer will give a warranty, or it will automatically be implied under the Uniform Commercial Code, that the product does not infringe any person's intellectual property rights. A U.S. exporter may be using the same type of documentation for export sales. If the U.S. exporter has not searched the foreign intellectual property registrations, and the product does infringe a foreign registration, the U.S. exporter will be in breach of warranty and may be unable to perform its sales agreement with its customer.

H. Confidentiality and Non-Disclosure Agreements

As a preliminary consideration, before exporting products to foreign countries or providing samples to potential customers, it is important to ask the foreign company to sign a confidentiality and non-disclosure agreement. In many countries, especially if the U.S. company has no patent registration there, the ability of the U.S. company to prohibit copying and piracy by reverse engineering is virtually nil. Some measure of protection can be obtained by requiring the foreign company to sign a confidentiality and non-disclosure agreement that commits it to not reverse engineer the product or engage in its manufacture itself or through third parties. Such agreements are not unusual, and any potential customer who refuses to sign one should be suspect.

I. Antiboycott Compliance

If you plan to make sales in the Middle East or you receive an order from a customer located there, before proceeding to accept and ship the order, you should be aware of the U.S. antiboycott regulations. Certain countries in the Middle East maintain international boycotts, usually of Israel, although there are times when other boycotts are in place. The Treasury Department updates the list of countries that participate in international boycotts on a quarterly basis. Currently those countries include Kuwait, Lebanon, Libya, Qatar, Saudi Arabia, Syria, United Arab Emirates, and Republic of Yemen. Iraq is not currently on the list, but it remains under review by the Department of Treasury.

U.S. law prohibits any U.S. company from refusing or agreeing to refuse to do business pursuant to an agreement or request from a boycotting country or to discriminate on the basis of race, religion, sex, or national origin. Perhaps more important, the law requires that if a U.S. company receives a request for information about its business relationships with blacklisted companies or boycotted countries, it must promptly report the request to the Bureau of Industry and Security at the U.S. Department of Commerce. Failure to do so can result in penalties including civil penalties of $250,000 per violation, criminal penalties for intentional violations, and denial of export privileges altogether. The forms for reporting requests for single and multiple transactions are shown in Figures 2–1 and 2–2, respectively.

The Internal Revenue Service also has antiboycott regulations under Sec. 999 of the I.R.S. Code. Section 999 prohibits U.S. taxpayers from participating in or cooperating with an international boycott by reducing certain foreign tax credits and other tax benefits that the U.S. company would be allowed to receive. The regulation requires that companies complete an I.R.S. Form 5713 reporting any operations relating to a boycotting country, and failure to file the appropriate forms will result in a $25,000 penalty, imprisonment for up to one year, or both. See Figures 2–3 and 2–3a.

J. Employee Sales Visits to Foreign Countries—Immigration and Customs Compliance and Carnets

In the course of developing export sales, it is likely that sales employees of the U.S. company will visit foreign countries to identify customers and evaluate markets. Another common export sales activity is exhibiting products in trade fairs sponsored by U.S. or foreign government agencies or trade associations. It is important that the U.S. company satisfy itself that its sales employees traveling to foreign countries comply with the immigration and customs laws of those countries. In particular, many countries require that individuals entering their country to engage in business activities obtain a different type of visa (which is stamped in the U.S. passport) to enter the country. Entering the country on a visitor's visa or engaging in activities inconsistent with the visa that has been issued can subject an employee to serious penalties and delay. With regard to the U.S. company's employees bringing samples of its products into a foreign country for display or sale, it is necessary that the regular customs duties be paid on the samples or that salespeople arrange for compliance with the local temporary importation procedures. Most countries have a temporary importation procedure whereby a bond must be posted to guarantee that the product that is being imported will be exported at a later time. For employees visiting a number of countries on sales visits, posting temporary importation bonds in a number of countries can be burdensome and must be arranged significantly in advance. One solution to this problem is the ATA Carnet developed by the Customs Cooperation Council and administered by the International Chamber of Commerce. In effect, the carnet is both a customs entry and a temporary importation bond that is honored by over ninety countries and that permits temporary entry of samples for order solicitation, display, and exhibition. Products entered by carnet must be exported and not sold. The carnet is obtained by applying to the International Chamber of Commerce and posting cash or a bond for 40 percent of the value with them. The application for a carnet is shown in Figure 2–4 and the bond in Figure 2–5. The carnet is shown in Figure 2–6. Additional information about carnets can be obtained from the U.S. Council for International Business in New York City, www.uscib.org. Applications for carnets are are available on the USCIB's web site. In order to avoid having to pay U.S. customs duties on the sample when the salesperson returns to the United States, the carnet should be signed by the U.S. Customs and Border Protection.

K. Utilization of Freight Forwarders and Foreign Customs Brokers

A competent freight forwarder can handle routing, inland and international transportation, containerization, scheduling of carriers, transshipments, bills of lading,

(*Text continues on page 34.*)

Figure 2–1. Report of request for restrictive trade practice or boycott—single transaction.

Form BIS-621P OMB No.0694-0012 U.S. DEPARTMENT OF COMMERCE
(REV 1-04) BUREAU OF INDUSTRY AND SECURITY

REPORT OF REQUEST FOR RESTRICTIVE TRADE PRACTICE OR BOYCOTT
SINGLE TRANSACTION

(For reporting requests described in Part 769 of the Export Administration Regulations)

NOTICE OF RIGHT TO PROTECT CERTAIN INFORMATION FROM DISCLOSURE

The Export Administration Act permits you to protect from public disclosure information regarding the quantity, description, and value of commodities or technical data supplied in item 11 of this report and in any accompanying documents. *If you do not claim this protection, all of the information in your report and accompanying documents will be made available for public inspection and copying.*

You can obtain this protection by certifying, in item 10 of the report, that disclosure of the information referred to above would place a United States company or individual involved in the report at a competitive disadvantage. If you make such a certification in item 10, you may remove information regarding the quantity, description, and value of the commodities or technical data supplied by you from item 11 of the inspection copy of the report form and from the public inspection copies of the accompanying documents.

The withholding of this information will be honored by the Department unless the Secretary determines that disclosure of the information would not place a United States company or individual at a competitive disadvantage or that it would be contrary to the national interest to withhold the information.

THIS SPACE FOR BIS USE

A BATCH__ __ __ __

MONTH/YEAR __ __ __ __

RSN __ __ __ __ __ SUBSET __ __

RTP __ __ __ __ __ __ __ __ __

CLASS __ FILING __ TAG __ __

This report required by law (50 U.S.C. App. § 2407 (b) (2) P.L. 96-72; E.O. 12214; 15 C.F.R. Part (769). Failure to report can result both in criminal penalties, including fines or imprisonment, and administrative sanctions.

Instructions: 1. Complete all items that apply. 2. Assemble original report form and accompanying documents as a unit, and submit intact and unaltered. 3. Assemble and submit the duplicate copy of the report form (marked Duplicate (Public Inspection Copy)) and additional copies of accompanying documents (marked with the legend "Public Inspection Copy.") 4. *If you certify, in item 10, that the disclosure of the information specified there would cause competitive disadvantage, edit the "Public Inspection Copy" of the report form relating to item 11.*

Public reporting for this collection of information is estimated to average one hour per request, including the time for reviewing instructions, searching existing data sources, gathering and maintaining the data needed, and completing and reviewing the collection o information. Send comments regarding this burden estimate or any other aspect of this collection of information, including suggestions for reducing the burden, to the Director of Administration, Bureau of Industry and Security, room 3889, U.S. Department of Commerce, Washington, DC 20230, and to the Office of Management and Budget, Paperwork Reduction Project (0694-0012), Washington, DC 20503.

1a. Identify firm submitting this report:

Name:

Address:

City: State: ZIP:

Country (if other than USA):

Telephone:

Firm Identification No. *(if known):*

Type an 'x' to specify firm type:

☐ Exporter
☐ Bank
☐ Forwarder
☐ Carrier
☐ Insurer
☐ Other

1b. Type an 'x' in any applicable box:

☐ Revision of a previous report (attach two copies of the previously submitted report)
☐ Resubmission of a deficient report returned by BIS (attach form letter that was returned with deficient report)
☐ Report on behalf of the person identified in item 2.
☐ Dual report on behalf of self and the person in item 2

2. If you are authorized to report and are reporting on behalf of another U.S. person, identify that person (e.g., domestic subsidiary, controlled Foreign subsidiary, exporter, beneficiary):

Name:
Address:
City: State: ZIP:
Country (If other than USA):
Type of firm: ***(see list in item 1a)***
Firm Identification No. *(if known)*:

3. Identify exporting firm, unless same as Item 1a or 2:

Name:
Address:
City: State: ZIP:
Country (If other than USA):
Firm Identification No. *(if known)*:

4. (a) Name of boycotting country from which request originated:

(b) Name of country directing inclusion of request, if different from (a) above:

5. Name of country or countries against which request is directed:

6. Reporting firm's reference number *(e.g., letter of credit, customer order, invoice)*:

7. Date firm received request: *(mm/dd/yyyy)*

8. Specify type(s) of document conveying this request by typing an 'x' in the appropriate box:

☐ Request to carrier for blacklist *certificate (submit two copies of blacklist certificate or transcript of request)*
☐ Unwritten, not otherwise provided for *(make transcript of request and submit copies)*
☐ Letter of credit
☐ Requisition/purchase order/accepted contract/shipping instruction
☐ Bid invitation/tender/proposal/trade opportunity
☐ Questionnaire *(not related to a particular dollar value transaction)*
☐ Other written (specify) ____________________

Submit two copies of each document or relevant page in which the request appears

9. Decision on request: *(select one by typing an 'x' in the appropriate box)*

☐ Have not taken and will not take the action requested.
☐ Have taken or will take the action requested.
☐ Have taken or will take the action requested but in a modified form *(attach detailed explanation)*
☐ Unable to report ultimate decision on the request at this time and will inform the Bureau of Industry and Security of the decision within ten days after decision is made.

Additional information: The firm submitting this report may, if it so desires, state on a separate sheet any additional information relating to the request reported or the response to that request. This statement will constitute a part of the report and will be made available for public inspection and copying, subject to the right to protect certain confidential information from disclosure described in item 10.

10. Protection of Certain Information from disclosure: (Type an 'x' in the appropriate boxes and sign below)

1. ☐ I (We) certify that disclosure to the public of the information regarding quantity, description, and value of the commodities or technical data contained in:

☐ Item 11 below (If you check this box, be sure to remove the bottom of the Duplicate (Public Inspection Copy) of the report form relating to Item 11.)

☐ Attached documents (If you check this box, be sure to edit the "Public Inspection Copy" of the documents submitted to exclude the specified information.) would place a United Sates person involved at a competitive disadvantage, and I (We) request that it be kept confidential.

2. ☐ I (We) authorize public release of all information contained in the report and in any attached documents. I (We) certify that all statements and information contained in this report are true and correct to the best of my (our) knowledge and belief.

Sign here in ink ________________ Type name ________________ Date ________

11. Describe the commodities or technical data involved, and specify quantity and value:

Description

Quantity:

Value to nearest whole dollar $

Submit the original and 1 copy to Office of Antiboycott Compliance, BIS, Room 6099C, U.S. Department of Commerce, Washington, D.C. 20230; Retain a copy for your records.

Figure 2–2. Report of request for restrictive trade practice or boycott—multiple transactions

FORM BIS-6051P
(REV 7-03)

U.S. DEPARTMENT OF COMMERCE
BUREAU OF INDUSTRY AND SECURITY

THIS SPACE FOR BIS USE

A BATCH ___ ___ ___ ___

MONTH/YEAR ___ ___ ___ ___

REPORT OF REQUEST FOR RESTRICTIVE TRADE PRACTICE OR BOYCOTT MULTIPLE TRANSACTIONS (Sheet No. 1)

(For reporting requests described in 769 of the Export Administration Regulations)

NOTICE OF RIGHT TO PROTECT CERTAIN INFORMATION FROM DISCLOSURE. The Export Administration Act permits you to protect from public disclosure information regarding the quantity, description, and value of the commodities or technical data supplied in item 9 of this report and in any accompanying documents. ***If you do not claim this protection, all of the information in your report and in accompanying documents will be made available for public inspection and copying***. You can obtain this protection by certifying, in Item 5 of the report, that disclosure of the information regarding the quantity, description and value of the commodities or technical data referred to above would place a United States company or individual involved in the report at a competitive disadvantage. If you make such a certification in Item 5, you may remove information regarding the quantity, description, and value of the commodities or technical data supplied by you from Item 9 of the public inspection copy of the report form and from the public inspection copies of the accompanying documents. The withholding of this information will be honored by the Department unless the Secretary determines that disclosure of the information would not place a United States company or individual at a competitive disadvantage or tat it would be contrary to the national interest to withhold the information.

This report is required by law (50 U.S.C. App. §2403-1a(b); P.L. 95-52; E.O. 12002; 15 CFR Part 769). Failure to report can result both in criminal penalties, including fines or imprisonment, and administrative sanctions.

INSTRUCTIONS: 1: This form may not include a transaction report that is filed late, nor indicate a decision on request other than those coded in item 4 below. 2. This form may be used to report on behalf of another United States person if all transactions apply to the person identified in item 2, but may not be considered as a dual report on behalf of both persons identified in item 1a and Item 2. 3. Limit each report to 75 transactions or less. 4. Attach as many continuation sheets as needed. Enter sheet number and name of reporting firm on each continuation sheet (starting with Sheet No. 2). 5. List each transaction across the continuation sheet, completing all items that apply. Use as many lines as necessary but separate transactions with a blank space or line. 6. Assemble original report form and accompanying documents as a unit, and submit intact and unaltered. 7. Assemble and submit the duplicate copy of report form (marked Duplicate (Public Inspection Copy)) and additional copies of accompanying documents (marked with the legend "Public Inspection Copy.") 8. *If you certify, in item 5, that the disclosure of the information specified tere would cause competitive disadvantage, edit the "Public Inspection Copy" of the documents submitted to exclude the specified information and remove the right hand portion of the Duplicate(Public Inspection Copy) of the continuation sheet(s) relating to Column 9.* **MULTIPLE TRANSACTIONS:** Public reporting for this collection of information is estimated to average one hour per reported request, including the time for reviewing instructions, searching existing data sources, gathering and maintaining the data needed, and completing and reviewing the collection o information. Send comments regarding this burden estimate or any other aspect of this collection of information, including suggestions for reducing this burden to Office of Administration, Bureau of Industry and Security, H3889, U.S. Department of Commerce, Washington, D.C. 20230; and to the Office of Management and Budget, Paperwork Reduction Project (0694-0012), Washington, D.C. 20503.

1a. Identify firm submitting this report:

Name: ________

Address: ________

City: ________ State: ____ ZIP: ____

Country *(if other than USA)*: ________

Telephone: ________

Firm: Identification No. *(If known)* ________

Specify firm type:

☐ Exporter ☐ Carrier

☐ Bank ☐ Insurer

☐ Forwarder ☐ Other

1b. Check any applicable box:

☐ Revision of a previous report (attach two copies of the previously submitted report)

☐ Resubmission of a deficient report returned by BTR (attach form letter that was returned with deficient report)

☐ Report on behalf of the person identified in item 2

2. If you are authorized to report and are reporting on behalf of another U.S. person, identify that person (e.g. domestic subsidiary, controlled foreign subsidiary, exporter, beneficiary):

Name: ________

Address: ________

City: ________ State: ____ ZIP: ____

Country *(if other than USA)*: ________

Type of firm: (see list in item 1a) ________

3. REQUESTING DOCUMENT CODES *(use to code Column 6 of continuation sheet)*

C Request to carrier for blacklist certificate (submit two copies of blacklist certificate or transcript of request)
U Unwritten, not otherwise provided for (make transcript of request and submit two copies)
L Letter of credit
R Requisition/purchase order/accepted contract/shipping instruction
B Bid invitation/tender/proposal/trade opportunity
Q Questionnaire (not related to a particular dollar value transaction)
9 Other written

} Submit two copies of each document or relevant page in which the request appears.

4. DECISION ON REQUEST CODES *(use to code Column 7 of continuation sheet)*

R Have not taken and will not take the action requested
T Have taken or will take the action requested

5. Protection of certain information from disclosure: *(Check appropriate boxes and sign below)*

☐ I (we) certify that disclosure to the public of the information regarding quantity, description, and value of the commodities or technical data contained in:

☐ Column 9 of the attached continuation sheets (If you check this box, be sure to remove column 9 from the Duplicate (Public Inspection Copy) of the continuation sheets.

☐ Attached documents (If you check this box, be sure to edit the "Public Inspection Copy" of the documents submitted to exclude the specified information.) would place a United States person involved at a competitive disadvantage, and I (we) request that it be kept confidential

☐ I (we) authorize public release of all information contained in the report and in any attached documents.

I (we) certify that all statements and information contained in this report are true and correct to the best of my (our) knowledge ~~and belief~~. ________

Sign here in ink ________ Type or print ________ Date ________

Submit original and 1 copy to Office of Antiboycott Compliance, BIS, Room 6099C, U.S. Department of Commerce, Washington, D.C. 20230; Retain a copy for your records.

Figure 2–3. International Boycott Report Form 5713

Form **5713** (Rev. December 2004)
Department of the Treasury
Internal Revenue Service

International Boycott Report

For tax year beginning ...., 20 ..... ,
and ending ...., 20 ..... .

▶ **Controlled groups, see page 3 of instructions.**

OMB No. 1545-0216
Attachment Sequence No. 123
File in Duplicate (See Instructions)

Name | **Identifying number**

Number, street, and room or suite no. (If a P.O. box, see page 2 of instructions.)

City or town, state, and ZIP code

Address of service center where your tax return is filed

Type of filer (check one):
☐ Individual ☐ Partnership ☐ Corporation ☐ Trust ☐ Estate ☐ Other

1 **Individuals**—Enter adjusted gross income from your tax return (see page 2 of instructions)

2 **Partnerships and corporations:**
a Partnerships—Enter each partner's name and identifying number.
b Corporations—Enter the name and employer identification number of each member of the controlled group (as defined in section 993(a)(3)). Do not list members included in the consolidated return; instead, attach a copy of Form 851. List all other members of the controlled group not included in the consolidated return.
If you list any corporations below or if you attach Form 851, you must designate a common tax year. Enter on line 4b the name and employer identification number of the corporation whose tax year is designated.

Name	Identifying number

If more space is needed, attach additional sheets and check this box . . . . ▶ ☐

	Code	Description
c Enter principal business activity code and description (see instructions)		
d IC-DISCs—Enter principal product or service code and description (see instructions)		

3 **Partnerships**—Each partnership filing Form 5713 must give the following information:
a Partnership's total assets (see instructions) . . . .
b Partnership's ordinary income (see instructions) . . . .

4 **Corporations**—Each corporation filing Form 5713 must give the following information:
a Type of form filed (Form 1120, 1120-F, 1120-FSC, 1120-IC-DISC, 1120-L, 1120-PC, etc.)
b Common tax year election (see page 2 of instructions)
(1) Name of corporation ▶ ....
(2) Employer identification number . . . .
(3) Common tax year beginning ...., 20 ....., and ending ...., 20 ..... .
c Corporations filing this form enter:
(1) Total assets (see instructions) . . . .
(2) Taxable income before net operating loss and special deductions (see instructions) . .

5 **Estates or trusts**—Enter total income (Form 1041, page 1) . . . .

6 Enter the total amount (before reduction for boycott participation or cooperation) of the following tax benefits (see instructions):
a Foreign tax credit . . . .
b Deferral of earnings of controlled foreign corporations . . . .
c Deferral of IC-DISC income . . . .
d FSC exempt foreign trade income . . . .
e Foreign trade income qualifying for the extraterritorial income exclusion . . . . . .

Please Sign Here
Under penalties of perjury, I declare that I have examined this report, including accompanying schedules and statements, and to the best of my knowledge and belief, it is true, correct, and complete.

Signature | Date | Title

For Paperwork Reduction Act Notice, see page 4 of the separate instructions. Cat. No. 12030E Form **5713** (Rev. 12-2004)

Figure 2–3. *(continued)*

Form 5713 (Rev. 12-2004) Page **2**

		Yes	No
7a	Are you a U.S. shareholder (as defined in section 951(b)) of any foreign corporation (including a FSC that does not use the administrative pricing rules) that had operations reportable under section 999(a)?		
b	If the answer to question 7a is "Yes," is any foreign corporation a controlled foreign corporation (as defined in section 957(a))?		
c	Do you own any stock of an IC-DISC?		
d	Do you claim any foreign tax credit?		
e	Do you control (within the meaning of section 304(c)) any corporation (other than a corporation included in this report) that has operations reportable under section 999(a)?		
	If "Yes," did that corporation participate in or cooperate with an international boycott at any time during its tax year that ends with or within your tax year?		
f	Are you controlled (within the meaning of section 304(c)) by any person (other than a person included in this report) who has operations reportable under section 999(a)?		
	If "Yes," did that person participate in or cooperate with an international boycott at any time during its tax year that ends with or within your tax year?		
g	Are you treated under section 671 as the owner of a trust that has reportable operations under section 999(a)?		
h	Are you a partner in a partnership that has reportable operations under section 999(a)?		
i	Are you a foreign sales corporation (FSC) (as defined in section 922(a), as in effect before its repeal)?		
j	Are you excluding extraterritorial income (defined in section 114(e)) from gross income?		

Part I **Operations in or Related to a Boycotting Country** (See instructions beginning on page 3.)

		Yes	No
8	**Boycott of Israel**—Did you have any operations in or related to any country (or with the government, a company, or a national of that country) associated in carrying out the boycott of Israel which is on the list maintained by the Secretary of the Treasury under section 999(a)(3)? (See **Boycotting Countries** on page 2 of the instructions.)		

If "Yes," complete the following table. If more space is needed, attach additional sheets using the exact format and check this box . . . ▶ ☐

	Name of country (1)	Identifying number of person having operations (2)	Principal business activity: Code (3)	Principal business activity: Description (4)	IC-DISCs only—Enter product code (5)
a					
b					
c					
d					
e					
f					
g					
h					
i					
j					
k					
l					
m					
n					
o					

Form **5713** (Rev. 12-2004)

Figure 2–3. *(continued)*

Form 5713 (Rev. 12-2004) Page **3**

	Yes	No
9 Nonlisted countries boycotting Israel—Did you have operations in any nonlisted country which you know or have reason to know requires participation in or cooperation with an international boycott directed against Israel?		

If "Yes," complete the following table. If more space is needed, attach additional sheets using the exact format and check this box . . . ▶ ☐

	Name of country (1)	Identifying number of person having operations (2)	Principal business activity: Code (3)	Principal business activity: Description (4)	IC-DISCs only—Enter product code (5)
a					
b					
c					
d					
e					
f					
g					
h					

	Yes	No
10 Boycotts other than the boycott of Israel—Did you have operations in any other country which you know or have reason to know requires participation in or cooperation with an international boycott other than the boycott of Israel?		

If "Yes," complete the following table. If more space is needed, attach additional sheets using the exact format and check this box . . . ▶ ☐

	Name of country (1)	Identifying number of person having operations (2)	Principal business activity: Code (3)	Principal business activity: Description (4)	IC-DISCs only—Enter product code (5)
a					
b					
c					
d					
e					
f					
g					
h					

	Yes	No
11 Were you requested to participate in or cooperate with an international boycott? . . .		
If "Yes," attach a copy (in English) of any and all such requests received during your tax year. If the request was in a form other than a written request, attach a separate sheet explaining the nature and form of any and all such requests. (See page 4 of instructions.)		
12 Did you participate in or cooperate with an international boycott? . . .		

If "Yes," attach a copy (in English) of any and all boycott clauses agreed to, and attach a general statement of the agreement. If the agreement was in a form other than a written agreement, attach a separate sheet explaining the nature and form of any and all such agreements. (See page 4 of instructions.)

Note: *If the answer to either question 11 or 12 is "Yes," you must complete the rest of Form 5713. If you answered "Yes" to question 12, you must complete Schedules A and C or B and C (Form 5713).*

Form **5713** (Rev. 12-2004)

Figure 2–3. *(continued)*

Form 5713 (Rev. 12-2004) Page **4**

Part II Requests for and Acts of Participation in or Cooperation With an International Boycott	Requests Yes	Requests No	Agreements Yes	Agreements No
13a Did you receive requests to enter into, or did you enter into, any agreement (see page 4 of instructions):				
(1) As a condition of doing business directly or indirectly within a country or with the government, a company, or a national of a country to—				
(a) Refrain from doing business with or in a country which is the object of an international boycott or with the government, companies, or nationals of that country?				
(b) Refrain from doing business with any U.S. person engaged in trade in a country which is the object of an international boycott or with the government, companies, or nationals of that country?				
(c) Refrain from doing business with any company whose ownership or management is made up, in whole or in part, of individuals of a particular nationality, race, or religion, or to remove (or refrain from selecting) corporate directors who are individuals of a particular nationality, race, or religion?				
(d) Refrain from employing individuals of a particular nationality, race, or religion?				
(2) As a condition of the sale of a product to the government, a company, or a national of a country, to refrain from shipping or insuring products on a carrier owned, leased, or operated by a person who does not participate in or cooperate with an international boycott?				

b Requests and agreements—If the answer to any part of 13a is "Yes," complete the following table. If more space is needed, attach additional sheets using the exact format and check this box. ▶ ☐

	Name of country (1)	Identifying number of person receiving the request or having the agreement (2)	Principal business activity: Code (3)	Principal business activity: Description (4)	IC-DISCs only—Enter product code (5)	Type of cooperation or participation — Number of requests: Total (6)	Number of requests: Code (7)	Number of agreements: Total (8)	Number of agreements: Code (9)
a									
b									
c									
d									
e									
f									
g									
h									
i									
j									
k									
l									
m									
n									
o									
p									

Printed on recycled paper Form **5713** (Rev. 12-2004)

Figure 2–3a. Schedule A—International Boycott Factor (Section 999(c)(1))

SCHEDULE A (Form 5713)

(Rev. December 2004)

Department of the Treasury Internal Revenue Service

International Boycott Factor (Section 999(c)(1))

Complete only if you are ***not*** *computing a loss of tax benefits using the specifically attributable taxes and income method on Schedule B (Form 5713)*

▶ Attach to Form 5713. ▶ See instructions on page 2.

OMB No. 1545-0216

Name | **Identifying number**

Name of country being boycotted (check one): ☐ Israel ☐ Other (identify) ▶ ....

Important: *If you are involved in more than one boycott, use a separate Schedule A for each boycott and attach to Form 5713.*

Name of Country (1)	Purchases, sales, and payroll attributable to boycotting operations, by operation		
	Boycott purchases (2)	Boycott sales (3)	Boycott payroll (4)
a			
b			
c			
d			
e			
f			
g			
h			
i			
j			
k			
l			
m			
n			
o			
Total			

1 Numerator of boycott factor (add totals of columns (2), (3), and (4)) . . . .

2 Denominator of boycott factor:

a Total purchases from countries other than United States . . . .

b Total sales to or from countries other than United States . . . .

c Total payroll paid or accrued for services performed in countries other than United States . . . .

d Total of lines 2a, b, and c . . . .

3 **International boycott factor** (divide line 1 by line 2d). Enter here and on Schedule C (Form 5713) (see instructions) . . . . ▶

For Paperwork Reduction Act Notice, see the instructions for Form 5713. Cat. No. 12050W **Schedule A (Form 5713) (Rev. 12-2004)**

Figure 2–3a. *(continued)*

Schedule A (Form 5713) (Rev. 12-2004) Page **2**

General Instructions

References are to the Internal Revenue Code.

Who Must File

Complete Schedule A (Form 5713) if:

- You participated in or cooperated with an international boycott and
- You are using the international boycott factor to figure the loss of tax benefits.

You must use the international boycott factor to figure the income qualifying for the extraterritorial income exclusion. To figure the loss of all other applicable tax benefits, you may either use the international boycott factor or you may specifically attribute taxes and income by operation on Schedule B (Form 5713).

Boycott Operations

All your operations in a boycotting country are considered to be boycott operations, unless you rebut the presumption of participating in or cooperating with the boycott (as explained below). In addition, your operations that are not in a boycotting country are boycott operations if they are connected to your participation in or cooperation with the boycott.

Rebutting the presumption of boycott participation or cooperation. One act of participation or cooperation creates the presumption that you participate in or cooperate with the boycott unless you rebut the presumption. The presumption applies to all your operations and those of each member of any controlled groups (defined in section 993(a)(3)) to which you belong, in each country that helps carry out the boycott.

You can rebut the presumption of participation in or cooperation with a boycott for a particular operation by demonstrating that the operation is separate from any participation in or cooperation with an international boycott. The presumption applies only to operations in countries that carry out the boycott. Therefore, you do not need to rebut the presumption for operations that are related to those countries if the operations take place outside of those countries.

International Boycott Factor

Your international boycott factor reflects boycott purchases, boycott sales, and boycott payroll.

Controlled groups. All members of a controlled group generally share one international boycott factor, which reflects all their purchases, sales, and payroll. However, if you belong to two or more controlled groups, your international boycott factor will reflect the purchases, sales, and payroll of all the controlled groups to which you belong.

Partnerships and trusts. You are deemed to have a prorated share of the purchases, sales, and payroll of each partnership in which you are a partner and of each trust of which you are treated as the owner under section 671. As a result, your international boycott factor may also reflect purchases, sales, and payroll of partnerships or trusts.

Specific Instructions

Compute a **separate** boycott factor and a separate schedule for **each** international boycott you participated in or cooperated with. Include your own operations and, if applicable, the operations of partnerships, trusts, and members of your controlled group.

See the instructions for lines 8 through 13, on page 3 of the Instructions for Form 5713, to determine the years for which you should report purchases, sales, and payroll for partnerships, trusts, and controlled groups.

Columns (1) Through (4)

In completing columns (1) through (4), show all boycott purchases, boycott sales, and boycott payroll from one operation on one line.

Partnerships. Complete **only** lines **a** through **o,** the total of columns (2), (3), and (4), and line 2. Do not complete line 3. Give this information to all partners so they can compute their own international boycott factor.

Column (1). Enter the name of the country that requires participation in or cooperation with an international boycott as a condition of doing business in that country. The country named in column (1) is not necessarily the country in which the operation takes place. For example, if you have an operation in Country Z that is not a boycotting country and the operation relates to Country X that is a boycotting country, enter the name of Country X in column (1). The Secretary maintains a list, under section 999(a)(3), of countries that require participation in or cooperation with an international boycott. See page 2 of the Instructions for Form 5713 for the current list of boycotting countries.

Column (2). Enter all purchases that are made from boycotting countries that are attributable to the operation reported on each line.

Column (3). Enter the sales that are made to or from boycotting countries and that are attributable to the operation reported on each line.

Column (4). Enter the total payroll that was paid or accrued for services performed in boycotting countries and that are attributable to the operation reported on each line.

Lines 1 Through 3

Line 1. Add the totals of columns (2), (3), and (4). This amount is the numerator of your international boycott factor.

Do not include amounts attributable to operations for which you rebutted the presumption of participating in or cooperating with the boycott.

Line 2. The denominator of the international boycott factor reflects all your purchases, sales, and payroll in or related to all countries other than the United States. If applicable, the denominator also reflects these items for your controlled groups, partnerships, and trusts. Include the amounts that are attributable to operations for which you rebutted the presumption of participating in or cooperating with the boycott.

Line 3. Enter the international boycott factor from line 3 of this form on the appropriate line of Schedule C (Form 5713) as follows.

IF you . . .	**THEN enter the international boycott factor on . . .**
Are required to reduce your foreign tax credit,	Line 2a(2).
Are denied a tax deferral on subpart F income,	Line 3a(4).
Are denied a tax deferral on IC-DISC income,	Line 4a(2).
Are denied an exemption of foreign trade income of a FSC,	Line 5a(2).
Are required to reduce foreign trade income qualifying for the extraterritorial income exclusion,	Line 6b.

Printed on recycled paper

consular certifications, legalizations, inspections, export licenses, marine and air insurance, warehousing, and export packing, either itself or through its agents. Unless the U.S. company is large enough to have a number of personnel who can perform the services in-house that are offered by freight forwarders, it is likely that the U.S. company will have to select and interface with a freight forwarder on export sales (and possibly a foreign customs broker on landed, duty-paid sales) in exporting its products to foreign countries. Transportation carriers are allowed to pay compensation (commissions) only to licensed freight forwarders for booking shipments. Freight forwarders have inherent conflicts of interest because they receive compensation from carriers and also receive freight-forwarding fees from shippers. Selection of the right freight forwarder is no small task, as freight forwarders have various levels of expertise, particularly in regard to different types of products and different country destinations. Some of the things that should be considered include reputation, size, financial strength, insurance coverage, fees, and automation. References should be checked. A list of freight forwarders can be obtained from the local commercial Yellow Pages or from the National Customs Brokers and Freight Forwarders Association of America in Washington, D.C., www.ncbfaa.org. Before selecting a freight forwarder, a face-to-face meeting with alternative candidates is recommended. At the outset of the relationship, the U.S. exporter will be asked to sign an agreement appointing the freight forwarder as its agent and giving it a power of attorney. It is important that the U.S. exporter ask its attorney to review such an agreement and make appropriate changes. (A simple sample power of attorney is shown in Figure 4–1.) Some exporters prefer to quote terms of sale where the exporter is responsible for the transportation and to control delivery by selection of and payment to their own freight forwarder. In other cases, the buyer selects the freight forwarder, known as a "routed" forwarder. The U.S. exporter should be aware that a freight forwarder and any foreign customs broker selected by it or by the freight forwarder are the exporter's agents, and any mistakes that they make will be the exporter's responsibility as far as third parties and government agencies are concerned. This is not always understood by companies that pay significant amounts of money to hire such persons. Where a freight forwarder is responsible for some loss or damage and refuses to make a reasonable settlement, the exporter may be able to proceed against the surety bond or even seek cancellation of the forwarder's Federal Maritime Commission license. Where the forwarder is bankrupt and has failed to pay transportation carriers amounts paid by the exporter, the exporter may be required to pay twice.

L. Export Packing and Labeling (Hazardous Materials)

It may be necessary for the U.S. company to have special packing for its products for long-distance ocean shipments. The packing used for domestic shipments may be totally inadequate for such shipping. Identification marks on the packages should be put in the packing list. Containers may be of various lengths and heights. Special types of containers may be needed, such as insulated, ventilated, open top, refrigerated ("reefers"), flat, and/or high-cube. Containerized shipments may be eligible for lower

(*Text continues on page 42.*)

Figure 2–4. Application for Carnet

United States Council
for International Business

ATA Carnet Application **(Please print out – fax or mail in)**

A. Applicant Information:

1. Carnet Holder (Corporate or Individual) ____________________

   Address ____________________ Phone No. ( ) ____________ Fax No. ( ) ____________

2. IRS NO./SS No. ____________________

3. ParentCompany ____________________ IRS No. ____________

4. Person Duly Authorized & Title ____________________ Phone No. ( ) ____________ Fax No. ( ) ____________

5. Authorized Representatives ____________________

B. Carnet Preparation Info:

6. Goods to be exported as: _______Commercial Samples (CS) ________ Professional Equipment (PE) ______ Exhibitions and Fairs (EF)

7. Approximate date of departure from U.S. : ____________________

8. Indicate the number of expected visits on the line provided beside each:

_____Algeria (AL)	_____Gibraltar (GI)	_____Luxembourg (UJ)	_____Slovakia (SK)
_____Andorra(AD)	_____Greece (GR)	_____Macedonia(MK)	_____Slovenia (SI)
_____Australia (AU)	_____Hong Kong (HK)	_____Malaysia (MY)	_____South Africa (ZA)
_____Austria (AT)	_____Hungary (HU)	_____Malta (MT)	_____Spain (ES)
_____Belgium (BE)	_____Iceland (IS)	_____Mauritius (MU)	_____Sri Lanka (LK)
_____Bulgaria (BO)	_____India (IN)**	_____Morocco(MA)	_____Sweden (SE)
_____China(CN)	_____Ireland (IE)	_____Netherlands (NL)	_____Switzerland (CH)
_____Croatia(HR)	_____Israel (IL)	_____New Zealand (NZ)	_____Taiwan(TW)*
_____Canada (CA)*	_____Italy (IT)	_____Norway (NO)	_____Thailand (TH)
_____Cyprus (CY)	_____Ivory Coast (CI)	_____Poland (PL)	_____Tunisia (TN)
_____Czech Republic (CZ)	_____Japan (JP)	_____Portugal (PT)	_____Turkey (TR)
_____Denmark (DK)	_____Korea (KR)	_____Romania (RO)	_____U.K. (GB)
_____Estonia(EE)	_____Lebanon(LB)	_____Senegal (SN)	_____ United States(US)
_____Finland (FI)	**only EF item will be admitted.	Singapore (SG)	Protectorates of above
_____France (FR)			
_____Germany (DE)			

9. Number of times leaving_________ and re-entering ________ the U.S

10. Transiting Countries : ____________________

C. Carnet Returned to you by:

11. ____ Regular Mail   12.______Messenger Pick-up   13. ____ Courier Service *(Be sure to attach a completed airway bill.)*

D. Processing Fees:

14. Basic Fee	$____________
15. Expedited Service Fee	____________
16. Additional Counterfoil/Voucher Fee	____________
17. Additional Continuation Sheets Fee	____________
18. Shipper's Export Declaration Fee *(see Carnet instruction Booklet for details)*	____________
19. Refundable Claim Deposit *(for government agencies only, see Step 4)*	____________
TOTAL PROCESSING FEE	$____________

1

Figure 2–4. *(continued)*

Carnet Application

E. Security:

20._____ Cash-Amount $__________ 21._____ Bond-Amount $__________ 22._____ Written Agreement (Members Only)

In connection with this security, I, as Carnet Holder, agree that the security I have posted as guarantee may be drawn upon to reimburse the U.S. Council for such duties, taxes, charges, and costs incurred by the U.S. Council as a result of my failure to comply with all U.S. Customs or Foreign Customs conditions as required by all ATA Conventions, and with all instructions issued by the U.S. Council on the use of my ATA Carnet, or as a result of any breach of the Carnet system. I further agree to reimburse the U.S. Council for any payments made on my behalf that may exceed my security amount. I also understand that if the Carnet is surrendered to the U.S. Council with all used and unused counterfoils/vouchers and the U.S. Council has determined that it has been correctly utilized, the U.S. Council may release me from the guarantee I have furnished prior to the 30 month period.

F. Obligation:

In connection with the use of this carnet, I, as the Holder of the Carnet and my representative(s), undertake to timely repatriate under Carnet all of the goods taken abroad, to produce satisfactory and timely evidence to cancel or mitigate any claim issued against my Carnet by a foreign guaranteeing association, to comply with all Customs regulations and requirements both in the United States and abroad, and to accept responsibility for the results of the negotiations or proceedings with any Customs Authority conducted by me as Holder or by the U.S. Council on my behalf. I further agree to return the Carnet to the U.S. Council with all used and unused counterfoils/vouchers within 15 days after my final trip by receipted mail and to retain a copy for my records

I declare that I have read all of the contents of the application package and that all my statements in connection with this application, and the descriptions and items on the General List, are true and correct.

23.__________________________________ Date____________________
(Corporate Officer or Duly Authorized Signature)

2

Figure 2–5. ATA Carnet Bond

ATA Carnet Bond

Carnet No. ______________________ Federal I.D. Number ______________________

KNOW ALL MEN BY THESE PRESENTS: That______________________________________

(Holder Name--Corporation, Individual, Sole Proprietorship or Partnership)

____

Street City State Zip

As **Principal** (hereinafter called **Principal**) and Allianz Marine and Aviation as **Surety** (hereinafter called **Surety**) are held and firmly bound unto the **UNITED STATES COUNCIL FOR INTERNATIONAL BUSINESS, INC.**, as **Obligee** (hereinafter called **Obligee**) in the amount of,

____ U.S. Dollars ____________

For payment whereof Principal and **Surety** bind themselves, their heirs, executors, administrators, successors and assigns, jointly and severally, firmly by these presents.

WHEREAS, **Obligee** has issued the Carnet as numbered above to the **Principal**; and

WHEREAS, the terms and conditions of said Carnet enable the **Principal** to enter the goods described therein into the Countries specified therein on a temporary basis and require the **Obligee** to make payment to said countries of any Customs duties, excise taxes or charges, which may be due as a result of Principal's failure to re-export, said goods Within the time period allowed; and

WHEREAS, **Principal**, by written application, has agreed to indemnify the **Obligee** against loss caused by **Principal's** Failure to so re-export said goods, and to reimburse **Obligee** for any payments made by **Obligee** for customs duties, Excise taxes and charges resulting from said failure, for which losses or payments **Obligee** shall be legally liable,

NOW, THEREFORE, THE CONDITION OF THIS OBLIGATION is such that if **Principal** shall re-export said goods in accordance with the terms of said Carnet, and shall reimburse the **Obligee** for any payments of customs duties, excise taxes or charges which may be imposed and for which the **Obligee** is legally liable, resulting from **Principal's** failure to so re-export said goods, then this obligation to be null and void; otherwise to remain in full force and effect,

SUBJECT, HOWEVER, TO THE FOLLOWING CONDITIONS:

(1) Notice of claim hereunder must be mailed by the **Obligee** or otherwise transmitted in a manner agreed upon, to the Home Office of the **Surety** within ninety (90) days from the date the **Obligee** shall receive its notice of a claim from any country specified in said Carnet. A claim shall be deemed received by the **obligee** upon receipt of a "G" letter, request for reimbursement.

(2) Regardless of the number of countries specified in said Carnet, and regardless of the periods of time spent in each said country, the liability of the **Surety** shall not extend to any temporary importation transactions occurring after the expiration of said Carnet.

(3) All suits at law or proceedings in equity to recover on this bond must be instituted within two (2) years of the date **Obligee** received notice of claim from any specified country.

(4) Regardless of the time for which this bond is in effect and regardless of the number of payments hereunder, the maximum liability of the **Surety** shall not exceed the penalty hereof.

(5) No right of action shall accrue upon or by reason hereof to, or for the use or benefit of, anyone other than the **Obligee** herein named.

(6) Payment by **Surety** of claims hereunder shall be due within 30 days from date demand amount shall be determined to be fixed and undisputed.

Signed and sealed this the ______________ day of ____________, 19__________

(Month) (Year)

____

(Holder Name-- Corporation, Individual, Sole Proprietorship or Partnership)

BY: ______________________________________ TITLE: ______________________________

(Authorized Officer or Individual; print or type)

______________________________________ BY: ______________________________

(Signature of above) (Authorized Signatory for Surety)

CERTIFICATE AS TO CORPORATE PRINCIPAL

I, ______________________, certify that I am the * ______________________ of the corporation named as **Principal** in the within bond; that ______________________, who signed the said bond on behalf of the **Principal** was then ______________________ of said corporation; that I know his/her signature, and his/her signature thereto is genuine; and that said bond was duly signed, sealed, and attested for in behalf of said corporation by authority of its governing body.

____

(Signature of Certifying Officer)

- May be executed by any other officer of the corporation.

This bond will be signed and executed electronically. There is no need to sign and return this form. You may wish to print it for your carnet records and for future reference.
Questions? Contact the CIB Carnet *HelpLine* at (800) ATA-2900.

Figure 2–6. ATA Carnet

Issuing Association
Association émettrice

USCIB

A.T.A. CARNET FOR TEMPORARY ADMISSION OF GOODS
CARNET A.T.A. POUR L'ADMISSION TEMPORAIRE DE MARCHANDISES
CUSTOMS CONVENTION ON THE A.T.A. CARNET FOR THE TEMPORARY ADMISSION OF GOODS
CONVENTION DOUANIERE SUR LE CARNET A.T.A. POUR L'ADMISSION TEMPORAIRE DE MARCHANDISES
CONVENTION ON TEMPORARY ADMISSION /*CONVENTION RELATIVE À L'ADMISSION TEMPORAIRE*
(Before completing the Carnet, please read Notes on cover page 3 /*Avant de remplir le carnet, lire la notice en page 3 de la couverture*)

INTERNATIONAL GUARANTEE CHAIN
CHAÎNE DE GARANTIE INTERNATIONALE
ICC W.C.F.

ATA CARNET / CARNET ATA

A. HOLDER AND ADDRESS / *Titulaire et adresse*
Sandler, Travis & Rosenberg
225 West Washington Street
Suite #1550
Chicago, IL, IL 60606

G. FOR ISSUING ASSOCIATION USE / *Réservé à l'association émettrice*
FRONT COVER / *Couverture*

a) A.T.A. CARNET No. / *Carnet A.T.A. N°* US 89/09-SAMPLE

Number of continuation sheets: / *Nombre de feuilles supplémentaires:* 0

B. REPRESENTED BY* / *Représenté par**
D.Bade, Corp. for Int'l Business 800-282-2900, Freight Forwarder's And/Or Any Authorized Representatives

b) ISSUED BY / *Délivré par*
United States Council for International Business

C. INTENDED USE OF GOODS / *Utilisation prévue des marchandises*
Commercial Samples,Exhibitions and Fairs,Professional Equipment

c) VALID UNTIL / *Valable jusqu'au*

2010	3	1
year *année*	month *mois*	day (inclusive) *jour (inclus)*

F. This Carnet may be used in the following countries/customs territories under the guarantee of the associations listed on page 4 of the cover:
Ce carnet est valable dans les pays/territoire douaniers ci-après, sous la garantie des associations reprises en page quatre de la couverture:

EUROPEAN UNION

AUSTRIA (AT)	FINLAND (FI)	LATVIA (LV)	ROMANIA (RO)
BELGIUM (BE)	FRANCE (FR)	LITHUANIA (LT)	SLOVAKIA (SK)
BULGARIA (BG)	GERMANY (DE)	LUXEMBOURG (LU)	SLOVENIA (SI)
CYPRUS (CY)	GREECE (GR)	MALTA (MT)	SPAIN (ES)
CZECH REPUBLIC (CZ)	HUNGARY (HU)	NETHERLANDS (NL)	SWEDEN (SE)
DENMARK (DK)	IRELAND (IE)	POLAND (PL)	UNITED KINGDOM (GB)
ESTONIA (EE)	ITALY (IT)	PORTUGAL (PT)	

OTHER COUNTRIES

ALGERIA (DZ)	ICELAND (IS)	MONGOLIA (MN)	SINGAPORE (SG)
ANDORRA (AD)	INDIA (IN)	MONTENEGRO (ME)	SOUTH AFRICA (ZA)
AUSTRALIA (AU)	ISRAEL (IL)	MOROCCO (MA)	SRI LANKA (LK)
BELARUS (BY)	IVORY COAST (CI)	NEW ZEALAND (NZ)	SWITZERLAND (CH)
CANADA (CA)	JAPAN (JP)	NORWAY (NO)	THAILAND (TH)
CHILE (CL)	KOREA (KR)	PAKISTAN (PK)	TUNISIA (TN)
CHINA (CN)	LEBANON (LB)	RUSSIA (RU)	TURKEY (TR)
CROATIA (HR)	MACEDONIA (MK)	SENEGAL (SN)	UKRAINE (UA)
GIBRALTAR (GI)	MALAYSIA (MY)	SERBIA (RS)	UNITED STATES (US)
HONG KONG, CHINA (HK)	MAURITIUS (MU)		

The Holder of this Carnet and his representative will be held responsible for compliance with the laws and regulations of the country/customs territory of departure and the countries/customs territories of importation. / *A charge pour le titulaire et son représentant de se conformer aux lois et règlements du pays/territoire douanier de départ et des pays/territoire douaniers d'importation.*

H. CERTIFICATE BY CUSTOMS AT DEPARTURE
Attestation de la douane, au départ

a) Identification marks have been affixed as indicated in column 7 against the following items No(s). of the General List
Apposé les marques d'identification mentionnées dans la colonne 7 en regard du (des) numéro(s) d'ordre suivant(s) de la liste générale

b) GOODS EXAMINED* / *Vérifié les marchandises**
Yes / *Oui* ☐ No / *Non* ☐

c) Registered under Reference No.*
*Enregistré sous le numéro**

d) ______ / / ______

Customs Office *Bureau de douane* Place *Lieu* Date (year/month/day) *Date (année/mois/jour)* Signature and Stamp *Signature it timbre*

I. Signature of authorized official and issuing Association stamp / *Signature du délégué et timbre de l'association émettrice*
Curt Wilson
Barrington 2009 / 3 / 2
Place and Date of Issue (year/month/day)
Lieu et date d'émission (année/mois/jour)

UNITED STATES COUNCIL FOR INTERNATIONAL BUSINESS

J.

X ______ X
Signature of Holder / *Signature du titulaire*

*If applicable / *S'il y a lieu*

N1 (11/3/08)

THIS CARNET IS THE PROPERTY OF USCIB. AFTER FINAL USE, RETURN IT TO USCIB.
1212 AVENUE OF THE AMERICAS, NEW YORK, NY 10036
(A RETOURNER A LA CHAMBRE EMETTRICE IMMEDIATEMENT APRES UTILISATION)

US 89/09-SAMPLE

Figure 2–6. *(continued)*

CONTINUATION SHEET GENERAL LIST No. 0
FEUILLE SUPPLEMENTAIRE LISTE GENERALE N°

CARNET No. *Carnet N°.* US 89/09-SAMPLE

ATA CARNET / *CARNET ATA*

Item No. / *N° d'ordre*	Trade description of goods and marks and numbers, if any / *Désignation commerciale des marchandises et, le cas échéant, marques et numéros*	Number of Pieces / *Nombre de Pièces*	Weight or Volume / *Poids ou Volume*	Value* / *Valeur**	**Country of Origin / **Pays d'origine	For Customs Use / *Réservé à la douane* Identification marks / *Marques d'identification*
1	2	3	4	5	6	7
1	Trade Show Booth	1		$10,000.00	US	
2	Professional Equipment, s/n:1234	[illegible]		$25,000.00	US	
3	Commercial Samples	5		$500.00	US	
	Totals	7		$35,500.00		
	NO CHANGES OR ADDITIONS ABOVE OR BELOW THIS LINE					
TOTAL or CARRIED OVER / *TOTAL ou À REPORTER*		7		$35,500.00		

UNITED STATES COUNCIL FOR INTERNATIONAL BUSINESS

(09/04)

*Commercial value in country/customs territory of issue and in its currency, unless stated differently. / *Valeur commerciale dans le pays/territoire douanier d'émission et dans sa monnaie, sauf indication contraire.*

** Show country of origin if different from country/customs territory of issue of the Carnet, using ISO country codes. / ** *Indiquer le pays d'origine s'il est différent du pays/territoire douanier d'émission du carnet, en utilisant le code international des pays ISO.*

Figure 2–6. (*continued*)

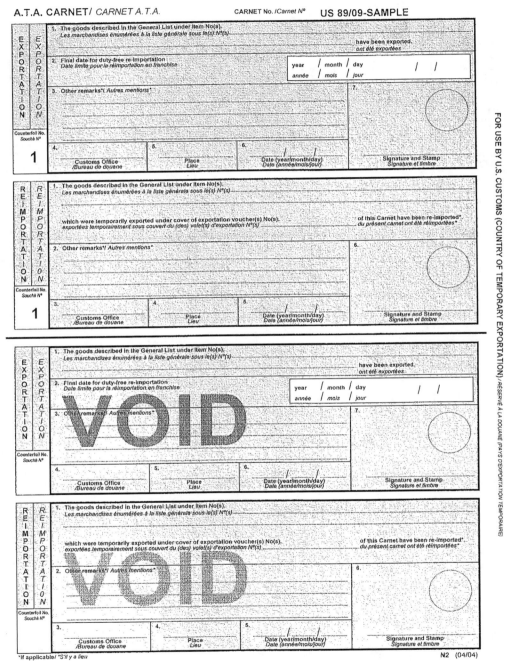

COUNTERFOIL

A.T.A. CARNET/ *CARNET A.T.A.* CARNET No. /*Carnet N°* US 89/09-SAMPLE

EXPORTATION / *EXPORTATION*

1. The goods described in the General List under item No(s). / *Les marchandises énumérées à la liste générale sous le(s) N°(s)* ... have been exported. / *ont été exportées*
2. Final date for duty-free re-importation / *Date limite pour la réimportation en franchise* — year / month / day; *année / mois / jour* — / /
3. Other remarks*/ *Autres mentions**
4. Customs Office /*Bureau de douane*
5. Place *Lieu*
6. Date (year/month/day) *Date (année/mois/jour)* / /
7. Signature and Stamp *Signature et timbre*

Counterfoil No. *Souche N°* 1

RE-IMPORTATION / *RE-IMPORTATION*

1. The goods described in the General List under item No(s). / *Les marchandises énumérées à la liste générale sous le(s) N°(s)* ... which were temporarily exported under cover of exportation voucher(s) No(s). / *exportées temporairement sous couvert du (des) volet(s) d'exportation N°(s)* ... of this Carnet have been re-imported*. / *du présent carnet ont été réimportées**
2. Other remarks*/ *Autres mentions**
3. Customs Office /*Bureau de douane*
4. Place *Lieu*
5. Date (year/month/day) *Date (année/mois/jour)* / /
6. Signature and Stamp *Signature et timbre*

Counterfoil No. *Souche N°* 1

EXPORTATION / *EXPORTATION* — VOID

1. The goods described in the General List under item No(s). / *Les marchandises énumérées à la liste générale sous le(s) N°(s)* ... have been exported. / *ont été exportées*
2. Final date for duty-free re-importation / *Date limite pour la réimportation en franchise* — year / month / day; *année / mois / jour* — / /
3. Other remarks*/ *Autres mentions**
4. Customs Office /*Bureau de douane*
5. Place *Lieu*
6. Date (year/month/day) *Date (année/mois/jour)* / /
7. Signature and Stamp *Signature et timbre*

Counterfoil No. *Souche N°*

RE-IMPORTATION / *RE-IMPORTATION* — VOID

1. The goods described in the General List under item No(s). / *Les marchandises énumérées à la liste générale sous le(s) N°(s)* ... which were temporarily exported under cover of exportation voucher(s) No(s). / *exportées temporairement sous couvert du (des) volet(s) d'exportation N°(s)* ... of this Carnet have been re-imported*. / *du présent carnet ont été réimportées**
2. Other remarks*/ *Autres mentions**
3. Customs Office /*Bureau de douane*
4. Place *Lieu*
5. Date (year/month/day) *Date (année/mois/jour)* / /
6. Signature and Stamp *Signature et timbre*

Counterfoil No. *Souche N°*

FOR USE BY U.S. CUSTOMS (COUNTRY OF TEMPORARY EXPORTATION) / *RÉSERVÉ À LA DOUANE (PAYS D'EXPORTATION TEMPORAIRE)*

*If applicable/ **S'il y a lieu* N2 (04/04)

DO NOT REMOVE FROM THE CARNET / *NE PAS DÉTACHER DU CARNET*

Figure 2–6. (*continued*)

COUNTERFOIL

A.T.A. CARNET/ *CARNET A.T.A.* CARNET No. /*Carnet N°* US 89/09-SAMPLE

FOR USE BY U.S. CUSTOMS (COUNTRY OF TEMPORARY EXPORTATION) / *RÉSERVÉ À LA DOUANE (PAYS D'EXPORTATION TEMPORAIRE)*

EXPORTATION / *EXPORTATION*

Counterfoil No. / *Souche N°*

1. The goods described in the General List under Item No(s). / *Les marchandises énumérées à la liste générale sous le(s) N°(s)* .... have been exported. / *ont été exportées*
2. Final date for duty-free re-importation / *Date limite pour la réimportation en franchise* year / *année* / month / *mois* / day / *jour* / /
3. Other remarks*/ *Autres mentions**

VOID

4. Customs Office / *Bureau de douane*
5. Place / *Lieu*
6. Date (year/month/day) / *Date (année/mois/jour)* / /
7. Signature and Stamp / *Signature et timbre*

REIMPORTATION / *RÉIMPORTATION*

Counterfoil No. / *Souche N°*

1. The goods described in the General List under Item No(s). / *Les marchandises énumérées à la liste générale sous le(s) N°(s)* .... which were temporarily exported under cover of exportation voucher(s) No(s). / *exportées temporairement sous couvert du (des) volet(s) d'exportation N°(s)* .... of this Carnet have been re-imported*. / *du présent carnet ont été réimportées**
2. Other remarks*/ *Autres mentions**

VOID

3. Customs Office / *Bureau de douane*
4. Place / *Lieu*
5. Date (year/month/day) / *Date (année/mois/jour)* / /
6. Signature and Stamp / *Signature et timbre*

EXPORTATION / *EXPORTATION*

Counterfoil No. / *Souche N°*

1. The goods described in the General List under Item No(s). / *Les marchandises énumérées à la liste générale sous le(s) N°(s)* .... have been exported. / *ont été exportées*
2. Final date for duty-free re-importation / *Date limite pour la réimportation en franchise* year / *année* / month / *mois* / day / *jour* / /
3. Other remarks*/ *Autres mentions**

VOID

4. Customs Office / *Bureau de douane*
5. Place / *Lieu*
6. Date (year/month/day) / *Date (année/mois/jour)* / /
7. Signature and Stamp / *Signature et timbre*

REIMPORTATION / *RÉIMPORTATION*

Counterfoil No. / *Souche N°*

1. The goods described in the General List under Item No(s). / *Les marchandises énumérées à la liste générale sous le(s) N°(s)* .... which were temporarily exported under cover of exportation voucher(s) No(s). / *exportées temporairement sous couvert du (des) volet(s) d'exportation N°(s)* .... of this Carnet have been re-imported*. / *du présent carnet ont été réimportées**
2. Other remarks*/ *Autres mentions**

VOID

3. Customs Office / *Bureau de douane*
4. Place / *Lieu*
5. Date (year/month/day) / *Date (année/mois/jour)* / /
6. Signature and Stamp / *Signature et timbre*

*If applicable/ **S'il y a lieu*

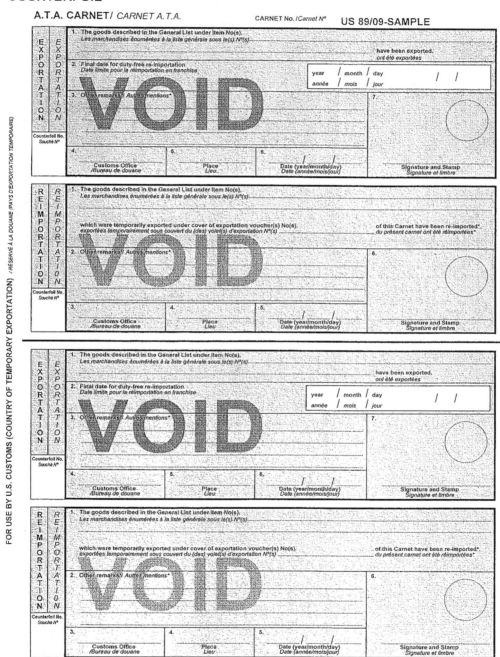

DO NOT REMOVE FROM THE CARNET / *NE PAS DÉTACHER DU CARNET*

insurance rates compared with breakbulk or palletized cargo. Specialized export packing companies exist and can often do the packing or can act as consultants in assisting the U.S. company with formulating packing that would be suitable for such shipments. Under the U.S. Uniform Commercial Code and the Convention on the International Sale of Goods (discussed in Chapter 3, Section B.2.m), unless expressly excluded, a seller makes a warranty that its products have been properly packaged. Under the Carriage of Goods by Sea Act, a steamship line is not responsible for damage to cargo due to insufficient packing. Improper packing can lead to disputes and claims for breach of warranty.

Under the Intermodal Safe Container Transportation Act as amended, a shipper arranging for intermodal transportation of a container or trailer carrying more than 29,000 pounds and traveling in any part by truck over the road must provide the initial carrier with a certificate of gross weight including a description of contents, which certificate must be transferred to each subsequent carrier.

All hazardous materials must be packed in accordance with the United Nations' Performance Oriented Packaging (POP) Standards. Shippers of hazardous materials must be registered with the Department of Transportation. "Hazmat employees," including those who handle, package, or transport hazardous materials and those who fill out shipping papers, must have training at least every three years (see discussion in Chapter 4, Section O).

Based on Transportation Security Administration requirements, passenger air carriers and air freight forwarders are required to obtain a "Shippers Security Endorsement" from the shipper certifying that the shipment does not contain any unauthorized explosive or destructive devices or hazardous materials and including a consent to search the shipment. Personal identification is required from the person tendering the shipment.

Labeling is equally important. If the product is a hazardous substance, special labeling and placarding is required. Furthermore, any product labeling may require printing in the foreign country's language. The types of information and disclosures required on such labeling may be prescribed by foreign law in the country of destination and should be confirmed as part of the pre-export planning. A European Union Directive that would have required that products sold in the European Union be labeled with only metric measurements after January 1, 2000, has been postponed indefinitely.

M. Terms of Sale

Although there are ordinarily many terms and conditions that the seller will include in its export sales agreements, one of the terms of sale upon which seller and buyer must agree is that relating to passage of title, risk of loss, price, and payment. Although a seller can sell on different terms of sale to different buyers in accordance with whatever terms are expressed in each buyer's purchase order, it is ordinarily much better for the seller to think about and formulate policies relating to its terms of sale in advance of receipt of orders. There are a number of considerations, the first of which relates to the use of abbreviations.

In order to standardize the understanding of the seller and buyer relating to their obligations in international sales agreements, various nomenclatures have been developed that use abbreviations, such as *ex-factory, ex-works, FOB plant, CIF, landed,* and so on. While these shorthand abbreviations can be useful, they can also be sources of confusion. The International Chamber of Commerce (INCO) has developed the "Incoterms," which were revised in 2000 (see Figure 2–7). There are also the Revised American Foreign Trade Definitions and the Warsaw Terms. Although these abbreviated terms of sale are similar, they also differ from nomenclature to nomenclature, and it is important to specify in the sales agreement which nomenclature is being used when an abbreviation is utilized. Under the Incoterms, however, the seller need provide war risk coverage only if requested by the buyer. Furthermore, even though it is assumed that sellers and buyers know the responsibilities and obligations that flow from utilizing specific terms such as *FOB plant*, the parties in fact may not always understand all of their rights and responsibilities in the same way, and disputes and problems may arise. For example, even though on an FOB seller's plant sale, the buyer is responsible for obtaining and paying for ocean insurance, often the buyer will expect the seller to obtain such insurance, which the buyer will reimburse the seller for paying. It is also possible that the seller will arrange for such insurance at the same time that the buyer does so, resulting in expensive duplication. Or, even though the buyer may be responsible for paying freight, the buyer may expect the seller to arrange

Figure 2–7. Examples of Incoterm usage.

Terms for Any Mode of Transport (including Intermodal)		
EXW	ex-works	South Bend, Indiana
FCA	free carrier	South Bend, Indiana
CPT	carriage paid to	Munich, Germany
CIP	carriage and insurance paid to	Munich, Germany
DAF	delivered at frontier	Amhof, Holland
DDU	delivered duty unpaid	Tubingen, Germany
DDP	delivered duty paid	Tubingen, Germany
Terms Limited to Sea and Inland Waterway Transport		
FAS	free alongside ship	Port of New Orleans
FOB	free on board	Port of New Orleans
CFR	cost and freight	Port of Rotterdam
CIF	cost, insurance & freight	Port of Rotterdam
DES	delivered ex-ship	Port of Rotterdam
DEQ	delivered ex-quay	Port of Rotterdam

Courtesy of Eugene J. Schreiber.

for shipment "freight collect." Finally, under the new Incoterms, certain traditional terms such as "C&F," "FOR," "FOT," and "FOB airport" have been abolished, and certain new terms such as "CFR," "DES," "DEQ," and "DDU" have been created. A diagram of the Incoterms is shown in Figure 2–8. In the author's experience, even if the parties choose to use an abbreviation to specify the way in which title will pass and delivery will be made, the author strongly recommends that the "who does what" be stated in detail in the sales agreement to avoid the possibility of a misunderstanding.

It is also important for the seller to realize that the price term may differ from the place of passage of title and risk of loss or time of payment. For example, under an INCO CFR or CIF term, the seller will be quoting a price to the buyer that includes the seller's cost of shipping the merchandise to the destination, but, in actuality, title and risk of loss will pass to the buyer when the merchandise is loaded on the ship at the time of export. Similarly, in a sales quotation, CIF means only that the price quoted by the seller will include all expenses to the point of destination—it does not mean that payment will be made upon arrival. Payment may be made earlier or later depending upon the agreement of the parties. Sellers should be sure that their export sales documentation distinguishes between price terms, title and risk of loss terms, and payment terms.

Figure 2–8. Diagram of the Incoterms.

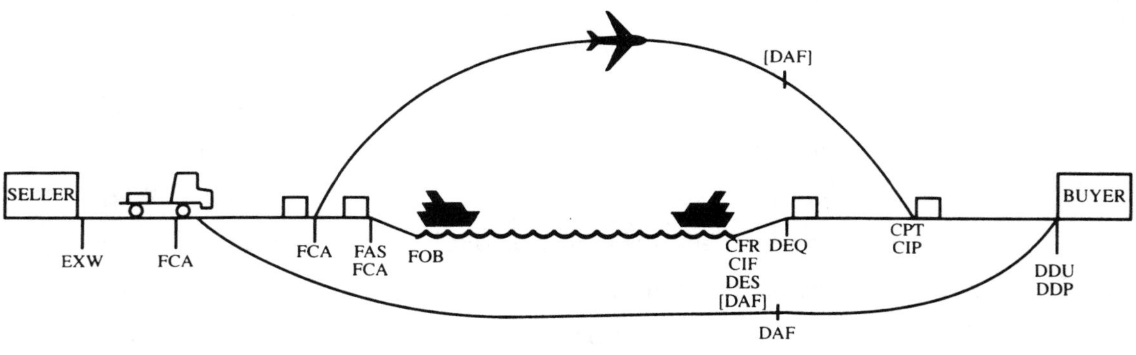

NOTES

1. On CFR, CIF, CPT, and CIP shipments, delivery and risk of loss transfer to the buyer at the port of *shipment*, although the seller is responsible for paying for costs of freight (CFR, CPT) and insurance (CIF, CIP).
2. Except for CIP and CIF sales (where insurance is part of the contract price), the seller is not required to purchase insurance but may do so up to the place of delivery, which becomes a cost to be factored into the seller's profitability and sales quotation.
3. Under CIF and CIP, the seller must provide only minimum coverage (110% of contract price) but no war risk or strike, riot, and civil commotion coverage unless the buyer agrees to bear the expense.
4. Packing costs for shipment to known ultimate destination are an expense of the seller (even on EXW sales).
5. Cost of pre-shipment inspections is always an expense of the buyer unless inspections are required by the country of exportation or otherwise agreed in the sales contract.

Under the Convention on the International Sale of Goods (discussed in Chapter 3, Section B.2.m), if the parties do not agree upon a place for the transfer of title and delivery in their sales agreement, title and delivery will transfer when the merchandise is delivered to the first transportation carrier.

Another consideration relates to tax planning. Under U.S. law, if title on the sale of inventory passes outside the United States, foreign source income is created, and in some situations, depending upon the seller's tax situation, the seller can reduce its U.S. income taxes by making sales in such a manner. It is usually advisable to ensure that title passes prior to customs clearance in the foreign country, however, to make sure that the seller is not responsible for payment of customs duties, which could include expensive antidumping or other special duties.

In most international transactions, the buyer will be responsible for importing the products to its own country, clearing customs, and paying any applicable customs duties. This is because the importer is liable for all customs duties, even antidumping duties. However, if the seller agrees to sell landed, duty paid, or delivered to the buyer's place of business (so-called "free domicile" or "free house" delivery), the seller will be responsible for such customs duties. Ordinarily, the seller cannot act as the importer of record in a foreign country unless it obtains a bond from a foreign bonding company and appoints an agent in that country for all claims for customs duties. Generally, a seller would not want to sell delivered, duty paid, but sometimes the buyer's bargaining leverage is such or competition is such that the seller cannot get the business unless it is willing to do so. If the buyer is wary of paying antidumping duties, it may refuse to act as the importer of record. Similarly, when the seller is selling to a related buyer, such as a majority or wholly owned subsidiary, the parent company may want to sell landed, duty paid, and assume such expenses.

In general, if the seller sells ex-factory (ex-works), it will have the least responsibility and risk. The buyer will then be responsible for arranging and paying for inland transportation to the port of export, ocean transportation, and foreign importation. In many cases, an ex-factory sale can result in the buyer's being able to avoid customs duties on the inland freight from the seller's factory to the port of export. In such instances, even though the buyer will have the responsibility for complying with all U.S. export laws, such as export control licenses, filing Electronic Export Information (formerly Shipper's Export Declarations) through the Automated Export System record, arranging insurance, and complying with foreign laws, it is a shortsighted seller who does not thoroughly discuss all of these items with the buyer during the formation of the sales agreement. If the buyer is unable to complete export or effect import, the fact that the seller is not legally responsible will be of little consolation and will lead to lawsuits, nonpayment, and loss of future business.

Even though selling ex-factory may be attractive to a seller, there are many reasons why the seller may want or need to sell on other terms. For example, the buyer may be inexperienced in arranging international shipments; the seller's competitors may be offering delivered terms; the seller may be selling to an affiliated company; the seller may need to control diversion back into the United States or other countries; the seller may be trying to assure delivery of goods subject to U.S. export controls; the seller may want to control the shipment until it is loaded on board the ship for letter of credit sales; the seller may want to control title and ownership until payment; or the seller may have warehouse-to-warehouse marine insurance under an open-cargo policy, and therefore, by agreeing to pay the insurance costs, can save the buyer some money; and sometimes the seller is in a better position to obtain lower ocean transportation or insurance rates. As already indicated, sometimes sales effected outside of the United States can lower the U.S. seller's income tax liability. For all of these reasons, a thorough discussion of the terms and conditions of sale between the seller and buyer, rather than simply following a set policy, may be advantageous.

N. Consignments

Unlike in sales transactions, where title to the merchandise transfers to the foreign buyer in the United States or sometime up to delivery in the foreign country in accordance with the terms of sale between the parties, in consignment transactions, the exporter/seller maintains ownership of the goods, and the consignee in the foreign country takes possession of the goods. The consignee then offers the goods for sale, and when a customer purchases the goods, title transfers from the exporter/seller to the importer/buyer and to the customer simultaneously. Such transactions have various procedural and documentary considerations. As the owner, the exporter/seller will be responsible for all transportation costs, insurance, filing of Electronic Export Information (Shipper's Export Declarations) through the Automated Export System, and obtaining export control licenses. While foreign customs regulations may permit the consignee to effect customs clearance, legally the goods are owned by the exporter/seller, and the exporter/seller will be liable for the foreign customs duties. Additional taxes may be assessed, such as personal property taxes assessed on the goods while they are awaiting sale and income taxes, because title will pass to the importer/buyer at the buyer's place of business in the foreign country. In addition, to avoid the inability to take possession of the goods in case of bankruptcy of the importer/buyer or other claims by the importer's creditors, special arrangements under the buyer's law, such as chattel mortgages, conditional sale agreements, public notices, or security interests, may be required. Because the export/import transaction is not a sale at the time of entry, transaction value cannot be used—the customs authorities will assess customs duties based upon an alternative valuation method.

O. Leases

In export transactions that are leases, no sales documentation should be used. The ability of the exporter/lessor to retain title and ownership, repossess the goods at the end of the lease, and obtain income tax benefits depends upon using lease documentation rather than sales agreements. As with consignments, the exporter/seller is legally responsible for all exporting and importing obligations, although those obligations can be delegated to the importer in the lease agreement. For customs valuation purposes, a lease is not a sale; therefore, transaction value will not be used, and the customs duties payable will depend upon an alternative valuation method. Whether the transaction will be subject to value-added taxes or other exactions depends upon the law of the destination country.

P. Marine and Air Casualty Insurance

Marine (or ocean) and air insurance is important on export shipments. Under the Carriage of Goods by Sea Act, ocean carriers are responsible for the seaworthiness of the vessel, properly manning the vessel, and making the vessel safe for carriage of the cargo. The ocean carrier is not responsible for negligence of the master in navigating the vessel, fires, perils, dangers, accidents of the sea, acts of God, acts of war, acts of public enemies, detention or seizures, acts or omissions of shippers, strikes or lockouts, riots and civil commotions, saving or attempting to save a life or property at sea, inherent defect, quality or vice of the goods, insufficiency of packing, quarantine restrictions, insufficiency or inadequacy of marks, latent defects not discoverable by due diligence, and any other causes arising without the actual fault and privity of the ocean carrier.

Without insurance, even when the carrier can be proven liable, responsibility is limited to $500 per "package" on ocean shipments and $28 per kilogram on air shipments unless a higher value is declared in advance and a higher transportation charge is paid. The seller may be responsible for (1) obtaining and paying for such insurance with no reimbursement by the buyer, or (2) obtaining and paying for such insurance with reimbursement by the buyer. Or, the buyer may be responsible for (1) obtaining and paying for such insurance with no reimbursement by the seller, or (2) obtaining and paying for such insurance with reimbursement by the seller. Although abbreviated trade terms, such as FOB port of shipment, are supposedly designed to clarify which parties are responsible for arranging and paying for various aspects of an export shipment, often confusion and misunderstandings occur. It is extremely important to clearly determine who will pay for such insurance and who will arrange for it. It is necessary for a seller or buyer to have an "insurable interest" in the merchandise in order to obtain insurance coverage. Depending on the terms of sale, the seller may have an ownership interest up to a particular point or a financial interest in the safe arrival of the shipment up until the time it is paid.

A U.S. company can buy an open or blanket cargo marine or air insurance policy that is in continuous effect for its shipments, or a special onetime cargo policy that insures a single shipment. Alternatively, it can utilize its freight forwarder's blanket policy. There are many advantages for a company to have its own open cargo policy, but the quantity of exports must justify it; otherwise, it is probably more appropriate to utilize the freight forwarder's blanket policy. Some insurance brokers recommend that a company have its own policy when exports and/or imports reach $500,000 to $1 million. When a blanket policy is used, a separate certificate is issued by the insurance company or the holder of the policy to evidence coverage for each shipment. (A sample marine insurance policy and certificate are shown in Chapter 4, Figures 4–10 and 4–11, respectively.)

Familiarizing oneself with such insurance policies is also important in the event that a casualty occurs and a claim needs to be filed. Generally, it is best to obtain "all risks" (rather than "named peril") and "warehouse-to-warehouse" (or "marine extension") coverage. Even "all risks" coverage does not include war risk or "strike, riot and civil commotion" coverage, and the seller should specifically determine whether these risks and others, such as delay in arrival and change in customs duties, should be covered by a rider and payment of an additional premium. Under the Incoterms, it is necessary to insure the shipment at 110 percent of the invoice value; in the case of some letter of credit sales, payment cannot be obtained unless insurance in that amount has been obtained. The filing of claims is discussed in Chapter 4, Section H.

In order to get paid under letters of credit or documentary collections through banking channels, it may be necessary for the seller to furnish a certificate to the bank evidencing that insurance coverage exists.

Marine insurance companies and insurance brokers can advise on the different types of coverage available and comparative premiums. The premium will depend on the type of merchandise, its value (risk of pilferage), its packing, the type of coverage (including riders), the method of transportation, the country of destination and routing, the loss history of the insured, the carriers used, whether transshipment will occur, etc.

Q. Methods of Transportation; Booking Transportation

In determining the general method by which the U.S. company will export, or in filling a specific shipment to a particular customer, marine transportation and air transportation must be evaluated. Obviously, air transportation is much quicker but is more expensive. Large shipments cannot be shipped by air. The exporter may choose to charter a vessel to obtain lower rates for bulk commodities. Inland transportation by truck, rail, or air must be selected. The booking of steamship lines, shipping schedules, any delays necessary to load a full container, and any intermediate stops for the ship must all be considered by the U.S. company or its freight forwarder before selecting the appropriate transportation method and carrier. Companies with small quantities or those unfamiliar with shipping internationally should work with a freight forwarder or a non-vessel-operating common carrier (NVOCC). These companies can arrange and book shipments with carriers, or they can arrange to consolidate small shipments to make up a full container, thus reducing the cost of transportation rates. One aspect to consider when consolidating cargo is that any delay by Customs or some other government agency would cause delays to other cargo in the same container. NVOCCs are companies that contract with the vessel-operating common carriers (VOCCs) to guarantee the purchase of a significant quantity of containers over a period of time. In exchange for the volume, the VOCC sells to the NVOCCs at reduced costs. In turn, the NVOCCs sell that container space to shippers at a profit. NVOCCs are considered the actual carriers to the shippers and they prepare their own "house" bills of lading, but they are considered shippers to the VOCCs, who prepare the "master" bill of lading. Both the ocean freight forwarders and the NVOCCs are required to be licensed by the Federal Maritime Commission and carry adequate insurance.

Both NVOCCs and VOCCs are required to maintain lists of service charges based upon commodity classifications called "tariffs" (not to be confused with the customs duties paid to governments on imported merchandise). These tariffs are subject to change and often contain numerous exceptions and surcharges. Tariffs must be filed with the Federal Maritime Commission electronically and be made publicly available. Links to the tariffs are available at the Federal Maritime Commission's web site: www.fmc.gov. All shipments are to be made in accordance with the tariffs on file unless the shipper has entered into a Confidential Service Agreement with the carrier. Both VOCCs and NVOCCs may enter into Service Agreements with shippers. Under these agreements, the shipper and the carriers may come to terms on rates, minimum quantities, and service commitments. Certain minimum elements of all service agreements must be made publicly available, but not the rates or service commitments. The exporter should be careful in recording quotations, dates, tariff classification numbers, rates, and the person making the quotation in order to avoid disputes over the details of the Service Agreement.

Airfreight rates are based on actual weight or dimensional weight, whichever is more. The size of the shipment (height x width x length in inches) divided by 166 equals the dimensional weight. Ocean freight rates will also be based on weight or measure, whichever is greater. Measure is calculated by multiplying the height by width by length in inches and dividing by 1,728 to get cubic feet. Sometimes the carrier's rates will be expressed in tons (short ton = 2,000 pounds, long ton = 2,240 pounds, or metric ton = 1,000 kilograms = 2,200 pounds) or in units of 40 cubic feet of volume. Miscellaneous freight shipped together is classified as "Freight All Kinds," which pays a higher rate than specific commodities. It is a violation of the Shipping Act of 1984 for a shipper to seek to obtain a lower shipping rate by misclassifying merchandise or stating false weights or measurements. Likewise, it is a violation for a steamship line to charge more or less than its publicly filed tariff rate (except under a service contract) or to pay rebates to shippers. If a shipper (exporter or importer) has satisfactory credit arrangements with a steamship line, it can ship "freight collect."

Shippers should also check into using courier services that can handle air, ground, and marine transportation for inclusive rates. Couriers also will handle the customs clearance. Unique to the courier services is that a courier will clear merchandise through customs in the country of import on its own bond, which allows it to clear merchandise more quickly. Unfortunately, the customs services may still hold the importer responsible for declarations made by couriers using their own bonds, which can result in issues for the importers.

Smaller shippers can join a shippers' association and obtain similar benefits. Shippers' associations are nonprofit transportation cooperatives. The associations arrange for domestic or international transportation for their members. For more information on shippers' associations, contact the American Institute for Shippers' Associations, a trade association, at www.shippers.org.

R. Country of Origin Marking

As in the United States, many foreign countries require that the product and the product packaging be marked with the country of manufacture or production before the product can enter the foreign country. The regulations may be quite specific, for example, requiring that the country of origin be die-stamped, cast-in-the-mold, etched, or engraved in the product at the time of production or otherwise permanently marked. The size and location of the marking may be specified, and exemptions from marking certain types of products may be available. Since the shipment cannot enter the country unless such marking has been done properly, it is important to check the foreign regulations prior to manufacture and shipment. The foreign country may also have specific requirements with respect to marking based on the product, such as pharmaceuticals, food products, textiles and apparel, etc. These requirements will generally be imposed not by the foreign customs service, but by the local consumer products agency.

S. Foreign Warehousing and Free Trade Zones

Many companies use a regional distribution center (for example, in Rotterdam or Hong Kong) for re-export to various countries in the region. Shipments to such regional distribution centers can be entered into that country temporarily for repackaging, relabeling, manipulation, modification, and sometimes further manufacturing without the payment of any customs duties if the product is going to be re-exported. Foreign countries often have certain bonded warehousing and free trade zone systems that permit such activities. If the U.S. exporter wishes to avail itself of those benefits, it must carefully check and comply with those procedures in order to obtain the duty-free treatment.

T. Export Financing and Payment Insurance

A number of government agencies, U.S. and foreign, provide financing for U.S. exporters. The U.S. Export-Import (EXIM) Bank has financing available for large exporters as well as a new program for smaller exporters. The Agency for International Development under its tied aid program, the Department of Agriculture, the International Development Cooperation Agency, the International Bank for Reconstruction and Development (World Bank), the Inter-American Development Bank, the Asian Development Bank, the African Development Bank, and the Small Business Administration all have programs designed to finance exports. Some foreign countries even finance the importation of products that they are seeking to obtain. Most recently, in the United States, the federal government has encouraged states to develop export financing programs. At last count, forty-eight states, including California and Illinois, have established successful programs, and a U.S. exporter should check with its state agencies or the National Association of State Development Agencies (www.naod.org.) to determine the availability and terms and conditions of financing prior to manufacture and export of its products. This is an important preliminary consideration because the buyer may have to provide documentation before the exporter can apply for such financing, and there may be longer lead times in completing the sale.

Related to this subject is insurance issued by the Foreign Credit Insurance Association and marketed by the U.S. Export-Import Bank, which has offices in major

U.S. cities. This association of U.S. insurance companies offers a policy that can protect an exporter against default in payment due to expropriation, foreign government political risks, and customer nonpayment due to commercial reasons. Several different types of policies are available covering 90 to 95 percent of the risk. Such insurance may be required in order to obtain certain export financing. A sample application is shown in Figure 2–9.

U. Tax Incentives

Up until September 2000, the United States had in place tax reduction programs for export profits called the Foreign Sales Corporation and Domestic International Sales Corporation programs. Then, based on findings by the World Trade Organization that these programs violated the world trading rules, the United States developed a replacement program. However, the WTO also found that the replacement program violated the same rules. Benefits under the old Foreign Sales Corporation program ended on December 31, 2001.

V. Export Trading Companies, Export Trade Certificates of Review, and Export Management Companies

In 1982, Congress enacted the Export Trading Company Act (ETC), which established two benefits: (1) banks are permitted to own all or part of exporting companies, and (2) exporting companies can obtain exemptions from the U.S. antitrust laws on their export activities. The latter benefit is of most interest to the individual exporter and can be useful in avoiding costly treble damage liability and expensive attorney's fees and court costs if the exporter obtains such a certificate. Certified activities often include the appointment of exclusive distributors and agents, and the imposition of restrictions on distributors, such as territories, prices, the handling of competitive products, and the termination of such distributors, all of which might normally violate U.S. antitrust laws. Furthermore, if a U.S. company wishes to cooperate with other companies in exporting, even with competitors, such activities can be protected under the certificate. Those certificates are issued by the U.S. Department of Commerce with the concurrence of the Department of Justice and are not difficult to apply for. However, the U.S. exporter should also check foreign law in the country of destination, as such certificates do not exempt the U.S. exporter from foreign law. A sample application and a certificate are shown in Figures 2–10 and 2–11, respectively.

An export management company, or EMC, is usually an export intermediary located in the United States that acts as a sales agent or representative for the manufacturer for exports to certain foreign markets. Typically, EMCs are paid a commission and may be helpful where the manufacturer is new to exporting or does not have its own distributor or sales agent in that foreign country. Theoretically, the difference between the EMC and the ETC is that ETCs are supposed to have sufficient capital to

(*Text continues on page 66.*)

Figure 2–9. Application for Export-Import Bank insurance.

OMB No. 3048-0023
Expires 08/31/2010

EXPORT IMPORT BANK OF THE UNITED STATES

SHORT-TERM MULTI-BUYER EXPORT CREDIT INSURANCE POLICY APPLICATION

Applicant: ______________________ dba: ______________________
Address: ______________________
Phone: ____________ Fax: ____________ E-Mail: ____________ Website: ____________
Contact: ____________ Title: ____________ E-Mail: ____________ Phone: ____________
Brokerage: ____________ Broker Contact: ____________

(optional) Is the majority ownership of your business represented by ___ women or ___ an ethnic minority?

How did you learn about Ex-Im Bank? ___ Ex-Im Bank Regional Office ___ Broker ___ Bank ___ U.S. Export Assistance Center ___ Ex-Im Bank City/State Partner ___ Other (describe***):*** ____________

1. Primary reason for application: ☐ risk mitigation ☐ financing ☐ extend more competitive terms
2. Do you have a credit line with a financial institution (exclude overdraft protection and credit cards) ☐ YES ☐ NO
3. Do you have an SBA or Ex-Im Bank Working Capital Loan or are you applying for one? SBA ☐ YES ☐ NO; EXIM ☐ YES ☐ NO
4. Total number of your employees and those at companies with whom you are affiliated: ______
5. Average total of annual export credit sales over the last two years for you and your affiliates:$ ____________
6. Do you wish to insure export credit sales made by your affiliates? (If yes, please refer to "additional named insured" eligibility criteria in question # 24. Answers to all remaining questions must include eligible affiliates you wish to add.)
7. Product and/or services to be exported & NAICS (if known): ____________
8. Do you sell Capital Goods to foreign manufacturers or producers? ☐ YES ☐ NO (if yes, attach explanation)
9. Are the products to be covered under the policy:
   - Manufactured or reconditioned in the U.S.? ☐Yes ☐No
   - Made or reconditioned with more than 50% U.S. content? ☐Yes ☐No
   - Shipped from the U.S.? ☐Yes ☐No
   - Sold to Military entities or Security Forces? ☐No ☐Yes
   - Used to support Nuclear Energy? ☐No ☐Yes
   - Environmentally Beneficial? ☐Yes ☐No
   - Supporting Renewable Energy? ☐Yes ☐No
   - On the U.S. Munitions List? (part 121 of title 22 of the Code of Federal Regulations) ☐No ☐Yes

Note: Your buyers, their guarantors (if any), and end users of the products must be in countries where Ex-Im Bank is able to provide support, see Ex-Im's Country Limitation Schedule (CLS) at www.exim,.gov . There may not be trade measures or sanctions against them under Section 201 Trade Act of 1974 . For a list of products and countries with Anti-Dumping or Countervailing Duty sanctions, see Anti-Dumping or Countervailing Sanctions).

10. Policy Payment Limit Requested: $ ____________ (maximum export credit receivables outstanding at any one time)
11. Buyer Types: ___% Manufacturers ___% Wholesalers/Traders ___% Retailers ___%Service Providers
12. Projected # of buyers to whom you will offer export credit terms: ______

EIB92-50 (04/06) **Page 1 of 4**

Figure 2–9. *(continued)*

OMB No. 3048-0023
Expires 08/31/2010

13. Enter the percentage of export credit sales by payment and term type projected for the next twelve months:

Payment Type	Terms (# of days) *(must total 100%, collectively)*							
	Sight	1-30	31-60	61-90	91-120	121-180	181-270	271-360
Unconfirmed L/C	___%	___%	___%	___%	___%	___%	___%	___%
Open account or Draft	___%	___%	___%	___%	___%	___%	___%	___%

(enter "Cash Against Documents" in the "Sight" column and "Open account/Draft" row)

14. Export Credit Portfolio (enter amounts for the next 12 months. If more than 9 countries, enter the balance in "all other").

Country	Export Credit Sales	Country	Export Credit Sales
	$		$
	$		$
	$		$
	$		$
	$	"all other countries"	$

15. Identify your three largest buyers:

Name	Country	Export Credit Sales (next 12 months)
____________	____________	$____________
____________	____________	$____________
____________	____________	$____________

16. Year you began: a) exporting? ______
b) exporting on credit terms (other than cash in advance or confirmed letters of credit)?_____

17. For the last three years what were your total export credit:
(include factored or insured receivables and attach any comments)

sales $____________
write-offs $____________
# of accounts written-off ____________

18. Highest average amount of export receivables outstanding over the last twelve months: $____________

19. Total export receivables outstanding: $____________ at ___/___/___ (date should be within 30 days of the application)

$________	$________	$________	$________	$________
current	1-60 days past due	61-90 days past due	91-180 days past due	> 180 days past due

20. Number of buyers past due more than 60 days for $10,000 or more: ____________

21. For each buyer over 60 days past due for $10,000 or more, attach an explanation including name of buyer, country, amount past due, due date, and reason for past due.

22. Name(s) of export credit decision maker(s):	Title(s):	Years of Credit Experience	Years of Foreign Credit Exp.
____________	____________	________	________
____________	____________	________	________

23. Please submit the following as Attachments:
- Credit Report on your company dated within 6 months of the application or attach a check for $35 payable to Ex-Im Bank.
- Your financial statements for the two most recent completed fiscal years (with notes if available)
- Descriptive product brochures (if available).
- Other pertinent information you wish to include.

EIB92-50 (04/06) **Page 2 of 4**

Figure 2–9. *(continued)*

OMB No. 3048-0023
Expires 08/31/2010

24. **Special Coverages** Required: If "none" check ☐ N/A

☐ **Add Additional Named Insureds (ANI's).** Credit decisions of each affiliate listed must be centralized with the Applicant and each affiliate must invoice export credit sales in their own name (or tradestyle); if either is not applicable, please attach an explanation. Questions 7-25 should include export sales of prospective ANI's.

Are the products of each affiliate the same as the applicant's products listed in question 4 of this application? ☐Yes ☐No

Affiliate Company/Trade style	Street Address/City / State / Country	NAICS Code	Relationship to Applicant

☐ **Services (Please attach a copy of your sample services contract)** Services must be: performed by U.S. based personnel or those temporarily domiciled overseas, and billed (invoiced) separately from any product sales.

☐ **Enhanced Assignment** of small business insurance policy proceeds. This is exporter performance risk protection that may be offered to lenders willing to finance Ex-Im Bank insured receivables. **Applicant Please Attach:**

- Written bank reference describing your relationship to date and size of existing credit line.
- 2 written trade references from principal commercial suppliers.
- For applications with policy limits over $500,000, financial statements must be audited or CPA reviewed with notes.

☐ **Other** (please specify):______________________________

25. Please complete the **Exclusion Worksheet on page 5** to request coverage exclusion of any export credit sales.

CERTIFICATIONS

The applicant certifies that neither it, nor its Principals, have within the past 3 years been a) debarred, suspended, declared ineligible from participating in, or voluntarily excluded from participation in, a Covered Transaction, b) formally proposed for debarment, with a final determination still pending, c) indicted, convicted or had a civil judgment rendered against it for any of the offenses listed in the Regulations, d) delinquent on any substantial debts owed to the U.S. Government or its agencies or instrumentalities as of the date of execution of this application; or e) the undersigned has received a written statement of exception from Ex-Im Bank attached to this certification, permitting participation in this Covered Transaction despite an inability to make certifications a) through d) in this paragraph.

The applicant further certifies that it has not and will not knowingly enter into any agreements, in connection with the products and services to be exported in the transaction described herein, with any individual or entity that has been debarred, suspended, declared ineligible from participating in, or voluntarily excluded from participation in a Covered Transaction. The term "Covered Transaction" shall have the meaning set forth in the Ex-Im Bank Debarment and Suspension Regulations at 12 C.F.R. Part 413 (Regulations).

In addition, the applicant further certifies that it has not, and will not, engage in any activity in connection with this transaction that is a violation of a) the Foreign Corrupt Practices Act of 1977, 15 U.S.C. 78dd-1 et seq. (which provides for civil and criminal penalties against individuals who directly or indirectly make or facilitate corrupt payments to foreign officials to obtain or keep business), b) the Arms Export Control Act, 22 U.S.C. 2751 et seq., c) the International Emergency Economic Powers Act, 50 U.S.C. 1701 et seq., or d) the Export Administration Act of 1979, 50 U.S.C. 2401 et seq.; nor been found by a court of the United States to be in violation of any of these statutes within the preceding 12 months, and to the best of its knowledge, the performance by the parties to this transaction of their respective obligations does not violate any other applicable law.

The applicant certifies that the representation made and the facts stated in this document and any attachments are true, to the best of its knowledge and belief, and it has not misrepresented or omitted any material facts, and if any of the certifications made herein become untrue, Ex-Im Bank will be promptly informed of such changes. The applicant further understands that these certifications are subject to the penalties for fraud against the U.S. Government (18 U.S.C. 1001 et seq.).

__________________ ________________________________

(Signature) (Print Name and Title) (Date)

EIB92-50 (04/06) **Page 3 of 4**

Figure 2–9. *(continued)*

OMB No. 3048-0023
Expires 08/31/2010

SMALL BUSINESS POLICIES APPLICANT CERTIFICATION

"We are an entity which **together with our affiliates** had **average annual export credit sales** during our preceding two fiscal years not exceeding **$5,000,000**, excluding sales made on terms of confirmed irrevocable letters of credit (CILC) or cash in advance (CIA)."

____
(Signature)

NOTICES

The applicant is hereby notified that information requested by this application is done so under authority of the Export-Import Bank Act of 1945, as amended (12 U.S.C. 635 et seq.); provision of this information is mandatory and failure to provide the requested information may result in Ex-Im Bank being unable to determine eligibility for support. The information provided will be reviewed to determine the participants' ability to perform and pay under the transaction referenced in this application. Ex-Im Bank may not require the information and applicants are not required to provide information requested in this application unless a currently valid OMB control number is displayed on this form (see upper right of each page).

Public Burden Statement: Reporting for this collection of information is estimated to average 1 hour per response, including reviewing instructions, searching data sources, gathering information, completing, and reviewing the application. Send comments regarding the burden estimate, including suggestions for reducing it, to Office of Management and Budget, Paperwork Reduction Project OMB# 3048-0009, Washington, D.C. 20503.

Send, or ask your insurance broker or city/state participant to review and send this application to the Ex-Im Bank Regional Office nearest you. Please refer to Ex-Im Bank's website at http://www.exim.gov for Regional Office addresses. Alternatively, email your application and attachments to Ex-Im Bank at exim.applications@exim.gov, or fax it to (202) 565-3675.

Ex-Im Bank reserves the right to request additional information upon review of the application. Please refer to Ex-Im Bank's Short Term Credit Standards (EIB 99-09) to determine the likelihood of approval of a policy.

EIB92-50 (04/06)

Page 4 of 4

Figure 2–10. Application for export trade certificate of review.

OMB Approved 0625-0125
Expires 09/30/2008

Form ITA-4093P LF
(6-05)

U.S. DEPARTMENT OF COMMERCE
International Trade Administration

APPLICATION FOR AN EXPORT TRADE CERTIFICATE OF REVIEW

No Export Trade Certificate may be issued unless a completed application form has been received (15 USC 4011-4021).

Special Action

☐ Application for Amendment

☐ Request for Expedited Review

See instructions below

DEPARTMENT OF COMMERCE USE ONLY

NAME OF APPLICANT	DATE RECEIVED	DATE DEEMED SUBMITTED
TRACKING SYSTEM NUMBER	MONITOR	

CONFIDENTIALITY OF APPLICATION

Information submitted by any person in connection with the issuance, amendment, or revocation of a Certificate of Review is exempt from disclosure under the Freedom of Information Act, Section 552, Title 5, United States Code.

Except as provided under Section 309(b)(2) of the Export Trading Company Act ("ACT") and 15 CFR 325.16(b)(3), no officer or employee of the United States shall disclose commercial or financial information submitted pursuant to the Act if the information is privileged or confidential and if disclosure of the information would cause harm to the person who submitted the information.

OTHER CONSIDERATIONS

NOTE: The exchange among competitors of competitively sensitive information may, in some circumstances, create risks that competition among the firms will be lessened and antitrust questions raised. The exchange of information about recent or future prices, production, sales or confidential business plans is especially sensitive. As a general matter, the danger that such exchanges will have anticompetitive effects is less when the firms involved have a small share of the market and greater if they have a substantial share.

Applicant may wish to consider seeking the advice of legal counsel on whether any steps would be advisable in the applicant's particular circumstances to avoid issues of this nature. One possible step that the applicant may wish to consider in preparing the application is to compile and submit these types of information through an unrelated third party, such as an attorney or consultant.

INSTRUCTIONS

The Department of Commerce urges applicants to read Title III of the Export Trading Company Act (P.L. 97-290, Section 4011-4021, Title 15, United States Code) and the accompanying regulations (Volume 15, Code of Federal Regulations, Part 325) and the guidelines (50 FR 1786) before completing this application form. These documents and additional information and guidance on the certification program are available free from Export Trading Company Affairs, Telephone (202) 482-5131, and can also be found at www.ita.doc.gov/oetca.

Space is provided on the attached form for some of the information requested. In most cases you are being asked to supply additional information on supplemental sheets or attachments. Please include the name of the applicant on each supplement or attachment, and specifically identify the item number to which the attachment refers. The two certifying statements on the last page of this form MUST be completed before your application will be deemed submitted.

Designate the documents or information which you consider privileged or confidential and disclosure of which would cause you harm.

File an original and two copies of the completed application either by first class mail, or registered mail to: Export Trading Company Affairs, International Trade Administration, Room 7021X, U.S. Department of Commerce, Washington, DC 20230; or by personal courier service during business hours to: U.S. Department of Commerce Courier Center, Room 1874.

In response to the questions in this application the applicant is requested to be as specific as possible.
Some information, in particular the identification of goods or services that the applicant exports or proposes to export, is requested in a certain form (North American Industry Classification System (NAICS) if reasonably available.) Where information does not exist in the requested form, an applicant is not required to create it, and may satisfy the request for information by providing it in some other convenient form.

NOTE:. It may not be necessary for every applicant to respond to every question on this form. If an applicant believes that certain information requested is not necessary for a determination on the application, the applicant may request a waiver prior to submitting the application. The applicant should contact Export Trading Company Affairs on (202) 482-5131.

AGENCY DISCLOSURE OF ESTIMATED BURDEN

Public reporting for this collection of information is estimated to be 32 hours per response, including the time for reviewing instructions, and completing and reviewing the collection of information. All responses to this collection are voluntary. Notwithstanding any other provision of law, no person is required to respond to nor shall a person be subject to a penalty for failure to comply with a collection of information subject to the requirements of the Paperwork Reduction Act unless that collection of information displays a current valid OMB Control Number. Send comments regarding the burden estimate or any other aspect of this collection of information, including suggestions for reducing this burden, to the Reports Clearance Officer, International Trade Administration, Department of Commerce, Room 4001, 14th and Constitution Avenue, N.W. Washington, DC 20230.

Figure 2–10. *(continued)*

ITEM 1: Applicant/Organizer Information

Name of Applicant:

Principal Address: ______________________________
Street Room or Suite

City State Zip

Name of Applicant's Controlling Entity, if any (if none enter "none"):

Principal Address:
Street Room or Suite

City State Zip

Individual(s) authorized by the applicant to submit application and to whom all correspondence should be addressed:

Name:

Title:

Address: ______________________________
Street Room or Suite

City State Zip

Telephone:

Relationship to Applicant:

ITEM 2: Name and principal address of each member, and of each member's controlling entity, if any.
(Attach your response to this application, clearly identifying the attachment as response to ITEM 2.)
Note - the members of a Certificate are all firms or entities that are covered by and receive the protection of the Certificate other than the applicant itself.

ITEM 3: A copy of any legal instrument under which the applicant is organized or will operate. Include copies, as appropriate, of its corporate charter, bylaws, partnership, joint venture, membership, or other agreements or contracts under which the applicant is organized.
(Attach your response to this application, clearly identifying the attachment as response to ITEM 3.)

ITEM 4: A copy of the applicant's most recent annual report, if any, and that of its controlling entity, if any.
(Attach your response to this application, clearly identifying the attachment as response to ITEM 4.)

To the extent the information is not included in the annual report, or in other documents submitted in connection with this application, attach a brief description of the applicant's domestic, import and export operations, including:
(a) The nature of its business; (Export facilitators or intermediaries who are available to export any type of product or service but who do not manufacture, produce, or directly provide any products or services may respond "all products and services." To the extent that a facilitator or intermediary specializes, please describe such products and/or services)
(b) The role of the applicant with respect to the proposed Certificate and the Certificate's members and methods of operations.
(c) The location(s) of its operations .
(d) The geographic location of its customers (foreign and domestic).

(This description may be supplemented by a chart or table.)

ITEM 5: A copy of each member's most recent annual report, if any, and that of its controlling entity, if any.

(continues)

Figure 2–10. *(continued)*

(Attach to this application, clearly identifying attachment as response to ITEM 5.)

To the extent the information is not included in the annual report, or in other documents submitted in connection with this application, attach a brief description of each member's domestic, import, and export operations, including:
(a) The nature of its business;
(b) The locations of its operations.
(c) The geographic location of its customers (foreign and domestic) .

(This description may be supplemented by a chart or table.)

ITEM 6:
(A) Names, titles, and responsibilities of the applicant's directors, officers, partners, and managing officials, and
(B) their business affiliations with the members or other businesses that produce or sell any of the types of goods or services described in ITEM 7, below.
(Attach your response to this application, clearly identifying the attachment as response to ITEM 6.)

ITEM 7(A): A description of the goods or services that the applicant exports or proposes to export under the Certificate. This description should reflect the industry's customary definitions of products and services and should include a description of the product's purpose or use. If the information is reasonably available, please identify the goods or services according to the North American Industry Classification System (NAICS) . Goods should normally be identified at the 6-digit level. Services should be identified at the most detailed level possible.
(Attach your response to this application clearly identifying the attachment as response to ITEM 7(A).)

ITEM 7(B): For each of the previous two fiscal years please provide the dollar value of the applicant's and each member's (i) total domestic sales, if any, and (ii) total export sales, if any. Include separately the value of sales of any controlling entities and all entities under their control.
(Attach your response to this application, clearly identifying the attachment as response to ITEM 7(B).)

ITEM 7(C) For *each* product or service to be covered by the Certificate, indicate the best information or estimate accessible to the applicant of the total value of sales in the United States by all companies (whether or not members of the proposed Certificate) for each of the last two (2) years. Identify the source of the information or the basis of the estimate. If the proposed Certificate will cover "all products and services" you may skip this item.
(Attach your response to this application, clearly identifying the attachment as response to ITEM 7(C).)

ITEM 7(D): Provide the following background information:
(a) For *each* product to be covered by the Certificate
1. The estimated number of domestic producers selling in the U.S. market;
2 . The estimated number of importers and/or foreign producers who directly supply product in the U.S. market;
3. A list of the top five competitors who are *not* proposed members of this Certificate, in terms of sales in the U.S. market, and an estimate of their respective (%) share in the U.S market;
4. The estimated share of the U.S. market accounted for by the firms to be covered by the Certificate;
(b) Other products with the same or similar purpose or use as the product to be covered by the proposed Certificate;
1. The estimated number of domestic producers selling in the U.S. market;
2. The estimated number of importers and/or foreign producers who directly supply product in the U.S. market;

Please provide any other background or industry information that the applicant believes will be necessary or helpful to a determination of whether to issue a Certificate under the standards of the Export Trading Company Act.
(Attach your response to this application, clearly identifying the attachment as response to ITEM 7(D).)

For each class of the goods, wares, merchandise, or services set forth in ITEM 7:

ITEM 8(A): Please provide the following information:

(a) for each class of the goods, wares, merchandise, or services set forth in ITEM 7(A), please provide the principal geographic areas or areas in the United States in which the applicant and each member sell their goods and services.
(b) for each class of the goods, wares, merchandise, or services set forth in ITEM 7(D)(a), please provide the principal geographic areas or areas in the United States in which these products are sold.
(Attach your response to this application, clearly identifying the attachment as response to ITEM 8 (A).)

ITEM 8(B): Identify the foreign geographic areas to which the applicant and each member intend to export their goods and services. If applicable state "worldwide".
(Attach your response to this application, clearly identifying the attachment as response to ITEM 8(B).)

ITEM 9: Describe the specific export conduct which the applicant seeks to have certified. Only the specific export conduct described in the application will be eligible for certification.

Examples of export conduct that applicants may seek to have certified include the manner in which goods and services will be obtained or provided; the manner in which prices or quantities will be set; exclusive agreements with U.S. suppliers or export intermediaries; territorial, quantity, or price agreements with U.S. suppliers or export intermediaries; and restrictions on membership or membership withdrawal.

(These examples are given only to illustrate the type of export conduct which might be of concern. The specific activities that the applicant may wish to have certified will depend on the applicant's particular circumstances or business plans.)
(Attach your response to this application, clearly identifying attachment as response to ITEM 9.)

ITEM 10: If the export trade, export trade activities, or methods of operation for which certification is sought will involve any agreement or

Figure 2–10. *(continued)*

any exchange of information among suppliers of the same or similar products or services with respect to domestic prices, production, sales, or other competitively sensitive business information, specify the nature of and need for the agreement or exchange of information.
(Attach your response to this application, clearly identifying the attachment as response to ITEM 11.)

ITEM 11: A statement whether the applicant intends or reasonably expects that any exported goods or services covered by the proposed Certificate will re-enter the United States, either in its original or modified form. If so, identify the goods or services and the manner in which they may re-enter the United States.
(Attach your response to this application, clearly identifying the attachment as response to ITEM 12)

ITEM 12: For the goods and services to be exported, provide (if known) the names and addresses of the suppliers (and the goods and services to be supplied by each) unless the goods and services to be exported are to be supplied by the applicant and/or its members only.
(Attach your response to this application, clearly identifying the attachment as response to ITEM 13.)

ITEM 13: (Optional) A proposed draft Certificate.
(Attach your response to this application, clearly identifying the attachment as response to ITEM 13.)

ITEM 14: If the applicant is requesting expedited review of its application, specify the facts and circumstances which warrant it in the space below. The justification should explain why expedited action is needed, such as bidding deadlines, infrequent shipping service to the point of destination, or other circumstances beyond the control of the applicant that require the applicant to act in less than 90 days, and that have significant impact on the applicant's export trade. The justification should include the dollar value of export sales that would be lost if an expedited review is not granted.
(If additional space is necessary, attach your response to this application, clearly identifying the attachment as response to ITEM 14.)

CERTIFICATIONS

I certify that the applicant named in ITEM 1 above and each of the members listed in ITEM 2 above has authorized me to submit this application and the attachments, and to represent the applicant and members, if any, in seeking an Export Trade Certificate of Review.

TYPED OR PRINTED NAME   SIGNATURE (SIGN IN INK)   DATE

I certify that to the best of my knowledge and belief that the information submitted in this application and the attachments is true and correct and fully responds to all items in the application.

TYPED OR PRINTED NAME   SIGNATURE (SIGN IN INK)   DATE

FORM ITA 4093-P (REV. 06-05)   USCOMM-DC 85-2 1655

Figure 2–11. Export trade certificate of review.

ExportTrade Certificate of Review Promotion Program   Page 1 of 6

Export Trading Company Affairs

HOME

News	Federal Register Notices	myEXPORTS	Certificate of Review	Application Instructions

Export Trade Certificate of Review-Sample 1

Company A, a limited liability company, has applied to the Secretary of Commerce for an Export Trade Certificate of Review under Title III of the Export Trading Company Act of 1982, 15 U.S.C. && 4011-4021, (the Act), and its implementing regulations, 15 C.F.R. pt. 325 (1999), (the Regulations).

The application was deemed submitted on XXXX, and a summary of the application was published in the Federal Register on XXXX.

The Secretary of Commerce and the Attorney General have reviewed the application and other information in their possession.

Based on analysis of this information, the Secretary of Commerce has determined, and the Attorney General concurs, that the Export Trade and Export Trade Activities and Methods of Operation set forth below meet the four standards set forth in Section 303(a) of the Act.

Accordingly, under the authority of the Act and the Regulations, Company A and its Members are certified to engage in the Export Trade Activities and Methods of Operation described below in the following Export Trade and Export Markets:

EXPORT TRADE

1. Products

California almonds in processed and unprocessed form.

2. Export Trade Facilitation Services (as they relate to the Export of Products)

All export trade-related facilitation services, including but not limited to: development of trade strategy; sales, marketing, and distribution; foreign market development; promotion; and all aspects of foreign sales transactions, including export brokerage, freight ; forwarding, transportation, insurance, billing, collection, trade documentation, and foreign exchange; customs, duties, and taxes; and inspection and quality control.

EXPORT MARKETS

The Export Markets include all parts of the world except the United States (the fifty states of the United States, the District of Columbia, the Commonwealth of Puerto Rico, the Virgin Islands, American Samoa, Guam, the Commonwealth of Northern Mariana Islands, and the Trust Territory of the Pacific Islands).

http://ita.doc.gov/td/oetca/sample1.htm   4/11/2009

Figure 2–11. *(continued)*

EXPORT TRADE ACTIVITIES AND METHODS OF OPERATION

1. Company A, on its own behalf or on behalf of all or less than all of its Members, through Company A or through Export Intermediaries (to the extent provided in section 1.g) may:

Sales Prices. Establish sale prices, minimum sale prices, target sale prices and/or minimum target sale prices, and other terms of sale;

Marketing and Distribution. Conduct marketing and distribution of Products;

Promotion. Conduct promotion of Products;

Quantities. Agree on quantities of Products to be sold, provided each Member shall be required to dedicate only such quantity or quantities as each such Member shall independently determine. Company A shall not require any Member to export a minimum quantity;

Market and Customer Allocation. Allocate geographic areas or countries in the Export Markets and/or customers in the Export Markets among Members;

Refusals to Deal. Refuse to quote prices for Products, or to market or sell Products, to or for any customers in the Export Markets, or any countries or geographical areas in the Export Markets;

Exclusive and Nonexclusive Export Intermediaries. Enter into exclusive and nonexclusive agreements appointing one or more Export Intermediaries (as defined under "Definitions" paragraph 1) for the sale of Products with price, quantity, territorial and/or customer restrictions as provided in sections 1.a through 1.f, inclusive, above; and

Non-Member Activities. Purchase Products from non-Members to fulfill specific sales obligations, provided that Company A and/or its Members shall make such purchases only on a transaction-by-transaction basis and when the Members are unable to supply, in a timely manner, the requisite Products at a price competitive under the circumstances. In no event shall a non-Member be included in any deliberations concerning any Export Trade Activities.

Company A and its Members may exchange and discuss the following information:

Information about sale and marketing efforts for the Export Markets, activities and opportunities for sales of Products in the Export Markets, selling strategies for the Export Markets, sales for the Export Markets, contract and spot pricing in the Export Markets, projected demands in the Export Markets for Products, customary terms of sale in the Export Markets, prices and availability of Products from competitors for sale in the Export Markets, and specifications for Products by customers in the Export Markets;

Information about the price, quality, quantity, source, and delivery dates of Products available from the Members to export;

Figure 2–11. *(continued)*

Information about terms and conditions of contracts for sale in the Export Markets to be considered and/or bid on by Company A and its Members;

Information about joint bidding or selling arrangements for the Export Markets and allocations of sales resulting from such arrangements among the Members;

Information about expenses specific to exporting to and within the Export Markets, including without limitation, transportation, trans- or intermodal shipments, insurance, inland freight to port, port storage, commissions, export sales, documentation, financing, customs, duties, and taxes;

Information about U.S. and foreign legislation and regulations, including federal marketing order programs, affecting sales for the Export Markets;

Information about Company A or its Members' export operations, including without limitation, sales and distribution networks established by Company A or its Members in the Export Markets, and prior export sales by Members (including export price information); and

Information about export customer credit terms and credit history.

Company A and its Members may prescribe the following conditions for admission of Members to Company A and termination of membership in Company A:

Membership shall be limited to Handlers as defined under "Definitions" paragraph 2.

Membership shall terminate on the occurrence of one or more of the following events:

i. Withdrawal or resignation of a Member;

Expulsion approved by a majority of all Members for a material violation of Company A's Operating Agreement, after prior written notice to the Member proposed to be expelled and an opportunity of such Member to appear and be heard before a meeting of the Members;

Death or permanent disability of a Member who is an individual or the dissolution of a Member other than an individual; and

The bankruptcy of a Member as provided in Company A's Operating Agreement.

Company A and its Members may meet to engage in the activities described in paragraphs 1 through 3 above.

DEFINITIONS

1. "Export Intermediary" means a person (including a Member) who acts as a distributor, sales representative, sales or marketing agent, or broker, or who performs similar functions, including providing, or arranging for the provision of,

Figure 2–11. *(continued)*

Export Trade Facilitation Services.

2. "Handler" means a person who handles almonds grown in California as defined in 7 C.F.R. § 981.13, under the Order Regulating Handling of Almonds Grown in California.

3. "Member," within the meaning of section 325.2(*l*) of the Regulations, means the members of Company A as set out in Attachment A and incorporated by reference.

TERMS AND CONDITIONS OF CERTIFICATE

1. Except as provided in paragraph 2(b) and (e) of the Export Trade Activities and Methods of Operation above, Company A and its Members shall not intentionally disclose, directly or indirectly, to any Handler (including Members) any information about its or any other Handler's costs, production, capacity, inventories, domestic prices, domestic sales, domestic orders, terms of domestic marketing or sale, or U.S. business plans, strategies or methods, unless: (1) such information is already generally available to the trade or public; (2) such disclosure is a necessary term or condition of an actual or potential bona fide sale or purchase of Products and the disclosure is limited to that prospective purchaser or seller; or (3) such disclosure is made in connection with the administration of the United States Department of Agriculture marketing order for almonds grown in California.

2. Each Member shall determine independently of other Members the quantity of Products the Member will make available for export or sell through Company A. Company A may not solicit from any Member specific quantities for export or require any Member to export any minimum quantity of Products.

3. Meetings at which Company A allocates export sales among Members and establishes export prices shall not be open to the public.

4. Participation by a Member in any Export Trade Activity or Method of Operation under this Certificate shall be entirely voluntary as to that Member, subject to the honoring of contractual commitments for sales of Products in specific export transactions. A Member may withdraw from coverage under this Certificate at any time by giving a written notice to Company A, a copy of which Company A shall promptly transmit to the Secretary of Commerce and the Attorney General.

5. Any agreements, discussions, or exchanges of information under this Certificate relating to quantities of Products available for Export Markets, Product specifications or standards, export prices, Product quality or other terms and conditions of export sales (other than export financing) shall be in connection only with actual or potential bona fide export transactions or opportunities and shall include only those Members participating or having a genuine interest in participating in such transactions or opportunities; provided that Company A and/or the Members may discuss standardization of Products for purposes of making bona fide recommendations to foreign governmental or private standard-

Figure 2–11. *(continued)*

setting organizations.

6. Company A and its Members will comply with requests made by the Secretary of Commerce, on behalf of the Secretary or the Attorney General, for information or documents relevant to conduct under the Certificate. The Secretary of Commerce will request such information or documents when either the Attorney General or the Secretary believes that the information or documents are required to determine that the Export Trade, Export Trade Activities and Methods of Operation of a person protected by this Certificate of Review continue to comply with the standards of section 303(a) of the Act.

PROTECTION PROVIDED BY CERTIFICATE

The Certificate protects Company A, its Members, and their directors, officers, and employees acting on their behalf, from private treble damage actions and government criminal and civil suits under U.S. federal and state antitrust laws for the export conduct specified in this Certificate and carried out during its effective period in compliance with its terms and conditions.

EFFECTIVE PERIOD OF CERTIFICATE

This Certificate continues in effect from the effective date indicated below until it is revoked or modified as provided in the Act and the Regulations.

OTHER CONDUCT

Nothing in this Certificate prohibits Company A and its Members from engaging in conduct not specified in this Certificate, but such conduct is subject to the normal application of the antitrust laws.

DISCLAIMER

The issuance of this Certificate of Review to Company A by the Secretary of Commerce with the concurrence of the Attorney General under the provisions of the Act does not constitute, explicitly or implicitly, an endorsement or opinion by the Secretary of Commerce or by the Attorney General concerning either (a) the viability or quality of the business plans of Company A or its Members or (b) the legality of such business plans of Company A or its Members under the laws of the United States (other than as provided in the Act) or under the laws of any foreign country.

The application of this Certificate to conduct in Export Trade where the United States Government is the buyer or where the United States Government bears more than half the cost of the transaction is subject to the limitations set forth in section V(D) of the "Guidelines for the Issuance of Export Trade Certificates of Review (Second Edition)," 50 Fed. Reg. 1786 (Jan. 11, 1985).

* * * * *

In accordance with the authority granted under the Act and Regulations, this

Figure 2–11. *(continued)*

Export Trade Certificate of Review is hereby issued to Applicant.

ATTACHMENT A

Members (within the meaning of section 325.2(*l*) of the Regulations):

8 members listed

purchase from the manufacturer, paying in advance and making their compensation through a resale markup rather than a commission. In actuality, some EMCs and ETCs do both.

W. Translation

An exporter should give sufficient forethought to the necessity of translating its advertising materials, instructions, warranties, and labeling into the language of the destination country. Not only will this be necessary in order to achieve sales, but failure to do so can lead to legal liabilities. For example, if a patent application is not properly translated, the rights may be lost. Some countries require that certain labeling be in their language. The location of a competent translator and completion of the translation may require significant lead time and, depending on the quantity of material, involve a significant expense.

X. Foreign Branch Operations, Subsidiaries, Joint Ventures, and Licensing

Sometimes the exporter will be exporting to its or its parent company's existing branch or subsidiary company in a foreign country. Or, rather than selling to an independent distributor, utilizing a sales agent, or selling directly to the end user, the exporter may decide to establish such a branch operation or subsidiary company. If personnel are available to staff the foreign branch or company, this step may increase the exporter's marketing penetration and may smooth export and import operations. Similarly, the exporter may form a joint venture with a foreign company to manufacture or market the exporter's products in one or more foreign countries. Where laws prohibit the importation of the exporter's products or where transportation costs or delays are unreasonable, the exporter may need to license a foreign company to manufacture the product and sell it in that market in return for payment of a royalty. All of these methods of doing business will require some modifications to the sales and other export and import documentation and procedures. For example, sales to affiliated companies often raise income tax issues involving transfer pricing and the related issue of proper customs valuation. License royalties may in certain circumstances be dutiable, and licensed technology may require export control approvals. A recent problem is the inadequacy of sales and purchase documentation for export audits due to simplified electronic ordering procedures between affiliated companies.

Y. Electronic Commerce

The development of the Internet and e-mail and the proliferation of web sites have created a revolution in electronic commerce. Because of the essentially worldwide availability of the Internet and access to web sites, new issues for cross-border exporting and importing have arisen. This has opened a new channel of direct marketing using electronic catalogs and has created conflict with the seller's traditional foreign distribution channels, such as distributors and sales agents. Sellers are more interested in marketing internationally and are forced to cope with the logistical issues that arise from purchase orders from abroad. Some of the more important issues that must be considered and managed include the following:

- *Validity and enforceability of electronic sales contracts.* This concern has required the consideration and development of legal terms of sale on the web site that are modified and appropriate for foreign as well as domestic customers. It has also forced the use of "click-wrap" agreements to record the purchaser's agreement to the sales terms and authentication procedures to confirm that the person purporting to place the order is actually that person. For low-price items, sellers may be willing to accept the risk of lack of enforceability of the sales contract, but for expensive items or ongoing business, this is not feasible. Many sellers have required their distributors and customers who are making ongoing purchases to sign hard-copy "umbrella" agreements at the outset of the relationship before undertaking electronic sales. This is a less satisfactory solution for onetime purchasers.
- *Delivery and logistics.* At least with direct sales to consumers, and for consumer goods, customers want and expect the convenience of direct delivery to their door. These "delivered duty paid" terms of sale are almost a necessity for this type of business. Customers also want prompt delivery, which is difficult to achieve if there is no stock of inventory in the buyer's country. For smaller products, delivery by international courier services such as UPS, Federal Express, and DHL has become more practical. In such cases, the transportation carrier is also able to act as the customs broker in the foreign country, paying customs duties and value-added taxes and billing them back to the seller. For large capital goods, however—such as in business-to-business (B2B) transactions, where the issues of containerized or other packaging, transportation booking, export licenses or permits, foreign customs clearance, and lack of skilled in-house personnel, require the use of a freight forwarder—have limited the expansion of Internet sales. Challenges continue to exist relating to establishing in-country inventory for immediate delivery without the expenses of establishing branch offices or subsidiary companies.
- *Price.* Since many customers want to have delivery to their door, when they see a price quotation on a Web site, they expect to see an "all-in" (delivered duty paid) price. The difficulty of maintaining up-to-date quotations online, including freight charges, insurance, duties, quotas, and value-added taxes for multiple countries of the world, has forced many sellers to hire software companies that offer such services.
- *Payment.* For low-price consumer goods, payment by credit card has enabled sellers to increase Internet sales. However, the fact that credit card purchases are not guaranteed payments and the virtual impossibility of pursuing a collection lawsuit overseas because of prohibitive cost has limited expansion. For expensive purchases or ongoing accounts, the seller may need the security of a letter of credit or documents against payment. On the other side, buyers dislike having to pay for purchases in advance without inspection of the goods. Where the seller has done business in the past on open account, or is willing to do so in the future, Internet sales can be practical.

- *Taxation.* Although one of the great spurs to the growth of electronic commerce in the past has been the ability to avoid certain taxes in certain countries, such as sales, value-added, corporate franchise, or personal property taxes, there is an increasing demand by governments to recover those tax revenues that are being lost. It is likely that some forms of taxation will increase and sellers may have to comply with foreign tax claims.
- *Information security.* Although there has been significant progress in maintaining the confidentiality of information transmitted over the Internet, the sophistication of "hackers" has also increased. For information from credit card numbers to purchase order numbers and customer lists, confidentiality, particularly from competitors and fraud artists, is crucial. The most secure current technologies using "key" systems are cumbersome, especially for small orders and onetime sales. Furthermore, exporting such software may require an export license.

Despite the foregoing difficulties, the outlook is good that more creative ways of dealing with these problems will evolve and that Internet sales will continue to expand.

Chapter 3

Exporting: Sales Documentation

The single most important document in the export sale is the sales agreement. Repeat: The single most important document in the export sale is the sales agreement! Most of the problems that occur in exporting can be eliminated or greatly reduced by using a suitable sales agreement. Generally, different types of sales agreements are used for isolated sales transactions and for ongoing sales transactions. I will discuss these as well as look at the important provisions in international sales agreements, distribution agreements, and sales agent agreements.

A. Isolated Sales Transactions

For the purposes of discussion in this chapter, isolated sales transactions are defined as situations where, for example, the customer purchases infrequently, or where sales are made on a trial basis in the anticipation of establishing an ongoing sales relationship, or when a customer is not being granted any credit until a satisfactory history of payment has been established. Sales agreements for such transactions should be in writing, and the seller and buyer may use a variety of common, preprinted forms. The seller should check carefully to try to eliminate as much as possible any conflicting provisions between the seller's forms and the forms received from the buyer.

1. *Importance of Written Agreements*

In some industries, for example, the commodities industry, it is common to conduct purchases and sales orally through telephone orders and acceptances. Sometimes oral agreements occur in international sales when the seller receives an order at a trade show, by long-distance telephone, or in a meeting. (Under the Convention on Contracts for the International Sale of Goods discussed in Section B.2.m, a sales agreement may be formed or modified orally.) It is highly advisable to formalize the purchase and sale agreement in a written document, even for domestic sales, and there are many additional reasons why export sales should be embodied in a written agreement. Under the Uniform Commercial Code applicable in the United States, if the sale exceeds $500 in value, an agreement to sell, and therefore to get paid for the sale, is enforceable by the seller only if the agreement is in writing. While there are some exceptions to this law, and sometimes even informal notes will be sufficient to create an enforceable sales agreement, by far the safest practice is to formalize the sales agreement in a written document signed by the parties.

In addition to legal issues, an old Chinese proverb states: "The lightest ink is better than the brightest memory." This is one way of saying that disputes in international sales transactions often arise because the parties did not record their agreement or failed to discuss an issue and reach agreement. A written sales agreement acts both as a checklist to remind the buyer and seller what they should discuss and agree upon and as a written record of their agreement. All modifications of the agreement should also be in writing.

2. *Email or Facsimile Orders*

While an email or facsimile order and acceptance can satisfy the legal requirements of written evidence of an agreement, such sales agreements commonly contain only the specification of the quantity, usually a price, and sometimes a shipment date. There are many other terms and conditions of sale that should be inserted in a good sales agreement, and a simple acceptance by the seller of such email or facsimile orders will fall far short of adequately protecting the seller in case of problems in the transaction. Consequently, acceptances of orders by email or facsimile should specifically and expressly state that the sale incorporates the seller's other standard terms and conditions of sale. Those additional terms and conditions of sale should be included in the seller's email or facsimile response to the buyer so that there can be no argument that the buyer was not aware of such terms and conditions of sale before proceeding with the transaction.

3. *The Formation of Sales Agreements*

The sales agreement is a formal contract governed by law. In general, a sales agreement is formed by agreement between the seller and the buyer and is the passing of title to and ownership of goods for a price. An agreement is a mutual manifestation of assent to the same terms. Agreements are ordinarily reached by a process of offer and acceptance. This process of offer and acceptance can proceed by the seller and the buyer preparing a sales agreement contained in a single document that is signed by both parties; by the exchange of documents such as purchase orders and purchase order acceptances; or by conduct, such as when the buyer offers to purchase and the seller ships the goods.

Particularly in light of the high-speed nature of business these days, from the point of view of clarity and reducing risks, preparation of a sales agreement contained in a single document is best. Both parties negotiate the agreement by exchanges of emails or faxes, or in person. Before proceeding with performance of any part of the transaction, both parties reach agreement and sign the same sales agreement. This gives both the seller and the buyer the best opportunity to understand the terms and conditions under which the other intends to transact business, and to negotiate and resolve any differences or conflicts. This type of sales agreement is often used if the size of the transaction is large; if the seller is concerned about payment or the buyer is concerned about manufacture and shipment; or if there are particular risks involved, such as government regulations or exchange controls, or differences in culture, language, or business customs that might create misunderstandings.

Quite often, however, the process of formation of the sales agreement is an exchange of documents that the seller and buyer have independently prepared and that, in the aggregate, constitute the sales agreement. These documents may contain differences and conflicts. Figure 3–1 shows the chronology of exchange and common documents used in many sales transactions. Although not all documents will be used in all sales transactions, these documents are in common use.

Several questions arise when a sales transaction is formed by such an exchange of documents. The first relates to the time of formation of the sales agreement. For example, a seller or buyer may send certain preliminary inquiries or information, such as a price list, without intending to actually offer to sell or place an order, but may find that the other party's understanding (or the applicable law) has created a binding sales agreement prior to the first party's intention. This can arise because under some countries' laws, an offer to sell or buy is accepted when the acceptance is dispatched, rather than when it is received. It can also arise because silence can be considered as acceptance if the parties are merchants.

Figure 3–1. Formation of sales agreements.

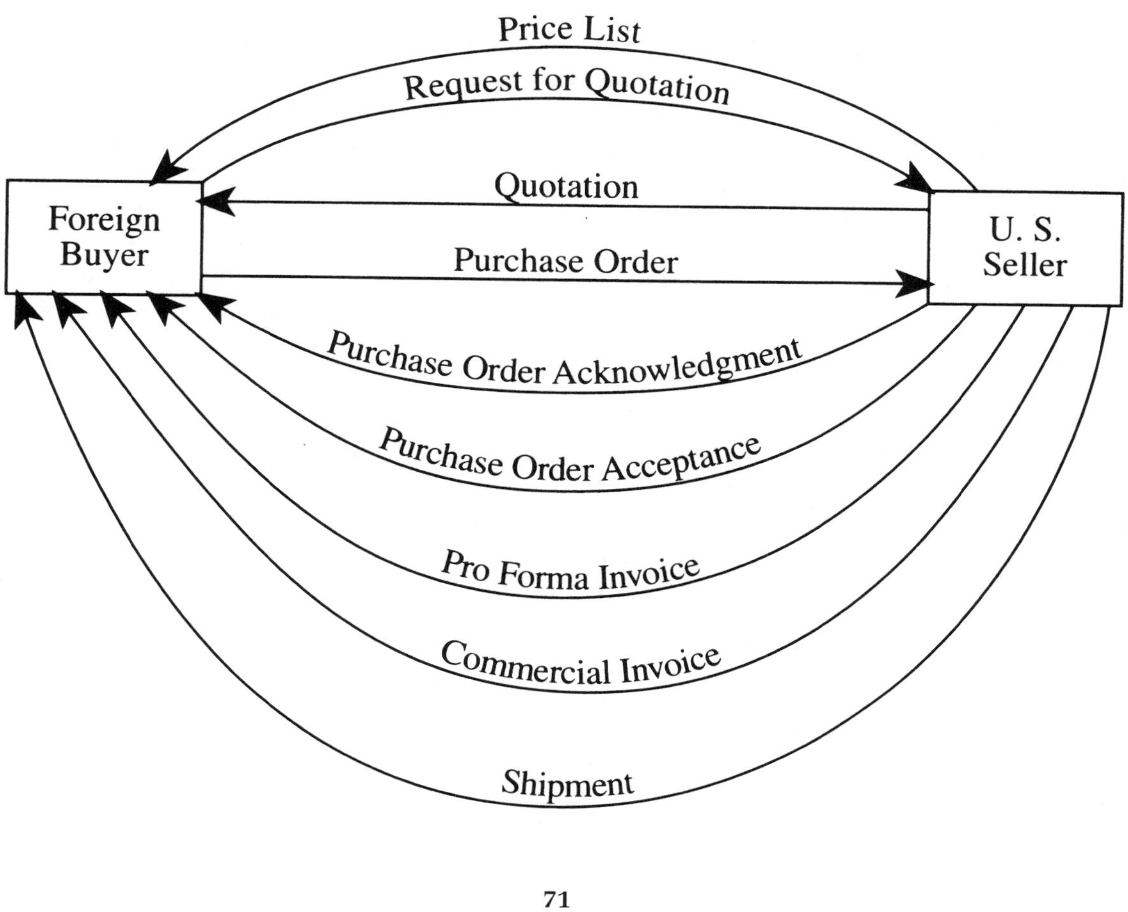

The second issue that arises relates to the governing law. Contracts are often governed by the law of the country where the contract is negotiated and performed or where the offer to sell or buy was accepted. Since an international agreement may be partly negotiated and partly performed in both countries, and since there may be a question as to whether the buyer accepted the offer to sell or the seller accepted the offer to purchase, situations can arise where the sales agreement is governed by the law of the buyer's country. Since foreign law may be quite different from U.S. law, the seller's rights and responsibilities may differ greatly from what she anticipated. Customary local ways of doing business, called trade usages, may unknowingly become a part of the sales agreement under the sales laws of some countries. Sellers and buyers sometimes try to resolve this problem by including a governing law term in their documents, but again, these may conflict.

A final method of formation of a sales agreement involves conduct. A simple example is where a buyer sends a purchase order and the seller, without communicating, simply ships the goods; or if the seller offers to sell the goods and the buyer simply sends payment. In such cases, the conduct in accepting the offer will include all of the terms and conditions of the offer. If the seller is not satisfied with the buyer's terms and conditions of purchase, he should send some communication to negotiate those terms before simply shipping the goods.

4. *Common Forms for the Formation of Sales Agreements*

There are a number of forms customarily used in the formation of sales agreements. In order to save time (and discourage changes by the other party), both buyers and sellers often purchase preprinted forms from commercial stationers or develop and preprint their own forms. Not all of the same documents are used by the seller or the buyer in all sales transactions. For example, a seller may submit a quotation to a potential buyer without receiving any request for quotation, or the first communication the seller receives may be a purchase order from the buyer. However, it is important to be familiar with the various forms and the role they play in bringing the negotiations to agreement.

a. Price Lists

Sometimes a seller will send a price list to a prospective buyer as its first communication. Ordinarily, such price lists would not be considered as an offer to sell, entitling the buyer to immediately accept. However, in order to prevent the unexpected formation of a sales agreement, such price lists should specify that this is not an offer to sell and no agreement will arise until a purchase order has been received and accepted. Such price lists should also specify their expiration date and that they are subject to change.

b. Requests for Quotations

Sometimes the first document involved in the formation of a sales agreement is a request from the buyer to the seller for a quotation (RFQ). Ordinarily, such a request—whether it be informal in an email or facsimile or formal in a printed form—will ask for a price quotation from the seller for a specific quantity and often a shipping date. (A sample printed form is shown in Figure 3–2.) When receiving such a request for

Figure 3–2. Quotation request.

QUOTATION REQUEST

From ______

Street Address ______

City and State ______

To

Inquiry No. ______

Date ______

Classification ______

PLEASE NOTE CAREFULLY

This inquiry implies no obligation on the part of the buyer.

Unless otherwise specified, there is no restriction on the number of items, that may be ordered.

In quoting, use duplicate copy of this form provided. Fill in complete information before returning.

Do not quote on articles you cannot supply. If substitutes are offered, make full explanation.

THIS IS AN INQUIRY—NOT AN ORDER

Delivery Point ______ By ☐ Parcel Post ☐ Express ☐ Rail Freight Line ______ ☐ Motor Freight Line ______ If not indicated, suggest most practical way.

Prices Quoted F.O.B. ______ Freight Allowance ______

Shipping Point ______

Terms: ______ % Discount ______ Days Net Cash ______ Days No charge to be made for packing, boxing crating or delivery to Transportation Co.

ITEM NO.	QUANTITY	ITEM AND SPECIFICATIONS	*	UNIT	LIST PRICE OF UNIT	DISCOUNT OFFERED	NET UNIT PRICE	ESTIMATED GROSS WT.

* Check-mark in this column indicates shipment can be made from stock.

Delivery of other items as follows: ______

Subject to withdrawal ______ Date returned ______

For Seller ______ For Buyer ______

CASCADE® L1-C2451 PRINTED IN U.S.A.

quotation, the seller should be particularly careful to ascertain whether the request contains other terms and conditions of purchase that are incorporated by reference to another document or are contained in the fine print "boilerplate" on the front or back of the request for quotation. If other terms are referenced, the best precaution is to ask the buyer to send such terms and conditions for the seller's review before replying. If additional terms of purchase are provided, they should be reviewed to determine if they conflict with the seller's usual terms and conditions of sale. This is particularly important in this day of email correspondence. The buyer should always request a copy of the seller's terms and conditions.

c. Quotations and Costing Sheets

In response to a request for a quotation, the seller ordinarily prepares and forwards a quotation. Before quoting a price for any specific quantity or any shipment date, it is extremely important that the seller accurately calculate its additional costs relating to an export sale and shipment before providing the quotation. The use of a costing sheet is highly recommended. (A sample costing sheet is shown in Figure 3–3.) By accurately completing the costing sheet, the seller can avoid quoting prices that will result in sales commitments with too little or no profit. In making quotations, the seller can use a printed form or prepare the quotations on a case-by-case basis. (A sample is shown in Figure 3–4.) If this is the first communication from the seller to the buyer, the seller should be careful to ensure that it contains all of the seller's terms and conditions of sale in addition to the price, quantity, and shipment date, or the quotation should specify that the seller will not be bound until he has received a written purchase order and has issued a written purchase order acceptance. Otherwise, when the buyer receives the quotation, she may find the price, quantity, and shipment date acceptable and accept that quotation when she receives it. This means that the sales agreements may be formed at that time in the buyer's country, or it may be formed when the buyer issues her purchase order (but before the purchase order is received by the seller). This may be so whether or not the seller designates his quotation as firm, because under the laws of some countries, quotations by merchants are deemed irrevocable for a certain period of time. When the sales agreement is formed under the law of the country of the buyer, the seller's rights and responsibilities under the sales agreement may be quite different from those under U.S. law. Sometimes it is necessary or acceptable to have a sales agreement governed by foreign law, but only after the seller has investigated the differences and has made an informed choice—not a mistaken one. Moreover, unless the seller has forwarded all of his terms and conditions of sale with his first communication (the quotation), the terms and conditions included in subsequent communications from the seller may not be binding on the buyer. Once again, as a seller, it is important to clearly state all terms and conditions at the time of quotation; even by email correspondence, attach a copy to any quotation.

d. Purchase Orders

The next document that may occur in a sales transaction is a purchase order (PO) issued by the buyer. Again, the purchase order may be informal, such as in an email or facsimile, or it may be on a printed form. Purchase orders are likely to contain

(*Text continues on page 78.*)

Figure 3–3. Export quotation worksheet.

EXPORT QUOTATION WORKSHEET

DATE ____________
COMMODITY ____________
CUSTOMER ____________
COUNTRY ____________
PAYMENT TERMS ____________

REF/PRO FORMA INVOICE NO. ____________
EXPECTED SHIP DATE ____________
PACKED DIMENSIONS ____________
PACKED WEIGHT ____________
PACKED CUBE ____________

PRODUCTS TO BE SHIPPED FROM ____________
TO ____________

SELLING PRICE OF GOODS: $________

SPECIAL EXPORT PACKING:
$________ quoted by ____________
$________ quoted by ____________
$________ quoted by ____________
$________

INLAND FREIGHT:
$________ quoted by ____________
$________ quoted by ____________
$________ quoted by ____________
$________

Inland freight includes the following charges:
☐ unloading ☐ pier delivery ☐ terminal ☐ ____________

OCEAN FREIGHT

	quoted by	tariff item
$____	________	#____
$____	________	#____
$____	________	#____

Ocean freight includes the following surcharges:
☐ Port congestion ☐ Heavy lift
☐ Currency adjustment ☐ Bunker
☐ Container rental ☐ Wharfage
☐ ________ ☐ ________

☐INSURANCE ☐includes war risk
rate: ________ per $100 or $________

TOTAL OCEAN CHARGES $________
notes:

AIR FREIGHT

	quoted by	spec code
$____	________	#____
$____	________	#____
$____	________	#____

Air freight includes the following surcharges:
☐ Fuel adjustment
☐ Container stuffing
☐ ________

☐INSURANCE ☐includes war risk
rate: ________ per $100 or $________

TOTAL AIR CHARGES $________ $________
notes:

SAMPLE

FORWARDING FEES: $________
Includes: ☐ Courier Fees ☐ Certification Fees ☐Banking Fees ☐ ________

CONSULAR LEGALIZATION FEES: $________

INSPECTION FEES: $________

DIRECT BANK CHARGES: $________

OTHER CHARGES: ____________ $________
____________ $________

TOTAL: ☐ FOB ________ ☐ C & F ________
☐ FAS ________ ☐ CIF ________ $________

Form No. 10-020 Printed and Sold by UNZCO 201 Circle Drive N, Suite 104, Piscataway, NJ 08854 (800) 631-3098 www.unzco.com

Figure 3–4. Quotation.

§2.4—Form 5

Quotation

[*Face side*]

SELLER COMPANY

____

____

Date: ______

BUYER COMPANY

____

____

We are pleased to quote as follows on your recent inquiry:

Quantity	Description	Price

Very truly yours,
SELLER COMPANY

By ____________________

THIS QUOTATION INCLUDES ALL OF THE PROVISIONS ON THE REVERSE SIDE HEREOF.

[*Reverse side*]

PROVISIONS

1. ANY PURCHASE ORDER PURSUANT TO THE ACCOMPANYING QUOTATION SHALL NOT RESULT IN A CONTRACT UNTIL IT IS ACCEPTED AND ACKNOWLEDGED BY SELLER AT SELLER'S OFFICE IN ____, ____.[1]

2. Payment terms are net ten (10) days after the rendering of seller's invoice.[2]

3. Delivery terms are f.o.b. cars at seller's

§ 2.4—Form 5

1. See § 2.5.

2. See § 9.6.

Figure 3–4. *(continued)*

plant in ____. Dates of delivery are determined from the date of seller's acceptance of any order or orders by buyer and are estimates of approximate dates of delivery, not a guaranty of a particular day of delivery.[3] Seller shall not be liable for failure or delay in shipping goods hereunder if such failure or delay is due to an act of God, war, labor difficulties, accident, inability to obtain containers or raw materials, or any other causes of any kind whatever beyond the control of seller.[4]

4. Any tax imposed by federal, state or other governmental authority on the sale of the merchandise and service referred to in this quotation shall be paid by buyer in addition to the quoted purchase price.

5. Buyer shall in respect of goods packaged by seller in accordance with designs, processes or formulas supplied, determined or requested by buyer, defend seller at buyer's expense and pay costs and damages awarded in any suit brought against seller for infringement of any letters patent by reason of use of such designs, processes or formulas, provided seller promptly notifies buyer in writing of any claim of or suit for infringement and tenders defense thereof to buyer. Seller is entitled to be represented in any suit at its own expense.[5]

6. Except for the warranty that the goods are made in a workmanlike manner and in accordance with the specifications therefor supplied or agreed to by buyer and are made or packaged pursuant to seller's customary manufacturing procedures, SELLER MAKES NO WARRANTY EXPRESS OR IMPLIED; AND ANY IMPLIED WARRANTY OF MERCHANTABILITY OR FITNESS FOR A PARTICULAR PURPOSE WHICH EXCEEDS THE FOREGOING WARRANTY IS HEREBY DISCLAIMED BY SELLER AND EXCLUDED FROM ANY AGREEMENT MADE BY ACCEPTANCE ANY ORDER PURSUANT TO THIS QUOTATION.[6] Seller will not be liable for any consequential damages, loss or expense arising in connection with the use of or the inability to use its goods for any purpose whatever. Seller's maximum liabil-

3. See § 9.4.

4. See § 9.19.

5. See §§ 8.1, 8.9.

6. See §§ 8.2 et seq.

(continues)

Figure 3–4. *(continued)*

ity shall not in any case exceed the contract price for the goods claimed to be defective or unsuitable.[7]

8. Buyer shall notify seller within ten days of receipt of merchandise of any complaint whatsoever buyer may have concerning such merchandise.[8]

9. There are no provisions with respect to this quotation which are not specified herein.[9] IF BUYER PLACES AN ORDER WITH SELLER BASED ON THIS QUOTATION, WHETHER IN WRITING OR ORALLY, THEN THIS QUOTATION AND BUYER'S ORDER AND SELLER'S ACCEPTANCE OR CONFIRMATION WILL CONSTITUTE THE ENTIRE CONTRACT BETWEEN BUYER AND SELLER WITH RESPECT TO THE SUBJECT MATTER OF THIS QUOTATION.[10] Any agreement so made shall be governed by the law of [*state*].[11]

SELLER COMPANY

COMMENT

This is a quotation, as distinguished from a firm offer. Since a quotation is only an invitation to submit an offer or to place an order, no power of acceptance is created in the addressee or recipient. See UCC § 2-205.

7. See §§ 8.12, 15.2.
8. See §§ 8.8, 9.9, 9.14, 9.15, 14.1.
9. See § 5.2.
10. See § 2.7.
11. See § 1.2.

many additional terms and conditions that the buyer wants to be a part of the sales agreement when the purchase order is accepted by the seller. (Samples are shown in Figures 3–5 and 3–6.) Even though the seller may expect that no sales agreement will be formed until he has received the buyer's purchase order, if he has previously sent a quotation to the buyer, the terms and conditions stated in the buyer's purchase order may govern the sales agreement. Of course, the terms and conditions contained in the buyer's purchase order are always written to be most favorable to the buyer. Another way in which the seller can try to guard against such a result is to expressly state in her quotation that the quotation is not an offer to sell and that no sales agreement will exist until such time as the seller has received a purchase order from the buyer and has issued its purchase order acceptance.

e. Purchase Order Acknowledgments, Acceptances, and Sales Confirmations

When a purchase order is received, some sellers prepare a purchase order acknowledgment form. A purchase order acknowledgment may state that the seller has received the purchase order from the buyer and is in the process of evaluating it,

(*Text continues on page 82.*)

Figure 3–5. Purchase order.

PURCHASE ORDER

UNITRAK™

VENDOR	PURCHASER
PRO FORMA INVOICE NO. / DATE	PURCHASE ORDER NO. / DATE
CONSIGNEE	NOTIFY/INTERMEDIATE CONSIGNEE

MFR. ITEM NO., SYMBOL, OR BRAND	QUANTITIES, FULL DESCRIPTION OF MERCHANDISE, AND PACKAGING INSTRUCTIONS	UNIT PURCHASE PRICE CURRENCY	TOTAL PURCHASE PRICE CURRENCY

SPECIAL PACKAGING REQUIREMENTS	OCEAN/AIR FREIGHT ______ INCLUDED COSTS ______ ______ ______ ______ TOTAL

RELEASE NO.	ITEM AND QUANTITY	DELIVERY DATE	PORT OF ENTRY	CARRIER

DOCUMENT REQUIREMENTS	TERMS OF PAYMENT

Form 16-310 Printed and Sold by UNZCO 190 Baldwin Ave., Jersey City, NJ 07306 • (800) 631-3098 • (201) 795-5400

VENDOR

Reprinted with permission from Bradford Stone's *West's Legal Forms,* Second Edition, copyright © 1985 by West Publishing Co.

Figure 3–6. Purchase order.

§ 2.6—Form 2

Buyer's Purchase Order—Another Form

Purchase Order No. ____________
Purchase Order Number
Must Appear on Invoices,
n/l. Packages and Packing
Slips.

BUYER COMPANY

P.O. Date

IMPORTANT
READ ALL INSTRUCTIONS, TERMS AND CONDITIONS ON FACE AND REVERSE SIDES.
ONLY SUCH INSTRUCTIONS, TERMS AND CONDITIONS SHALL CONSTITUTE THE AGREEMENT BETWEEN THE PARTIES.

TO:

SELLER COMPANY

Ship via	f.o.b.	terms	ship to

as per your quotation — promised delivery date at destination

Please Enter Our Purchase Order of Above No. Subject to All Instructions, Terms and Conditions on Face and Reverse Side Hereof.

QUANTITY	**DESCRIPTION**	**Price Per**	**AMOUNT**
		TOTAL	

ADDITIONAL INSTRUCTIONS, TERMS AND CONDITIONS ON REVERSE SIDE

INSTRUCTIONS, TERMS AND CONDITIONS:

BUYER COMPANY

By ____________

1. **Acceptance Copy** must be signed and returned immediately.
2. **Packing Slips** must be included in all shipments and last copy must state "ORDER COMPLETED."
3. **Order Number** must be shown on each package, packing slip and invoice.
4. **Invoices** must be rendered in duplicate not later than the day following shipment. Attach bill of lading or express receipt to each invoice.[1]
5. **Deliveries** must be made to Buyer's receiving room, not to individuals or departments.[2]
6. **Extra Charges.** No additional charges of any kind, including charges for boxing, packing, cartage, or other extras will be allowed unless specifically agreed to in writing in advance by Buyer.
7. **Payment.** It is understood that the cash discount period will date from the receipt of

§2.6—Form 2

1. UCC §§ 2-503, 2-504(b) and (c). See § 9.4. 2. UCC §§ 2-308, 2-309(1), 2-503. See § 9.4.

Figure 3–6. *(continued)*

the goods or from the date of the invoice, whichever is later. C.O.D. shipments will not be accepted. Drafts will not be honored.[3]

8. **Quantities.** The specific quantity ordered must be delivered in full and not be changed without Buyer's consent in writing. Any unauthorized quantity is subject to our rejection and return at Seller's expense.[4]
9. **Price.** If price is not stated in this order, it is agreed that the goods shall be billed at the price last quoted, or billed at the prevailing market price, whichever is lower. This order must not be filled at a higher price than last quoted or charged without Buyer's specific authorization.[5]
10. **Applicable Laws.** Seller represents that the merchandise covered by this order was not manufactured and is not being sold or priced in violation of any federal, state or local law.
11. **Fair Labor Standards Act.** Seller agrees that goods shipped to Buyer under this order will be produced in compliance with the Fair Labor Standards Act.[6]
12. **Warranty Specifications.** Seller expressly warrants that all the materials and articles covered by this order or other description or specification furnished by Buyer will be in exact accordance with such order, description or specification and free from defects in material and/or workmanship, and merchantable. Such warranty shall survive delivery, and shall not be deemed waived either by reason of Buyer's acceptance of said materials or articles or by payment for them. Any deviations from this order or specifications furnished hereunder, or any other exceptions or alterations must be approved in writing by Buyer's Purchasing Department.[7]
13. **Cancellation.** Buyer reserves the right to cancel all or any part of the undelivered portion of this order if Seller does not make deliveries as specified, time being of the essence of this Contract, or if Seller breaches any of the terms hereof including, without limitation, the warranties of Seller.[8]
14. **Inspection and Acceptance.** All goods shall be received subject to Buyer's right of inspection and rejection. Defective goods or goods not in accordance with Buyer's specifications will be held for Seller's instruction at Seller's risk and if Seller so directs, will be returned at Seller's expense. If inspection discloses that part of the goods received are not in accordance with Buyer's specifications, Buyer shall have the right to cancel any unshipped portion of the order. Payment for goods on this order prior to inspection shall not constitute acceptance thereof and is without prejudice to any and all claims that Buyer may have against Seller.[9]
15. **Patents.** Seller warrants the material purchased hereunder does not infringe any letters patent granted by the United States and covenants and agrees to save harmless and protect Buyer, its successors, assigns, customers and users of its product, against any claim or demand based upon such infringement, and after notice, to appear and defend at its own expense any suits at law or in equity arising therefrom.[10]
16. **Interpretation of Contract and Assignments.** This contract shall be construed according to the laws of the State of [*state*]. This contract may not be assigned by Seller without Buyer's written consent.[11]

3. UCC §§ 2-310, 2-511. See § 9.6.
4. UCC §§ 2-307, 2-601, 2-602. See §§ 9.4, 9.8 et seq.
5. UCC § 2-305. See § 2.3.
6. 29 U.S.C.A. § 215.
7. UCC §§ 2-313, 2-316. See §§ 8.2, 8.10.
8. UCC § 2-703(f); see UCC §§ 2-612, 2-719, 2-720. See §§ 9.16, 13.2, 15.2.
9. UCC §§ 2-512, 2-513, 2-601 through 2-607. See §§ 9.5, 9.7, 9.8 et seq.
10. UCC § 2-312(3). See §§ 8.1, 8.9.
11. UCC §§ 1-105, 2-210. See §§ 1.2, 6.1 et seq.

such as checking on the credit of the buyer or determining the availability of raw materials for manufacture, but that the seller has not yet accepted the purchase order and will issue a purchase order acceptance at a later date. In other cases, the language of the purchase order acknowledgment indicates that it is also an acceptance of the order, and no further communication is issued. Sales confirmations usually perform the same role as purchase order acceptances. The seller will normally include its detailed terms and conditions of sale in its purchase order acknowledgment or purchase order acceptance. If the buyer's request for a quotation or purchase order does not contain detailed terms and conditions of purchase, the seller can feel reasonably comfortable that its terms and conditions of sale will control if they are included in the purchase order acknowledgment or acceptance form. If the buyer has previously sent detailed terms and conditions of purchase, however, the seller is at risk that those terms and conditions will control unless it expressly states that the order is accepted and the sale is made *only* on the seller's terms and conditions of sale *and* thereafter (prior to production and shipment) the buyer confirms its acceptance of the seller's terms. (A sample purchase order acceptance is shown in Figure 3–7.) The purchase order acceptance should specify that the agreement cannot be modified except in writing signed by the seller. As many sales confirmations occur through email correspondence these days, it is important to ensure that the seller include the terms and conditions in its confirmation.

f. Pro Forma Invoices

If the buyer is in a country that has foreign exchange controls, he may need to receive a pro forma invoice from the seller in order to get government approval to make payment, and the seller may want to receive such approval before commencing production. This is an invoice that the buyer will submit to the central bank to obtain permission and clearance to convert foreign currency into U.S. dollars in order to make payment to the seller. The seller should exert some care in preparing this invoice, because it may be extremely difficult to change the price in the final invoice due to changes in costs or specifications. Sometimes, a pro forma invoice is used as the first document sent by the seller in response to a buyer's request for quotation. (A sample pro forma invoice is shown in Figure 3–8.) It should contain the complete terms and conditions of sale. This type of pro forma invoice should not be confused with that used by an importer when the seller has not provided a commercial invoice (see Figure 8–2).

g. Commercial Invoices

Later, when manufacture is complete and the product is ready for shipment, ordinarily the seller will prepare a commercial invoice, which is the formal statement for payment to be sent directly to the buyer or submitted through banking channels for payment by the buyer. Such invoices may also contain the detailed terms or conditions of sale on the front or back of the form. (A sample is shown in Figure 3–9.) However, if this is the first time that the seller has brought such terms to the attention of the buyer, it is likely that they will not be binding on the buyer because the seller has already accepted the buyer's order by the seller's conduct in manufacturing and/or

(*Text continues on page 87.*)

Figure 3–7. Purchase order acceptance.

§ 2.6—Form 8

Seller's Sales Order—Another Form

[*Face side*]

SELLER COMPANY

PRODUCT

TO: [*Buyer Company*]

GENTLEMEN:

We thank you for the order listed below which we are pleased to have accepted subject to only those terms and conditions of sale which are set forth below and on the reverse side hereof.[1]

Trusting that we have your assent to these terms and conditions we accordingly have entered your order in our mill schedules.

DATE

YOUR ORDER:

TERMS OF DELIVERY:[2]

§ 2.6—Form 8

1. UCC § 2-207(1). These terms probably will not ribbon match those on buyer's purchase order form. See discussion and forms at § 2.7 below.

2. UCC §§ 2-307, 2-308, 2-309(1), 2-319 et seq., 2-503. See § 9.4.

(*continues*)

Figure 3–7. *(continued)*

TERMS OF PAYMENT:[3]

PLEASE ADDRESS CORRESPONDENCE RELATING TO THIS ORDER TO OUR DISTRICT SALES OFFICE AT

VERY TRULY YOURS,
SELLER COMPANY

By ________________________
[*Manager of Sales*]

[*Reverse side*]

TERMS AND CONDITIONS OF SALE

In accordance with the usage of trade, your assent to the terms and conditions of sale set forth below and on the reverse side hereof shall be conclusively presumed from your failure seasonably to object in writing and from your acceptance of all or any part of the material ordered.[4]

All proposals, negotiations, and representations, if any, regarding this transaction and made prior to the date of this acknowledgment are merged herein.[5]

PRICES—All prices, whether herein named or heretofore quoted or proposed, shall be adjusted to the Seller's prices in effect at the time of shipment.[6]

If transportation charges from point of origin of the shipment to a designated point are included in the prices herein named or heretofore quoted—

(a) any changes in such transportation charges shall be for the account of the Buyer;

3. UCC § 2-310; see UCC § 2-511. See § 9.6.

4. See § 2.6—Form 7 and Comment. See also § 2.7.

5. UCC § 2-202. See § 5.2.

6. UCC § 2-305. See § 2.3.

Figure 3–7. *(continued)*

(b) except as otherwise stated in the Seller's quotation, the Seller shall not be responsible for switching, spotting, handling, storage, demurrage or any other transportation or accessorial service, nor for any charges incurred therefor, unless such charges are included in the applicable tariff freight rate from shipping point to the designated point.

TAXES—Any taxes which the Seller may be required to pay or collect, under any existing or future law, upon or with respect to the sale, purchase, delivery, storage, processing, use or consumption of any of the material covered hereby, including taxes upon or measured by the receipts from the sale thereof, shall be for the account of the Buyer, who shall promptly pay the amount thereof to the Seller upon demand.

DELAY—The Seller shall be excused for any delay in performance due to acts of God, war, riot, embargoes, acts of civil or military authorities, fires, floods, accidents, quarantine restrictions, mill conditions, strikes, differences with workmen, delays in transportation, shortage of cars, fuel, labor or materials, or any circumstance or cause beyond the control of the Seller in the reasonable conduct of its business.[7]

INSPECTION—The Buyer may inspect, or provide for inspection, at the place of manufacture. Such inspection shall be so conducted as not to interfere unreasonably with the manufacturer's operations, and consequent approval or rejection shall be made before shipment of the material. Notwithstanding the foregoing, if, upon receipt of such material by the Buyer, the same shall appear not to conform to the contract between the Buyer and the Seller, the Buyer shall immediately notify the Seller of such condition and afford the Seller a reasonable opportunity to inspect the material. No material shall be returned without the Seller's consent.[8]

EXCLUSION OF WARRANTIES—The Implied Warranties of Merchantability and Fitness for Purpose Are Excluded From This Contract.[9]

BUYER'S REMEDIES—If the material furnished to the Buyer shall fail to conform to this contract or to any express or implied warranty, the Seller shall replace such non-conforming material at the original point of delivery and shall furnish instructions for its disposition. Any transportation charges involved in such disposition shall be for the Seller's account.

The Buyer's exclusive and sole remedy on account or in respect of the furnishing of material that does not conform to this contract, or to any express or implied warranty, shall be to secure replacement thereof as aforesaid. The Seller shall not in any event be liable for the cost of any labor expended on any such material or for any special, direct,

7. UCC § 2-615. See § 9.19.
8. UCC §§ 2-512, 2-513. See § 9.7.
9. UCC §§ 2-314, 2-315, 2-316. See §§ 8.4, 8.5, 8.6, 8.11.

(continues)

Figure 3–7. *(continued)*

indirect, incidental or consequential damages to anyone by reason of the fact that such material does not conform to this contract or to any express or implied warranty.[10]

PERMISSIBLE VARIATIONS, STANDARDS AND TOLERANCES—Except in the particulars specified by Buyer and expressly agreed to in writing by Seller, all material shall be produced in accordance with Seller's standard practices. All material, including that produced to meet an exact specification, shall be subject to tolerances and variations consistent with usages of the trade and regular mill practices concerning: dimension, weight, straightness, section, composition and mechanical properties; normal variations in surface, internal conditions and quality; deviations from tolerances and variations consistent with practical testing and inspection methods; and regular mill practices concerning over and under shipments.[11]

PATENTS—The Seller shall indemnify the Buyer against any judgment for damages and costs which may be rendered against the Buyer in any suit brought on account of the alleged infringement of any United States patent by any product supplied by the Seller hereunder, unless made in accordance with materials, designs or specifications furnished or designated by the Buyer, in which case the Buyer shall indemnify the Seller against any judgment for damages and costs which may be rendered against the Seller in any suit brought on account of the alleged infringement of any United States patent by such product or by such materials, designs or specifications; provided that prompt written notice be given to the party from whom indemnity is sought of the bringing of the suit and that an opportunity be given such party to settle or defend it as that party may see fit and that every reasonable assistance in settling or defending it shall be rendered. Neither the Seller nor the Buyer shall in any event be liable to the other for special, indirect, incidental or consequential damages arising out of or resulting from infringement of patents.[12]

CREDIT APPROVAL—Shipments, deliveries and performance of work shall at all times be subject to the approval of the Seller's Credit Department. The Seller may at any time decline to make any shipment or delivery or perform any work except upon receipt of payment or security or upon terms and conditions satisfactory to such Department.

TERMS OF PAYMENT—Subject to the provisions of CREDIT APPROVAL above, terms of payment are as shown on the reverse side hereof and shall be effective from date of invoice. A cash discount shall not be allowed on any transportation charges included in delivered prices.[13]

10. UCC §§ 2-508, 2-714, 2-715, 2-719. See §§ 9.17, 14.1, 14.2, 15.2.

11. UCC §§ 1-205, 2-208, 2-313, 2-314(2)(d). See §§ 5.1, 8.2, 8.4.

12. UCC § 2-312(3). See §§ 8.1, 8.9.

13. UCC §§ 2-310, 2-511. See § 9.6.

Figure 3–7. *(continued)*

COMPLIANCE WITH LAWS—The Seller intends to comply with all laws applicable to its performance of this order.[14]

RENEGOTIATION—The Seller assumes only such liability with respect to renegotiation of contracts or subcontracts to which it is a party as may be lawfully imposed upon the Seller under the provisions of any Renegotiation Act applicable to this order.[15]

NON-WAIVER BY SELLER—Waiver by the Seller of a breach of any of the terms and conditions of this contract shall not be construed as a waiver of any other breach.[16]

14. UCC § 1-103. See § 1.1.

15. See, e.g., Renegotiation Act (Renegotiation of Contracts), 50 U.S.C.A.App. §§ 1211 et seq.

16. UCC § 1-107; see UCC §§ 2-209, 1-207. See §§ 3.3, 10.2.

shipping the products. (See also the discussion of commercial invoices in Chapter 4, Section C.)

h. Conflicting Provisions in Seller and Buyer Sales Documentation

It is common in international trade for sellers and buyers to use preprinted forms designed to reduce the amount of negotiation and discussion required for each sales agreement. Undoubtedly, such forms have been drafted by attorneys for each side and contain terms and conditions of purchase or terms and conditions of sale that are favorable to the buyer and seller, respectively. Consequently, it is not unusual for sellers and buyers intent on entering into a sales transaction to routinely issue such documentation with little or no thought regarding the consistency of those provisions. Afterward, if the sales transaction breaks down and either the buyer or the seller consults its attorney regarding its legal rights and obligations, the rights of the parties may be very unclear. In the worst case, the seller may find that a sales agreement has been validly formed on all of the terms and conditions of the buyer's purchase order and is governed by the law of the buyer's country. In order to reduce or eliminate this problem, often the seller's attorney drafts requests for quotations, purchase order acknowledgments, and acceptances and invoices with language stating that, notwithstanding any terms or conditions that might be contained in the buyer's request for quotation or purchase order, the seller agrees to make the sale only on its own terms and conditions. While this can be of some help, sometimes the buyer's requests for quotation and purchase orders also contain such language, and consequently, the buyer's terms and conditions may win out. If the buyer was the last to send its terms and conditions of purchase, and the seller did not object, the seller's conduct in shipping the goods can result in an agreement under the buyer's terms and conditions. In fact, the only way to be comfortable regarding the terms and conditions of sale that will govern a sales agreement is to actually review the terms and conditions contained in the buyer's forms and compare them with the terms and conditions that the seller desires

(Text continues on page 90.)

Figure 3–8. Pro forma invoice.

PROFORMA INVOICE/EXPORT ORDER **UNITRAK**(TM)

CUSTOMER:

SHIP TO (Consignee):

NOTIFY (Intermediate Consignee):

IN-HOUSE ORDER NO.	DATE
PRO FORMA INVOICE NO.	DATE
COMMERCIAL INVOICE NO.	DATE
CUSTOMER PURCHASE ORDER NO.	DATE
CUSTOMER ACCOUNT NO.	
PURCHASER'S NAME	TITLE
SHIP VIA	EST. SHIP DATE
TELEPHONE NO.	
TELEX/FAX/CABLE NO.	

PART NUMBER	UNIT OF MEASURE	QUANTITY	DESCRIPTION	UNIT PRICE	TOTAL PRICE

SPECIAL INSTRUCTIONS:

ADDITIONAL CHARGES			TERMS OF PAYMENT	
FREIGHT	☐ Ocean	☐ Air	☐ LETTER OF CREDIT	Bank
CONSULAR/LEGALIZATION			☐ DRAFT	Terms
INSPECTION/CERTIFICATION			☐ OPEN ACCOUNT	Terms
SPECIAL PACKING			☐ OTHER	
			CURRENCY OF PAYMENT	

Form 15-330 Printed and Sold by UNZCO 190 Baldwin Ave., Jersey City, NJ 07306 • (800) 631-3098 • (201) 795-5400

PROFORMA INVOICE

Reprinted with permission of Unz & Co., 190 Baldwin Ave., Jersey City, NJ 07306, USA.

Figure 3–9. Commercial invoice.

COMMERCIAL INVOICE

SHIPPER/EXPORTER	COMMERCIAL INVOICE NO. / DATE
	CUSTOMER PURCHASE ORDER NO. / B/L, AWB NO.
	COUNTRY OF ORIGIN / DATE OF EXPORT
CONSIGNEE	TERMS OF PAYMENT
NOTIFY: INTERMEDIATE CONSIGNEE	EXPORT REFERENCES
FORWARDING AGENT	AIR/OCEAN PORT OF EMBARKATION
	EXPORTING CARRIER/ROUTE

Terms of Sale and Terms of Payment under this offer are governed by Incoterms # 322, "Uniform Rules For The Collection Of Commercial Paper" and # 400 "Uniform Customs And Practice For Documentary Credits"

PKGS.	QUANTITY	NET WT. *(Kilos)*	GROSS WT. *(Kilos)*	DESCRIPTION OF MERCHANDISE	UNIT PRICE	TOTAL VALUE

PACKAGE MARKS:	MISC. CHARGES *(Packing, Insurance, etc.)*	
	INVOICE TOTAL	

CERTIFICATIONS

AUTHORIZED SIGNATURE

Form 15-320 Printed and Sold by UNZCO 190 Baldwin Ave., Jersey City, NJ 07306 • (800) 631-3098 • (201) 795-5400

Reprinted with permission of Unz & Co., 190 Baldwin Ave., Jersey City, NJ 07306, USA.

to utilize. Where specific conflicts exist or where the buyer's terms and conditions of purchase differ from the seller's terms and conditions of sale, the seller should expressly bring that to the attention of the buyer, the difference should be negotiated to the satisfaction of the seller, and appropriate changes should be made in the form of a rider to the standard form or a letter to clarify the agreement that has been reached between the parties (which should be signed by both parties).

In some isolated sales transactions where the quantities are small, the seller may simply choose to forgo this effort and accept the risk that the transaction will be controlled by the buyer's terms and conditions of sale. However, the seller should establish some dollar limit over which a review is to be made and should not continue a practice that might be appropriate for small sales but would be very dangerous for large sales.

i. Side Agreements

Occasionally, the buyer may suggest that the seller and buyer enter into a side or letter agreement. In some cases, the suggestion may be innocent enough, for example, where the parties wish to clarify how they will interpret or carry out a particular provision of their sales agreement. Even then, however, it is better practice to incorporate all of the agreements of the parties in a single document. Unfortunately, more often the buyer's proposal of a side agreement is designed to evade the buyer's foreign exchange control, tax, customs, or antitrust laws. Sellers should be wary of entering into such agreements unless they fully understand the consequences. Such agreements may be unenforceable, the seller may not be able to get paid on its export sale, and/or the seller may be prosecuted as a co-conspirator for violating such laws.

B. Ongoing Sales Transactions

When a customer begins to purchase on a regular basis, or when the seller desires to make regular sales to a particular end user or reseller, the seller and the buyer should enter into a more comprehensive agreement to govern their relationship. Often these types of agreements are a result of the buyer's being willing to commit to regular purchases, and, therefore, to purchase a larger quantity of the goods, in return for obtaining a lower price. Or, they may result from the buyer's desire to "tie up," that is, to obtain more assurance from the seller to commit to supply the buyer's requirements, or from the seller's desire to plan its production. The three major types of agreements used in ongoing sales transactions are (1) international sales agreements, that is, supply agreements where the seller sells directly to an end-user customer who either incorporates the seller's product as a component into a product the buyer manufactures, or consumes the product and does not resell the product; (2) distributor agreements, where the seller sells the product to a purchaser, usually located in the destination country, who resells the product in that country, usually in the same form but sometimes with modifications; and (3) sales agent or sales representative agreements, where a person, usually located in the destination country, is appointed to solicit orders from potential customers in that country. In the last case, the sale is not made to the sales agent, but is made directly to the customer, with payment of a commission or other compensation to the sales agent.

In any of the three foregoing agreements, there is a correlation between the documentation used in isolated sales transactions and the documentation used in ongoing sales transactions. Furthermore, there are a number of important provisions that are not relevant to domestic sales that should be included in international sales, distributor, and sales agent agreements.

1. Correlation With Documentation for Isolated Sales Transactions

As discussed in Section A.4 above, it is common for sellers and buyers to use forms such as requests for quotation, purchase orders, purchase order acknowledgments, purchase order acceptances, sales confirmations, pro forma invoices, and invoices during the course of ordering and selling products. When an ongoing sales relationship is being established with a particular customer, it is usual to enter into an umbrella or blanket agreement that is intended to govern the relationship between the parties over a longer period of time, for example, one year, five years, or longer. Sometimes the parties will enter into a trial marketing agreement that will last for a short period of time, such as one year, before deciding to enter into a longer-term agreement. In any event, the international sales (supply) agreement, the distributor agreement, and the sales agent (representative) agreement define the rights and obligations of the parties over a fairly long period of time and commit the seller and the buyer to doing business with each other so that both sides can make production, marketing, and advertising plans and expenditures. Special price discounts in return for commitments to purchase specific quantities are common in such agreements. Such agreements may contain a commitment to purchase a specific quantity over the life of the agreement and may designate a specific price or a formula by which the price will be adjusted over the life of the agreement. To this extent, these agreements serve as an umbrella over the parties' relationship, with certain specific acts to be accomplished as agreed by the parties from time to time. For example, it is usually necessary during the term of such agreements for the buyer to advise the seller from time to time of the specific quantity that it wishes to order at that time, to be applied against the buyer's overall purchase commitment. This will be done by the issuance of a purchase order.

If the price of the product is likely to fluctuate, no price may be specified in the umbrella agreement. Instead, the price may be changed from time to time by the seller depending on the seller's price at the time the buyer submits a purchase order, perhaps with a special discount from such price because the buyer has committed to buy a substantial quantity over the life of the agreement. In such cases, depending upon whether or not a specific price has been set in the umbrella agreement, the buyer will send a request for a quotation and the seller will provide a quotation, or a purchase order will be sent describing the specific quantity the buyer wishes to order at that time, a suggested shipment date, and the price. The seller will still use a purchase order acknowledgment and/or a purchase order acceptance form to agree to ship the specific quantity on the specific shipment date at the specific price. The seller will continue to provide pro forma invoices if they are necessary for the buyer to obtain a foreign exchange license to make payment, as well as a commercial invoice against which the buyer must make payment.

In summary, where the seller and the buyer wish to enter into a longer-term agreement, they will define their overall relationship in an umbrella agreement, but the usual documentation utilized in isolated sales transactions will also be utilized to set specific quantities, prices, and shipment dates. Sometimes conflicts can arise between the terms and conditions in the umbrella agreement and the specific documentation. Usually the parties provide that in such cases, the umbrella agreement will control, but this can also lead to problems in situations where the parties wish to vary the terms of their umbrella agreement for a specific transaction.

2. *Important Provisions in International Sales Agreements*

There are numerous terms and conditions in an international sales agreement that require special consideration different from the usual terms and conditions in a domestic sales agreement. Unfortunately, sometimes sellers simply utilize sales documentation that was developed for U.S. domestic sales, only to discover that it is woefully inadequate for international sales. A simple sample international sales agreement (export) is included as Appendix B.

a. Selling and Purchasing Entities

In entering into an international sales agreement, it is important to think about who the seller and buyer will be. For example, rather than the U.S. company acting as the seller in the international sales agreement, it may wish to structure another company as the seller, primarily for potential tax savings. There are two main structures available to take advantage of such tax savings: the commission agent structure and the buy-sell structure. In the commission agent structure, the exporter will incorporate another company (in the United States or abroad, depending upon the tax incentive being utilized) and pay that company a commission on its export sales (which is, of course, a payment to a related company). In the buy-sell structure, an exporter would sell and transfer title to a related company that it sets up (in the United States or abroad), and the related company would act as the seller for export sales in the international sales agreement. If the exporter is not manufacturing products but is instead buying from an unrelated manufacturing company and reselling to unrelated companies, such activities sometimes can be more profitably conducted if the company incorporates a subsidiary in a low-tax jurisdiction, such as the Cayman Islands or Hong Kong.

If the seller and the buyer are related entities, such as a parent and subsidiary corporation, the foreign customs treatment may be different, for example, in the valuation of the merchandise or the assessment of antidumping duties. Some transactions may be structured to involve the use of a trading company, either on the exporting side, the importing side, or both. Depending upon whether the trading company takes title or is appointed as the agent (of either the buyer or the seller), or whether the trading company is related to the seller or the buyer, the foreign customs treatment may be different. For example, commissions paid to the seller's agent are ordinarily subject to customs duties in the foreign country, but commissions paid to the buyer's agent are not.

In the instance where the purchaser is in the United States and where a third-party intermediary is used from the manufacturer, it may be possible to use the sale price from the manufacturer to the third party as the dutiable value for the assessment of U.S. customs duties providing the transaction is structured correctly. This is commonly referred to as a "first-sale" transaction. See Chapter 6, Part F for more information on this program.

b. Quantity

The quantity term is even more important than the price. Under U.S. law, if the parties have agreed on the quantity, the sales agreement is enforceable even if the parties have not agreed on price—a current, or market, price will be implied. When no quantity has been agreed upon, however, the sales agreement will not be enforceable.

One reason for forming a formal sales agreement is for the buyer to obtain a lower price by committing to purchase a large quantity, usually over a year or more. The seller may be willing to grant a lower price in return for the ability to plan ahead, schedule production and inventory, develop economies of scale, and reduce shipping and administrative costs. The seller should be aware that price discounts for quantity purchases may violate some countries' price discrimination laws, unless the amount of the discount can be directly related to the cost savings of the seller for that particular quantity.

Quantity agreements can be for a specific quantity or a target quantity. Generally, if the commitment is a target only, failure to actually purchase such amount will not justify the seller in claiming damages or terminating the agreement (although sometimes the buyer will agree to a retroactive price increase). Failure to purchase a minimum purchase quantity, however, will justify termination and a claim for breach.

Sometimes the buyer may wish to buy the seller's entire output or the seller may seek a commitment that the buyer will purchase all of its requirements for the merchandise from the seller. Usually such agreements are lawful, but in certain circumstances they can violate the antitrust laws, such as when the seller is the only supplier or represents a large amount of the supply, or the buyer is the only buyer or represents a large segment of the market.

c. Pricing

There are a number of considerations in formulating the seller's pricing policy for international sales agreements. In addition to the importance of using a costing sheet to identify all additional costs of exporting to make sure that the price quoted to a customer results in a net profit acceptable to the seller (see Section A.4.c), the seller has to be aware of several constraints in formulating its pricing policy.

The first constraint relates to dumping. Many countries of the world are parties to the GATT Antidumping Code or have domestic legislation that prohibits dumping of foreign products in their country. This generally means that the price at which products are sold for export to their country cannot be lower than the price at which such products are sold in the United States. The mere fact that sales are made at lower prices for export does not automatically mean that a dumping investigation will be initiated or that a dumping finding will occur. Under the laws of most countries, no dumping will occur if the price to that market is above that country's current market price, even if the seller's price to that country is lower than its sales price in its own country.

On the other hand, there are essentially no U.S. legal constraints on the extent to which a price quoted for export can exceed the price for sale in the United States. The antitrust laws in the United States (in particular the price discrimination provisions of the Robinson-Patman Act) apply only when sales are being made in the United States. Consequently, a seller may charge a higher or lower price for export without violating U.S. law. However, if the seller is selling to two or more customers in the same foreign country at different prices, such sales may violate the price discrimination provisions of the destination country's law.

If the price is below the seller's total cost of production, there is always a risk that such sales will be attacked as predatory pricing in violation of the foreign country's antitrust laws. The accounting calculation of cost is always a subject of dispute, particularly where the seller may feel that the costs of domestic advertising or other costs should not be allocated to export sales. However, in general, any sales below total, fully allocated costs are at risk.

Another very important pricing area relates to rebates, discounts, allowances, and price escalation clauses. Sometimes the buyer will ask for and the seller will be willing to grant some form of rebate, discount, or allowance under certain circumstances, such as the purchase of large quantities of merchandise. Such price concessions generally do not, in and of themselves, violate U.S. or foreign law, but if such payments are not disclosed to the proper government authorities, both the U.S. exporter and the foreign buyer can violate various laws, and the U.S. exporter also may be charged with conspiracy to violate, or aiding and abetting the buyer's violation of those laws. For example, the U.S. exporter must file a Shipper's Export Declaration (Electronic Export Information) on each shipment (see discussion in Chapter 4, Section T), and must declare the price at which the goods are being sold. If, in fact, this price is false (because the exporter has agreed to grant some rebate, discount, or allowance, or, in fact, does so), the U.S. exporter will violate U.S. law and be subject to civil and criminal penalties. Similarly, when the buyer imports the goods to the destination country, the buyer will be required to state a value for customs and foreign exchange control purposes in its country and will receive U.S. dollars through the central bank to pay for the goods and must pay customs duties on the value declared. In addition, the buyer will probably use that value to show a deduction from its sales or revenues as a cost of goods sold, that is, as a tax deduction. Consequently, the true prices must be used. If the buyer requests the seller to provide two invoices for different amounts or if the buyer asks the seller to pay the rebate, discount, or allowance outside of its own country (for example, by deposit in a bank account in the United States, Switzerland, or some other country), there is considerable risk that the intended action of the buyer will violate the buyer's foreign exchange control laws, tax laws, and/or customs laws. If the seller cooperates by providing any such documentation or is aware of the scheme, the seller can also be charged with conspiracy to violate those foreign laws and can risk fines, arrest, and imprisonment in those countries. Similarly, retroactive price increases (for example, due to currency fluctuations) or price increases or decreases under escalation clauses may cause a change in the final price that may have to be reported to the customs, foreign exchange, or tax authorities. Before agreeing to grant any price rebate, discount, or allowance, or before agreeing to use a price escalation clause, or to implement a retroactive price increase or decrease, or to make any payment to the buyer in any place except the buyer's own country, the seller should satisfy itself that its actions will not result in the violation of any U.S. or foreign law.

If the sale is to an affiliated company, such as a foreign distribution or manufacturing subsidiary, additional pricing considerations arise. Because the buyer and seller are related, pricing can be artificially manipulated. For example, a U.S. exporter that is taxable on its U.S. manufacturing and sales profits at a rate of 35 percent when selling to an affiliated purchaser in a country that has a higher tax rate may attempt to minimize taxes in the foreign country by charging a high price to its foreign affiliate. Then, when the foreign affiliate resells the product, its profit will be small. Or, if the foreign affiliate uses the product in its manufacturing operation, the deduction for cost of materials will be high, thereby reducing the profits taxable in that country. When the sale is to a country where the tax rate is lower than in the United States, the considerations are reversed and the transfer price is set at a low rate, in which case the U.S. profits will be low. These strategies are well known to the tax authorities in foreign countries and to the Internal Revenue Service in the United States. Consequently, sales between affiliated companies are always susceptible to attack by the tax authorities. In general, the tax authorities in both countries will require that the seller sell to its affiliated buyer at an arm's-length price, as if it were selling to an unaffiliated buyer. Often, preserving evidence that the seller was selling to its unaffiliated customers at the same price as its affiliated customers will be very important in defending a tax audit. When the U.S. seller is selling to an affiliated buyer in a country with a lower tax rate, the customs authorities in the foreign country will also be suspicious that the transfer price is undervalued, and, therefore, customs duties may be underpaid.

Another consideration in the pricing of goods for export concerns parallel imports or gray market goods. If buyers in one country (including the United States) are able to purchase at a lower price than buyers in another country, an economic incentive will exist for customers in the lower-price country to divert such goods to the higher-price country in hopes of making a profit. Obviously, the seller's distributor in the higher-price country will complain about such unauthorized imports and loss of sales. The laws of many countries, however, such as the European Community (EC) and Japan, encourage such parallel imports as a means of encouraging competition and forcing the authorized distributor to reduce its price. In the EC, attempts to prohibit a distributor from selling outside of its country (but within the EC) can violate the law. Unfortunately, maintaining pricing parity is not always easy because of floating exchange rates, not only between the United States and other countries, but among those other countries.

d. Currency Fluctuations

Related to the issue of pricing are the currency fluctuations that occur between the markets of the seller and the buyer. If the U.S. exporter quotes and sells only in U.S. dollars, the fluctuation of the foreign currency will not affect the final U.S. dollar amount that the exporter receives as payment. However, if the buyer is a much larger company than the seller and has more negotiating and bargaining leverage, or if the seller is anxious to make the sale, it may be necessary to agree to a sale denominated in foreign currency, such as Japanese yen or European euros. In such a case, if the foreign currency weakens between the time of the price agreement and the time of payment, the U.S. exporter will receive fewer U.S. dollars than it had anticipated when it quoted the price and calculated the expected profit. In such a case, the exporter is assuming the foreign exchange fluctuation risk. Sometimes, when the term of the agreement is long, or when major currency fluctuations are anticipated, neither the seller nor the buyer is comfortable in entirely assuming such risk. Consequently, they may agree to some sharing of the risk, such as a 50/50 price adjustment for changes due to any exchange fluctuations that occur during the life of the agreement, or some other formula that attempts to protect both sides against such fluctuations.

e. Payment Methods

In a domestic sales transaction, the seller may be used to selling on open account, extending credit, or asking for cash on delivery. In international agreements, it is more customary to utilize certain methods of payment that are designed to give the seller a greater level of protection. The idea is that if the buyer fails to pay, it is much more difficult for a seller to go to a foreign country, institute a lawsuit, attempt to attach the buyer's assets, or otherwise obtain payment. When sellers are dealing with buyers who are essentially unknown to them, with whom they have no prior payment experience, or who are small or located in countries where there is significant political upheaval or changing economic circumstances, the seller may insist that the buyer pay by cash in advance. This is particularly important if the sale is of specially manufactured goods. Where a seller wants to give the buyer some credit but also to have security of payment, the seller often requires the buyer to obtain a documentary letter of credit from a bank in the buyer's country. The seller may also require that the letter of credit be confirmed by a bank in the seller's country, which guarantees payment by the buyer's bank. The seller may still sell on terms with payment to be made at the time of shipment, or the seller may give the buyer some period of time (for example, from 30 days to 180 days) to make payment, but the letter of credit acts as an umbrella obligation of the bank guaranteeing the buyer's payment. In some cases, however, the buyer will be unable to obtain a letter of credit, for example, because the buyer's bank does not feel comfortable with the buyer's financial solvency. Furthermore, issuance of letters of credit involves the payment of bank fees, which are normally paid for by the buyer, and the buyer usually does not wish to incur such expenses in addition to the cost of purchasing the goods. In such cases, particularly if the seller is anxious to make the sale or if other competitors are willing to offer more liberal payment terms, the seller may be forced to give up a letter of credit and agree to make the sale on some other, less secure, method of payment.

The next best method of payment is by sight draft documentary collection, commonly known as documents against payment or D/P transactions. In this case, the exporter uses the services of a bank to effect collection, but neither the buyer's bank nor a U.S. bank guarantees payment by the buyer. The seller will ship the goods, and the bill of lading and a draft (that is, a document like a check in the amount of the sale drawn on the buyer—rather than a bank—and payable to the seller) will be forwarded to the seller's bank. The seller's bank will forward such documents to a correspondent bank in the foreign country (sometimes the seller or its freight forwarder sends the documents directly to the foreign bank—this is known as direct collection), and the foreign bank will collect payment from the buyer prior to the time that the goods arrive. If payment is not made by the buyer, the correspondent bank does not release the bill of lading to the buyer, and the buyer will be unable to take possession of the goods or clear customs. Although it can still be a significant problem for the seller if the buyer does not make payment and the shipment has already gone, the seller should still be able to control the goods upon arrival, for example, by asking the bank to place them in a warehouse or by requesting that they be shipped to a third country or back to the United States at the seller's expense. Direct collections are often used for air shipments to avoid delays through the seller's bank and, also, because air waybills are non-negotiable.

The next least secure payment method is to utilize a time draft, commonly known as documents against acceptance or D/A transactions. Like the sight draft transaction, the bill of lading and time draft are forwarded through banking channels, but the buyer agrees to make payment within a certain number of days (for example, 30 to 180) after she receives and accepts the draft. Normally, this permits the buyer to obtain possession of the goods and may give the buyer enough time to resell them before her obligation to pay comes due. However, documents against acceptance transactions are a significantly greater risk for the seller because, if the buyer does not pay at the promised time, the seller's only recourse is to file a lawsuit—the goods have already been released to the buyer. Where the buyer is financially strong, sometimes such acceptances can be discounted by the seller, however, permitting the seller to get immediate payment but giving the buyer additional time to pay. This discounting may be done with recourse or without recourse depending upon the size of the discount the seller is willing to accept. There may also be an interest charge to the buyer for the delay in payment, which the seller may decide to waive in order to make the sale. The buyer's bank may also agree to add its "aval." This then becomes a bank guaranty of payment equivalent to a letter of credit.

The least secure payment method is sale on open account, where the seller makes the sale and the shipment by forwarding the bill of lading and a commercial invoice directly to the buyer for payment. Because the bill of lading is sent directly to the buyer, once it leaves the possession of the seller, the seller will be unable to control what happens to the goods and the buyer will be able to obtain the goods whether or not payment is made. When a seller agrees to sell on open account, it must look to an alternative method, for example, a security interest under foreign law (see subsection g, below), to protect its right to payment in case the buyer fails to pay at the agreed time. For this method of payment and for documents against acceptance, the seller should definitely consider obtaining commercial risk insurance through the Foreign Credit Insurance Association (see Chapter 2, Section S).

Another type of letter of credit transaction that adds security is the standby letter of credit. If a buyer opens a standby letter of credit in favor of the seller, invoices, bills of lading, and similar documentation are forwarded directly to the buyer without using a bank for collection, but the issuing bank's guaranty is there in case of default by the buyer.

Sometimes a seller will begin selling to a particular customer under letters of credit, but as the seller becomes more familiar with the customer (the customer honors its obligations, increases its purchases, or enters into an ongoing sales agreement), the seller will be willing to liberalize its payment terms.

In addition, in international transactions, the seller will have to consider alternative payment methods, such as wire transfers via banking channels, since payment by check will often involve an inordinate length of time if the check is first sent to the seller in the United States and then sent back to the foreign country to be collected from the buyer's bank. Direct telegraphic transfer from bank account to bank account is a highly efficient and useful way to deal with international payments. However, buyers may be unwilling to wire the money to the seller until they are satisfied that the goods have been sent or until after arrival and inspection. Other methods of payment, such as cash payments made by employees traveling from the buyer to the seller or vice versa, or payments made in third countries, all carry the risk of violating the buyer's foreign exchange control, tax, and/or customs laws, and should be agreed to only after detailed investigation of the possible risks. A chart comparing these various methods of payment is shown in Figure 3–10.

Another method of payment that may arise in international sales is countertrade. Countertrade describes a variety of practices, such as barter (an exchange of goods), counterpurchase (where the seller must agree to purchase a certain amount from the buyer or from another seller in the buyer's country), or offset (where the seller must reinvest some of the sales profits in the buyer's country). The risks and complications of such sales are higher. Sometimes, of course, the seller may have to agree to such arrangements in order to get the business, but specialized sales agreements adequately addressing many additional concerns must be utilized. Countertrade is further discussed in Part IV, Chapter 9.

Finally, an additional method of obtaining payment is the factoring of export accounts receivable. While many banks and some factors are reluctant to accept receivables on foreign sales due to the greater risks and uncertainties of collection, other factors are willing to do so. This may represent an opportunity for an exporter to obtain its money immediately in return for accepting a lesser amount, some discount from the sales price. If the factor buys the accounts receivable with recourse, that is, the right to charge back or get back the money paid to the exporter in case of default in payment by the customer, the factor's charge or discount should be correspondingly lower.

f. Export Financing

The substantive aspects of export financing were discussed in Chapter 2, Section T. If export financing is going to be utilized, it should be discussed in the international sales agreement.

The buyer will thus be clearly aware that the seller intends to use such export financing. The documentation that the buyer is required to provide in order for the seller to obtain such financing should be specified in the agreement, and the seller's obligation to sell and make shipment at specific dates should be subject to obtaining such export financing in a timely manner.

g. Security Interest

If the seller intends to sell on open account or on documents against acceptance, the seller should carefully investigate obtaining a security interest under the law of

(*Text continues on page 101.*)

Figure 3–10. International credit terms/payment methods.

FIRST CHICAGO

INTERNATIONAL CREDIT TERMS/PAYMENT METHODS

TERM	DEFINITION	APPLICATION	ADVANTAGES	DISADVANTAGES
Open Account	Exporter makes shipment and awaits payment direct from importer. Any documents needed by importer sent when sale is invoiced.	1. Importer has excellent credit rating. 2. Importer is long-time, well-known customer. 3. Importer is subsidiary of exporter or vice versa. 4. Small shipments to good customers. 5. Low-risk country.	1. Simple bookkeeping for exporter. 2. Easy documentation. 3. Competitive. 4. Low cost. 5. May be insured.	1. Full brunt of financing falls on exporter. 2. In matters of dispute, no interested third party involved. 3. Problems of availability of foreign exchange. 4. Exporter assumes credit risk of importer and risk of importer's country's political condition.
Consignment or Extended Terms	Exporter makes shipment and receives payment as goods are sold or used by importer.	1. Normally used only between subsidiaries of the same company. 2. Promissory notes may be used along with trust receipts and other legal agreements.	1. Exporter may retain title until goods are sold and/or paid for. 2. Competitive.	1. Same as Open Account. 2. Subject to local laws and customs. 3. Requires periodic inventorying of goods.
Time or Date Draft, Documents against Acceptance (D/A)	Exporter makes shipment and presents draft and documents to bank with instructions that documents are to be released to importer upon importer's acceptance of the draft (importer's acknowledgment of his debt and promise to pay at a future date).	1. Importer has excellent and/or good credit rating. 2. Low-risk country. 3. Extended terms necessary to make sale.	1. Draft is evidence of indebtedness. 2. Receivable may be discountable by exporter's bank with or without recourse. 3. Gives importer time to sell goods before having to pay for them. 4. Interested third party involved in case of dispute (bank). 5. Low cost. 6. May be insured.	1. Exporter is financing shipment until maturity of draft. 2. Problems of availability of foreign exchange. 3. Exporter assumes credit risk of importer and risk of importer's country's political condition. 4. Exporter assumes risk of refused shipment.

(continues)

Figure 3–10. *(continued)*

[reverse]

TERM	DEFINITION	APPLICATION	ADVANTAGES	DISADVANTAGES
Sight Draft, Documents against Payment (D/P), Cash against Documents	Exporter makes shipment and presents documents to bank with instructions that documents be released to importer only upon payment of draft.	1. Importer has excellent and/or good credit rating. 2. Small shipments. 3. Medium volume. 4. Low-risk country. 5. May be used in countries having foreign exchange restrictions not allowing open account purchases or sales.	1. Evidence of indebtedness. 2. Documents not released to importer before payment. (Exporter may retain title to merchandise until paid.) 3. Interested third party involved (bank). 4. Low cost. 5. May be insured.	1. Exporter must wait until draft has been received and paid. 2. Exporter assumes credit risk of importer and risk of importer's country's political condition. 3. Exporter assumes risk of refused shipment.
C.O.D.	Cash on delivery, collected by the carrier.	1. Importer's credit is excellent or good. 2. Small shipments. 3. Carrier accepts such shipments.	1. Exporter assured of payment before delivery of goods to importer by carrier.	1. Importer must have cash available. 2. Someone must pay C.O.D. charges. 3. Service not available to all countries. 4. Discourages repeat sales. 5. Exporter assumes risk of refused shipment.
Irrevocable L/C	Instrument issued by importer's bank in favor of exporter, payable against presentation to the issuing bank of specified documents.	1. Importer's credit rating may be excellent, good, fair, or unknown. 2. First-time sale. 3. Large sale. 4. Sale to country that requires L/Cs. 5. Low-risk country.	1. Exporter looks to bank for payment if documents are proper and in order. 2. Credit is irrevocable and may be amended only upon concurrence of all parties. 3. May be insured at preferred rate. 4. Banks may be willing to offer engagements to negotiate.	1. Cost of L/C. 2. Documents must be carefully prepared by exporter. 3. Exporter's credit risk is the foreign bank: foreign exchange and political risk still exist. 4. Importer exposed to possibilities of fraud.
Confirmed Irrevocable Letter of Credit	Same as above, except importer's bank asks advising bank to add its confirmation. Payable upon presentation of documents to the advising/confirming bank.	1. Importer's credit rating may be excellent, good, fair, or unknown. 2. First-time sale. 3. Large sale. 4. Country that requires L/Cs. 5. High-risk country.	1. Exporter looks to confirming bank for payment immediately upon shipment if documents are proper. 2. Credit is irrevocable and may be amended only upon concurrence of all parties. 3. Exporter's credit risk is confirming bank; confirming bank takes credit of issuing bank.	1. Cost of L/C. 2. Documents must be carefully prepared by exporter. 3. Importer exposed to possibility of fraud.
Cash in Advance	Importer sends good funds before exporter ships.	1. Importer is good, fair, or unknown credit risk. 2. One-time sale. 3. Small shipment. 4. High-risk country.	1. Exporter may use funds to prepare shipment. 2. No risk to exporter. 3. Low cost.	1. Importer bears costs of financing as well as risk of never receiving goods. 2. Uncompetitive; may preclude repeat business. 3. Some countries prohibit payment in advance.

the buyer's country to protect its rights to payment. Under the laws of most countries, unless the seller has registered its lien or security interest with a public agency, if the buyer goes into bankruptcy or falls into financial difficulties, the seller will be unable to repossess the merchandise that it sold, even if the merchandise is still in the possession of the buyer. Also, the seller may be unable to obtain priority over other creditors, and after such creditors are paid, nothing may remain for the seller. For example, through an attorney, the seller should investigate the availability of a security interest in the buyer's country and the requirements for establishing a security interest. The seller may need to retain title or a chattel mortgage or make a conditional sale. Then, in the international sales agreement, the fact that the buyer is granting a security interest to the seller and the documents that will be furnished by the buyer for public registration should be discussed and specified. The security interest normally should be established, including public registration, prior to delivery to the buyer, whether such transfer occurs in the United States (for example, ex-factory sales) or in the foreign country (for example, landed sales). The attorney would conduct a search of the public records in the buyer's country, and if other security interests have been granted, the seller should require the buyer to obtain a written subordination agreement from the other creditors before going forward.

h. Passage of Title, Delivery, and Risk of Loss

Ownership is transferred from the seller to the buyer by the passage of title. Under U.S. law, title will pass at the time and place agreed to by the parties to the international sales agreement. It can pass at the seller's plant; at the port of export; upon arrival in the foreign country; after clearance of customs in the foreign country; upon arrival at the buyer's place of business; or at any other place, time, or manner agreed to by the parties. Under the new Convention on the International Sale of Goods (discussed in subsection m), if the parties do not agree on the time and place for transfer of title and delivery, title will pass when the merchandise is transferred to the first transportation carrier. Usually the risk of loss for any subsequent casualty or damage to the products will pass to the buyer at the same time the title passes. However, it is possible to specify in the sales agreement that it will pass at a different time. Up to the point where the risk of loss passes to the buyer, the seller should be sure that the shipment is insured against casualty loss.

i. Warranties and Product Defects

From the seller's point of view, next to the payment provision, perhaps the most important single provision in an international sales agreement is the one that specifies the warranty terms. Under the laws of most countries and the Convention on Contracts for the International Sale of Goods (discussed in subsection *m*), unless the seller limits its warranty expressly in writing in its international sales agreement, the seller will be responsible and liable for foreseeable consequential damages that result to the buyer from defective products. Since such consequential damages can far exceed the profits that the seller has made on such sales, unless the seller expressly limits its liabilities, the risk of engaging in the sales transaction can be too great. The sales agreement should specify exactly what warranty the seller is giving for the products, whether the products are being sold "as is" with no warranty, whether there is a limited warranty such as repair or replacement, whether there is a dollar limit on the warranty, whether there is a time period within which the warranty claim must be made, and/or whether there is any limitation on consequential damages. In many countries, as a matter of public policy, the law prohibits certain types of warranty disclaimers or exclusions. Consequently, in drafting the warranty limitation, the seller may need to consult with an attorney to make sure that the warranty will be effective in the destination country. In addition, of course, the buyer will be seeking the strongest warranty possible, so this is an area in which the seller must be particularly careful. If the sales agreement is formed by a mere exchange of preprinted forms, as discussed in Section A.4 above, the seller may find that the buyer's terms or conditions control the sale and that no limitation of warranty has been achieved. In such cases, the seller must negotiate a warranty acceptable to both sides before going ahead with the sale. One related point is that the Magnuson-Moss Warranty Act, which prescribes certain warranties and is applicable to merchandise sold in the United States, including imported merchandise, is not applicable to export sales. Laws in the foreign country may be applicable, however.

j. Preshipment Inspections

A number of countries, particularly in South America and Africa (see list in Chapter 4, Section G), require that before companies located in their country purchase products from a foreign seller, the foreign seller submit to a preshipment inspection. The ostensible purpose of such inspections is to eliminate a situation where a dishonest seller ships defective products or even crates of sawdust, but obtains payment through a letter of credit or banking channels because the seller has provided a fraudulent bill of lading and draft to the bank, and the buyer has not yet been able to inspect the goods. Even if the buyer has not paid in advance, if the products arrive in the foreign country and are defective, the buyer may be faced with substantial losses or the necessity of re-exporting the merchandise to the seller. Consequently, it is not unreasonable for a buyer to request and for a seller to agree to a preshipment inspection, but the terms and conditions of such an inspection should be specified in the international sales agreement. In particular, in recent years, some of the inspection agencies have been reviewing more than the quality of the goods and have been requiring sellers to produce documentation relating to sales of the same product to other customers to ascertain the prices at which sales were made. If the particular customer that is getting the preshipment inspection determines that the price that it is paying is higher than the prices that the seller has charged other customers, the customer may refuse to go forward with the transaction or attempt to renegotiate the price. Consequently, in an international sales agreement, if the seller simply agrees to a preshipment inspection satisfactory to the buyer, the inspection company's report may be an unfavorable one based upon price, and the buyer would be excused from going forward with the purchase. In summary, the type of preshipment inspection that will be permitted, its scope, its terms, and the consequences if the inspection is unfavorable should be specified in the international sales agreement.

The seller (and buyer) should also realize that providing for a preshipment inspection will usually delay the shipment anywhere from twenty to forty days.

k. Export Licenses

The importance of an export license was touched upon in Chapter 2, Section F, and is discussed in detail in Chapter 5. If an export license will be required in an international sales agreement, the exporter should state that it is required and should require the buyer to provide the necessary documentation to apply for the license. If the buyer fails to provide such documentation, the seller would be excused from making the export sale and could claim damages. Furthermore, in order to protect the seller from a violation of U.S. export control laws, the international sales agreement and the provisions therein relating to any export license would be evidence that the seller had fulfilled its responsibilities to inform the buyer that the products cannot be re-exported from the buyer's own country without obtaining a re-export license from the U.S. authorities. Finally, the sales agreement should provide that if the seller cannot obtain the export license, the seller's performance of the sales agreement will be excused without the payment of damages to the buyer. (Under the Incoterms, the buyer is responsible for obtaining the export license on "ex-works" sales, but recent changes to U.S. law make the seller responsible unless the buyer has specifically agreed to such responsibility and has appointed a U.S. agent.)

l. Import Licenses and Foreign Government Filings

An international sales agreement should specify that the buyer will be responsible for obtaining all necessary import licenses and making any foreign government filings. The buyer should state exactly what licenses must be obtained and what filings must be made. The sales agreement should specify that the buyer will obtain such licenses sufficiently in advance, for example, prior to manufacture or shipment, so that the seller can be comfortable that payment will be forthcoming. In regard to the applications for such licenses or any foreign government filings, the exporter should insist upon and should obligate the buyer in the international sales agreement to provide copies of those applications prior to their filing. In this way, the seller can confirm that the information in the application is correct; for example, that the prices being stated to the government agencies are the same as those that the seller is quoting to the buyer, or if there is any reference to the seller in the applications, that the seller will know what is being said about it. This will also permit the seller to know the exact time when such applications are being made and, therefore, whether the approval will delay or interfere with the anticipated sales shipment and payment schedule.

m. Governing Law

In any international sales agreement, whether the agreement is formed by a written agreement between the parties or whether it is an oral agreement, the rights and obligations of the parties will be governed by either the law of the country of the seller or the law of the country of the buyer. The laws of most countries permit the seller and buyer to specifically agree on which law will apply, and that choice will be binding upon both parties whether or not a lawsuit is brought in either the buyer's or the seller's country. Of course, whenever the subject is raised, the seller will prefer the agreement to be governed by the laws of the seller's country, and the buyer will prefer it to be governed by the laws of the buyer's country. If the bargaining leverage of the parties is approximately equal, it is fair to say that it is more customary for the buyer to agree that the seller's law will govern the agreement. However, if the buyer has more bargaining leverage, the seller may have to agree that the buyer's foreign law applies. Before doing so, however, the seller should check on what differences exist between the foreign law and U.S. law so that the seller can fully appreciate the risks it is assuming by agreeing to the application of foreign law. The seller can also determine whether or not the risk is serious enough to negotiate a specific solution to that particular problem with the buyer. Frequently, however, the parties do not raise, negotiate, or expressly agree upon the governing law. This may occur as a result of an exchange of preprinted forms wherein the buyer and seller have each specified that its own law governs, which results in a clear conflict between these two provisions. It may also occur when the parties have not agreed upon the governing law, as in a situation where an oral agreement of sale has occurred, or when the email, facsimile, or other purchase or sale documentation does not contain any express specification of the governing law. In such cases, if a dispute arises between the parties, it will be extremely difficult to determine with any confidence which law governs the sales agreement. Often the seller believes that the law of the country where the offer is accepted will govern. However, the laws of the two countries may be in conflict on this point, and it may be unclear whether this means an offer to sell or an offer to buy and whether or not the acceptance must be received by the offeror before the formation of the sales agreement.

An additional development relating to this issue is the Convention on Contracts for the International Sale of Goods (the Convention). On January 1, 1988, this multinational treaty went into effect among the countries that signed it, including the United States. The following list includes the parties to the Convention as of February 2009.

Parties to the Convention on Contracts for the International Sale of Goods (as of February 5, 2009)

Argentina	Cuba	Guinea
Armenia	Cyprus	Honduras
Australia	Czech Rep.	Hungary
Austria	Denmark	Iceland
Belarus	Ecuador	Iraq
Belgium	Egypt	Israel
Bosnia-Herzegovina	El Salvador	Italy
Bulgaria	Estonia	Japan
Burundi	Finland	South Korea
Canada	France	Kyrgyzstan
Chile	Gabon	Latvia
China (PRC)	Georgia	Lebanon
Colombia	Germany	Lesotho
Croatia	Greece	Liberia

Lithuania	Paraguay	Spain
Luxembourg	Peru	Sweden
Macedonia	Poland	Switzerland
Mauritania	Romania	Syria
Mexico	Russian Federation	Uganda
Moldova	Saint Vincent & Grenadines	Ukraine
Mongolia	Serbia	United States
Montenegro	Singapore	Uruguay
Netherlands	Slovakia	Uzbekistan
New Zealand	Slovenia	Zambia
Norway		

The Convention is a detailed listing of over one hundred articles dealing with the rights and responsibilities of the buyer and the seller in international sales agreements. It is similar in some respects to Article 2 of the Uniform Commercial Code in the United States. Nevertheless, there are many concepts, such as fundamental breach, avoidance, impediment, and nonconformity, that are not identical to U.S. law.

The Convention permits buyers and sellers located in countries that are parties to the Convention to exclude the application of the Convention (by expressly referring to it) and to choose the law of either the seller or the buyer to apply to the international sales agreement. However, for companies located in any of the countries that are parties to the convention (including U.S. companies), if the seller and buyer cannot or do not agree on which law will apply, the provisions of the Convention will automatically apply. In general, this may be disadvantageous for the U.S. seller because the Convention strengthens the rights of buyers in various ways.

In summary, the seller should include provisions on governing law in its international sales agreement, and if the buyer disagrees, the seller should negotiate this provision. The seller should also determine what differences exist between the Convention and U.S. law in case the parties cannot agree and the Convention thereby becomes applicable.

n. Dispute Resolution

One method of resolving disputes that may arise between the parties is litigation in the courts. For a U.S. exporter, the most likely dispute to arise is the failure of the buyer to make payment. In such a case, the exporter may be limited to going to the courts of the buyer's country in order to institute litigation and seek a judgment to obtain assets of the buyer. Even if the parties have agreed that U.S. law will govern the sales agreement, there is a risk that a foreign court may misapply U.S. law, disregard U.S. law, or otherwise favor and protect the company located in its own country. Furthermore, there can be significant delays in legal proceedings (from two to five years), court and legal expenses can be high, and the outcome may be unsatisfactory. In order to reduce such risks, the exporter can specify in the international sales agreement that all disputes must be resolved in the courts of the seller's country, and that the buyer consents to jurisdiction there, and to the commencement of any such lawsuit by the simple forwarding of any form of written notice by the seller. Of course, buyers may resist such provisions, and whether or not the seller will be able to finally obtain this agreement will depend upon the negotiating and bargaining strength of the parties. The seller does need to realize that even if it obtains a judgment in the United States, if the buyer has no assets in the United States, its judgment may be of limited value.

Another form of dispute resolution that is common in international sales agreements is arbitration. In many foreign countries, buyers take a less adversarial approach to the resolution of contractual disputes, and they feel more comfortable with a less formal proceeding, such as arbitration. While arbitration can be included in an international sales agreement, an exporter should thoroughly understand the advantages and disadvantages of agreeing to resolve disputes by arbitration.

First, arbitration is unlikely to save much in expenses, and quite often may not involve a significantly shorter time period to resolve the dispute. In fact, from the point of view of expense, in some cases, if the buyer refuses to go forward with the arbitration, the seller will have to advance the buyer's portion of the arbitration fees to the arbitration tribunal; otherwise, the arbitrators will not proceed with the dispute. Furthermore, in litigation, of course, the judges or juries involved are paid at the public expense, whereas in arbitration, the parties must pay the expenses of the arbitrators, which can be very substantial.

Second, the administering authority must be selected. The International Chamber of Commerce is commonly designated as the administering authority in arbitration clauses, but the fees it charges are very high. The American Arbitration Association also handles international disputes, but the foreign buyer may be unwilling to agree to arbitration by a U.S. administering authority. Other administering authorities, such as the Inter-American Commercial Arbitration Commission, the London Court of International Arbitration, the Stockholm Chamber of Commerce Arbitration Institute, the British Columbia International Arbitration Centre, or an arbitration authority in the buyer's country, may be acceptable.

Third, the number of arbitrators should be specified. Since the parties will be paying for them, I recommend that one arbitrator be utilized and specified in the agreement to resolve disputes of a smaller amount (a specified dollar figure) and that three arbitrators be utilized for larger disputes.

Fourth, the place of arbitration must be specified. Again, the seller and buyer will have a natural conflict on this point, so some third country or intermediate location is probably most likely to be mutually agreeable. Another variation that has developed, although its legal validity has been questioned, is an agreement that if the exporter commences the arbitration, arbitration will be conducted in the buyer's country, and if the buyer commences the arbitration, the arbitration will be conducted in the exporter's country. This has the effect of discouraging either party from bringing arbitration and forcing the parties to reach amicable solutions to their disputes.

Finally, the seller should ascertain beforehand whether an arbitral award would be enforced in the courts of the buyer's country. Some fifty-five countries have become parties to a multinational treaty known as the New York Convention, which commits them to enforcing the arbitral awards of other member countries. Without this assurance, the entire dispute may have to be relitigated in the buyer's country.

o. Termination

Termination of an international sales agreement or distributor or sales agent agreement may prove to be much more difficult than termination of a domestic agreement. Many countries have enacted laws that as a matter of public policy are designed to protect buyers, distributors, and sales agents located in their country against unfair terminations. The rationale for these laws is generally that the U.S. seller has significant economic leverage by virtue of its position, and that after a buyer has invested a great deal of time in purchasing products or building up a market for resale of such products, the sellers should not be permitted to terminate the agreement on short notice or without payment of some compensation. Of course, such rationale may be totally inconsistent with the facts, such as when the seller is a small company or when the buyer is breaching the agreement. In any event, before engaging in an ongoing sales relationship with any customer in a foreign country or appointing a distributor or sales agent there, the seller should get specific legal advice and determine what protective legislation exists. Often, avoidance of such legislation or reduction in the amount of compensation that must be paid at the time of termination is highly dependent upon inserting in the international sales agreement at the outset certain specific provisions (which will vary from country to country) limiting the seller's termination liability. For example, the seller's right to terminate without any payment of compensation when the buyer is in breach should be specified. The right of the seller to appoint another distributor in the country and to require the former distributor to cooperate in transferring inventory to the new distributor and the right to terminate for change in control, bankruptcy, or insolvency of the buyer should be specified.

Related thereto is the term of the agreement. Often agreements will be set up for a one-year term with automatic renewal provisions. Such agreements are treated as long-term agreements or indefinite or perpetual agreements under some laws and can result in the payment of maximum termination compensation. The term of the agreement that will best protect the seller's flexibility and reduce the compensation payable should be inserted after review of the buyer's law.

C. Export Distributor and Sales Agent Agreements

In addition to the foregoing provisions, which arise in all international sales agreements, there are other, specific provisions that arise in export distributor agreements and sales agent agreements.

1. Distinction Between Distributor and Sales Agent

A distributor is a company that buys products from a seller, takes title thereto, and assumes the risk of resale. A distributor will purchase at a specific price and will be compensated by reselling the product at a higher price. Under the antitrust laws of most countries, the seller cannot restrict or require a distributor to resell the product at any specific price, although it may be able to restrict the customers or territories to which the buyer resells.

A sales agent does not purchase from the seller. The sales agent or representative locates customers and solicits offers to purchase the product from them. In order to avoid tax liability for the seller in a foreign country, the sales agent normally will not have any authority to accept offers to purchase from potential customers in that country. Instead, the offers from the customer are forwarded to the seller for final acceptance, and shipment and billing is direct between the seller and the customer. For such services, the sales agent is paid a commission or some other type of compensation. Because no sale occurs between the seller and the sales agent, the seller can specify the price at which it will sell to customers, and the sales agent can be restricted to quoting only that price to a potential customer. Likewise, the sales agent can be restricted as to its territory or the types of customers from which it can solicit orders. Sometimes the sales agent will guarantee payment by the customers or perform other services, such as after-sales service or invoicing of the customers. A chart summarizing these differences is shown in Figure 3–11.

The financial returns and accounting will differ when using a distributor versus a sales agent.

The main reason is that the sales price will be direct to the customer, which will be higher than the sale price to a distributor. A comparison of these revenues and expenses is shown in Figure 3–12.

2. *Export Distributor Agreements*

As previously indicated, when a distributor agreement is utilized, such agreement will act as an umbrella agreement, and specific orders for specific quantities, shipment dates, and, possibly, prices will be stated in purchase orders, purchase order

Figure 3–11. Legal comparison of distributors and agents.

COMPARISON OF DISTRIBUTORS AND AGENTS

		Distributor	Agent
1.	Compensation	Markup	Commission
2.	Title	Owner	Not owner
3.	Risk of loss	On distributor	On seller
4.	Price control	Cannot control	Can control
5.	Credit risk	On distributor	On seller
6.	Tax liability in foreign country	On distributor	Potentially on seller if agent given authority to accept orders or if distributor maintains inventory for local delivery

Figure 3–12. Financial comparison of using distributors and sales agents.

Seller's Profit and Loss	*Distributor*	*Sales Agent*
Net sales	$2,000,000	$4,000,000
Gross profit	$1,000,000	$3,000,000
Commission (10%)		$ 400,000
Possible need to warehouse inventory in foreign country		$ 400,000
Advertising		$ 400,000
Customer service, after-sales service		$ 300,000
General, selling, and administrative	$ 200,000	$ 200,000
Operating income	$ 800,000	$ 900,000
Operating income/net sales	40%	22.5%

acceptances, and similar documentation. A checklist for negotiation issues for the appointment of a distributor is shown in Figure 3–13. The important provisions in an international distributor agreement include the following:

a. Territory and Exclusivity

The distributor will normally want to be the exclusive distributor in a territory, whereas the seller would generally prefer to make a nonexclusive appointment so that if the distributor fails to perform, it can appoint other distributors. Also, the seller may simply wish from the outset to appoint a number of distributors in that country to adequately serve the market. A possible compromise is that the appointment will be exclusive unless certain minimum purchase obligations are not met, in which case the seller has the right to convert the agreement to a nonexclusive agreement.

Usually the country or part of the country that is granted to the distributor is specified. The distributor agrees not to solicit sales from outside the territory, although under the laws of some countries, it may not be possible to prohibit the distributor from reselling outside the territory. In such cases, the distributor may be prohibited from establishing any warehouse or sales outlet outside the territory.

b. Pricing

As previously indicated, normally it will be illegal to specify the price at which the foreign distributor can resell the merchandise. This may present some problems because the distributor may mark the product up very substantially, gouging end

(*Text continues on page 112.*)

Figure 3–13. Foreign distributorship appointment checklist.

1. Appointment
   - (a) Appointment
   - (b) Acceptance
   - (c) Exclusivity
   - (d) Subdistributors

2. Territory

3. Products

4. Sales Activities
   - (a) Advertising (optional)
   - (b) Initial purchases (optional)
   - (c) Minimum purchases (optional)
   - (d) Sales increases (optional)
   - (e) Purchase orders
   - (f) Distributor's resale prices
   - (g) Direct shipment to customers
   - (h) Product specialist (optional)
   - (i) Installation and service
   - (j) Distributor facilities (optional)
   - (k) Visits to distributor premises
   - (l) Reports
   - (m) Financial condition

5. Prices
   - (a) Initial
   - (b) Changes
   - (c) Taxes

6. Acceptance of Orders and Shipment
   - (a) Acceptance
   - (b) Inconsistent terms in distributor's order
   - (c) Shipments
   - (d) No violation of U.S. laws
   - (e) Passage of title, risk of loss

7. Payments
   - (a) Terms
   - (b) Letter of credit
   - (c) Deposits
   - (d) Payments in dollars
   - (e) No setoff by distributor
   - (f) Security interest

8. Confidential Information

Figure 3–13. *(continued)*

9. Sales Literature
    - (a) Advertising literature
    - (b) Quantities
    - (c) Mailing lists
10. Patents, Trademarks, and Copyrights; Agency Registrations
11. No Warranty Against Infringement
12. No Consequential Damages
13. Product Warranty, Defects, Claims, Returns
14. Relationship Between Parties
15. Effective Date and Duration
    - (a) Effective date and term
    - (b) Early termination
        - (i) Breach
        - (ii) Insolvency
        - (iii) Prospective breach
        - (iv) Change in ownership or management
        - (v) Foreign protective law
        - (vi) Unilateral (reciprocal) on agreed notice (without cause)
16. Rights and Obligations Upon Termination
    - (a) No liability for seller
    - (b) Return of promotional materials
    - (c) Repurchase of stock
    - (d) Accrued rights and obligation
17. Non-Competition
18. No Assignment
19. Government Regulation
    - (a) Foreign law
    - (b) U.S. law
    - (c) Foreign Corrupt Practices Act compliance
20. Force Majeure
21. Separability
22. Waiver
23. Notices
    - (a) Written notice
    - (b) Oral notice

users and resulting in less sales and market penetration for the seller's products. Consequently, in some countries it is possible to restrict the maximum resale price but not the minimum resale price. In addition, because of the gray market problem, the price at which the seller sells to the distributor must be set very carefully. Depending on the price at which the distributor buys or whether or not the distributor can be legally prohibited from exporting, the distributor may resell products that will create a gray market in competition with the seller's other distributors or even the seller in its own markets. This can occur especially as a result of exchange rate fluctuations, where the distributor is able to obtain a product at a lower price in its own currency than is available in other markets where the product is being sold.

The seller must monitor currency fluctuations and retain the right to make price adjustments in the distributor agreement to make sure that the seller is fairly participating in the profits being created along the line of distribution. For example, if the U.S. seller sells a product for $1 at a time when the Japanese exchange rate is ¥250 to $1, the buyer will be paying ¥250 for the $1 product and perhaps marking it up to ¥400. However, if the yen strengthens and the buyer can purchase a $1 product by paying only ¥150, and if the buyer continues to resell at ¥400, the buyer will make inordinate profits. Sometimes the buyer will continue to ask for price reductions from the seller even though the buyer has had a very favorable exchange rate movement. Normally the seller's interest is that the buyer reduce the resale price (for example, to ¥250) in order to make more sales, increase volume, increase market penetration, and capture the long-term market. When the distributor will not agree to reduce its resale price, the price from the seller should be raised to make sure that part of the profits that the distributor is making on resales in its own country are recovered by the seller.

c. Minimum Purchase Quantities

In most long-term sales agreements or distributor agreements, one of the reasons for entering into such agreements is that the seller expects a commitment for a significant quantity to be purchased and the buyer is requesting some price discount for such a commitment. Consequently, before a seller agrees to give a distributor an exclusive appointment in a territory or to grant any price reductions, a provision relating to the minimum purchase quantities (which may be adjusted from time to time according to some objective formula or by agreement of the parties) should be inserted in the distributor agreement. Distributors will ordinarily be required to commit to using their best efforts to promote the sale of the merchandise in the territory, but since best efforts is a somewhat vague commitment, minimum purchase quantities (or dollar amounts) are important supplements to that commitment.

d. Handling Competing Products

Normally a seller will want a provision wherein the distributor agrees not to handle competing products. If the distributor is handling any competing products (either manufacturing them or purchasing them from alternative sources), it is likely that the distributor will not always promote the seller's products, especially if the buyer is getting larger markups or margins on the other products. In addition, if the seller grants an exclusive distribution right to the distributor, the seller has given up the opportunity to increase its sales by appointing more distributors in the territory. Under such circumstances, the distributor should definitely agree not to handle any competing products. In some countries, the distributor can be restricted from handling competing products only if an exclusive appointment is given by the seller.

e. Effective Date and Government Review

In some countries it is necessary to file distributor or long-term sales agreements with government authorities. Sometimes there is a specific waiting period before the agreement can become effective or government review will be completed. In any event, the distributor agreement should provide that it does not become effective until government review is completed. If the distributor's government suggests changes to the agreement, for example, the elimination of minimum purchase quantities, the seller should have the opportunity to renegotiate the agreement or withdraw from the agreement without being bound to proceed. In that respect, the seller must be careful not to ship a large amount of inventory or accept a large initial order while government review is pending.

f. Appointment of Subdistributors

Whether or not a distributor has the right to appoint subdistributors should be expressly stated in the distributor agreement. If this right is not discussed, the distributor may have the right under its own law to appoint subdistributors. This can cause various problems for the seller. Not only will the seller have no immediate direct contact with the subdistributors, but it may not even be aware of who such subdistributors are, their location, or the territories into which they are shipping. Soon the seller's products may show up in territories granted to other distributors or be imported back into the United States, or significant gray market sales or counterfeits may develop. If the right to appoint subdistributors is granted, the distributor should remain responsible for its activities, including payment for any goods sold to such subdistributors, and for providing the names of such subdistributors to the seller in advance so that the seller will have the opportunity to investigate the financial strength, creditworthiness, and business reputation of all persons who will be distributing its products.

g. Use of Trade Names, Trademarks, and Copyrights

As discussed in Chapter 2, Section G, there are risks that the seller's intellectual property rights will be lost. Sometimes distributors are the biggest offenders. In an effort to protect their market position, they use the seller's name or trademark in their own business or corporate name or register the seller's intellectual property in their own country. This is a particular disadvantage for the seller, because if the distributor does not perform properly and the seller wishes to terminate the distributor and to appoint a new distributor, the past distributor may own the intellectual property rights or have a registered exclusive license to distribute the products in that country. Until the distributor consents to the assignment of the intellectual property rights to the seller or the new distributor or deregisters its exclusive license, any sales into the territory by the seller or by the new distributor will be an infringement of the intellectual property rights owned by the former distributor and cannot proceed. This puts the former distributor in a very strong bargaining position to negotiate a substantial termination compensation payment. Even when the distributor is granted an exclusive territory, the distributor agreement should provide that the distributor is granted a nonexclusive patent, trademark, and/or copyright license to sell the products (but not to manufacture or cause others to manufacture the products), and should obligate the distributor to recognize the validity of the intellectual property rights and to take no steps to register them or to otherwise interfere with the ownership rights of the seller. Of course, the seller should register its intellectual property rights directly in the foreign country in its own name and not permit the distributor to do so on the seller's behalf or in the distributor's name.

h. Warranties and Product Liability

In addition to the considerations discussed above, the seller should require the distributor to maintain product liability insurance in its own name and to name the seller as an additional insured in amounts that are deemed satisfactory by the seller. Although product liability claims are not as common overseas as they are in the United States, they are increasing substantially, and under most product liability laws, even though the distributor sold the product to the customer, the customer will have a right to sue the manufacturer (or supplier) directly. Furthermore, the fact that the manufacturer was aware that its product was being sold in that country will make it foreseeable that a defective product will be sold there and the U.S. manufacturer may be subject to the jurisdiction of the courts in that country. The seller should also make sure that the distributor does not modify or add any additional warranties in the resale of the product beyond those that the manufacturer or U.S. seller has given. Practically, this means that the distributor should be obligated to provide a copy of its warranty in advance of resale for approval by the seller. The distributor may also be authorized or required to perform after-sales service, but the seller will need an opportunity to audit the books and service records from time to time to prevent abuses and warranty compensation reimbursement claims by the distributor for service that has not actually been performed.

3. Export Sales Agent Agreements

Like distributor agreements, sales agent agreements often contain many of the same provisions included in an international sales agreement, but there are certain provisions that are peculiar to the sales agent agreement that must be considered. A checklist for negotiation issues for the appointment of a sales agent is shown in Figure 3–14.

a. Commissions

The sales agent is compensated for its activities by payment of a commission by the seller. The sales agent is appointed to solicit orders, and when such orders are accepted by the seller, the agent may be paid a commission. Sometimes payment of the commission is deferred until such time as the customer actually makes payment to the seller. Generally, the seller should not bill the agent for the price of the product (less commission) because such a practice could result in characterizing the relationship as a distributorship rather than a sales agency. Generally, any commissions

(*Text continues on page 117.*)

Figure 3–14. Foreign sales representative appointment checklist.

1. Appointment—Acceptance
   - (a) Exclusivity
   - (d) Subrepresentatives
2. Territory
3. Product
4. Responsibilities
   - (a) Promotional efforts
   - (b) Price quotations
   - (c) Minimum orders (optional)
   - (d) Increase in orders (optional)
   - (e) Representative's facilities
5. Confidential Information
6. Reports
   - (a) Operations report
   - (b) Credit information
7. Visits to Representative's Premises by Supplier
8. Promotional Literature
9. Trademarks and Copyrights
10. Acceptance of Orders and Shipments
    - (a) Acceptance only by supplier
    - (b) No violation of U.S. laws
    - (c) Direct shipment to customers
11. Commissions
    - (a) Commission percentage or fee
    - (b) Accrual
    - (c) Refund
12. Discontinuation of Products
13. Repair and Rework
14. Relationship Between Parties
15. No Warranty Against Infringement

(*continues*)

Figure 3–14. *(continued)*

16. Product Warranty (to customers)

17. Effective Date and Duration
    - (a) Effective date and term
    - (b) Early termination
        - (i) Breach
        - (ii) Insolvency
        - (iii) Prospective breach
        - (iv) Change in ownership or management
        - (v) Foreign protective law
        - (vi) Unilateral (reciprocal) on agreed notice (without cause)

18. Rights and Obligations Upon Termination
    - (a) No liability of supplier
    - (b) Commission
    - (c) Return of promotional materials
    - (d) Accrued rights and obligation

19. Non-Competition

20. No Assignment

21. Government Regulation
    - (a) Foreign law
    - (b) U.S. law
    - (c) Foreign Corrupt Practices Act compliance

22. Force Majeure

23. Separability

24. Waiver

25. Notices
    - (a) Written notice
    - (b) Oral notice

26. Governing Law

27. Dispute Resolution

28. Entire Agreement
    - (a) Entire agreement
    - (b) Modifications

payable should be made by wire transfer directly to the sales agent's bank account in the foreign country. Payments in cash, checks delivered in the United States, or payments in third countries may facilitate violation of the foreign exchange control or tax laws of the foreign country, and the seller may be liable as an aider and abettor of the violation.

b. Pricing

Because there is no sale between the seller and the sales agent, the seller can lawfully require the sales agent to quote only prices that the seller has authorized. For sellers who wish to establish uniform pricing on a worldwide basis, eliminate gray markets, and control markups, use of the sales agent appointment can be highly beneficial. However, the trade-off is that the seller will ordinarily assume the credit risk and will have to satisfy itself in regard to the ability of the customer to pay. This sometimes presents difficulties in obtaining sufficient information, although the sales agent can be given the responsibility for gathering and forwarding such information to the seller prior to acceptance of any orders. In addition, some sales agents are willing to be appointed as del credere agents, whereby the sales agent guarantees payment by any customer from whom it solicits an order. Obviously, sales agents will require higher commissions for guaranteeing payment, but it can reduce the seller's risks in having to investigate the customer's credit while permitting the seller to specify the price that the sales agent quotes.

c. Shipment

Shipment is not made to the sales agent; it is made directly to the customer from whom the sales agent has solicited the order. Generally there will be problems associated with trying to maintain an inventory at the agent's place of business in the foreign country. Under the laws of many countries, if the seller maintains an inventory abroad in its own name or through an agent, the seller can become taxable on its own sales profits to customers in that country. If the customer cannot wait for shipment from the United States, or if it is important to maintain an inventory in the country, the appropriate way to do so while using sales agents must be investigated with an attorney knowledgeable in foreign law.

d. Warranties

It is important to keep in mind that product warranties should be made only to customers (purchasers). Since sales agents are not purchasers, the inclusion of warranty provisions in a sales agency agreement can cause confusion unless it is made clear that the warranty in the agreement with the sales agent is for the purpose of informing the sales agent as to what warranty it is authorized to communicate to prospective purchasers.

e. Relationship of the Parties

Although businesspersons frequently refer to intermediaries as distributors and "agents," legally, it is dangerous for a seller to enter into a principal-agent relationship. In such cases, the seller may become legally responsible for the acts and omissions of the agent. Generally, the "agent" should be an independent contractor, and that should be clearly expressed in the agreement. For this reason, it is usually better to designate the intermediary as a sales "representative." Furthermore, the seller should make clear that it does not control the day-to-day activities of the agent; otherwise, he may be deemed an agent or even an employee (if he is an individual), with corresponding liability risks and potential tax obligations.

D. Foreign Corrupt Practices Act Compliance

Another provision that should be included in the agreement relates to the Foreign Corrupt Practices Act (FCPA). In the United States, the FCPA makes it a violation of U.S. law for an agent of a U.S. exporter to pay any money or compensation to a foreign government agency, official, or political party for the purpose of obtaining or retaining business. If this occurs, the U.S. exporter will have violated the law if it knew that the foreign agent was engaged in such activities. Obviously, whether the exporter "knew" can be a matter of dispute, but if unusual circumstances occur, for instance, a distributor or agent asks for a special discount, allowance, or commission, or that payment be made to someone other than the distributor or agent, the exporter can be charged with knowledge of unusual circumstances that should have caused it to realize that something improper was occurring. One way to help avoid such liability is to specify expressly in the agreement that the agent recognizes the existence of the FCPA and commits and agrees not to make any payments to foreign government officials or political parties for the purpose of gaining business, or at least not to do so without consultation with the seller and receiving confirmation that such activity will not violate the FCPA. Distributors and agents should also be informed and agree not to make such payments to the buyer's employees, even if the buyer is not a government agency, as such payments will usually violate foreign commercial bribery laws.

As of March 2009, when Israel became a signatory, thirty-eight countries have ratified the Organization of Economic Cooperation and Development Anti-Bribery Convention. The OECD monitors enforcement in order to ensure that all member countries continue to fight against bribery.

Chapter 4

Exporting: Other Export Documentation

Although the sales agreement is by far the most important single document in an export sales transaction, there are numerous other documents with which the exporter must be familiar. In some cases, the exporter may not actually prepare such documents, especially if the exporter utilizes the services of a freight forwarder. Nevertheless, as discussed in Chapter 2, Section K, relating to the utilization of freight forwarders, the exporter is responsible for the content of the documents prepared and filed by its agent, the freight forwarder. Since the exporter has legal responsibility for any mistakes of the freight forwarder, it is very important for the exporter to understand what documents the freight forwarder is preparing and for the exporter to review and be totally comfortable with the contents of such documents. Furthermore, the documents prepared by the freight forwarder are usually prepared based on information supplied by the exporter. If the exporter does not understand the documents or the information that is being requested and a mistake occurs, the freight forwarder will claim that the mistake was due to improper information provided by the exporter.

A. Freight Forwarder's Power of Attorney

A freight forwarder may provide a form contract that specifies the services it will perform and the terms and conditions of the relationship. Among other things, the contract will contain a provision appointing the freight forwarder as an agent to prepare documentation and granting a power of attorney for that purpose. A sample power of attorney form is shown in Figure 4–1. The freight forwarder is required to have a power of attorney or other written authorization in order to prepare and file the Electronic Export Information (Shipper's Export Declaration) through the Automated Export System. In many instances, the freight forwarder may only ask for the power of attorney up front, and the terms and conditions for the exporter/forwarder relationship appear on the back of its invoice. The exporter and the forwarder should clearly define the services that are expected and any terms and conditions in advance of beginning their relationship together. A sample written authorization is shown in Figure 4–2.

(*Text continues on page 122.*)

Figure 4–1. Power of attorney.

U.S. Census Bureau

SAMPLE FORMAT: Power of Attorney

POWER OF ATTORNEY
EXPORTER (U.S. PRINCIPAL PARTY IN INTEREST)/FORWARDING AGENT

Know all men by these presents, That ___________________________, the (USPPI)
(Name of U.S. Principal Party in Interest (USPPI))
organized and doing business under the laws of the State or Country of ________________
and having an office and place of business at ______________________________________
(Address of USPPI)
hereby authorizes _______________________________, the (Forwarding Agent)
(Forwarding Agent)
of ____
(Address of Forwarding Agent)
to act for and on its behalf as a true and lawful agent and attorney of the U.S. Principal Party in Interest for and in the name, place and stead of the U.S. Principal Party in Interest, from this date, in the United States either in writing, electronically, or by other authorized means to:

Act as Forwarding Agent for Export Control, Census Reporting and Customs purposes. Make, endorse or sign any Shipper's Export Declaration or other documents or to perform any act which may be required by law or regulation in connection with the exportation or transportation of any merchandise shipped or consigned by or to the U.S. Principal Party in Interest and to receive or ship any merchandise on behalf of the U.S. Principal Party in Interest.

The U.S. Principal Party in Interest hereby certifies that all statements and information contained in the documentation provided to the Forwarding Agent relating to exportation are true and correct. Furthermore, the U.S. Principal Party in Interest understands that civil and criminal penalties, may be imposed for making false or fraudulent statements or for the violation of any United States laws or regulations on exportation.

This power of attorney is to remain in full force and effect until revocation in writing is duly given by the U.S. Principal Party in Interest and received by the Forwarding Agent.

IN WITNESS WHEREOF, ______________________________ caused these
(Full Name of USPPI/USPPI Company)
presents to be sealed and signed:

Witness: ________________________ Signature: ________________________
Capacity: ________________________
Date: ________________________

Regulations, Outreach, & Eduation Branch, Foreign Trade Division: 301-457-2238

Figure 4–2. Written authorization.

U.S. Census Bureau

SAMPLE FORMAT: Written Authorization

WRITTEN AUTHORIZATION TO PREPARE OR TRANSMIT SHIPPER'S EXPORT INFORMATION

I __________________________________, authorize

Exporter (U.S. Principal Party in Interest)

______________________________, to act as forwarding agent for

(Forwarding Agent)

export control and customs purposes and to sign any Shipper's Export Declaration (SED), or transmit such export information electronically, which may be required by law or regulation in connection with the exportation or transportation of any merchandise on behalf of said U.S. Principal Party in Interest. The U.S. Principal Party in Interest certifies that necessary and proper documentation to accurately complete the SED or transmit the information electronically is and will be provided to the said Forwarding Agent. The U.S. Principal Party in Interest further understands that civil and criminal penalties may be imposed for making false or fraudulent statements or for the violation of any United States laws or regulations on exportation and agrees to be bound by all statements of said agent based upon information or documentation provided by exporter to said agent.

Signature: __________________________________

(U.S. Principal Party in Interest)

Capacity: __________________________________

Date: ______________

Regulations, Outreach, & Eduation Branch, Foreign Trade Division: **301-457-2238**

B. Shipper's Letters of Instructions

On each individual export transaction, the freight forwarder will want to receive instructions from the exporter on how the export is to be processed. The terms or conditions of sale agreed upon between the seller and the buyer may vary from sale to sale. Consequently, in order for the freight forwarder to process the physical export of the goods and prepare the proper documentation, it is necessary for the exporter to advise the freight forwarder as to the specific agreement between the seller and buyer for that sale, including the International Commerce Terminology (INCOTERMS), the parties, the value, the delivery destination, inland carriers, etc. Freight forwarders often provide standard forms containing spaces to be filled in by the exporter for the information that it needs. Commercial stationers also sell forms that are designed to fit most transactions. (An example of such a form is shown in Figure 4–3.) As previously noted, the exporter should take special care in filling out this form, since any mistakes will be the basis on which the freight forwarder avoids responsibility.

C. Commercial Invoices

When the merchandise is ready to be shipped, the exporter must prepare a commercial invoice, which is a statement to the buyer for payment. Usually English is sufficient, but some countries require the seller's invoice to be in their language. Multiple copies are usually required, some of which are sent with the bill of lading and other transportation documents. The original is forwarded through banking channels for payment (except on open account sales, where it is sent directly to the buyer). On letter of credit transactions, the invoice must be issued by the beneficiary of the letter of credit and addressed to the applicant for the letter of credit. Putting the commercial invoice number on the other shipping documents helps to tie the documents together. The customs laws of most foreign countries require that a commercial invoice be presented by the buyer (or the seller if the seller is responsible for clearing customs), and the price listed on it is used as the value for the assessment of customs duties where the customs duties are based upon a percentage of the value (ad valorem rates). Perhaps the most important thing to note here is that many countries, like the United States, have special requirements for the information that, depending upon the product involved, must be contained in a commercial invoice. It is extremely important that, before shipping the product and preparing the commercial invoice, the exporter check through either an attorney, the buyer, or the freight forwarder to determine exactly what information must be included in the commercial invoice in order to clear foreign customs. In addition, often certain items, such as inland shipping expenses, packing, installation and service charges, financing charges, international transportation charges, insurance, assists, royalties, or license fees, may have to be shown separately because some of these items may be deducted from or added to the price in calculating the customs value and the payment of duties. Many countries in the Middle East and Latin America require that commercial invoices covering shipments to their countries be "legalized." This means that the country's U.S. embassy

Figure 4–3. Shipper's letter of instructions.

SHIPPER'S LETTER OF INSTRUCTIONS

1a. EXPORTER *(Name and address including ZIP CODE)*

b. EXPORTER'S EIN (IRS) NO.

c. PARTIES TO TRANSACTION ☐ Related ☐ Unrelated

2. DATE OF EXPORTATION

3. BILL OF LADING/AIR WAYBILL NO.

4a. ULTIMATE CONSIGNEE

SHIPPER'S REFERENCE

b. INTERMEDIATE CONSIGNEE

5. FORWARDING AGENT

6. POINT (STATE) OF ORIGIN OR FTZ NO.

7. COUNTRY OF ULTIMATE DESTINATION

8. LOADING PIER *(Vessel only)*

9. MODE OF TRANSPORT *(Specify)*

10. EXPORTING CARRIER

11. PORT OF EXPORT

12. PORT OF UNLOADING *(Vessel and air only)*

13. CONTAINERIZED *(Vessel only)* ☐ Yes ☐ No

14. SHIPPER REQUESTS INSURANCE ☐ Yes ☐ No

SHIPPER MUST CHECK

☐ C.O.D. $ ______ ☐ AIR ☐ OCEAN

☐ PREPAID ☐ COLLECT ☐ DIRECT ☐ CONSOLIDATE

SHIPPER'S INSTRUCTIONS IN CASE OF INABILITY TO DELIVER CONSIGNMENT AS CONSIGNED

☐ ABANDON ☐ RETURN TO SHIPPER

☐ DELIVER TO

SCHEDULE B DESCRIPTION OF COMMODITIES

- - - - - - - - - - - - - - - - - - } *(Use Columns 17-19)*

15. MARKS AND NOS. AND KINDS OF PACKAGES

D/F (16)	SCHEDULE B NUMBER (17)	CHECK DIGIT	QUANTITY SCHEDULE B UNITS (18)	SHIPPING WEIGHT *(Kilos)* (19)	VALUE *(U.S. dollars, omit cents)* *(Selling price or cost if not sold)* (20)

SHIPPER'S NOTE:

IF YOU ARE UNCERTAIN OF THE SCHEDULE B COMMODITY NO. DO NOT TYPE IT IN - WE WILL COMPLETE WHEN PROCESSING THE 7525V.

WE HAVE FORWARDED TO YOU THE SHIPMENT DESCRIBED BELOW VIA:

☐ YOUR TRUCK, OR

☐ OTHER CARRIER (LISTED BELOW)

TRUCK LINE NAME

RECEIPT (PRO) NUMBER

DECLARED VALUE FOR CARRIAGE

$

21. VALIDATED LICENSE NO./GENERAL LICENSE SYMBOL

22. ECCN *(When required)*

PLEASE SIGN THE FIRST EXPORT DECLARATION IN BOX 23 WITH PEN AND INK

23. Duly authorized officer or employee

The exporter authorizes the forwarder named above to act as forwarding agent for export control and customs purposes.

DOCUMENTS ENCLOSED

24. I certify that all statements made and all information contained herein are true and correct and that I have read and understand the instructions for preparation of this document, set forth in the "Correct Way to Fill Out the Shipper's Export Declaration." I understand that civil and criminal penalties, including forfeiture and sale, may be imposed for making false or fraudulent statements herein, failing to provide the requested information or for violation of U.S. laws on exportation (13 U.S.C. Sec. 305; 22 U.S.C. Sec. 401; 18 U.S.C. Sec. 1001; 50 U.S.C. App. 2410).

Signature

Confidential - For use solely for official purposes authorized by the Secretary of Commerce (13 U.S.C. 301 (g)).

SPECIAL INSTRUCTIONS

Title

Export Shipments are subject to inspection by U. S. Customs Service and/or Office of Export Enforcement.

Date

25. AUTHENTICATION *(When required)*

NOTE: The Shipper or his authorized agent hereby authorizes the above named Company, in his name and on his behalf, to prepare any export documents, to sign and accept any documents relating to said shipment and forward this shipment in accordance with the conditions of carriage and the tariffs of the carriers employed. The shipper guarantees payment of all collect charges in the event the consigned refuses payment. Hereunder the sole responsibility of the Company is to use reasonable care in the selection of carriers, forwarders, agents and others to whom it may entrust the shipment.

STF EX10026F

or consulate must stamp the invoice. All exports require a destination control statement to appear on the commercial invoice and on the bill of lading, air waybill, or other export documentation.

> These commodities, technology or software were exported from the United States in accordance with the Export Administration Regulations. Diversion contrary to U.S. law is prohibited.

(See discussion in Chapter 5, Section J.) (Commercial invoices are also discussed in Chapter 3, Section A.4.g, and a sample is shown in Figure 3–9.) While there is no international standard for the contents of invoices, Figure 4–4 summarizes typical requirements.

D. Bills of Lading

Bills of lading are best understood if considered as bills of loading. These documents are issued by transportation carriers as evidence that they have received the shipment and have agreed to transport it to the destination in accordance with their usual tariffs (rate schedule). Separate bills of lading may be issued for the inland or domestic portion of the transportation and the ocean (marine) or air transportation, or a through bill of lading covering all transportation to the destination may be issued. The domestic portion of the route will usually be handled by the trucking company or railroad transporting the product to the port of export. Such transportation companies have their own forms of bills of lading, and, again, commercial stationers make available forms that can be utilized by exporters, which generally say that the exporter agrees to all of the specific terms or conditions of transport normally contained in the carrier's usual bill of lading and tariff. The inland bill of lading should be prepared in accordance with the freight forwarder's or transportation carrier's instructions.

The ocean transportation will be covered by a marine bill of lading prepared by the exporter or freight forwarder and issued by the steamship company. Information in bills of lading (except apparent condition at the time of loading), such as marks, numbers, quantity, weight, and hazardous nature, is based on information provided to the carrier by the shipper, and the shipper warrants its accuracy. Making, altering, negotiating, or transferring a bill of lading with intent to defraud is a criminal offense. If the transportation is by air, the airline carrier will prepare and issue an air waybill. A freight consolidator will issue house air waybills, which are not binding on the carrier but are given to each shipper to evidence inclusion of its shipment as part of the consolidated shipment. In such cases, the freight consolidator becomes the "shipper" on the master bill of lading.

Bills of lading, whether inland or ocean, can be issued either in non-negotiable (straight) form or in negotiable form. (Air waybills are issued only in a non-negotiable form.) (The Uniform Commercial Code requires bills of lading to be negotiable unless the seller and buyer expressly agree otherwise.) If the bill of lading is specified as non-negotiable, the transportation carrier must deliver it only to the consignee

Figure 4–4. Contents of a commercial invoice.

1. Full name of seller, including address and telephone number, on letterhead or printed form.
2. Full name of buyer and buyer's address (or, if not a sale, the consignee).
3. The place of delivery (for example, ex-works, FOB port of export, CIF).
4. The sale price and grand total for each item, which includes all charges to the place of delivery. "Assists," royalties, proceeds of subsequent resale or use of the products, and indirect payments, if any, must also be included in the sale price. If it is not a sale, list the fair market value, a statement that it is not a sale, and that the value stated is "For Customs Purposes Only."
5. A description of the product(s) sufficiently detailed for the foreign customs authorities to be able to confirm the correct Harmonized Tariff classification, including the quality or grade.
6. The quantities (and/or weights) of each product.
7. A date for the invoice (on or around the date of export).
8. The currency of the sale price (or value) (U.S.$ or foreign).
9. The marks, numbers, and symbols on the packages.
10. The cost of packaging, cases, packing, and containers, if paid for by the seller, which is not included in the sales price and being billed to the buyer.
11. All charges paid by the seller, separately identified and itemized, including freight (inland and international), insurance, and commissions, etc., which are not included in the price and being billed to the buyer.
12. The country of origin (manufacture).
13. CHECK WITH THE BUYER OR IMPORTER BEFORE FINALIZING THE INVOICE TO CONFIRM THAT NO OTHER INFORMATION IS REQUIRED.

named in the bill of lading, and the bill of lading serves more as a record of the receipt of the goods and the agreement to transport them to a specific destination and consignee in return for payment of the transportation charges. If the bill of lading is a negotiable bill of lading, however, the right to receive delivery and the right to reroute the shipment are with the person who has ownership of the bill of lading properly issued or negotiated to it. Such bills of lading are issued to the shipper's order, rather than to a specific, named consignee. Where collection and payment is through banking channels, such as under a letter of credit or documentary collection governed by the Uniform Customs and Practices, negotiable bills of lading are required (except for air shipments). The exporter must endorse the bill of lading and deliver it to the bank in order to receive payment. Ocean bills of lading are usually issued in three originals, any of which may be used by the buyer to obtain possession.

Inland bills and air waybills are issued in only one original. Where a negotiable bill of lading cannot be produced at the time of delivery, the steamship line may agree to make delivery if it receives a "letter of indemnity" from the exporter or importer (or both). Letters of credit require that before payment can be made, the exporter must furnish evidence to the bank that the goods have been loaded "on board" a steamship, and the bill of lading must be "clean." This latter term means that the steamship company has inspected the goods and found no damage to them at the time they were loaded on board. Steamship companies also issue "received for shipment" bills of lading. Steamship companies will hold such shipments in storage for some time until one of their steamships is going to the designated destination, but, until such bill of lading is stamped "on board," it is not clear when the shipment will actually depart and when it will arrive in the country of destination. When a U.S. export control license is needed for the shipment (and on some other types of shipments), a destination control statement must be put on the bill of lading. (See discussion in Chapter 5, Section J.) (Samples of an inland bill of lading, an ocean bill of lading, and an air waybill are shown in Figures 4–5, 4–6, and 4–7, respectively.)

E. VOCCs and NVOCCs

The Federal Maritime Commission (FMC) regulates all ocean transportation in commerce with the United States. It is governed under the statutory provisions and regulations of the Shipping Act of 1984, the Foreign Shipping Practices Act of 1988, section 19 of the Merchant Marine Act, 1920, and Public Law 89-777 and the Ocean Shipping Reform Act of 1998.

The FMC regulates the steamship lines, or the vessel-operating common carriers (VOCCs). The Shipping Act of 1916 granted immunity from the antitrust laws in order to stabilize shipping rates and services. As a result, the carriers formed conferences that were able to discuss and set rates for all ocean transportation. In exchange, the carriers were required to publish their rates with the Commission and make them available to all similarly situated shippers. With the passage of the Ocean Shipping Reform Act of 1998, steamship lines were allowed to enter into confidential service contracts with shippers and publish only limited information. The rates and service commitments remained confidential. The VOCCs now publish these tariffs on the Internet, where anyone may access them for a fee.

The FMC also regulates and licenses all ocean transportation intermediaries (OTI), which are the ocean freight forwarders and the non-vessel-operating common carriers (NVOCCs). NVOCCs purchase large quantities of container space from the VOCCs on specific trade lanes, and since they buy in bulk, they obtain highly favorable rates. In turn, the NVOCCs sell that space to shippers at a higher cost. They issue their own bills of lading and are required to make their tariffs publicly available. In addition, they are able to enter into confidential service agreements with their shippers. The NVOCC plays a unique position in the transportation of goods; it is a shipper to the VOCCs and a carrier to its shippers.

(*Text continues on page 132.*)

Figure 4–5. Inland bill of lading.

STRAIGHT BILL OF LADING—SHORT FORM—ORIGINAL—NOT NEGOTIABLE

RECEIVED, subject to the classifications and tariffs in effect on the date of the issue of this Bill of Lading, the property described above in apparent good order, except as noted (contents and condition of contents of packages unknown), marked, consigned, and destined as indicated above which said carrier (the word carrier being understood throughout this contract as meaning any person or corporation in possession of the property under the contract) agrees to carry to its usual place of delivery at said destination, if on its route, otherwise to deliver to another carrier on the route to said destination. It is mutually agreed as to each carrier of all or any of said property over all or any portion of said route to destination and as to each party at any time interested in all or any said property, that every service to be performed hereunder shall be subject to all the bill of lading terms and conditions in the governing classification on the date of shipment.

Shipper hereby certifies that he is familiar with all the bill of lading terms and conditions in the governing classification and the said terms and conditions are hereby agreed to by the shipper and accepted for himself and his assigns.

From ____________________

DESIGNATE WITH AN (X)

At ____________________ 20 ____ BY TRUCK ☐ FREIGHT ☐ Shipper's No. __________

Carrier ____________________ Agent's No. __________

(Mail or street address of consignee—For purposes of notification only.)

Consigned to ____________________

Destination ____________________ State of __________ County of __________

Route ____________________

Delivering Carrier ____________________ Vehicle or Car Initial __________ No. __________

No. Packages	Kind of Package, Description of Articles, Special Marks, and Exceptions	*Weight (Sub. to Cor.)	Class or Rate	Check Column
TOTAL PIECES				

SAMPLE

Subject to Section 7 of conditions of applicable bill of lading, if this shipment is to be delivered to the consignee without recourse on the consignor, the consignor shall sign the following statement:

The carrier shall not make delivery of this shipment without payment of freight and all other lawful charges.

Per __________
(Signature of Consignor.)

If charges are to be prepaid, write or stamp here, "To be Prepaid."

Received $ __________ to apply in prepayment of the charges on the property described hereon.

____
Agent or Cashier

Per __________
(The signature here acknowledges only the amount prepaid.)

Charges Advanced:

C.O.D. SHIPMENT

Prepaid ☐
Collect ☐ $ __________

Collection Fee __________

Total Charges __________

*If the shipment moves between two ports by a carrier by water, the law requires that the bill of lading shall state whether it is "Carrier's or Shipper's weight."

†Shipper's imprint in lieu of stamp; not a part of bill of lading approved by the Department of Transportation.

NOTE—Where the rate is dependent on value, shippers are required to state specifically in writing the agreed or declared value of the property.

THIS SHIPMENT IS CORRECTLY DESCRIBED. CORRECT WEIGHT IS

__________ LBS.

Subject to verification by the Respective Weighing and Inspection Bureau According to Agreement.

Per __________

† The fibre containers used for this shipment conform to the specifications set forth in the box maker's certificate thereon, and all other requirements of Rule 41 of the Uniform Freight Classification and Rule 5 of the National Motor Freight Classification. †Shipper's imprint in lieu of stamp, not a part of bill of lading approved by the Interstate Commerce Commission.

If lower charges result, the agreed or declared value of the within described containers is hereby specifically stated to be not exceeding 50 cents per pound per article.

__________ Shipper, Per

__________ Agent, Per __________

This is to certify that the above-named materials are properly classified, described, packaged, marked and labeled and are in proper condition for transportation according to the applicable regulations of the Department of Transportation.

Form 35-643H Printed and Sold by UNZ&CO www.unzco.com • (800) 631-3098

1

Figure 4–6. Ocean bill of lading.

Ocean Bill of Lading

Exporter	Booking Number	Document Number
	Export References	
Ultimate Consignee	Forwarding Agent	
Notify Party	Also Notify	

Pre-Carriage By	Place of Receipt	Domestic Routing
Exporting Carrier	Port of Loading	Loading Pier/Terminal
Port of Discharge	Place of Receipt on Carrier	Type of Move

Marks and Numbers	No. of Pkgs	HM	Description	Weight	Measurements

Ship Ref No. There are: pages, including attachments to this Ocean Bill of Lading

These commodities, technology or software were exported from the United States in accordance with the Export Administration Regulations. Diversion contrary to U.S. law prohibited.

Carrier has a policy against payment solicitation, or receipt of any rebate, directly or indirectly, which would be unlawful under the United States Shipping Act, 1984 as amended.

FREIGHT RATES, CHARGES, WEIGHTS AND/OR MEASUREMENTS

Received by Carrier for shipment by ocean vessel between port of loading and port of discharge, and for arrangement or procurement of pre-carriage from place of receipt and on-carriage to place of delivery, where stated above, the goods as specified above in apparent good order and condition unless otherwise stated. The goods to be delivered at the above mentioned port of discharge or place of delivery, whichever is applicable.

IN WITNESS WHEREOF original Bills of Lading have been signed, not otherwise stated above, one of which being accomplished the others shall be void.

DATED AT

BY

Agent

Mo. Day Year

B/L No.

This document created using Shipping Solutions Professional export software, www.shipsolutions.com.

Figure 4–6. *(continued)*

BILL OF LADING–TERMS AND CONDITIONS

1. (a) Except as otherwise provided herein this Bill of Lading shall have effect subject to the provisions of the Carriage of Goods by Sea Act of the United States of America, approved April 16, 1936, which shall be deemed to be incorporated herein, and nothing herein contained shall be deemed a surrender by the Carrier of any of its rights or immunities or an increase of any of its responsibilities or liabilities under said Act. The provisions stated in said Act (except as otherwise specifically provided herein) shall govern before loading on and after discharge from the vessel and throughout the entire time the Goods are in the custody of the Carrier if this Bill of Lading is issued or delivered in a locality where there is in force a compulsorily applicable Carriage of Goods by Sea Act, ordinance or statute of a nature similar to the International Convention for the Unification of Certain Rules Relating to Bills of Lading dated at Brussels, August 25, 1924. It shall be subject to the provisions of said Act, ordinance or statute and rules thereto annexed.
(b) The Carrier shall be entitled to the full benefit of, and right to, all limitations of, or exceptions from, liability authorized by any provisions of Sections 4281 to 4288, inclusive, of the Revised Statutes of the United States and amendments thereto and of any other provisions of the laws of the United States or of any other country whose laws shall apply.

2. In this Bill of Lading
(a) "Carrier" means the Carrier named on the face side hereof, the vessel, her owner, Master, operator, demise charterer, and if bound hereby, the time charterer, and any substitute Carrier whether the owner, operator, charterer or Master shall be acting as carrier or bailee;
(b) "Vessel" means and includes the ocean vessel on which the Goods are shipped, named on the face hereof, or any substitute vessel, also any leadership, ferry, barge, lighter or any other watercraft used by the Carrier in the performance of this contract.
(c) "Merchant" means and includes the shipper, the consignee, the receiver, the holder of this bill of lading, the owner of the Goods or person entitled to the possession of the Goods and the servants or agents of any of these.
(d) "Charges" means and includes freight and all expenses and money obligations incurred and payable by the Merchant.
(e) "Goods" means and includes the cargo received from the shipper and described on the face side hereof and any Container not supplied by or on behalf of the Carrier.
(f) "Container" means and includes any container, van, trailer, transportable tank, flat, pallet or any similar article of transport.
(g) "Person" means and includes an individual, corporation, partnership or other entity as the case may be.
(h) "Participating Carrier" means and shall include any other water, land or air carrier performing any stage of the Combined Transport.

3. It is understood and agreed that other than the said Carrier no person whatsoever (including the Master, officers and crew of the vessel, all servants, agents, employees, representatives, and all stevedores, terminal operators, crane operators, watchmen, carpenters, ship cleaners, surveyors and other independent contractors whatsoever) is or shall be deemed to be liable with respect to the goods as carrier, bailee or otherwise howsoever, in contract or in tort. If, however, it should be adjudged that any other than said carrier is under any responsibility with respect to the Goods, all limitations of the exonerations from liability provided by law or by the terms hereof shall be available to such other persons as herein described in contracting for the foregoing exemptions, limitations and exonerations from liability, the Carrier is acting as agent and trustee for and on behalf of all persons described above, all of whom shall to this extent be deemed to be a party to this contract evidenced by this Bill of Lading, it being always understood that said beneficiaries are not entitled to any greater or further exemptions, limitations or exonerations from liability than those that the Carrier has under this Bill of Lading in any given situation.

4. Subject to all rights, privileges and limitations of and exonerations from liability granted to the ocean carrier under this Bill of Lading or by law, any liability by the respective participating carriers for loss or damage to the Goods or packages carried hereunder shall be governed by the following:
(a) If loss or damage occurs while the goods or packages are in the custody of the ocean carrier, only the ocean carrier shall be responsible therefor, and any liability of the ocean carrier shall be determined by the terms and conditions of this Bill of Lading and any law compulsorily applicable.
(b) If loss or damage occurs while the Goods or packages are in the custody of a participating domestic or foreign Carrier, only the participating domestic or foreign Carrier(s) shall be responsible therefor, and any liability of such participating domestic or foreign Carrier(s) shall be determined, in respective order, by the terms, conditions and provisions of the applicable participating domestic or foreign Carrier's Bill(s) of Lading, whether issued or not, tariff(s) and law compulsorily applicable in the circumstances.
(c) Notwithstanding subdivision (a) and (b) hereof, it is contemplated that the Goods or packages will from time to time be carried in through transportation that will include inland transportation within the United States by railroad and sea carriage by one or more of the other Carriers above defined. (When used on or endorsed on this Bill of Lading the words "on board" shall mean and include on board the original carrying vessel when the Goods or packages are being transported from a foreign port or place to the continental United States, but when the Goods or packages are being transported from the continental United States to a foreign port or place "on board" shall mean and include on board a rail car operated by the originating carrier and en route by rail to the port of loading for loading on board the Carrier's or participating Carrier's vessel.)
(d) If loss or damage occurs after receipt of the Goods or packages hereunder, and it cannot be determined from the records of the ocean Carrier or participating domestic or foreign Carrier(s) whether such damage or loss occurred during ocean, domestic or foreign carriage, it shall be conclusively presumed that the loss or damage occurred on board the vessel and while the Goods or packages were in the custody of the ocean Carrier.
(e) At all times when the Goods or packages are in the custody of the above mentioned participating domestic or foreign Carriers, such Carriers shall be entitled to all the rights, defenses, exceptions from or limitations of liability and immunities of whatsoever nature referred to or incorporated herein applicable or granted to the Carrier as herein defined, to the full extent permitted to such domestic and foreign Carriers under this Bill(s) of Lading, tariffs and any other laws applicable or relating thereto, provided however, that nothing contained in this Bill of Lading shall be deemed a surrender by these domestic or foreign Carriers of any of their rights and immunities or an increase of any of their limitations of and exonerations from liability under their said Bill(s) of Lading, tariffs or laws applicable or relating to said carriage.
(f) In making any arrangements for transportation by participating domestic or foreign Carriers of the Goods or packages carried hereunder, either before or after ocean carriage, it is understood and agreed that the ocean Carrier acts solely as agent of the Merchant, without any other responsibility whatsoever, and it assumes no responsibility as Carrier for such domestic or foreign transportation.
(g) Notice of loss or damage and claim against the ocean Carrier, where applicable, shall be given to the ocean Carrier, and suit commenced as provided for in Clauses 30 and 31 hereof. Notice of loss or damage against the participating domestic or foreign Carrier(s), where applicable, shall be filed with the participating domestic or foreign Carrier(s) and suit commenced as provided for in the terms, conditions and provisions of said Carrier(s) Bill(s) of Lading or by law applicable thereto. It is understood by the Merchant that such terms, conditions and provisions, as they pertain to notice of, and claim for, loss or damage and commencement of suit, contain different requirements than those requirements pertaining to ocean Carriage as contained in Clauses 30 and 31 hereof.

5. The goods carried hereunder are subject to all the terms and provisions of the Carrier's applicable Tariff or Tariffs on file with the Federal Maritime Commission, Interstate Commerce Commission or any other regulatory body which governs a particular portion of this carriage, and the terms and provisions of the said Tariff or Tariffs are hereby incorporated herein as part of the Terms and Conditions of this Bill of Lading. Copies of the relevant provisions of the applicable Tariff or Tariffs are obtainable from the Carrier, Federal Maritime Commission, Interstate Commerce Commission or other regulatory body upon request. In the event of any conflict between the terms and provisions of such Tariff or Tariffs and the Terms and Conditions of this Bill of Lading, this Bill of Lading shall prevail.

6. The Merchant warrants that in agreeing to the Terms and Conditions hereof, he is, or has the authority of the person owning or entitled to the possession of the Goods and this Bill of Lading.

7. (a) The Carrier shall be entitled to sub-contract on any terms the whole or any part of the carriage, loading, unloading, storing, warehousing, handling and any and all duties whatsoever undertaken by the Carrier in relation to the Goods.
(b) As to through transportation, the Carrier undertakes to procure such services as necessary and shall have the right at its sole discretion to contract any mode of land, sea or air transportation and to arrange participation by other Carriers to accomplish the combined transport from place of receipt to place of delivery. Whenever any stage of the combined transport is accomplished by any land or air Carrier or any other water Carrier, each such stage shall be controlled according to any law compulsorily applicable to such stage and according to the contracts, rules and tariffs of each participating Carrier, the same as if such contracts, rules and tariffs were fully set forth herein.

8. The Carrier shall be entitled but under no obligation to open any Container at any time and to inspect the contents unless applicable law prohibits same. If it thereupon appears that the contents or any part thereof cannot safely or properly be carried or carried further, either at all or without incurring any additional expense or taking any measures in relation to the Container or its contents or any part thereof, the Carrier may abandon the transportation thereof and/or take any measures and/or incur any reasonable additional expense to carry or to continue the carriage or to store the same ashore or afloat under cover or in the open, at any place, which storage shall be deemed to constitute due delivery under this Bill of Lading. The Merchant shall indemnify the Carrier against any reasonable additional expense so incurred.

9. Carrier may containerize any Goods or packages. Containers may be stowed on deck or under deck and when so stowed shall be deemed for all purposes to be stowed under deck, including for General Average and U.S. Carriage of Goods by Sea Act, 1936 and similar legislation.

10. Deck cargo (except goods carried in containers on deck) and live animals are received and carried solely at Merchant's risk (including accident or mortality of animals) and the Carrier shall not in any event be liable for any loss or damage thereto arising or resulting from any matters mentioned in Section 4, Sub-Section 2(a) to (p), inclusive, of the United States Carriage of Goods by Sea Act or from any other cause whatsoever not due to the fault of the Carrier, any warranty of seaworthiness in the premises being hereby waived, and the burden of proving liability being in all respects upon the Merchant. Except as provided above, such shipments shall be deemed Goods and shall be subject to all terms and provisions of this Bill of Lading relating to Goods.

11. Special containers with heating or refrigeration units will not be furnished unless contracted for expressly in writing at time of booking and, when furnished, may entail an increased freight rate or charge. Shipper shall advise Carrier of desired temperature range when delivering Goods to Carrier, and Carrier shall exercise due diligence to maintain the temperature within a reasonable range while the containers are in its custody or control. The Carrier does not, however, accept any responsibility for the functioning of heated or refrigerated containers not owned or leased by Carrier.

12. The scope of the voyage herein contracted for shall include usual or customary or advertised ports of call whether named in this contract or not, also ports in or out of the advertised, geographical or usual route or order, even though in proceeding thereto the vessel may sail beyond the port of discharge named herein or in a direction contrary thereto or return to the original port, or depart from the direct or customary route and includes all canals, straits, and other waters. The vessel may call at any port for the purpose of the current, prior or subsequent voyages. The vessel may omit calling at any port whether scheduled or not, and may call at the same port more than once, may discharge the goods during the first or subsequent call at the port of discharge, may for matters occurring before or after loading, and either with or without the goods on board, and before or after proceeding towards the port of discharge, adjust compasses, drydock with or without cargo on board, stop for repairs, shift berths, make trial trips or tests, take fuel or stores, remain in port, be on bottom, aground or at anchor, sail with or without pilots, tow and be towed, and save or attempt to save life or property, and all of the foregoing are included in the contract voyage. The vessel may carry contraband, explosives, munitions, warlike stores, hazardous cargo, and sail armed or unarmed, and with or without convoy.

The Carrier's sailing schedules are subject to change without notice both as to the sailing date and date of arrival. If this is a Through Bill of Lading, no Carrier is bound to transport the shipment by any particular train, truck, aircraft, vessel or other means of conveyance, or in time for any particular market or otherwise. No Carrier shall be liable for delay and any Carrier shall have the right to forward the goods by substitute Carrier.

13. If at any time the performance of the contract evidenced by this Bill of Lading is or is likely to be affected by any hindrance, risk, delay, difficulty, or disadvantage of whatsoever kind which cannot be avoided by the exercise of reasonable endeavors, the Carrier (whether or not the transport is commenced) may without notice to the Merchant treat the performance of this contract as terminated and place the Goods or any part of them at the Merchant's disposal at any place or port which the Carrier may deem safe and convenient, whereupon the responsibility of the Carrier in respect of such Goods shall cease. The Carrier shall nevertheless be entitled to full freight and charges on Goods received for transportation and the Merchant shall pay any additional costs of carriage to and delivery and storage at such place or port.

14. If the Carrier makes a special agreement, whether by stamp hereon or otherwise, to deliver the Goods at a specified dock or place, it is mutually agreed that such agreement shall be construed to mean that the Carrier is to make such delivery only if, in the sole judgment of the Carrier, the vessel can get to, be at, and leave said dock or place, always safely afloat, and only if such dock or place is available for immediate receipt of the Goods and that otherwise the Goods shall be discharged as otherwise provided in this Bill of Lading, whereupon all responsibility of Carrier shall cease.

15. The port authorities are hereby authorized to grant a general order for discharging immediately upon arrival of the vessel and the Carrier, without giving notice either of arrival or discharge, may, immediately upon arrival of the vessel at the designated destination, discharge the goods continuously, Sundays and holidays included, at all such hours by day or by night as the Carrier may determine no matter what the state of the weather or custom of the port may be.

The Carrier shall not be liable in any respect whatsoever if heat or refrigeration or special cooling facilities shall not be furnished during loading or discharge or any part of the time that the Goods are upon the wharf, craft or other loading or discharging place.

Landing and delivery charges and pier dues shall be at the expense of the Goods unless included in the freight herein provided for. If the Goods are not taken away by the consignee by the expiration of the next working day after the Goods are at his disposal, the Goods may, at Carrier's option and subject to Carrier's lien, be sent to store or warehouse or be permitted to lie where landed, but always at the expense and risk of the Goods. The responsibilities of the Carrier in any capacity shall altogether cease and the Goods shall be considered to be delivered and at their own risk and expense in every respect when taken into the custody of Customs or other Authorities, or into that of any municipal or governmental concessionaire or depository. The Carrier shall not be required to give any notification of disposition of the Goods, except as may be otherwise provided in this Bill of Lading.

16. At ports or places where, by local law, authorities, or custom, the Carrier is required to discharge cargo to lighters or other craft, or where it has been so agreed, or where wharves are not available which the ship can get to, lie at, or leave, always safely afloat, or where conditions prevailing at the time render discharge at a wharf dangerous, imprudent, or likely to delay the vessel, the Merchant shall promptly furnish lighters or other craft to take delivery alongside the ship, at the risk and expense of the Goods. If the Merchant fails to provide such lighters or other craft, Carrier, acting solely as agent for the Merchant, may engage such lighters or other craft at the risk and expense of the Goods. Discharge of the Goods into such lighters or other craft shall constitute proper delivery, and any further responsibility of Carrier with respect to the goods shall thereupon terminate.

17. The Carrier shall have liberty to comply with any order or directions or recommendations in connection with the transport under this contract of carriage given by any Government or Authority or anyone acting or purporting to act on behalf of such Government or Authority, or having, under the terms of the mortgage or insurance on the vessel or other transport, the right to give such orders, directions or recommendations. Discharge or delivery of the Goods in accordance with the said order or directions or recommendations shall be deemed a fulfillment of the contract. Any extra expense incurred in connection with the exercise of the Carrier's liberty under this clause shall be paid by the Merchant in addition to freight and charges.

18. Whenever the Carrier or Master may deem it advisable, or in any case where goods are destined for port(s) or place(s) at which the vessel or participating carriers will not call, the Carrier may, without notice, forward the whole or any part of the shipment, before or after loading at the original port of shipment, or any other place or places even though outside the scope of the voyage or the route to or beyond the port of discharge or the destination of the Goods, by water, by land or by air or by any combination thereof, whether operated by the Carrier or others and whether departing or arriving or scheduled to depart or arrive before or after the ship expected to be used for the transportation of the shipment. The Carrier may delay forwarding awaiting a vessel or conveyance in its own service or with which it has established connections in all cases where the shipment is delivered to another Carrier or to a lighter, Port Authority, warehouseman or other bailee for transshipment, the liability of this Carrier shall absolutely cease when the Goods are out of its exclusive possession and shall not resume until the Goods again come into its exclusive possession, and the responsibility of this Carrier during any such period shall be that of an agent of the Merchant, and this Carrier shall be without any other responsibility whatsoever. The carriage by any transshipping or on-Carrier and all transshipment or forwarding shall be subject to all the terms whatsoever in the regular form of bill of lading, consignment note, contract or other shipping document used at the time by the Carrier performing such transshipment or forwarding.

19. In any situation whatsoever and wheresoever occurring and whether existing or anticipated before commencement of or during the combined transport, which in the judgment of the Carrier or the Master is likely to give rise to risk of capture, seizure, detention, damage, delay or disadvantage of loss to the Carrier of any part of the Goods to make it unsafe, imprudent or unlawful for any reason to receive, keep, load, or carry the goods, or commence or proceed on or continue the transport or to enter or discharge the goods or disembark passengers at the port of discharge, or the usual or agreed or intended place of discharge or delivery, or to give rise to delay, or difficulty in proceeding by the usual or intended route, the Carrier or the Master may decline to receive, keep, load or carry the Goods or may devan container(s) contents or any part thereof and may require the Merchant to take delivery of Goods at the place of receipt or any other point in the combined transport and upon failure to do so, may warehouse the Goods at the risk and expense of the Goods, or the vessel, whether or not proceeding toward or entering or attempting to enter a port of discharge, or reaching or attempting to reach a usual place of discharge therein or attempting to discharge the shipment may discharge the Goods and/or devan the contents of any container(s) at another port depot, lighter craft or other place or may forward or transship them as provided in this Bill of Lading, or the Carrier or the Master may retain the Goods vanned or unvanned, on board until the return of the vessel to the port of loading or to the port of discharge or until such time as the Carrier or the Master thinks advisable and discharge the Goods at any place whatsoever as herein provided. The Carrier or the Master is not required to give notice of such devanning or of discharge of the Goods or of the forwarding thereof as herein provided. When the Goods are discharged from the ship as herein provided, such shall be at the risk and expense of the Goods. Such discharging shall constitute complete delivery and performance under this contract and the Carrier shall be free from any further responsibility, unless it be shown that any loss or damage to the Goods arose from Carrier's negligence in the discharge and delivery as herein provided, the burden of establishing such negligence being on the Merchant. For any service rendered to the Goods as hereinabove provided or for any delay or expense to the vessel caused as a result thereof, the Carrier shall be entitled to a reasonable extra compensation, and shall have a lien on the goods for such carriage. Notice of disposition of the Goods shall be mailed to shipper or consignee named in this Bill of Lading. Goods shut out from the vessel named herein for any cause may be forwarded on a subsequent vessel of this type or at Carrier's option, on a vessel of another type or by other mode of transportation.

20. Notwithstanding the foregoing, the Carrier shall neither be liable therefor, nor concluded as to the correctness of any such marks, descriptions or representations.

When any cargo unit owned or leased by Carrier is packed or loaded by shipper or its agent, or discharged by consignee or its agent, shipper, consignee, receiver, holder of this Bill of Lading, owners of the Goods and person entitled to the possession of the Goods shall be and remain liable, jointly and severally, for any loss or damage to the cargo unit during such loading or discharge, howsoever occurring, until the cargo unit is returned to Carrier's custody and, at tariff rates, for any delay beyond the time allowed for such loading or discharge, and for any loss, damage or expense incurred by Carrier as a result of the failure to return the cargo unit to the Carrier in the same, sound condition and state of cleanliness as when received by shipper. Such loss, damage, expense or delay shall constitute a lien on the Goods.

Where a cargo unit is to be unpacked or unloaded by consignee or its agent, consignee or its agent shall promptly unpack or unload such cargo unit and take delivery of its contents, irrespective of whether the Goods are damaged or not. Carrier shall not be liable for loss or damage caused to the Goods by or during such unpacking or unloading.

21. When containers, vans, trailers, transportable tanks, flats, palletized units, and all other packages (all hereinafter referred to generically as "cargo units") are not packed or loaded by Carrier, such cargo units shall be deemed shipped as "Shipper's weight, load and count." Carrier has no reasonable means of checking the quantity, weight, condition or existence of the contents thereof, does not represent the quantity, weight, condition or existence of such contents, as furnished by the shipper and inserted in this Bill of Lading, to be accurate, and shall not be liable for nonreceipt or misdescription of such contents. Carrier shall have no securing and/or stowage of contents of such cargo units, or for loss or damage caused thereby or resulting therefrom, or for the physical suitability or structural adequacy of such cargo units properly to contain their contents.

The Merchant, whether principal or agent, by packing or loading the cargo unit and/or by allowing the cargo unit to be so packed or loaded, represents, guarantees and warrants (a) that the Goods are properly described, marked and safely packed in their respective cargo units, that such cargo units are physically suitable, sound and structurally adequate properly to contain and support the Goods during handling and on the transport and that the cargo units may be handled in the ordinary course without damage to themselves or to their contents, or to the vessel or conveyance or to their other cargo, or property, or persons, (b) that all particulars with regard to the cargo units and their contents and the weight of each said cargo unit, are in all respects correct, and (c) that they have ascertained and fully disclosed in writing to the Carrier and all participating Carriers on or prior to shipment, any condition, ingredient or characteristic of the Goods which might indicate that they are inflammable, explosive, corrosive, radioactive, noxious, hazardous or dangerous in nature, or which might cause damage, injury or detriment to the Goods, or to the vessel, conveyance or other cargo or to property or persons and that they have complied fully with all statutes, ordinances and regulations of the Department of Transportation of the United States of America and all other regulatory bodies with respect to labeling, packing and preparation of shipment of all such Goods.

The shipper, consignee, receiver, holder of this Bill of Lading, owner of the Goods and person entitled to the possession of the Goods jointly and severally agree fully to protect and indemnify Carrier and to hold it harmless in respect to any injury or death of any person, or loss or damage to cargo or cargo unit of any other property or to the vessel or conveyance or expense or fine arising out of damage to cargo or cargo unit or any other property, or to the vessel or conveyance or expense or fine arising out of or in any way connected with breach of any of the foregoing representations or warranties, howsoever occurring, even without fault of shipper, consignee and/or owner of the Goods, and even though such injury, death, loss or damage is caused in whole or in part by fault of the Carrier or unseaworthiness.

22. The Merchant and the Goods themselves shall be liable for and shall indemnify the Carrier, and the Carrier shall have a lien on the Goods for all expenses of mending, repairing, fumigating, repacking, coopering, baling, reconditioning of the Goods and gathering of loose contents of packages, also for expenses for repairing containers damaged while in the possession of the Merchant for demurrage on containers and any payment, expense, fine, dues, duty, tax, impost, loss, damage or detention sustained or incurred by or levied upon the Carrier, vessel or conveyance in connection with the Goods, howsoever caused, including any action or requirement of any government or governmental authority or person purporting to act under the authority thereof, seizure under legal process or attempted seizure, incorrect or insufficient marking, numbering or addressing of containers, packages or description of the contents, failure of the Merchant to procure consular, Board of Health or other certificates to accompany the Goods or to comply with laws or regulations of any kind imposed with respect to the Goods by the authorities at any port or place or any act or omission of the Merchant. The Carrier's lien shall survive delivery and may be enforced by private or public sale and without notice.

23. Freight shall be payable, at Carrier's option, on actual gross intake weight or measurement or on actual gross discharge weight or measurement or on a value or other basis. Freight may be calculated on the basis of the particulars of the Goods furnished by the shipper herein, but the Carrier may, as previously stated herein, at any time open the packages or containers and examine, weigh, measure and value the Goods (unless applicable law prohibits same). In case shipper's particulars are found to be erroneous and additional freight payable, the Merchant and the Goods shall be liable for any expense incurred for examining, weighing, measuring and valuing the Goods. Full freight shall be paid on damaged or unsound goods. Full freight hereunder to place of delivery named herein and advance charges (including on-Carrier's) shall be considered completely earned on receipt of the Goods by the Carrier, whether the freight be stated or intended to be prepaid or to be collected at destination, and the Carrier shall be entitled to all freight and charges, extra compensation, demurrage, detention, General Average, claims and any other payments made and liability incurred with respect to the Goods, whether actually paid or not, and to receive and retain them irrevocably under all circumstances whatsoever, vessel, conveyance and/or cargo lost, damaged or otherwise, or the combined transport changed, frustrated or abandoned. In case of forced abandonment or interruption of the combined transport for any cause, any forwarding of the goods or any part thereof shall be at the risk and expense of the Goods. All unpaid charges shall be paid in full, without any offset, counterclaim or deduction in the currency of the place of receipt, or, at Carrier's option, in the currency of the place of delivery at the demand rate of New York exchange as quoted on day of arrival of the Goods at the place of delivery.

The Merchant shall be jointly and severally liable to the Carrier for the payment of all freight charges and the amount due to the Carrier, and for any failure of either or both to perform his or their obligations under the provisions of this Bill of Lading, and they shall indemnify the Carrier against, and hold it harmless from, all liability, loss, damage and expense which the Carrier may sustain or incur arising or resulting from any such failure of performance by the Merchant. Any person, firm or corporation engaged by any party to perform forwarding services with respect to the cargo shall be considered the exclusive agent of the Merchant for all purposes and any payment of freight to such person, firm or corporation shall not be considered payment to the Carrier in any event. Failure of such person, firm or corporation to pay any part of the freight to the Carrier shall be considered a default by the Merchant in the payment of the freight.

The Carrier shall have a lien on the Goods and any documents relating thereto, which shall survive delivery, for all freight charges and damages of any kind whatsoever, and for the costs of recovering same, including expenses incurred in preserving this lien, and may enforce this lien by public or private sale and without notice. The shipper, consignee, receiver, holder of this Bill of Lading, owner of the Goods and person entitled to the possession of the Goods shall be jointly and severally liable to the Carrier for the payment of all freight charges and damages as aforesaid and for the performance of the obligations of each of them hereunder.

24. Carrier shall not be liable for any consequential or special damages and shall have the option of replacing lost Goods or repairing damaged Goods.

25. The weight or quantity of any bulk cargo inserted in this Bill of Lading is the weight or quantity as ascertained by a third party other than the Carrier and Carrier makes no representation with regard to the accuracy thereof. This Bill of Lading shall not be deemed evidence against the Carrier of receipt of goods of the weight or quantity so inserted in the Bill of Lading.

26. Neither the Carrier nor any corporation owned by, subsidiary to or associated or affiliated with the Carrier shall be liable to answer for or make good any loss or damage to the goods occurring at any time and even though before loading on or after discharge from the ship, by reason or by means of any fire whatsoever, unless such fire shall be caused by its design or neglect, or by its actual fault or privity. In any case where this exemption is not permitted by law, Carrier shall not be liable for loss or damage by fire unless shown to have been caused by Carrier's negligence.

27. If the vessel comes into collision with another vessel as a result of the fault or negligence of the other vessel and any act, neglect or default of the Carrier, Master, mariner, pilot or the servants of the Carrier in the navigation or in the management of the vessel, the Merchant will indemnify the Carrier against all loss or liability to the other or non-carrying vessel or her owners insofar as such loss or liability represents loss of, or damage to, or any claim whatsoever of the Merchant, paid or payable by the other or non-carrying vessel or her owners to the Merchant and set-off, recouped or recovered by the other or non-carrying vessel or her owners as part of their claim against the carrying vessel or Carrier.

The foregoing provisions shall also apply where the owners, operators or those in charge of any vessel or vessels or objects other than, or in addition to the colliding vessels or objects are at fault in respect of a collision, contact, stranding or other accident.

This provision is to remain in effect in other jurisdictions even if unenforceable in the Courts of the United States of America.

28. General average shall be adjusted, stated and settled according to York Antwerp Rules 1974, except Rule XII thereof, at such port or place as may be selected by the Carrier and as to matters not provided for by these Rules, according to the laws and usages of New York.

In such adjustment, disbursements in foreign currencies shall be exchanged into United States money at the rate prevailing on the dates made and allowances for damage to cargo claimed in foreign currency shall be converted at the rate prevailing on the last day of discharge at the port or place of final discharge of such damaged cargo from the ship. Average agreement or bond and such additional security as may be required by the Carrier must be furnished before delivery of the goods. Such cash deposit as the Carrier or his agents may deem sufficient as additional security for the contribution of the goods and for any salvage and special charges thereon shall, if required, be made by the Goods, shippers, consignees or owners of the goods to the Carrier before delivery of the Goods. Notwithstanding anything hereinbefore contained, such deposit shall at the option of the Carrier be payable in United States currency, and be remitted to the adjuster pending settlement of the General Average and refunds of credit balances, if any, shall be paid in United States currency. In addition to the circumstances dealt with in the 1974 York Antwerp Rules, it is agreed that if the Carrier has used due diligence in the stowage of cargo and if the safe prosecution of the voyage is thereafter imperiled in consequence of the disturbance of stowage, the costs of handling, discharge, reloading and restowing cargo shall be allowed in General Average, even though the handling of cargo is not necessary for the purpose of effecting repairs to the vessel.

In the event of accident, danger or disaster, before or after commencement of the voyage resulting from any cause whatsoever, whether due to negligence or not for which or for the consequence of which, the Carrier is not responsible by statute, contract or otherwise, the Goods, the shipper, consignee, receiver, holder of this Bill of Lading, owner of the Goods and person entitled to the possession of the Goods, jointly and severally, shall contribute with the Carrier in General Average to the payment of any sacrifices, losses or expenses of a General Average nature that may be made or incurred and shall pay salvage and special charges incurred in respect of the Goods. If a salving ship is owned or operated by the Carrier, salvage shall be paid for as fully and in the same manner as if such salving ship or ships were owned or operated by strangers. Cargo's contribution in General Average shall be paid to the ship owner even when such average is the result of fault, neglect or error of the Master, pilot, officers or crew. The Merchant expressly renounces any and all codes, statutes, laws or regulations which might otherwise apply.

29. In case of any loss or damage to or in connection with Goods exceeding in actual value the equivalent of $500 lawful money of the United States, per package, or in case of Goods not shipped in packages, per shipping unit, the value of the Goods shall be deemed to be $500 per package or per shipping unit. The Carrier's liability, if any, shall be determined on the basis of a value of $500 per package or per shipping unit or pro rata in case of partial loss or damage unless the nature of the Goods and a valuation higher than $500 per package or per shipping unit shall have been declared by the shipper before shipment and inserted in this Bill of Lading, and extra freight paid if required. In such case, if the actual value of the Goods per package or per shipping unit shall exceed such declared value, the value shall nevertheless be deemed to be declared value and the Carrier's liability, if any, shall not exceed the declared value and any partial loss or damage shall be adjusted pro rata on the basis of such declared value. The words "shipping unit" shall mean each physical unit or piece of cargo not shipped in a package, including articles or things of any description whatsoever, except goods shipped in bulk, and irrespective of the weight or measurement unit employed in calculating freight charges.

Where containers, vans, trailers, transportable tanks, flats, palletized units and other such packages are not packed by the Carrier, each individual such container, van, trailer, transportable tank, palletized unit and other such package including in each instance its contents, shall be deemed a single package and Carrier's liability, limited to $500 with respect to each such package.

30. As to loss or damage to the Goods or packages occurring or presumed to have occurred during ocean voyage, unless notice of loss of or damage and the general nature of it be given in writing to the Carrier or its agent at the port of delivery before or at the time of the removal of the Goods or packages into the custody of the person entitled to delivery thereof under this Bill of Lading or, if the loss or damage be not apparent, within three consecutive days after delivery at the port of discharge, such removal shall be prima facie evidence of the delivery by the Carrier of the Goods or packages as described in this Bill of Lading.

31. As to loss or damage to the Goods or package occurring or presumed to have occurred during ocean carriage, the Carrier and the vessel shall be discharged from all liability in respect of loss, damage, misdelivery, delay or in respect of any other breach of this contract and any claim whatsoever with respect to the Goods or packages, unless suit is brought within one year after delivery of the Goods or package or the date when the Goods or package should have been delivered. Suit shall not be deemed brought unless jurisdiction shall have been obtained over the Carrier and/or the vessel by service of process or by an agreement to appear.

32. Gold, silver, specie, bullion or other valuables, including those named or described in Sec. 4281 of the Revised Statutes of the United States, will not be received by the Carrier unless their true character and value are disclosed to the Carrier and a special written agreement therefor has been made in advance, and will not, in any case, be loaded or landed by the Carrier. No such valuables shall be considered received by or delivered to the Carrier until brought aboard the ship by the shipper and put in the actual possession of and a written receipt therefor is given by the Master or other officer in charge. Such valuables will only be delivered by the Carrier aboard the ship on presentation of bills of lading properly endorsed and upon such delivery on board the Carrier's responsibility shall cease. If delivery is not so taken promptly after the ship's arrival at the port of discharge, the goods may be retained aboard or landed or carried on, solely at the risk and expense of the goods.

33. It is agreed that superficial rust, oxidation or any like condition due to moisture, is not a condition of damage but is inherent to the nature of the cargo, and acknowledgement of receipt of the Goods in apparent good order and condition is not a representation that such conditions of rust, oxidation and the like did not exist on receipt.

34. Nothing in this Bill of Lading shall operate to deprive the Carrier of any statutory protection or exemption from, or limitation of, liability, contained in the laws of the United States, or in the laws of any other country which may be applicable. This Bill of Lading shall be construed according to the laws of the United States and the Merchant agrees that any suits against the Carrier shall be brought in the Federal Courts of the United States. The terms of this Bill of Lading shall be separable, and if any part or term hereof shall be held invalid, such holding shall not affect the validity or enforceability of any other part or term hereof.

Figure 4–7. Air waybill.

Shipper's Name and Address	Shipper's Account Number	Not negotiable **Air Waybill** Issued by Copies 1, 2 and 3 of this Air Waybill are originals and have the same validity
Consignee's Name and Address	Consignee's Account Number	It is agreed that the goods described herein are accepted in apparent good order and condition (except as noted) for carriage SUBJECT TO THE CONDITIONS OF CONTRACT ON THE REVERSE HEREOF. ALL GOODS MAY BE CARRIED BY ANY OTHER MEANS INCLUDING ROAD OR ANY OTHER CARRIER UNLESS SPECIFIC CONTRARY INSTRUCTIONS ARE GIVEN HEREON BY THE SHIPPER, AND SHIPPER AGREES THAT THE SHIPMENT MAY BE CARRIED VIA INTERMEDIATE STOPPING PLACES WHICH THE CARRIER DEEMS APPROPRIATE. THE SHIPPER'S ATTENTION IS DRAWN TO THE NOTICE CONCERNING CARRIERS' LIMITATION OF LIABILITY. Shipper may increase such limitation of liability by declaring a higher value for carriage and paying a supplemental charge if required.
Issuing Carrier's Agent Name and City		Accounting Information
Agent's IATA Code	Account No.	
Airport of Departure (Addr. of First Carrier) and Requested Routing		

to	By first Carrier	Routing and Destination	to	by	to	by	Currency	CHGS Code	WT/VAL PPD	WT/VAL COLL	Other PPD	Other COLL	Declared Value for Carriage	Declared Value for Customs

Airport of Destination	Flight/Date	For Carrier Use only	Flight/Date	Amount of Insurance	INSURANCE: If Carrier offers insurance and such insurance is requested in accordance with conditions thereof, indicate amount to be insured in figures in box marked "amount of

Handling Information

SCI

These commodities licensed by the U.S. for ultimate destination

Diversion contrary to U.S.law prohibited.

No. of Pieces RCP	Gross Weight	kg lb	Rate Class / Commodity Item No.	Chargeable Weight	Rate / Charge	Total	Nature and Quantity of Goods (incl. Dimensions or Volume)

Prepaid	Weight Charge	Collect	Other Charges
0.00		0.00	
	Valuation Charge		
0.00		0.00	
	Tax		
0.00		0.00	
	Total Other Charges Due Agent		Shipper certifies that the particulars on the face hereof are correct and that insofar as any part of the consignment contains dangerous goods, such part is properly described by name and is in proper condition for carriage by air according to the applicable Dangerous Goods Regulations.
0.00		0.00	
	Total Other Charges Due Carrier		
0.00		0.00	
			Signature of Shipper or his Agent
Total Prepaid		Total Collect	
0.00		0.00	
Currency Conversion Rates	CC Charges in Dest. Currency		Executed on (Date) at (Place) Signature of Issuing Carrier or its Agent
For Carriers Use only at Destination	Charges at Destination	Total Collect Charges	

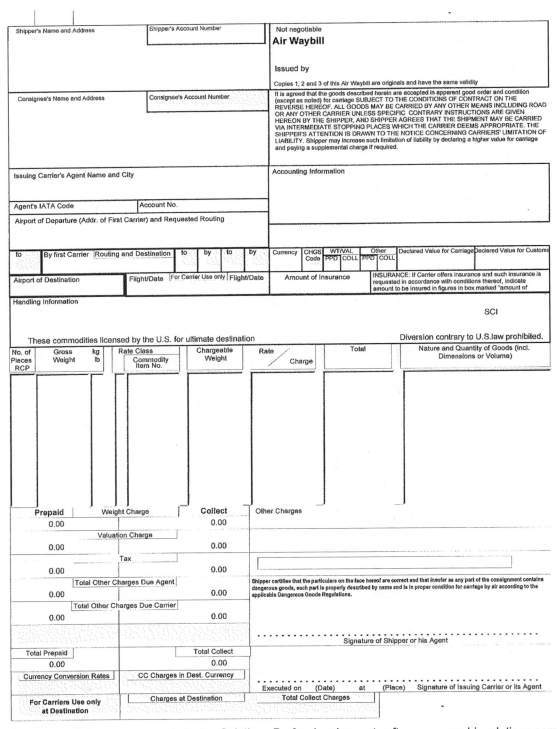

This document created using Shipping Solutions Professional export software, www.shipsolutions.com.

Figure 4–7. *(continued)*

NOTICE CONCERNING CARRIER'S LIMITATION OF LIABILITY

IF THE CARRIAGE INVOLVES AN ULTIMATE DESTINATION OR STOP IN A COUNTRY OTHER THAN THE COUNTRY OF DEPARTURE, THE WARSAW CONVENTION MAY BE APPLICABLE AND THE CONVENTION GOVERNS AND IN MOST CASES LIMITS THE LIABILITY OF THE CARRIER IN RESPECT OF LOSS, DAMAGE, OR DELAY TO CARGO TO 250 FRENCH GOLD FRANCS PER KILOGRAM, UNLESS A HIGHER VALUE IS DECLARED IN ADVANCE BY THE SHIPPER AND A SUPPLEMENTARY CHARGE PAID IF REQUIRED.
THE LIABILITY LIMIT OF 250 FRENCH GOLD FRANCS PER KILOGRAM IS APPROXIMATELY USD 20.00 PER KILOGRAM ON THE BASIS OF USD 42.22 PER OUNCE OF GOLD.

CONDITIONS OF CONTRACT

1. As used in this contract 'carrier' means all air carriers that carry or undertake to carry the goods hereunder or perform any other services incidental to such air carriage, 'Warsaw Convention' means the Convention for the Unification of certain rules relating to International Carriage by Air, signed at Warsaw, 12 October 1929, or that Convention as amended at The Hague, 28 September 1955, which ever may be applicable, and French gold francs means francs consisting of 65 1/2 milligrams of gold with a fineness of nine hundred thousandths.

2. 2.1. Carriage hereunder is subject to the rules relating to liability established by the Warsaw Convention unless such carriage is not 'international carriage' as defined by that Convention.
   2.2. To the extent not in conflict with the foregoing, carriage hereunder and other services performed by each carrier are subject to:
   2.2.1. applicable laws (including national laws implementing the Convention), government regulations, orders and requirements;
   2.2.2. provisions herein set forth, and
   2.2.3. applicable tariffs, rules, conditions of carriage, regulations and timetables (but not the times of departure and arrival therein) of such carrier, which are made part hereof and which may be inspected at any of its offices and at airports from which it operates regular services. In transportation between a place in the United States or Canada and any place outside thereof the applicable tariffs are the tariffs in force in those countries.

3. The first carrier's name may be abbreviated on the face hereof, the full name and its abbreviation being set forth in such carrier's tariffs, conditions of carriage, regulations and timetables. The first carrier's address is the airport of departure shown on the face hereof. The agreed stopping places (which may be altered by carrier in case of necessity) are those places, except the place of departure and the place of destination, set forth on the face hereof or shown in carrier's timetables as scheduled stopping places for the route. Carriage to be performed hereunder by several successive carriers is regarded as a single operation.

4. Except as otherwise provided in carrier's tariffs or conditions of carriage, in carriage to which the Warsaw Convention does not apply carrier's liability shall not exceed USD 20.00 or the equivalent per kilogram of goods lost, damaged or delayed, unless a higher value is declared by the shipper and a supplementary charge paid.

5. If the sum entered on the face of the air waybill as 'Declared Value for Carriage' represents an amount in excess of the applicable limits of liability referred to in the above Notice and in these Conditions and if the shipper has paid any supplementary charge that may be required by the carrier's tariffs, conditions of carriage or regulations, this shall constitute a special declaration of value and in this case carrier's limit of liability shall be the sum so declared. Payment of claims shall be subject to proof of actual damages suffered.

6. In cases of loss, damage or delay of part of the consignment, the weight to be taken into account in determining carrier's limit of liability shall be only the weight of the package or packages concerned.
   Note:
   Notwithstanding any other provision, for foreign air transportation as defined in the U.S. Federal Aviation Act as amended, in case of loss or damage or delay of a shipment or part thereof, the weight to be used in determining the carrier's limit of liability shall be the weight which is used (or a pro rata share in the case of a part shipment loss, damage or delay) to determine the transportation charge for such shipment.

7. Any exclusion or limitation of liability applicable to carrier shall apply to and be for the benefit of carrier's agents, servants and representatives and any person whose aircraft is used by carrier for carriage and its agents, servants and representatives. For purpose of this provision carrier acts herein as agent for all such persons.

8. 8.1. Carrier undertakes to complete the carriage hereunder with reasonable dispatch. Carrier may use alternate carriers or aircraft and may without notice and with due regard to the interests of the shipper use other means of transportation.
   Carrier is authorized by shipper to select the routing and all intermediate stopping places that it deems appropriate or to change or deviate from the routing shown on the face hereof.
   This Sub-paragraph is not applicable to/from USA.
   8.2. Carrier undertakes to complete the carriage hereunder with reasonable dispatch. Except within USA where carrier tariffs will apply, carrier may use alternate carriers or aircraft and may without notice and with due regard to the interests of the shipper use other means of transportation. Carrier is authorized by shipper to select the routing and all intermediate stopping places that it deems appropriate or to change or deviate from the routing shown on the face hereof.
   This Sub-paragraph is applicable only to/from USA.

9. Subject to the conditions herein, the carrier shall be liable for the goods during the period they are in its charge or the charge of its agent.

10. 10.1. Except when the carrier has extended credit to the consignee without the written consent of the shipper, the shipper guarantees payment of all charges for carriage due in accordance with carrier's tariffs, conditions of carriage and related regulations, applicable laws (including national laws implementing the Convention), government regulations, orders and requirements.
    10.2. When no part of the consignment is delivered, a claim with respect to such consignment will be entertained even though transportation charges thereon are unpaid.

11. Notice of arrival of goods will be given promptly to the consignee or to the person indicated on the face hereof as the person to be notified. On arrival of the goods at the place of destination, subject to the acceptance of other instructions from the shipper prior to arrival of the goods at the place of destination, delivery will be made to, or in accordance with the instructions of the consignee. If the consignee declines to accept the goods or cannot be communicated with, disposition will be in accordance with instructions of the shipper.

12. 12.1. The person entitled to delivery must make a complaint to the carrier in writing in the case;
    12.1.1. of visible damage to the goods, immediately after discovery of the damage and at the latest within fourteen (14) days from receipt of the goods;
    12.1.2. of other damage to the goods, within fourteen (14) days from the date of receipt of the goods;
    12.1.3. of delay, within twenty-one (21) days of the date the goods are placed at his disposal; and
    12.1.4. of non-delivery of the goods, within one hundred and twenty (120) days from the date of the issue of the air waybill.
    12.2. For the purpose of 12.1. complaint in writing may be made to the carrier whose air waybill was used, or to the first carrier or to the last carrier or to the carrier who performed the transportation during which the loss, damage or delay took place.
    12.3. Any rights to damages against carrier shall be extinguished unless an action is brought within two years from the date of arrival at the destination, or from the date on which the aircraft ought to have arrived, or from the date on which the transportation stopped.

13. The shipper shall comply with all applicable laws and government regulations of any country to, from, through or over which the goods may be carried, including those relating to the packing, carriage or delivery of the goods, and shall furnish such information and attach such documents to this air waybill as may be necessary to comply with such laws and regulations. Carrier is not liable to the shipper for loss or expense due to the shipper's failure to comply with this provision.

14. No agent, servant or representative of carrier has authority to alter, modify or waive any provisions of this contract.

15. If carrier offers insurance and such insurance is requested, and if the appropriate premium is paid and the fact recorded on the face hereof, the goods covered by this air waybill are insured under an open policy for the amount requested as set out on the face hereof (recovery being limited to the actual value of goods lost or damaged provided that such amount does not exceed the insured value). The insurance is subject to the terms, conditions and coverage (from which certain risks are excluded) of the open policy, which is available for inspection at an office of the issuing carrier by the interested party. Claims under such policy must be reported immediately to an office of carrier.

Carrier maintains cargo liability insurance to protect itself against claims for which it is legally liable.

F. Packing Lists

Packing lists are used to describe the way the goods are packed for shipment, such as how many packages are in the shipment, the types of packaging used, the weight of each package, the size of each package, and any markings that may be on the packages. Forms for packing lists are available through commercial stationers or are provided by packing companies who prepare export shipments. Sometimes packing lists are required by the customs laws of foreign countries, but even if they are not, an important use of the packing list is for filing insurance claims if there is damage or casualty to the shipment during transportation and for locating specific freight should Customs decide it wants to examine the cargo. (see Figure 4–8).

G. Inspection Certificates

In some situations, the buyer may request and the seller may agree to a preshipment inspection; in other cases, preshipment inspection may be required by the buyer's government (see discussion in Chapter 3, Section B.2.j). If there will be preshipment inspection, one of the documents provided as part of the export documentation is the certificate issued by the inspection company. Sometimes the inspection certificate will be furnished directly to the buyer (or the buyer's government) by the inspection company, but other times the seller must provide the inspection certificate to the bank, as for example in a letter of credit transaction specifying that an inspection certificate is required in order to obtain payment. (A sample certificate issued by an inspection company is shown in Figure 4–9.)

Although the list tends to change frequently, countries requiring preshipment inspection include Angola, Bangladesh, Benin, Burkina Faso, Bumndi, Burundi, Cambodia, Cameroon, Central African Republic, Comoros, Republic of Congo, Democratic Republic of Congo, Cote d'Ivoire, Ecuador, Ethiopia, Guinea, Iran, Liberia, Madagascar, Malawi, Mali, Mauritania, Mexico (certain goods), Mozambique, Niger, Saudi Arabia, Senegal, Sierra Leone, Togo, and Uzbekistan.

H. Marine and Air Casualty Insurance Policies and Certificates

As discussed in Chapter 2, Section P, it is extremely important to identify both who is arranging for the transportation insurance (to guard against casualty and loss) and who is going to pay for it. Even when the buyer is responsible for paying for such insurance, the buyer may be expecting the seller to arrange for it and to provide an insurance policy or certificate at the time of shipment as evidence that the shipment is properly covered. The usual practice is to insure for 110 percent of the CIF or invoice value of the goods (in order to cover loss, as well as any incidental surveying, inspection, or other expenses) and to obtain a policy or certificate in negotiable form and covering "all risks." "Warehouse-to-warehouse" coverage is best. Large exporters usually issue their own certificates under their open cargo policy. Others may obtain

(*Text continues on page 135.*)

Figure 4–8. Packing list.

Packing List

Exporter

Invoice Date

PO Number

Order Number

Exporting Carrier

Invoice Number

Ultimate Consignee

Quantity	Unit of Measure	Product ID	Description

	Gross Wgt		Net Wgt				Cube	
	Lb		Lb	In L	W	H		Ft
	Kg		Kg	Cm L	W	H		Mt
Total Number of Pkgs								

TOTALS			Gross Wgt		Net Wgt	Cube	
	Pieces	Lb		Lb			Ft
	Pkgs	Kg		Kg			Mt

Special Instruction

Authorized Signature: ____________________

Page of

This document created using Shipping Solutions Professional export software, www.shipsolutions.com.

Figure 4–9. Preshipment inspection certificate.

SGS SGS Control Services Inc.

CERTIFICATE OF INSPECTION

42 Broadway
New York, N.Y. 10004
Tel. (212) 482-8700
Telex: 426974
426975
426976
Cables: Supervise

January 29, 1990

John Doe Co., Inc.
P.O. Box 789
Chicago, IL 60601

REF: 12345/CONTRACT I.K. 678

Inspection, Testweighing and Sampling were carried out at Warehouse 2D, Municipal Docks, Houston, Texas on January 26, 1990 on a shipment of 10,000 bags of Wheat Flour marked

ABC Flour Mills
Wheat Flour
Product of U.S.A.
100 lbs. net

PACKING: In polypropylene bags in good condition

WEIGHT: Testweighing of 500 bags (or 5%) selected at random, and test-taring of 5 empty bags, indicated:

Average per bag 100.5 lbs. gross
0.5 lbs. tare
100.0 lbs. net

SPECIMEN

On this basis 10,000 bags would weigh
1,005,000 lbs. gross
5,000 lbs. tare
1,000,000 lbs. or 453.597 tonnes net

SAMPLING & ANALYSIS: Representative sampling of 500 bags (or 5%) selected at random yielded 10 samples, a composite of which was analyzed by our Houston Laboratory with these results, which meet contract specifications:

(14% Moisture Basis)

Protein	11.27
Ash	0.46%
Moisture	13.30%

LOADING: Shipment loaded aboard MV "MARY LOU," Lower Hold and Tweendeck No. 1, January 28, 1990 under our supervision.

SPECIMEN

SGS CONTROL SERVICES INC.

Member of the **SGS** Group (Société Générale de Surveillance)

ALL INSPECTIONS ARE CARRIED OUT TO THE BEST OF OUR KNOWLEDGE AND ABILITY AND OUR RESPONSIBILITY IS LIMITED TO THE EXERCISE OF REASONABLE CARE

Courtesy of SGS Government Programs Inc.

insurance certificates issued by the freight forwarder under its open cargo policy or individual policies from insurance agents for individual shipments. Letters of credit may require that an insurance policy or certificate be provided by the exporter in order to obtain payment. The exporter may receive the actual policy (see Figure 4–10) or a separate certificate (see Figure 4–11) certifying that the insurance has been issued. A sample form for presentation of loss or damage claims is shown in Figure 4–12. Under the Carriage of Goods by Sea Act, shortages must be notified to the steamship line at the time of delivery and concealed damage within three days after delivery. Any lawsuit against the steamship line for loss or damage must be made within one year of delivery of the goods.

I. Dock and Warehouse Receipts

Upon completion of the inland transportation to the port of export, the inland carrier may deliver the goods to a warehouse company or to a warehouse operated by the steamship company as arranged by the freight forwarder. A dock receipt (see Figure 4–13) is often prepared by the freight forwarder on the steamship company's form and is signed by the warehouseman or agent of the steamship company upon receipt of the goods as evidence of the receipt. The inland carrier then provides a signed copy of the dock receipt to the freight forwarder as evidence that it has completed the delivery.

J. Consular Invoices

In addition to a commercial invoice, some countries, including Panama, Bolivia, Haiti, the Dominican Republic, and Honduras, also require that a consular invoice be prepared. A consular invoice is usually prepared from the information in the commercial invoice, but it must be signed by a representative of the country of destination stationed at that country's embassy or consulate located in the United States nearest the exporter. One reason for requiring such invoices is that the country of destination may deduct certain charges from the price of the goods in order to determine the value for customs duties. If the commercial invoice does not contain all of the information necessary, the foreign customs service would be unable to complete the duty assessment. The consular invoice (see Figure 4–14) lists the specific items about which that country requires information. The consul charges a fee for this service.

K. Certificates of Origin

Some countries require that goods shipped to the country be accompanied by a certificate of origin designating the place of manufacture or production of the goods. This is signed by the exporter, and, usually, a local chamber of commerce that is used to performing this service (again, for a fee) certifies to the best of its knowledge that the products are products of the country specified by the exporter. The exporter may

(*Text continues on page 158.*)

Figure 4–10. Marine insurance policy.

MARINE POLICY «PolicyNo»

1. **ASSURED**
hereinafter referred to as the Company, in consideration of premiums to be paid at rates hereinafter stated, does insure, lost or not lost

«Assured»
«Address1»
«Address2»
«City», «State» «PostalCode»

Hereinafter referred to as the Assured. For account of whom it may concern.

2. **LOSS PAYABLE**

Loss, if any, payable to the Assured or order.

3. **GOODS INSURED:**

To cover on lawful goods and/or merchandise of every description (under and/or On Deck) but consisting principally of **INSERT COMMODITY DESCRIPTIONS , and other merchandise incidental to the business of the Assured and** consigned and/or shipped by or to the Assured or by or to others for the Assured's account or control or in which the Assured may have an interest, but excluding shipments sold on F.O.B., F.A.S., C.&F. or similar terms whereby the Assured is not obliged to furnish marine insurance and excluding shipments purchased on terms which include insurance to destination; also to cover all shipments for the account of others on which the Assured may receive instructions to insure, such instructions being given in writing prior to sailing of vessel and prior to any known or reported loss or accident.

4. **INSURABLE INTEREST**

This insurance is to cover all shipments made by or to the Assured or by or to others for the Assured's account or control, or in which the Assured may have an interest, also to cover all shipments for the account of others on which the Assured may receive instructions to insure or deem themselves responsible to insure, prior to sailing of vessel and prior to any known or reported loss or accident. This Policy does not and is not intended to provide any legal liability coverage, except as explicitly agreed, absent a specific endorsement herein to the contrary.

5. **ATTACHMENT:**

To attach and cover for 100 (one hundred) percent interest on goods and/or merchandise of every description shipped on and after **«EffDate»** and to remain in force continuously thereafter until cancelled by either party giving the other 30 days written notice; such cancellation, however, not to affect any transit risk on which this insurance has attached prior to the effective date of said cancellation. Notwithstanding the above, coverage provided hereunder on any risks insured on a time basis or insured for coverage at any location shall terminate as of the effective date of the cancellation.

Policy No. «PolicyNo» **Page 1 of 17** **Assured: «Assured»**

Figure 4–10. *(continued)*

6. **CONVEYANCES**
By:
a. Metal self-propelled vessels and connecting conveyances;
b. Aircraft and connecting conveyances;
c. Mail or express

7. **CRAFT CLAUSE (February 1949)**

Including transit by craft and/or lighter to and from the vessel. Each craft and/or lighter to be deemed a separate insurance. The Assured are not to be prejudiced by any agreement exempting lightermen from liability.

8. **LIMITS OF LIABILITY**

In respect of the above stated interest, however, this policy shall not be liable for more than:

A. $«VesselLimit»	any one vessel or conveyance or in any one place at any one time;
B. $«OnDeckLimit»	any one vessel subject to an On-Deck bill(s) of lading;
C. $«AirLimit»	any one aircraft or connecting conveyance;
D. $«perBarge»	any one barge, except as a connecting conveyance, but not exceeding
E. $«PerTow»	any one tow;
F. $«PostalLimit»	any one package by parcel post, mail, Express Courier or similar parcel delivery service;
G.$«DomesticLimit»	any one land or air conveyance in any one place at any one time Domestic Transit)

Note: Wherever the words "ship, vessels, seaworthiness or vessel owner" appear in this policy, they are deemed to also include the words "aircraft, airworthiness and aircraft owner."

9. **ACCUMULATION**

Should there be an accumulation of interest beyond the limits expressed in this policy by reason of any interruption of transit and/or occurrence beyond the control of the Assured, or by reason of any casualty and/or at a transshipping point, and/or on a connecting steamer or conveyances, these Underwriters shall hold covered such excess interest and shall be liable for the full amount at risk, but in no event to exceed twice the applicable policy limit, provided notice be given to Underwriters as soon as known to the Assured.

10. **GEOGRAPHICAL LIMITS**

At and from ports and or places in the World to ports and or places in the World (but excluding to/from Russia and other C.I.S. countries, former Yugoslavia, Afghanistan, Bolivia, Paraguay, Angola, Nigeria and Iraq) with privilege of transshipment by land and/or water and including domestic shipments that are shipped directly between points within a country and pass through coastal and/or international waters or international airspace. All other domestic shipments are excluded unless specifically endorsed hereon.

11. **VALUATION**

A. Commercial Goods and/or Merchandise (under invoice): Valued at amount of invoice, including all charges therein, plus any prepaid and/or advanced and/or guaranteed freight, if any, plus 10%

B. Commercial Goods and/or Merchandise (not under invoice): Valued and insured for the fair market value at place of shipment or arrival, provided such declaration be made prior to shipment. It is further agreed that irrespective of the value insured, claims for repairs shall be payable for the fair market costs of such repairs but in no event for more than the insured value.
In no event shall claims exceed the value declared prior to shipment and declared for premium purposes.

Foreign currency to be converted into U.S. dollars at rate of exchange current in New York on date of invoice.

Policy No. «PolicyNo» **Page 2 of 17** **Assured: «Assured»**

Figure 4–10. *(continued)*

12. **FULL VALUE REPORTING**

If the total value at risk exceeds the limit of liability provided by this insurance, the Assured shall nevertheless, as soon as known, report the full amount at risk to Underwriters and shall pay full premium thereon, in consideration of which the principle of co-insurance is waived by Underwriters.

Acceptance of such reports and premium shall not alter or increase the limit of liability of Underwriters but Underwriters shall be liable for the amount of covered loss up to but not exceeding the applicable limit of liability.

13. **SHORE COVERAGE**

Including while on docks, wharves or elsewhere on shore and/or during land transportation, risks of collision, derailment, fire, lightning, sprinkler leakage, wind, hail, flood, earthquake, landslide, volcanic eruption, aircraft, objects falling from aircraft, the rising of navigable waters, or any accident to the conveyance and/or collapse and/or subsidence of docks and/or structures, and to pay loss or damage caused thereby, even though the insurance is otherwise F.P.A.

14. **AVERAGE TERMS AND CONDITIONS**

A. Except while on deck of ocean vessel subject to an On Deck Bill of Lading, the following average terms and conditions will apply, via steamer and/or aircraft to shipments of NEW GOODS AND/OR MERCHANDISE AS PER CLAUSE 4 OF THIS Policy (UNLESS OTHERWISE AGREED UPON AS PER CLAUSE 14.A.1 BELOW) ARE INSURED:

Against all risks of physical loss or damage from any external cause, excepting those risks excluded by the F.C.& S., Nuclear and S.R. & C.C. warranties of this Policy, subject to:

Deductible Amount of: **Insert Deductible Amt**

1) **OPTIONAL TERMS**

Option is hereby granted the Assured (except while on deck of ocean vessel), when exercised and so declared to these Underwriters prior to sailing of vessel and before any known or reported loss or accident, of insuring approved general merchandise in approved overseas packing subject to one of the following Terms of Average.

F.P.A.: Warranted free from Particular Average unless the vessel or craft be stranded, sunk or burnt, but notwithstanding this warranty Underwriters are to pay any loss or damage to the interest insured which may reasonably be attributed to fire, collision or contact of the vessel and/or conveyance with any external substance (ice included) other than water, or to discharge of cargo at port of distress.

If shipment by aircraft - FPA AIR PERILS: This insurance covers only loss of or damage to the interest insured which may be reasonably attributed to crash of aircraft, fire, lightning or explosion, collision, forced landing, jettison or throwing overboard for the safety of aircraft, crew or passengers.

Note: Wherever the above F.P.A. terms appear in the Policy, they are deemed to also include the F.P.A. Air Perils as written above, *including the risks of theft of or non-delivery of an entire shipping package, jettison, washing or loss overboard.*

2) **USED GOODS/MERCHANDISE is insured:**

Warranted free from Particular Average unless the vessel or craft be stranded, sunk or burnt, but notwithstanding this warranty Underwriters are to pay any loss or damage to the interest insured which may reasonably be attributed to fire, collision or contact of the vessel and/or conveyance with any external substance (ice included) other than water, or to discharge of cargo at port of distress; and also to pay the insured value of any merchandise and/or goods jettisoned and/or washed or lost overboard, and the risks of theft of or non-delivery of an entire shipping package.

Policy No. «PolicyNo» **Page 3 of 17** **Assured: «Assured»**

Figure 4–10. *(continued)*

B. Goods on Deck Subject to an On-Deck Bill of Lading are insured subject to the following terms and conditions: Warranted free of particular average unless caused by stranding, sinking, burning and/or collision of the vessel; but to pay the insured value of any merchandise and/or goods jettisoned and/or washed overboard, irrespective of percentage. Notwithstanding the foregoing, merchandise and/or goods shipped On Deck under an Under-Deck Bill of Lading, without the knowledge and consent of the shipper, shall be treated as under-deck cargo and insured as per Sub-division A of this clause.

15. IMPROPER PACKING

In no case shall this insurance cover loss, damage or expense caused by the insufficiency or unsuitability of packing or preparation of the subject-matter insured. For the purpose of this clause "packing" shall be deemed to include stowage in a container or liftvan but only when such stowage is carried out prior to attachment of this insurance or by the Assured or their servants.

16. DELAY

Warranted free of claim for loss of market or for loss, damage or deterioration arising from delay, whether caused by a peril insured against or otherwise.

17. GENERAL AVERAGE

General average and salvage charges payable according to United States laws and usage and/or as per foreign statement and/or as per York-Antwerp rules (as prescribed in whole or in part) if in accordance with the contract of affreightment. Payable in full irrespective of insured or contributory values, but in no event for amounts greater than the applicable limit of liability shown elsewhere in this Policy.

18. WAREHOUSE TO WAREHOUSE CLAUSE

This insurance attaches from the time the goods leave the Warehouse and/or Store at the place named in the Policy, certificate or declaration for the commencement of the transit and continues during the ordinary course of transit, including customary transshipment, if any, until the goods are discharged overside from the overseas vessel at the final port. Thereafter the insurance continues whilst the goods are in transit and/or awaiting transit until delivered to final warehouse at the destination named in the Policy, certificate or declaration or until the expiry of 15 days (or 30 days if the destination to which the goods are insured is outside the limits of the port) whichever shall first occur. The time limits referred to above to be reckoned from midnight of the day on which the discharge overside of the goods hereby insured from the overseas vessel is completed. Held covered at a premium to be arranged in the event of transshipment, if any, other than as above and/or in the event of delay in excess of the above time limits arising from circumstances beyond the control of the Assured. It is necessary for the Assured to give prompt notice to Underwriters when they become aware of an event for which they are "held covered" under this Policy and the right to such cover is dependent on compliance with this obligation.

Policy No. «PolicyNo» **Page 4 of 17** **Assured: «Assured»**

Figure 4–10. *(continued)*

19. MARINE EXTENSION CLAUSES

Notwithstanding anything to the contrary in this Policy, it is understood and agreed that the following terms, extension and conditions shall apply to all shipments which become at risk under this Policy.

A. This insurance attaches from the time the goods leave the warehouse at the place named in the Policy, Certificate or Declaration for the commencement of the transit and continues until the goods are delivered to the final warehouse at the destination named in the Policy, Certificate, or Declaration, or substituted destination as provided in Clause C hereunder.

B. This insurance specially to cover the goods during

1) Deviation, delay, forced discharge, reshipment and transshipment.

2) any other variation of the adventure arising from the exercise of a liberty granted to the shipowner or charterer under the contract of affreightment.

C. In the event of the exercise of any liberty granted to the shipowner or charterer under the contract of affreightment whereby such contract is terminated at a port or place other than the originally insured destination, the insurance continues until the goods are sold and delivered at such port or place; or, if the goods not be sold but are forwarded to the originally insured destination or to any other destination, this insurance continues until the goods have arrived at final warehouse as provided in Clause A above.

D. If while this insurance is still in force before the expiry of 15 days from midnight of the day on which the discharge overside of the goods hereby insured from overseas vessel at the final port of discharge is complete, the goods are re-sold (not being a sale within the terms of Clause C) and are to be forwarded to a destination other than that covered hereunder while deposited at such port of discharge until again in transit or until the expiry of the aforementioned 15 days whichever shall first occur. If a sale is effected after the expiry of the aforementioned 15 days whilst this insurance is still in force the protection afforded hereunder shall cease as from the time of the sale.

E. Held covered at a premium to be arranged in case of change of voyage or of any omission or error in the description of the interest, vessel or voyage.

F. This insurance shall in no case be deemed to extend to cover loss, damage or expense proximately caused by delay or inherent vice or nature of the subject matter insured.

G. It is a condition of this Insurance that there shall be no interruption or suspension of transit unless due to circumstances beyond the control of the Assured.

Nothing in the forgoing shall be construed as overruling the F.C. & S. Clause or as extending this insurance to cover any risks of war or consequences of hostilities.

20. SOUTH AMERICAN CLAUSE

It is hereby understood and agreed that the following clause will apply to all shipments to South America.

Notwithstanding anything contained elsewhere herein to the contrary, (particularly the Warehouse to Warehouse and Marine Extension Clauses) the insurance provided hereunder shall continue to cover the goods for sixty (60) days on shipments via the Magdalena River) after completion of discharge from the overseas vessel at port of destination or until the goods are delivered to the final warehouse at destination, whichever may first occur, and shall then terminate.

The time limit referred to above to be reckoned from midnight of the day on which the discharge from the overseas vessel is completed.

Policy No. «PolicyNo» **Page 5 of 17** **Assured: «Assured»**

Figure 4–10. *(continued)*

21. PARAMOUNT WARRANTIES

THE FOLLOWING WARRANTIES SET FORTH IN CLAUSE 21, SHALL BE PARAMOUNT AND SHALL NOT BE MODIFIED OR SUPERSEDED BY ANY OTHER PROVISION INCLUDED HEREIN OR STAMPED OR ENDORSED HEREON UNLESS SUCH OTHER PROVISION REFERS TO RISKS EXCLUDED BY SUCH WARRANTIES AND EXPRESSLY ASSUMES THE SAID RISKS.

F.C. & S.

Notwithstanding anything herein contained to the contrary, this insurance is warranted free from capture, seizure, arrest, restraint, detainment, confiscation, preemption, requisition or nationalization, and the consequences thereof or any attempt thereat, whether in time or peace or war and whether lawful or otherwise; also warranted free, whether in time of peace or war, from all loss, damage or expense caused by any weapon of war employing atomic or nuclear fission and/or fusion or other reaction or radioactive force or matter or by any mine or torpedo, also warranted free from all consequences of hostilities or warlike operations (whether there by declaration of war or not), but this warranty shall not exclude collision or contact with aircraft, rockets or similar missiles or with any fixed or floating object (other than a mine or torpedo), stranding, heavy weather, fire or explosion unless caused directly (and independently of the nature of the voyage or service which the vessel concerned or, in the case of a collision, any other vessel involved therein, is performing) by a hostile act by or against a belligerent power; and for the purposes of this warranty "power" includes any authority maintaining naval, military or air forces in association with a power.

Further warranted free from the consequences of civil war, revolution, rebellion, insurrection or civil strife arising therefrom, or piracy.

NUCLEAR EXCLUSION

Notwithstanding anything contained to the contrary herein, it is hereby understood and agreed that this Policy shall not apply to any loss, damage or expense due to or arising out of, whether directly or indirectly, nuclear reaction, radiation or radioactive contamination, regardless of how it was caused. However, subject to all provisions of this Policy, if this Policy insures against fire, then direct physical damage to the property insured located within the United States or Puerto Rico by fire directly caused by the above excluded perils, is insured, provided that the nuclear reaction, radiation, or radioactive contamination was not caused, whether directly or indirectly, by any of the perils excluded by the F.C. & S. Warranty of this Policy.

Nothing in this clause shall be construed to cover any loss, damage, liability or expense caused by nuclear reaction, radiation or radioactive contamination arising directly or indirectly from the fire mentioned above.

S.R. & C.C.

Notwithstanding anything herein to the contrary, this insurance is warranted free from loss, damage or expense caused by or resulting from:

A. Strikes, lockouts, labor disturbances, riots, civil commotions, or the acts of any person or persons taking part in any such occurrences or disorders.

B. Vandalism, sabotage or malicious act, which shall be deemed also to encompass the act or acts of one or more persons, whether or not agents of a sovereign power, carried out for political, terroristic or ideological purposes and whether any loss, damage or expenses resulting therefrom is accidental or intentional.

DELAY (d) Warranted free of claim or loss of market or for loss, damage or deterioration arising from delay whether caused by a peril insured against or otherwise.

INHERENT VICE(e) Warranted free from claim for loss or damage or expense caused by or resulting from inherent vice or nature of the subject matter insured.

Policy No. «PolicyNo» **Page 6 of 17** **Assured:** «Assured»

Figure 4–10. *(continued)*

22. **BILL OF LADING, ETC., CLAUSE**

The Assured is not to be prejudiced by the presence of the negligence clause and/or latent defect clause in the Bill of Lading and/or charter party. The seaworthiness of the vessel as between the Assured and these Underwriters is hereby admitted and the wrongful act or misconduct of the shipowner or his servants causing a loss is not to defeat the recovery by an innocent Assured if the loss in the absence of such wrongful act of misconduct would have been a loss recoverable under this Policy. With leave to sail with or without pilots and to tow and assist vessels or craft in all situations, and to be towed.

23. **EXPLOSION**

Including the risk of explosion, however or wheresoever occurring during the currency of this insurance unless excluded by the F.C. & S. warranty or the SR & CC. warranty set forth herein or unless proximately caused by inherent vice or nature of the subject matter insured or by the personal negligence or act of the Assured.

24. **BOTH TO BLAME**

Where goods are shipped under a Bill of Lading containing the so called "both to blame collision" clause, these Underwriters agree as to all losses covered by this insurance, to indemnify the Assured for this Policy's proportion of any amount (not exceeding the amount insured) which the Assured may be legally bound to pay to the shipowners under such clause. In the event that such liability is asserted, the Assured agrees to notify these Underwriters who shall have the right at their own cost and expense to defend the Assured against such claim.

25. **INCHMAREE CLAUSE**

This insurance is also specially to cover any loss of or damage to the interest insured hereunder, through the bursting of boilers, breakage of shafts or through any latent defect in the machinery, hull or appurtenances, or from faults or errors in the navigation and/or management of the vessel by the master, mariners, mates, engineers or pilots.

26. **SUE AND LABOR**

In case of any imminent or actual loss or misfortune, it shall be lawful and necessary to and for the Assured, his or their factors, servants and assigns, to sue, labor and travel for, in and about the defense, safeguard and recovery of the said goods and merchandise, or any part thereof, without prejudice to this insurance, to the charges whereof, Underwriters will contribute according to the rate and quantity of the sum hereby insured; nor shall the acts of the Assured or Underwriters, in recovering, saving and preserving the property insured, in case of disaster, be considered a waiver or an acceptance of abandonment.

27. **CONSTRUCTIVE TOTAL LOSS**

No recovery for a constructive total loss shall be had hereunder unless the property insured is reasonably abandoned on account of its actual total loss appearing to be unavoidable, or because it cannot be preserved from actual total loss without an expenditure which would exceed its value when the expenditure had been incurred.

28. **CARRIER CLAUSE**

Warranted that this insurance shall not inure, directly or indirectly, to the benefit of any carrier or bailee.

29. **WAREHOUSING/FORWARDING CHARGES**

Notwithstanding any average warranty contained herein, Underwriters agree to pay any landing, warehousing, forwarding or other expenses and/or particular charges should same be incurred following any instance recoverable hereunder, as well as any partial loss arising from transshipment. Underwriters also agree to pay

Policy No. «PolicyNo» **Page 7 of 17** **Assured: «Assured»**

Figure 4–10. *(continued)*

the insured value of any package, piece, or unit totally lost in loading, transshipment and/or discharge and to pay for any loss or damage to the interest insured which may be reasonably attributed to discharge of cargo at port of distress.

30. DEVIATION

This insurance shall not be vitiated by an unintentional error in description of vessel, voyage or interest, or by deviation, over carriage, change of voyage, transshipment or any other interruption in the ordinary course of transit from causes beyond the control of the Assured. It is agreed, however, that any such error, deviation or other occurrence mentioned above shall be reported to these Underwriters as soon as known to the Assured and additional premium paid if required.

31. CHANGE OF DESTINATION

In case of voluntary change of destination and/or deviation and/or delay, within the Assured's control, the insured goods are held covered at an additional premium, if any, to be agreed upon; the Assured agreeing to report, as soon as possible, all events to these Underwriters.

32. INSOLVENCY

In no case shall this insurance cover loss, damage or expense arising from insolvency or financial default of the owners, managers, charterers or operators of the vessel where, at the time of loading of the subject matter insured on board the vessel, the Assured is aware, or in the ordinary course of business should be aware, that such insolvency or financial default could prevent the normal prosecution of the voyage.

33. FUMIGATION

In the event that any vessel, conveyance, wharf or warehouse is fumigated by order of properly constituted authority and loss or damage to goods and/or merchandise insured hereunder results therefrom Underwriters hereon agree to indemnify the Assured for such loss or damage and the Assured agrees to subrogate to Underwriters any recourse that the Assured may have for recovery of such loss or damage from others.

34. DUTY

This insurance also covers, subject to Policy terms of average, the risk of partial loss by reason of perils insured against on import duties imposed on goods imported into the United States or Canada insured hereunder, and collect freight (unless guaranteed or payable "vessel lost or not lost") it being understood and agreed however, that when the risk upon the goods continues beyond the time of discharge from the overseas vessel (including lighterage, if any) or, if received into bond, upon the release of said bond, the increased value consequent upon the payment of such duties and/or freight shall attach as additional insurance upon the goods from the time such duty and/or freight is paid or becomes due, to the extent of the amounts actually paid or payable.

Any limit of liability expressed in this Policy shall be applied separately to such increased value.

The Assured warrants that on each shipment insured under this clause, a separate amount shall be reported sufficient to cover said import duty and/or freight, upon which premium shall be payable at an agreed percentage of the merchandise rate.

The Assured agrees in all cases to use reasonable efforts to obtain abatement or refund of duties paid or claimed in respect of goods lost, damaged or destroyed. It is further agreed that the Assured shall, when these Underwriters so elect, surrender the merchandise to the Customs Authorities and recover import duties thereon as provided by law, in which event the claim under the Policy shall be only for total loss of the merchandise so surrendered, and expenses.

This insurance on import duty and/or freight shall terminate at the end of the import movement covered under the Policy (including the Warehouse to Warehouse an/or Marine Extension Clauses), but nothing contained in these clauses shall alter or effect any coverage granted elsewhere in the Policy during the storage or transit subsequent thereto.

Policy No. «PolicyNo» **Page 8 of 17** **Assured: «Assured»**

Figure 4–10. *(continued)*

35. CONSOLIDATION

Notwithstanding anything contained herein to the contrary, (particularly the Warehouse to Warehouse and Marine Extension Clauses) this insurance is extended to cover the property insured hereunder wherever same is stopped in transit, anywhere in the world, short of final destination, whether prior to loading and/or after discharge from overseas vessel or at any transshipment point for the purpose of consolidation, deconsolidation, packing, repacking, containerization, decontainerization, distribution, redistribution, on or at the premises of freight forwarders, consolidators, truckers, warehousemen, or others anywhere in the world for a period not exceeding thirty (30) days after receipt of the insured merchandise at such premises. Held covered in excess of the above time limit upon approval of Underwriters and at an additional premium if required.

36. DEMURRAGE CHARGES

If the Assured is instructed by Underwriters to hold a container, and the Assured is assessed a late penalty and/or demurrage charge for holding the container past the return date, Underwriters will pay the late penalties and/or demurrage charges. The amount Underwriters will pay shall be the charges assessed from the time Underwriters direct the Assured to hold the container until the time Underwriters inform the Assured that the container can be released.

37. MACHINERY

At the option of the Assured in case of loss or damage to any part of a machine, Underwriters will pay the proportion that the part lost or damaged bears to the insured value; or Underwriters will pay for the cost and expense including labor and forwarding charges of replacing or repairing the lost or damaged part. Loss, if any, sustained by payment of additional duty on replacement parts shipped for damaged machinery shall only be recoverable if duty was insured with the original shipment of machinery.

In no event, however, shall Underwriters be liable for more than the insured value of the complete machine.

38. REPLACEMENT CLAUSE (USED/REFURBISHED MACHINERY)

In the event of a claim for loss of or damage to any part of parts of the interest insured, in consequence of a peril covered by this Policy, the amount recoverable hereunder shall not exceed such proportion of the cost of replacement of the part or parts lost or damaged as the insured value bears to the value of a new machine, plus additional charges for forwarding and refitting the new part or parts if incurred, but excluding duty unless the full duty is included in the amount insured, in which case loss, if any, sustained by payment of additional duty shall also be recoverable.

Provided always that in no case shall the liability of Underwriters exceed the insured value of the complete machine.

Furthermore constructive total loss of the machine reasonably attributable to obsolescence of part or parts is specifically excluded.

39. EXPEDITING EXPENSE CLAUSE

In the event of loss of or damage to the subject-matter insured, Underwriters agree to pay the costs of airfreighting the damaged parts to manufacturers for repair and return, or the airfreighting of replacement parts from suppliers to destination, notwithstanding that the insured goods were not originally dispatched by airfreight.

40. REFUSED OR RETURNED SHIPMENTS

In the event of refusal or inability of the Assured or other consignee to accept delivery of goods or merchandise insured hereunder, this insurance is extended to cover such shipments subject to original insured value and insuring conditions while awaiting shipment or reshipment and/or return or until otherwise disposed. The

Policy No. «PolicyNo» **Page 9 of 17** **Assured: «Assured»**

Figure 4–10. *(continued)*

Assured agrees to report all such shipments as soon as practicable after they have knowledge of them and to pay premium if required, at rates to be agreed.

41. BRANDS

In case of damage to property bearing a Brand or Trade Mark, the sale of which in any way carries or implies a guarantee of the supplier or Assured, the salvage value of such damaged property shall be determined after removal of all Brands and any Trade Marks. On containers from which the Brand or TradeMark cannot be removed, contents shall be transferred to plain bulk containers. With respect to any merchandise, and/or containers from which it is impracticable to destroy all evidence of the Assured's connection therewith, these Underwriters agree to consult with the Assured with respect to the disposition of said merchandise and/or containers.

42. LABELS

A. In case of damage affecting labels, capsules or wrappers, Underwriters, if liable therefore under the terms of this Policy, shall not be liable for more than an amount sufficient to pay the cost of new labels, capsules or wrappers and the cost of reconditioning the goods, but in no event shall Underwriters be liable for more than the insured value of the damaged merchandise.

B. This Policy is extended to indemnify the Assured for actual expenses incurred in the reconditioning of or the replacing of, at final point of destination, the package of goods and/or merchandise insured under this Policy during transit to such destination provided:

1) The type of package would normally withstand the transit without damage.
2) Packing is free from damage at inception of transit risk as evidenced by issuance of a clean Bill of Lading (without a letter of indemnity to the shipper) or otherwise proven by the Assured.
3) Damage to packing is due to a peril insured against.
4) Reconditioning of packing or repacking is actually necessary.

In no event, however, shall Underwriters be liable for more than the insured value of the damaged goods.

43. PAIRS AND SETS

In the event of loss of or damage to one or more pieces of a set consisting, when complete for sale or use, of two or more component pieces, the liability of Underwriters shall be to pay the insured value of the total set.

44. DELIBERATE DAMAGE / POLLUTION HAZARD

This Policy covers, but only while the property insured is on board a waterborne conveyance, loss of or damage to property directly caused by governmental authorities acting for the public welfare to prevent or mitigate a pollution hazard or threat thereof, provided that the accident or occurrence creating the situation which required such governmental action would have resulted in a recoverable claim under the Policy (subject to all of its terms, conditions and warranties) if the property insured would have sustained physical loss or damage as a direct result of such accident or occurrence.

The coverage afforded hereunder shall not increase the Limits of Liability provided herein.

45. DELIBERATE DAMAGE BY CUSTOMS SERVICE

This insurance is also specially to cover physical loss of or damage to goods insured arising out of the performance of inspection duties of Customs Services or another duly constituted governmental agency.

46. ADDITIONAL FREIGHT/DUTY

This insurance also covers, subject to Policy terms, the risk of partial loss by reason of perils insured against on the freight payable at port of destination (unless guaranteed or payable "vessel lost or not lost") and/or on duties

Policy No. «PolicyNo» **Page 10 of 17** **Assured:** «Assured»

Figure 4–10. *(continued)*

imposed on goods insured hereunder, it being understood and agreed, however, that when the risk upon goods continues beyond the time of landing from the overseas vessel, the increased value, consequent upon the payment of such freight and/or duties, shall attach as an additional insurance upon the goods from the time such freight and/or duty is paid or becomes due to the extent of the amounts thereof actually paid or payable.

This clause shall not increase the Limits of Liability provided for elsewhere herein.

The Assured will, in all cases, use reasonable efforts to obtain abatement or refund of duties paid or claimed in respect of goods lost, damaged or destroyed. It is further agreed that the Assured shall, when the Underwriters so elect, surrender the merchandise to the Customs authorities and recover duties thereon as provided by law, in which event the claim under this Policy shall be only for a total loss of the merchandise so surrendered and expenses.

This insurance on freight and/or duty shall terminate at the end of the import movement covered under this Policy, but nothing contained in these clauses shall alter or affect any coverage granted elsewhere in the Policy during the storage or transit subsequent thereto.

47. INCREASED VALUE

With respect to goods and/or merchandise and/or property purchased by the Assured on C.I.F. or other similar terms whereby insurance is provided by the Seller or purchased by the Assured while still afloat on such terms prior to any known report of loss or accident, this Policy is extended to cover increased value, to be valued at the difference between the amount of insurance furnished by the Seller as evidenced by certificates or policies of insurance or otherwise, and valuation provided in this Policy applying to shipments purchased on C.I.F. or similar terms.

This insurance to pay the same percentage of loss on increased value or original Underwriters would pay on cargo subject to the Average Terms and Conditions contained in Clause 15 of this Policy; However, all references to deductibles appearing in this policy shall not be applicable to this insurance. In the event that the merchandise is short delivered or sold unidentifiable in consequences of perils insured against, this insurance is to pay a total loss on the increased value on the part short delivered or sold unidentifiable. Free of General Average and/or Salvage Charges except on the excess of contributory value over the original amount insured if uncollectible under original insurance on cargo.

48. F.O.B./F.A.S. SALES

1) In consideration of premiums to be paid at rates set forth in the Schedule of Rates in this Policy, subject to all its terms and conditions, the insurance is hereby extended to cover shipments originating in the Continental United States and sold by the Assured to others on F.A.S., F.O.B. or similar terms.

2) This Policy shall cover such F.A.S./F.O.B. shipments from the time of leaving store, warehouse or factory at interior point of shipment and continue while in due course of transit to the port of export and while there, until loaded on board overseas vessel or until Assured's interest and responsibility cease in accordance with the terms of sale, whichever shall first occur.

3) It is expressly understood and agreed that this insurance on F.A.S./F.O.B. shipments shall apply only as excess insurance placed by the Assured's suppliers or buyers which may have attached at the time of loss or damage.

49. F.O.B./F.A.S. PURCHASES

Notwithstanding anything to the contrary herein, it is agreed that this Cover's liability to the Assured commences from time the goods leave the suppliers' factory, warehouse, store or mill, notwithstanding the goods and/or interest may have been purchased Free on Board, Free Alongside Ship or Cost and Freight, and the Assured subrogating their right or recourse against suppliers for any loss or damage that may occur prior to delivery at the point designated in the applicable Free on Board, Free Alongside Ship or Cost and Freight terms.

Policy No. «PolicyNo» **Page 11 of 17** **Assured: «Assured»**

Figure 4–10. *(continued)*

The Assured agrees to report, the total value of all such shipments and pay premium thereon at rates set forth in the Schedule of Rates in this Cover Note.

50. CONTINGENT INSURANCE

This insurance is also specially to cover goods sold by the Assured on terms which do not obligate them to provide insurance, if there is loss or damage from a peril insured herein, and

A. The Assured cannot collect from the consignee or other party because of a refusal or inability to pay;
B. The Assured has been paid but remains contractually obligated to replace the loss or damaged goods.

Underwriters shall advance to the Assured, as a loan, the amount of loss as provided herein. Such loss to be repayable upon remittance of the purchase price by the buyer or otherwise. Goods insured under this coverage shall be valued at the amount of the Assured's invoice, plus freight and other charges (if not included in the invoice). This insurance is for the sole account of the Assured and in no event is it to inure to the benefit of buyers, consignees or any other party.

It is a condition precedent to this coverage that the Assured shall not divulge the existence of this coverage to any party. Such disclosure shall void coverage provided by this clause.
The Assured shall preserve their rights against the buyer or other parties and, upon receipt of payment from Underwriters, shall subrogate to Underwriters all rights and shall give all assistance, other than pecuniary, in enforcing them.

The Assured agrees to report the total value of all such shipments and pay premium thereon at rates set forth in the Schedule of Rates named in this Policy.

51. DEBRIS REMOVAL

This insurance is extended to cover, in addition to any other amount recoverable under this insurance, extra expenses reasonably incurred by the Assured for the removal and disposal of debris of the subject matter insured, or part thereof, by reason of damage thereto caused by an insured risk, but excluding absolutely:

A. Any expenses incurred in consequence of or to prevent or mitigate pollution or contamination, or any threat or liability therefore

B. The cost of removal of cargo from any vessel or craft.

In no case shall Underwriters be liable under this clause for more than 10% of the insured value under this Policy of the damaged subject-matter removed.

52. ATMOSPHERIC CONDITIONS

In the event of the goods insured hereunder being wetted or exposed to any odor occurring during the period of the insurance provided in this Cover Note, and the quality of the goods is thereby affected, the extra expenses of drying and/or reconditioning will be reimbursed by Underwriters. In the event the goods cannot be reconditioned, the liability of Underwriters shall be to pay the insured value of the affected goods.

53. NOTICE OF LOSS

In case of actual or expected loss of or damage to the goods insured, it shall be reported to the Underwriters or their claim representatives as soon as practicable upon knowledge by the Assured of the actual or expected loss.

54. PAYMENT ON ACCOUNT

Policy No. **«PolicyNo»** **Page 12 of 17** **Assured:** **«Assured»**

Figure 4–10. *(continued)*

Underwriters agree that where claim papers submitted demonstrate that only the quantum of the claim is in question, they will make a "payment on account" equal to 75% of the lower of the amounts claimed and agreed by Underwriters.

55. SUBROGATION

It is agreed that, on payment of any loss, the Assured shall assign and subrogate to Underwriters all their rights against third parties to the extent of such payments and shall permit suit to be brought in their name but at the Underwriters expense. The Assured further agrees to render all reasonable assistance in the prosecution of any suit. Should the sound market value of the damaged or lost goods exceed the amount insured, any recovery obtained will be pro-rated between Underwriters and the Assured as their respective interests bear to the sound market value of the goods. However, except in General Average, Underwriters shall not be subrogated to any rights and/or claims against the Assured's affiliates or subsidiaries.

56. CONTROL OF DAMAGED GOODS

It is agreed that in the event of damage to goods insured under this policy, the Assured shall retain control of all damaged goods. The Assured, however, agrees whenever practicable to recondition and sell such goods after removal of all brands and trademarks, the Company being entitled to the proceeds from such sale.

57. WAIVER AND/OR RELEASE

Privilege is hereby given to the Assured to accept from Carriers' bills of lading, receipts or contracts of transportation containing a release or limitation of liability as to the value of the goods, without prejudice to this insurance.

Further, in the event of loss or damage to property covered hereunder the Assured shall immediately make claim in writing against the carriers, bailees, or others involved.

58. MULTIPLE RECOVERY

No loss shall be paid hereunder if the Assured has collected the same from others

59. OTHER INSURANCE

If at the time of loss or damage there is available to the Assured or any other interested party, any other insurance which would apply in the absence of this Policy (excepting such insurance as may be arranged by the shipper or consignee), the insurance provided for hereunder shall apply only as excess insurance over such other insurance.

60. CONCEALED DAMAGE CLAUSE

Should delay occur in the opening of any package after arrival of goods at the final destination or should the goods be placed in bond or warehouse or any other place of deposit by the Assured or ultimate consignee prior to unpacking; if loss or damage is found when such packages are eventually opened, such loss shall be paid or adjusted by the Underwriters in the same manner as though the packages had been opened immediately upon their arrival, provided that:

a. It is no later than **30 days** after arrival at final destination and which can be reasonably shown to have occurred prior to delivery into such places of deposit.
b. Such loss or damage is recoverable under the terms of the policy.

Packages showing external damage are to be opened immediately upon arrival.

61. UNEXPLAINED SHORTAGES

This insurance is also specially to cover unexplained shortages of goods insured shipped in sealed container(s) whether or not the original seals are intact upon arrival at the final destination, provided that:

Policy No. «PolicyNo» **Page 13 of 17** **Assured: «Assured»**

Figure 4–10. *(continued)*

A. The coverage for the shipment includes loss caused by theft;
B. The Assured makes every attempt to recover the loss from anyone who may have been responsible for the shortage through involvement in stuffing the container.

It is a condition precedent to this coverage that the Assured shall not divulge the existence of this coverage to any party. Such disclosure shall void coverage provided by this clause.

62. FRAUDULANT BILL OF LADING CLAUSE

This policy covers physical loss or damage to merchandise insured under this Policy occasioned through the acceptance by the Assured and/or their agents or shippers of fraudulent Bills of Lading and/or shipping receipts and/or messenger receipt.

Also loss or damage caused by the utilization of legitimate bills of lading and/or other shipping documents without the authorization and/or consent of the Assured or its agents.

In no event, however, does this Policy cover loss or damage arising from the shipper's fraud or misstatement.

63. ERRORS & OMISSIONS

It is, however, agreed that this insurance shall not be prejudiced by any unintentional delay or inadvertent omission in reporting hereunder or any unintentional error in the description of the interest, vessel or voyage, if prompt notice be given Underwriters in all such cases as soon as said delay and/or omission and/or error becomes known to the Assured and adjustment of premium be made if and as required.

64. MISREPRESENTATION AND FRAUD

This policy shall be void if the Assured has concealed or misrepresented any material fact or circumstance concerning this insurance or the subject thereof or in case of any fraud, attempted fraud or false swearing by the Assured touching any matter relating to this insurance or the subject thereof, whether before or after the loss.

65. LETTERS OF CREDIT

Notwithstanding the conditions of this Policy, it is agreed that Certificates and/or Policies may be issued hereunder to the Assured to comply with the insurance requirements of any letter of credit and/or sales contract concerned, provided the cover required is not wider than that provided by the current Policy Wording. In the event that wider coverage is required, prior agreement of Underwriters is to be obtained at an additional premium to be agreed.

66. CERTIFICATES OF INSURANCE

Underwriters agree to issue "Claims Payable Abroad" and "Claims Payable to London" certificates as required subject to the inclusion of the following clause:

The Clauses referred to herein are those current at the inception of this open cover but should such clauses be revised during the period of this open cover and provided that Underwriters shall have given at least 30 days notice thereof, then the revised Clauses shall apply to risks attaching subsequent to the date of expiry of said notice."

67. AUTHORITY TO ISSUE CERTIFICATES

Authority is hereby granted the Assured to issue Underwriters' certificates hereunder, provided such certificates shall conform to the terms and conditions of this Policy and/or any written instructions that are or may be given by Underwriters and/or Roanoke Trade Insurance, Inc. from time to time. All such certificates issued shall be countersigned by a duly authorized representative of the Assured.

Policy No. «PolicyNo» **Page 14 of 17** **Assured: «Assured»**

Figure 4–10. *(continued)*

68. REPORTING

It is warranted that the Assured by acceptance of this Policy agrees to report all shipments in respect of which insurance is provided hereunder to

for transmission to Underwriters as soon as known to the Assured, or as soon thereafter as may be practicable.

70. INSPECTION OF RECORDS

Underwriters or their duly appointed representative shall be permitted at any time during business hours during the time this Policy is in force, or within a year after its termination, to inspect the records of the Assured as respects goods insured within the terms of this Policy.

71. BROKERS

(a) It is understood that for the purposes of this insurance the Assured's Broker of Record is

(b) It is a condition of this policy that the above brokers, or any substituted brokers, shall be deemed to be exclusively the agents of the Assured and not of this company in any and all matters related to, connected with, or affecting t his insurance. Any notice given or mailed by or on behalf of this Company to the above brokers in connection with or affecting this insurance, or its cancellation, shall be deemed to have been delivered to the Assured.

72. NOTICE OF SUIT

No suit, action or proceeding against this Company for recovery of any claim shall be sustainable unless commenced within one year from the date of the happening of the accident out of which the claim arises, provided that if such limitation is invalid by the laws of the state within which the policy is issued then such suit, action or proceeding shall be barred unless commenced within the shortest limit of time permitted by the laws of such state.

73. CANCELLATION

This Policy shall be subject to 30 days Notice of Cancellation, by either party, giving the other party written notice to that effect, but such cancellation shall not affect any risk on which this insurance has attached prior to the effective date of such notice.

Notwithstanding the foregoing notice period, Underwriters may effect immediate cancellation by giving written notice thereof at any time when premiums have been due and unpaid for a period of sixty (60) days or more.

74. CLASSIFICATION CLAUSE

Rates are for shipments of merchandise as specified herein, made Under Deck without transshipment unless otherwise state specifically. Shipped on:

1) Metal-hull, self-propelled vessels which are not over 20 years of age nor less than 1,000 net registered tons and which are classed A1 American Record or equivalent by a member of the International Association of Classification Societies; or

Policy No. «PolicyNo» **Page 15 of 17** **Assured: «Assured»**

Figure 4–10. *(continued)*

2) Vessels over 20 years of age which are approved by Underwriters, and which are not less than 1,000 net registered tons and classed as in (1) above, but while operating in their regular trades;

3) but in either case excluding vessels built:

   a) for service on the Great Lakes;
   b) solely for Military or Naval Service; or
   c) for carriage of dry bulk or liquid bulk cargoes, and which are more than 15 years of age, unless specifically approved by Underwriters.

Shipments by vessel which are not described in (1) or (2) above or which are excluded in (3) above are subject to additional rates to be quoted by Underwriters at the time of the reporting of shipment.

IN WITNESS WHEREOF, this Policy shall not be valid unless countersigned by an authorized representative of this Company and Roanoke Trade Insurance, Inc.

Countersigned at Boston, Massachusetts on this date: 4/28/2009

By: ______________________________
Authorized Representative

By: ______________________________
Authorized Representative

Policy No. «PolicyNo» **Page 16 of 17** **Assured: «Assured»**

Figure 4–10. *(continued)*

Dated: «EffDate»

Part of Policy No. «PolicyNo»
of the

American Institute
Strikes, Riots & Civil Commotions (Cargo)
(December 2, 1992)

S.R. & C.C. ENDORSEMENT

This insurance also covers:

1. Physical loss of or damage to the property insured directly caused by strikers, locked-out workmen, or persons taking part in labor disturbances or riots or civil commotions and,

2. Physical loss of or damage to the property insured directly caused by vandalism, sabotage or malicious act, which shall be deemed also to encompass the act or acts of one or more persons, whether or not agents of a sovereign power, carried out for political, terroristic or ideological purposes and whether any loss, damage or expense resulting therefrom is accidental or intentional; PROVIDED that any claim to be recoverable under this sub-section (2) be not excluded by the FC&S Warranty in the Policy to which this endorsement is attached.

   While the property insured is at risk under the terms and conditions of this insurance within the United States of America, the Commonwealth of Puerto Rico, the U.S. Virgin Islands and Canada, this insurance is extended to cover physical loss of or damage to the property insured directly caused by acts committed by an agent of any government, party or faction engaged in war, hostilities or other warlike operations, provided such agent is acting secretly and not in connection with any operation of military or naval armed forces in the country where the described property is situated.

   Nothing in this clause shall be construed to include or cover any loss, damage, deterioration or expense directly or indirectly arising from, contributed to or caused by any of the following, whether due to a peril insured against or otherwise:

   A. Change in temperature or humidity.

   B. The absence, storage, or withholding of power, fuel, or labor of any description whatsoever during any strike, lockout, labor disturbance, riot or civil commotion.

   C. Loss of market or loss, damage or deterioration arising from delay;

   D. Hostilities, warlike operations, civil war, revolution, rebellion or insurrection, or civil strife arising therefrom, except to the limited extent that the acts of certain agents acting secretly have been expressly covered above; or,

   E. Any weapon of war employing atomic or nuclear fission and/or fusion or other like reaction or radioactive force or matter.

   The Assured agrees to report all shipments attaching under this cover and to pay premiums therefore at the rates established by Underwriters from time to time.

Notwithstanding the Cancellation Clause provided herein, the coverage provided under this clause may be cancelled by either party upon forty-eight hours written or telegraphic notice to the other party, but such cancellation shall not affect any risks which have already attached hereunder.

Policy No. «PolicyNo» **Page 17 of 17** **Assured: «Assured»**

Figure 4–11. Marine insurance certificate.

Special Marine Policy

No. ____________

Open Policy No. ______________________ of | SERVICE OFFICE: | **ORIGINAL** (ORIGINAL AND DUPLICATE ISSUED ONE OF WHICH BEING ACCOMPLISHED, THE OTHER TO BE NULL AND VOID)

$ ______________________ (PLACE & DATE) ______________________

This Company, in consideration of a premium as agreed, and subject to the Terms and Conditions printed or stamped hereon and/or attached hereto, does insure, lost or not lost ______________________

For account of whom it may concern; to be shipped by the vessel ______________________

______________________, and connecting conveyances.

MARKS AND NUMBERS

From ______________________

To ______________________

Lawful Goods Consisting Of ______________________,

______________________, Number of ______________________

Valued at **Sum hereby Insured**

____

Inv. #

B/L #

Loss, if any, payable to **Assured** or order.

TERMS AND CONDITIONS - SEE ALSO BACK HEREOF

WAREHOUSE TO WAREHOUSE: This insurance attaches from the time the goods leave the Warehouse and/or Store at the place named in the Policy for the commencement of the transit and continues during the ordinary course of transit, including customary transshipment if any, until the goods are discharged overside from the overseas vessel at the final port. Thereafter the insurance continues whilst the goods are in transit and/or awaiting transit until delivered to final warehouse at the destination named in the Policy or until the expiry of 15 days (or 30 days if the destination to which the goods are insured is outside the limits of the port) whichever shall first occur. The time limits referred to above to be reckoned from midnight of the day on which the discharge overside of the goods hereby insured from the overseas vessel is completed. Held covered at a premium to be arranged in the event of transshipment, if any, other than as above and/or in the event of delay in excess of the above time limits arising from circumstances beyond the control of the Assured. NOTE -- IT IS NECESSARY FOR THE ASSURED TO GIVE PROMPT NOTICE TO THESE ASSURERS WHEN THEY BECOME AWARE OF AN EVENT FOR WHICH THEY ARE "HELD COVERED" UNDER THIS POLICY AND THE RIGHT TO SUCH COVER IS DEPENDENT ON COMPLIANCE WITH THIS OBLIGATION.

SHORE CLAUSE: Where this insurance by its terms covers while on docks, wharves or elsewhere on shore, and/or during land transportation, it shall include the risks of collision, derailment, overturning or other accident to the conveyance, fire, lightning, sprinkler leakage, cyclones, hurricanes, earthquakes, floods (meaning the rising of navigable waters), and/or collapse or subsidence of docks or wharves, even though the insurance be otherwise F.P.A.

BOTH TO BLAME CLAUSE: Where goods are shipped under a Bill of Lading containing the so-called "Both to Blame Collision" Clause, these Assurers agree as to all losses covered by this insurance, to indemnify the Assured for this Policy's proportion of any amount (not exceeding the amount insured) which the Assured may be legally bound to pay to the shipowners under such clause. In the event that such liability is asserted the Assured agrees to notify these Assurers who shall have the right at their own cost and expense to defend the Assured against such claim.

MACHINERY CLAUSE: When the property insured under this Policy includes a machine consisting when complete for sale or use of several parts, then in case of loss or damage covered by this insurance to any part of such machine, these Assurers shall be liable only for the proportion of the insured value of the part lost or damaged, or at the Assured's option, for the cost and expense, including labor and forwarding charges, of replacing and repairing the lost or damaged part; but in no event shall these Assurers be liable for more than the insured value of the complete machine.

LABELS CLAUSE: In case of damage affecting labels, capsules or wrappers, these Assurers, if liable therefor under the terms of this policy, shall not be liable for more than an amount sufficient to pay the cost of new labels, capsules or wrappers, and the cost of reconditioning the goods, but in no event shall these Assurers be liable for more than the insured value of the damaged merchandise.

DELAY CLAUSE: Warranted free of claim for loss of market or for loss, damage or deterioration arising from delay, whether caused by a peril insured against or otherwise, unless expressly assumed in writing hereon.

AMERICAN INSTITUTE CLAUSES: This insurance, in addition to the foregoing, is also subject to the following American Institute Cargo Clauses, current forms:
1. CRAFT, ETC. 2. DEVIATION 3. WAREHOUSE & FORWARDING CHARGES, PACKAGES TOTALLY LOST LOADING, ETC. 4.GENERAL AVERAGE 5.EXPLOSION 6. BILL OF LADING, ETC. 7. INCHMAREE 8. CONSTRUCTIVE TOTAL LOSS 9. CARRIER 10. EXTENDED R.A.C.E. 11. CHEMICAL, BIOLOGICAL, ELECTROMAGNETIC EXCLUSION

PERILS CLAUSE: Touching the adventures and perils which this Company is contented to bear, and takes upon itself, they are of the seas, assailing thieves, jettisons, barratry of the master and mariners, and all other like perils, losses and misfortunes (illicit or contraband trade excepted in all cases), that have or shall come to the hurt, detriment or damage of the said goods and merchandise, or any part thereof.

AVERAGE TERMS: ON DECK AND SUBJECT TO AN "ON DECK" BILL OF LADING -- (which must be so declared by the Assured): Free of Particular Average unless caused by the vessel being stranded, sunk, burnt, on fire or in collision, but including jettison and/or washing overboard irrespective of percentage. EXCEPT WHILE SUBJECT TO AN "ON DECK" BILL OF LADING:

ALL RISK STANDARD WORDING: To cover against all risks of physical loss or damage from any external cause irrespective of percentage, but excluding, nevertheless, the risks of war, strikes, riots, seizure, detention and other risks excluded by the F.C. & S. (Free of Capture & Seizure) Warranty and the S.R. & C.C. (Strikes, Riots, and Civil Commotions) Warranty policy, excepting to the extent that such risks are specifically covered by endorsement.

This Policy is extended to include the provisions of the following clauses as if the current form of each were endorsed hereon:

American Institute Clauses -

F.C. & S. Warranty
Marine Extension Clauses
S.R.&C.C. Endorsement
War Risk Insurance
Nuclear Exclusion

Where appropriate -
South America 60-Day Clause

PARAMOUNT WARRANTIES: THE FOLLOWING WARRANTIES SHALL BE PARAMOUNT AND SHALL NOT BE MODIFIED OR SUPERSEDED BY ANY OTHER PROVISION INCLUDED HEREIN OR STAMPED OR ENDORSED HEREON UNLESS SUCH OTHER PROVISION REFERS SPECIFICALLY TO THE RISKS EXCLUDED BY THESE WARRANTIES AND EXPRESSLY ASSUMES THE SAID RISKS C.& S.(a) NOTWITHSTANDING ANYTHING HEREIN CONTAINED TO THE CONTRARY THIS INSURANCE IS WARRANTED FREE FROM: (a) capture, seizure, arrest, restraint, detainment, confiscation, preemption, requisition or nationalization, and the consequences thereof or any attempt thereat, whether in time of peace or war and whether lawful or otherwise; (b) all loss, damage or expense, whether in time of peace or war, caused by (i) any weapon or war employing atomic or nuclear fission and/or fusion or other reaction or radioactive force or matter or (ii) any mine or torpedo; (c) all consequences of hostilities or warlike operations (whether there be a declaration of war or not), but this warranty shall not exclude collision or contact with aircraft, or with rockets or similar missiles (other than weapons of war) or with any fixed or floating object (other than a mine or torpedo), stranding, heavy weather, fire or explosion unless caused directly (and independently of the nature of the voyage or service which the vessel concerned or, in the case of a collision, any other vessel involved therein, is performing) by a hostile act by or against a belligerent power; and for the purposes of this warranty "power" includes any authority maintaining naval, military or air forces in association with a power; (d) the consequences of civil war, revolution, rebellion, insurrection, or civil strife arising therefrom; or from the consequences of the imposition of martial law, military or usurped power; or piracy. S.R.&C.C. (b) Notwithstanding anything herein contained to the contrary, this insurance is warranted free from loss, damage or expense caused by or resulting from: (1) strikes, lockouts, labor disturbances, riots, civil commotions, or the acts of any person or persons taking part in any such occurrences or disorders, (2) vandalism, sabotage or malicious act, which shall be deemed also to encompass the act or acts of one or more persons, whether or not agents of a sovereign power, carried out for political, terroristic or ideological purposes and whether any loss, damage or expense resulting therefrom is accidental or intentional.

ECONOMIC SANCTIONS AND EMBARGO PROGRAMS OF THE UNITED STATES: This policy excludes loss otherwise payable to an individual, organization, or authority that is the subject of any trade embargo or other trade sanction imposed by the United States Government; or that arises out of any trade in, or shipment of, any goods or merchandise prohibited by such embargo or sanction, whether or not deemed lawful under the laws of another nation

DRAFT

Figure 4–11. *(continued)*

Insurance Document (or Certificate)

Definition

A document indicating the type and amount of insurance coverage in force on a particular shipment. In documentary credit transactions the insurance document is used to assure the consignee that insurance is provided to cover loss of or damage to cargo while in transit subject to policy terms and conditions.

A completed insurance document includes the following elements:

1. The name of the insurance company
2. Policy number
3. Description of the merchandise insured
4. Points of origin and destination of the shipment. Coverage is indicated by the terms of sale. For example, for goods sold "FOB," coverage commences once the cargo is on board the vessel and continues until the consignee takes possession at either the seaport or in-land port of destination.
5. Conditions of coverage, exclusions, and deductible, if applicable.
6. A signature by the insurance carrier, underwriter or agent for same
7. Indication that the cover is effective at the latest from the date of loading of the goods on board a transport vessel or the taking in charge of the goods by the carrier, as indicated by the transport document (bill of lading, etc.)
8. Statement of the sum insured
9. In a documentary letter of credit, specifies coverage for at least 110 percent of either: (a) the CIF or CIP value of the shipment, if such can be determined from the various documents on their face, otherwise, (b) the amount of the payment, acceptance or negotiation specified in the documentary credit, or (c) the gross amount of the commercial invoice
10. Is presented as the sole original, or if issued in more than one original, the full set of originals

Cautions & Notes

In documentary credit transactions the insurance currency should be consistent with the currency of the documentary credit.

Documentary credit transactions indicating CIF (Cost Insurance Freight) or CIP (Carriage and Insurance Paid) pricing should list an insurance document in the required documentation.

"Cover notes" issued by insurance brokers (as opposed to insurance companies, underwriters, or their agents) are not accepted in letter of credit transactions unless authorized specifically by the credit terms.

In Case of Loss or Shortfall

The consignee should always note on the delivery document any damage or shortfall prior to signing for receipt of the goods. The consignee has the responsibility to make reasonable efforts to minimize loss. This includes steps to prevent further damage to the shipment. Expenses incurred in such efforts are almost universally collectible under the insurance policy. Prompt notice of loss is essential.

The original copy of the insurance certificate is a negotiable document and is required in the filing of a claim.

Copies of documents necessary to support an insurance claim include the insurance policy or certificate, bill of lading, invoice, packing list, and a survey report (usually prepared by a claims agent).

Figure 4–12. Standard form for presentation of loss or damage claim.

General Order No. 41 P. OF. D.G. D.G.

STANDARD FORM FOR PRESENTATION OF LOSS OR DAMAGE CLAIMS

Approved by
THE INTERSTATE COMMERCE COMMISSION
THE NATIONAL INDUSTRIAL TRAFFIC LEAGUE
THE FREIGHT CLAIM ASSOCIATION

______________________ (Address of Claimant)

______________________ (Date)

______________________ Claimant's Number §

______________________ Carrier's Number

______________________ (Name of person to whom claim is presented)

(Name of carrier) ______________________

(Address) ______________________

This claim for $__________ is made against the carrier named above by (Name of claimant) ______________________

______________________ for (Loss or damage) __________ in connection with the following described shipment:

Description of shipment ______________________

Name and address of consignor (shipper) ______________________

Shipped from (City, town or station) __________, To (City, town or station) __________

Final destination (City, town or station) __________ Routed via __________

Bill of Lading issued by __________ Co.; Date of Bill Lading __________

Paid Freight Bill (Pro) Number __________. Original Car number and Initial __________

Name and address of consignee (to whom shipped) ______________________

If shipment reconsigned enroute, state particulars: ______________________

DETAILED STATEMENT SHOWING HOW AMOUNT CLAIMED IS DETERMINED
(Number and description of articles, nature and extent of loss or damage, invoice price of articles, amount of claim, etc.)

SAMPLE

Total Amount Claimed

IN ADDITION TO THE INFORMATION GIVEN ABOVE, THE FOLLOWING DOCUMENTS ARE SUBMITTED IN SUPPORT OF THIS CLAIM.*

( ) 1. Original bill of lading, if not previously surrendered to carrier.
( ) 2. Original paid freight ("Expense") bill.
( ) 3. Original invoice or certified copy.
4. Other particulars obtainable in proof of loss or damage claimed.

Remarks: ______________________

The foregoing statement of facts is hereby certified to as correct.

______________________ (Signature of claimant)

§ Claimant should assign to each claim a number, inserting same in the space provided at the upper right hand corner of this form. Reference should be made thereto in all correspondence pertaining to this claim.

* Claimant will please check (x) before such of the documents mentioned as have been attached, and explain under "Remarks" the absence of any of the documents called for in connection with this claim. When for any reason it is impossible for claimant to produce original bill of lading, if required, or paid freight bill, claimant should indemnify† carrier or carriers against duplicate claim supported by original documents.

† Indemnity agreement for lost bill of lading. Form 71, Unz & Co.

Form 30-048 Printed and Sold by UNZ&CO 190 Baldwin Ave., Jersey City, NJ 07306 • (800) 631-3098

Figure 4–13. Dock receipt.

(SPACES IMMEDIATELY BELOW ARE FOR SHIPPERS MEMORANDA--NOT PART OF DOCK RECEIPT)

DELIVERING CARRIER TO STEAMER:	CAR NUMBER—REFERENCE
FORWARDING AGENT—REFERENCES	EXPORT DEC. No.

DOCK RECEIPT
NON-NEGOTIABLE

SHIPPER . . . .

SHIP	VOYAGE NO.	FLAG	PIER	PORT OF LOADING
FOR. PORT OF DISCHARGE *(Where goods are to be delivered to consignee or on-carrier)*			For TRANSSHIPMENT TO *(If goods are to be transshipped or forwarded at port of discharge)*	

PARTICULARS FURNISHED BY SHIPPER OF GOODS

MARKS AND NUMBERS	No. of PKGS.	DESCRIPTION OF PACKAGES AND GOODS	MEASURE-MENT	GROSS WEIGHT

SAMPLE

DIMENSIONS AND WEIGHTS OF PACKAGES TO BE SHOWN ON REVERSE SIDE

DELIVERED BY:

LIGHTER
TRUCK } . . . .

ARRIVED— DATE . . . . TIME . . . .

UNLOADED— DATE . . . . TIME . . . .

CHECKED BY . . . .

PLACED IN SHIP / ON DOCK LOCATION . . . .

RECEIVED THE ABOVE DESCRIBED MERCHANDISE FOR SHIPMENT AS INDICATED HEREON, SUBJECT TO ALL CONDITIONS OF THE UNDERSIGNED'S USUAL FORM OF DOCK RECEIPT AND BILL OF LADING. COPIES OF THE UNDERSIGNED'S USUAL FORM OF DOCK RECEIPT AND BILL OF LADING MAY BE OBTAINED FROM THE MASTER OF THE VESSEL, OR THE VESSEL'S AGENT

AGENT FOR MASTER

BY . . . .
RECEIVING CLERK

DATE . . . .

Form 35-586 • 700 Central Ave., New Providence, N.J. 07974 • (800) 631-3098

Figure 4–14. Consular invoice.

FACTURE CONSULAIRE **CONSULAT DE LA** **REPUBLIQUE D'HAITI** **CONSULAR INVOICE**

B. L. No. ________

Marks (Marques) and Country of Origin

Merchandise Shipped on the S. S.: ________ on ________
Marchandises expédiées sur le SS. Nationality - Name (nom) le Date of Sailing
Sailing from the Port of ________ for ________, Haiti
Partant du port de Pour
Name and Address of Shipper ________
Nom et adresse de l'expéditeur
Consigned to order of ________ of ________
Consignées à l'ordre de
Notify ________ of ________, Haiti
Notifier de

Numbers Numéros	Number of pieces Nombre de colis	Nature of Packing Nature de l'emballage	Denomination and Details of Each Article (Quantity, Quality, Measure, Yardage, etc.) in Terms of the Haitian Tariff. Dénomination et détails de chaque article (quantité, qualité, mesure, yardage, etc.) dans les termes du Tarif Haïtien.	Weights in / Poids en: Gross Brut	Net Net	Values in U.S. Currency Valeur en Monnaie des E.U.

We affirm that this invoice is a correct and faithful expression of the truth, J'affirme que cette facture est l'expression sincère et fidèle de la vérité, that it corresponds in every particular with our books, and that neither the qu'elle est en tout conforme à mes livres, qu'aucune dénomination usuelle, usual designation, nor the weights, nor the quantity or quality, nor the value ni le poids, ni la quantité ou la qualité, ni la valeur, ni l'origine des articles and origin named therein are in any way altered, and are thereof exactly the qui y sont portés, n'ont été altérés et sont, en conséquence, les mêmes que same than those appeared on our Export Declaration No.
of (date) submitted to the U. S. Custom House.
ceux accusés sur ma déclaration No.
du soumise à la Douane des Etats-Unis.

________ Date ________ 19 ____

________ For Account of
Name of forwarding agent, broker or commissioner, etc.

Shippers ________
Expéditeurs

Per: ________
Signature

NOTE:—In all cases where the merchandise is taxed at net weight, the weight to be taxed of said merchandise will include all interior or immediate packing, including the paste board boxes or objects made of paste board, not subject to a higher tax. (Article 29, Law of July 26, 1926.)

Dans tous les cas où les marchandises sont taxées au poids net, le poids imposable des dites marchandises comprendra tous les emballages antérieurs ou immédiats, y compris les cartons ou objets en carton, non soumis à un droit plus élevé (Article 29, loi du 26 Juillet, 1926.)

ARRANGEMENT OF DOCUMENTS:

3 Consular Invoices and 3 Original Bills of lading clipped or stapled together, the invoice on top.

To each of the remaining Consular invoices a copy of signed B/L must be stapled and the whole set clipped together.

Value of merchandise / Valeur des marchandises		
Packing (if not included in the value of the merchandise) / Emballage (s'il n'est pas compris dans la valeur des marchandises)		
Inland Freight. Bill of Lading. Wharfage and Trucking Charges / Frêt et frais du connaissement, embarquement et camionnage.		
Total F. O. B. Value		
Brokerage fees / Commission d'achat		
Interest / Intérêts		
Export Duties paid at Port of Origin / Droits d'exportation acquittés au port d'origine		
Ocean Freight and Bill of Lading Expenses (including embarking and disembarking) / Frêt et frais du connaissement, embarquement et débarquement compris		
Insurance / Assurance		
Consular fees / Droits consulaires: *2% of F O B value $		
Stamp on Inv. ($1.20)		
B/L visa ($2.00)		
Stamp on B/L ($1.20)		
Other expenses / Autres frais		
Total amount of invoice / Montant total de la facture		

CONSULAR INVOICE FEES

*For any merchandise being shipped by boat to Haiti and whose value FOB is inferior to $200.00 — the fee is $3.00 plus B/L visa and Stamps ________ 7.40
Over $200.00 — the fee is 2% on the value FOB plus B/L visa and Stamps
Visa for Certificate of Origin $2.00 plus Stamps $1.20 ________ 3.20
Visa for Commercial Invoice if requested $2.00 plus Stamp $1.20 ________ 3.20
ADDITIONAL FEES:
Visa on Consular Invoice requested after 4 p. m. ________ 2.00*
Visa on Consular Invoice requested on holidays ________ 4.00*

request the freight forwarder to ascertain and advise it whether a certificate of origin is required, but prior thereto, the exporter should check with the buyer for a list of all documents required to make customs entry in the country of destination. Certificates of origin must be distinguished from country of origin marking. Many countries require that the products themselves and the labels on the packages specify the country of origin (see discussion in Chapter 2, Section R). The country of origin certificate may be in addition to or in lieu of that requirement. (A generic sample, to be executed by a local chamber of commerce, is shown in Figure 4–15.)

In some instances, a certificate of origin is required in order to claim preferential duty rates such as the one required under the North American Free Trade Agreement (NAFTA). NAFTA contains product-specific country of origin criteria that must be met to qualify for reduced duty treatment on exports to or imports from Canada or Mexico. In general, in order to be eligible for the duty-free or reduced duty rates under NAFTA, all items imported from outside of North America must have undergone the "tariff shift" specified in Annex 401 during the manufacturing process for that product. In addition, some products must contain a specified "regional value content," usually 50 or 60 percent. Finished goods and sometimes raw materials purchased from others often must be traced backward to establish their country of origin. (A sample of the NAFTA Certificate of Origin and Instructions is shown in Figure 4–16.) The United States has entered into a number of free trade agreements similar to NAFTA, such as the Dominican Republic–Central America–United States Free Trade Agreement (CAFTA-DR), the U.S.-Chile Free Trade Agreement, the U.S.-Australia Free Trade Agreement, the U.S.-Singapore Free Trade Agreement, the U.S.-Bahrain Free Trade Agreement, the U.S.-Morocco Free Trade Agreement, the U.S.-Oman Free Trade Agreement, and the U.S.-Malaysia Free Trade Agreement. Others are in negotiation. (Other sample certificates of origin are shown in Figures 4–17 and 4–18).

L. Certificates of Free Sale

Sometimes an importer will request that an exporter provide a certificate of free sale. Loosely speaking, this is a certification that a product being purchased by the importer complies with any U.S. government regulations for marketing the product and may be freely sold within the United States. Sometimes, depending upon the type of product involved, the importer will be able to accept a self-certification by the exporter. Frequently, however, the importer seeks the certificate of free sale because the importer's own government requires it. For example, these requests are common with regard to food, beverages, pharmaceuticals, and medical devices. The foreign government may or may not require the importer to conduct its own testing of the products for safety but may, either as a primary source or as backup for its own testing, seek confirmation that the products are in compliance with the U.S. Food, Drug and Cosmetics Act. The U.S. Food and Drug Administration has procedures for issuing a Certificate for Products for Export certifying that the product is registered with the FDA in the United States and is in compliance with U.S. law. (A sample certificate is shown in Figure 4–19; an FDA Application Form 3613-e is shown in

(*Text continues on page 165.*)

Figure 4–15. Certificate of origin.

Certificate of Origin

The undersigned ____
(Owner or Agent)

for ____
(Name and Address of Shipper)

declares the following listed goods shipped on ______________________
(Name of Carrier)

on ______________________ consigned to ______________________
(Shipment Date) (Recipient's Name)

____
(Recipient's Name and Address)

are the products of the United States of America.

Marks & Numbers	No. of Packages, Boxes or Cases	Weight in Kilos Gross	Net	Full Description of Item

State of ______________________ County of ______________________

Sworn to me ____

this __________ day of __________, 20____ ______________________
(Signature of Owner or Agent)

____

The ______________________, a recognized Chamber of Commerce Under the laws of the State of ______________________, has examined the manufacturer's invoice or shipper's affidavit concerning the origin of the merchandise and, according to the best of its knowledge and belief, finds that the products named originated in the United States of North America.

Secretary ______________________

Figure 4–16. NAFTA certificate of origin and instructions.

DEPARTMENT OF HOMELAND SECURITY
U.S. Customs and Border Protection

OMB No. 1651-0098
Exp. 02-28-2009
See back of form for Paperwork Reduction Act Notice.

NORTH AMERICAN FREE TRADE AGREEMENT
CERTIFICATE OF ORIGIN
19 CFR 181.11, 181.22

Please print or type

1. EXPORTER NAME AND ADDRESS TAX IDENTIFICATION NUMBER:	2. BLANKET PERIOD FROM TO
3. PRODUCER NAME AND ADDRESS TAX IDENTIFICATION NUMBER:	4. IMPORTER NAME AND ADDRESS TAX IDENTIFICATION NUMBER:

5. DESCRIPTION OF GOOD(S)	6. HS TARIFF CLASSIFICATION NUMBER	7. PREFERENCE CRITERION	8. PRODUCER	9. NET COST	10. COUNTRY OF ORIGIN

I CERTIFY THAT:

- THE INFORMATION ON THIS DOCUMENT IS TRUE AND ACCURATE AND I ASSUME THE RESPONSIBILITY FOR PROVING SUCH REPRESENTATIONS. I UNDERSTAND THAT I AM LIABLE FOR ANY FALSE STATEMENTS OR MATERIAL OMISSIONS MADE ON OR IN CONNECTION WITH THIS DOCUMENT;
- I AGREE TO MAINTAIN AND PRESENT UPON REQUEST, DOCUMENTATION NECESSARY TO SUPPORT THIS CERTIFICATE, AND TO INFORM, IN WRITING, ALL PERSONS TO WHOM THE CERTIFICATE WAS GIVEN OF ANY CHANGES THAT COULD AFFECT THE ACCURACY OR VALIDITY OF THIS CERTIFICATE;
- THE GOODS ORIGINATED IN THE TERRITORY OF ONE OR MORE OF THE PARTIES, AND COMPLY WITH THE ORIGIN REQUIREMENTS SPECIFIED FOR THOSE GOODS IN THE NORTH AMERICAN FREE TRADE AGREEMENT AND UNLESS SPECIFICALLY EXEMPTED IN ARTICLE 411 OR ANNEX 401, THERE HAS BEEN NO FURTHER PRODUCTION OR ANY OTHER OPERATION OUTSIDE THE TERRITORIES OF THE PARTIES; AND
- THIS CERTIFICATE CONSISTS OF [   ] PAGES, INCLUDING ALL ATTACHMENTS.

11.	11a. AUTHORIZED SIGNATURE		11b. COMPANY	
	11c. NAME *(Print or Type)*		11d. TITLE	
	11e. DATE *(MM/DD/YYYY)*	11f. TELEPHONE NUMBER ▶	*(Voice)*	*(Facsimile)*

CBP Form 434 (04/97)

Figure 4–16. *(continued)*

PAPERWORK REDUCTION ACT NOTICE: This information is needed to carry out the terms of the North American Free Trade Agreement (NAFTA). NAFTA requires that, upon request, an importer must provide CBP with proof of the exporters written certification of the origin of the goods. The certification is essential to substantiate compliance with the rules of origin under the Agreement. You are required to give us this information to obtain a benefit.

The estimated average burden associated with this collection of information is 15 minutes per respondent or recordkeeper depending on individual circumstances. Comments concerning the accuracy of this burden estimate and suggestions for reducing this burden should be directed to U.S. Customs and Border Protection, Information Services Branch, Washington, DC 20229, and to the Office of Management and Budget, Paperwork Reduction Project (1651-0098), Washington DC 20503.

NORTH AMERICAN FREE TRADE AGREEMENT CERTIFICATE OF ORIGIN INSTRUCTIONS

For purposes of obtaining preferential tariff treatment, this document must be completed legibly and in full by the exporter and be in the possession of the importer at the time the declaration is made. This document may also be completed voluntarily by the producer for use by the exporter. Please print or type:

FIELD 1: State the full legal name, address (including country) and legal tax identification number of the exporter. Legal taxation number is: in Canada, employer number or importer/exporter number assigned by Revenue Canada; in Mexico, federal taxpayer's registry number (RFC); and in the United States, employer's identification number or Social Security Number.

FIELD 2: Complete field if the Certificate covers multiple shipments of identical goods as described in Field #5 that are imported into a NAFTA country for a specified period of up to one year (the blanket period). "FROM" is the date upon which Certificate becomes applicable to the good covered by the blanket Certificate (it may be prior to the date of signing this Certificate). "TO" is the date upon which the blanket period expires. The importation of a good for which preferential treatment is claimed based on this Certificate must occur between these dates.

FIELD 3: State the full legal name, address (including country) and legal tax identification number, as defined in Field #1, of the producer. If more than one producer's good is included on the Certificate, attach a list of additional producers, including the legal name, address (including country) and legal tax identification number, cross-referenced to the good described in Field #5. If you wish this information to be confidential, it is acceptable to state "Available to CBP upon request". If the producer and the exporter are the same, complete field with "SAME". If the producer is unknown, it is acceptable to state "UNKNOWN".

FIELD 4: State the full legal name, address (including country) and legal tax identification number, as defined in Field #1, of the importer. If the importer is not known, state "UNKNOWN"; if multiple importers, state "VARIOUS".

FIELD 5: Provide a full description of each good. The description should be sufficient to relate it to the invoice description and to the Harmonized System (H.S.) description of the good. If the Certificate covers a single shipment of a good, include the invoice number as shown on the commercial invoice. If not known, indicate another unique reference number, such as the shipping order number.

FIELD 6: For each good described in Field #5, identify the H.S. tariff classification to six digits. If the good is subject to a specific rule of origin in Annex 401 that requires eight digits, identify to eight digits, using the H.S. tariff classification of the country into whose territory the good is imported.

FIELD 7: For each good described in Field #5, state which criterion (A through F) is applicable. The rules of origin are contained in Chapter Four and Annex 401. Additional rules are described in Annex 703.2 (certain agricultural goods), Annex 300-B, Appendix 6 (certain textile goods) and Annex 308.1 (certain automatic data processing goods and their parts). **NOTE: In order to be entitled to preferential tariff treatment, each good must meet at least one of the criteria below.**

Preference Criteria

A The good is "wholly obtained or produced entirely" in the territory of one or more of the NAFTA countries as referenced in Article 415. **Note: The purchase of a good in the territory does not necessarily render it "wholly obtained or produced".** If the good is an agricultural good, see also criterion F and Annex 703.2. *(Reference: Article 401(a) and 415)*

B The good is produced entirely in the territory of one or more of the NAFTA countries and satisfies the specific rule of origin, set out in Annex 401, that applies to its tariff classification. The rule may include a tariff classification change, regional value-content requirement, or a combination thereof. The good must also satisfy all other applicable requirements of Chapter Four. If the good is an agricultural good, see also criterion F and Annex 703.2. *(Reference: Article 401(b))*

C The good is produced entirely in the territory of one or more of the NAFTA countries exclusively from originating materials. Under this criterion, one or more of the materials may not fall within the definition of "wholly produced or obtained", as set out in article 415. All materials used in the production of the good must qualify as "originating" by meeting the rules of Article 401(a) through (d). If the good is an agricultural good, see also criterion F and Annex 703.2. *Reference: Article 401(c).*

D Goods are produced in the territory of one or more of the NAFTA countries but do not meet the applicable rule of origin, set out in Annex 401, because certain non-originating materials do not undergo the required change in tariff classification. The goods do nonetheless meet the regional value-content requirement specified in Article 401(d). This criterion is limited to the following two circumstances:

1. The good was imported into the territory of a NAFTA country in an unassembled or disassembled form but was classified as an assembled good, pursuant to H.S. General Rule of Interpretation 2(a), or
2. The good incorporated one or more non-originating materials, provided for as parts under the H.S., which could not undergo a change in tariff classification because the heading provided for both the good and its parts and was not further subdivided into subheadings, or the subheading provided for both the good and its parts and was not further subdivided.

NOTE: This criterion does not apply to Chapters 61 through 63 of H.S. ***(Reference: Article 401(d))***

E Certain automatic data processing goods and their parts, specified in Annex 308.1, that do not originate in the territory are considered originating upon importation into the territory of a NAFTA country from the territory of another NAFTA country when the most-favored-nation tariff rate of the good conforms to the rate established in Annex 308.1 and is common to all NAFTA countries. *(Reference: Annex 308.1)*

F The good is an originating agricultural good under preference criterion A, B, or C above and is not subject to a quantitative restriction in the importing NAFTA country because it is a "qualifying good" as defined in Annex 703.2, Section A or B (please specify). A good listed in Appendix 703.2B.7 is also exempt from quantitative restrictions and is eligible for NAFTA preferential tariff treatment if it meets the definition of "qualifying good" in Section A of Annex 703.2. **NOTE 1: This criterion does not apply to goods that wholly originate in Canada or the United States and are imported into either country. NOTE 2: A tariff rate quota is not a quantitative restriction.**

FIELD 8: For each good described in Field #5, state "YES" if you are the producer of the good. If you are not the producer of the good, state "NO" followed by (1), (2), or (3), depending on whether this certificate was based upon: (1) your knowledge of whether the good qualifies as an originating good; (2) your reliance on the producer's written representation (other than a Certificate of Origin) that the good qualifies as an originating good; or (3) a completed and signed Certificate for the good, voluntarily provided to the exporter by the producer.

FIELD 9: For each good described in field #5, where the good is subject to a regional value content (RVC) requirement, indicate "NC" if the RVC is calculated according to the net cost method; otherwise, indicate "NO". If the RVC is calculated over a period of time, further identify the beginning and ending dates (MM/DD/YYYY) of that period. *(Reference: Article 402.1, 402.5).*

FIELD 10: Identify the name of the country ("MX" or "US" for agricultural and textile goods exported to Canada; "US" or "CA" for all goods exported to Mexico; or "CA" or "MX" for all goods exported to the United States) to which the preferential rate of CBP duty applies, as set out in Annex 302.2, in accordance with the Marking Rules or in each party's schedule of tariff elimination.

For all other originating goods exported to Canada, indicate appropriately "MX" or "US" if the goods originate in that NAFTA country, within the meaning of the NAFTA Rules of Origin Regulations, and any subsequent processing in the other NAFTA country does not increase the transaction value of the goods by more than seven percent; otherwise indicate "JNT" for joint production. *(Reference: Annex 302.2)*

FIELD 11: This field must be completed, signed, and dated by the exporter. When the Certificate is completed by the producer for use by the exporter, it must be completed, signed, and dated by the producer. The date must be the date the Certificate was completed and signed.

CBP Form 434 (04/97)(Back)

Figure 4–17. U.S.–Chile FTA certificate of origin.

UNITED STATES - CHILE FREE TRADE AGREEMENT
TRATADO DE LIBRE COMERCIO CHILE - ESTADOS UNIDOS
CERTIFICATE OF ORIGIN

1. EXPORTER NAME AND ADDRESS: TAX IDENTIFICATION NUMBER:	2. BLANKET PERIOD *(DD/MM/YYYY)* FROM: TO:
3. PRODUCER NAME AND ADDRESS TAX IDENTIFICATION NUMBER:	4. IMPORTER NAME AND ADDRESS TAX IDENTIFICATION NUMBER:

5. DESCRIPTION OF GOOD(S)	6. HS TARIFF CLASSIFICATION NUMBER	7. PREFERENCE CRITERIA	8. PRODUCER	9. NET COST	10. COUNTRY OF ORIGIN

I CERTIFY THAT:

• THE INFORMATION ON THIS DOCUMENT IS TRUE AND ACCURATE AND I ASSUME THE RESPONSIBILITY FOR PROVING SUCH REPRESENTATIONS. I UNDERSTAND THAT I AM LIABLE FOR ANY FALSE STATEMENTS OR MATERIAL OMISSIONS MADE ON OR IN CONNECTION WITH THIS DOCUMENT;

• I AGREE TO MAINTAIN, AND PRESENT UPON REQUEST, DOCUMENTATION NECESSARY TO SUPPORT THIS CERTIFICATE, AND TO INFORM, IN WRITING, ALL PERSONS TO WHOM THE CERTIFICATE WAS GIVEN OF ANY CHANGES THAT COULD AFFECT THE ACCURACY OR VALIDITY OF THIS CERTIFICATE;

• THE GOODS ORIGINATED IN THE TERRITORY OF THE PARTIES, AND COMPLY WITH THE ORIGIN REQUIREMENTS SPECIFIED FOR THOSE GOODS IN THE UNITED STATES - CHILE FREE TRADE AGREEMENT, AND UNLESS SPECIFICALLY EXEMPTED IN ARTICLE 4.11, THERE HAS BEEN NO FURTHER PRODUCTION OR ANY OTHER OPERATION OUTSIDE THE TERRITORIES OF THE PARTIES.

• THIS CERTIFICATE CONSISTS ____ PAGES, INCLUDING ALL ATTACHMENTS.

11.	11a. AUTHORIZED SIGNATURE:		11b. COMPANY:	
	11c. NAME (print or type):		11d. TITLE:	
	11e. DATE: (DD/MM/YYYY)	11f. TELEPHONE	*(Voice)*	*(Facsimile)*

This document created using Shipping Solutions Professional export software, www.shipsolutions.com.

Figure 4–18. CAFTA-DR certificate of origin.

Central America-Dominican Republic-United States Free Trade Agreement

Tratado de Libre Comercio entre Centroamérica, República Dominicana y los Estados Unidos

1 Exporter's name, address and tax identification number: **Nombre, dirección y número de registro fiscal del exportador:** **Tax Identification Number:**	**2. Blanket Period:** **Periodo que cubre:** **From / De** | *D* | *M* | *Y-A* **To / A** | *D* | *M* | *Y-A*
3. Producer's name, address and tax identification number: **Nombre, dirección y número de registro fiscal del productor:** **Tax Identification Number:**	**4. Importer's name, address and tax identification number:** **Nombre, dirección y número de registro fiscal del importador:** **Tax Identification Number:**

5. Description of Good(s) - Descripción de la(s) mercancia(s)	6. HS Tariff Classification Clasificación arancelaria	7. Preferential tariff treatment criteria Criterio para trato arancelario preferencial	8. Other criteria Otros criterios	9.Producer Productor

10. Remarks:
Observaciones:

11. Under oath I certify that:

- The information on this document is true and accurate and I assume the responsibility for proving such representations. I understand that I am liable for any false statements or material omissions made on or in connection with this document.

- I agree to maintain, and present upon request, documentation necessary to support this certification, and to inform, in writing, all persons to whom the certification was given of any changes that would affect the accuracy or validity of this Certification.

- The goods originated in the territory of one or more of the Parties, and comply with the origin requirements specified for those goods in the Central America-Dominican Republic - United States Free Trade Agreement, and that there has been no further processing or any other operation outside the territories of the Parties, other than unloading, reloading, or any other operation necessary to preserve the goods in good condition or to transport the good to the territory of a Party.

Declaro bajo juramento que:

- La información contenida en este documento es verdadera y exacta y me hago responsable de comprobar lo aquí certificado. Estoy consciente que soy responsable por cualquier declaración falsa u omisión material hecha en o relacionada con el presente documento.

- Me comprometo a conservar y presentar, en caso de ser requerido, los documentos necesarios que respalden el contenido de la presente certificación, así como a notificar por escrito a todas las personas a quienes se ha entregado la presente certificación, de cualquier cambio que pudiera afectar la exactitud o validez del mismo.

- Las mercancias son originarias del territorio de una o más Partes y cumplen con todos los requisitos de origen que les son aplicables conforme al Tratado de Libre Comercio entre Centroamérica, República Dominicana y Estados Unidos, y que no han sido objeto de procesamiento ulterior o de cualquier otra operacion fuera de los territorios de las Partes, excepto la descarga, recarga o cualquier otra operación necesaria para mantener la mercancia en buena condición o para transportarla a terrirtorio de una Parte.

This Certification consists of ____ pages, including all attachments.
Esta Certificacion se compone, de ____ hojas incluyendo todos sus anexos.

Authorized Signature - Firma autorizada		**Company - Empresa**
Name - Nombre		**Title - Cargo**
Date - Fecha | D | M | Y-A	**Telephone Telefono**	**Fax**

This document created using Shipping Solutions Professional export software, www.shipsolutions.com.

Figure 4–19. Certificate of free sale.

DEPARTMENT OF HEALTH & HUMAN SERVICES — Public Health Service

Food and Drug Administration
2098 Gaither Road
Rockville MD 20850

CERTIFICATE FOR PRODUCTS FOR EXPORT

The Food and Drug Administration certifies that the products as described below are subject to its jurisdiction. Products which are legally distributed in accordance with the Federal Food, Drug, and Cosmetic Act within the United States may be exported without restriction.

21 CFR 820 of the Food and Drug Administration regulations requires the manufacturer to follow Good Manufacturing Practices. The plant in the United States where these products are manufactured is subject to periodic inspections by the Food and Drug Administration.

This certificate is not valid unless the Foreign Country Certification Statement is completed by a responsible individual of the exporting firm.

PRODUCTS	MANUFACTURING PLANT LOCATION
See Attached List (one page)	

Marilyn K. Schoenfelder
Acting Branch Chief
Information Processing and
Office Automation Branch
Division of Program Operations
Office of Compliance

COUNTY OF MONTGOMERY
STATE OF MARYLAND

Subscribed and sworn to before me this 1st day of June, 1994.

MARY JO O'DONNELL
NOTARY PUBLIC STATE OF MARYLAND
My Commission Expires October 19, 1997

Figure 4–20; and guidance from the FDA on the information needed to request a certificate of free sale is shown in Figure 4–21.)

M. Delivery Instructions and Delivery Orders

The delivery instructions (see Figure 4–22) form is usually issued by the freight forwarding company to the inland transportation carrier (the trucking or rail company), indicating to the inland carrier which pier or steamship company has been selected for the ocean transportation and giving specific instructions to the inland carrier as to where to deliver the goods at the port of export. This must be distinguished from the delivery order (see Figure 4–23), which is a document used to instruct the customs broker at the foreign port of destination what to do with the goods, in particular, the method of foreign inland transportation to the buyer's place of business.

N. Special Customs Invoices

In addition to the commercial invoice, some countries require a special customs invoice (see Figure 4–24) designed to facilitate clearance of the goods and the assessment of customs duties in that country. Such an invoice lists specific information required under the customs regulations of that country. It is similar in some ways to the consular invoice, except that it is prepared by the exporter and need not be signed or certified by the consulate.

O. Shipper's Declarations for Dangerous Goods

Under the U.S. Hazardous Materials Transportation Act, the International Air Transport Association Dangerous Goods Regulations, and the International Maritime Dangerous Goods Code, exporters are required to provide special declarations or notices to the inland and ocean transportation companies when the goods are hazardous. This includes explosives, radioactive materials, etiological agents, flammable liquids or solids, combustible liquids or solids, poisons, oxidizing or corrosive materials, and compressed gases. These include aerosols, dry ice, batteries, cotton, antifreeze, cigarette lighters, motor vehicles, diesel fuel, disinfectants, cleaning liquids, fire extinguishers, pesticides, animal or vegetable fabrics or fibers, matches, paints, and many other products. The shipper must certify on the invoice that the goods are properly classed, described, packaged, marked, and labeled, and are in proper condition for transportation in accordance with the regulations of the Department of Transportation (see Chapter 2, Section L). The hazardous materials regulations are extremely detailed, and an exporter who has any doubt must check to determine whether its product is listed. If it is, the required declarations, invoicing, and labeling must be completed. (A sample declaration is shown in Figure 4–25.) Sometimes the exporter will be required to certify that the shipment is *not* a hazardous material (see Figure 4–26).

(*Text continues on page 176.*)

Figure 4–20. FDA Form 3613e—food export certificate application.

Form Approved: OMB No. 0910-0498; Expiration Date: 3/31/09

Department of Health and Human Services Food and Drug Administration Center for Food Safety and Applied Nutrition	**FOOD EXPORT CERTIFICATE APPLICATION**	Date

1. Food Manufacturer Information

Manufacturer name	Doing business as name *(If other than "Manufacturer name" to left, and you wish this name to appear on the export certificate)*
State License/Registration number	Postal Address
Contact person name	
Contact phone/fax	City / State / ZIP/postal code
Contact email	Country

2. Exporting Company Information (if applicable)

Export company name	
State License/Registration number	Address
Contact person name	City / State / ZIP/postal code
Contact phone/fax/or email	Country

3. Shipment Description

Product	*Common Name*	*Manufacturer*	*Description/Comments*

Continue on additional page(s) as needed.

4. Intended Destination of Shipment (Country)

Name of country

5. Send Certificate To ☐ Manufacturer ☐ Distributor ☐ Other *(provide the following information)*

Firm name	Address
	City / State / ZIP/postal code
Contact person name	Country

6. Send Certificate Via

Carrier name *(U.S. Mail, FedEx, etc.)*	Account number *(If applicable)*

7. Fees

Fees are $10 per certificate, and will be billed upon receipt of this application.	☐ Copies of certificate: ______ *Number* x ______ *Fee/copy* = Total $______

FORM FDA 3613e (2/06) Page 1 of 2 PSC Graphics: (301) 443-1090 EF

Figure 4–20. *(continued)*

8. Label(s)

Attach an original or an electronic copy of any applicable product label(s). A fax copy is acceptable only if it is readable.

9. Verification

The undersigned verifies that all ingredients are approved for use by FDA or appear on the GRAS list, and each product is intended for human consumption and is available for sale in the U.S. without restriction.

Signature	Name and Title	Date

Department of Health and Human Services
Food and Drug Administration
Center for Food Safety and Applied Nutrition

FOOD EXPORT CERTIFICATE APPLICATION
Instructions

For Manufacturers/Distributors

1. The Manufacturer/Distributor fills out the application information describing the consignment, manufacturer (note that different processing facilities of the manufacturer may be listed on the table describing the foods), where and how to send the certificate, optional information as needed, and applicant signature, name and date.
2. The Manufacturer/Distributor submits the application (by mail, fax, email), along with labels as applicable. *The label must be legible.*

For FDA Officials

3. FDA official reviews the application to be sure all the blanks are filled in properly, verifies manufacturer's license or registration, and investigates inspection data on the listed products.
4. The Official may require an inspection prior to issuance of the export certificate.
5. The Official prints the Certificate on watermarked Department letterhead, assigns a unique registration number and expiration date, signs, dates, seals and issues the Certificate as indicated.
6. The Official maintains in his records an identical copy of the signed Certificate, marked "Copy" *for a period of at least two years.*
7. In the event that the Manufacturer fails to comply with the law as stated on the Certificate, the Official will reject the application and promptly notify the Manufacturer that the Certificate cannot be issued.

After the Certificate Has Been Issued

8. The Manufacturer/Distributor forwards the Certificate to the foreign Importer and verifies that it is acceptable.
9. If the Certificate is not acceptable, the Exporter notifies the FDA Official that the certificate has not been accepted by the Importer, and the Official will promptly attempt to reconcile the issue with the Importer.
10. If an original certificate is destroyed or lost, the Manufacturer/Distributor can request an identical replacement, bearing the unique identification number and same expiration date, to be issued by the Official and marked "Replacement."

Paperwork Reduction Act Statement

Public reporting burden for this collection of information is estimated to average 1 hour per response, including the time for reviewing instructions, searching existing data sources, gathering and maintaining the data needed, and completing and reviewing the collection of information. Send comments regarding this burden estimate or any other aspect of this collection of information, including suggestions for reducing this burden, to the address below.

Food and Drug Administration
Center for Food Safety and Applied Nutrition (HFS-550)
5100 Paint Branch Parkway
College Park, MD 20740

An agency may not conduct or sponsor, and a person is not required to respond to, a collection of information unless it displays a currently valid OMB control number.

FORM FDA 3613e (2/06) **Page 2 of 2**

Figure 4–21. FDA guidelines for criteria needed with request for certificate of free sale.

US FDA/CFSAN - Criteria in Request for Certificate of Free Sale Page 1 of 2

FDA U.S. Food and Drug Administration — Department of Health and Human Services

CENTER FOR FOOD SAFETY AND APPLIED NUTRITION

FDA Home Page | CFSAN Home | Search/Subject Index | Q & A | Help

CFSAN/Office of Nutritional Products, Labeling and Dietary Supplements
June 23, 2000; Updated January 1, 2006 and December 7, 2006

CRITERIA NEEDED WITH REQUEST FOR CERTIFICATE OF FREE SALE FOR DIETARY SUPPLEMENT(S), INFANT FORMULA(S), & MEDICAL FOOD(S)

(Certificates are only issued for products manufactured in the United States.)

1. Letter requesting certificate of free sale.
2. List product or products.
3. List the country or countries certificate of free sale is going to.
4. State how many certificates you are requesting.
5. State whether you want all products together on each certificate, or one product on a separate certificate.
6. Original label or labels for each product. **(Note: No photocopies unless product is distributed in BULK FORM ONLY; if labeling is in a foreign language, we need the label/labels in English; the labels must be flat, do not send round containers with label applied)**.
7. The cost per certificate is $10.00. You do not have to mail the $10.00; you will be billed.
8. Mail all submissions to:

   Certificate Program
   Food and Drug Administration
   Office of Nutritional Products, Labeling, and Dietary Supplements, HFS-810
   5100 Paint Branch Parkway
   College Park, MD 20740-3835

Note: There is no need to mail the request to anyone's attention as long as you have the office's certificate program mail code as listed above.

The Certificate of Free Sale is issued on official Department of Health and Human Services (DHHS) letterhead along with a DHHS seal, and cannot be notarized.

Current processing time is approximately 8 weeks.

If you have any questions please feel free to call (301) 436-2375 (or fax your question to (301) 436-2639)) and ask to speak with someone concerning certificates of free sale.

Dietary Supplements

CFSAN Home | CFSAN Search/Subject Index | CFSAN Disclaimers & Privacy Policy | CFSAN Accessibility/Help

http://vm.cfsan.fda.gov/~dms/ds-cert.html 4/28/2009

Figure 4–21. *(continued)*

US FDA/CFSAN - Criteria in Request for Certificate of Free Sale   Page 2 of 2

FDA Home Page | Search FDA Site | FDA A-Z Index | Contact FDA

FDA/Center for Food Safety & Applied Nutrition
Hypertext updated by ear/cjm/shm December 7, 2006

http://vm.cfsan.fda.gov/~dms/ds-cert.html   4/28/2009

Figure 4–22. Delivery instructions.

ENTRY NO.

DATE | OUR REF. NO.

IMPORTING CARRIER | LOCATION | FROM PORT OF / ORIGIN AIRPORT

B/L OR AWB NO. | ARRIVAL DATE | FREE TIME EXP. | LOCAL DELIVERY OR TRANSFER BY (DELIVERY ORDER ISSUED TO)

DELIVER TO

PICK-UP BY

THE CARRIER OR CARTMAN TO WHOM THIS ORDER IS ASSIGNED WILL BE HELD RESPONSIBLE FOR ANY STORAGE AND DEMURRAGE CHARGES RESULTING FROM NEGLIGENCE.

IMPORTANT: NOTIFY US AT ONCE IF DELIVERY CANNOT BE EFFECTED AS INSTRUCTED.

MARKS & NOS. | DESCRIPTION & WT.

SAMPLE

CUSTOMS PERMIT
☐ ATTACHED
LODGED WITH
☐ U.S. CUSTOMS

PKG. NOS. HELD BY U.S. CUSTOMS—TO FOLLOW

GO #

DOCUMENTS ATTACHED
☐ DEL. ORDER: ☐ B/L: ☐ DOCK REC.
☐

DELIVERY CHGS.

PER

Form 15-515 Printed and Sold by UNZCO 700 Central Ave., New Providence, NJ 07974 • 800-631-3098

DELIVERY INSTRUCTIONS

Figure 4–23. Delivery order.

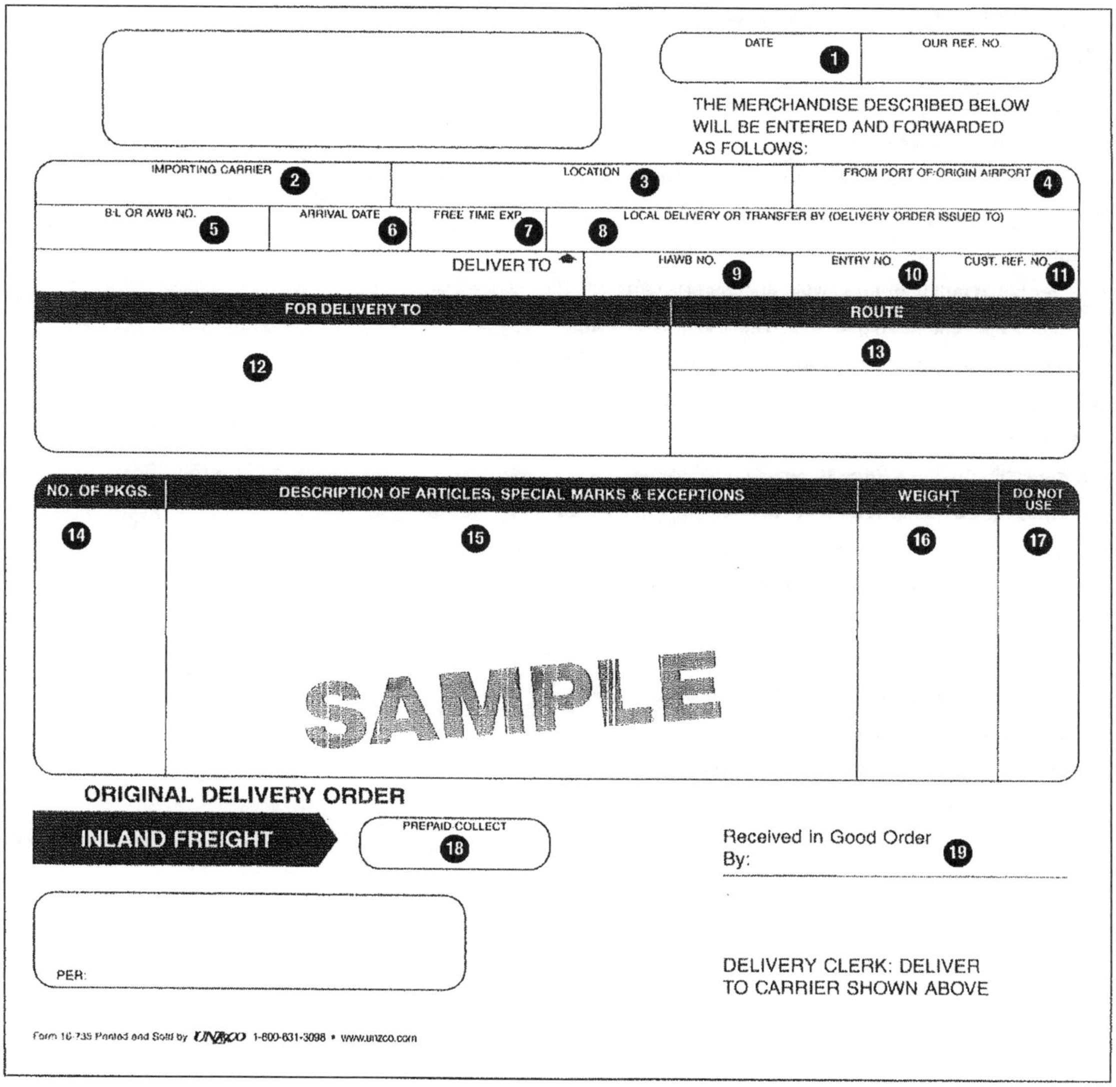

DATE 1 | OUR REF. NO.

THE MERCHANDISE DESCRIBED BELOW
WILL BE ENTERED AND FORWARDED
AS FOLLOWS:

IMPORTING CARRIER 2 | LOCATION 3 | FROM PORT OF/ORIGIN AIRPORT 4

B/L OR AWB NO. 5 | ARRIVAL DATE 6 | FREE TIME EXP. 7 | 8 LOCAL DELIVERY OR TRANSFER BY (DELIVERY ORDER ISSUED TO)

DELIVER TO | HAWB NO. 9 | ENTRY NO. 10 | CUST. REF. NO. 11

FOR DELIVERY TO 12 | ROUTE 13

NO. OF PKGS. 14 | DESCRIPTION OF ARTICLES, SPECIAL MARKS & EXCEPTIONS 15 | WEIGHT 16 | DO NOT USE 17

SAMPLE

ORIGINAL DELIVERY ORDER

INLAND FREIGHT

PREPAID COLLECT 18

Received in Good Order
By: 19

PER:

DELIVERY CLERK: DELIVER
TO CARRIER SHOWN ABOVE

Form 16-735 Printed and Sold by UNZCO 1-800-631-3098 • www.unzco.com

Figure 4–23. *(continued)*

Instructions for completing the Delivery Order

1. **Date of form preparation**
2. **Enter the name of the importing carrier, shipping line, or air line as applicable.**
3. **Enter the location of the port of entry.**
4. **Enter the shipment city and state or country** of the port of origin or airport name and location.
5. **Enter bill of lading or air waybill number** of the shipment.
6. **Specify the scheduled date of arrival** at the seaport or airport.
7. **Enter estimated expiration date of "free time" period** before storage charges are assessed.
8. **Specify name of local delivery or cartage agent** if applicable.
9. **Enter the house air waybill number** for airfreight shipments.
10. **Enter the Customs Entry Number** if applicable.
11. **Enter the customer reference number** specified by the shipper.
12. **Enter the complete delivery name and address of the consignee** (recipient) of the freight.
13. **Specify the carrier's, forwarder's, or agent's delivery routing.**
14. **Enter the total number of packages** to be delivered.
15. **Enter the description of the freight** to include packaging and contents.
16. **Enter the gross weight of the shipment** (indicate whether pounds or kilograms).
17. **Leave this column blank.**
18. **Specify if the shipment is freight prepaid or collect.**
19. **Consignee signature** to verify delivery.

Figure 4–24. Special customs invoice (Canada)

Revenue Canada | Revenu Canada

CANADA CUSTOMS INVOICE

FACTURE DES DOUANES CANADIENNES

Page of/de

1. Vendor (Name and Address)/Vendeur (Nom et adresse)

2. Date of Direct Shipment to Canada/Date d'expédition directe vers le Canada

3. Other References (Include Purchaser's Order No.)
Autres références (Inclure le n° de commande de l'acheteur)

4. Consignee (Name and Address)/Destinataire (Nom et adresse)

5. Purchaser's Name and Address (if other than Consignee)
Nom et adresse de l'acheteur (S'il differe du destinataire)

6. Country of Transhipment/Pays de transbordement

7. Country of Origin of Goods/Pays d'origine des merchandises — If shipment includes goods of different origins, enter origins against items 12. Si l'expédition comprend des marchandises d'origines différentes, préciser leur provenance en 12

8. Transportation: Give Mode and Place of Direct Shipment to Canada
Transport: Préciser mode et point d'exedition direct vers le canada

9. Conditions of Sale and Terms of Payment (i.e. Sale, Consignment Shipment, Leased Goods, etc.)
Conditions de vente et modalités de paiement (p. ex. vente, expédition en consignation, location de marchandises, etc.)

10. Currency of Settlement/Devises du paiement

11. No. of Pkgs/Nbre de colis	12. Specification of Commodities (Kind of Packages, Marks and Numbers, General Description and Characteristics, i.e. Grade, Quality) - Désignation des articles (Nature des colis, marques et numéros, description générale et caractéristiques, p. ex. classe, qualité)	13. Quantity (State Unit) - Quantite (Preciser l'unite)	Selling Price / Prix de vente: 14. Unit Price/Prix unitaire	15. Total

18. If any of fields 1 to 17 are included on an attached commercial invoice, check this box ☐
Si les renseignements des zones 1 à 17 figurent sur la facure commerciale, cocher cette boite.
Commercial Invoice No. *N de facure commerciale*

16. Total Weight (KILOS) *Poids total* — Net | Gross (Brut)

17. Invoice Total
Total de la facture

19. Exporter's Name and Address (If other than vendor)
Nom et adresse de l'exportateur (S'il diffère du vendeur)

20. Originator (Name and Address) *Expéditeur d'origine (Nom et adresse)*

21. CCRA ruling (If applicable) *Décision de l'Agence (S'il y a lieu)*

22. If fields 23 to 25 are not applicable, check this box ☐
Si les zones 23 à 25 sone sans objet, cocher cette boite

23. If included in Field 17 indicate amount:
Si compris dans le total à la zone 17, préciser:
(i) Transportation charges, expenses and insurance from the place of direct shipment to Canada
Les frais de transport, dépenses et assurances à partir du point d'expédition directe vers le Canada ______
(ii) Costs of construction, erection and assembly incurred after importation into Canada
Les coûts de contruction, d'érection et d'assemblage après importation au Canada ______
(iii) Export packing (Le coût de l'emballage d'exportation) ______

24. If not included in field 17 indicate amount:
Si compris dans le total à la zone 17, préciser.
(i) Transportation charges, expenses and insurance to the place of direct shipment to Canada
Les frais de transport, dépenses et assurances jusq'au point d'expédition directe vers le Canada
(ii) Amount for commissions other than buying commissions
Les commissions autres que celles versées pour l'achat ______
(iii) Export packing (Le coût de l'emballage d'exportation) ______

25. Check (if applicable:)
Cocher (S'il y a lieu:)
(i) Royalty payments or subsequent proceeds are paid or payable by the purchaser
Des redevances ou produits ont été ou seront versés par l'acheteur ☐
(ii) The purchaser has supplied goods or services for use in the production of these goods
L'acheteur a fourni des marchandises ou des services pour la production des marchandises ☐

This document created using Shipping Solutions Professional export software, www.shipsolutions.com.

Figure 4–25. Shipper's declaration for dangerous goods.

SHIPPER'S DECLARATION FOR DANGEROUS GOODS

Shipper

Air Waybill No.

Page of Pages

Shipper's Reference Number
(optional)

Consignee

Two completed and signed copies of this Declaration must be handed to the operator.

WARNING

Failure to comply in all respects with the applicable Dangerous Goods Regulations may be in breach of the applicable law, subject to legal penalties.

TRANSPORT DETAILS

This shipment is within the limitations prescribed for:
(delete non-applicable)

PASSENGER AND CARGO AIRCRAFT	CARGO AIRCRAFT ONLY

Airport of Departure:

Airport of Destination:

Shipment type: *(delete non-applicable)*

NON-RADIOACTIVE	RADIOACTIVE

NATURE AND QUANTITY OF DANGEROUS GOODS

Dangerous Goods Identification						
UN or ID No.	Proper Shipping Name	Class or Division (Subsidiary Risk)	Packing Group	Quantity and type of packing	Packing Inst.	Authorization

SAMPLE

Additional Handling Information

24 HR. Emergency Contact Telephone____________

I hereby declare that the contents of this consignment are fully and accurately described above by the proper shipping name, and are classified, packaged, marked and labelled/placarded, and are in all respects in proper condition for transport according to applicable international and national governmental regulations. I declare that all of the applicable air transport requirements have been met.

Name and Title of Signatory

Place and Date

Signature
(see warning above)

Form No. 30-062L Printed and Sold by UNZ&CO www.unzco.com • (800) 631-3098

Figure 4–26. Shipper's certification of articles not restricted.

SHIPPER'S CERTIFICATION OF ARTICLES NOT RESTRICTED

WARNING: Failure to comply in all respects with Government and IATA restricted articles regulations may be a violation of the law, subject to fines, imprisonment, or both. This certification shall in no circumstance be signed by an employee of a forwarder, carrier or cargo agent.

NUMBER OF PACKAGES	ARTICLE AND DESCRIPTION Specify each article separately.	NET QUANTITY PER PACKAGE	FLASH POINT (for liquids)	
			°C.	°F.
	SAMPLE			

I hereby certify that the contents of this consignment, in spite of product name or appearance, are not restricted for air transportation by the Air Transport Restricted Articles Tariff No. 6-D, Government Hazardous Material Regulations or IATA Restricted Articles regulations. I acknowledge that I may be liable for damages resulting from any misstatement or omission and I further agree that any air carrier involved in the shipment of this consignment may rely upon this Certification.

Name and full address of shipper	Name and title of person signing
Date	Signature of shipper

FOR CARRIER'S USE ONLY

Air Waybill No.	Airport of Departure	Airport of Destination

THIS CERTIFICATION IS NOT A REQUIREMENT OF U.S. DEPT. OF TRANS.

Form 30-070L Printed and Sold by UNZ&CO (800) 631-3098 • www.unzco.com

P. Precursor and Essential Chemical Exports

Those who export (or import) "precursor" chemicals and "essential" chemicals that can be used to manufacture illegal drugs are required to file Drug Enforcement Administration (DEA) Form 486 (see Figure 4–27). In some cases, this form must be filed fifteen days in advance of exportation (or importation).

Q. Animal, Plant, and Food Export Certificates

The U.S. Department of Agriculture is supportive of companies that want to export livestock, animal products, and plants and plant products. Often, the destination country will have specific requirements in order to permit import to that country, but sometimes the foreign country will accept or require inspections performed and certificates issued in the United States. In general, the U.S. Department of Agriculture offers inspection services and a variety of certificates to enable exporters to satisfy foreign government requirements. One example is an "Export Certificate/Health Certificate—Animal Products" issued by the Veterinary Services Division (VS Form 17-140; see Figure 4–28) to certify that animals and poultry are free from communicable disease and meet the requirements of the importing country. Another type of certification is a "Federal Phytosanitary Certificate" (PPQ Form 577) to certify that live plants are free from plant pests. An exporter may apply for an export certificate to the Food Safety Inspection Service on Form 9060-6 and a "Meat and Poultry Export Certificate of Wholesomeness" will be issued.

R. Drafts for Payment

If payment for the sale is going to be made under a letter of credit or by documentary collection, such as documents against payment ("D/P" or sight draft) or documents against acceptance ("D/A" or time draft), the exporter will draw a draft on the buyer's bank in a letter of credit transaction or the buyer in a documentary collection transaction payable to itself (sometimes it will be payable to the seller's bank on a confirmed letter of credit) in the amount of the sale. This draft will be sent to the seller's bank along with the instructions for collection, or sometimes the seller will send it directly to the buyer's bank (direct collection). If the payment agreement between the seller and the buyer is at sight, the buyer will pay the draft when it is received, or if it is issued under a letter of credit, the buyer's bank will pay the draft when it is received. If the agreement between the seller and the buyer is that the buyer will have some grace period before making payment, the amount of the delay, called the usance, will be written on the draft (time draft), and the buyer will usually be responsible for payment of interest to the seller during the usance period unless the parties agree otherwise. The time period may also be specified as some period after a fixed date, such as ninety days after the bill of lading or commercial invoice date, or payment simply may be due on a fixed date. (Samples of a sight

(*Text continues on page 180.*)

Figure 4–27. DEA import/export declaration.

U.S. Department of Justice

Import / Export Declaration for List I and List II Chemicals

Drug Enforcement Administration

SEE REVERSE INSTRUCTIONS FOR PRIVACY ACT | OMB Approval No. 1117-0023

1a. Type of Transaction: ☐ IMPORT ☐ EXPORT ☐ INTERNATIONAL | 1b. Type of Submission: ☐ ORIGINAL ☐ AMENDED ☐ WITHDRAWAL

1c. **WARNING!** 15-day advance notice required for initial shipment or for company that has lost regular importer or regular customer status. See 21 C.F.R. Part 1313 for further details.
☐ I certify I have met the conditions for the waiver of 15-day advance notice requirement.

DEA Transaction Number

2a. U.S. IMPORTER/ U.S. EXPORTER / U.S. BROKER
(Name, address, telephone, and fax no.)

DEA Registration Number (for List I only):__________

Purchase/Invoice no. (optional)__________

2b. IF IMPORT, LIST FOREIGN CONSIGNOR; IF EXPORT OR INTERNATIONAL TRANSACTION, LIST FOREIGN TRANSFEREE.
(Name, address, telephone, and fax no.)

Foreign permit no. (if applicable)__________

3. Listed Chemicals to be Imported / Exported / Brokered

3a. Name and Description of chemical appearing on label or container. For drug products, show dosage strength and dosage size.	3b. Name of chemicals as designated by Title 21 C.F.R. 1310.02	3c. Number of containers, size, net weight of each chemical (kg). For drug products, show number of dosage units. Show net total weight per chemical.	3d. DATE OF ACTUAL IMPORT/EXPORT AND ACTUAL QUANTITY (To be completed by person named in (2a).) If same as 3c, write "same as 3c."

4a. ☐ FOREIGN ☐ DOMESTIC
PORT OF EXPORTATION:__________
APPROX. DEPARTURE DATE:

4b. ☐ FOREIGN ☐ DOMESTIC
PORT OF IMPORTATION: __________
APPROX. ARRIVAL DATE:

5. MODE OF TRANSPORTATION, NAME OF VESSEL, OR NAME OF CARRIER:

SIGNATURE OF AUTHORIZED INDIVIDUAL (Print or Type Name below Signature)

Print Name:

DATE:

DEA form - 486 (Previous version obsolete.)
September 2006

Copy 1

(*continues*)

Figure 4–27. *(continued)*

6. **RETURN DECLARATION FOR EXPORTS AND INTERNATIONAL TRANSACTIONS** (Name & Quantity of List I and List II Chemicals exported to the Transferee or resulting from International Transaction. MUST be returned within 30 days from actual date of export (3d). If same as 3d, write "same as 3d."

SIGNATURE: DATE:

For IMPORTS: List TRANSFEREE(S) UPON INITIAL APPLICATION (Names, address, telephone, and fax no.) Fill in 7 through 9. USE SEPARATE SHEET IF MORE THAN 3 TRANFEREES. **For INTERNATIONAL TRANSACTIONS:** Show foreign supplier in 7a and 7b only.

7a. NAME OF TRANSFEREE OF IMPORT	7b. ADDRESS OF TRANSFEREE OF IMPORT
7c. Name & Quantity of List I and List II chemical to be Imported for this transferee. (Enter names as shown on labels; numbers and sizes of packages; and strength.)	7d. Name & Quantity of List I and List II Chemical Actually Imported and Date Imported for this Transferee

7e. **RETURN DECLARATION** (Name & Quantity of List I and List II Chemical Distributed to the Transferee. MUST be returned within 30 days of date of actual import (7d) If amount not completely distributed, send a Return Declaration 30 days from the next distribution.). If the whole order was distributed, may say "all import distributed" and the date.

SIGNATURE: DATE:

8a. NAME OF TRANSFEREE OF IMPORT	8b. ADDRESS OF TRANSFEREE OF IMPORT
8c. Name & Quantity of List I and List II chemical to be Imported for this transferee. (Enter names as shown on labels; numbers and sizes of packages; and strength.)	8d. Name & Quantity of List I and List II Chemical Actually Imported and Date Imported for this Transferee.

8e. **RETURN DECLARATION** (Name & Quantity of List I and List II Chemical Distributed to the Transferee. MUST be returned within 30 days from actual date of import (8d) If amount not completely distributed, send a Return Declaration 30 days from the next distribution.). If the whole order was distributed, may say "all import distributed" and the date.

SIGNATURE: DATE:

9a. NAME OF TRANSFEREE OF IMPORT	9b. ADDRESS OF TRANSFEREE OF IMPORT
9c. Name & Quantity of List I and List II chemical to be Imported for this transferee. (Enter names as shown on labels; numbers and sizes of packages; and strength.)	9d. Name & Quantity of List I and List II Chemical Actually Imported and Date Imported for this Transferee.

9e. **RETURN DECLARATION** (Name & Quantity of List I and List II Chemical Distributed to the Transferee. MUST be returned within 30 days of date of actual import (9d) If amount not completely distributed, send a Return Declaration 30 days from the next distribution.). If the whole order was distributed, may say "all import distributed" and the date.

SIGNATURE: DATE:

DEA form - 486 (Previous version obsolete.)
September 2006

Copy 1

Figure 4–28. Export certificate—animal products.

UNITED STATES DEPARTMENT OF AGRICULTURE ANIMAL AND PLANT HEALTH INSPECTION SERVICE **HEALTH CERTIFICATE EXPORT CERTIFICATE ANIMAL PRODUCTS**	FOR OFFICIAL USE ONLY PORT DATE AND NO.

This certificate is for Veterinary purposes only. It is valid for 30 days after the date of signature (in the case of transport by ship or rail, the time is prolonged by the time of the voyage).

This is to certify that rinderpest, foot-and-mouth disease, classical swine fever, swine vesicular disease, African swine fever, and contagious bovine pleuropneumonia do not exist in the United States of America.

ADDITIONAL DECLARATION

The United States has been free of foot-and-mouth disease, rinderpest, and African swine fever for over 2 years prior to shipping. This office has on file a notarized affidavit from ____ (exporting company) verifying the accuracy of the statements below.

The products for export contain animal origin ingredients derived from animals that were presented for examination by government veterinarians at slaughterhouses approved by the competent government authority and evaluated favorably for inclusion in the certified materials, and were slaughtered under standards existing in the United States or in the State of origin. These hides originate from

________________________ (species of origin) animals.

(SIGNATURE OF ENDORSING OFFICIAL)	(TYPED NAME)	(TITLE OF ENDORSING OFFICIAL)

DESCRIPTION OF THE CONSIGNMENT

NAME AND ADDRESS OF EXPORTER		NAME AND ADDRESS OF CONSIGNEE
PRODUCT (quantity, unit of measure, and kind) name of the product: number of packs: gross weight:	number of pieces: net weight:	
IDENTIFICATION individual lot number(s): container seal number(s):	container number(s): shipping date:	CONVEYANCE Name of vessel or aircraft:

VS FORM 16-4
(MAR 2004)

draft and a time draft under a letter of credit are shown in Figures 4–29 and 4–30, respectively.)

S. Letters of Credit

When the buyer has agreed to provide a letter of credit as part of the payment terms, the buyer will apply to its local bank in its home country and a letter of credit will be issued. The seller should send instructions to the buyer before the letter of credit is opened, advising the seller as to the terms and conditions it desires. (A sample set of instructions and documentation checklist is shown in Figure 4–31.) The seller should always specify that the letter of credit must be irrevocable. The bank in the buyer's country is called the issuing bank. The buyer's bank will contact a correspondent bank near the seller in the United States, and the U.S. bank will send a notice or advice to the exporter that the letter of credit has been opened. If the letter of credit is a confirmed letter of credit, the U.S. bank is called the confirming bank; otherwise, it is called the advising bank. The advice will specify the exact documents that the exporter must provide to the bank in order to receive payment. Since the foreign and U.S. banks are acting as agent and subagent, respectively, for the buyer, the U.S. bank will refuse to pay unless the exact documents specified in the letter of credit are provided. The banks never see the actual shipment or inspect the goods; therefore, they are extremely meticulous about not releasing payment unless the documents required have been provided. The issuing bank and advising bank each have up to seven banking days to review the documents presented before making payment. When the exporter receives the advice of the opening of a letter of credit, the exporter should review in detail the exact documents required in order to be paid under the letter of credit. A list of common "discrepancies" that may prevent payment is shown in Figure 4–32. A checklist that the exporter (beneficiary of the letter of credit) should follow in reviewing the letter of credit and other documents is shown in Figure 4–33. Sometimes, if an exporter is a good customer of the advising bank, the bank may be willing to make payment even when there are discrepancies if the exporter signs a letter of indemnity (see Figure 4–34). The buyer can also instruct the bank to waive discrepancies. If, for any reason, the exporter anticipates that it cannot provide a document exactly as required, it should contact the buyer immediately and have the buyer instruct its bank and the U.S. correspondent bank to amend the letter of credit. If this is not done, even though the exporter has shipped the goods, payment will not be made by the bank. It is also important to note the date for presentation of documents and the expiration date of the letter of credit, and if for any reason shipment cannot be made within the time period, the seller should contact the buyer, and the buyer must instruct the banks to amend the letter of credit to extend the presentation and/or expiration date. (A sample advice for an irrevocable letter of credit is shown in Figure 4–35.) Sometimes letters of credit are issued in "SWIFT," which is the Society for Worldwide Interbank Financial Telecommunication. SWIFT is a member-owned cooperative through which the financial world conducts its business operations with speed, certainty, and confidence.

Figure 4–29. Sight draft.

SOLE BILL OF EXCHANGE

US $ 250,000 DATE March 1, 1990 NO. 1

TENOR At sight

PAY TO THE ORDER OF ABC Export Company — Payee must endorse draft on reverse side prior to payment

Two hundred fifty thousand and no/100 U.S. Dollars

DRAWN UNDER LETTER OF CREDIT NO. 2738 DATED January 31, 1990

ISSUED BY The Mitsui Bank, Ltd.

DRAWN ON XYZ Import Company

2-3, Toranomon 1-chome

Tokyo, Japan

ABC Export Company

AUTHORIZED SIGNATURE

Courtesy of The First National Bank of Chicago.

Figure 4–30. Time draft.

SOLE BILL OF EXCHANGE

US $ $250,000 DATE March 1, 1990 NO. 2

TENOR 90 days after sight

PAY TO THE ORDER OF ABC Export Company — Payee must endorse draft on reverse side prior to payment

Two hundred fifty thousand and no/100 U.S. Dollars

DRAWN UNDER LETTER OF CREDIT NO. 2021 DATED January 31, 1990

ISSUED BY The Mitsui Bank, Ltd.

DRAWN ON XYZ Import Company

2-3, Toranomon 1-chome

Tokyo, Japan

ABC Export Company

AUTHORIZED SIGNATURE

Courtesy of The First National Bank of Chicago.

T. Electronic Export Information

Export shipments require the filing of the Electronic Export Information (EEI) through the Automated Export System (AES). The EEI is electronically transmitted through the Internet to the Census Bureau and to U.S. Customs and Border Protection in advance of the shipment.

The U.S. Principal Party in Interest (USPPI) is generally the party responsible for filing the EEI through the AES. The USPPI is the party in the United States that receives the primary benefit, financial or otherwise, from the export transaction. Only in a routed export transaction, such as an ex-works sale, is the Foreign Principal Party in Interest (FPPI) responsible for ensuring that the information is filed. To do so, the

(*Text continues on page 183.*)

Figure 4–31. Letter of credit instructions.

Letter of Credit Instructions

Date: ____________ Re: Our Pro Forma Invoice/Sales Contract Number ______________ Dated: ____________

To (Importer):	From:

Please instruct your bank to issue a letter of credit by teletransmission in accordance with the following terms and conditions and subject to the current revision of the Uniform Customs and Practice for Documentary Credits (1993 Revision) ICC Publication No. 500.

1. The Letter of Credit must be irrevocable.

2. The Credit must be advised to us through:

   ☐ With their confirmation.
   ☐ Without their confirmation.
   (Please check one box)

   Name and Address of Advising Bank

3. The credit should expire on the date ____________ at the counters of the Advising/Confirming bank in (insert place of expiry): ______________________________.

4. The Beneficiary's name and address must read exactly as:

   Exact Name and Address of Beneficiary

SAMPLE

5. The credit must be issued in the amount of U.S. Dollars $ ____________________,
   ☐ approximately, or ☐ plus/minus ________ percent (please check one).

6. The credit must be available with the Advising/Confirming Bank by ☐ payment, or ☐ acceptance, or ☐ deferred payment, or ☐ negotiation (please check one).

7. Drafts are to be drawn on ______________________________, ☐ at sight, or
   ☐ at ______ days sight, or ☐ at ________ days date (please check one). **Note:** the draft is to be dated the same date as the date of shipment.

8. Partial shipments are ☐ allowed, ☐ not allowed (please check one). Transshipments are ☐ allowed, ☐ not allowed (please check one).

9. Shipments to be effected from : ______________________________, for transportation to: ______________________________, not later than the date: ____________.

10. The following documents are to be required:

    TRANSPORT DOCUMENT(S) (It is very important that you select the appropriate transport document for the mode of shipment being used. Refer to Articles 23 through 30 of UCP 500).

Form 10-026 Printed and Sold By Unz & Co, Inc. 700 Central Ave, New Providence, NJ 07974 (800) 631-3098

Figure 4–32. Common discrepancies in letters of credit.

- Documents presented after the expiration date of the letter of credit.
- Documents presented more than twenty-one days after shipment (or other date specified in the letter of credit).
- Missing documents, such as a full set of bills of lading, insurance certificates, and inspection certificates.
- Description of merchandise on the invoice differs from the description in the letter of credit (such as being written in a different language or different wording in the same language).
- Shipment terms and charges (ex-works, CFR, CIF) on the invoice differ from the terms specified in the letter of credit.
- Transshipment when it is not allowed.
- Shipment made after the date specified in the letter of credit.
- On board stamp on bills of lading not dated and signed or initialed by the carrier or his agent.
- Bills of lading improperly consigned, not endorsed, or show damage to goods.
- Documents inconsistent with one another (e.g., weights or packing information not the same on all documents presented).
- Insurance document not as per the credit terms, not in a sufficient amount, not endorsed, or after the shipment date.
- Drafts drawn on wrong person or for wrong amount or not signed or endorsed.
- Invoice not made out in the name of the applicant shown on the letter of credit.

FPPI must appoint an agent, such as the freight forwarder, to file the EEI on its behalf. With a valid power of attorney, freight forwarders may file the EEI information through the AES on behalf of the USPPI or the FPPI. When the transaction is a routed export transaction, the USPPI is still responsible for providing information about the shipment, including any export control information such as the Export Control Classification Number (see Chapter 5) or license requirements to the FPPI or its agent so that the EEI may be completed fully and accurately (see Figure 4–36).

The EEI must be electronically filed in advance of the export. Once it is transmitted, the exporter receives an Internal Transaction Number (ITN). The ITN must be provided to the exporting carrier in advance of the export. The specific time frames differ based on the mode of transport as follows:

- For vessel exports, the EEI must be filed and the ITN provided to the carrier 24 hours prior to loading.
- For air exports, including courier shipments, the EEI must be filed and the ITN provided to the carrier no later than 2 hours prior to the departure of the aircraft.

(*Text continues on page 188.*)

Figure 4–33. Checklist for a letter of credit beneficiary.

CHECKLIST FOR A COMMERCIAL LETTER OF CREDIT BENEFICIARY

The following checklist identifies points that a beneficiary of a commercial letter of credit should consider when receiving the letter of credit and when preparing required documents.

Letters of Credit

1. Are the names and addresses of the buyer and seller spelled correctly?
2. Is the credit irrevocable and issued in accordance with the latest International Chamber of Commerce (ICC) publication of the Uniform Customs and Practice for Documentary Credits (UCP)?
3. Which bank issued the credit? Is this bank satisfactory, or should a U.S. bank add its confirmation?
4. Do the terms of the letter of credit agree with the terms of the contract? Can you meet these terms?
5. Is the shipping schedule, as stipulated in the letter of credit, realistic? If necessary, is partial shipment or transshipment allowed?
6. Is the merchandise described correctly, including unit price, weight, and quantities?
7. Can presentation of documents be made on time? Will documents arrive before the expiration date and any other time limits indicated in the letter of credit?
8. Are the points of shipment and destination as agreed?
9. Are the terms of sale regarding freight charges and insurance as agreed?
10. If necessary, is the credit transferable?
11. Are the payment terms as agreed? If time payment terms are stated, which party is responsible for discount and acceptance charges?
12. Which party is responsible for banking charges?

Drafts

1. Are the drafts drawn by the beneficiary for the amount shown on the commercial invoice and in accordance with the tenor indicated?
2. Are drafts properly identified with the letter of credit?
3. Are the drafts drawn on (addressed to) the proper drawee and signed by authorized parties, with their titles indicated?

Courtesy of Continental Bank N.A. (Bank of America Illinois).

Figure 4–33. *(continued)*

4. Are the drafts endorsed in blank if made out "to order" of the beneficiary (drawer)?

Commercial Invoices

1. Is the commercial invoice in the name of the beneficiary?
2. Is the commercial invoice addressed to the applicant named in the letter of credit?
3. Did you sign the commercial invoice if required?
4. Was the commercial invoice countersigned by any other party if required in the letter of credit?
5. Does the commercial invoice conform to the letter of credit's terms relative to the following items:
   - Total amount?
   - Unit prices and computations?
   - Description of merchandise and terms (FOB, CFR, CIF, and so on)?
   - Foreign language used for the merchandise description, if used in the letter of credit?
   - Description of packing, if required?
   - Declarations or clauses properly worded?
6. Do the shipping marks on the commercial invoice agree with those appearing on the bill of lading?
7. Do the shipping charges on the commercial invoice agree with those on the bill of lading?
8. If partial shipments are prohibited, is all merchandise shipped? Or, if partial shipments are permitted, is the value of the merchandise invoiced in proportion to the quantity of the shipment when the letter of credit does not specify unit prices?

Consular Invoices (If Required)

1. Does the consular invoice match the commercial invoice and bill of lading?
2. Is the description of merchandise in a foreign language, if it is shown that way in the letter of credit?
3. Is the official form completed in all the indicated places?
4. Are there no alterations, except by a Letter of Correction issued by the consulate?
5. If legalized commercial invoices are required, have the required number of copies been properly legalized?

(continues)

Figure 4–33. *(continued)*

Marine Bills of Lading (Ocean Shipments)

1. Are bills of lading in negotiable form if required in the letter of credit?
2. Are all originals being presented to the bank or accounted for?
3. Are all originals properly endorsed when consigned "to the order" of the shipper?
4. Are bills of lading clean (no notation showing defective goods or packaging)?
5. Do bills of lading indicate that merchandise was loaded on board and loaded within the time specified in the letter of credit? If this provision is not part of the text but in the form of a notation, is the notation dated and signed (initialed) by the carrier or its agent?
6. Are the bills of lading made out as prescribed in the letter of credit (in other words, with names and addresses of beneficiary, applicant, notify parties, and flag, if any)?
7. If freight was prepaid, is this payment clearly indicated by either "FREIGHT PREPAID" or "FREIGHT PAID"?
8. If charter party, sailing vessel, on deck, forwarder's, or consolidator's bills of lading are presented, does the credit specifically allow for them?
9. Do marks and numbers, quantities, and the general description of goods agree with the commercial invoice and letter of credit, with no excess merchandise shipped?
10. Does the bill of lading show transshipment if prohibited in the letter of credit?
11. Is the document signed by the carrier or its agent? Are corrections, if any, signed or initialed by the carrier or agent?

Insurance Documents

1. Are you presenting an insurance policy or a certificate? (Acknowledgments or a broker's cover are acceptable only if expressly allowed in the letter of credit.)
2. Is the insured amount sufficient?
3. Is the insurance coverage complete and in conformity with the letter of credit as it relates to:
   - Special risks where required?
   - Coverage of destination and time (in other words, carried through to the proper point and covering the entire period of shipment)?
   - Proper warehouse clauses?
4. Has the insurance document been countersigned where required?

Figure 4–33. *(continued)*

5. Was the insurance document endorsed in blank if payable to the shipper?
6. Are shipping marks identical to those on the commercial invoice and bill of lading?
7. Are all corrections signed or initialed, and are riders or binders attached or cross-referenced?

Other Shipping Documents—Air Waybills, Inland Bills of Lading, Parcel Post Receipts

1. Do marks and numbers, quantities, and the general description of goods agree with the invoice and letter of credit, with no excess merchandise shipped?
2. Are the documents made out as prescribed by the letter of credit (including names and addresses of beneficiary, applicant, notify parties, flag, flight number, and visa, if any)?
3. If freight or dispatch expenses were to be prepaid, is this clearly indicated?
4. Are the documents dated within the terms specified by the letter of credit?
5. Are the bills of lading signed by the carrier or its agent? Are corrections, if any, initialed by the carrier or agent?

Certificates of Origin, Weight, Inspection, and Analysis

1. Are names and addresses as per the commercial invoice and letter of credit?
2. Is the country of origin, if required, as per the commercial invoice and letter of credit?
3. Have they been issued by the proper party and signed?
4. Do they show a description relative to the commercial invoice and letter of credit?
5. Are they in exact compliance with the letter of credit and dated with a reasonably current date?

Packing and Weight List

1. Does the packing type shown agree with the commercial invoice?
2. Does the quantity, or do the units, match the commercial invoice?
3. Is the exact breakdown of merchandise per individual packages shown, if required?

Have you made a final comparative check of all documents to make sure they are consistent with one another?

Figure 4–34. Letter of indemnity.

(Company letterhead)

ABC Bank
Export Services Department
111 Main St.
Chicago, IL 60606

BLANKET INDEMNITY

Gentlemen:

In consideration of your honoring/negotiating our drawings presented to you under any and all letters of credit issued in our favor notwithstanding any discrepancies that might exist therein, we hereby agree to indemnify and hold you harmless, on demand, for the amount of each such drawing, together with any costs and expenses incurred in connection therewith, in the event that the documents included in the drawing are refused by the issuing bank.

- For truck, the EEI must be filed and the ITN provided no later than one hour prior to the arrival of the exporting truck at the border.
- For rail exports, the EEI must be filed and the ITN provided no later than two hours prior to the train's arrival at the border.

To register for filing through the AES system, the terms and conditions state that that any false or misleading statements transmitted through the AES system (which is interpreted to include accidentally false statements as well as intentionally false statements) will subject the exporter to various civil and criminal penalties, including a $10,000 fine and up to five years' imprisonment. Consequently, the exporter has a real interest in making sure that any agent, such as the freight forwarder, prepares the EEI correctly and that the information being submitted to U.S. Customs and Border Protection is accurate. If the exporter discovers that the EEI that it or its freight forwarder has prepared is inaccurate, it should electronically file an amended EEI through the AES system.

There is an exemption from filing an EEI where the value of the shipment is $2,500 or less per Schedule B number and for most shipments to Canada. Any shipment that requires an export license (see discussion in Chapter 5) is not exempt even if the value is less than $2,500.

Specific information is required for completion of the EEI. If the seller is a corporation, it requires its Federal Employer Identification Number issued by the Internal Revenue Service. The EEI also requires that the seller specify whether the transaction is a related-party transaction. This means that the seller has a 10 percent or more stockholding or similar interest in the foreign consignee, or vice versa.

(*Text continues on page 193.*)

Figure 4–35. Advice of irrecovable letter of credit (confirmed)

ABC BANK

MAR 05, 2009

1000 ABC BANK CENTER
CHICAGO, IL 60606

XYZ EXPORT COMPANY
111 MAIN STREET
SPRINGFIELD, IL 62111

ATTENTION : EXPORT DEPARTMENT

EXPORT IRREVOCABLE LC.

OUR REF :	12345678
LETTER OF CREDIT NO :	IC09/1234
ISSUED BY :	JKL BANK, BEIRUT LEBANON
EXPIRY DATE :	MAY 26, 2009
BY ORDER OF :	BEIRUT BUYING COMPANY
AMOUNT:	USD50,000.00

GENTLEMEN:

AT THE REQUEST OF THE JKL BANK, BEIRUT LEBANON, WE ENCLOSE HEREWITH THE ORIGINAL LETTER OF CREDIT OR A COPY THEREOF, AS INDICATED HEREIN. ABC BANK IS SOLELY PROVIDING AN ADVICE AND CONVEYS NO ENGAGEMENT ON OUR PART.

ALL PRESENTATIONS UNDER THIS LETTER OF CREDIT MUST BE IN FULL COMPLIANCE WITH THE TERMS AND CONDITIONS OF THIS CREDIT AND IF YOU CANNOT FULFILL ONE OR MORE OF THEM, PLEASE CONTACT YOUR CUSTOMER IMMEDIATELY TO ARRANGE FOR NECESSARY AMENDMENTS. WHEN PRESENTING YOUR DRAFT(S) AND DOCUMENTS OR WHEN COMMUNICATING WITH US, PLEASE QUOTE OUR REFERENCE NUMBER SHOWN ABOVE.

ORIGINAL CREDIT AND SUBSEQUENT AMENDMENTS, IF ANY, SHOULD ACCOMPANY ALL DRAFT(S) AND DOCUMENTS.

ADDITIONAL INFORMATION:
ABC BANK ADVISING CHARGES USD $75.00
ANY BANK NEGOTIATING DOCUMENTS MUST DEDUCT OUR CHARGES AND REMIT TO ABC BANK AT THE BELOW ADDRESS.

BY RECEIVING AND ACCEPTING PAYMENT UNDER THIS CREDIT, YOU CERTIFY THAT YOU ARE IN COMPLIANCE WITH THE UNITED STATES EXPORT CONTROL REGULATIONS AND OTHER TRADE RELATED LAWS AND REGULATIONS, IF ANY.

ALL PARTIES TO THIS LETTER OF CREDIT ARE ADVISED THAT THE U.S. GOVERNMENT HAS IN PLACE SANCTIONS AGAINST CERTAIN COUNTRIES, RELATED ENTITIES AND INDIVIDUALS UNDER THESE SANCTIONS. ABC BANK IS PROHIBITED FROM ENGAGING TRANSACTIONS THAT VIOLATE ANY OF SUCH SANCTIONS.

IF THE DOCUMENTS PRESENTED DO NOT COMPLY WITH THE TERMS AND CONDITIONS OF THIS LETTER OF CREDIT, A DOCUMENT DISCREPANCY FEE OF $25.00 WILL BE DEDUCTED FROM ANY REMITTANCE MADE UNDER THIS LETTER OF CREDIT.

(*continues*)

Figure 4–35. *(continued)*

ABC BANK

BENEFICIARY AS PER THE LC:

XYZ EXPORT COMPANY
111 MAIN ST.
SPRINGFIELD, IL 62111 USA

THIS ADVICE IS SUBJECT TO THE UNIFORM CUSTOMS AND PRACTICE FOR DOCUMENTARY CREDITS CURRENTLY IN FORCE.

ABC BANK'S OBLIGATIONS, IF ANY, UNDER THIS LETTER OF CREDIT SHALL BE GOVERNED BY THE LAWS OF THE STATE OF ILLINOIS.

PLEASE DIRECT INQUIRIES ALONG WITH OUR REFERENCE NUMBER TO:

CUSTOMS SERVICE DEPARTMENT
ABC BANK
1000 ABC BANK CENTER
CHICAGO IL 60606
TEL: 312.111.1000 EXT. 100 (CUSTOMER SERVICE)
FAX: 312.111.1105 EXT. 105 (CUSTOMER SERVICE)
CUSTOMERSERVICE@ABCBANK.COM

WE CONFIRM THIS LETTER OF CREDIT AND THEREBY UNDERTAKE THAT ALL DRAWINGS DRAWN UNDER AND IN COMPLIANCE WITH THE TERMS AND CONDITIONS OF THIS LETTER OF CREDIT WILL BE DULY HONORED BY US ON DELIVERY OF DOCUMENTS AS SPECIFIED IF PRESENTED AT THIS OFFICE ON OR BEFORE THE EXPIRY DATE.

____

ABC BANK (AUTHORIZED REPRESENTATIVE)

Figure 4–35. *(continued)*

ABC BANK

REFERENCE NUMBER 12345678

UVR 2222 PSS 4321
CHLCE
.CHMITAB 1233333 400567

0509 40ABCBUS11RXXX11111
0509 40ORSTUS1TTXXX22222
700 00

:27 SEQUENCE OF TOTAL : 1/2

:40B FORM OF DOC CREDIT: IRREVOCABLE WITHOUT OUR CONFIRMATION

:20 OUR REF NUMBER: A00666666

:21 DOC CREDIT NUM: IC009/1234

:31C DATE OF ISSUE: 090305

:40E LC SUBJECT TO: UCP LATEST VERSION

:31D DATE AND PLACE OF EXPIRY: 090430 CHICAGO, ILLINOIS USA

:50 APPLICANT:

BEIRUT BUYING COMPANY
222-A KASLIK STREET
BEIRUT LEBANON

:59 BENEFICIARY:

XYZ EXPORT COMPANY
111 MAIN ST.
SPRINGFIELD, IL 62111 USA

:32B CURRENCY: USD50,000

:39C ADDITIONAL AMTS COVERED: NOT EXCEEDING

:41D AVAILABLE WITH..BY.. THE BANK OF CHICAGO, CHICAGO
BY ACCEPTANCE

:42C DRAFTS AT: DRAFTS AT 120 DAYS FROM B/L DATE

:42D DRAWEE: DRAWN ON BANK OF CHICAGO, CHICAGO

:43P PARTIAL SHIPMENT: NOT ALLOWED

:43T TRANS SHIPMENT: NOT ALLOWED

:44E PORT OF LOADING: ANY US SEAPORT

(continues)

Figure 4–35. *(continued)*

ABC BANK

:44F: PORT OF DISCHARGE: BEIRUT PORT, LEBANON

:44G LATEST DATE OF SHIPMENT: 090415

:48 PERIOD FOR PRESENTATION: DRAFTS AND DOCUMENTS MUST BE PRESENTED 21 DAYS AFTER SHIPMENT DATE AND WITHIN L/C VALIDITY

:49 CONFIRM INSTRUCTIONS: CONFIRM

:57D "ADV THRU BANK"
ABC BANK
1000 ABC BANK CENTER
CHICAGO, IL 60606 USA

:45B DESCRIPTION OF GOODS: PAPER MAKING MACHINERY
CIF BEIRUT PORT, LEBANON

:46B DOCUMENTS REQUIRED: OUR CORRESPONDENT STATES THE FOLLOWING DOCUMENTS ARE REQUIRED UNDER THEIR CREDIT ISSUED ON JANUARY 3, 2009.

1-BENEFICIARIES' HANDSIGNED AND DATED COMMERCIAL INVOICE IN ONE ORIGINAL AND 2 COPIES, SHOWING NAME OF MANUFACTURER OR EXPORTER OF GOODS, FULL DESCRIPTION OF GOODS AND ITS QUANTITY, NET AND GROSS WEIGHT, UNIT AND TOTAL PRICE, THEIR MARKS AND SERIAL NUMBER AND BEARING BENEFICIARIES' FOLLOWING STATEMENT: 'WE CERTIFY THAT THIS INVOICE IS TRUE AND AUTHENTIC, THAT IT IS THE ONLY ONE ISSUED BY US FOR THE GOODS DESCRIBED HEREIN, THAT IT SHOWS THEIR EXACT VALUE WITHOUT ANY DEDUCTION OR ADVANCE PAYMENT AND THAT THEIR ORIGIN IS FROM THE UNITED STATES OF AMERICA'. ORIGINAL COMMERCIAL INVOICE SHOULD BE CERTIFIED BY THE CHAMBER OF COMMERCE.

2-CERTIFICATE OF ORIGIN IN 1 ORIGINAL AND 2 COPIES ISSUED BY THE CHAMBER OF COMMERCE.

3-FULL SET OF CLEAN 'SHIPPED ON BOARD' MARINE BILLS OF LADING ISSUED TO THE ORDER OF JKL BANK, BEIRUT LEBANON MARKED FREIGHT PREPAID, NOTIFY APPLICANTS.

4-FULL SET OF INSURANCE CERTIFICATE/POLICY ISSUED TO THE ORDER OF JKL BANK, BEIRUT LEBANON, MARKED PREMIUM PAID, INDICATING THEIR PAYING AGENT'S NAME AND ADDRESS IN LEBANON, THE NAME OF THE CARRYING VESSEL AND COVERING GOODS AGAINST THE FOLLOWING RISK: INSTITUTE CARGO CLAUSES (A)1.1.82 FIRE, THEFT IN THE CUSTOMS HOUSE, RIOTS AND CIVIL COMMOTION CLAUSES. TRANSHIPMENT RISKS IF ANY VALID FOR 6- DAYS AFTER DISCHARGE OF GOODS AT FINAL DESTINATION.

5-PACKING LIST IN 3 COPIES.

6-WEIGHT LIST IN 3 COPIES.

7-CERTIFICATE ISSUED AND SIGNED BY THE SHIPPING COMPANY OR ITS AGENT CERTIFYING THE FOLLOWING: WE CERTIFY THAT THE VESSEL CARRYING THE GOODS UNDER SUBJECT CREDIT IS SELF PROPELLED OF STEEL CONSTRUCTION CLASSED WITH A CLASSIFICATION SOCIETY WHICH IS A MEMBER OF THE INTERNATIONAL ASSOCIATION OF CLASSIFICATION SOCIETY (IACS) MENTIONED IN IACS WEBSITE WWW.IACS.ORG.UK. WE ALSO CERTIFY THAT, AT THE TIME OF LOADING, THE CARRYING VESSEL NAMED (TO BE INDICATED) IS ISM CODE CERTIFIED AND HOLDS A VALID INTERNATIONAL SAFETY MANAGEMENT CERTIFICATE, AS WELL AS A VALID ISM CODE DOCUMENT OF COMPLIANCE AS REQUIRED BY THE SOLAS' CONVENTION 1974 AS AMENDED.

:47B ADDITIONAL CONDITIONS:

OUR CORRESPONDENT STATES THE FOLLOWING CONDITIONS ARE REQUIRED UNDER

Figure 4–35. *(continued)*

ABC BANK

THEIR CREDIT ISSUED ON JANUARY 3, 2009.
ALL THE DOCUMENTS TO BE ISSUED IN THE NAME OF THE APPLICANT AS THE BUYER UNLESS OTHERWISE REQUESTED.
TRANSPORT DOCUMENTS SHOWING NAME OF A THIRD PARTY AS SHIPPER ARE NOT ACCEPTABLE.
DOCUMENTS INCLUDING B/L ISSUED OR DATED PRIOR TO THE ISSUANCE OF THE L/C ARE NOT ACCEPTABLE.
PAYMENT UNDER RESERVE IS PROHIBITED.
THIS CREDIT NUMBER, DATE AND OUR BANK'S NAME MUST BE QUOTED ON ALL REQUIRED DOCUMENTS.
A DISCREPANCY FEE FOR USD $25 IS TO BE BORNE BY BENEFICIARIES FOR EACH SET OF DOCUMENTS PRESENTED TO US WITH DISCREPANCIES.
PHOTOCOPIES OF DOCUMENTS PRESENTED FOR NEGOTIATION ARE NOT ACCEPTABLE EVEN IF STAMPED ORIGINAL.
ALL BANKING CHARGES AND COMMISSIONS OUTSIDE LEBANON PLUS REIMBURSING BANK CHARGES ARE ON BENEFICIARIES' ACCOUNT UNQUOTE.
PLEASE NOTE THAT IF THE CREDIT PROVIDES THE OPTION OF HAVING THE PORT ELIGIBILITY CERTIFICATION SUBMITTED BY AN AGENT, PURSUANT TO U.S. DEPARTMENT OF COMMERCE REGULATIONS, WE ARE PROHBITED FROM ACCEPTING, AND WILL NOT ACCEPT, THE AGENT'S CERTIFICATE.

The seller must specify the Schedule B Commodity Number for the product being exported. Schedule B classifications are available on the Census Bureau's web site at www.census.gov. Since the adoption of the Harmonized Tariff System (HTS) on January 1, 1989, in the United States, with only a few exceptions, the HTS number may be used instead of the Schedule B classification number. However, the HTS specifically identifies that certain commodities are still required to use the Schedule B number. See the "Notice to Exporters" section in the General Notes of the HTS available at the U.S. International Trade Commission web site: http://hotdocs.usitc.gov/docs/tata/hts/bychapter/0901n2x.pdf.

The seller must designate whether the product being shipped is "D" (domestic) or "F" (foreign). Domestic products are those grown, produced, or manufactured in the United States or imported and enhanced in value. Foreign products are those that have been imported into the United States and exported in the same condition as when imported.

For the EEI form, the seller must declare the value of the goods. This is defined to mean the selling price, or if not sold, the cost, including the inland freight, insurance, and other charges, to the U.S. port of export. It does not include unconditional discounts and commissions. This value declaration is extremely important, because if it varies from the selling price stated in the commercial invoice, consular invoice, special customs invoice, insurance certificate, or, especially, any forms filed by the buyer with the foreign customs or exchange control authorities, a charge of false statement may arise, subjecting the exporter and/or the foreign buyer to civil or criminal penalties.

Finally, the EEI calls for an export license number or exception symbol, and the Export Control Classification Number (ECCN). This information relates to the export licensing system applicable in the United States. A detailed discussion of that system follows in Chapter 5. The important thing to note at this point is that prior to clearance for shipment from the United States, the exporter or its agent must declare, under penalty of perjury, that no export license is required; or that the export can be made under a license exception, and the correct license exception symbol must be inserted in the EEI; or that a license is required and has been obtained, and the license number issued by the U.S. Department of Commerce is stated in the EEI. When an individual license is required, there will be an ECCN that also must be inserted in the EEI. If this information is not put in the form, the shipment will be detained and will not be permitted to clear. Under the revised regulations, the seller will be responsible for making the license determination unless the buyer has expressly agreed in writing to accept such responsibility and has appointed a U.S. agent (such as a freight forwarder) to share such responsibility.

U. Freight Forwarder's Invoices

The freight forwarder will issue a bill to the exporter for its services. Sometimes the forwarder will include certain services in its standard quotation, while other services will be add-ons. It is important to make clear at the outset of the transaction which services will be performed by the exporter, the freight forwarder, and others, such as the bank.

V. Air Cargo Security and C-TPAT

1. Air Cargo Security

Recent security threats and airline disasters have increased the demand for greater transparency regarding shippers and cargo. This necessitates advance information about the shipment, the parties, the routing, and the destination. The Transportation Security Administration (TSA) is the agency responsible for screening passengers prior to boarding a plane, but it is also responsible for the Indirect Air Carrier Cargo Security Program (IACCSP), which oversees air freight forwarders and all cargo that is destined for passenger planes.

Air freight forwarders are considered Indirect Air Carriers (IAC) and are required to register for this confidential program. The program requires the development of internal procedures regarding the acceptance of air cargo from "known" shippers and screening all cargo prior to lading. A "known" shipper is one that has an ongoing shipping relationship with the IAC forwarder, and the IAC forwarder has visited the shipper to ensure that it is a legitimate business. Once a shipper has been substantiated as a known shipper, its name is entered into a national databank that only IACs may access. Shipments from any unknown shipper require specific documentation and identification from the driver delivering the cargo to the forwarder as well as screening before it may be shipped on a cargo-only aircraft. Additional measures include restricted access to cargo facilities, ongoing training for staff, and background checks for certain personnel. TSA continuously changes and updates the program, and that information may be disseminated on a need-to-know basis only.

Figure 4–36. Exporter AES & Shipper Instructions

EASI-SLI™ **Exporter AES & Shipper Instructions™ (EASI-SLI™)**

1. U.S.P.P.I (complete name and addess + Zip) 1a. EIN or ID No.	4. Exporter's Reference No. **6. AES XTN**	5. Date Prepared **7. AES ITN / Filing Exemption**
2. Ultimate Consignee 2a. Related Party: ☐ Yes ☐ No	8. Dangerous Goods ☐ Yes ☐ No 10. Point/State of Origin	9. Routed Export Transaction ☐ Yes ☐ No 11. Ultimate Destination
3. Intermediate Consignee	12. Forwarding Agent 13. Special Instructions	

Schedule B Description of Commodities

14. D/F or M	15. Schedule B No.	16. Description License No. Exception/Exemption ECCN/ITAR Category	17. Schedule B Quantity	18. Shipping Wt (kg)	19. Value (U.S. $)
		SAMPLE			

20. Shipment Mode	21. Containerized ☐ Yes ☐ No	22. Consolidate ☐ Yes ☐ No	23. Freight Charges: ☐ Prepaid ☐ Collect	24. If unable to deliver: ☐ Abandon ☐ Return ☐ Notify Shipper

25. Inland Carrier	26. Ship Date	27. B/L No.	The U.S.P.P.I. authorizes the Forwarding Agent named above to act as an authorized agent on behalf of the U.S.P.P.I. for export control, Customs & Border Protection, and Census Bureau purposes to transmit export information electronically through the Automated Export System.
28. Exporting Carrier	29. Export Date	30. B/L No.	

31. Shipper requests insurance: ☐ Yes $________ ☐ No If insurance is requested, shipment is insured to the amount indicated. Recovery is limited to actual loss in acceptance with the carrier's tariff.	32. Duly authorized office r or employee of U.S.P.P.I. Name: Signature	Date: Telephone: Email: DDTC Registration No.

Form No. 15-306 Printed and Sold by UNZ&CO 800-631-3098 • www.unzco.com

EXPORTER COPY

2. Customs and Trade Partnership Against Terrorism (C-TPAT)

U.S. Customs and Border Protection has developed an extensive program to combat terrorism through a voluntary program known as the Customs and Trade Partnership Against Terrorism, or C-TPAT. Although the program is voluntary, Customs has indicated that participating importers will receive fewer intensive exams as the carrot for joining. Many large importers have signed on, and as Customs has expanded the programs along the supply chain, those importers have required all of their business partners to join as well, so it has become widespread.

To participate in the program, a company needs to file a Memorandum of Intent (MOI) with Customs that it will establish controls to restrict access to cargo. Then it needs to document what procedures it has in place to ensure that it complies, including controlled access, identification cards, escorting of guests throughout property, a seven-point check of all containers, no empty containers left unlocked, tracking mechanisms, etc. Customs has developed "best practices" for companies to use as guidelines. Once the MOI has been filed and the company's procedures have been submitted, it becomes a "certified" participant. Customs will visit the company to review the procedures and make suggestions for improvement. Customs will also visit an importer's foreign vendors to ensure that security procedures are in place from the initial point of sale. Once the verifications have been made, the importer is designated as a Tier 2 or Tier 3 participant. The higher the tier, the more benefits the importer is supposed to receive.

Customs has rolled the program out to forwarders, customs brokers, carriers, and warehouses. And all parties that have been certified are published in a data bank that can be accessed by companies to ensure that they use C-TPAT certified providers in their supply chain.

Should Customs determine that there has been a breakdown in the security and foreign articles have been introduced into a shipment, the importer or other party may be removed from the program and be subject to additional screening at additional cost. At this point, there are no penalties, as the program is still considered a voluntary program.

Chapter 5
Export Controls and Licenses

A. Introduction

There are a number of laws that control exports from the United States, including the Arms Export Control Act, the Atomic Energy Act of 1954, the International Emergency Economic Powers Act, the Trading with the Enemy Act, the Munitions Act, the Food, Drug and Cosmetic Act, and the Comprehensive Anti-Apartheid Act. The Department of State, Office of Defense Trade Controls; the Drug Enforcement Administration; the Food and Drug Administration; the Department of Interior; the Department of Treasury, Office of Foreign Assets Control; the Department of Energy; the Nuclear Regulatory Commission; the Department of Commerce, Patent and Trademark Office; the Department of Transportation; and the U.S. Maritime Administration all have responsibilities regarding the regulation and control of exports. The law that is of most general application to the broadest range of commodities is known as the Export Administration Act and is administered by the Department of Commerce. In March 1996, the Department of Commerce issued completely rewritten regulations interpreting the responsibilities under the Export Administration Act. Although one of the important changes under the new regulations is that products are controlled only if they are listed on the Commerce Control List, in fact, for every export shipment from the United States, the exporter must determine that the product does not require a license or that a license exception applies and indicate that on the Electronic Export Information. If the exporter neglects this task, the shipment could be seized and the exporter subjected to serious penalties. Not only must an exporter do this once, but it must be constantly alert to product modifications that may make a product that was previously eligible for export without a license subject to an export license requirement.

How, then, does one determine whether the product requires an export license, may be shipped "No License Required," or is eligible for a license exception? Under the new Export Administration Regulations (EAR), an exporter may be shocked to learn, the regulations require the exporter to proceed through a twenty-nine-step analysis for each of its products. These can be summed up in four major steps: First, analyzing the scope of the EAR; second, determining the applicability of the Ten General Prohibitions; third, determining the applicability of the various license exceptions; and fourth, complying with the export documentation requirements. The following discussion is divided between the export of products, on the one hand, and the export of technology, software, and technical assistance, on the other. It also distinguishes between the initial export from the United States and re-exports of U.S.-origin products from one foreign country to another. The following discussion is a summary of over 350 pages under the new EAR, and exporters should seek legal advice for specific export transactions.

B. Scope of the EAR

The first step in determining whether or not an export license is required is to determine whether the contemplated activity is "subject to" (that is, within the scope of), the EAR. In general, the coverage of the EAR is very broad. Items subject to the EAR include all items in the United States no matter where they originated, including any located in a U.S. foreign trade zone or moving in transit through the United States; all U.S.-origin items wherever located; U.S.-origin parts, components, materials, or other commodities incorporated abroad in foreign-made products (in quantities exceeding de minimis levels); and certain foreign-made direct products of U.S.-origin technology. Items not subject to the EAR include prerecorded phonograph records reproducing the content of printed books, pamphlets, newspapers and periodicals, children's picture and painting books, music books, sheet music, calendars and calendar blocks, paper, maps, charts, atlases, gazetteers, globes and covers, exposed and developed microfilm reproducing the contents of any of the foregoing, exposed and developed motion picture film and soundtrack, and advertising printed matter exclusively related thereto. Step 1 is to determine whether or not the item being exported is subject to the exclusive export control jurisdiction of another government agency. If it is, the item is outside the scope of the EAR and administrative control of the Department of Commerce but will be subject to the regulations and administration of that other government agency. Steps 4 and 5 relate to determining whether or not a product manufactured in a foreign country contains more than the permitted (de minimis) level of U.S.-origin parts, components, or materials. For embargoed countries, the U.S.-origin parts, components, or materials cannot exceed 10 percent of the total value of the foreign-made product; for all other countries, the limit is 25 percent. If an exporter is unsure whether or not its proposed transaction is within the scope of the EAR, it may request an advisory opinion, which would normally be answered within thirty calendar days after receipt. (Steps 2 and 6, pertaining to technology and software exports, and Step 3, pertaining to re-export of U.S.-origin items, are discussed below.)

C. Commerce Control List

The first of the Ten General Prohibitions is concerned with exporting (or re-exporting) controlled items to countries listed on the Country Chart without a license. All products manufactured or sold in the United States are classified somewhere in the Commerce Control List. The Commerce Control List states that it is not all-inclusive, so exporters should carefully review their items in conjunction with the list to identify any similar products. Specific products that are of concern for various reasons are specifically listed by name in great detail using scientific and engineering specifications. At the end of each category or commodity group classification, there is a catch-all, or basket, category, "EAR 99," which applies to all other commodities not specifically named but that fall within that general commodity category.

The general commodity categories are:

0—Nuclear materials, facilities, and equipment and miscellaneous products
1—Materials, chemicals, microorganisms, and toxins
2—Materials processing
3—Electronics
4—Computers
5—Telecommunications and information security
6—Lasers and sensors
7—Navigation and avionics
8—Marine
9—Propulsion systems, space vehicles, and related equipment

Within each of the foregoing categories, controlled items are arranged by group. Each category contains the same five groups. The groups are as follows:

A—Equipment, assemblies, and components
B—Test, inspection, and production equipment
C—Materials
D—Software
E—Technology

It should be noted that with the rewrite of the EAR, the numbering system has changed and products that were previously classified under one number in the Commerce Control List may now be classified under a new number or deleted, or additional items may be included.

Additionally, the Commerce Department has issued "interpretations" relating to various products, including anti-friction bearings and parts; parts of machinery, equipment, or other items; wire or cable cut to length; telecommunications equipment and systems; numerical control systems; parts, accessories, and equipment exported as scrap; scrap arms, ammunition, and implements of war; military automotive vehicles and parts for such vehicles; aircraft parts, accessories, and components; civil aircraft inertial navigation equipment; "precursor" chemicals; technology and software; and chemical mixtures. An alphabetical index to the Commerce Control List is included in the EAR but, in fact, it is not very helpful in actually finding a product. It is much more useful to conduct a computerized search of the EAR. A further complication is that technology changes constantly, and new products do not fit well into the old classifications.

The descriptions in the Commerce Control List are extremely detailed, containing engineering and scientific language, and it is unlikely that a person in the export sales or traffic department will be able to determine whether his company's products are covered by a particular description without the assistance of company engineers. If it is unclear whether a product falls under one of the classifications, the exporter can request a commodity classification through the Simplified Network Application Process–Revised (SNAP-R) program. Such requests will ordinarily be answered within 30 days after receipt. (See more about the SNAP-R program below in Section H).

Step 7 is the process of reviewing the Commerce Control List and determining whether or not the item being exported falls under a specific classification number and reviewing the "Reasons for Control" specified within the Commerce Control List for that item. Items are controlled for one of the following fourteen reasons:

AT—Anti-Terrorism
CB—Chemical and Biological Weapons
CC—Crime Control
CW—Chemical Weapons Convention
EC—Encryption Items
FC—Firearms Convention
MT—Missile Technology
NS—National Security
NP—Nuclear Nonproliferation
RS—Regional Stability
SS—Short Supply
UN—United Nations
SI—Significant Items
SL—Surreptitious Listening

For each product listed in the Commerce Control List, the reason for control is specified. Some products are subject to multiple reasons for control, and some reasons apply to only some of the products listed within the Export Control Classification Number (ECCN). In order to proceed with the analysis, it is necessary to obtain the Reason for Control and "column" shown for the controlled product within the ECCN for that product.

Certain products are controlled because they are in short supply within the United States and are listed on the Commerce Control List. But for these, unlike other products, the Commerce Control List does not specify the "column," or possible license exceptions. These products include crude oil, petroleum products (which is rather an extensive list), unprocessed western red cedar, and horses exported by sea for slaughter. For such products, the applicable licensing requirements and exceptions are specified under part 754 of the EAR.

Sample pages from the Commerce Control List for ECCN 2A001, "Anti-friction bearings and bearing systems, as follows, (see List of Items Controlled) and components therefor," are shown in Figure 5–1. In reviewing this, an exporter will learn that certain specified bearings are a controlled commodity, that the reasons for control include "NS" (National Security), "AT" (Anti-Terrorism), and, for certain items within the classification, "MT" (Missile Technology). It also indicates that certain common

(*Text continues on page 203.*)

Figure 5–1. Sample pages from the Commerce Control List (ECCN 2A001).

CATEGORY 2 - MATERIALS PROCESSING

Note: *For quiet running bearings, see the U.S. Munitions List.*

A. SYSTEMS, EQUIPMENT AND COMPONENTS

2A001 Anti-friction bearings and bearing systems, as follows, (see List of Items Controlled) and components therefor.

License Requirements

Reason for Control: NS, MT, AT

Control(s)	*Country Chart*
NS applies to entire entry	NS Column 2
MT applies to radial ball bearings having all tolerances specified in accordance with ISO 492 Tolerance Class 2 (or ANSI/ABMA Std 20 Tolerance Class ABEC-9, or other national equivalents) or better and having all the following characteristics: an inner ring bore diameter between 12 and 50 mm; an outer ring outside diameter between 25 and 100 mm; and a width between 10 and 20 mm.	MT Column 1
AT applies to entire entry	AT Column 1

License Exceptions

LVS: $3000, N/A for MT
GBS: Yes, for 2A001.a and 2A001.b, N/A for MT
CIV: Yes, for 2A001.a and 2A001.b, N/A for MT

List of Items Controlled

Unit: $ value
Related Controls: (1) See also 2A991. (2) Quiet running bearings are subject to the export licensing authority of the Department of State, Directorate of Defense Trade Controls. (See 22 CFR part 121.)
Related Definitions: Annular Bearing Engineers Committee (ABEC).
Items:

Note: *2A001 does not control balls with tolerance specified by the manufacturer in accordance with ISO 3290 as grade 5 or worse.*

Note: *2A001 does not control balls with tolerance specified by the manufacturer in accordance with ISO 3290 as grade 5 or worse.*

a. Ball bearings and solid roller bearings having all tolerances specified by the manufacturer in accordance with ISO 492 Tolerance Class 4 (or ANSI/ABMA Std 20 Tolerance Class ABEC-7 or RBEC-7, or other national equivalents), or better, and having both rings and rolling elements (ISO 5593) made from monel or beryllium;

Note: *2A001.a does not control tapered roller bearings.*

b. Other ball bearings and solid roller bearings having all tolerances specified by the manufacturer in accordance with ISO 492 Tolerance Class 2 (or ANSI/ABMA Std 20 Tolerance Class ABEC-9 or RBEC-9, or other national equivalents), or better;

Note: *2A001.b does not control tapered roller bearings.*

c. Active magnetic bearing systems using any of the following:

c.1. Materials with flux densities of 2.0 T or greater and yield strengths greater than 414 MPa;

c.2. All-electromagnetic 3D homopolar bias

Figure 5–1. *(continued)*

designs for actuators; *or*

c.3. High temperature (450 K (177°C) and above) position sensors.

2A225 Crucibles made of materials resistant to liquid actinide metals, as follows (see List of Items Controlled).

License Requirements

Reason for Control: NP, AT

Control(s)	*Country Chart*
NP applies to entire entry	NP Column 1
AT applies to entire entry	AT Column 1

License Exceptions

LVS: N/A
GBS: N/A
CIV: N/A

List of Items Controlled

Unit: $ value
Related Controls: See ECCNs 2E001 ("development"), 2E002 ("production"), and 2E201 ("use") for technology for items controlled under this entry.
Related Definitions: N/A
Items:

a. Crucibles having both of the following characteristics:

a.1. A volume of between 150 cm^3 and 8,000 cm^3; *and*

a.2. Made of or coated with any of the following materials, having a purity of 98% or greater by weight:

a.2.a. Calcium fluoride (CaF_2);

a.2.b. Calcium zirconate (metazirconate) ($CaZrO_3$);

a.2.c. Cerium sulphide (Ce_2S_3);

a.2.d. Erbium oxide (erbia) (Er_2O_3);

a.2.e. Hafnium oxide (hafnia) (HfO_2);

a.2.f. Magnesium oxide (MgO);

a.2.g. Nitrided niobium-titanium-tungsten alloy (approximately 50% Nb, 30% Ti, 20% W);

a.2.h. Yttrium oxide (yttria) (Y_2O_3); *or*

a.2.i. Zirconium oxide (zirconia) (ZrO_2);

b. Crucibles having both of the following characteristics:

b.1. A volume of between 50 cm^3 and 2,000 cm^3; *and*

b.2. Made of or lined with tantalum, having a purity of 99.9% or greater by weight;

c. Crucibles having all of the following characteristics:

c.1. A volume of between 50 cm^3 and 2,000 cm^3;

c.2. Made of or lined with tantalum, having a purity of 98% or greater by weight; *and*

c.3. Coated with tantalum carbide, nitride, boride, or any combination thereof.

2A226 Valves having all of the following characteristics (see List of Items Controlled).

License Requirements

license exceptions are available; e.g., "LVS" (Low Value Shipment) is available if the value is not over $3,000, but it is not available to those countries designated for MT controls. "GBS" and "CIV" are available, but only for certain items and not to countries designated for MT controls. If the item being exported is not specifically described on the Commerce Control List, it thereby falls within EAR 99 and no license will be required for export, but records analyzing and demonstrating that the item falls outside of any of the classifications must be maintained, and proper export documentation must be completed (see Section J below).

D. Export Destinations

If an item is listed in the Commerce Control List, it is prima facie subject to an export license requirement. However, to determine whether or not an export license will actually be required, it is necessary to proceed to determine the country of ultimate destination (Step 8). Products being exported may pass through one or more countries (except certain prohibited countries), but licenses are issued based on the country of ultimate destination—the country that, according to the representation of the purchaser, is the last country of delivery and use.

The Commerce Country Chart is divided into four main groups: Groups A (four subgroups), B, D (four subgroups), and E (two subgroups). These country listings overlap and are different depending upon the Reason for Control (see Figures 5–2 through 5–5).

Using the Reason for Control listed in the Commerce Control List for the product being exported and the column listed there, the exporter can review the Commerce Country Chart by country of destination. Wherever the exporter observes that an "X" is shown for that country in the same Reason for Control and columns specified in the ECCN for that product, an export license will be required (Step 9). For example, under the 2A001 category listed above, if the item being exported is a radial ball bearing having all tolerances specified in Figure 5–1, then it is controlled for Missile Technology and may not be exported to any country listed on the Country Chart (see Figure 5–6) with an "X" under MT column 1 without a license. A license may or may not be granted depending on the consignee and the intended use (see Section E below).

Where the item being exported is not a finished good but is a part or component being exported for incorporation into a product being manufactured abroad, if the part or component being exported is described in an entry on the Commerce Control List and the Country Chart requires a license to the intended export destination, then a license will be required unless the parts or components meet the de minimis 10 percent or 25 percent standards (Step 10).

Where the export is to certain embargoed destinations, it is unlikely that a license will be granted. Presently, the EAR prohibits exports to Cuba, Iran, Syria, and Sudan. All exports to North Korea require a license. The Department of Treasury, Office of Foreign Assets Control, also maintains controls on the foregoing destinations plus to persons or entities on the Specially Designated Nationals list who participate

(*Text continues on page 211.*)

Figure 5–2. Country group A.

Country Group A

Country	[A:1]	[A:2] Missile Technology Control Regime	[A:3] Australia Group	[A:4] Nuclear Suppliers Group
Argentina		X	X	X
Australia	X	X	X	X
Austria[1]		X	X	X
Belarus				X
Belgium	X	X	X	X
Brazil		X		X
Bulgaria		X	X	X
Canada	X	X	X	X
Croatia			X	
Cyprus			X	X
Czech Republic		X	X	X
Denmark	X	X	X	X
Estonia			X	
Finland[1]		X	X	X
France	X	X	X	X
Germany	X	X	X	X
Greece	X	X	X	X
Hong Kong[1]				
Hungary		X	X	X
Iceland		X	X	
Ireland[1]		X	X	X
Italy	X	X	X	X
Japan	X	X	X	X
Kazakhstan				X
Korea, South[1]		X	X	X
Latvia			X	X
Lithuania			X	
Luxembourg	X	X	X	X
Malta			X	
Netherlands	X	X	X	X
New Zealand[1]		X	X	X
Norway	X	X	X	X
Poland		X	X	X
Portugal	X	X	X	X
Romania			X	X
Russia		X		X
Slovakia			X	X
Slovenia			X	X
South Africa		X		X

Figure 5–3. Country group B.

Country Group B

Countries

Afghanistan
Algeria
Andorra
Angola
Antigua and Barbuda
Argentina
Aruba
Australia
Austria
The Bahamas
Bahrain
Bangladesh
Barbados
Belgium
Belize
Benin
Bhutan
Bolivia
Bosnia & Herzegovina
Botswana
Brazil
Brunei
Bulgaria
Burkina Faso
Burundi
Cameroon
Canada
Cape Verde
Central African Republic
Chad
Chile
Colombia
Comoros
Congo (Democratic Republic of the)
Congo (Republic of the)
Costa Rica
Cote d'Ivoire
Croatia
Cyprus
Czech Republic
Denmark
Djibouti
Dominica
Dominican Republic
East Timor
Ecuador
Egypt
El Salvador
Equatorial Guinea
Eritrea
Estonia
Ethiopia
Fiji
Finland
France
Gabon
Gambia, The
Germany
Ghana
Greece
Grenada
Guatemala
Guinea
Guinea-Bissau
Guyana
Haiti
Honduras
Hong Kong
Hungary
Iceland
India
Indonesia
Ireland
Israel
Italy
Jamaica
Japan
Jordan
Kenya
Kiribati
Korea, South
• Kosovo
Kuwait
Latvia
Lebanon
Lesotho
Liberia
Liechtenstein
Lithuania

(*continues*)

Figure 5–3. *(continued)*

Country Group B
Countries

Luxembourg
Macedonia, The Former Yugoslav Republic of
Madagascar
Malawi
Malaysia
Maldives
Mali
Malta
Marshall Islands
Mauritania
Mauritius
Mexico
Micronesia, Federated States of
Monaco
Montenegro
Morocco
Mozambique
Namibia
Nauru
Nepal
Netherlands
Netherlands Antilles
New Zealand
Nicaragua
Niger
Nigeria
Norway
Oman
Pakistan
Palau
Panama
Papua New Guinea
Paraguay
Peru
Philippines
Poland
Portugal
Qatar
Romania
Rwanda
Saint Kitts & Nevis
Saint Lucia
Saint Vincent and the Grenadines
Samoa
San Marino
Sao Tome & Principe
Saudi Arabia
Senegal
Serbia
Seychelles
Sierra Leone
Singapore
Slovakia
Slovenia
Solomon Islands
Somalia
South Africa
Spain
Sri Lanka
Surinam
Swaziland
Sweden
Switzerland
Taiwan
Tanzania
Thailand
Togo
Tonga
Trinidad & Tobago
Tunisia
Turkey
Tuvalu
Uganda
United Arab Emirates
United Kingdom
United States
Uruguay
Vanuatu
Vatican City
Venezuela
Western Sahara
Yemen
Zambia
Zimbabwe

Figure 5–4. Country group D.

Country Group D

Country	[D: 1] National Security	[D: 2] Nuclear	[D: 3] Chemical & Biological	[D: 4] Missile Technology
Afghanistan			X	
Albania	X			
Armenia	X		X	
Azerbaijan	X		X	
Bahrain			X	X
Belarus	X		X	
Burma	X		X	
Cambodia	X			
China (PRC)	X		X	X
Cuba		X	X	
Egypt			X	X
Georgia	X		X	
India		X	X	X
Iran		X	X	X
Iraq	X	X	X	X
Israel		X	X	X
Jordan			X	X
Kazakhstan	X		X	
Korea, North	X	X	X	X
Kuwait			X	X
Kyrgyzstan	X		X	
Laos	X			
Lebanon			X	X
Libya	X	X	X	X
Macau	X		X	X
Moldova	X		X	
Mongolia	X		X	
Oman			X	X
Pakistan		X	X	X
Qatar			X	X
Russia	X		X	
Saudi Arabia			X	X

(*continues*)

Figure 5–4. *(continued)*

License Exceptions **Supplement No. 1 to Part 740–page 6**

Country	[D: 1] National Security	[D: 2] Nuclear	[D: 3] Chemical & Biological	[D: 4] Missile Technology
Syria			X	X
Taiwan			X	
Tajikistan	X		X	
Turkmenistan	X		X	
Ukraine	X			
United Arab Emirates			X	X
Uzbekistan	X		X	
Vietnam	X		X	
Yemen			X	X

Figure 5–5. Country group E.

Country Group E [1]

Country	[E:1] Terrorist Supporting Countries [2]	[E:2] Unilateral Embargo
Cuba	X	X
Iran	X	
Korea, North	X	
Sudan	X	
Syria	X	

[1] In addition to the controls maintained by the Bureau of Industry and Security pursuant to the EAR, note that the Department of the Treasury administers:

(a) A *comprehensive embargo* against Cuba, Iran, and Sudan; and

(b) An *embargo against certain persons,* e.g., Specially Designated Terrorists (SDT), Foreign Terrorist Organizations (FTO), Specially Designated Global Terrorists (SDGT), and Specially Designated Narcotics Traffickers (SDNT). Please see part 744 of the EAR for controls maintained by the Bureau of Industry and Security on these and other persons.

[2] The President made inapplicable with respect to Iraq provisions of law that apply to countries that have supported terrorism.

Figure 5–6. Excerpt from Commerce Country Chart.

Commerce Country Chart

Reason for Control

Countries	Chemical & Biological Weapons			Nuclear Nonproliferation		National Security		Missile Tech	Regional Stability		Firearms Convention	Crime Control			Anti-Terrorism	
	CB 1	CB 2	CB 3	NP 1	NP 2	NS 1	NS 2	MT 1	RS 1	RS 2	FC 1	CC 1	CC 2	CC 3	AT 1	AT 2
Spain	X					X		X	X							
Sri Lanka	X	X		X		X	X	X	X	X		X		X		
Sudan	X	X		X		X	X	X	X	X		X		X	X	X
Suriname	X	X		X		X	X	X	X	X	X	X		X		
Swaziland	X	X		X		X	X	X	X	X		X		X		
Sweden	X					X		X	X	X		X		X		
Switzerland	X					X		X	X	X		X		X		
Syria	X	X	X	X		X	X	X	X	X		X		X	X	
Taiwan	X	X	X	X		X	X	X	X	X		X		X		
Tajikistan	X	X	X	X		X	X	X	X	X		X	X			
Tanzania	X	X		X		X	X	X	X	X		X		X		
Thailand	X	X		X		X	X	X	X	X		X		X		
Togo	X	X		X		X	X	X	X	X		X		X		
Tonga	X	X		X		X	X	X	X	X		X		X		

in Terrorist Activities, Nuclear Proliferation Activities, and Narcotics Trafficking. The analysis of whether or not the intended export is subject to control under those regulations is Step 14.

Related to the country of destination, BIS established the Transshipment Country Export Control Initiative, whose goal is to strengthen export controls in countries and companies that are transshipment hubs, where legally exported goods are transshipped to prohibited destinations. Currently these areas include Panama, Malta, Cyprus, United Arab Emirates, Singapore, Malaysia, Thailand, Taiwan, and Hong Kong. Most of these areas are working with the U.S. government to strengthen controls for legitimate trade. There are certain countries through which the goods cannot transit on the way to their ultimate destination. These countries include the following: Albania, Armenia, Azerbaijan, Belarus, Bulgaria, Cambodia, Cuba, Estonia, Georgia, Kazakhstan, Kyrgyzstan, Laos, Latvia, Lithuania, Mongolia, North Korea, Russia, Tajikistan, Turkmenistan, Ukraine, Uzbekistan, and Vietnam (Step 8).

E. Customers, End Users, and End Uses

The Commerce Department issues and updates on an ongoing basis the "Denied Persons List." This list identifies persons who have previously violated U.S. export control laws and who are prohibited from engaging in export activities. The Department of Treasury maintains a similar list of "Specially Designated Nationalists and Terrorists." It is a violation of the export control laws for a person on such lists to be involved in any export as a purchaser, consignee, freight forwarder, or any other role. Whenever an exporter is engaged in a transaction, it is incumbent upon the exporter to check the Denied Persons List and the List of Specially Designated Nationalists and Terrorists to avoid potential serious export violations (Step 12). A complete list of the all the prohibited parties published by the various agencies with control over exports is available at http://www.bis.doc.gov/complianceandenforcement/liststocheck.htm. In addition, there are a number of vendors with software that will scan export documentations against these lists for exporters.

Even where an export may be ordinarily made, if the product being exported will be used in certain end-use activities, a license may be required or the license may be unavailable. These include nuclear explosive activities; unsafeguarded nuclear activities; exports of items for nuclear end uses that are permitted for countries in Supplement Number 3 to part 744; design, development, production, or use of missiles in a country listed in Country Group D:4; and design, development, production, stockpiling, or use of chemical or biological weapons.

Finally, "U.S. persons" are prohibited from engaging in, facilitating, or supporting proliferation activities. This includes the design, development, production, or use of nuclear explosive devices in or by a country listed in Country Group D:2; the design, development, production, or use of missiles in or by a country listed in Country Group D:4; and the design, development, production, stockpiling, or use of chemical and biological weapons in any country listed in Country Group D:3. This includes any action such as financing, employment, transportation, and/or freight forwarding. The definition of "U.S. person" includes any individual who is a citizen of the United

States, a permanent resident alien of the United States, or a protected individual; any juridical person organized under the laws of the United States, including foreign branches; and any person in the United States. This prohibition relates to any activities, including products produced entirely abroad without any U.S.-origin parts, components, or technology, and services provided entirely abroad—it need not involve a U.S. export or import. Confirming that the intended transaction does not violate the prohibition on proliferation activities is Step 15.

The Commerce Department expects exporters to know their customer. Step 18 involves deciding whether there are any "red flags" in the transaction. If there are red flags, the exporter is under a duty to inquire further, employees must be instructed how to handle red flags, and the exporter must refrain from the transaction or advise the Department of Commerce, Bureau of Industry and Security and wait for its guidance. The red flags are listed in Figure 5–7.

F. Ten General Prohibitions

Step 19 involves a review of the "Ten General Prohibitions" to confirm whether or not the intended export violates any of the prohibitions. Proceeding with the transaction with knowledge that a violation has occurred or is about to occur is itself prohibited. This prohibition includes selling, transferring, exporting, re-exporting, financing, ordering, buying, removing, concealing, storing, using, loaning, disposing of, transferring, transporting, forwarding, or otherwise servicing any item subject to the EAR.

The Ten General Prohibitions are as follows:

1. Exporting or re-exporting controlled items to listed countries without a license
2. Re-exporting and exporting from abroad foreign-made items incorporating more than a de minimis amount of controlled U.S. content
3. Re-exporting and exporting from abroad the foreign-produced direct product of U.S. technology and software to Cuba or a destination in Country Group D:1
4. Engaging in actions prohibited by Denial Orders
5. Exporting or re-exporting to prohibited end uses or end users
6. Exporting or re-exporting to embargoed destinations
7. Support of proliferation activities
8. Shipping goods through, transiting, or unloading in prohibited countries
9. Violating any order, terms, and conditions of the EAR or any license or exception
10. Proceeding with transactions with knowledge that a violation has occurred or is about to occur

If none of the Ten General Prohibitions will be violated by the intended export transaction, then no license is required (Step 20).

Figure 5–7. Red flags.

1. The customer or its address is similar to one of the parties found on the Commerce Department's [BIS's] list of denied persons.
2. The customer or purchasing agent is reluctant to offer information about the end use of the item.
3. The product's capabilities do not fit the buyer's line of business, such as an order for sophisticated computers for a small bakery.
4. The item ordered is incompatible with the technical level of the country to which it is being shipped, such as semiconductor manufacturing equipment being shipped to a country that has no electronics industry.
5. The customer is willing to pay cash for a very expensive item when the terms of sale would normally call for financing.
6. The customer has little or no business background.
7. The customer is unfamiliar with the product's performance characteristics but still wants the product.
8. Routine installation, training, or maintenance services are declined by the customer.
9. Delivery dates are vague, or deliveries are planned for out of the way destinations.
10. A freight forwarding firm is listed as the product's final destination.
11. The shipping route is abnormal for the product and destination.
12. Packaging is inconsistent with the stated method of shipment or destination.
13. When questioned, the buyer is evasive and especially unclear about whether the purchased product is for domestic use, for export, or for re-export.

G. License Exemptions and Exceptions

If an item is outside of the scope of the EAR, that is, it is not subject to the EAR, then, assuming that it is not subject to licensing by and the requirements of any other agency, it can be exported "No License Required" (NLR). In addition, an item that is subject to the EAR because it is a U.S. export or a certain type of re-export but is not specifically identified on the Commerce Control List (therefore falling into the basket category "EAR 99"), can also be exported NLR provided it is not subject to any of the Ten General Prohibitions. Finally, if the item is listed on the Commerce Control List but there is no "X" in the country box of ultimate destination, it may be exported NLR provided, again, that it does not violate any of the Ten General Prohibitions.

Assuming, however, that the foregoing analysis indicates that a license will be required for export, before applying for a license, the exporter can review the license exceptions designated in the EAR. Although there are numerous license exceptions specified, Step 21 involves reviewing a list of restrictions that apply to all license exceptions contained in Section 740.2 of the EAR. Again, assuming that none of those restrictions apply, the exporter may review each of the available license exceptions and assess whether or not the intended export transaction qualifies for one of the specific exceptions.

One large group of exceptions is based upon the Commerce Control List. As discussed above in regard to the Commerce Control List, identifying a product intended for export on the list will also show various types of license exceptions that may be available under the ECCN. For example, LVS (Low Value Shipments) may be available for small shipments, GBS may be available for shipments to Country Group B, CIV may be available for shipments to civil (nonmilitary) end users, TSR may be available for certain restricted technology and software destined for countries in Group B, and APP may be available for certain computers when exported to certain Computer Tier countries that are listed in Section 740.7. All the foregoing license exceptions are based on the Commerce Control List. Another exception, TMP, encompasses both temporary exports (TMP) and temporary imports (TSU). Likewise, RPL includes both replacement parts and service and repair exports. Exports to government end users may qualify for GOV. GFT covers gifts and humanitarian donations. BAG covers the export of commodities and software that are personal effects, household effects, vehicles, and tools of trade. (They must be owned by the individual and intended for and necessary and appropriate for the use of the individual. Such items must accompany the traveler, or in certain cases may be shipped within three months before or after the individual's departure.) AVS is an exception for the export of aircraft and vessels, and APR (Additional Permissive Re-exports) is a license exception for re-exports from Country Group A:1 destined for cooperating countries provided that: (1) the export is in compliance with the export control regulations of the exporting country and (2) that the reason for control is not NP, CB, MT, SS, or SI reasons. The export must be to either a country in Country Group B *that is not also included* in Country Group D:2, D:3, D:4, Cambodia, or Laos, and the commodity being re-exported is both controlled for national security reasons and not controlled for export to Country Group A:1; or a country in Country Group D:1 other than Cambodia, Laos, or North Korea and the commodity being re-exported is controlled for national security reasons.

In addition, certain commodities and software may be exempted from licensing under ENC if either the products are exported to countries other than those listed under E1 on the country chart, they are destined for private-sector end users who are headquartered in certain countries (Australia, Austria, Belgium, Bulgaria, Canada, Cyprus, Czech Republic, Denmark, Estonia, Finland, France, Germany, Greece, Hungary, Iceland, Ireland, Italy, Japan, Latvia, Lithuania, Luxembourg, Malta, Netherlands, New Zealand, Norway, Poland, Portugal, Romania, Slovakia, Slovenia, Spain, Sweden, Switzerland, Turkey, and United Kingdom), and the products are used for development or production of new products; or they are destined for foreign subsidiaries of U.S. companies. In other instances, the ENC exception may be used after a one-time review by BIS. Exports using this exception may require quarterly reporting to BIS.

One other exemption, for exports of agricultural products including food and beverages to Cuba, is available under the AGR exemption provided that the contract, financing, and export transportation meet certain requirements. However, it should be noted that no U.S.-origin good (or foreign-origin good with greater than 10%

U.S.-origin content) may be exported to Cuba from any other country using this exception. Recently, consumer communication devices (CCDs) was added for the export of computers, monitors, printers, modems, and cell phones to Cuba.

Analyzing whether an export qualifies for an exception comprises Steps 22 and 23. If the exporter believes that an exception applies, it must export in accordance with the terms and conditions of the exception (Steps 17 and 24).

In completing the export documentation, including specifically the Electronic Export Information, designation of NLR license exception is made under penalty of perjury and subjects any false or inaccurate designation to the penalties described in Section N below.

H. License Applications and Procedures

If the transaction is subject to the EAR, the product is on the Commerce Control List, there is an "X" in the Country Chart for the intended destination, and no exception applies, the exporter will have to apply for a license (see Figure 5–8). The first step in applying for a license is determining what documentation is required from the buyer.

1. Documentation From Buyer

If the item being exported is controlled for national security reasons, valued at over $50,000, and destined for one of the following countries, an import or end-user certificate from the buyer's government is required: Argentina, Australia, Austria, Belgium, Bulgaria, Czech Republic, Denmark, Finland, France, Germany, Greece, Hong Kong, Hungary, India, Republic of Ireland, Italy, Japan, Republic of Korea, Liechtenstein, Luxembourg, Netherlands, New Zealand, Norway, Pakistan, Poland, Portugal, Romania, Singapore, Slovakia, Spain, Sweden, Switzerland, Taiwan, Turkey, and United Kingdom. A list of government agencies issuing import certificates is contained in the EAR. For exports destined for the People's Republic of China, an import or end-user certificate is required for all transactions exceeding $50,000 involving items that require a license for any reason.

A sample of the form used for U.S. imports is shown in Figure 5–9. In a number of situations, no support documentation is required from the buyer to apply for an export license. These include exports and re-exports involving ultimate consignees located in any of the following countries: Bahamas, Barbados, Belize, Bermuda, Bolivia, Brazil, Canada, Chile, Colombia, Costa Rica, Dominican Republic, Ecuador, El Salvador, French Guiana, French West Indies, Greenland, Guatemala, Guyana, Haiti, Honduras, Jamaica, Leeward and Windward Islands, Mexico, Miquelon and Saint Pierre Islands, Netherlands Antilles, Nicaragua, Panama, Paraguay, Peru, Surinam, Trinidad and Tobago, Uruguay, and Venezuela. No support documentation is required for license applications where the ultimate consignee or purchaser is a foreign government or foreign government agency except for the People's Republic of China. Likewise, no support documentation is required for items exported for temporary exhibit, demonstration, or testing purposes; the application is filed by or on behalf of, a relief agency registered

(*Text continues on page 218.*)

Figure 5–8. Decision tree for exporters.

Steps for Using the EAR **Supplement No. 1 to Part 732**

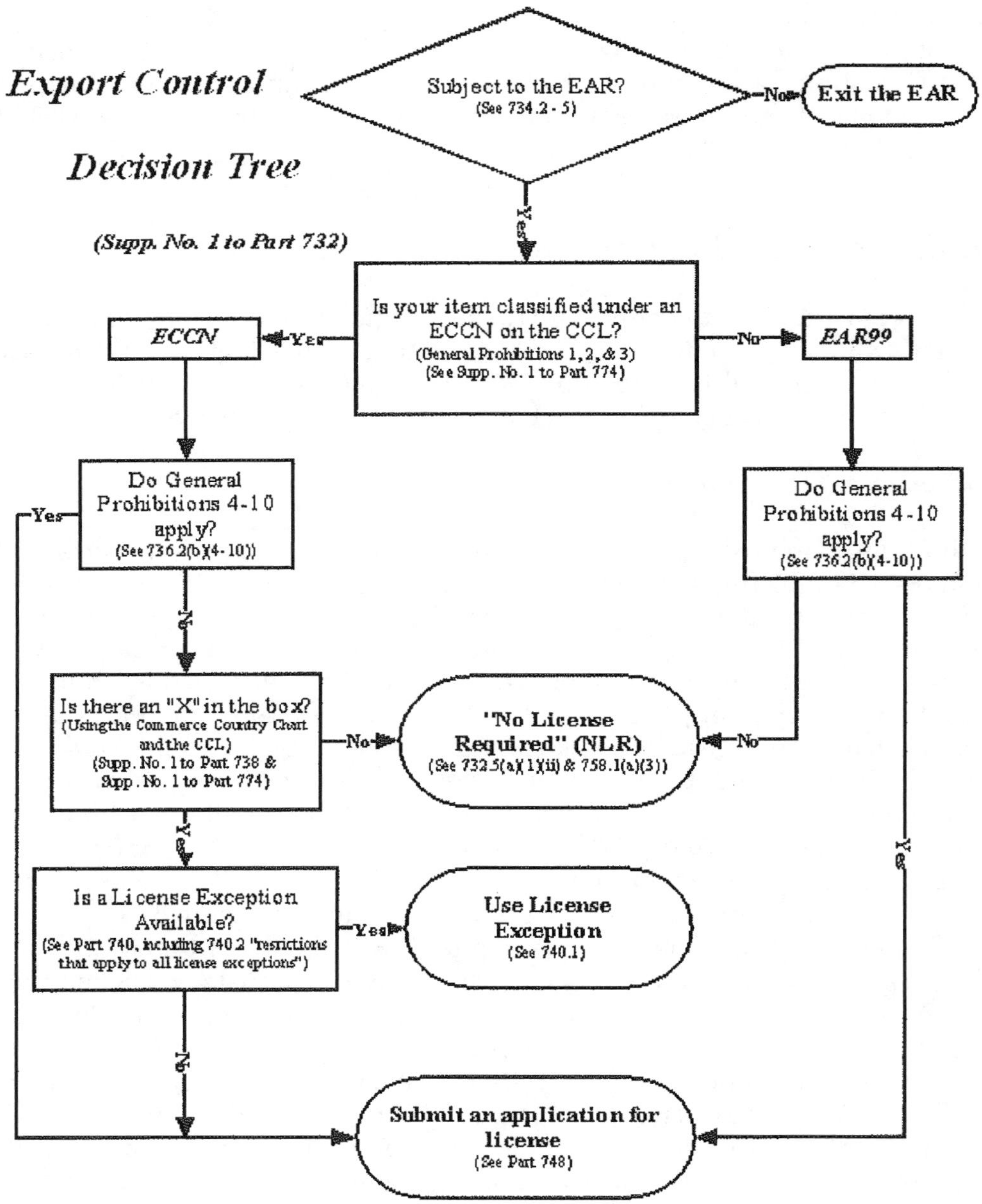

Figure 5–9. Import certificate (U.S.).

FORM BIS-645P/ATF-4522/DPS-53 (REV 8/02)

Form Approved: OMB No. 0694-0017 - Modele approuvé: OMB No. 0694-0017

U.S. DEPARTMENT OF COMMERCE
Bureau of Industry and Security
U.S. DEPARTMENT OF THE TREASURY
Bureau of Alcohol, Tobacco and Firearms
U.S. DEPARTMENT OF STATE
Office of Munitions Control

INTERNATIONAL IMPORT CERTIFICATE
(CERTIFICAT INTERNATIONAL D'IMPORTATION)

NOTE: **Read instructions on the reverse side before completing and submitting this form.** (Lire les instructions au verso avant de remplir et de presenter la présente formule.)

Certificate Number

1. U.S. **Importer/Importateur** (Name and address—Nom et adresse)

FOR U.S. GOVERNMENT USE (Réservé pour le Gouvernment des Etats-Unis)

2. **Exporter/Exportateur** (Name and address—Nom et adresse)

If this form has been approved by the Department of Commerce or the Department of State, it is not valid unless the official seal of the Department of Commerce, or the Department of State, appears in this space. If this form is approved by the Treasury Department, a seal is not required. (Si ce formulaire a été approuvé par le Ministère du Commerce, ou le Ministère des Affaires Etrangères, il n'est pas valide à moins qu'un sceau officiel du Ministère du Commerce ou du Ministère des Affaires Etrangères soit apposé sur le document. Si ce formulaire est approuvé par le Ministère des Finances, un sceau officiel n'est pas nècessaire.

3. Description of goods (Désignation de la Marchandise)	TSUS Anno. No. (Numéro de la liste)	Quantity (Quantité)	Value (Valeur) (FOB, CIF, etc.)

4. Representation and undertaking of U.S. importer or principal

The undersigned hereby represents that he has undertaken to import into the United States of America under a U.S. Consumption Entry or U.S. Warehouse Entry the commodities in quantities described above, or, if the commodities are not so imported into the United States of America, that he will not divert, transship, or reexport them to another destination except with explicit approval of the Department of Commerce, the Department of State, or the Department of the Treasury, as appropriate. The undersigned also undertakes to notify the appropriate Department immediately of any changes of fact or intention set forth herein. If a delivery verification is required, the undersigned also undertakes to obtain such vertification and make disposition of it in accordance with such requirement. **Any false statement willfully made in this declaration is punishable by fine and imprisonment.** (See experts from U.S. Code on reverse side.)

Déclaration et engagement de l'importateur ou du commettant des Etats-Unis

Le soussigné déclare par la présente qu'il a pris l'engagement d'importer aux Etats-Unis d'Amérique, en vertu d'une Déclaration américaine de Mise en Consommation, ou d'une Declaration américaine d'Entrée en entrepôt, la quantité de produits ci-dessus et que, dans le cas ou ces produits ne seraient pas ainsi importés aux Etats-Unis d'Amérique, il ne le détournera, ne les transbordera, ni les réexportera a destination d'un autre lieu, si ce n'est avec l'approbation explicite du Ministère du Commerce, du Ministère des Affaires Etrangères ou du Ministère des Finances, comme il est requis. Le soussigné prend également l'èngagement d'aviser le Ministère intéressé des Etats-Unis de tous changements survenus dans les actes ou les intentions énoncés dans la présente déclaration. Si demande est faite d'une confirmation de la livraison le soussignè prend également l'engagement d'obtenir cette confirmation et d'en disposer de la manière prescrite par cette demande. **Toute fausee déclaration faite intentionnellement espose l'auteur aux pénalités prévues par la loi.** (Voir Extrait du Code des Etats-Unis au verso.)

Type or Print (Prière d'écrire a la machine ou en caractères d imprimerie)

Name of Firm or Corporation (Nom de la Firme ou de la Societé)

Type or Print (Prière d'écrire a la machine ou en caractères d imprimerie)

Name and Title of Authorized Official (Nom et titre de l'agent ou employé autorisé)

Signature of Authorized Official (Signature de l'agent ou employé autorisé)

Date of Signature (Date de la signature)

This document ceases to be valid unless presented to the competent foreign authorities within six months from its date of issue. (Le présent document perd sa validité s'il n'est pas remis aux autorités étrangères compétentes dans un délai de six mois à compter de sa délivrance.)

No import certification may be obtained unless this International Import Certificate has been completed and filed with the appropriate U.S. Government agency (Department of Commerce: 50 U.S.C. app. §2411, E.O. 12214 15 C.F.R. §368; Department of the Treasury; 22 U.S.C. §2778, E.O. 11959, 27 C.F.R. §47; Department of State: 22 U.S.C. 2778, 2779, E.O. 11958, 22 C.F.R. §123). Information furnished herewith is subject to the provisions of Section 12(c) of the Export Administration Act of 1979, 50 U.S.C. app. 2411(c), and its unauthorized disclosure is prohibited by law.

FOR U.S. GOVERNMENT USE (Réservé au Gouvernement des Etats-Unis)

Certification: This is to certify that the above declaration was made to the U.S. Department of Commerce, State, or Treasury through the undersigned designated official thereof and a copy of this certification is placed in the official files.

Certification : Il est certifié par la présente que la déclaration ci-dessus a été faite au Ministère du Commerce, des Affaires Etrangères, ou des Finances des Etats-Unis par l'intermédiaire du fonctionnaire autorisé sousssigné de ce Ministère et qu'une copie de ce certificat a été conservée dans les archives officielles.

Signature____________________ **Date**__________

Designated Commerce, State, or Treasury Official (Fonctionnaire competent du Ministère du Commerce, d'Etat, ou du Trésor) Date

USCOMM DC 89-24414

ORIGINAL COPY

with the Advisory Committee on Voluntary Foreign Aid, U.S. Agency for International Development, for export to a member agency in the foreign government; the license is for the export or re-export of items for temporary exhibit, demonstration, or testing purposes; the license is for items controlled for short supply reasons; the license application is for the export or re-export of software or technology; the license application is submitted for certain encryption items; or the license application is submitted under the Special Comprehensive License procedures (see Section K below).

All other export transactions require a "Statement by Ultimate Consignee and Purchaser." This is a revised form, BIS-711. A sample is shown in Figure 5–10. No Statement by Ultimate Consignee and Purchaser is required where the transaction is valued at $5,000 or less. If the country of ultimate destination is listed in either Country Group D:2, D:3, or D:4, a copy of the Statement must be submitted with the license application. Otherwise, the Statement must be maintained in the records of the applicant for the license.

2. *License Application Form*

Figure 5–11 shows the online license application form through the Simplified Network Application Program-Revised (SNAP-R) system. All licenses must now be filed electronically through the SNAP-R system by a registered party, either the exporter or an agent for the exporter. The instructions for completion of the form are on the website at http://www.bis.doc.gov/snapr/snapr_exporter_user_manual.pdf. In addition to the general instructions, specific information must be provided for certain items or types of transactions ("unique license application requirements"). These include the export of chemicals, medicinals, and pharmaceuticals; communications intercepting devices; computers; telecommunications, information security items, and related equipment; gift parcels; goods transiting the United States; goods transiting other countries; nuclear nonproliferation items and end uses; numerical control devices; motion control boards; numerically controlled machine tools; dimensional inspection machines; direct numerical control systems; specially designed assemblies and specially designed software; parts, components, and materials incorporated abroad in foreign-made products; ship stores and plane stores, supplies, and equipment; regional stability controlled items; re-exports; robots; short supply controlled items; technology; temporary exports or re-exports; exports of chemicals controlled for CW reasons by ECCN 1C350 to countries not listed on Supplement No. 2 to Part 745 of the EAR; encryption review requests; foreign national review requests; aircraft and vessels on temporary sojourn; and in-country transfers.

The specific instructions for such items and transactions are contained in the EAR. Completion of the license application form comprises Steps 25 and 26.

3. *Procedures*

As indicated earlier, the license application form must be filed electronically through the SNAP-R program. Once it is filed, the registered party will receive email notices that there are messages from BIS on the SNAP-R web site when further action

(*Text continues on page 224.*)

Figure 5–10. Statement by ultimate consignee and purchaser.

FORM **BIS-711** FORM APPROVED UNDER OMB CONTROL NO. 0694-0021, 0694-0093	U.S. DEPARTMENT OF COMMERCE BUREAU OF INDUSTRY AND SECURITY Information furnished herewith is subject to the provisions of Section 12(c) of the Export Administration Act of 1979, as amended, 50 U.S.C. app 2411(c) and its unauthorized disclosure is prohibited by law.	DATE RECEIVED (Leave Blank)

STATEMENT BY ULTIMATE CONSIGNEE AND PURCHASER

1. ULTIMATE CONSIGNEE	CITY	
ADDRESS LINE 1	COUNTRY	
ADDRESS LINE 2	POSTAL CODE	TELEPHONE OR FAX

2. DISPOSITION OR USE OF ITEMS BY ULTIMATE CONSIGNEE NAMED IN BLOCK 1

We certify that the items: *(left mouse click in the appropriate box below)*

A. ☐ Will be used by us (as capital equipment) in the form in which received in a manufacturing process in the country named in Block 1 and will not be reexported or incorporated into an end product.

B. ☐ Will be processed or incorporated by us into the following product (s) ____________________
to be manufactured in the country named in Block 1 for distribution in ____________________

C. ☐ Will be resold by us in the form in which received in the country named in Block 1 for use or consumption therein.
The specific end-use by my customer will be____________________

D. ☐ Will be reexported by us in the form in which received to ____________________

E. ☐ Other (describe fully)____________________

NOTE: If BOX (D) is checked, acceptance of this form by the Bureau of Industry and Security as a supporting document for license applications shall not be construed as an authorization to reexport the items to which the form applies unless specific approval has been obtained from the Bureau of Industry and Security for such export.

3. NATURE OF BUSINESS OF ULTIMATE CONSIGNEE NAMED IN BLOCK 1

A. The nature of our usual business is____________________

B. Our business relationship with the U.S. exporter is ____________________

and we have had this business relationship for ____ year(s).

4. ADDITIONAL INFORMATION

5. ASSISTANCE IN PREPARING STATEMENT

STATEMENT OF ULTIMATE CONSIGNEE AND PURCHASER

We certify that all of the facts contained in this statement are true and correct to the best of our knowledge and we do not know of any additional facts which are inconsistent with the above statement. We shall promptly send a supplemental statement to the U.S. Exporter, disclosing any change of facts or intentions set forth in this statement which occurs after the statement has been prepared and forwarded, except as specifically authorized by the U.S. Export Administration Regulations (15 CFR parts 730-774), or by prior written approval of the Bureau of Industry and Security, we will not reexport, resell, or otherwise dispose of any items approved on a license supported by this statement (1) to any country not approved for export as brought to our attention by means of a bill of lading, commercial invoice, or any other means, or(2) to any person if we know that it will result directly or indirectly, in disposition of the items contrary to the representations made in this statement or contrary to Export Administration Regulations.

6. SIGNATURE OF OFFICIAL OF ULTIMATE CONSIGNEE	**7.** NAME OF PURCHASER	
NAME OF OFFICIAL	SIGNATURE OF PURCHASER	
TITLE OF OFFICIAL	NAME OF OFFICIAL	
DATE *(mmmm,dd,yyyy)*	TITLE OF OFFICIAL	
CERTIFICATION FOR USE OF U.S. EXPORTER - We certify that no corrections, additions, or alterations were made on this form by us after the form was signed by the (ultimate consignee)(purchaser).	DATE *(mmmm,dd,yyyy)*	
8. NAME OF EXPORTER	SIGNATURE OF PERSON AUTHORIZED TO CERTIFY FOR EXPORTER	
NAME OF PERSON SIGNING THIS DOCUMENT	TITLE OF PERSON SIGNING THIS DOCUMENT	DATE *(mmmm,dd,yyyy)*

We acknowledge that the making of any false statements or concealment of any material fact in connection with this statement may result in imprisonment or fine, or both and denial, in whole or in part, of participation in U.S. exports and reexports.

Public reporting burden for this collection of information is estimated to average 15 minutes per response plus one minute for recordkeeping, including the time for reviewing instruments, searching existing data sources, gathering and maintaining the data needed, and completing and reviewing the collection of information. Send comments regarding this burden estimate or any other aspect of this collection of information, including suggestions for reducing this burden, to the Director of Administration, Room 3889, Bureau of Industry and Security, U.S. Department of Commerce, Washington, DC 20230, and to the Office of Management and Budget Paperwork Reduction Project (0694-0021, 0694-0093), Washington, D.C. 20503. Notwithstanding any other provision of law, no person is obligated to respond to nor shall a person be subject to a penalty for failure to comply with a collection of information subject to the Paperwork Reduction Act unless that collection of information displays a currently valid OMB Control Number.

Figure 5–11. SNAP-R application.

Edit Work Item | Page 1 of 4

SNAP- R

SNAP-R HOME
CREATE WORK ITEM
LIST WORK ITEMS
SEARCH WORK ITEMS
SEARCH DOCUMENTS
VIEW MESSAGES
MANAGE USER PROFILE
HELP
LOGOUT

Export License Application | BIS-748P
Reference Number: ABC1111 | Status: DRAFT

Edit Export License Application

Please click **Save Draft** to save your unfinished work. Required fields are marked with an asterisk (*). The numbers [?] next to the fields are only for reference to the paper version of this form and do not need to be considered to complete this application.
To delete this Work Item: Delete Work Item

To grant or delete rights to others to view, edit, or submit this Work Item: Manage User Rights [?]

[Collapse All]

Contact Information*

Reference Number*(AAA9999) [?] ABC1111
1. Contact Person (First, Last)* [?]
2. Telephone Number* (999-999-9999) [?]
3. Fax Number (999-999-9999) [?]
Email [?]
4. Creation Date [?] 04/18/2009
5. Type Of Application Export License Application

Save Draft

Document Checklist

6. Documents submitted with application [?]
Export Items (BIS-748P-A) [?]
End Users (BIS-748P-B) [?]
☐ BIS-711
☐ Import/End-User Certificate
☐ Technical Specification
☐ Letter of Explanation
☐ Foreign Availability
☐ Other

7. Documents on file with applicant [?]
☐ BIS-711
☐ Letter of Assurance
☐ Import/End-User Certificate
☐ Nuclear Certification
☐ Other

Save Draft

License Information

9. Special Purpose [?]
10. Resubmission ACN [?]
11. Replacement License Number [?]
13. Import Certificate Country [?] Please Select
Import Certificate Number

Save Draft

Applicant Information* [?]
* Required field
14. CIN (Applicant ID)*
Applicant*
Address Line 1*
Address Line 2
City*

https://snapr.bis.doc.gov/snapr/exp/WorkItem/168297?action=Edit%20Work%20Item | 4/18/2009

Figure 5–11. *(continued)*

Edit Work Item Page 2 of 4

State/Province* (Required for US address) [ ]
Postal Code* [ ]
Country* Please Select
EIN [ ]
Save Draft

Other Party Information
* Required field (only if entering an Other Party). Otherwise leave blank.
15. Other Party ID
Other Party*
Address Line 1*
Address Line 2
City*
State/Province* (Required for US address)
Postal Code*
Country*
Telephone or Fax* [ ]
Save Draft

Purchaser Information
* Required field (only if entering a Purchaser). Otherwise leave blank.
16. Purchaser* [ ]
Address Line 1* [ ]
Address Line 2 [ ]
City* [ ]
Postal Code [ ]
Country* Please Select
Telephone or Fax [ ]
Save Draft

Intermediate Consignee Information
* Required field (only if entering an Intermediate Consignee). Otherwise leave blank.
17. Intermediate Consignee* [ ]
Address Line 1* [ ]
Address Line 2 [ ]
City* [ ]
Postal Code [ ]
Country* Please Select
Telephone or Fax [ ]
Save Draft

Ultimate Consignee Information*
* Required field
18. Ultimate Consignee* [ ]
Address Line 1* [ ]
Address Line 2 [ ]
City* [ ]
Postal Code [ ]
Country* Please Select
Telephone or Fax [ ]
Save Draft

https://snapr.bis.doc.gov/snapr/exp/WorkItem/168297?action=Edit%20Work%20Item 4/18/2009

Figure 5–11. *(continued)*

Edit Work Item

Page 3 of 4

End User Information

Enter information for a new End User

* Required field (only if entering an End User). Otherwise leave blank.

19. End User*

Address Line 1*

Address Line 2

City*

Postal Code

Country* Please Select

Telephone or Fax

Add End User

Specific End Use*

21. Specific End Use*

Save Draft

Export Item Information*

Enter information for a new Export Item

22. a. ECCN* Please Select

b. APP(9.9999999)

c. Product/Model Number

d. CCATS Number

e. Quantity* 0

f. Units each

g. Unit Price

h. Total Price* 0.0

i. Manufacturer

j. Technical Description*

Add Export Item

Total Application Dollar Value

23. Total Application Dollar Value $0.00

Additional Information

24. Additional Information

https://snapr.bis.doc.gov/snapr/exp/WorkItem/168297?action=Edit%20Work%20Item 4/18/2009

Figure 5–11. *(continued)*

Save Draft

Documents attached to application

To upload a new supporting document or view or delete attached supporting documents: View and Manage Supporting Documents

Title	Author	Type
There are no documents attached.		

Please remember to **Save Draft** before leaving this form to avoid losing work

Save Draft | Check For Errors | Preview Work Item to Submit

FOIA | Disclaimer | Privacy Policy Statement | Information Quality
Department of Commerce | Contact Us

is required or when it is available. If the license application is not complete, it will be returned without action ("RWA"). If the Department of Commerce intends to deny the license ("ITD"), it will inform the applicant, specifying the reasons, and permit the applicant to respond before finally denying the license application. In some cases, the Commerce Department can hold the application without action ("HWA"). If the exporter desires to know the status of a license application, it can telephone the BIS's system for tracking export license applications ("STELA").

When the license is issued, the registered party prints the license from the SNAP-R web site. The licenses will carry a license number and validation date (a sample is shown in Figure 5–12). Usually the license will be issued for a period of two years. The license number must be entered in the Electronic Export Information form filed through the Automated Export System for export clearance. When a license has been issued, the export must be carried out in accordance with the terms and conditions of the license (Step 17).

I. Re-Exports

Items that originated in the United States and were originally exported with or without a license continue to potentially be subject to the EAR. Step 3 requires a person engaging in a re-export transaction to determine whether the re-export can be made without a license, whether a license exception applies, or whether a license must be obtained.

As explained above, if a transaction is subject to the EAR, it is necessary to assess whether or not the transaction is also prohibited by one of the Ten General Prohibitions. General Prohibition 1 includes re-export of controlled items to listed countries; 2 includes re-export from abroad of foreign-made items incorporating more than the de minimis amount of controlled U.S. content (parts and components of re-exports); 3 includes re-exports from abroad of the foreign-produced direct product of U.S. technology and software; 4 includes re-export to prohibited end uses or end users; and 5 includes re-exports to embargoed destinations without a license.

J. Export Documentation and Record-Keeping

In order to complete the exportation, whether a license is required or not, it is necessary for the exporter to complete certain export documentation and maintain certain records. The EAR requires an exporter to complete the Electronic Export Information filing through the Automated Export System declaring the eligibility of the export. The exporter will be required to enter "NLR" when no license is required; the license exception symbol where the export qualifies for a license exception, for example, GBS; or the license number where a license has been obtained. In general, the ECCN number must also be shown in EEI.

In addition to the Electronic Export Information, a destination control statement must be entered on all copies of the bill of lading, the air waybill, and the commercial

(*Text continues on page 227.*)

Figure 5–12. Sample export license.

EXPORT LICENSE
VALIDATED: MAR 22 2008
EXPIRES: MAR 31 2010

UNITED STATES DEPARTMENT OF COMMERCE
BUREAU OF INDUSTRY AND SECURITY
P.O. Box 273, Ben Franklin Station
Washington, DC 20044

THIS LICENSE AUTHORIZES THE LICENSEE TO CARRY OUT THE EXPORT TRANSACTION DESCRIBED ON THE LICENSE (INCLUDING ALL ATTACHMENTS). IT MAY NOT BE TRANSFERRED WITHOUT PRIOR WRITTEN APPROVAL OF THE OFFICE OF EXPORT LICENSING. THIS LICENSE HAS BEEN GRANTED IN RELIANCE ON REPRESENTATIONS MADE BY THE LICENSEE AND OTHERS IN CONNECTION WITH THE APPLICATION FOR EXPORT AND IS EXPRESSLY SUBJECT TO ANY CONDITIONS STATED ON THE LICENSE, AS WELL AS ALL APPLICABLE EXPORT CONTROL LAWS, REGULATIONS, RULES, AND ORDERS. THIS LICENSE IS SUBJECT TO REVISION, SUSPENSION, OR REVOCATION WITHOUT PRIOR NOTICE.

APPLICANT REFERENCE NUMBER:

PURCHASER:

ULTIMATE CONSIGNEE:

INTERMEDIATE CONSIGNEE:

APPROVED END USER(S):

;A

COMMODITIES:

QTY	DESCRIPTION	ECCN	TOTAL PRICE
30		1C107	
:			
180		1C107	

(*continues*)

Figure 5–12. *(continued)*

EXPORT LICENSE
VALIDATED: MAR 22 2008
EXPIRES: MAR 31 2010

UNITED STATES DEPARTMENT OF COMMERCE
BUREAU OF INDUSTRY AND SECURITY
P.O. Box 273, Ben Franklin Station
Washington, DC 20044

---

8 1C107

TOTAL:

THE EXPORT ADMINISTRATION REGULATIONS REQUIRE YOU TO TAKE THE FOLLOWING ACTIONS WHEN EXPORTING UNDER THE AUTHORITY OF THIS LICENSE.

A. RECORD THE EXPORT COMMODITY CONTROL NUMBER IN THE BLOCK PROVIDED ON EACH SHIPPER'S EXPORT DECLARATION (SED).

B. RECORD YOUR VALIDATED LICENSE NUMBER IN THE BLOCK PROVIDED ON EACH SED.

C. PLACE A DESTINATION CONTROL STATEMENT ON ALL BILLS OF LADING, AIRWAY BILLS, AND COMMERCIAL INVOICES.

RIDERS AND CONDITIONS:

1. STATED END USE ONLY. NOT FOR USE IN MISSILE, SPACE LAUNCH VEHICLES, UNMANNED AIR VEHICLES, RESEARCH, DEVELOPMENT, PRODUCTION OR ANY MISSILE RELAT ED END USES.

2. APPLICANT MUST INFORM CONSIGNEE OF ALL LICENSE CONDITIONS.

3. NO RESALE, TRANSFER, OR REEXPORT OF THE ITEMS LISTED ON THIS LICENSE IS AUTHORIZED WITHOUT PRIOR AUTHORIZATION BY THE U.S. GOVERNMENT.

invoice for an export. If the export requires a license; the export is made under the license exceptions GBS, CIV, LVS, RPL, or TEMP (TMP, TSU, ENC, AGR); or the export is made under NLR (if the Reason for Control of the item as stated on the entry in the Commerce Control List is NS or NP), at a minimum, the destination control statement "These commodities, technology or software were exported from the United States in accordance with the Export Administration Regulations. Diversion contrary to law is prohibited" must be entered on such documents.

An additional document that may be required is a delivery verification (see Figures 5–13 and 5–14). When an export is being made to a country where an import certificate issued by the government of a foreign country is required for application for the export license, the Department of Commerce will on a selective basis require the exporter to obtain a delivery verification. If verification of delivery is required, the requirement will appear as a condition on the face of the license when issued. The list of countries issuing import certificates and delivery verification is contained in Supplement Number 4 to part 748 of the EAR.

Where an Electronic Export Information was filed incorrectly or the transaction is altered, a corrected Electronic Export Information must be filed with the customs director at the port of exportation.

Exporters are required to maintain the originals of all documents pertaining to export transaction, including license applications, memoranda, notes, correspondence, contracts, invitations to bid, books of account, and financial records. If the exporter complies with certain specific requirements, the exporter may maintain the records electronically. The system must be able to record and reproduce all marks, information, and other characteristics of the original record, including both sides of the paper; the system must preserve the initial image and record all changes, who made them, and when they were made; and this information must be stored in such a manner that none of it may be altered once it is initially recorded. The records must be maintained for a period of five years from the time of the export from the United States, any known re-export, or any other termination of the transaction. The record-keeping requirement extends to records maintained outside the United States if they pertain to any U.S. export transaction or any re-export. Any person subject to the jurisdiction of the United States may be required to produce the records in response to an inquiry from the Department of Commerce. (In some cases, a request for records located abroad may conflict with the laws and regulations of a foreign country.)

K. Special Comprehensive Licenses

Formerly, under the previous EAR, an exporter could apply for a Distribution License, a Service Supply License (SSL), or a Project License. Under the new EAR, all such licenses are combined as a Special Comprehensive License (SCL). Ordinary licenses granted by the Bureau of Industry and Security cover only single export transactions. With an SCL, multiple exports and re-exports can be authorized. The SCL authorizes specific exports and re-exports that are otherwise prohibited by General

(*Text continues on page 230.*)

Figure 5–13. Notification of delivery verification requirement.

Form Approved: OMB No. 0694-0016

FORM BIS-648P *(formerly form BXA-648P)*
(REV.4-03)

U.S. DEPARTMENT OF COMMERCE
BUREAU OF INDUSTRY AND SECURITY

NOTIFICATION OF DELIVERY VERIFICATION REQUIREMENT

Date *(mmmm,dd,yyyy)*	
Export License No.	
Applicant's Reference No.	
International Import Certificate No.	

Information furnished herewith is subject to the provisions of Section 12(c) of the Export Administration Act of 1979. 50 U.S.C app. 2411 (c), and its unauthorized disclosure is prohibited by law. Your failure to complete and return this form along with required delivery verification(s) may subject you to administrative action under the Export Administration Act.

IMPORTANT NOTICE

LICENSEE: You are required to provide the Bureau of Industry and Security with a document verifying the delivery of each shipment made against the attached license. For your information, instructions on what you must do about obtaining and submitting delivery verification documents will be found of the last page of this form.

AGENT OR FREIGHT FORWARDER: When this form BIS-648P is attached to a license which has been forwarded by the Bureau of Industry and Security to an agent or freight forwarder of the licensee, it is the responsibility of the agent or freight forwarder to notify the licensee that verification of delivery is required for exports made against the license.

Select item 1, 2, or 3, as applicable, using the letter 'X', and complete the item. The ORIGINAL of this form must be returned to the Bureau of Industry and Security, P.O. Box 273, Washington, DC 20044, as soon as you have received all delivery verification documents for shipments made against the attached license. (See paragraph A3 on the back of the Duplicate Copy.)

1. ☐ The total quantity authorized for export by this license has been exported and all delivery verification documents are attached hereto.

2. ☐ A part of the quantity authorized for export by this license will not be exported. Delivery verification documents covering all commodities exported are attached hereto.

3. ☐ No shipment has been made against this license and none is contemplated.

4. The License:

a. ☐ is returned herewith for cancellation.

b. ☐ was returned to the Bureau of Industry and Security as required by 386.2(d) of the Export Administration Regulations.

Remarks:

Print or type name of Licensee	Print or type name and title of authorized representative
Date signed *(mmmm,dd,yyyy)*	Signature of authorized representative

(See instructions on page 3)

Figure 5–14. Delivery verification certificate.

Form Approved: OMB No. 0694-0016, 0694-0093

FORM BIS-647-P
(REV.4/03)

U.S. DEPARTMENT OF COMMERCE
Bureau of Industry and Security

DELIVERY VERIFICATION CERTIFICATE

Public reporting burden for this collection of information is estimated to average 15 minutes per response,, including the time for reviewing instructions, searching existing data sources, gathering and maintaining the data needed, and completing and reviewing the collection of information. Send comments regarding this burden estimate or any other aspect of this collection of information, including suggestions for reducing the burden, to the Director of Administration, room-3889, Bureau of Industry and Security, U.S. Department of Commerce, Washington, D.C. 20230; and to the Office of Management and Budget Paperwork Reduction Project (0694-0016, 0694-0093) Washington, DC 20503.

Notwithstanding any other provision of law, no person is required to respond to nor shall a person be subject to a penalty for failure to comply with a collection of information subject to the requirements of the Paperwork Reduction Act unless that collection of information displays a currently valid OMB Control Number.

Instructions- When required to obtain a delivery verification, the U.S. Importer shall submit this form in duplicate, to the Customs Office. U.S. importer is required to complete all items on this form except the portion to be completed by the U.S. Customs Service. The Customs Office will certify a Delivery Verification Certificate only after the import has been delivered to the U.S. importer. The duly certified form shall then be dispatched by the U.S. importer to the foreign exporter or otherwise disposed of in accordance with instructions of the exporting country.

No delivery verification may be obtained unless a completed application form has been received. (50 U.S.C App § 2401 et seq.,15 C.F.R. §748)

EXPORTER *(Name and Address)*

Name

Address

City *State/Country* *Zip/ Postal Code*

This certification applied to the goods described below, shown on U.S. Department of Commerce International Import Certificate

No.__________

ARRIVED *(Name of Port)*

DATE OF ARRIVAL *(mm/dd/yyyy)*

IMPORTER *(Name and Address)*

Name

Address

City *State/Country* *Zip/ Postal Code*

NAME OF SHIP, AIRCRAFT, OR CARRIER *(Include numbers on bills of lading, airways bills, etc.)*

DESCRIPTION OF GOODS	QUANTITY	VALUE *(FOB, CIR, etc)*

TO BE COMPLETED BY U.S. CUSTOMS SERVICE

REGION NO.

(Custom's Seal)

CERTIFICATION-It is hereby certified that the importer has produced evidence that the goods specified above have been delivered and brought under the Export Administration Regulations of the United States.

Signature

Date

ENTRY	☐ WAREHOUSE	☐ CONSUMPTION	NUMBER	DATE

Prohibitions 1, 2, and 3. All items subject to the EAR are eligible for export under an SCL except the following:

1. Items controlled for missile technology reasons that are identified by the letters MT in the applicable Reason for Control paragraph of the Commerce Control List
2. Items controlled by ECCN 1C351, 1C352, 1C353, 1C354, 1C991, 1E001, 2B352, 2E001, 2E002, and 2E301 on the Commerce Control List that can be used in the production of chemical and biological weapons
3. Items controlled by ECCN 1C350, 1C355, 1D390, 2B350, and 2B351 on the Commerce Control List that can be used in the production of chemical weapons, precursors, and chemical warfare agents to destinations listed in Country Group D:3
4. Items controlled for short supply reasons that are identified by the letters SS in the applicable Reason for Control paragraph on the Commerce Control List
5. Items controlled for EI reasons on the Commerce Control List
6. Maritime (civil) nuclear propulsion systems or associated design or production
7. Communications intercepting devices and related software and technology controlled by ECCN 5A980, 5D980, or 5E980 on the Commerce Control List
8. Hot section technology for the development, production, or overhaul of commercial aircraft engines controlled under ECCN 9E003.a.1 through a.12.f and related controls
9. Items specifically identified as ineligible by the Bureau of Industry and Security on the SCL
10. Additional items consistent with international commitments

Shipments under an SCL may be made to all countries specified in the SCL except Cuba, Iran, Iraq, North Korea, Sudan, and Syria and other countries that the Bureau of Industry and Security may designate on a case-by-case basis. Servicing items owned or controlled by or under the lease of entities in the foregoing countries is also prohibited.

In order to apply for an SCL, an exporter must have an internal control program (ICP), and the SCL consignee must assure that any exports or re-exports are not made contrary to the Export Administration Regulations. The exporter files the regular license application, through the SNAP-R filing. In addition, the applicant must submit a comprehensive narrative statement containing the information specified in the EAR; a Form BIS-752, "Statement by Consignee in Support of Special Comprehensive License"; Form BIS-752-A, "Export Territories"; certain certifications by the consignee on its company letterhead; and the description of its ICP. The ICP must state the procedures and safeguards that have been put in place by the exporter and the consignee to ensure compliance with the U.S. export and re-export control laws. It must address thirteen specific items specified in the EAR. The consignee must agree to maintain records and make them available for inspection by the U.S. Department of Commerce. The EAR contains additional instructions for completing all these forms.

An SCL, when issued, is valid for four years and may be extended for an additional four years. Certain changes in the export relationship or procedures require prior written approval from the Bureau of Industry and Security, whereas other changes must be reported to the Bureau of Industry and Security within thirty days after their occurrence.

L. Technology, Software, and Technical Assistance Exports

A significant portion of the EAR is concerned with the export of technology, software, and technical assistance. Within each category of the Commerce Control List, there is a "group" that includes software ("D") and technology ("E") pertaining to that category. Such exports would normally take place pursuant to a license agreement between the U.S. licensor and the foreign licensee. However, in fulfillment of a license agreement, tangible documents as well as oral information may be communicated. The definition of "export" includes an actual shipment or transmission of items subject to the EAR out of the United States and, with regard to the export of technology or software, includes any "release" of technology or software subject to the EAR in a foreign country or any release of technology or source code subject to the EAR to a foreign national, in the United States or in another country. The release of technology or software includes visual inspection by foreign nationals of U.S.-origin equipment and facilities, the oral exchange of information in the United States or abroad, or the application to situations abroad of personal knowledge or technical experience acquired in the United States. This is considered a "deemed export." "Technology" is defined as information necessary for the development, production, or use of a product. Information may take the form of "technical data" or "technical assistance." Controlled technology is defined in the General Technology Note (Supplement Number 1 to part 774). Technical data may include blueprints, plans, diagrams, models, formulas, tables, engineering designs, specifications, manuals, and instructions written or recorded on other media or devices such as disk, tape, or read-only memories. Technical assistance may take the form of instruction, skills training, working knowledge, or consulting services.

Two steps in analyzing the scope of the EAR, Step 2 and Step 6, pertain to technology. Step 2 exempts from control of the EAR publicly available technology and software. This is both for exports and for re-exports. Publicly available technology and software includes that which has already been published or will be published, which includes software generally accessible to the interested public in any form either free or at a price that does not exceed the cost of reproduction and distribution; patents and open, published patent applications; information readily available at libraries open to the public; and/or information released at an "open" conference meeting, seminar, or trade show. The EAR contains questions and answers further developing and clarifying what type of technology and software is publicly available. It also includes information arising from "fundamental" (as opposed to "proprietary") and educational research. Step 6 of the EAR pertains to foreign-made items produced with certain U.S. technology. If the foreign-produced item is described in an entry on the Commerce Control List, and the Country Chart requires a license for a direct export from the United States for national security reasons, or if the destination is Cuba or a country in Group D:1 and the technology or software that was used to create the foreign-produced direct product required a written assurance from the licensee as a supporting document for the license or as a condition to utilizing license exception TSR, a license is required. This restriction also applies to direct products of a complete plant. In addition to the exemption for publicly available technology and software, several exceptions from license requirements are also available. License exception TSR (Technology and Software under Restriction) permits exports and re-exports of technology and software when so specified on the specific entry in the Commerce Control List and the export is to destinations in Country Group B. The exporter must receive written assurances from the consignee prior to export that the technology or software will not be released to a national in Country Group D:1 or E:2 and will not export to those same countries the direct product of the technology if the product is subject to national security controls.

Another license exception, TSU (Technology and Software Unrestricted), permits the export of "operating technology and software" (OTS) and "sales technology" (STS). Operating technology is the minimum technology necessary for the installation, operation, maintenance (checking), and repair of products lawfully exported.

It must be in object code and exported to the destination to which the equipment for which it is required has been legally exported. Sales technology is data supporting a prospective or actual quotation, bid, or offer to sell, lease, or otherwise supply any item. It does not include information that discloses the design, production, or manufacture of the item being offered for sale. Software updates that are intended for and are limited to correction of errors are also authorized. Finally, "mass market" software may be exported under this exception. Generally, this is software sold from stock at retail selling points or by mail order and designed for installation by the user without further substantial support by the supplier.

License exception TMP authorizes temporary exports. Within that exception is included exports of "beta test" software (BETA). This pertains only to software that the producer intends to market to the general public, is provided free of charge or at a price that does not exceed the cost of reproduction and distribution, does not require further substantial support from the supplier, and for which the importer provides a certification that it will not be transferred. The software must be returned or destroyed within thirty days after completion of the test.

An Interpretation has been issued by the Bureau of Industry and Security for the purposes of clarifying what technology and software may be exported to Country Group D:1. Under the controls relating to end users and end use, technology pertaining to maritime nuclear propulsion plants may not be exported without a license.

M. Validated End-User Program

The Validated End-User program (VEU) allows for the export, re-export, and transfer to validated end users of any eligible items that are destined to a specific eligible destination without a license. Currently only China and India are eligible under the

VEU program. Companies in the country of destination request authorization to become a VEU. The Office of Exporter Services reviews the companies for such things as the entity's exclusive engagement in civil end-use activities, its compliance with U.S. export controls, the ability to comply with the VEU requirements, the entity's agreement to on-site reviews by U.S. government officials, and the entity's relationship with both U.S. and foreign companies. Items that are controlled under the Missile Technology (MT) or Crime Control (CC) reasons are ineligible for authorization under this program. In addition, there are end-use restrictions to the VEU's own facility in the eligible destination. There are certification, record-keeping, reporting, and review requirements. U.S. subsidiaries in these destinations are ideal candidates for the VEU program.

N. Violations and Penalties

For violation of the Export Administration Act, penalties can be assessed of up to $1 million or five times the value of the exports involved, whichever is greater, and/or violators can be imprisoned for up to ten years. The Export Administration Act expired many years ago and to date has not been renewed; however, the president annually authorizes application of the EAA regulations under the International Emergency Economic Powers Act (IEEPA). Penalties under IEEPA were raised in 2007 to $250,000 per violation or twice the amount of the transaction in question. In addition, export privileges can be denied for up to ten years. Since these are extremely serious penalties, it is important to make every effort not to violate the law, even accidentally. Exports in violation of the law may be seized by the U.S. Customs and Border Protection. A Customs Export Enforcement Subpoena is shown in Figure 5–15. If the exporter, its freight forwarder, or any other of the exporter's agents receives such a subpoena or even an informal inquiry from Customs or the Office of Export Enforcement, Bureau of Industry and Security, the exporter should take it very seriously and make sure that it is in compliance with the law before responding.

O. Munitions and Arms Exports

Under the Arms Export Control Act, exports and imports of defense articles and services without a license are prohibited. Export licenses are issued by the Department of State, Directorate of Defense Trade Controls (DDTC), under the International Traffic in Arms Regulations. Import licenses are issued by the Department of Justice, Bureau of Alcohol, Tobacco and Firearms. Items that are inherently military in character or that have substantial military applicability and have been specifically designed or modified for military purposes are included in the U.S. Munitions List.

Prior to exporting any such item, the exporter must register with the DDTC on Form DS-2032 (see Figure 5–16), which must be accompanied by a Transmittal Letter (see Figures 5–17 and 5–18) attesting to the fact that none of the officers of the registrant nor any member of the board of directors has ever been indicted for or

(*Text continues on page 235.*)

Figure 5–15. Customs export enforcement subpoena.

CUSTOMS EXPORT ENFORCEMENT SUBPOENA

1 TO (Name, Address, City, State, ZIP)	DEPARTMENT OF THE TREASURY UNITED STATES CUSTOMS SERVICE **SUBPOENA** TO APPEAR AND/OR PRODUCE RECORDS

By the service of this subpoena upon you, YOU ARE HEREBY SUMMONED AND REQUIRED TO:

(A) ☐ APPEAR before the Customs officer named in Block 2 below at the place, date, and time indicated, to testify and give information.

(B) ☐ PRODUCE the records (including statements, declarations, and other documents) indicated in Block 3 below, before the Customs officer named in Block 2 at the place, date, and time indicated.

Your testimony and/or the production of the indicated records is required in connection with an investigation or inquiry to insure compliance with: 1) the Export Administration Act of 1979, as amended; 2) the Arms Export Control Act; and/or 3)____________________; and to determine liability for any penalty, forfeiture, or other sanction arising thereunder.

Failure to comply with this subpoena will render you liable to proceedings in a U.S. District Court to enforce compliance with this subpoena as well as other sanctions.

2 (A) NAME, TITLE, ADDRESS, AND TELEPHONE NUMBER OF CUSTOMS OFFICER BEFORE WHOM YOU ARE TO APPEAR	(B) DATE (C) TIME

3 RECORDS REQUIRED TO BE PRODUCED FOR INSPECTION

Issued under authority of: section 12(a) of the Export Administration of 1979, as amended, 50 USC, App. 2411(a)(1); the Arms Export Control Act, 22 USC 2778(e); or ____________________.

4 NAME OF PERSON AUTHORIZED TO SERVE SUBPOENA: or any other Customs officer.	5 DATE OF ISSUE COMMISSIONER OF CUSTOMS BY (Signature):
If you have any questions regarding this subpoena, contact the Customs officer identified in Block 2.	6 NAME, TITLE, ADDRESS, AND TELEPHONE NUMBER OF PERSON ISSUING THIS SUBPOENA

Customs Form 337 (041886)

Figure 5–15. *(continued)*

[*reverse*]

CERTIFICATE OF SERVICE AND ACKNOWLEDGMENT OF RECEIPT

A. CERTIFICATE OF SERVICE OF SUBPOENA

I certify that I served the subpoena on the front of this form as follows:

☐	I delivered a copy of the subpoena to the person to whom it was directed, as follows:	ADDRESS OR LOCATION	DATE TIME
☐	*(For corporations, partnerships, and unincorporated associations which may be sued under a common name)* I delivered a copy of the subpoena to an officer, managing or general agent, or agent authorized to accept service of process as follows:	PERSON TO WHOM SUBPOENA WAS DELIVERED: NAME / Title ADDRESS OR LOCATION	DATE TIME
☐	I left a copy of the subpoena at the last and usual dwelling or place of abode of the person to whom it was directed as follows:	ADDRESS OR LOCATION NAME OF PERSON WITH WHOM SUBPOENA LEFT (If Any)	DATE TIME

SIGNATURE	TITLE	DATE

B. ACKNOWLEDGMENT OF RECEIPT

I acknowledge receipt of a copy of the subpoena on the front of this form.

SIGNATURE	TITLE	
X	DATE	TIME

Customs Form 337 (041886) (Back)

☆U.S. GOVERNMENT PRINTING OFFICE: 1988 - 542-156/61130

convicted of violating any U.S. criminal statutes; or is ineligible to contract with or to receive a an import or export license from any agency of the U.S. government. Even if the manufacturer is not exporting, if it manufactures articles under the U.S. Munitions List, it must be registered with the DDTC.

Once registered, an exporter must enroll in the D-Trade electronic licensing system in order to obtain a license for the permanent export, temporary export, or temporary import of U.S. Munitions List items. This requires the user to purchase access to the D-Trade system, which allows for individual digital certificates. The application for permanent export of U.S. Munitions List items is filed through D-Trade on a DSP-5 (see Figure 5–19). For some items, specified as "significant military equipment," the applicant must obtain a signed Nontransfer and Use Certificate (DSP-83) from the consignee and end user prior to making application. (See Figure 5–20.) In some cases, as a condition of granting the license, the DDTC may require that the applicant obtain

(*Text continues on page 247.*)

Figure 5–16. Statement of Registration

OMB APPROVAL NO 1405-0002
EXPIRATION DATE 11/30/2011
*ESTIMATED BURDEN 2 Hours

U.S. Department of State

STATEMENT OF REGISTRATION

(SEE INSTRUCTIONS PAGE)
(Attach additional sheet if necessary)

PM/DDTC Date Received *(mm/dd/yyyy)*

Registrant Code

1. Registrant's Company Name and Address:
   a. Name
   b. Doing Business As
   c. Physical Street Address
   d. Apt. (no P.O. Box)
   e. City
   f. State/Province
   g. Country
   h. Zip/Postal Code

   Telephone Number (Country/Area Code)

   Fax Number (Country/Area Code)

2. Current Registration Code (if applicable):
   - ☐ Manufacturer/Exporter
   - ☐ Broker

3. Enclosed (for 12 month registration)

4. Registrant Is:
   - ☐ Individual
   - ☐ Corporation
   - ☐ Partnership
   - ☐ Company
   - ☐ Other

5. Registrant Is:
   - ☐ Broker: US Person
   - ☐ Broker: Foreign Person
   - ☐ Manufacturer
   - ☐ Manufacturer/Exporter

6. Incorporation or Commencement of Business:
   Date *(mm/dd/yyyy)*

   In

   City, County, State, and Country

7. Directors, Officers, Partners, Owners:

<u>Name</u>
a. Last
b. First
c. Middle
d. Citizenship(s)
e. Social Security Number
f. Position

<u>Place of Birth</u>
a. City
b. State/Province
c. Country

<u>Date of Birth</u>
(mm/dd/yyyy)

<u>Home Address</u>
a. Physical Street Address
b. Apt. (no P.O. Box)
c. City
d. State/Province
e. Country
f. Zip/Postal Code

☐ Additional page(s) attached

DS-2032
11-2011

Page 1 of 2

Figure 5–16. *(continued)*

8. U.S. Munitions List Articles Manufactured and/or Exported, Brokered, or Defense Services Provided:

Category	Commodity/Service	Purchasing U.S. Government Agency *(if any)*

☐ Additional page(s) attached

9. Names and Address of Registrant's Wholly- and Partially-Owned U.S. Subsidiaries/ Affiliates:

☐ Yes *(Specify)* ☐ No

a. Name ______

b. Physical Street Address (no P.O. Box) ______

c. City ______

d. State/Province ______

e. Zip/Postal Code ______

f. Telephone Number (Country/Area Code) ______

☐ Additional page(s) attached

10. Names and Address of Registrant's Wholly- and Partially-Owned Foreign Subsidiaries/ Affiliates:

☐ Yes *(Specify)* ☐ No

a. Name ______

b. Physical Street Address (no P.O. Box) ______

c. City ______

d. State/Province ______

e. Country ______

f. Zip/Postal Code ______

g. Telephone Number (Country/Area Code) ______

☐ Additional page(s) attached

11. Name, Address, and Telephone Number of Registrant's Parent Company *(if any)*:

a. Name ______

b. Physical Street Address (no P.O. Box) ______

c. City ______

d. State/Province ______

e. Country ______

f. Zip/Postal Code ______

g. Telephone Number (Country/Area Code) ______

☐ Additional page(s) attached

12. Is the Registrant:

☐ Owned

☐ And/Or Controlled

By Foreign Persons *(22 CFR 122.2(c))*:

☐ Yes (Specify) ☐ No

13. Does Registrant Submit Federal Income Tax Forms Separately From Company in Block 11?

☐ Yes

☐ No

14. Registrant's Statement:

Under Penalty According to Federal Law *(see 22 CFR 127; 22 USC 2778, 18 USC 1001)*

I, ______ Warrant the Truth of All Statements Made Herein

Type Full Name

______ Signature ______ Date *(mm/dd/yyyy)*

______ Title/Position of Senior Officer ______ Email

DS-2032
11-2011

(DESTROY PREVIOUS EDITIONS)

Page 2 of 2

Figure 5–16. *(continued)*

STATEMENT OF REGISTRATION INSTRUCTIONS

General Notes:
- Complete all items. If "none" applies to an item, so state.
- If more space is required to complete an item, electronic attachment pages are available for most items.
- Important: Changes in the information contained in this application by law must be reported promptly in accordance with 22 CFR 122.4. Clearly identifying or otherwise highlighting the changed information will facilitate analysis.

Block 1. Show the legal business name, physical office address, and telephone number of the registrant. No P.O. Box address accepted.

Block 2. If you have been, or are currently, registered with the Directorate of Defense Trade Controls (PM/DDTC), give your PM/DDTC registrant code number.

Block 3. For renewals, registrants will be notified of their annual fee via mail 60 days prior to expiration date. Payment must be submitted by check and must be in U.S. currency, payable through a U.S. financial institution. Cash and foreign currency will not be accepted. Make check payable to "U.S. Department of State." Send to one of the addresses provided below. Enter the fee amount on the line provided and the check number may be inserted, in parenthesis, following the fee amount.

Block 4. Give the most applicable legal organizational description. If "other" is selected, explain legal organizational structure. Select one.

Block 5. Indicate the nature of your business as a Manufacturer, Manufacturer/Exporter, or Broker of Defense Articles and Services (e.g., hardware, data, software, services) and select only one. Separate registration required for Broker. Manufacturer or Manufacturer/Exporter must be a U.S. person. Broker may be a U.S. person or a foreign person and the appropriate entry marked in Block 5.

Block 6. Enter the date (mm/dd/yyyy), city, county, state, and country where your legal business, as listed in Item 1, commenced doing business. You must attach a copy of the document(s) issued by the government authority enabling you to engage in business in the U.S. (e.g. Articles of Incorporation) or foreign country, as appropriate.

Block 7. Enter the full name, title, date (mm/dd/yyyy), place of birth (city, state, & country), social security number, complete physical home address, and country of citizenship (list all citizenships held, actual or pending, including whether or not you are a U.S. person under 22 CFR 120.15). No P.O. Box address accepted.

Block 8. Enter U.S. Munitions List (USML) category (22 CFR 121), generic name, in addition the U.S. Government agency (if applicable) for USML articles manufactured, and/or exported, brokered, or defense services provided.

Block 9. List U.S. defense-related subsidiaries/affiliates, wholly or partially owned by registrant for USML articles manufactured, and/or exported, or defense services provided. Telephone number is not mandatory but could facilitate analysis.

Block 10. List defense-related foreign subsidiaries/affiliates, wholly or partially owned by registrant for USML articles manufactured, and/or exported, or defense services provided. Telephone number is not mandatory but could facilitate analysis.

Block 11. Give complete name, address, and telephone number of parent company.

Block 12. Is the registrant owned and/or controlled by foreign (non U.S.) person(s)? See 22 CFR 122.2 (c) for definition of ownership or control. If "Yes," you must explain in the transmittal letter the specific percentages of ownership and control held by each foreign (non U.S.) person.

Block 13. Company entities or subsidiaries may not register separately.

Block 14. The individual signing this form must be a senior officer empowered by the registrant. The signer must be a U.S. person unless the signer is a broker, which includes U.S. and non-U.S. persons. Violations and penalties are explained in 22 CFR 127.

Send to: Postal Mailing Address
U.S. Department of State
Directorate of Defense Trade Controls
Compliance and Registration Division
2401 E Street, NW, SA-1, Room H1 200
Washington, DC 20522-0112

Send to: Express Mailing Address and Courier Delivery Address
U.S. Department of State
Directorate of Defense Trade Controls
Compliance and Registration Division
2401 E Street, NW, SA-1, Room H1 200
Washington, DC 20037

PRIVACY ACT AND PAPERWORK REDUCTION ACT STATEMENTS

AUTHORITIES U.S. Department of State's authorities to register persons engaged in the business of manufacturing, exporting, or importing any defense article or defense service are 22 USC 2778 (b) (1) (A) (i) and 22 CFR Part 122. The authorities to register brokers are 22 USC 2778 (b) (1) (A) (ii) (I) and 22 CFR 129.3 and 129.4.

PURPOSE The purpose of registration is to provide the U.S. Government with necessary information on individuals and entities engaged in certain manufacturing, exporting, and brokering activities.

ROUTINE USES The information solicited on this form is made available as a routine use to appropriate agencies whether Federal, State, local or foreign, for intelligence, law enforcement, and administrative purposes, or pursuant to a court order. It may also be used to send required reports to Congress about certain defense trade transactions.

SOCIAL SECURITY NUMBER Disclosure of the social security number(s) is voluntary and for the purpose of facilitating coordination with the Department of Treasury to review the registration statement for law enforcement concerns in accordance with 22 USC 2778 (b) (1) (B). Refusal to provide requested social security number, by itself, will not result in registration being denied, but may result in delays in the processing of a registration request.

*Public reporting burden for this collection of information is estimated to average 2 hours per response, including time required for searching existing data sources, gathering the necessary data, providing the information required, and reviewing the final collection. Send comments on the accuracy of this estimate of the burden and recommendations for reducing it to: U.S. Department of State (A/ISS/DIR) Washington, DC 20520.

DS-2032
11-2011

Instruction Page 1 of 1

Figure 5–17. Transmittal Letter Format

Transmittal Letter Format

Instructions

The letter MUST be:

1. Copied verbatim except for the sections in parentheses and italicized. In those sections, add specific information.
2. Prepared on the Registrant company letterhead. The format will satisfy the requirements of 22 CFR 122.2(b) when there is no conviction, indictment or ineligibility to declare. If any such considerations apply, their full particulars must be provided in the body of the letter.
3. Signed by an authorized senior officer that is listed in Block 7 of the DS-2032 form.
4. Prepared using the same business legal name as that in the documentation of incorporation (e.g. business license, articles of incorporation).
5. Included with new registration packages, renewal packages (and material change notifications).

Postal Mailing Address:

U.S. Department of State

Directorate of Defense Trade Controls
Compliance & Registration Division
2401 E Street NW, SA-1, Room H1200
Washington, DC 20522-0112

Express Mailing Address and Courier Delivery Service:

U.S. Department of State

Directorate of Defense Trade Controls
Compliance & Registration Division
2401 E Street NW, SA-1, Room H1200
Washington, DC 20037

Figure 5–18. Sample Transmittal Letter

Dear Mr. Trimble:

In compliance with 22 CFR 122.2(b)(1) and (b)(2), I hereby state that I am an authorized senior official of *(insert the name of the Registrant as listed in Block 1 of the DS-2032 form)*. Furthermore, I hereby state that:

Neither the intending registrant, chief executive officer, president, vice-presidents, other senior officers or officials (e.g., comptroller, treasurer, general counsel) nor any member of the board of directors:

(i) has ever been indicted for or convicted of violating any of the U.S. criminal statues enumerated in 22 CFR 120.27; or

(ii) is ineligible to contract with, or to receive a license or other approval to import defense articles or defense services from, or to receive an export license or other approval from, any agency of the U.S. Government.

In accordance with 22 CFR 122.2(b) (2), I state that *(insert the name of the Registrant as listed in Block 1 of the DS-2032 form)* is neither owned nor controlled by foreign persons (as defined in 22 CFR 120.16) *(and if owned or controlled by foreign persons, enter that explanation of ownership and control here, and pay particular attention to foreign persons, or their representatives, referenced in 22 CFR 126.1).*

(Signature, in ink, of Senior Officer as their name appears in Block 7 of DS-2032 form. Also print full name and official title).

Figure 5–19. Application/License for permanent export

Electronic Form Version Number: 2.3

OMB APPROVAL NO. 1405-0003
EXPIRATION DATE: 09-30-2008
*ESTIMATED BURDEN: 1 HOUR

* PAPERWORK REDUCTION ACT STATEMENT: Public reporting burden for this collection of information is estimated to average 1 hour per response, including time required for searching existing data sources, gathering the necessary data, providing the information required, and reviewing the final collection. Send comments on the accuracy of this estimate of the burden and recommendations for reducing it to: Department of State (A/RPS/DIR) Washington, D.C. 20520.

U.S. DEPARTMENT OF STATE

DIRECTORATE OF DEFENSE TRADE CONTROLS

APPLICATION/LICENSE FOR PERMANENT EXPORT OF UNCLASSIFIED DEFENSE ARTICLES AND RELATED UNCLASSIFIED TECHNICAL DATA

*Transaction Number: [ ]

Please note that an Asterisk (*) next to a field in the documents designates a mandatory field.

No classified information can be included in this application. Classified information must be sent separately to PM/DDTC in accordance with Defense Security Service guidelines.

Classified information is being sent under separate cover ☐

To select and open a document, highlight a form and select the "Open Document" button. The document that you selected will open.

Required Documents

DSP-5

Included Documents

Optional Documents

126.13 Eligibility Letter
Basic Ordering Agreement
Contract
DSP-83
Firearms and Ammunitions Import Permit
Firearms and Ammunitions Letter of Explanation
Letter of Intent
Other Amplifying Data
Part 130 Report
PM/DDTC Sec 126.8 Prior Approval
Precedent (identical/similar) Cases
Product Brochures
Purchase Order
Supplementary Explanation of Transaction
Technical Data to Support Hardware License
Technical Drawings, Schematics, or Blue Prints
Transaction Exception Request

DSP-5
Revised 02-2006

Figure 5–19. *(continued)*

DSP-5, Page 1 of 4

SEAL

Signature

License is hereby granted to the applicant for the described commodity to be permanently exported from the United States. This license may be revoked, suspended or amended by the Secretary of State without prior notice whenever the Secretary deems such action advisable.

DATE ISSUED

LICENSE NO.

LICENSE VALID FOR **MONTHS FROM ABOVE DATE**

UNITED STATES OF AMERICA DEPARTMENT OF STATE

APPLICATION/LICENSE FOR PERMANENT EXPORT OF UNCLASSIFIED DEFENSE ARTICLES AND RELATED UNCLASSIFIED TECHNICAL DATA

*1. Date Prepared

*** 2. PM/DDTC Applicant/ Registrant Code**

*** 3. Country of Ultimate Destination:**

NOTE: You may only select 1 country as the ultimate destination if the commodity(ies) being shipped include Hardware type.

*** 4. Probable Port of Exit from U.S.:**

5. Applicant's Name, Address, ZIP Code, Telephone Number

*Applicant is: ☐ Government ☐ Manufacturer ☐ Exporter ☐ Subsidiary

*Name

*Attention

*Address

*City

*State * ZIP Code

*Telephone # Ext.

6. Name, agency and telephone number of U.S. Government personnel (not PM/DDTC) familiar with the commodity.

Name

Telephone # Ext.

Agency

Add

*** 7. Name and telephone numbers of applicant contact if U.S. Government needs additional information.**

*Name

*Telephone # Ext.

Add

8. Description of Transaction:

*a. This application represents: ☐ ONLY completely new shipment ☐ ONLY the unshipped balance under license numbers

b. This application has related license numbers: ☐

c. This application is in reference to an agreement: ☐

*d. Commodity is being financed under: ☐ Foreign Military Sale ☐ Foreign Military Financing ☐ Grant Aid Program ☐ Not Applicable

Line Item # 1

***9. Quantity**

Unit Type

***10. Commodity**

Defense Article Type

*** 11. USML Category Number**

Category

Item is SME and DSP-83 is required ☐

Is a DSP-83 attached?

If SME, and DSP-83 is not attached, state why.

***12. $ Value**

Unit Price Line Item Total

Add ☐

*13. TOTAL VALUE (Sum of All Pages) $

Figure 5–19. *(continued)*

DSP-5, Page 2 of 4

14. Name and address of foreign end-user

* Name

*Address

*City

*Country

Add ☐

15. Manufacturer of Commodity

☐ Same as Block 5

*Name

*Address

*City

State | ZIP Code

*Country

Add ☐

16. Name and address of foreign consignee

☐ Same as Block 14

*Name

*Address

*City

*Country

Add ☐

17. Source of Commodity

☐ Same as Block 5 ☐ Same as Block 15

*Name

*Address

*City

State | ZIP Code

*Country

Add ☐

18. Name and address of foreign intermediate consignee

☐ None

* Name

*Address

*City

*Country

*Role

Add ☐

19. Name and address of Seller in United States

☐ Same as Block 5 ☐ Same as Block 15 ☐ Same as Block 17

* Name

*Address

*City

*State | *ZIP Code

Add ☐

*** 20. Specific purpose for which the material is required, including specific Program/End Item.**

Select at least one:

☐ Off-Shore ☐ Request for Prior Approval (22 CFR 126.8)

☐ Brokering (22 CFR 129) ☐ Other (Please Provide Details)

21. Name and address of consignor and/or freight forwarder in United States

☐ Same as Block 5

* Name

*Address

*City

*State | *ZIP Code

Add ☐

Figure 5–19. *(continued)*

DSP-5

22. Applicant's statement

I [ ]

an empowered official (ITAR 120.25) or an official of a foreign government entity in the U.S., hereby apply for a license to complete the transaction described above; warrant the truth of all statements made herein; and acknowledge, understand and will comply with the provisions of Title 22 CFR, 120-130, and any conditions and limitations imposed.

I am authorized by the applicant to certify the following in compliance with 22 CFR 126.13:

(1) Neither applicant, its chief executive officer, president, vice presidents, other senior officers or officials (e.g., comptroller, treasurer, general counsel) nor any member of its board of directors is:

(a) the subject of an indictment for or has been convicted of violating any of the U.S. criminal statutes enumerated in 22 CFR120.27 since the effective date of the Arms Export Control Act, Public Law 94-329, 90 Stat. 729 (June 30, 1976); or

(b) ineligible to contract with, or to receive a license or other approval to import defense articles or defense services from, or to receive an export license or other approval from any agency of the U.S. Government;

(2) To the best of the applicant's knowledge, no party to the export as defined in 22 CFR 126.7 (e) has been convicted of violating any of the U.S. criminal statutes enumerated in 22 CFR 120.27 since the effective date of the Arms Export Control Act, Public Law 94-329, 90 Stat. 729 (June 30, 1976); or is ineligible to contract with, or to receive a license or other approval to import defense articles or defense services from, or to receive an export lisence or other approval from any agency of the U.S. Government.

***22 CFR 126.13 Certification (Select one)**

☐ I am authorized by the applicant to certify that the applicant and all the parties to the transaction can meet in full the conditions of 22 CFR 126.13 as listed above.

☐ I am authorized by the applicant to certify to 22 CFR 126.13. The applicant or one of the parties of the transaction cannot meet one or more of the conditions of 22 CFR 126.13 as listed above. A request for an exception to policy is attached.

☐ I am not authorized by the applicant to certify the conditions of 22 CFR 126.13 as listed above. The applicant and all the parties to the transaction can meet in full the conditions of 22 CFR 126.13 as listed above. Please see the attached letter for such certification.

☐ I am not authorized by the applicant to certify the conditions of 22 CFR 126.13 as listed above. The applicant or one of the parties of the transaction cannot meet one or more of the conditions of 22 CFR 126.13 as listed above. A letter of such certification and request for an exception to policy is attached.

***Compliance with 22 CFR 130 (Select one)**

☐ This transaction does not meet the requirements of 22 CFR 130.2

☐ This transaction meets the requirements of 22 CFR 130.2. The applicant or its vendors have not paid, nor offered, nor agreed to pay, in respect of any sale for which a license or approval is requested, political contributions, fees or commissions in amounts as specified in 22 CFR 130.9(a).

☐ The applicant or its vendors have paid, or offered, or agreed to pay, in respect of any sale for which a license or approval is requested, political contributions, fees or commissions in amounts as specified in 22 CFR 130.9(a). Information required under 22 CFR 130.10 is attached.

☐ I am not authorized by the applicant to certify the conditions of 22 CFR 130.9(a). Please see the attached for such certification.

*Signature

[Signature]

23. License to be to: (Enter name, address and phone number)

[This block is inactive on electronic form.]

☐ Same as Block 5 ☐ Hold for Pickup

Name [ ]

Address [ ]

City [ ]

State [ ] ZIP Code [ ]

Telephone # [ ]

Figure 5–19. *(continued)*

DSP-5, Page 4 of 4

CONDITIONS OF ISSUANCE

1. This license is issued under the conditions cited in 22 CFR 120 - 130, including the provisos as applicable, that:

   A. It shall not be construed as implying U.S. Government approval or commitment to authorize future exports of any article (equipment or technical data) on the Munitions List, or a U.S. Government commitment with regard to any proposed manufacturing license or technical assistance agreements which may result from an authorized export.

   B. If a license is issued for technical data only, it does not authorize the export of any hardware; if a license is issued for hardware only, it does not authorize the export of any technical data, unless specifically covered by an exemption.

   The issuance of this license does not release the licensee from complying with other requirements of U.S. law and regulations.

2. The prior written approval of the Department of State must be obtained before U.S. Munitions List articles exported from the U.S. under license or other approval may be resold, diverted, transferred, transshipped, reshipped, reexported to, or used in any country, or by any end-user, other than that described on the license or other approval as the country of ultimate destination or the ultimate end-user.

RETURN OF LICENSE

This license must be returned to PM/DDTC, SA-1, 12th Floor, Directorate of Defense Trade Controls, Bureau of Political-Military Affairs, U.S. Department of State, Washington, DC 20522-0112 when: (1) the total value authorized has been shipped; (2) the applicant states that there will be no further shipments; (3) the date of expiration is reached; or (4) when requested by the Directorate of Defense Trade Controls.

ENDORSEMENT

Indicate below which ITEM on the face of the license is BEING EXPORTED and maintain a CONTINUING BALANCE of the remaining value:

SHIPMENT DATE	QUANTITY	COMMODITY (Include classification)	SHIPMENT VALUE	SED NO.	INITIALS	PORT OF EXIT/ENTRY
	TOTAL AUTHORIZED VALUE:					
	REMAINING BALANCE:					

NOTE: Continuation of additional shipments must be authenticated by use of continuation sheets in the U.S.Customs handbook.

Figure 5–20. Nontransfer and Use Certificate

U.S. Department of State
UNITED STATES OF AMERICA
NONTRANSFER AND USE CERTIFICATE

1. This certificate is submitted in connection with export application no. ____________

OMB No. 1405 0021
EXPIRATION DATE: 09-30-2008
*ESTIMATED BURDEN: 1 Hour
(Instruction Page)

2. Name of United States applicant	3. Name of foreign end-user	4. Country of ultimate destination

5. Articles/data
We certify that we have placed an order with the person named in item 2 for the following articles/data in the quantity and value shown below:

QUANTITY	ARTICLES/DATA DESCRIPTION	VALUE (U.S. $)

6. Certification of foreign consignee
We certify that we are importing the articles/data listed in item 5 for delivery to the end-user in item 3. Except as specifically authorized by prior written approval of the U.S. Department of State, we will not re-export, resell, or otherwise dispose of any of those articles/data (1) outside the country in item 4 above, or (2) to any person, including the end-user, if there is reason to believe that it will result, directly or indirectly, in disposition of the articles/data contrary to the representations made in this certificate by any party. We further certify that all of the facts contained in this certificate are true and correct to the best of our knowledge and belief and we do not know of any additional facts that are inconsistent with this certificate. We will promptly send a supplemental certificate to the U.S. applicant in item 2 disclosing any change of facts or intentions set forth in this statement.

Sign here in ink ____________________ Signature of Official, Foreign Consignee ____________ Date Signed *(mm-dd-yyyy)*

Type or print ____________________ Name and Title of Signer — Seal

7. Certification of foreign end-user
We certify that we are the end-user of the articles/data in item 5. Except as specifically authorized by prior written approval of the U.S. Department of State, we will not re-export, resell, or otherwise dispose of any of those articles/data (1) outside the country in item 4 above, or (2) to any other person. If the end-user is a foreign government, we certify that we will observe the assurances contained in item 8. We further certify that all of the facts contained in this certificate are true and correct to the best of our knowledge and belief and we do not know of any additional facts that are inconsistent with this certificate.

Sign here in ink ____________________ Signature of Official, End-User ____________ Date Signed *(mm-dd-yyyy)*

Type or print ____________________ Name and Title of Signer — Seal

8. Certification of foreign government
We certify that we will not authorize the re-export, resales or other disposition of the articles/data authorized in item 5 outside the country in item 4 without prior written approval of the U.S. Government. If the articles/data are for use by our "armed forces" (i.e., army, navy, marine, air force, coast guard, national guard, national police, and any military unit or military personnel organized under or assigned to an international organization), we certify that we will use the authorized articles/data only: (a) for the purposes specified in the Mutual Defense Assistance Agreement, if any, between the U.S. Government and this government; (b) for the purposes specified in any bilateral or regional defense treaty to which the U.S. Government and this government are both parties, if subparagraph (a) is inapplicable; or (c) for internal security, individual self-defense, and/or civic action, if subparagraphs (a) and (b) are inapplicable.

Sign here in ink ____________________ Signature of Government Official ____________ Date Signed *(mm-dd-yyyy)*

Type or print ____________________ Name and Title of Signer — Seal

9. We certify that no corrections, additions or alterations were made on this form by us after it was signed by the foreign consignee, foreign end-user or foreign government.

Sign here in ink ____________________ Signature of Applicant ____________ Date Signed *(mm-dd-yyyy)*

Type or print ____________________ Name and Title of Signer — Seal

DSP-83
10-2005

Page 1 of 1

Figure 5–20. *(continued)*

INSTRUCTIONS FOR DSP-83

The U.S. Department of State requires that this completed form DSP-83 be included as a part of an application for authorization to export significant military equipment and classified equipment or data (22 CFR §§123.10(a), 124.10 and 125.7.) Failure to submit will result in the application being returned without action. The form DSP-83 must be completed by the appropriate foreign persons (e.g., consignee, end-user, government) and forwarded to the U.S. Department of State through the U.S. person making the application.

1. *Item 1.* The U.S. Department of State will enter the application number when the form DSP-83 is submitted with the application. The U.S. applicant must provide the application number when form DSP-83 is submitted separately from the application.

2. *Item 2.* Show the name of the U.S. person submitting the application to the U.S. Department of State.

3. *Item 3.* Show the foreign person that will receive the articles/data for end-use. A bank, freight forwarding agent, or other intermediary is not acceptable as an end-user.

4. *Item 4.* Show the country in which the articles/data will ultimately receive end-use.

5. *Item 5.* Show precise quantities of the articles/data. List each article/data clearly, giving type, model number, make and (if known) U.S. military designation or national stock number. When components and spare parts are involved, fully identify the minor component, major component and end item in which they will be used (e.g., turbine blades for C-34 jet engine for F24B aircraft). Give a separate value for each major component. Values must represent only the selling price and not include supplementary costs such as packing and freight.

6. *Item 6.* To be completed by the foreign person who has entered into the export transaction with the applicant to purchase the articles/data for delivery to the end-user. This item shall be completed only if the foreign consignee is not the same as the foreign end-user.

7. *Item 7.* To be completed by the foreign person, in the country of ultimate designation, who will make final use of the articles/data.

8. *Item 8.* When requested by the U.S. Department of State, this item is to be completed by an official of the country of ultimate destination having the authority to so commit the government of that country.

9. *Item 9.* Certification of U.S. applicant.

*Public reporting burden for this collection is estimated to average 1 hour per response, including time required for searching existing data sources, gathering the necessary data, providing the information required, and reviewing the final collection. Send comments on the accuracy of this estimate of the burden and recommendations for reducing it to: U.S. Department of State (A/RPS/DIR) Washington, DC 20520.

DSP-83
10-2005

Instruction Page 1 of 1

an import certificate signed by the government of the foreign country and/or provide verification of delivery of the item to the foreign country. Different procedures and license forms apply to classified articles and technical data. Different procedures and forms also apply to direct, commercial sales and to sales to the U.S. Department of Defense for resale to foreign countries under the Foreign Military Assistance program. Before appointing any foreign distributors who are authorized to resell the products, the exporter must submit the distributorship agreement to the DDTC for approval. Agreements to grant manufacturing licenses or provide technical assistance must also be approved in advance through Technical Assistance Agreements and Manufacturing License Agreements. Applications for licenses will be denied for exports to Afghanistan, Belarus, Burma, Cote d'Ivoire, China (PRC), Cuba, Democratic Republic of Congo, Haiti, Iran, Iraq, Liberia, Libya, North Korea, Rwanda, Sierra Leone, Somalia, Sri Lanka, Sudan, Syria, Venezuela, Vietnam, and Zimbabwe. Those who broker sales of defense articles are also required to register with the DDTC.

An area of particular sensitivity is the requirement that if the amount of the export sales is $500,000 or more, the license applicant must disclose to the DDTC the names and detailed payment information on any fees or commissions of $1,000 or more paid to any person to promote or secure the sale of a defense article or service to the armed forces of a foreign country. The applicant must also report any political contributions of $1,000 or more to any government employee, political party, or candidate. The applicant must also survey its suppliers, subcontractors, and agents to ascertain whether they have paid or agreed to make any such payments. In addition to the disclosure to the DDTC, such payments may violate foreign law.

Persons who violate the Arms Export Control Act are subject to the civil and criminal penalties under the Export Administration Regulations (see Section N, above) and can be debarred from exporting for a period of up to three years. The DDTC's policy is that persons engaged in the export of defense articles and services should maintain an export procedures manual containing DDTC-specified policies and procedures to reduce the risk of violations.

Part III

Importing: Procedures and Documentation

Chapter 6

Importing: Preliminary Considerations

Before beginning to import, and on each importation, the importer/buyer should consider a number of preliminary matters that will make a great deal of difference in smooth and efficient importing.

A. Products

Before actually importing, or whenever the importer is considering importing a new item, the characteristics of that item should be reviewed. That is, is the product being imported as a raw material or component to be used in the manufacturing process? Is it a finished product that is going to be resold in the form imported or with some slight or significant modification? Is it a replacement or spare part? Is the item sold singly or as a part of a set or system? Does the product need to be modified, such as in size, weight, or color, to be suitable for the U.S. market? Often the appropriate methods of manufacturing and marketing, the appropriate purchase and import documentation, the appropriate procedures for importation, and the treatment under U.S. law, including U.S. customs law, will depend upon these considerations (for example, whether or not the product may be imported duty-free or what the correct classification and duty will be).

In addition to the general procedures and documents, some products are subject to special import restrictions, permits, licenses, standards, and/or procedures. These include foods, drugs, cosmetics, alcoholic beverages, tea, medical devices, certain energy-using commercial and industrial equipment, civil aircraft and parts, educational and scientific apparatus, children's products including toys and books, products containing phthalates, wood products, ethyl alcohol, master records and matrices, vegetable oils, seed potatoes and corn, works of art, antiques, engines for vehicles and off-road, bolting cloths, purebred animals for breeding, products subject to quotas, certain radiation-producing electronic products, wildlife, pets, certain mammals, fish, snails, clams, crustaceans, mollusks and amphibians, migratory birds, meat and meat products, watches and watch movements, sugar, textiles, wool, cheese, milk and dairy products, fruits, vegetables, nuts, insects, livestock and animals, plants and plant products, poultry and poultry products, seafood, seeds, arms, ammunition and explosives, cigarette lighters, radioactive materials and devices, household appliances, flammable fabrics, animal rugs, narcotic drugs, drug paraphernalia, certain fireworks, monetary instruments in excess of $10,000, bicycles and bicycle helmets, lead paint, precursor chemicals, automobiles, boats, pesticides, toxic and hazardous substances, postage stamps, petroleum and petroleum products, archaeological and ethnological material, pre-Columbian sculpture and murals, and "foreign excess property." Importation of white or yellow phosphorous matches; certain fireworks; "cultural property"; switchblades; lottery tickets; most endangered species; African elephant ivory and articles; counterfeit articles; treasonable or obscene material; and products of convict, child, and forced labor is prohibited.

B. Volume

What is the expected volume of imports of the product? Will this be an isolated purchase of a small quantity or an ongoing series of transactions amounting to substantial quantities? Small quantities may be imported under purchase orders and purchase order acceptance documentation. Large quantities may require more formal international purchase agreements; more formal methods of payment; special shipping, packing, and handling procedures; an appointment as the U.S. sales agent and/or distributor from the foreign exporter; or commitments to perform after-sales service. (See the discussion in Chapter 7, Section B.)

C. Country Sourcing

One of the principal preliminary considerations will be to identify those countries that have the products that the importer is seeking to purchase. If the importer seeks to import a raw material or natural resource, the importer may be limited to purchasing from those countries where such products are grown or mined. If the importer is looking for a manufactured product, it is likely that the number of countries where such products are available for sale will be much greater; however, identifying the low-cost countries based upon proximity to raw materials, labor costs of manufacturing, current exchange rates with the United States, or transportation costs may require considerable study and analysis. This information is not always easy to obtain. Since the U.S. government is more interested in promoting exports, it does not regularly collect such information and make it available to U.S. companies wishing to import. Importers will probably have to contact foreign governments directly (or through their U.S. embassies and consulates), foreign chambers of commerce, and foreign trade associations. Sometimes, foreign banks operating in the United States, U.S. accounting firms or law firms that have offices in the foreign country, or U.S. banks with offices in the foreign country can be helpful in supplying information. The United Nations publishes its *International Trade Statistics Yearbook* showing what countries are selling and exporting all types of products. In identifying the potential country, the importer should ascertain whether the products of that country are eligible for duty-free or reduced duty treatment under the Generalized System of Preferences, the Caribbean Basin Economic Recovery Act, the North American Free Trade Agreement, the Dominican Republic–Central America–United States Free Trade Agreement, the African Growth and Opportunity Act, or any other of the numerous new free trade agreements, including those with Australia, Bahrain, Chile, Morocco, Oman, and Singapore. Under the U.S. Foreign Assets Control Regulations, importation from Cuba, Burma (Myanmar), Iran (except for certain carpets and food), Sudan, and Syria is prohibited without a license or approval from the Department of the Treasury (with a general policy of denial), and imports from such countries will be immediately seized by U.S. Customs and Border Protection. Imports from North Korea must be approved by the Office of Foreign Assets Control, but unless the imports are from persons or the government of North Korea and relating to certain satellite, electronic, or missile technology, they are likely to be approved. Rough diamonds may be imported into or exported from the United States only from or to countries participating in the Kimberly Process Certification Scheme. It should also be noted that importers are prohibited from making or receiving any funds, goods, or services from parties that are identified in the Specially Designated Nationals List who are sponsors of terrorism, narcotics drug trafficking, or the proliferation of weapons of mass destruction (see Chapter 5, Section E).

D. Identification of Suppliers

Once the countries with the products available for supply have been identified, of course, the importer still needs to identify a specific supplier. This will be just as important as identifying which countries can provide the products at the lowest cost. An unreliable supplier or one that has poor product quality control will certainly result in disaster for the importer. The importer should spend a significant amount of time in evaluating the potential supplier if there are going to be ongoing purchase transactions. The importer should ascertain the business reputation and performance of the potential supplier. If possible, the importer should inspect the plant and manufacturing facilities of the supplier. The importer should determine whether there are other customers within its own country who might be able to confirm the quality and supply reliability of the potential supplier. Related thereto, if the importer will be acting as the distributor or sales agent for the foreign manufacturer, the importer needs to ascertain whether the supplier has already appointed (on either an exclusive or a nonexclusive basis) other U.S. distributors or sales agents. The importer should also determine if a supplier is acting as an agent for the manufacturer or if the supplier will be acting as the buying agent for the buyer. If the latter, the buyer should enter into a separate agency agreement and pay all commissions separately, since the importer need not pay customs duties on buying commissions but must do so on commissions paid to the seller's agent.

Once potential suppliers have been identified, if an ongoing relationship is contemplated, a personal visit to evaluate the supplier is essential. One efficient way that the author has used is to arrange a schedule of interviews at its foreign law office so that the U.S. importer can meet with numerous potential suppliers in that country in the course of a two- or three-day period. Based on such meetings, one or more suppliers can be selected and the capabilities of those suppliers can be clearly understood. In evaluating potential suppliers, it is important to obtain a credit report. International credit reports are available from Dun & Bradstreet, www.dnb.com/us; Graydon America, www.graydon-group.com; Teikoku Data Bank America, Inc. [Japan], www.teikoku.com; Owens Online, www.owens.com; and local offices of the U.S. Department of Commerce (International Company Profiles).

E. Compliance With Foreign Law

Prior to importing from a foreign country or even agreeing to purchase from a supplier in a foreign country, a U.S. importer should be aware of any foreign laws that might affect the purchase. Information about foreign law can often be obtained from the supplier from whom the importer intends to purchase. However, if the supplier is incorrect in the information that it gives to the importer, the importer may have to pay dearly for having relied solely upon the advice of the supplier. Incorrect information about foreign law may result in the prohibition of importation of the supplier's product, or it may mean that the importer cannot resell the product as profitably as expected. Unfortunately, suppliers often overlook those things that may be of the greatest concern to the importer. As a result, it may be necessary for the U.S. importer to confirm its supplier's advice with third parties, including attorneys, banks, or government agencies, to feel confident that it properly understands the foreign law.

1. *Foreign Export Controls*

A number of countries, particularly those that are politically allied with the United States, enforce a system of export controls on dual-use items. The previous COCOM controls have been superseded by the "Wassenaar Arrangement." Currently, forty countries are members of the agreement. In order to export certain dual-use products from those countries, even to the United States, certain procedures of the foreign country must be followed. The first step is for the importer to ascertain whether or not the product is a controlled commodity under the foreign country's laws. If it is, the U.S. importer will be required to furnish a document to the foreign supplier to enable the foreign supplier to obtain a license from its own government to export the product to the United States. The importer will have to identify the documents required either through the potential supplier or directly from the foreign government agency, but in most cases an import certificate (see Chapter 5, Figure 5–9) will be required. The U.S. importer must have this document signed by the U.S. Department of Commerce, and it must be forwarded to the foreign supplier to enable it to apply for and obtain the necessary foreign government license for exporting the product. In addition, there may be other documents that the supplier must provide to its own government in order to obtain an export license. When an export license will be required, the importer should clearly ascertain the time period required in order to adequately plan its import schedule. The importer should also take certain steps in its purchase and sale documentation with the supplier to adequately obligate the supplier to obtain the necessary export licenses. (See discussion in Chapter 7, Section B.2.k.)

2. *Exchange Control Licenses*

Many countries of the world control their foreign exchange. Consequently, before an exporter can export valuable products produced or manufactured in its own country to a U.S. importer, the exporter's government will insist that the exporter have adequate assurance of payment by the U.S. importer. The foreign exporter will need a license in order to convert U.S. dollars received from the U.S. importer into its local currency to obtain payment. This is important for the importer to confirm in order to make sure that the products are not detained prior to export because the necessary exchange control license has not been obtained. Of significant importance to the importer is the requirement by the exporter's country that payment must be made by certain means, such as confirmed irrevocable letter of credit. In order to protect their companies against nonpayment, some governments impose strict payment requirements on foreign trade contracts. If the importer is unable or unwilling to pay by letter of credit, importation from that country may be practically impossible.

3. *Export Quotas*

Generally, the importing country establishes quotas for imported products. These are discussed in Section F.6 below. However, the U.S. government, through its negotiating representatives such as the U.S. Trade Representative's office, often requires the foreign government to agree to impose export quotas on products destined for the United States. These are sometimes designated Voluntary Restraint Agreements (VRA), and foreign government "visas" are required. (This "visa" should not be confused with the visa required by the immigration laws of foreign countries in order to travel there.)

Ordinarily, the foreign supplier should be aware of any export quotas or export visa requirements, but if the foreign supplier has been selling only domestically in the past, the supplier may not be familiar with those requirements. The U.S. importer should double-check on the existence of any foreign government quotas or visas prior to entering into purchase transactions that cannot be fulfilled. Sometimes these export visas or export rights are auctioned in the foreign country, and a potential exporter must participate in the government auction at the correct time in order to get an allocation for the coming year. Where export quotas or VRAs have been established, competition for such export visas is usually intense, and an importer will be unable to enter into spot transactions on short notice for the purchase of the products from suppliers who have not obtained the necessary government visas.

The United States does not have any VRAs or any commodities requiring import visas at this time. However, in order to track volumes of certain sensitive commodities, the International Trade Administration does monitor those commodities. For example, currently steel is monitored through the requirement of a license for every steel import. See additional information in Appendix K.

F. U.S. Customs Considerations

Various aspects of the U.S. Customs and Border Protection laws as they affect potential importers will be discussed in greater detail throughout subsequent chapters; however, there are a number of items that should be part of the importer's preliminary planning.

1. *Utilization of Customs Brokers*

Whether or not an importer should utilize a customs broker primarily depends upon the amount of imports the importer will have, and the number and expertise of its own personnel. If the importer has sufficient personnel with sufficient expertise, these people can be trained to handle the importing procedures and documentation themselves. Even large importers, however, often use the services of a customs broker. The most difficult problem may be the selection of a customs broker. There are many customs brokers with varying levels of expertise and various levels of financial stability. More important, some customs brokers are more familiar with certain types of products. Today, it is becoming increasingly important that the customs broker have an automated electronic interface with U.S. Customs and Border Protection and the ability to process documentation electronically. Interviews with a number of potential brokers and a frank discussion of the products and quantities that the importer intends to import, the source countries, and the brokers' capabilities are worthwhile. A visit to the brokers' premises may be even more helpful.

This concern and effort is more than merely academic. The broker acts as the agent for the importer, and, therefore, even though the importer may pay a fee to the broker, expecting to obtain the broker's expertise, if the broker makes a mistake or an error, U.S. Customs and Border Protection will attribute the responsibility for it to the importer, the principal. For example, if the broker fails to pay customs duties to Customs that were paid to the broker by the importer, the importer may be required to pay twice. In performing its services, the broker will require a power of attorney from the importer. (A sample power of attorney acceptable to U.S. Customs and Border Protection is shown in Figure 6–1.) However, the importer should be aware that many customs brokers expand upon the standard power of attorney and include a number of other provisions (which are designed to protect the broker and not the importer) in the form that they furnish to the importer. The importer should review the power of attorney and make appropriate modifications. The broker should at least agree to indemnify and hold the importer harmless from any penalties, costs, or damages due to the broker's negligence or errors. Another form that is useful in instructing the broker what services the importer desires on each importation is an importer's letter of instruction (see Figure 6–2).

(*Text continues on page 259.*)

Figure 6–1. Power of attorney for customs broker.

Department of the Treasury
U.S. Customs Service
19 CFR 141.32

POWER OF ATTORNEY

Check appropriate box:
☐ Individual
☐ Partnership
☐ Corporation
☐ Sole Proprietorship

KNOW ALL MEN BY THESE PRESENTS: That, ______________________________
(Full Name of person, partnership, or corporation, or sole proprietorship; Identify)

____

a corporation doing business under the laws of the State of ______________________ or a ______________________

doing business as ______________________ residing at ______________________

having an office and place of business at ______________________, hereby constitutes and appoints each of the following persons

____
(Give full name of each agent designated)

____

as a true and lawful agent and attorney of the grantor named above for and in the name, place, and stead of said grantor from this date and in Customs Port__________, and in no other name, to make, endorse, sign, declare, or swear to any entry, withdrawal, declaration, certificate, bill of lading, or other document required by law or regulation in connection with the importation, transportation, or exportation of any merchandise shipped or consigned by or to said grantor; to perform any act or condition which may be required by law or regulation in connection with such merchandise; to receive any merchandise deliverable to said grantor;

To make endorsements on bills of lading conferring authority to make entry and collect drawback, and to make, sign, declare, or swear to any statement, supplemental statement, schedule, supplemental schedule, certificate of delivery, certificate of manufacture, certificate of manufacture and delivery, abstract of manufacturing records, declaration of proprietor on drawback entry, declaration of exporter on drawback entry, or any other affidavit or document which may be required by law or regulation for drawback purposes, regardless of whether such bill of lading, sworn statement, schedule, certificate, abstract, declaration, or other affidavit or document is intended for filing in said port or in any other customs port;

To sign, seal, and deliver for and as the act of said grantor any bond required by law or regulation in connection with the entry or withdrawal of imported merchandise or merchandise exported with or without benefit of drawback, or in connection with the entry, clearance, lading, unlading or navigation of any vessel or other means of conveyance owned or operated by said grantor, and any and all bonds which may be voluntarily given and accepted under applicable laws and regulations, consignee's and owner's declarations provided for in section 485, Tariff Act of 1930, as amended, or affidavits in connection with the entry of merchandise;

To sign and swear to any document and to perform any act that may be necessary or required by law or regulation in connection with the entering, clearing, lading, unlading, or operation of any vessel or other means of conveyance owned or operated by said grantor;

And generally to transact at the customhouses in said port any and all customs business, including making, signing, and filing of protests under section 514 of the Tariff Act of 1930, in which said grantor is or may be concerned or interested and which may properly be transacted or performed by an agent and attorney, giving to said agent and attorney full power and authority to do anything whatever requisite and necessary to be done in the premises as fully as said grantor could do if present and acting, hereby ratifying and confirming all that the said agent and attorney shall lawfully do by virtue of these presents; the foregoing power of attorney to remain in full force and effect until the _____ day of ______________, 19 _____, or until notice of revocation in writing is duly given to and received by the Port Director of Customs of the port aforesaid. If the donor of this power of attorney is a partnership, the said power shall in no case have any force or effect after the expiration of 2 years from the date of its receipt in the office of the Port Director of Customs of the said port.

IN WITNESS WHEREOF, the said ______________________________

has caused these presents to be sealed and signed: (Signature) ______________________________

(Capacity) ______________________________ (Date) ______________

WITNESS: ______________________________

Customs Form 5291 (120195) (Corporate seal)*(Optional) **(SEE OVER)**

INDIVIDUAL OR PARTNERSHIP CERTIFICATION *(Optional)

CITY ______________________
COUNTY ______________________ } SS:
STATE ______________________

On this ________ day of ______________, 19 ____, personally appeared before me ______________________

residing at ______________________, personally known or sufficiently identified to me, who certifies that

______________________(is)(are) the individual(s) who executed the foregoing instrument and acknowledge it to be ______________________ free act and deed.

(Notary Public)

CORPORATE CERTIFICATION *(Optional)

(To be made by an officer other than the one who executes the power of attorney)

I, ______________________, certify that I am the ______________________

of ______________________, organized under the laws of the State of ______________________

that ______________________, who signed this power of attorney on behalf of the donor, is the ______________________

of said corporation; and that said power of attorney was duly signed, sealed, and attested for and on behalf of said corporation by authority of its governing body as the same appears in a resolution of the Board of Directors passed at a regular meeting held on the ________ day of ______________, now in my possession or custody. I further certify that the resolution is in accordance with the articles of incorporation and bylaws of said corporation.

IN WITNESS WHEREOF, I have hereunto set my hand and affixed the seal of said corporation, at the City of ______________________ this ________ day of ______________________, 19 ______

______________________ (Signature) ______________________ (Date)

If the corporation has no corporate seal, the fact shall be stated, in which case a scroll or adhesive shall appear in the appropriate, designated place.

Customs powers of attorney of residents (including resident corporations) shall be without power of substitution except for the purpose of executing shipper's export declarations. However, a power of attorney executed in favor of a licensed customhouse broker may specify that the power of attorney is granted to the customhouse broker to act through any of its licensed officers or any employee specifically authorized to act for such customhouse broker by power of attorney.

NOTE: The corporate seal may be omitted. Customs does not require completion of a certification. The grantor has the option of executing the certification or omitting it.

☆GOVERNMENT PRINTING OFFICE: 1998 – 606-491

Customs Form 5291 (120195)(Back)

Figure 6–2. Importer's letter of instruction.

INSTRUCTIONS TO CUSTOMS BROKER

Dear customs broker:

Please arrange for Customs clearance of the following merchandise. Please note that failure to follow the instructions below will result in an incorrect entry. Please forward a copy of the CF7501 for our review prior to submission to Customs:

SHIPPING DETAILS:

Air waybill/Ocean bill of lading: ______________________________

Scheduled Arrival Date: ______________________________

Carrier: ______________________________

In-Bond Carrier: ______________________________

Exporting Country: ______________________________

CUSTOMS DETAILS:

HTS Numbers: ______________________________

Descriptions: ______________________________

Values: ______________________________

Origin of goods: ______________________________

Manufacturer/Shipper: ______________________________

Other Government Agency requirements: ______________________________

Payment of duties:______________________________

DELIVERY INFORMATION:

Deliver to: ______________________________

____

Carrier:______________________________

Other Instructions:______________________________

Please contact ____________________ at ____________________ or email ____________________ if you have **any** additional questions prior to taking action on our behalf.

In the event that a broker is intransigent and refuses to perform its services as required by law, an importer can request that license revocation proceedings be initiated by U.S. Customs and Border Protection.

2. Importation Bonds

In order to import merchandise into the United States, it is necessary for the importer to obtain a bond from a surety company. This is to guarantee that all customs duties, customs penalties, and other charges assessed by Customs will be properly paid, even if the importer goes bankrupt. There are essentially two types of bonds: the single transaction bond and the continuous bond. Single transaction bonds cover single importations, may be for as much as three times the value of the goods depending upon the goods, and are practical only for an importer who is engaged in very few importations. Continuous bonds are issued to cover all of the importations of an importer for a particular time period, usually one year. The amount is usually equal to 10 percent of the total customs duties paid for the previous year or reasonably estimated for the current year, but not less than $50,000. Obviously, before a surety company will provide the importation bond, it will be necessary for the importer to make application, undergo a credit investigation, and show financial stability. Customs brokers have their own customs bonds, and will sometimes handle imports for importers under the coverage of their bond, although this is the exception more than the rule. An application to file a continuous bond and the bond must be filed with the Revenue Division of U.S. Customs and Border Protection in Indianapolis, IN. (A sample customs bond is shown in Figure 6–3.)

3. Importer's Liability and Reasonable Care

The company that intends to import should fully comprehend that liability for all U.S. customs duties, penalties, and charges is the responsibility of the importer. U.S. Customs and Border Protection generally will not have jurisdiction (or it will be too much trouble for it to obtain jurisdiction) over the foreign supplier to collect or assess any customs penalties. Ordinarily, the importer may feel that there is a reasonable risk in importing and paying the normal (for example, 5 percent) customs duties. However, if certain events occur, such as the imposition of antidumping duties, or if false documents, even documents furnished by the foreign supplier (such as commercial invoices), are filed with U.S. Customs and Border Protection in connection with the importation, whether intentionally or accidentally, the importer's liability can dramatically escalate, including the imposition of substantial criminal fines and civil penalties amounting to the full domestic value of—not just the customs duties on—the merchandise. This liability can extend backward up to five years from the date of violation or, in the case of fraud, five years from the date of discovery of the violation by U.S. Customs and Border Protection. Under the Customs Modernization Act, the importer is now required to use "reasonable care" in determining the value, classification, and admissibility of imported merchandise. A checklist released by U.S. Customs is shown in Appendix D.

(*Text continues on page 262.*)

Figure 6–3. Customs bond.

DEPARTMENT OF HOMELAND SECURITY
U.S. Customs and Border Protection
CUSTOMS BOND
19 CFR Part 113

OMB No. 1651-0050 Exp. 12-31-2010

CBP USE ONLY	BOND NUMBER 1 (Assigned by CBP)
	FILE REFERENCE

In order to secure payment of any duty, tax or charge and compliance with law or regulation as a result of activity covered by any condition referenced below, we, the below named principal(s) and surety(ies), bind ourselves to the United States in the amount or amounts, as set forth below. | Execution Date

SECTION I—Select Single Transaction **OR** Continuous Bond (not both) and fill in the applicable blank spaces.

☐ SINGLE TRANSACTION BOND	Identification of transaction secured by this bond (e.g., entry no., seizure no., etc.)	Date of transaction	Port code
☐ CONTINUOUS BOND	Effective date	This bond remains in force for one year beginning with the effective date and for each succeeding annual period, or until terminated. This bond constitutes a separate bond for each period in the amounts listed below for liabilities that accrue in each period. The intention to terminate this bond must be conveyed within the period and manner prescribed in the Customs Regulations.	

SECTION II-- This bond includes the following agreements. 2 (Check one box only, except that, 1a may be checked independently or with 1, and 3a may be checked independently or with 3. Line out all other parts of this section that are not used.

Activity Code	Activity Name and Customs Regulations in which conditions codified	Limit of Liability	Activity Code	Activity Name and Customs Regulations in which conditions codified	Limit of Liability
☐ 1	Importer or broker 113.62		☐ 5	Public Gauger. 113.67	
☐ 1a	Drawback Payments Refunds 113.65		☐ 6	Wool & Fur Products Labeling Acts Importation (Single Entry Only) 113.68	
☐ 2	Custodian of bonded merchandise. . . . . .113.63 (Includes bonded carriers, freight forwarders, cartmen and lightermen, all classes of warehouse, container station operators)		☐ 7	Bill of Lading (Single Entry Only) 113.69	
			☐ 8	Detention of Copyrighted Material (Single Entry Only). 113.70	
☐ 3	International Carrier. 113.64		☐ 9	Neutrality (Single Entry Only) 113.71	
☐ 3a	Instruments of International Traffic 113.66				
☐ 4	Foreign Trade Zone Operator. 113.73		☐ 10	Court Costs for Condemned Goods (Single Entry Only) 113.72	

SECTION III– List below all tradenames or unincorporated divisions that will be permitted to obligate this bond in the principal's name including their CBP identification Number(s). 3 (If more space is needed, use Section III (Continuation) on back of form.)

Importer Number	Importer Name	Importer Number	Importer Name
		Total number of importer names listed in Section III:	

Principal and surety agree that any charge against the bond under any of the listed names is as though it was made by the principal(s).

Principal and surety agree that they are bound to the same extent as if they executed a separate bond covering each set of conditions incorporated by reference to the Customs Regulations into this bond.

If the surety fails to appoint an agent under Title 6, United States Code, Section 7, surety consents to service on the Clerk of any United States District Court or the U.S. Court of International Trade, where suit is brought on this bond. That clerk is to send notice of the service to the surety at:

Mailing Address Requested by the Surety

PRINCIPAL 4	Name and Address	Importer No. 3 SIGNATURE 5	SEAL
PRINCIPAL 4	Name and Address	Importer No. 3 SIGNATURE 5	SEAL
SURETY 4, 6	Name and Address 6	Surety No. 7 SIGNATURE 5	SEAL
SURETY 4, 6	Name and Address 6	Surety No. 7 SIGNATURE 5	SEAL

SURETY AGENTS	Name 8	Identification No. 9	Name 8	Identification No. 9

PART 1 - CBP, PART 2 - SURETY, PART 3 - PRINCIPAL

CBP Form 301 (05/98)

Figure 6–3. *(continued)*

Note: Turn carbons over before writing on back of form.

SECTION III (Continuation)

Importer Number	Importer Name	Importer Number	Importer Name

WITNESSES	SIGNED, SEALED, and DELIVERED in the PRESENCE OF:	
Two witnesses are required to authenticate the signature of any person who signs as an individual or partner; however a witness may authenticate the signatures of both such non-corporate principals and sureties. No witness is needed to authenticate the signature of a corporate official or agent who signs for the corporation.	Name and Address of Witness for the Principal SIGNATURE:	Name and Address of Witness for the Surety SIGNATURE:
	Name and Address of Witness for the Principal SIGNATURE:	Name and Address of Witness for the Surety SIGNATURE:

EXPLANATIONS AND FOOTNOTES

1 The CBP Bond Number is a control number assigned by CBP to the bond contract when the bond is approved by an authorized CBP official.

2 For all bond coverage available and the language of the bond conditions refer to Part 113, subpart G, Customs Regulations.

3 The Importer Number is the CBP identification number filed pursuant to section 24.5, Customs Regulations. When the Internal Revenue Service employer identification number is used the two-digit suffix code must be shown.

4 If the principal or surety is a corporation, the name of the State in which incorporated must be shown.

5 See witness requirement above.

6 Surety Name, if a corporation, shall be the company's name as it is spelled in the Surety Companies Annual List published in the Federal Register by the Department of the Treasury (Treasury Department Circular 570).

7 Surety Number is the three digit identification code assigned by CBP to a surety company at the time the surety company initially gives notice to CBP that the company will be writing CBP bonds.

8 Surety Agent is the individual granted a Corporate Surety Power of Attorney, CBP 5297, by the surety company executing the bond.

9 Agent Identification No. shall be the individual's Social Security number as shown on the Corporate Surety Power of Attorney, CBP 5297, filed by the surety granting such power of attorney.

Paperwork Reduction Act Notice: The Paperwork Reduction Act says we must tell you why we are collecting this information, how we will use it, and whether you have to give it to us. We ask for this information to carry out U.S. Customs and Border Protection laws and regulations of the United States. We need it to ensure that persons transacting business with CBP have the proper bond coverage to secure their transactions as required by law and regulation. Your response is required to enter into any transaction in which a bond is a prerequisite under the Tariff Act of 1930, as amended. The estimated average burden associated with this collection of information is 15 minutes per respondent or recordkeeper depending on individual circumstances. Comments concerning the accuracy of this burden estimate and suggestions for reducing this burden should be directed to U.S. Customs and Border Protection, Information Services Branch, Washington, DC 20229, and to the Office of Management and Budget, Paperwork Reduction Project (1651-0050), Washington, DC 20503.

Privacy Act Statement: The following notice is given pursuant to section 7(b) of the Privacy Act of 1974 (5 U.S.C. 552a). Furnishing the information of this form, including the Social Security Number, is mandatory. The primary use of the Social Security Number is to verify, in the CBP Automated System, at the time an agent submits a CBP bond for approval that the individual was granted a Corporate Surety Power of Attorney by the surety company. Section 7 of Act of July 30, 1947, chapter 390, 61 Stat. 646, authorizes the collection of this information.

CBP Form 301 (05/98)(Back)

In order to avoid some of these risks, the buyer may decide to insist that the exporter act as the importer of record. This can be done if the exporter establishes a branch office or subsidiary company in the United States, or if the exporter obtains a bond from a surety company incorporated in the United States and the exporter appoints a person in the United States in the state of the port of entry who is authorized to accept service of process in the event of any court action commenced against the exporter. The broker can also act as the importer of record but, because of the potential liability, it will normally seek to relieve itself from this responsibility by asking the importer to sign a Declaration of Consignee, Customs Form 3347A (see Figure 6–4).

4. *Application for Importer's Number*

As a general rule, U.S. Customs and Border Protection will use the importer's Federal Employer Identification Number (FEIN) to track the company's imports or, in the case of an individual importer, her social security number. However, companies without an FEIN that have not previously engaged in importing must file an application for an importer's number with U.S. Customs and Border Protection. (When the importer's name or address changes, it should file an amendment to this application.) A sample application is shown in Figure 6–5. Thereafter, Customs will notify the applicant of its assigned importer's number. This number must be used on many documents that the importer or its broker will file with U.S. Customs and Border Protection on future importations

5. *Ports of Entry*

The importer should determine what the appropriate ports of entry in the United States should be. If goods are traveling by air or by ship, it will be easy enough to determine their place of arrival. However, where the goods are unloaded is not necessarily the place where customs entry will be made. Goods can be unloaded on the East or West Coast and transported in-bond to an inland port of entry for the filing of entry documents and release from Customs custody. Because of the congestion that may occur at certain ports, efficient importing may sometimes mandate the use of ports that would not normally be considered. In addition, there are situations where different U.S. Customs offices will treat importations differently. This port shopping is not illegal; however, if an importer has sought a determination of a classification and proper duty for a prospective import at one port, under new Customs regulations, the importer must disclose its inquiry and answer to any other port where it may enter merchandise. Finally, in some cases, such as the importation of goods subject to U.S. Department of Agriculture or Fish and Wildlife requirements, entry is permitted only at certain designated ports of entry.

6. *Import Quotas*

Through legislation, enacted as often as yearly, the U.S. Congress imposes quotas on different types of imported merchandise. Quotas may be worldwide or related to

(*Text continues on page 267.*)

Figure 6–4. Owner's declaration.

DEPARTMENT OF HOMELAND SECURITY
U.S. Customs and Border Protection

OMB No. 1651-0093
Exp. 02-28-2009

DECLARATION OF CONSIGNEE WHEN ENTRY IS MADE BY AN AGENT

19 CFR 141.19(B)(2)

If this declaration is made by an agent who does not present with the entry the declaration of the consignee, or who does not have proper authority to execute such declaration for this principal, bond must be given to produce such declaration in accordance with Section 485(c), Tariff Act of 1930.

THIS DECLARATION MUST BE PRESENTED TO THE PORT DIRECTOR OF CBP AT THE PORT OF ENTRY WITHIN SIX MONTHS AFTER THE DATE OF THE BOND GIVEN THEREFORE, UNLESS AN EXTENSION OF TIME IS GRANTED BY THE PORT DIRECTOR.

1. NAME OF CONSIGNEE	2. ADDRESS (STREET, CITY, STATE, ZIP CODE)

3. VESSEL/CARRIER ARRIVED FROM	4. NAME OF VESSEL/CARRIER	5. ENTRY NUMBER	6. DATE

7. NUMBER OF PACKAGES	8. SELLER OR SHIPPER	9. PLACE AND DATE OF INVOICE	10. AMOUNT PAID OR TO BE PAID IN FOREIGN CURRENCY	11. RATE OF EXCHANGE	12. ENTERED VALUE (FOREIGN CURRENCY)	13. ENTERED VALUE (U.S. DOLLARS)

COMPLETE SECTION I, OR SECTION II, OR SECTION III (CHECK ONE) AND SECTION IV.

☐ SECTION I — DECLARATION OF NOMINAL CONSIGNEE

14. NAME OF OWNER	15. ADDRESS (STREET, CITY, STATE, ZIP CODE)

I, the undersigned, herewith declare that the consignee in whose name the entry covering the merchandise described herein was made, is not the actual owner of the said merchandise, but that such entry exhibits a full and complete account of all the merchandise imported in the vessel indicated therein by the above name person who is the actual owner for CBP purposes of the said merchandise except as listed below.

☐ SECTION II — DECLARATION OF CONSIGNEE FOR MERCHANDISE OBTAINED IN PURSUANCE OF A PURCHASE OR AGREEMENT TO PURCHASE

I, the undersigned, representing the above name consignee, herewith declare that they are the consignees for CBP purposes of the merchandise described herein, that the entry covering the said merchandise exhibits a full and complete account of all the merchandise imported by them in the vessel indicated in the said entry and that the said merchandise was obtained by them in pursuance of a purchase or an agreement to purchase, except as listed below.

☐ SECTION III — DECLARATION OF CONSIGNEE FOR MERCHANDISE OBTAINED OTHERWISE THAN IN PURSUANCE OF A PURCHASE OR AGREEMENT TO PURCHASE

I, the undersigned, representing the above name consignee, herewith declare that they are the consignees for CBP purposes of the merchandise described herein, that the entry covering the said merchandise exhibits a full and complete account of all the merchandise imported by them in the vessel indicated in the said entry and that the said merchandise was obtained by them in pursuance of a purchase or an agreement to purchase, except as listed below.

16. EXCEPTIONS (IF ANY)

☐ SECTION IV — GENERAL DECLARATION

I also declare, to the best of my knowledge and belief, that all statements appearing in the entry and in the invoice or invoices and other documents presented herewith and in accordance with which the entry is made, are true and correct in every respect; that the entry and invoices set forth the true prices, values, quantities, and all information as required by the law and the regulations made in pursuance thereof, that the invoices and other documents are in the same state as when received; that I have not received and do not know of any other invoices, paper, letter, document, or information showing a different currency, price, value, quantity, or description of the said merchandise, and that if at any time hereafter I discover any information showing a different state of facts, I will immediately make the same known to the port director of CBP at the port of entry.

17. SIGNATURE	18. ADDRESS	19. DATE

20. TITLE (CHECK ONE)

☐ PRINCIPAL ☐ MEMBER OF THE FIRM ☐ PRINCIPAL OFFICER OF THE CORPORATION: TITLE ____________ ☐ AUTHORIZED AGENT

CBP Form 3347A (12/02)

(*continues*)

Figure 6–4. *(continued)*

PAPERWORK REDUCTION ACT NOTICE: The Paperwork Reduction Act says we must tell you why we are collecting this information, how we will use it, and whether you have to give it to us. We ask for the information to carry out the U.S. Customs and Border Protection laws. We need it when an agent of the consignee has knowledge of the facts and is authorized by that consignee to execute the declarations on the entry or entry summary, in compliance with Section 484 of the Tariff Act of 1930, as amended. Your response is required to obtain a benefit.

Statement required by 5 CFR 1320.21: The estimated average burden associated with this collection of information is 6 minutes per respondent or recordkeeper depending on individual circumstances. Comments concerning the accuracy of this burden estimate and suggestions for reducing this burden should be directed to U.S. Customs and Border Protection, Information Services Branch, Washington DC 20229, and to the Office of Management and Budget, Paperwork Reduction Project (1651-0093), Washington, DC 20503.

CBP Form 3347A (Back)(12/02)

Figure 6–5. Application for importer's number and instructions.

Approved OMB NO. 1651-0064
Exp. 09-30-2009
See back of form for Paperwork Reduction Act Notice.

DEPARTMENT OF HOMELAND SECURITY
U.S. Customs and Border Protection

IMPORTER ID
INPUT RECORD

19 CFR 24.5

1. TYPE OF ACTION *(Mark all applicable)*

☐ Notification of importer's number
☐ Change of address*
☐ Change of name*
☐ Check here if you also want your address updated in the Fines, Penalties, and Forfeitures Office

*NOTE--If a continuous bond is on file, a rider must accompany this change document.

2. IMPORTER NUMBER *(Fill in one format)*:--

2A. I.R.S. Number

2B. Social Security Number

2C. ☐ Check here if requesting a CBP-assigned number and indicate reason(s). *(Check all that apply.)* ☐ I have no IRS No. ☐ I have no Social Security No. ☐ I have not applied for either number. ☐ I am not a U.S. resident

2D. CBP-Assigned Number

3. Importer Name

4. DIV/AKA/DBA ☐ DIV ☐ AKA ☐ DBA

5. DIV/AKA/DBA Name

6. Type

☐ Corporation ☐ Partnership ☐ Sole Proprietorship ☐ Individual ☐ U.S. Government ☐ State/Local Governments ☐ Foreign Governments

7. Importer Mailing Address *(2 32-character lines maximum)*

8. City

9. State Code

10. ZIP

11. Country ISO Code *(Non-U.S. Only)*

12. Importer Physical Location Address *(2 32-character lines maximum, see instructions)*

13. City

14. State Code

15. ZIP

16. Country ISO Code *(Non-U.S. Only)*

17a. Has importer ever been assigned a CBP Importer Number using the same name as in Block 3?

☐ No ☐ Yes *(List number(s) and/or name(s) in Block 17c.)*

17b. Has importer ever been assigned a CBP Importer Number using a name different from that in Block 3?

☐ No ☐ Yes *(List number(s) and/or name(s) in Block 17c.)*

17c. If "Yes" to 17a and/or 17b, list number(s) and/or name(s)

I CERTIFY: That the information presented herein is correct; that if my Social Security Number is used it is because I have no IRS Employer Number, that if my CBP assigned number is used it is because I have neither a Social Security Number nor an IRS Employer Number, that if none of these numbers is used, it is because I have none, and my signature constitutes a request for assignment of a number by CBP.

18. Printed or Typed Name and Title

19. Telephone No. Including Area Code

20. Signature

X

21. Date

22. Broker Use Only

Previous Editions are Obsolete

CBP Form 5106 (03/99)

(*continues*)

Figure 6–5. (*continued*)

Paperwork Reduction Act Notice: We need this information to establish the Importer's name, address, and importer number. We will use this information as basis for establishing bond coverage, release and entry of merchandise, liquidation, issuance of bills and refunds, and processing of drawback and FP&F actions. Your response is mandatory. The estimated average burden associated with this collection of information is 6 minutes per respondent or recordkeeper depending on individual circumstances. Comments concerning the accuracy of this burden estimate and suggestions for reducing this burden should be directed to U.S. Customs and Border Protection, Information Services Branch, Washington, DC 20229 and to the Office of Management and Budget, Paperwork Reduction Project (1651-0064) Washington, DC 20503.

PRIVACY ACT STATEMENT: Pursuant to the requirements of Public Law 93-579 (Privacy Act of 1974, notice is hereby given that 19 CFR 24.5 authorizes the disclosure of Social Security numbers (SSN) on the CBP Form 5106. The principal purpose for disclosure of the Social Security number is to assure maintenance of records that have a high degree of usefulness in regulatory investigations or proceedings. The information collected may be provided to those officers and employees of the CBP and any constituent unit of the Department of the Homeland Security who have a need for the records in the performance of their duties. The records may be referred to any department or agency of the federal government upon the request of the head of such department or agency. The authority to collect the SSN is 31 CFR 103.25. The SSN will be used to identify the individuals conducting business with the CBP.

BLOCK 1 - TYPE OF ACTION

Notification of Importer's Number - Check this box if you are a first time importer, using an importer number for the first time, or if you have not engaged in CBP business within the last year.

Change of Name - Check this box if this importer number is on file but there is a change in the name on file.

Change of Address - Check this box if this importer number is on file but there is a change in the address on file.

BLOCK 2 - IMPORTER

2A *-IRS Number - Complete this block if you are assigned an Internal Revenue Service employer identification number.*

2B *-Social Security Number - Complete this block if no Internal Revenue Service employer identification number has been assigned. The Social Security number should belong to the principal or owner of the company or the individual who represents the importer of record.*

2C *-Requesting a CBP Assigned Number - Complete this block if no Internal Revenue Service employer identification number has been assigned, or no Social Security number has been assigned. If this box is checked, all corresponding boxes in 2C must also be marked. PLEASE NOTE. A CBP Assigned Number is for CBP use* ***only*** *and does not replace a Social Security number or Internal Revenue Service employer identification number. In general, a CBP Assigned Number will only be issued to foreign businesses or individuals, provided no IRS or Social Security number exists for the applicant. If Block 2C is completed, this form must be submitted in duplicate. CBP will issue an Assigned Number and return a copy of the completed form with the Assigned Number to the requester. This identification number will be used for all future CBP transactions when an importer number is required. If an Internal Revenue Service employer identification number and/or a Social Security number are obtained after an importer number has been assigned by CBP, the importer will continue to use the assigned number unless otherwise instructed.*

2D *-CBP Assigned Number - Complete this block if you are assigned a CBP Assigned Number but there is an Action change (Block 1).*

BLOCK 3 - IMPORTER NAME

If the name is an individual, input the last name first, first name, and middle initial. Business names should be input first name first.

BLOCK 4 - DIV/AKA/DBA

Complete this block if an importer is a division of another company (DIV), is also known under another name (AKA), or conducts business under another name (DBA).

BLOCK 5 - DIV/AKA/DBA NAME

Complete this block only if Block 4 is used.

BLOCK 6 - TYPE OF COMPANY

Check applicable box. *Please Note:* Place an "X" after U.S. Gov't **only** for a U.S. federal government department, agency, bureau or office. All federal agencies are assigned I.R.S. numbers which should be used for any CBP transactions by that agency.

BLOCK 7 - IMPORTER MAILING ADDRESS

This block must always be completed. It may or may not be the importer's business address. Insert a post office box number, or a street number representing the first line of the importer's mailing address (up to 32 characters). For a U.S. or Canadian mailing address, additional mailing address information may be inserted (up to 32 characters). If a P.O. box number is given for the mailing address, a second address (physical location) must be provided in Block 12.

BLOCK 8 - CITY

Insert the city name of the importees mailing address.

BLOCK 9 - STATE

For a U.S. mailing address, insert a valid 2-position alphabetic U.S. state postal code (see list below). For a Canadian mailing address, insert a 2-character alphabetic code representing the province of the importer's mailing address (see list below).

BLOCK 10 - ZIP CODE

For a U.S. mailing address, insert a 5 or 9 digit numeric ZIP code as established by the U.S. Postal Service. For a Canadian mailing address, insert a Canadian postal routing code. For a Mexican mailing address, leave blank. For all other foreign mailing addresses, a postal routing code may be inserted.

BLOCK 11 -COUNTRY ISO CODE

For a U.S. mailing address, leave blank. For any foreign mailing address, including Canada and Mexico, insert a 2 character alphabetic International Standards Organization (ISO) code representing the country. Please Note: Valid ISO codes may be found in Annex B of the Harmonized Tariff Schedule of the United States; Customs Directive 099 5610-002, "Standard Guidelines for the Input of Names and Addresses into ACS Files"; or CBP Form 7501 Instructions".

BLOCK 12 - SECOND IMPORTER ADDRESS

If the importer's place of business is the same as the mailing address, leave blank. If different from the mailing address, insert the importer's business address in this space. A second address representing the importer's place of business is to be provided if the mailing address is a post office box or drawer.

BLOCK 13 - CITY

Insert the city name for the importer's business address.

BLOCK 14 - STATE

For a U.S. address, insert a 2 character alphabetic U.S. state postal code (see list below). For a Canadian address, insert a 2 character alphabetic code representing the province of the importer's business address (see list below).

BLOCK 15 - ZIP CODE

For a U.S. business address, insert a 5 or 9 digit numeric ZIP code as established by the U.S. Postal Service. For a Canadian address, insert a Canadian postal routing code. For a Mexican address, leave blank. For all other foreign addresses, postal routing code may be inserted.

BLOCK 16 - COUNTRY ISO CODE

For a U.S. address, leave blank. For any foreign address, including Canada and Mexico, insert a 2 character alphabetic ISO code representing the country.

BLOCK 17 - PREVIOUSLY ASSIGNED CUSTOMS IMPORTER NUMBER

Indicate whether or not importer has previously been assigned a CBP Importer Number under the same name or a different name. If "Yes" to either question, list name(s) and/or number(s) in Block 17c.

OFFICIAL UNITED STATES POSTAL SERVICE
TWO-LETTER STATE AND POSSESSION ABBREVIATIONS

AL	Alabama	MT	Montana
AK	Alaska	NE	Nebraska
AZ	Arizona	NV	Nevada
AR	Arkansas	NH	New Hamsphire
AS	American Samoa	NJ	New Jersey
CA	California	NM	New Mexico
CO	Colorado	NY	New York
CT	Connecticut	NC	North Carolina
DE	Delaware	ND	North Dakota
DC	Distric of Columbia	MP	Northern Mariana Islands
FM	Federated States of Micronesia	OH	Ohio
FL	Florida	OK	Oklahoma
GA	Georgia	OR	Oregon
GU	Guam	PW	Palau
HI	Hawaii	PA	Pennsylvania
ID	Idaho	PR	Puerto Rico
IL	Illinios	RI	Rhode Island
IN	Indiana	SC	South Carolina
IA	Iowa	SD	South Dakota
KS	Kansas	TN	Tennessee
KY	Kentucky	TX	Texas
LA	Louisiana	UT	Utah
ME	Maine	VT	Vermont
MH	Marshall Islands	VA	Virginia
MD	Maryland	VI	Virgin Islands
MA	Massachusetts	WA	Washington
MI	Michigan	WV	West Virginia
MN	Minnesota	WI	Wisconsin
MS	Mississippi	WY	Wyoming
MO	Missouri		

OFFICIAL TWO-LETTER CANADIAN PROVINCE CODES

AB	Alberta	NS	Nova Scotia
BC	British Columbia	ON	Ontario
MB	Manitoba	PE	Prince Edward Island
NB	New Brunswick	QC	Quebec
NL	Newfoundland (Incl. Labrador)	SK	Saskatchewan
NT	Northwest Territories	YT	Yukon Territory

CBP Form 5106 (03/99)(Back)

specific countries. Some quotas are absolute; that is, once a specific quantity has been entered into the United States, no further imports are permitted.

Most quotas are tariff-rate quotas, meaning that a certain quantity of the merchandise is entered at one duty rate, and once that quantity has been exceeded—for the United States as a whole, not for the specific importer—the tariff duty rate increases. Thus, the importer can continue to import, but it will have to pay a higher tariff duty. Examples of tariff-rate quotas are certain milks and creams, upland cotton, and tobacco.

Additionally, there are specific tariff-rate quotas for products under the jurisdiction of the U.S. Department of Agriculture, which require the importer to have an import license. With a license, the importer may import at a lower duty rate; without a license, the importer may still import the product, but it must pay a higher duty rate. Examples of the Department of Agriculture quotas are certain butters, sour creams, dried milks or creams, butter substitutes, blue-molded cheese, cheddar cheese (except Canadian cheddar), American-type cheese, Edam and Gouda cheeses, Italian-type cheeses, Swiss or Emmentaler cheese, and cheese substitutes.

Under the NAFTA agreement, there are also specific tariff-rate quotas for products imported from Mexico, including certain dried milks and creams, condensed and evaporated milks and creams, cheese, tomatoes, onions and shallots, eggplants, chili peppers, watermelons, peanuts, sugars derived from sugarcane or sugar beets, orange juice, cotton, and brooms. Imports of some products from both Canada and Mexico are subject to tariff-rate quotas, such as certain cotton, man-made fiber, or wool apparel and cotton or man-made fiber fabrics and yarns.

Following the Uruguay Round negotiations of the General Agreement on Tariffs and Trade (GATT), specific tariff-rate quotas on certain products were also implemented.

These quotas include beef, milk and cream, dried milk and cream, dairy products, condensed or evaporated milk and cream, dried whey, Canadian cheddar cheese, peanuts, sugar (including sugarcane), certain articles containing sugar, blended syrups, cocoa powder, chocolate, chocolate crumb, infant formula, mixes and doughs, peanut butter and paste, mixed condiments and seasonings, ice cream, animal feed, cotton, card strips made from cotton, and fibers of cotton.

Finally, so as not to harm U.S. farm production, there are tariff-rate preferences for certain vegetables and fresh produce when entered during the peak growing season in the United States. Importers of produce during peak season will be assessed a lower duty rate. However, in the off season, the tariff classification and associated duty rate are higher.

Before agreeing to purchase products for importation and in planning the cost of the product, the importer must ascertain in advance whether any absolute or tariff-rate quotas exist on the merchandise.

7. Antidumping, Countervailing, and Other Special Duties

Before entering into an agreement to purchase products for importation, the importer should specifically confirm whether those products are subject to an antidumping or countervailing duty order of the U.S. Department of Commerce (administered by U.S. Customs and Border Protection) or to a special duty imposed under Section 201 or 406 of the Trade Act of 1974. When goods are subject to one of these orders, the amount of customs duties (which are payable by the importer) can be much greater than on ordinary importations. While in recent years manufactured items have been subject to a relatively low rate of normal duty (in the range of 3 to 5 percent), cases under these laws exist where duties of as much as 300 percent of the value of the goods have been assessed. Furthermore, U.S. Customs regulations prohibit the reimbursement of the U.S. importer by the foreign supplier if the U.S. importer pays antidumping or countervailing duties. Where goods are subject to an antidumping or countervailing duty order, the importer will be required to sign a certificate for U.S. Customs and Border Protection under penalty of perjury that it has not entered into any agreement for reimbursement of such duties. When an importer is negotiating the price for purchase from the foreign supplier, it is important for the importer to ascertain the price at which the foreign supplier is selling in its own country and for export to third countries. This will help the importer determine whether there is a risk that an antidumping investigation can be initiated in the future on the imports of the product being purchased. Furthermore, if the importer determines that the goods are already subject to an antidumping order, it can take certain steps, such as insisting that the exporter act as the importer of record, becoming a related party to the seller, or substantially transforming the merchandise in a third country, to reduce or eliminate the dumping risks.

8. Classification

Before importing and during the time that the importer is trying to calculate the potential duties payable on the imported product, it will be necessary for the importer to ascertain the correct customs classification for the product. Under the Customs Modernization Act, an importer must use "reasonable care" in classifying the product. As of January 1, 1989, the United States became a party to the Harmonized Tariff System (HTS), a new commodity classification system that has been adopted in one hundred and thirty-five countries. This is an attempt to standardize among those countries a common classification system for all merchandise. The HTS classification system is extensive. A copy of the table of contents of the HTS, the General Rules of Interpretation used to classify merchandise, the symbols for special tariff reduction programs, and a sample page relating to women's coats are included in Appendix F. All merchandise is classified in some provision of this tariff system, including a catch-all provision for items not elsewhere specified. Only by identifying the appropriate classification in the HTS can the importer ascertain the duty that will be payable on the imported product. Sometimes, in order to attempt to classify the merchandise, the importer will have to obtain information from the exporter—for example, which material constitutes the chief value when the goods are classified by component material.

Unfortunately, identification of the correct classification is not always easy. Not only can an item be classified under two or more classifications (such as individual items or as a set or system), but in some cases, such as the development of new commercial products, no classification may be immediately apparent. In that event, it may be necessary to request a classification ruling from U.S. Customs and Border Protection. Some rulings are informal and can provide useful guidance for planning purposes. However, if the importer wants to have assurance of a certain duty rate (and not a surprise duty increase at some later date), it is necessary to seek a binding, formal ruling from U.S. Customs and Border Protection. (See subsection 18, below.) It goes without saying that tariff classification opinions offered by customs brokers are not binding on U.S. Customs and Border Protection and can be regarded only as knowledgeable guesses. The classification should be checked each year, since products are sometimes reclassified by Customs.

9. *Valuation*

When the importer imports merchandise, it is generally required to state a value for the merchandise on the documents filed with U.S. Customs and Border Protection, and the seller will be required to furnish the buyer with a commercial invoice evidencing the sales price. Under the Customs Modernization Act, an importer must use "reasonable care" in determining the value of the merchandise. Even when the item is duty-free, for U.S. import balance of payments statistical purposes, the Department of Commerce, through U.S. Customs and Border Protection, wants to know the value of the merchandise. Where the goods are dutiable at an ad valorem duty, that is, a percentage of the value, obviously it makes a great deal of difference whether the value is $100 or $100,000. In general, the value will be the price of the merchandise paid or payable by the importer/buyer to the exporter/seller. This is known as the transaction value. This must include any indirect payments, such as when the merchandise is being provided free or at a reduced price to satisfy a previous debt. There are a number of deductions permitted from the invoice price, such as foreign inland freight from the seller's factory to the port of export if such charges are separately identified on the invoice and shipment is made on a through bill of lading, and ocean or air international transportation charges and insurance. Similarly, the law requires certain additions to the price paid or payable in order to arrive at the transaction value, such as packing costs incurred by the buyer; selling commissions incurred by the buyer; assists, royalties, or license fees that the buyer is required to pay as a condition of the sale; and any proceeds accruing to the seller upon subsequent resale, disposal, or use of the merchandise, provided that such amounts were not included in the original price. This means that the value for customs purposes may be different from the price that the buyer and the seller have negotiated.

One area of concern occurs when the buyer and the seller are related parties. That is, if the buyer or the seller owns 5 percent or more of the stock or a similar interest in the other, or if the buyer and the seller are commonly owned by a third party, U.S. Customs and Border Protection suspects that the price paid between the buyer and the seller may not be a true arm's-length value. Customs assumes that the price may have been manipulated, for example, to reduce income taxes in the seller's country or to avoid antidumping duties in the buyer's country. Consequently, when the importation is between a related seller and buyer, Customs will ordinarily request, and the importer will be required to furnish, information designed to establish to Customs' satisfaction that the price paid or payable is equivalent to a true arm's-length price.

In certain circumstances, for example, where Customs has determined that the transaction value is not equivalent to a true arm's-length price, or any element of the price cannot be determined, Customs will use other valuation methods to calculate the customs value. Customs may use the transaction value of identical or similar merchandise, the deductive value, or the computed value. When Customs determines that one of these alternative valuation methods is required, the importer can often be surprised by a retroactive increase in customs duties that can substantially and adversely affect the importer.

Where the purchase is in a foreign currency, Customs requires the price to be converted to U.S. dollars for valuation of the merchandise on the date of export, even though the date of payment will probably be different. Customs uses quarterly exchange rates based on the average of the exchange rates for that particular country during the first three business days of the quarter. Should the daily exchange rate vary by 5 percent from the quarterly rate, Customs will switch to the daily rate based on the date of export.

10. Duty-Free and Reduced Duty Programs

Before importing, the importer should ascertain whether or not the product is eligible for one of the special duty-free or reduced duty programs that Congress has allowed.

The largest program is known as the Generalized System of Preferences (GSP). This program was designed to encourage the economic development of less-developed countries by permitting the importation of those countries' products duty-free. The HTS contains a list of the approximately 101 countries eligible for this program. (See Appendix F.) The fact that a product will be imported from one of the GSP beneficiary countries, however, does not guarantee duty-free treatment. Some specific products even from eligible countries have been excluded, and it is necessary for the importer to identify whether the particular product is on the exclusion list. In addition, at least 35 percent of the final appraised value must be added in that country. The importer must claim the duty-free status by putting an "A" in the Entry Summary and, if requested by Customs, obtaining evidence from the supplier that the goods meet the criteria.

For imports from the twenty-four countries located in the Caribbean Basin, a similar duty-free program is available. Similar programs are available for imports from Israel under the Israel Free Trade Agreement; imports from Jordan under the Jordan Free Trade Agreement; imports from Colombia, Peru, and Ecuador under the Andean Trade Preference Act; and imports from forty countries under the African Growth and Opportunity Act. Some of the programs allow 15 percent U.S.-origin content to be calculated into the 35 percent origin criteria for preferential duty purposes.

Under the North American Free Trade Agreement, implemented on January 1, 1994, products of Canadian and Mexican origin eventually can be imported duty-free to the United States if various requirements are met. Usually, this means that the product must be of Canadian or Mexican origin under one of six eligibility rules and the exporter must provide the importer with a certificate of origin (see Figure 4–16). Many items were granted duty-free status immediately, but other items had their duties reduced over a 15-year phase-out period. All eligible items are now duty free. Thus, if the importer can comply with the requirements, the duty will be less than on ordinary imports from Canada or Mexico.

Recently the United States has entered into free trade agreements with Singapore, Chile, Morocco, Australia, Dominican Republic–Central America–United States Free Trade Agreement (DR-CAFTA), Bahrain, Oman, and Peru. Other free trade agreements, such as those with Korea, Colombia, and Panama, are all pending approval. (See Figures 4–17 and 4–18 for samples of other certificates of origin).

11. Column 2 Imports

The HTS presently classifies imports according to their source. Products coming from nations that are members of the General Agreement on Tariffs and Trade (GATT) are entitled to be imported at the lowest duty rates ("Normal Tariff Rate [NTR]"—generally 0 to 10 percent). Products from Cuba and North Korea are assessed duties at much higher rates, in the range of 20 to 110 percent. (Importations from certain countries—Cuba, Iran, Sudan, and Syria—are prohibited without a license from the Office of Foreign Assets Control, Department of Treasury. Imports from North Korea require approval from the Office of Foreign Assets Control.)

In addition, under Section 406 of the Trade Act of 1974, if there is a substantial increase in products from a Communist country that causes market disruption and injury to the U.S. industry, the International Trade Commission, with the approval of the president, can impose quotas or assess additional duties. An importer contemplating importation from a Communist country should confirm whether such quotas or duties have been imposed.

12. Deferred Duty Programs (Bonded Warehousing and Foreign Trade Zones)

An importer may wish to plan its importations in a manner that defers the payment of duties. Two possible programs exist for this purpose. The first is bonded warehouse importations. Importers can apply for and obtain authorization from U.S. Customs and Border Protection to establish a bonded warehouse on their own premises, or they can utilize the services of a public warehouse that has received similar Customs authorization. When such authorization has been received, goods can be imported and placed in such warehouses, to be withdrawn for use or consumption at a later date (up to five years) with a warehouse entry. In the meantime, no customs duties are payable. When the goods are withdrawn for consumption, the goods will be dutiable at the value at the time of withdrawal rather than the time of entry into the warehouse. A bond must be secured to prevent loss of duties in case the merchandise is accidentally or intentionally released into U.S. commerce. The importer can manipulate, mark, re-label, repackage, and perform a number of other operations (except manufacturing) on the merchandise. A warehouse entry is made on the regular Entry Summary form by designating the correct type code. (See Chapter 8, Section K.)

The second program for the deferral of duties is the use of a foreign trade zone. Foreign trade zones are operations authorized by the U.S. Foreign Trade Zones Board and are operated on a charge basis for importers using them. In authorized locations, importers may place imported merchandise for manipulation, and, more importantly, actual manufacturing operations can occur there. (Further manufacturing is not permitted in bonded warehouse operations.) The merchandise can then be entered for consumption in the United States or exported. While the merchandise is in the foreign trade zone (there is no time limit), no duty is payable, and if the merchandise is exported, no U.S. duties will be paid at all. A number of importers, such as automobile manufacturers, have established very large foreign trade zone operations on their own premises, called subzones, and customs duties are reduced by importing components and raw materials and finishing them into final products in the subzone. The final product is then entered into the United States at the classification and duty rate applicable to the final product, which is often lower than that for the raw materials and components. The establishment of bonded warehousing and foreign trade zone operations requires significant lead time and record-keeping, and the importer should take this into account in its pre-importation planning. (Samples of applications to admit merchandise to a foreign trade zone and to perform activities there are shown in Figures 8–6 and 8–7.) Other agency requirements, such as Food & Drug requirements, are not waived at the time of importation for entry into foreign trade zones.

13. Temporary Importations

In some situations, an importer may intend to import merchandise only temporarily. For example, an importer may be importing samples for testing, inspection, or making purchasing decisions; an importer may wish to display a sample at a trade fair or other sales show; or an importer may wish to import merchandise and to further manufacture it and then export the finished product. In such cases, the importer can enter the goods under a temporary importation bond (TIB). Under a TIB entry, the importer establishes a bond covering the imported merchandise and guarantees that it will be exported within one year, unless extended (up to two more years). If the goods are not exported, the bond is forfeited, usually in the amount of twice the value of the customs duties that would have been payable on the products. TIBs are not available for merchandise that is subject to an absolute quota. The importer should be aware of its obligation to account for the exportation of products prior to the deadline, and should file an Application for Exportation of Articles under Special Bond, Form 3495 (see Figure 6–6) with Customs prior to the export so that Customs can inspect it and confirm that the exportation indeed occurs. Without this, the importer will be unable to cancel the bond and avoid payment of double duties.

14. Country of Origin

Determination of the proper country of origin can affect the duty rate payable on imported goods or whether they are subject to quotas. In addition, Section 304 of the Tariff Act of 1930 requires that imported merchandise be clearly and conspicuously marked in a permanent manner with the English name of the foreign country of origin. Some types of merchandise are exempt from the marking requirement, but, in such cases, the outermost container that will go to the end user must usually be marked. This is an important preliminary planning consideration because the

Figure 6–6. Application for Exportation of Articles Under Special Bond.

DEPARTMENT OF HOMELAND SECURITY
U.S. Customs and Border Protection

Form Approved OMB No. 1651-0004
Exp. 09-30-2007

APPLICATION FOR EXPORTATION OF ARTICLES UNDER SPECIAL BOND

19 CFR 10.38

TO CBP PORT DIRECTOR

1. TO: CBP Port Director *(Address)*	2. FROM: *(Name and Address of Importer or Agent)*

ATTACH COPY OF EXPORT INVOICE DESCRIBING ARTICLES TO BE EXPORTED

3. Name of Exporting Carrier	4. Date of Departure	5. Country of Origin	6. No. of Export Packages
7. Port of Entry	8. Entry Number	Date	9. Date Bonded Period Expires
10. Date Articles Available for CBP Examination	11. Signature of Importer or Agent		12. Date

(FOR CBP USE ONLY)
NOTICE TO IMPORTER TO DELIVER ARTICLES TO BE EXAMINED AND IDENTIFIED FOR EXPORTATION

13. Place of CBP Examination	Date
14. Date	15. CBP PORT DIRECTOR BY:

REPORT OF EXAMINATION

☐ 16. The articles covered by this application have been examined and agree with the invoice in content and No. of export pkgs. and are approved for export.

17. No. of Export Packages	18. Date of Delivery for Exportation	19. Marks and Numbers on Export Packages

☐ 20. The articles covered by this application do not agree with the invoice in content or in number of packages as follows

21. SIGNATURE OF EXAMINING CBP OFFICER	22. DATE

REPORT OF EXPORTATION

23. Home of Exporting Conveyance *(Vessel, Railroad, Airline and Flight Number)*

24. Date of Departure	PAPERWORK REDUCTION ACT NOTICE: The Paperwork Reduction Act says we must tell you why we are collecting this information, and whether you have to give it to us. We need this information to ensure that importers and exporters are complying with the Customs laws of the United States and allow us to figure and collect the right amount of revenue. Your response is mandatory. The estimated average burden associated with this collection of information is 8 minutes per respondent or record keeper depending on individual circumstances. Comments concerning the accuracy of this burden estimate and suggestions for reducing this burden should be directed to U.S. Customs and Border Protection, Information Services Group, Washington, DC 20229, and to the Office of Management and Budget, Paperwork Reduction Project (1651-0004), Washington, DC 20503.
25. Manifest No.	
26. SIGNATURE OF CBP OFFICER	

(CBP officer must return one copy of this form to port of origin upon exportation.)

(Previous Editions are Obsolete)

CBP Form 3495 (08/99)

Customs regulations specify that certain types of products must be marked in certain ways, such as die-stamping, cast-in-the-mold lettering, or etching, during the manufacturing process. The importer should check the country of origin regulations prior to purchasing products to ascertain whether or not it must advise the supplier or seller of any special marking methods prior to the manufacture of the products. Sometimes off-the-shelf inventory manufactured in a foreign country cannot be modified after manufacture to comply with the U.S. country of origin marking requirements. Merchandise that is not properly marked may be seized by U.S. Customs and Border Protection. In some cases, the products can be marked after such seizure, but only upon payment of a marking penalty of 10 percent, which increases the cost of importing the products. More seriously, sometimes Customs will release the merchandise to the importer, and the importer may resell it. Then, Customs may issue a notice of redelivery of the products (see Figure 8–17). If the importer is unable to redeliver the products, a substantial customs penalty may be payable. The marking must remain on the product (including after any repacking) until it reaches the ultimate purchaser, which is usually the retail customer. Recently, penalties for any intentional removal of markings were raised to a $100,000 fine and/or imprisonment for one year.

15. Assists

One of the situations in which U.S. Customs and Border Protection can increase the value of imported merchandise and assess additional customs duties is where the importer has provided an "assist" to the manufacturer/exporter. This may occur when the importer furnishes tooling, dies or molds, raw materials or components, or other items used in the manufacture of the product to the seller at a reduced price or free of charge. Any technical data, such as engineering drawings or know-how, furnished by the importer to the supplier that was not produced in the United States is also an assist. If the importer will be providing any assists, this should be considered at the time the seller makes up the commercial invoices and sales documentation, and the importer should determine the appropriate way to pay customs duties on the value thereof.

16. Specialized Products

Certain products imported into the United States must comply with the regulations of various U.S. government agencies. For example, foods, drugs, cosmetics, and medical devices must comply with the Food, Drugs and Cosmetics Act; electronic products must comply with the Federal Communications Commission regulations; hazardous materials and dangerous goods must comply with the regulations of the Environmental Protection Agency and the Department of Transportation; wood products require submission of certificates regarding the origin of the wood; children's products and phthalates require testing certifications; wood packaging requires evidence of fumigation. Foods must also comply with the Department of Agriculture regulations. Specialized forms must be filed upon importation of such products, and the importer may need to get the information from the exporter to complete such forms prior to arrival of the goods. (Sample forms are shown in Figures 8–9 through 8–15.)

17. Record-Keeping Requirements

Under the U.S. Customs regulations, importers are required to keep copies of all documents relating to their importations for a period of five years. In the event of any question, Customs has the right to inspect such records (on reasonable advance notice) to ascertain that the importer has complied with U.S. customs laws. Prior to engaging in importing, the importer should establish record retention policies and procedures; this will ensure that the relevant records are kept for the appropriate period of time. (See the fuller discussion of this issue in Chapter 1, Section E.)

18. Customs Rulings

Where the importer has questions about the proper application of the customs laws, it may be necessary for the importer to seek a ruling from U.S. Customs and Border Protection. Without such rulings, the importer may take the risk that it is violating customs laws. For example, rulings may be requested relating to the proper classification of merchandise, the proper valuation of merchandise, whether merchandise qualifies for a duty-free or deferred duty treatment, or the proper country of origin marking. As a general rule, classification rulings are issued within approximately 30 days, but more complicated rulings may take from several months to one year. In the event of a substantial volume of planned importations and significant ambiguity regarding the appropriate method of compliance, a ruling may be advisable, and enough lead time to obtain the ruling must be allowed.

G. Import Packing and Labeling

Prior to the exportation of the purchased products, the importer should ascertain the type of packaging and labeling that the exporter will use. Different packaging is often required to withstand the rigors of international transportation and to ensure that the importer is going to receive the products in an undamaged condition. Generally, container transportation will protect best against damage and pilferage. Certain types of containers may be needed, such as ventilated, refrigerated, flat, open top, or high-cube. If the merchandise is a hazardous material, it cannot be transported unless it complies with the International Maritime Dangerous Goods Code or the International Air Transportation Association Dangerous Goods regulations depending on the mode of transport. In addition, the U.S. Department of Transportation has harmonized the U.S. hazardous materials regulations with the international standards. (Hazardous material is discussed in Chapter 2, Section L.) The packing, labeling, and invoicing requirements for such hazardous materials must be communicated to the seller before shipment. Where the supplier sells FOB factory or on any term or condition of sale other than delivered to the buyer, the buyer/importer will be taking the risk of loss during the transportation. Under the Carriage of Goods by Sea Act, steamship lines are not responsible for damage to cargo that is insufficiently packed. Even with insurance, the importer should make an effort to prevent losses due to improper packing. Identification marks on the packages should be put in the packing list. Containerized shipments may be eligible for lower insurance rates compared to breakbulk cargo. The buyer should keep in mind that upon arrival, the goods will have to be examined by U.S. Customs and Border Protection. Packing that facilitates such examination will minimize delays in release from Customs custody. The buyer should ascertain the classification and duty rates of different goods and instruct the buyer to segregate the merchandise prior to shipment. As of July 5, 2006, all wood packaging material (WPM), including pallets, crates, boxes, and pieces of wood used to support or brace cargo, must meet the import requirements and be free of timber pests before entering or transiting the United States. WPM must be heat treated or fumigated with methyl bromide and must be marked with an approved international logo according to the *International Standards for Phytosanitary Measures: Guidelines for Regulating Wood Packaging Material in International Trade* (ISPM 15). U.S. Customs and Border Protection will refuse import to any WPM without the appropriate logo. It cannot be brought into compliance after arrival in the United States. It must be exported. Importers of plant and wood products must declare country of harvest beginning in 2009 (See Figure 6–7.).

Similarly, in order to sell or transport some merchandise after its arrival in the United States, it must be labeled in a certain way. Through its own investigation or through consultation with third parties, the importer should determine if any special labeling is required and should notify the exporter of this prior to exportation of the merchandise. For example, the Consumer Product Safety Act; the regulations of the Bureau of Alcohol, Tobacco and Firearms; the Energy Policy Conservation Act; the Food, Drugs, and Cosmetics Act; the Wool Products Labeling Act; the Textile Fiber Products Identification Act; the Hazardous Substances Act; and the Fur Product Labeling Act are some U.S. laws that impose requirements relating to the proper labeling of imported products. Shipments that are not properly labeled may be refused entry.

H. U.S. Commercial Considerations

There are several commercial considerations that the importer must take into account.

1. *Prevailing Market Price*

In planning its import purchases, the importer must pay attention to the prevailing market price. Obviously, if raw materials or components can be purchased in the United States at a lower price than they can be purchased abroad, depending upon the source country, importation will not be economically feasible. In purchasing for resale, if the purchase price is not sufficiently low to permit an adequate markup when the product is resold at the prevailing U.S. market price, the importation will not be economic. If the product is resold in the U.S. market below the prevailing market price, competitors may charge that the sales are predatory pricing (sales below fully allocated costs) or dumping (sales below the price at which the same products are sold to customers in the country of origin).

2. *Buy American Policies*

In planning import transactions, the importer should determine if there are any Buy American policies applicable to the resale of the products. In particular, in sales to the U.S. federal or state governments or their agencies, there may be certain preferences given to U.S. manufactured products. Sometimes there is a maximum foreign content limitation or there are price preferences. If the importer expects to make such sales, it may be necessary to determine if the cost savings of the foreign product is sufficient to overcome the potential sales differential under Buy American policies. The proliferation of the various free trade agreements with bilateral provisions for nondiscrimination in government procurement contracts has made the use of foreign-origin materials from those countries acceptable, if the contract meets certain criteria. It is important to clarify the origin of the merchandise under the Buy American Act or the Trade Agreements Act to be certain before entering into a government contract.

3. *U.S. Industry Standards*

Merchandise manufactured abroad may not comply with standards adopted by U.S. trade associations or enacted into law, such as local building codes. Prior to agreeing to purchase foreign products, the importer should check any applicable U.S. industry standards to make sure that the products will comply. The importer may need to advise the manufacturer of the appropriate specifications so that the products can be manufactured to meet U.S. industry standards.

I. Terms of Purchase

Although there are ordinarily many terms and conditions that the buyer will include in its import purchase agreements, the terms of purchase upon which seller and buyer must agree is that relating to passage of title, risk of loss, price, and payment. Although a buyer can purchase on different terms of sale from different sellers in accordance with whatever terms are expressed in each seller's quotation or purchase order acceptance, it is ordinarily much better for the buyer to think about and formulate policies relating to its terms of purchase in advance of placing its order. There are a number of considerations, the first of which relates to the use of abbreviations.

In order to standardize the understanding of the seller and buyer relating to their obligations in international purchase agreements, various nomenclatures have been developed that use abbreviations such as *ex-factory, FOB plant, CIF,* and *landed.* While these shorthand abbreviations can be useful, they can also be sources of confusion.

The International Chamber of Commerce developed the "Incoterms," which were revised in 2000 (see Chapter 2, Figures 2–7 and 2–8). Even though it is assumed that sellers and buyers know the responsibilities and obligations that flow from utilizing specific terms such as *FOB plant,* the parties in fact may not always understand all of their rights and responsibilities in the same way, and disputes and problems may arise. For example, even though on an FOB seller's plant sale, the buyer is responsible for obtaining and paying for ocean insurance, often the buyer will want the seller to obtain such insurance, which the buyer will reimburse the seller for paying. It is also possible that the seller will arrange for such insurance at the same time that the buyer does so, resulting in expensive duplication. Or, even though the buyer may be responsible for paying freight, the buyer may expect the seller to arrange for shipment "freight collect." Finally, under the new Incoterms, certain traditional terms such as "C&F," "FOR," "FOT," and "FOB airport" have been abolished and certain new terms such as "CFR," "DES," "DEQ," and "DDU" have been created. In the author's experience, even if the parties choose to use an abbreviation to specify the way in which title will pass, the author strongly recommends that the "who does what" be stated in detail in the purchase agreement to avoid the possibility of a misunderstanding.

It is also important for the buyer to realize that the price term may differ from the place of passage of title and risk of loss or time of payment. For example, under an Inco CFR or CIF term, the seller will be quoting a price to the buyer that includes the seller's cost of shipping the merchandise to the destination, but, in actuality, title and risk of loss will pass to the buyer when the merchandise is loaded on the ship at the time of export. Similarly, in a sales quotation, CIF means only that the price quoted by the seller will include all expenses to the point of destination—it does not mean that payment will be made upon arrival. Payment may be made earlier or later, depending upon the agreement of the parties. Buyers should be sure that their import purchase documentation distinguishes between price terms, title and risk of loss terms, and payment terms.

Under the new Convention on Contracts for the International Sale of Goods (discussed in Chapter 7, Section B.2.l), if the parties do not agree upon a place for transfer of title and delivery in their sale agreement, title and delivery will transfer when the merchandise is delivered to the first transportation carrier, and payment by the buyer will be due at that time.

In most international transactions, the buyer will be responsible for importing the products to its own country, clearing customs, and paying any applicable customs duties. This is because the importer is liable for all customs duties, even antidumping duties. However, if the seller agrees to sell landed, duty paid, or delivered to the buyer's place of business (so-called "free domicile" or "free house" delivery), the seller will be responsible for such customs duties. Ordinarily, the seller cannot act as the importer of record in the United States unless it obtains a bond from a U.S. surety company and appoints an agent in the United States for all claims for customs duties. Generally, a seller would not want to sell delivered, duty paid, but sometimes the buyer's bargaining leverage is such or competition is such that the seller cannot get the business unless it is willing to do so. Similarly, if the buyer is wary of paying dumping duties, she may insist that the seller act as the importer of record. Another situation is when the buyer is buying from a related seller, such as a parent company. In such a case, the parent company may want to sell landed, duty paid and assume such expenses.

In general, if the seller sells ex-factory, it will have the least responsibilities and risks. The buyer will then be responsible for arranging and paying for inland transportation to the port of export, ocean transportation, and U.S. importation. In some cases, an ex-factory purchase can result in the buyer's being able to avoid U.S. customs duties on the inland freight from the seller's factory to the port of export. In such cases, the buyer will have the responsibility for complying with all foreign export laws, such as obtaining export control licenses, export visas, and exchange control licenses; arranging insurance; and complying with foreign laws. In order to ensure that the seller has the responsibility to complete all of these requirements of foreign law, ordinarily the buyer should not buy ex-factory, but FOB port of export, CIF, or landed. If the buyer buys landed, it should discuss with the seller and make sure that the seller understands its responsibilities during the formation of the purchase agreement. If the seller is unable to effect import, the fact that the buyer is not legally responsible will be of little consolation and will lead to lawsuits, nondelivery, and loss of future supply.

Even though purchasing on a landed, delivered duty-paid basis may be attractive to the buyer, there are many reasons why the buyer may need or want to purchase on other terms. For example, the seller may be inexperienced in arranging international shipments, the buyer's competitors may be willing to purchase ex-factory, the buyer may be buying from an affiliated company, or the buyer may have warehouse-to-warehouse marine insurance under a blanket policy and, therefore, by agreeing to pay the insurance costs, can save the seller some money. Sometimes the buyer is in a better position to obtain lower ocean transportation or insurance rates. For all of these reasons, a thorough discussion of the terms and conditions of purchase between the seller and the buyer, rather than simply following a set policy, may be advantageous.

J. Consignments

In addition to purchase transactions, where title to the merchandise transfers to the U.S. buyer in the foreign country or sometime up to delivery in the United States in accordance with the terms of purchase between the parties, in consignment transactions the exporter/seller maintains ownership of the goods and the consignee in the United States takes possession of the goods. The consignee then offers the goods for sale, and when a customer purchases the goods, title transfers from the exporter/seller to the importer/buyer and to the customer simultaneously. Such transactions have various procedural and documentary considerations. As the owner, the exporter/seller will be responsible for all transportation costs, insurance, filing of export declaration, and obtaining foreign export control license. While U.S. Customs regulations may permit the consignee to effect customs clearance, legally the goods are owned by the exporter/seller, and the exporter/seller will be liable for the U.S. customs duties. Additional taxes may be assessed, such as personal property taxes assessed on the goods while they are awaiting sale and income taxes, because title will pass to the importer/buyer at the buyer's place of business in the United States. In addition, to avoid the inability to take possession of the goods in case of bankruptcy of the importer/buyer or other claims by the importer's creditors, special arrangements under the buyer's law, such as public notices or security interests, may be required. Because the export/import transaction is not a sale at the time of entry, transaction value cannot be used—U.S. Customs and Border Protection will assess customs duties based upon an alternative valuation method.

K. Leases

In import transactions that are leases, no purchase documentation should be used, although a commercial "invoice" declaring the names of the parties, the commodity, the quantity, and the value for Customs purposes must be provided at the time of importation. The ability of the exporter/lessor to retain title and ownership, repossess the goods at the end of the lease, and obtain income tax benefits depends upon using lease documentation rather than sales agreements. Similar to the consignment situation, the exporter/seller is legally responsible for all exporting and importing obligations, although those obligations can be delegated to the importer in the lease agreement. For U.S. customs valuation purposes, a lease is not a sale; therefore, transaction value will not be used, and the customs duties payable will depend upon an alternative valuation method.

L. Marine and Air Casualty Insurance

If the supplier sells FOB factory or port of export, the importer will be responsible for the ocean (marine) or air insurance covering the shipment. The importer should make arrangements for the insurance or make sure that it is properly obtained prior to exportation. Without such insurance, even when the carrier can be proven liable, responsibility is limited to $500 per "package" on ocean shipments and $20 per kilogram on air shipments unless a higher value is disclosed in advance and a higher transportation charge paid. The importer's letter of credit or payment instructions should require insurance unless the importer already has its own or, under the terms of purchase, the importer has agreed to be responsible for the insurance. Even when the importer believes that the terms of sale are clear, the importer should coordinate with the exporter to avoid a situation in which both the importer and exporter obtain such insurance and the importer is billed twice, or neither party obtains the insurance. Importers can obtain single shipment insurance or use open cargo policies covering all of their imports during a specific time period. "Warehouse-to-warehouse" and "all risk" rather than "named peril" coverage is best. Even "all risk" coverage does not include war risk or "strike, riot, and civil commotion" coverage, and the buyer must specifically request the seller to obtain such coverage if the buyer desires it. (A sample marine insurance policy and certificate are shown in Figures 4–10 and 4–11, respectively.) For additional information, see Chapter 2, Section P, and Chapter 4, Section H.

M. Method of Transportation; Booking Transportation

When the importer is responsible for the transportation of the merchandise from the foreign country to the United States, the importer will have to make a decision concerning the mode of transportation and arrange for shipment. Transportation may be made by air or by ship. Transportation can be arranged directly with air carriers or steamship companies or through freight forwarders and NVOCCs (see Chapter 4, Section E for more information). Air transportation is obviously much quicker, but is more expensive. Large shipments cannot be shipped by air. In obtaining quotations from various carriers, it is important to record and confirm any such quotations to avoid future increases and discrepancies. When checking with transportation carriers, the name of the person making the quotation, the date, the rate, and the appropriate tariff classification number used by the carrier should be recorded. (Additional information is contained in Chapter 2, Section Q.)

N. Import Financing

Some foreign governments offer financing assistance to U.S. importers who are purchasing merchandise from exporters in their countries. Some state government agencies even offer financing to purchase imported components if the finished products will be exported. If the importer intends to utilize any import financing program, the program should be investigated sufficiently in advance of commencing imports. The necessary applications and documentation must be filed and approvals obtained prior to importation of the merchandise.

O. Patent, Trademark, and Copyright Registrations and Infringements

In purchasing foreign products for importation to the United States, the importer should satisfy itself that the products will not infringe the patent, trademark, and/or copyright registration (sometimes called intellectual or industrial property rights) of another person. If the trademark or copyright has been registered with U.S. Customs and Border Protection, entry of the merchandise may be prohibited and the merchandise seized. Under the Anti-Counterfeiting Consumer Protection Act of 1996, importing or trading in counterfeit goods is punishable by a fine of up to $1 million. Even though the foreign manufacturer may have a patent, trademark, or copyright in its own country, unless such patent, trademark, or copyright has been registered in the United States, importation of the product may infringe a valid right of another person. That person may be a U.S. manufacturer or a foreign company that has registered its rights in the United States. Under the new Convention on Contracts for the International Sale of Goods (discussed in Chapter 7, Section B.2.l) and contrary to U.S. law, there is no implied warranty that a foreign-manufactured product will not infringe on U.S. intellectual property rights as long as the foreign seller was not aware of an infringement. The importer should initiate a patent, trademark, or copyright search to make sure that the patent, trademark, or copyright has not been registered in the United States, and in its purchase documentation, the importer should receive warranties and representations from its supplier that it will indemnify and hold the importer harmless from any such infringement actions. Obviously, if the supplier is a small company without much financial strength or has no offices in the United States and is not subject to the jurisdiction of the U.S. courts, the complaining party may proceed only against the importer in an infringement action. The importer will be unable to obtain indemnification from the supplier unless the supplier has consented to jurisdiction in the United States in the purchase agreement or the importer files another lawsuit against the supplier in the foreign country.

If the foreign supplier has not registered its patents, trademarks, or copyrights in the United States, the importer may wish to do so. To avoid disputes, generally the importer should do so only with the authorization of the foreign supplier. If the supplier is manufacturing the product with the importer's brand or trademark in a private branding arrangement, the importer should register such trademark and the supplier should disclaim all rights therein.

A related area concerns gray market imports. Even though the importer may have obtained an exclusive purchase right, distributorship, or sales agency in the United States, products manufactured by the supplier may be diverted from other customers in the manufacturer's home country or third countries for sale in the United States. Such situations will occur only where the price at which the manufacturer sells in its home market or to third countries is below the prevailing market price in the United States, and, therefore, third persons can make a profit by buying at the lower price and reselling in the United States. However, this may arise as a result of exchange rate fluctuations rather than intentional disregard of the importer's exclusive rights. Under current U.S. Customs regulations, trademarks and copyrights can be registered with U.S. Customs and Border Protection, and products that are counterfeit will be seized. Genuine products manufactured by the original manufacturer or its authorized licensee (gray market goods) will also be seized unless they were manufactured by a foreign affiliated company of the U.S. trademark or copyright owner.

P. Confidentiality and Non-Disclosure Agreements

If the importer will be furnishing any samples to the exporter, for example, when the foreign manufacturer is manufacturing products in accordance with specifications of the importer in a contract manufacturing arrangement, or when the importer will be providing other confidential or proprietary information regarding its business or products, the importer should require the manufacturer/exporter to sign a confidentiality and non-disclosure agreement in advance of disclosure of any proprietary information. In some countries where laws against counterfeiting are weak, this contractual agreement may be the importer's only protection against unauthorized copying or unfair competition by the manufacturer/exporter or dishonest third parties.

Q. Payment

An importer may be required to pay for merchandise it purchases by cash in advance or a letter of credit, unless the exchange control regulations of the government of the buyer do not require it or the buyer has sufficient bargaining leverage to purchase on more liberal terms. The buyer's methods of payment are discussed in Chapter 7, Section B.2.e. If a letter of credit is required, the seller will often provide instructions to the importer (see Chapter 4, Figure 4–31), and the importer will have to make an application in the nature of a credit application to a bank that offers letter of credit services. A sample application is shown in Figure 6–8. An applicant's checklist for a commercial letter of credit is shown in Figure 6–9. A sample of an advice of letter of credit as it will be issued to the seller is shown in Chapter 4, Figure 4–35. A sample credit notification sent by the importer's bank to a correspondent bank in the seller's country (who will advise the seller that the letter of credit has been opened) is shown in Figure 6–10. For payment by documentary collection, a sample of the seller's instructions to the bank is shown in Chapter 4, Figure 4–31. Sample sight or time drafts that the seller will present to the correspondent bank under a letter of credit to obtain payment when the goods are shipped are shown in Figures 4–29 and 4–30, respectively.

A buyer using a letter of credit should realize that the bank does not verify the quantity, the quality, or even the existence of the goods. The bank will make payment as long as the seller presents documents that appear on their face to be in compliance with the terms of the letter of credit. For this reason, a buyer may wish to arrange for a preshipment inspection by an inspection service.

R. Translation

The importer must also give consideration to the necessity of translating into English any foreign language documents, such as advertising materials, instruction manuals, warranties, and labeling. The importer may be able to get the seller to agree to perform such translations and bear the cost. These translations may be necessary to achieve sales and adequately protect the importer's rights. For example, if a patent application is incorrectly translated, the patent owner may lose its rights. The location of a competent translator and completion of the translation may require significant lead time and, depending on the volume of material, may involve significant expense.

S. Foreign Branch Operations, Subsidiaries, Joint Ventures, and Licensing

Sometimes the importer will be importing from its or its parent company's existing branch or subsidiary company in a foreign country. Or, rather than purchasing from an independent manufacturer or distributor, the importer may decide to establish such a branch operation or subsidiary company. If personnel are available to staff the foreign branch or company, this may increase the importer's sourcing capability and may smooth export and import operations. Similarly, the importer may form a

(*Text continues on page 289.*)

Figure 6–7. Lacey Act Certification.

According to the Paperwork Reduction Act of 1995, no persons are required to respond to a collection of information unless it displays a valid OMB control number. The valid OMB control number for this information collection is 0579-0349. The time required to complete this information collection is estimated to average 1.5 hours per response, including the time for reviewing instructions, searching existing data sources, gathering and maintaining the data needed, and completing and reviewing the collection of information.

FORM APPROVED
OMB No. 0579-0349

Plant and Plant Product Declaration Form

Section 3: Lacey Act Amendments of 2008 (16 U.S.C. 3372)

APHIS **U.S. DEPARTMENT OF AGRICULTURE**
ANIMAL AND PLANT HEALTH INSPECTION SERVICE
PLANT PROTECTION AND QUARANTINE

Applicability of Declaration:

You are required to complete this form if you are importing any of the following:
Any wild member of the plant kingdom, including roots, seeds, parts, or products thereof, and including trees from either natural or planted forest stands, except:

1. Common cultivars, except trees, and common food crops (including roots, seeds, parts, or products thereof);
2. * Scientific specimens of plant genetic material (including roots, seeds, germplasm, parts, or products thereof) that are to be used only for laboratory or field research;
3. * Plants that are to remain planted or to be planted or replanted; or
4. Plants used exclusively as packaging material to support, protect, or carry another item, unless the packaging material itself is the item being imported.

* You must still complete this form if you are importing plants described under 3. and 4. that are listed:

- In an appendix to the Convention on International Trade in Endangered Species of Wild Fauna and Flora (27 UST 1087; TIAS 8249);
- As an endangered or threatened species under the Endangered Species Act of 1973 (16 U.S.C. 1531 et seq.); or
- Pursuant to any State law that provides for the conservation of species that are indigenous to the State and are threatened with extinction.

SECTION 1 - Shipment Information

1. ESTIMATED DATE OF ARRIVAL: (MM/DD/YYYY)	
2. ENTRY NUMBER:	3. CONTAINER NUMBER:
4. BILL OF LADING:	5. MID:
6. IMPORTER NAME:	8. CONSIGNEE NAME:
7. IMPORTER ADDRESS:	9. CONSIGNEE ADDRESS:

I certify under penalty of perjury that the information furnished is true and correct:

Signature | Type or Print Name | Date

Knowingly making a false statement in this Declaration for Importation may subject the declarant to criminal penalties in accordance with 16 U.S.C. 3373(d).

PPQ FORM 505
MARCH 2009

Version 03-26-2009-0856 Page 1

Figure 6–7. *(continued)*

Plant and Plant Product Import Declaration (cont.)

SECTION 2 - Compliance with Lacey Act Requirements (16 U.S.C. 3372(f))

10. DESCRIPTION OF MERCHANDISE:	11. HTSUS NUMBER: (no dashes/symbols)
	12. ENTERED VALUE: (in U.S. Dollars)

For each article or component of an article, provide the following:

13. ARTICLE/ COMPONENT OF ARTICLE	14. PLANT SCIENTIFIC NAME: (Genus and Species)	15. COUNTRY OF HARVEST:	16. QUANTITY OF PLANT MATERIAL:	17. UNIT OF MEASURE:	18. % RECYCLED MATERIAL:

I certify under penalty of perjury that the information furnished is true and correct:

Signature   Type or Print Name   Date

Knowingly making a false statement in this Declaration for Importation may subject the declarant to criminal penalties in accordance with 16 U.S.C. 3373(d).

PPQ FORM 505
MARCH 2009

Version 03-26-2009-0856

Page 2

Figure 6–7. *(continued)*

Version 03-26-2009-0856

1. **Estimated Date of Arrival:** Enter the date (MM/DD/YYYY) that the product is expected to enter the United States of America.

2. **Entry Number:** Enter the U. S. Customs entry number assigned to this shipment. (Format: xxx-xxxxxxx-x)

3. **Container Number:** Enter the number of the shipping container in which the product is being shipped - available from your shipping company. If there is no container number, please leave this section blank.

4. **Bill of Lading:** Enter the Bill of Lading (BOL) number assigned to this shipment - available from the shipping company. If there is no Bill of Lading number, please leave this section blank.

5. **MID:** Manufacturer Identification Code - available from the manufacturer or customs broker (19 CFR Appendix to Part 102).

6. **Importer Name:** Enter the name of the import company or individual for the product.

7. **Importer Address:** Enter the address of the import company or individual in #6.

8. **Consignee Name:** Name of the individual or company who ordered and will ultimately receive the shipment.

9. **Consignee Address:** Enter the address of the individual or company in #8.

10. **Description of the Merchandise:** Enter the name of the plant or plant product, and its use (example: wooden spoons for kitchenware). If the use is unknown, enter only the name of the product (example: lumber).

11. **HTSUS Number:** Enter the Harmonized Tariff Code for the merchandise described in #10 - available at http://www.usitc.gov/tata/hts/.

12. **Entered Value (in U.S. Dollars):** Write the entered value of the imported merchandise described in #10 in U.S. Dollars.

13. **Article/Component of Article:** Enter a brief description of each article, or component of an article, that is manufactured from plants or plant parts. (Example: A decorative item including a wood frame and 100 % recycled paperboard - enter the frame as a line item, and record the percent recycled material in the paperboard in section #13.)

14. **Plant Scientific Name:** For each article/component in #14 enter the scientific name (example: See next page). If the species of plant used to produce the product varies, and the species used to produce the product is unknown, enter each species that may have been used to produce the product.

1

Figure 6–7. *(continued)*

Version 03-26-2009-0856

15. **Country of Harvest:** Enter the country of origin (where the plant was harvested) (example: See below). If the country of harvest varies, and is unknown, enter all countries from which the plant material in the product may have been harvested.

16. **Quantity of Material:** How much product/merchandise is in the shipment (example: See below).

17. **Unit of Measure:** Use the drop down box on the form to enter the units for #17. (example: See below).

 doz - dozen
 kg - kilograms
 m - meter
 m^2 - square meters
 m^3 - cubic meters
 No. - number
 pcs - pieces
 t - metric tons
 bf - board feet

18. **% Recycled Material:** If the product is paper or paperboard, enter the percentage of recycled material it contains (0 - 100%). If the percentage of recycled material varies, enter the average percentage of recycled material used in the product (example: If the percentage of recycled material used is between 25% and 45%, enter 35%).

13. ARTICLE/COMPONENT OF ARTICLE:	14. PLANT SCIENTIFIC NAME: (Genus and Species)	15. COUNTRY OF HARVEST:	16. QUANTITY OF PLANT MATERIAL:	17. UNIT OF MEASURE:	18. % RECYCLED MATERIAL
Tables made of Mahogany	*Swietenia macrophylla*	Indonesia	500	No.	0
European ash lumber (2" x 4')	*Fraxinus excelsior*	Switzerland	352,000	BF	0

19. **Submission of Paper Declaration:** Importers should have the form available for Customs and Border Protection (CBP) to review at the port of entry. After CBP clears the shipment, the importer must mail the form to the USDA at the following address:

 The Lacey Act
 c/o U.S. Department of Agriculture
 Box 10
 4700 River Road
 Riverdale, MD 20737

Note: Sign and Print your name, and write the date on both sections of the form.

SPECIAL NOTE: IF YOU HAVE FILED A LACEY ACT DECLARATION ELECTRONICALLY THROUGH THE CUSTOMS SYSTEM, THERE IS NO NEED TO FILE A PAPER DECLARATION.

2

Figure 6–8. Applicant's checklist for letter of credit.

CHECKLIST FOR A COMMERCIAL LETTER OF CREDIT—APPLICANT

The following checklist identifies points that an applicant for a commercial letter of credit should consider when making an agreement with the seller (beneficiary) and completing an application for a letter of credit.

1. Does the beneficiary agree that the letter of credit should be irrevocable?
2. Do you have the complete name and address of the beneficiary, including street address and postal code, if applicable? If the beneficiary is a large company, what is the name of the person to whom correspondence should be addressed?
3. Is the letter of credit to be delivered to the beneficiary by the issuing bank through its correspondent bank, by the issuing bank directly, or by you directly?
4. How is the letter of credit to be delivered to the beneficiary—by air mail or by telex?
5. Do you or the beneficiary wish to designate an advising bank to deliver the letter of credit to the beneficiary, or do you want the issuing bank to choose the advising bank? If you wish to designate the advising bank, do you have its complete name and address?
6. Is the advising bank or another bank going to confirm the letter of credit? Or does the beneficiary wish another bank to act as the confirming bank? Do you have the complete name and address of the confirming bank, if any?
7. What is the total amount of credit, and in what currency is it to be denominated? If you want to approximate the total value of the transaction, is the credit amount preceded by a qualification such as "not exceeding" or "approximately" (meaning 10 percent more or less)?
8. What is the expiration date of the letter of credit?
9. What is the location for presentation of documents?
10. To what bank (nominated bank) is the beneficiary going to present documents?
11. How many days does the beneficiary have after shipment of goods to present documents to the nominated bank?
12. What is the method of payment under the letter of credit—sight draft, time draft, deferred payment?
13. What is the tenor of the draft(s), and what percentage of the invoice value is each draft to cover?
14. Is (are) the draft(s) to be drawn on you or another drawee?
15. How many copies of the commercial invoice should the beneficiary present to the nominated bank?
16. What is the agreed-upon description of the merchandise and/or services to be itemized in the commercial invoice? (Include quantity and unit price, if applicable.)
17. What are the origin and destination of the shipment?
18. What are the terms of shipment (FOB, CFR, CIF, other)?

Courtesy of Continental Bank N.A. (Bank of America Illinois).

Figure 6–8. *(continued)*

19. Are the freight charges to be collect or prepaid?
20. What is the last date on which the beneficiary can ship in order to comply with the shipping terms?
21. Are partial shipments allowed?
22. Are transshipments allowed?
23. What transportation document(s) do you require the beneficiary to present to the nominated bank? How many copies of each do you require?
24. Do you require that an extra set of transportation documents accompany an air shipment?
25. What is the name, address, and phone number of the person to be notified when the shipment arrives?
26. Is the beneficiary responsible for insuring the shipment, or are you? What percentage of the invoice value is the insurance to cover? Where are the risks to be covered?
27. What other documents do you require the beneficiary to present? How many copies of each do you require? When appropriate, who is to issue each document, and what should its wording be?
28. Who is responsible for the bank charges other than those of the issuing bank?
29. Who is responsible for discount charges, if any?
30. What is the complete name and address of the person to whom the nominated bank should send the documents submitted by the beneficiary?
31. Is the credit transferable?

joint venture with a foreign company to manufacture or export the importer's desired product to the United States and perhaps other countries. Where the laws prohibit the establishment of branches, subsidiaries, or satisfactory joint ventures, the importer may need to license to or contract with a foreign company to manufacture the product for sale to the importer. All of these methods of doing business will require some modifications to the purchase and other export and import documentation and procedures. For example, purchases from affiliated entities often raise income tax issues of transfer pricing and the related issue of proper customs valuation. License royalties may in certain circumstances be dutiable, and licensed technology may require export control approvals.

T. Electronic Commerce

The development of the Internet and email and the proliferation of web sites have created a revolution in electronic commerce. Because of the essentially worldwide availability of the Internet and access to web sites, new issues for cross-border importing and exporting have arisen. This has opened a new channel of direct marketing using electronic catalogs and has created conflict with the seller's traditional foreign distribution channels, such as distributors and sales agents. Sellers are more

Figure 6–10. Instructions by importer's bank to correspondent bank in seller's country regarding opening of letter of credit.

ABC BANK

P.O. Box 100, Chicago, IL 60606
Swift Address: ABCBAS100
Fax: 312.111.1000

IRREVOCABLE NEGOTIABLE CREDIT

ADVISING BANK: DATE:

ALL DRAFTS MUST BE MARKED
ABC BANK REFERENCE NO:
ADVISING BANK REFERENCE NO.

GENTLEMEN:

BY THE ORDER OF: WE HEREBY ISSUE
THROUGH YOU IN FAVOR
OF:

OUR IRREVOCABLE CREDIT FOR THE ACCOUMT OF FOR AN AMOUNT NOT TO EXCEED, IN THE AGGREGATE, U.S. DOLLARS AVAILABLE BY YOUR DRAFTS AT ON ABC BANK, CHICAGO, ILLINOIS, U.S.A., WHEN ACCOMPANIED BY THE DOCUMENTS INDICATED BELOW, EFFECTIVE AND EXPIRING ON

THIS CREDIT IS SUBJECT TO THE FOLLOWING:

SHIP FROM: SHIP TO:

DOCUMENTS REQUIRED:

COVER SHIPMENT OF:

SHIPPING TERMS:

NEGOTIATING BANK MUST AIRMAIL OR COURIER ONE ORIGINAL COMMERCIAL INVOICE, CUSTOMS INVOICE, AND BILL OF LADING TO FOR OUR ACCOUNT AND A CERTIFICATE TO THIS EFFECT MUST BE SUBMITTED WITH THE REMAINING DOCUMENTS

WE HEREBY ENGAGE WITH THE DRAWERS AND WITH NEGOTIATING BANKS AND BANKERS THAT EACH DRAFT DRAWN UNDER AND IN COMPLIANCE WITH THE TERMS OF THIS CREDIT WILL BE DULY HONORED IF PRESENTED FOR NEGOTIATION ON OR BEFORE THE EXPIRY DATE.

THE AMOUNT OF EACH DRAFT MUST BE ENDORSED ON THE REVERSE OF THIS CREDIT BY THE NEGOTIATING BANK.

THIS CREDIT IS SUBJECT TO THE UNIFORM CUSTOMS AND PRACTICE FOR DOCUMENTARY CREDITS (2007 EDITION), INTERNATINAL CHAMBER OF COMMERCE PUBLICATION 600.

VERY TRULY YOURS,
ABC BANK

ADVISING BANK'S NOTIFICATION

____
(AUTHORIZED SIGNATURE)

____
PLACE, DATE, NAME AND SIGNATURE

____
(AUTHORIZED SIGNATURE)

interested in marketing internationally and are forced to cope with the logistical issues that arise from purchase orders from abroad. Some of the more important issues that must be considered and managed include the following:

- *Validity and enforceability of electronic sales contracts.* This concern has required the consideration and development of legal terms of sale on the web site that are modified and appropriate for foreign as well as domestic customers. It has also forced the use of "click-wrap" agreements to record the purchaser's agreement to the sales terms and authentication procedures to confirm that the person purporting to place the order is actually that person. For low-price items, sellers may be willing to accept the risk of lack of enforceability of the sales contract, but for expensive items or ongoing business, this is not feasible. Many sellers have required their distributors and customers who are making ongoing purchases to sign hard-copy "umbrella" agreements at the outset of the relationship before undertaking electronic sales. This is a less satisfactory solution for one-time purchasers.
- *Delivery and logistics.* At least with direct sales to consumers, and for consumer goods, the customer wants and expects the convenience of direct delivery to his door. These "delivered duty paid" terms of sale are almost a necessity for this type of business. Customers also want prompt delivery, which is difficult to achieve if there is no stock of inventory in the buyer's country. For smaller products, delivery by international courier services such as UPS, Federal Express, and DHL has become more practical. In such cases, the transportation carrier is also able to act as the customs broker in the United States, paying customs duties and value-added taxes and billing them back to the seller. For large capital goods, however, such as in B2B transactions, the issues of containerized or other packing, transportation booking, export licenses or permits, U.S. customs clearance, and lack of skilled in-house personnel, thereby requiring the use of a freight forwarder, have limited the expansion of Internet sales. Challenges continue to exist relating to establishing in-country inventory for immediate delivery without the expenses of establishing branch offices or subsidiary companies.
- *Price.* Since many customers want to have delivery to their door, when they see a price quotation on a web site, they expect to see an "all-in" (delivered duty paid) price. The difficulty of maintaining up-to-date quotations online, including freight charges, insurance, duties, quotas, and value-added taxes for multiple countries, has forced many sellers to hire software companies that offer such services.
- *Payment.* For low-price consumer goods, payment by credit card has enabled sellers to increase Internet sales. However, since credit card purchases do not guarantee payment to the seller (the buyer can instruct the credit card company not to pay the seller in certain circumstances, such as a dispute over quality), the seller is always at risk when payment is by credit card. That fact, together with the virtual impossibility of pursuing a collection lawsuit against the buyer overseas due to prohibitive costs, has limited the expansion of Internet sales. For expensive purchases or ongoing accounts, the seller may need the security of a letter of credit or documents against payment. On the other side, buyers dislike having to pay for purchases in advance without inspection of the goods. Where the seller has done business in the past on open account, or is willing to do so in the future, Internet sales can be practical.

- *Taxation.* Although one of the great spurs to the growth of electronic commerce in the past has been the ability to avoid certain taxes in certain countries, such as sales, value-added, corporate franchise, or personal property taxes, there is an increasing demand by governments to recover those tax revenues that are being lost. It is likely that some forms of taxation will increase and that sellers and buyers may have to comply with U.S. and foreign tax claims.
- *Information security.* Although there has been significant progress in maintaining the confidentiality of information transmitted over the Internet, the sophistication of "hackers" has also increased. For information from credit card numbers to purchase order numbers and customer lists, confidentiality, particularly from competitors and fraud artists, is crucial. The most secure current technologies using "key" systems are cumbersome, especially for small orders and one-time sales. Furthermore, exporting such software may require an export license.

Despite the foregoing difficulties, the outlook is good that more creative ways of dealing with these problems will evolve and that Internet sales will continue to expand.

Chapter 7

Importing: Purchase Documentation

The single most important document in importing is the purchase agreement. Just as in exporting, most of the problems that occur in importing can be eliminated or greatly reduced by using a suitable purchase agreement. Generally, different types of documentation are used for isolated purchase transactions as opposed to ongoing purchase transactions. The various types of documentation, including the important provisions in international purchase agreements, import distribution agreements, and import sales agent agreements, will be discussed. (In order to understand how the seller views the transaction, you may wish to read Chapter 3.)

A. Isolated Purchase Transactions

For the purposes of discussion in this chapter, isolated purchase transactions are defined as situations where, for example, the importer purchases infrequently or purchases are made on a trial basis in anticipation of establishing an ongoing purchase relationship, or when the exporter is unwilling to grant any credit to the importer until a satisfactory history of payment has been established. Purchase agreements for such transactions should be in writing, and the seller and buyer may use a variety of common, preprinted forms. The importer/buyer should check carefully to try to eliminate as much as possible any conflicting provisions between the seller/exporter's forms and the forms used by the buyer.

1. Importance of Written Agreements

In some industries (for example, the commodities industry), it is common to conduct purchases and sales orally through telephone orders and acceptances. Sometimes oral agreements occur in international purchasing when the buyer gives an order at a trade show, by long-distance telephone, or in a meeting. Under the new Convention on Contracts for the International Sale of Goods (discussed in Section B.2.l), a sales agreement may be formed or modified orally. It is highly advisable to formalize the purchase and sale agreement in a written document even for domestic purchases, and there are many additional reasons why import purchases should be memorialized in a written agreement. Under the Uniform Commercial Code applicable in the United States, an agreement to purchase, and therefore to require delivery, is enforceable by the buyer only if the agreement is in writing if the purchase exceeds $500 in value. While there are some exceptions to this law, and sometimes even informal notes will be sufficient to create an enforceable purchase agreement, by far the safest practice is to formalize the purchase agreement in a written document.

In addition to legal issues, an old Chinese proverb states: "The lightest ink is better than the brightest memory." This is one way of saying that disputes in international purchase transactions often arise because the parties did not record their agreement or failed to discuss an issue and reach agreement. A written purchase agreement acts both as a checklist to remind the buyer and seller of what they should discuss and agree upon and as a written record of their agreement. All modifications of the agreement should also be in writing.

2. *Email or Facsimile Orders*

While a email or facsimile order and acceptance can satisfy the legal requirements as written evidence of an agreement, such communications commonly contain only the specification of the quantity, sometimes an offering price, and possibly a shipment date. There are many other terms and conditions of purchase that should be inserted in a good purchase agreement, and a simple order by the buyer in response to such email or facsimile offers to sell will fall far short of adequately protecting the buyer in the event of problems in the transaction. Consequently, acceptances of offers to sell by email or facsimile should specifically and expressly state that the purchase incorporates the buyer's other standard terms and conditions of purchase. Those additional terms and conditions of purchase should be included in the buyer's earliest email or facsimile response to the seller, so that there can be no argument that the seller was not aware of such terms and conditions of purchase before proceeding with the transaction.

3. *The Formation of Purchase Agreements*

The purchase agreement is a formal contract governed by law. In general, a purchase agreement is formed by agreement between the seller and the buyer and is the passing of title and ownership to goods for a price. An agreement is a mutual manifestation of assent to the same terms. Agreements are ordinarily reached by a process of offer and acceptance. This process of offer and acceptance can proceed by the seller and the buyer preparing a purchase agreement contained in a single document that is signed by both parties, by the exchange of documents such as purchase orders and purchase order acceptances, or by conduct, such as when the buyer offers to purchase and the seller ships the goods.

From the view of clarity and reducing risks, preparation of a purchase agreement contained in a single document is best. Both parties negotiate the agreement by exchanges of letters, emails, or faxes or in person. Before proceeding with the performance of any part of the transaction, both parties reach agreement and sign the same purchase agreement. This gives both the seller and the buyer the best opportunity to understand the terms and conditions under which the other intends to transact business, and to negotiate and resolve any differences or conflicts. This type of purchase agreement is often used if the size of the transaction is large, if the seller is concerned about payment or the buyer is concerned about manufacture and shipment, or if there are particular risks involved, such as government regulations or exchange controls, or differences in culture, language, or business customs that might create misunderstandings.

Quite often, however, the process of formation of the purchase agreement is an exchange of documents that the seller and buyer have independently prepared, and that, in the aggregate, constitute the purchase agreement. These documents may contain differences and conflicts. Figure 3–1 in Chapter 3 shows the chronology of this exchange and common documents used in many purchase transactions. Although not all documents will be used in every purchase transaction, these documents are in common use.

Several questions arise when a purchase transaction is formed by such an exchange of documents. The first relates to the time of formation of the purchase agreement. For example, a seller or buyer may send certain preliminary inquiries or information, such as a price list, without intending to actually offer to sell or place an order, but may find that the other party's understanding (or the applicable law) has created a binding purchase agreement prior to the first party's intention to do so. This can arise because under some countries' laws, an offer to sell or buy is accepted when the acceptance is dispatched, rather than when it is received. It can also arise because silence can be considered as acceptance if the parties are merchants.

The second issue that arises relates to the governing law. Contracts are often governed by the law of the country in which the contract is negotiated and performed or in which the offer to sell or buy was accepted. Since an international agreement may be partly negotiated and partly performed in both countries, and since there may be a question as to whether the buyer accepted the offer to sell or the seller accepted the offer to purchase, situations can arise in which the purchase agreement is governed by the law of the seller's country. Since foreign law may be quite different from U.S. law, the buyer's rights and responsibilities may differ greatly from what he anticipated. Customary local ways of doing business, called trade usages, may unknowingly become a part of the purchase agreement under the sales laws of some countries. Sellers and buyers sometimes try to resolve this problem by including a governing law term in their documents, but again, these may conflict.

A final method of formation of a purchase agreement involves conduct. A simple example is where a buyer sends a purchase order, and the seller, without communicating, simply ships the goods, or where the seller offers to sell the goods and the buyer simply sends payment. In such cases, the conduct in accepting the offer will include all of the terms and conditions of the offer. If the buyer is not satisfied with the seller's terms and conditions of sale, she should send some communication to negotiate those terms before simply sending an order or making payment.

4. Common Forms for the Formation of Purchase Agreements

There are a number of forms that are customarily used in the formation of purchase agreements. In order to save time (and discourage changes by the other party), both buyers and sellers often purchase preprinted forms from commercial stationers or develop and preprint their own forms. Not all of these documents are used by the seller or the buyer in all purchase transactions. For example, a seller may submit a quotation to a potential buyer without receiving any request for quotation, or the first communication the seller receives may be a purchase order from the buyer. However, it is important to be familiar with the various forms.

a. Price Lists

Sometimes a seller will send a price list to a prospective buyer as its first communication. Ordinarily, a buyer should not consider such lists as offers to sell that entitle the buyer to accept. The buyer should ordinarily communicate with the seller (specifying that he is not making an order), asking for a quotation and confirming that the terms of the price list are still current.

b. Requests for Quotations and Offers to Purchase

Sometimes the first document involved in the formation of a purchase agreement is a request from the buyer to the seller for a quotation (RFQ) (see Figure 3–2). Ordinarily, such a request—whether it be informal, in an email, facsimile, or letter, or formal, in a printed form—will ask for a price quotation from the seller for a specific quantity and often a shipping date. When requesting a quotation, the buyer should be particularly careful to specify that its request is not an offer to purchase and that such an offer will be made only by the buyer's subsequent purchase order. Another method is to expressly state that the buyer's request is subject to or incorporates all of the buyer's standard terms and conditions of purchase. The most cautious approach is for the buyer to print all of its terms and conditions of purchase in its request for quotation. In that way, there is absolutely no argument that the seller was not aware of all the terms and conditions on which the buyer is willing to purchase, and if the seller has any objection thereto, it should so state in its quotation to the buyer. The buyer should request that the seller's quotation be in writing.

c. Quotations

In response to a request for a quotation, the seller ordinarily prepares and forwards a quotation or a pro forma invoice. In making quotations, the seller may use a printed form that may contain all of its terms and conditions of sale on the front or back thereof (see Figures 3–4 and 3–8). If this is the first communication from the seller to the buyer, the buyer should be careful to ascertain whether the quotation contains other terms and conditions of sale in addition to the price, quantity, and shipment date. This may be expressly stated in fine print boilerplate provisions on the front or back or by reference to the seller's terms and conditions of sale being incorporation by reference. If the seller refers to terms and conditions that are not expressly stated in the quotation, the best course is for the buyer to ask the seller to provide a copy of such terms and conditions of sale prior to sending any order. If such terms and conditions are stated, the buyer should carefully review them to determine if there are any discrepancies between the buyer's standard terms and conditions of purchase or if there are any terms and conditions that are objectionable to the buyer. If there are objectionable terms, it is far better to negotiate and resolve these items before placing any order.

The quotation may expressly state that the offer is firm or irrevocable for a certain period of time, and it may also state that it is not an offer to sell and that the seller is not agreeing to sell until it has received a purchase order from the buyer and has issued an acceptance of the order. If the quotation does not state that it is firm for a certain period of time, the buyer may wish to immediately inquire if this is so; otherwise, the seller is generally free to withdraw its quotation anytime before acceptance, which could mean even after the buyer has sent a purchase order, especially if the seller has reserved the right not to sell until it accepts the buyer's purchase order.

d. Purchase Orders

The next document that may occur in a purchase transaction is a purchase order (PO) issued by the buyer. Again, the purchase order may be informal, such as in an email, facsimile, or letter, or it may be on a printed form. This is the most important document for the buyer because it should contain all of the additional terms and conditions that the buyer wants to be a part of the purchase agreement when the purchase order is accepted by the seller. (See samples in Figures 3–5 and 3–6.) Before issuing a purchase order in response to a quotation, the buyer should carefully calculate its costs. The buyer should determine whether the quotation is ex-factory, FOB port, CIF, or delivered, since all expenses of transportation from the point quoted will be expenses of the buyer, including U.S. customs duties. If the buyer intends to resell the product in its imported form, it should determine whether the quoted price plus additional expenses of importation will still permit the buyer to sell at the prevailing U.S. market price with a reasonable profit or, if the product will be used as a raw material or component, that its delivered cost will be lower than that from U.S. suppliers (compare Figure 3–3). If the price is unacceptable, the buyer should make a counteroffer at a lower price before sending a purchase order. Even though the buyer may expect that no purchase agreement will be formed until she has sent a purchase order, if the seller has previously sent a quotation to the buyer, the terms and conditions stated in the seller's quotation may govern the purchase agreement. Of course, the terms and conditions contained in the seller's quotation or purchase order acceptance are always written to be most favorable to the seller. An important way in which the buyer can try to guard against such a result is for the buyer to specify in its purchase order that its purchase order is an offer to purchase only on the terms and conditions stated therein and that any acceptance with different terms and conditions will be void unless expressly accepted by the buyer in writing. The purchase order should also limit acceptance to a certain time period so that the offer to purchase is not open indefinitely. Finally, the purchase order should specify that any acceptance and purchase agreement will be governed by the law of the buyer's state and the United States, excluding the Convention on Contracts for the International Sale of Goods, to avoid a purchase order acceptance being issued in the foreign country and the formation of a purchase agreement governed by foreign law.

e. Purchase Order Acknowledgments and Acceptances and Sales Confirmations

When a purchase order is received, some sellers prepare a purchase order acknowledgment, purchase order acceptance, or sales confirmation form (see sample in Figure 3–7). A purchase order acknowledgment may state that the seller has received the purchase order from the buyer and is in the process of evaluating it, such as checking on the credit of the buyer or determining the availability of raw materials for manufacture, but that the seller has not yet accepted the purchase order and will issue a purchase order acceptance at a later date. In other cases, the language of the purchase order acknowledgment is also clearly an acceptance of the order, and no further communication is issued. Sales confirmations usually perform the same role as purchase order acceptances. The seller will normally include its detailed terms and conditions of sale in its purchase order acknowledgment or purchase order acceptance. If this is the first time that the buyer has seen such terms and conditions of sale (that is, if they were not included in the seller's earlier quotation), even if the buyer has stated in its purchase order that it is offering to purchase only on its own terms and conditions, the buyer should confirm that there is no conflict and that the seller has not purported to accept the purchase order only on its own terms and conditions. If a conflict exists, the buyer should immediately negotiate and resolve the conflict; otherwise, the seller may proceed with manufacture and shipment, and the buyer may be bound by the seller's terms and conditions. If the seller's quotation and purchase order acceptance do not contain detailed terms and conditions of sale, the buyer can feel reasonably comfortable that its terms or conditions will control.

f. Commercial Invoices

Later, when manufacture is complete and the product is ready for shipment, ordinarily the seller will prepare a commercial invoice, which is the formal statement for payment to be sent directly to the buyer or submitted through banking channels for payment by the buyer. Such invoices may also contain the detailed terms or conditions of sale on the front or back of the form (see sample in Figure 3–9). However, if this is the first time that the seller has brought such terms to the attention of the buyer, and the buyer has previously advised the seller of its detailed terms and conditions of purchase in its request for quotation or purchase order, the buyer should immediately object if the seller's terms and conditions are in conflict.

g. Conflicting Provisions in Seller and Buyer Sales Documentation

It is common in international trade for sellers and buyers to use preprinted forms that are designed to reduce the amount of negotiation and discussion required for each sales agreement. Undoubtedly, such forms have been drafted by attorneys for each side and contain terms and conditions of purchase or terms and conditions of sale that are favorable to the buyer and the seller, respectively. Consequently, it is not unusual for sellers and buyers who are intent on entering into a sales transaction to routinely issue such documentation with little or no thought being given to the consistency of those provisions. Afterward, if the sales transaction breaks down and either the buyer or the seller consults its attorney regarding its legal rights and obligations, the rights of the parties may be very unclear. In the worst case, the buyer may find that a purchase agreement has been validly formed on all of the terms and conditions of the seller's quotation or purchase order acceptance and is governed by the law of the seller's country. In order to reduce or eliminate this problem, often the buyer's attorney drafts requests for quotations and purchase orders with language that states that, notwithstanding any terms or conditions that might be contained in the seller's quotation or purchase order acceptance, the buyer agrees to make the purchase only on its own terms or conditions. While this can be of some help, sometimes the seller's quotation and purchase order acceptance also contain such language, and consequently, the buyer's terms and conditions may not win out. In fact, the only way to be comfortable regarding the terms or conditions of sale that will govern a purchase agreement is to actually review the terms or conditions contained in the seller's forms and compare them with the terms and conditions that the buyer desires to utilize. Where specific conflicts exist or where the seller's terms or conditions of purchase differ from the buyer's terms or conditions of purchase, the buyer should expressly bring that to the attention of the seller, the differences should be negotiated to the satisfaction of the buyer, and appropriate changes should be made in the form of a rider to the purchase agreement or a letter to clarify the agreement reached between the parties (which should be signed by both parties).

In some isolated sales transactions where the quantities are small, the buyer may simply choose to forgo this effort and accept the risk that the transaction will be controlled by the seller's terms and conditions of sale. However, the buyer should establish some dollar limit over which a review is to be made and should not continue a practice that might be appropriate for small purchases but would be very dangerous for large purchases.

h. Side Agreements

Occasionally, the seller may suggest that the seller and buyer enter into a side or letter agreement. In some cases, the suggestion may be innocent enough, for example, where the parties wish to clarify how they will interpret or carry out a particular provision of the purchase agreement. Even then, however, it is better practice to incorporate all of the agreements of the parties in a single document. Unfortunately, more often the seller's proposal of a side agreement is designed to evade the seller's foreign exchange control, tax, or antitrust laws. Buyers should be wary of entering into such agreements unless they fully understand the consequences. Such agreements may be unenforceable, the buyer may not be able to get delivery of the goods for which it paid, and/or the buyer may be prosecuted as a co-conspirator for violating such laws.

B. Ongoing Purchase Transactions

When an importer begins to purchase on a regular basis, or when the importer desires to make regular purchases from a particular supplier, the buyer and the seller should enter into a more comprehensive agreement to govern their relationship. Often these types of agreements are a result of the buyer's being willing to commit to regular purchases, and, therefore, to purchase a larger quantity of the goods, in return for obtaining a lower price. Or, they may result from the buyer's desire to tie up, that is, to obtain more assurance from the seller to commit to supply the buyer's requirements, or from the seller's desire to plan its production. The three major types of agreements used in ongoing sales transactions are (1) international purchase agreements, that is, supply agreements where the seller sells directly to the buyer, who either incorporates the seller's product as a component into a product that the buyer manufactures or consumes the product itself and does not resell the product; (2) distributor agreements, where the buyer buys the product from a foreign seller and resells the product in the United States or for export, usually in the same form but sometimes with modifications; and (3) sales agent or sales representative agreements, where a U.S. person is appointed to solicit orders from potential customers in the United States for a foreign seller. In the last case, the sale is not made to the sales agent, but is made directly to the U.S. customer, with payment of a commission or other compensation to the sales agent.

In any of the three foregoing agreements, there is a correlation between the documentation used in isolated purchase transactions and the documentation used in ongoing purchase transactions. Furthermore, there are a number of important provisions in international purchase, distributor, and sales agent agreements that are not relevant to domestic purchases but should be included in such agreements.

1. Correlation With Documentation for Isolated Purchase Transactions

As discussed in Section A.4, it is common for sellers and buyers to use forms such as requests for quotation, purchase orders, purchase order acknowledgments, purchase order acceptances, sales confirmations, and invoices during the course of buying and selling products. When an ongoing purchase relationship with a particular seller is being established, it is usual to enter into an umbrella or blanket agreement that is intended to govern the relationship between the parties over a longer period of time, for example, one year, five years, or longer. Sometimes the parties will enter into a trial purchase agreement that will last for a short period of time, such as one year, before deciding to enter into a longer-term agreement. In any event, the international purchase (supply) agreement, the distributor agreement, and the sales agent (representative) agreement define the rights and obligations of the parties over a fairly long period of time and commit the buyer and the seller to doing business with each other so that both sides can make production, marketing, and advertising plans and expenditures. Special price discounts in return for commitments to purchase specific quantities are common in such agreements. Such agreements may contain a commitment to purchase a specific quantity over the life of the agreement and may designate a specific price or a formula by which the price will be adjusted over the life of the agreement. To this extent, these agreements serve as an umbrella over the parties' relationship, with certain specific acts to be accomplished as agreed to by the parties. For example, it is usually necessary during the term of such agreements for the buyer to advise the seller as to the specific quantity it wishes to order at that time, to be applied against the buyer's overall purchase commitment.

If the price of the product is likely to fluctuate, no price may be specified in the umbrella agreement. Instead, the price may be changed from time to time by the seller depending upon the seller's price at the time the buyer submits an order, perhaps with a special discount from such price because the buyer has committed to buy a substantial quantity over the life of the agreement. In such cases, depending upon whether or not a specific price has been set in the umbrella agreement, the buyer will send a request for quotation and the seller will provide a quotation, or a purchase order will be sent describing the specific quantity that the buyer wishes to order at that time, a suggested shipment date, and the price. The seller will still use a purchase order acknowledgment and/or a purchase order acceptance form to agree to ship the specific quantity on the specific shipment date at the specific price. The seller will continue to provide a commercial invoice against which the buyer must make payment.

In summary, when the seller and the buyer wish to enter into a longer-term agreement, they will define their overall relationship in an umbrella agreement, but the usual documentation utilized in isolated purchase transactions will also be utilized to order specific quantities and to confirm prices and shipment dates. Sometimes conflicts can arise between the terms and conditions in the umbrella agreement and those in the specific documentation. Usually the parties provide that, in such cases, the umbrella agreement will control, but this can also lead to problems in situations where the parties wish to vary the terms of their umbrella agreement for a specific transaction.

2. *Important Provisions in International Purchase Agreements*

There are numerous terms and conditions in an international purchase agreement that require special consideration different from the usual terms and conditions in a domestic purchase agreement. A sample international purchase agreement is included as Appendix F.

a. *Purchasing and Selling Entities*

One consideration that may arise in an international purchase agreement is the identity of the purchasing and selling entities. In some cases, the buyer may want to organize a separate company to handle all importations. One reason for this is to insulate the U.S. company's assets against claims related to the imported article, such as product liability claims. If the U.S. company will be reselling the products, it may wish to conduct such business in a separate subsidiary company that conducts the importing and resale operations. (Ordinarily, unless the parent corporation is in the chain of ownership and takes title to the products, it would not be liable for product liability claims.) Generally, however, a U.S. company will not be able to protect its assets against unforeseen U.S. Customs liability by organizing a subsidiary to act as the importer. That usually will make no difference, as the importer will be required to post a bond to guarantee payment of all customs duties and penalties. If the importing company has limited assets, the bonding company will not issue the bond unless the parent company guarantees the debts of the subsidiary/importer.

If the seller and the buyers are related entities, such as a subsidiary and parent corporation, the U.S. Customs treatment may be different, for example, in the valuation of the merchandise or assessment of antidumping duties. Some transactions may be structured to involve the use of a trading company on the exporting side, the importing side, or both. Depending upon whether the trading company takes title or is appointed as the agent (of either the buyer or the seller), or whether the trading company is related to the seller or the buyer, the customs value may be different. For example, commissions paid to the seller's agent are ordinarily subject to customs duties in the United States, but commissions paid to the buyer's agent are not.

b. Quantity

The quantity term is even more important than the price. Under U.S. law, if the parties have agreed on the quantity, the purchase agreement is enforceable even if the parties have not agreed on the price—a current, or market, price will be implied. When no quantity has been agreed upon, however, the purchase agreement will not be enforceable.

One reason for forming a formal purchase agreement is for the buyer to obtain a lower price by committing to purchase a large quantity, usually over a year or more. The seller may be willing to grant a lower price in return for the ability to plan ahead, schedule production and inventory, develop economies of scale, and reduce shipping and administrative costs. The buyer should be aware that price discounts based on quantity may violate U.S. price discrimination laws unless the amount of the discount can be directly related to the cost savings of the seller for that particular quantity.

Quantity agreements can be for a specific quantity or a target quantity. Generally, if the commitment is a target only, failure to actually purchase such an amount will not justify the seller in claiming damages or terminating the agreement (although sometimes the buyer may agree to a retroactive price increase). Failure to purchase a minimum purchase quantity, however, will justify termination and a claim for breach. Sometimes the buyer may wish to buy the seller's entire output or the seller may seek a commitment that the buyer will purchase all of its requirements for the merchandise from the seller. Usually, such agreements are lawful, but in certain circumstances they can violate the U.S. antitrust laws, such as when the seller is the only supplier or represents a large amount of the supply, or the buyer is the only buyer or represents a large segment of the market.

c. Pricing

There are a number of considerations in formulating the buyer's pricing policy for international purchase agreements. A delivered price calculation sheet will identify all additional costs of importing to make sure that the price of resale results in a net profit that is acceptable to the buyer. The buyer also has to be aware of several constraints in formulating its pricing policy.

The first constraint relates to dumping. The United States has laws prohibiting dumping. This generally means that the price at which products are sold for export to the United States cannot be lower than the price at which such products are sold for domestic consumption in the country from which they are exported. However, the mere fact that sales to the United States are made at lower prices does not automatically mean that a dumping investigation will be initiated or that a dumping finding will occur. Under the laws of the United States, no dumping will occur if the price to the United States is above the current U.S. market price, even if the seller's price to the United States is lower than its sale price in its own country.

Additionally, there are U.S. legal constraints on the extent to which a price quoted for import can vary from buyer to buyer. The antitrust laws in the United States (in particular, the price discrimination provisions of the Robinson-Patman Act) apply when two or more sales to two or more buyers are being made in the United States. If the seller is selling to two or more buyers in the United States at different prices, such sales may violate the price discrimination provisions of U.S. law. The buyer who is paying the higher price may sue the foreign seller. Moreover, if the buyer purchasing at the lower price induced the price discrimination, the buyer would also violate U.S. law. In order to gain some assurance that it is getting the best price, sometimes a buyer will obtain a covenant from the seller in the purchase agreement that the seller agrees to grant the buyer the best price that it grants to any other purchaser during the term of the agreement. Such covenants may be helpful, but the buyer must have the right to inspect the sales records of the seller to confirm that it is getting the best price.

If the price is below the seller's total cost of production, there is a risk that such purchases will be attacked as predatory pricing in violation of U.S. antitrust laws. The accounting calculation of cost is always a subject of dispute, particularly where the seller may feel that the costs of foreign advertising or other costs should not be allocated to export sales. However, in general, any sales below total, fully allocated costs are at risk. Obviously, it will be the importer's competitors who will object to, and sue to stop, such sales.

Another very important pricing area relates to rebates, discounts, allowances, and price escalation clauses. Sometimes the buyer will ask for and the seller will be willing to grant some form of rebate, discount, or allowance under certain circumstances, such as the purchase of large quantities of merchandise. Such price concessions generally do not, in and of themselves, violate U.S. or foreign law, but if such payments are not disclosed to the proper government authorities, both the U.S. importer and the foreign seller may violate various U.S. and foreign laws and may be charged with conspiracy to violate or aiding and abetting the other's violation of those laws. For example, the U.S. importer must file customs entry documents on each shipment and must declare the price at which the goods are being purchased. If, in fact, this price is false (because the exporter has agreed to grant some rebate, discount, or allowance or, in fact, does so), the U.S. importer will violate U.S. law and be subject to civil and criminal penalties. Similarly, when the seller exports the goods to the United States, the seller will be required to state a value for export purposes in its country. If the seller sends the buyer two invoices for different amounts, or if the seller asks the buyer to pay any part of the purchase price outside of the seller's country (for example, by deposit in a bank account in the United States, Switzerland, or some other country), there is considerable risk that the intended action of the seller will violate the seller's foreign exchange control, tax, and/or customs laws. If the buyer cooperates by making any such payment, or is aware of the scheme, the buyer can also be charged with conspiracy to violate those foreign laws and can risk fines, arrest, and imprisonment in that country. Similarly, retroactive price increases (for example, due to currency fluctuations) or price increases under escalation clauses may cause a change in the final price, which may have to be reported to foreign exchange authorities or to U.S. Customs. Before agreeing to accept any price rebate, discount, or allowance; to use a price escalation clause; to implement a retroactive price increase; or to make any payment to the seller in any place except the seller's own country by check or wire transfer (not cash), the buyer should satisfy itself that its actions will not result in the violation of any U.S. or foreign law.

If the purchase is from an affiliated company, such as a foreign parent or subsidiary, additional pricing considerations arise. Because the buyer and the seller are related, pricing can be artificially manipulated. For example, a U.S. importer whose U.S. profits are taxable at a rate of 35 percent may, when purchasing from an affiliated seller in a country that has a higher tax rate, attempt to minimize taxes in the foreign country by purchasing from its foreign affiliate at a low price. Thus, when the foreign affiliate sells the product, its profit will be small and its taxes reduced. When the purchase is from a country where the tax rate is lower than that in the United States, the considerations are reversed and the transfer price is set at a high rate, in which case the U.S. profits will be low. These strategies are well known to the tax authorities in foreign countries and to the Internal Revenue Service in the United States. Consequently, purchases from affiliated companies are always susceptible to attack by the tax authorities. In general, the tax authorities in both countries require that the buyer purchase from its affiliated seller at an arm's-length price, as if it were purchasing from an unaffiliated seller. Often, preserving evidence that the seller was selling to its unaffiliated customers at the same price as its affiliated customers will be very important in defending a tax audit. When the U.S. buyer is purchasing from a country with a higher tax rate, the U.S. Customs authorities will also be suspicious that the transfer price is undervalued, and, therefore, customs duties may be underpaid. Under U.S. tax regulations, the U.S. importer cannot claim any income tax deduction for cost of goods greater than the value declared for U.S. Customs purposes.

Another consideration in the pricing of goods for import concerns parallel imports or gray market goods. If buyers in one country are able to purchase at a lower price than that in the United States, an economic incentive will exist for customers in the lower-price country to divert such goods to the United States in hopes of making a profit. Obviously, the seller's distributor in the United States will complain about such unauthorized imports and loss of sales. Recently, the U.S. Supreme Court has held that genuine goods, that is, those that are made by the same manufacturer and are not mere copies or imitations, can be imported into the United States under the U.S. Customs laws. An importer who experiences such gray market goods may have other legal remedies available to stop or prevent such imports, but the best remedy is to make sure that the seller is not selling at lower prices in other markets. Unfortunately, maintaining pricing parity is not always easy because of floating exchange rates, not only between the United States and other countries, but also among those other countries.

Finally, the import price as shown in the seller's invoice and as declared to the U.S. Customs for duty purposes affects the "cost of goods" for U.S. income tax purposes, as specified in section 1059A of the Internal Revenue Code.

d. Currency Fluctuations

Related to the issue of pricing are the currency fluctuations that occur between the countries of the seller and the buyer. If the U.S. importer purchases only in U.S. dollars, the fluctuations of the foreign currency will not affect the final U.S. dollar amount that the importer makes as payment. However, if the seller is a much larger company than the buyer and has more negotiating and bargaining leverage, or if the buyer is anxious to make the purchase, it may be necessary to agree to a purchase agreement denominated in foreign currency, such as the Japanese yen or the euro. In such cases, if the foreign currency strengthens between the time of the price agreement and the time of payment, the U.S. importer will have to pay more U.S. dollars than it had anticipated when it agreed to the price and calculated the expected cost. In such cases, the importer is assuming the foreign exchange fluctuation risk. Sometimes, when the term of the agreement is long, or when major currency fluctuations are anticipated, neither the seller nor the buyer is comfortable in entirely assuming such risk. Consequently, they may agree to some sharing of the risk, such as a 50/50 price adjustment due to any exchange fluctuations that occur during the life of the agreement, or some other formula that attempts to protect both sides against such fluctuations. If the two parties have agreed to a currency exchange formula and documented that formula in writing prior to import, U.S. Customs and Border Protection will accept that methodology for calculating the value for duty purposes instead of using the standard quarterly exchange rate.

e. Payment Methods

In a domestic sales transaction, the buyer may be used to purchasing on open account, receiving credit, or paying cash on delivery. In international purchases, it is more customary to utilize certain methods of payment that are designed to give the overseas seller a greater level of protection. The idea is that if the buyer fails to pay, it is much more difficult for a seller to come to the United States, institute a lawsuit, attempt to attach the buyer's assets, or otherwise obtain payment. When a seller is dealing with a buyer who is essentially unknown to it, with whom it has no prior payment experience, or who is small, the seller often requires that the buyer pay cash in advance or obtain a documentary letter of credit from a bank in the buyer's country. The seller may also require that the letter of credit be confirmed by a bank in the seller's country to guarantee payment by the buyer's bank. The seller may still sell on terms with payment to be made at the time of arrival, or the seller may give the buyer some longer period of time (for example, from 30 days to 180 days) to make payment, but the letter of credit acts as an umbrella obligation of the bank guaranteeing such payment, and the buyer does not pay the seller directly, but through the bank that issues the letter of credit. In some cases, however, the buyer will be unable to obtain a letter of credit, for example, because the buyer's bank does not feel comfortable with the buyer's financial solvency. Furthermore, the issuance of letters of credit involves the payment of bank fees, which are normally paid by the buyer, and the buyer usually does not wish to incur such expenses in addition to the cost of purchasing the goods. Another disadvantage to the buyer is that it will be unable to inspect the goods before its bank is obliged to make payment. In such cases, particularly if the seller is anxious to make the sale, or if other sellers are willing to offer more liberal payment terms, the buyer may be able to force the seller to give up a letter of credit and agree to make the sale on some other, more liberal, method of payment.

The best method of purchase for the buyer is on open account, where the seller makes the sale and the shipment by forwarding the bill of lading and a commercial invoice directly to the buyer for payment. Because the bill of lading is sent directly to the buyer, once it leaves the possession of the seller, the seller will be unable to control what happens to the goods, and the buyer will be able to obtain the goods whether or not payment is made. This also gives the buyer an opportunity to inspect the goods prior to making payment. When a seller agrees to sell on open account, the seller may request that the buyer open a standby letter of credit or grant a security interest under

U.S. law to protect the seller's right to payment in case the buyer goes bankrupt or otherwise fails to pay at the agreed time (see subsection g, below).

The next best method of payment for the buyer is to utilize a time draft, commonly known as a document against acceptance or D/A transaction. The bill of lading and time draft (that is, a document like a check in the amount of the sale drawn by the seller on the buyer—rather than a bank—and payable to the seller) are forwarded through banking channels, but the buyer agrees to make payment within a certain number of days (for example, 30 to 180) after it receives and accepts the draft. Normally, this permits the buyer to obtain possession of the goods and may give the buyer enough time to resell them before its obligation to pay comes due. However, documents against acceptance transactions are a significantly greater risk for the seller because, if the buyer does not pay at the promised time, the seller's only recourse is to file a lawsuit—the goods have already been released to the buyer. Where the buyer is financially strong, however, sometimes such acceptances can be discounted by the seller, permitting the seller to get immediate payment but giving the buyer additional time to pay. This discounting may be done with recourse or without recourse, depending upon the size of the discount the seller is willing to accept. The seller may decide to waive the interest charge for the delay in payment in order to make the sale.

The next best method of payment for the buyer is by sight draft documentary collection, commonly known as documents against payment or D/P transactions. In this case, the seller uses the services of a bank to effect collection, but neither the buyer's bank nor the seller's bank guarantees payment by the buyer. The seller will ship the goods, and the bill of lading and a draft will be forwarded to the seller's bank. The seller's bank will forward such documents to a correspondent bank in the United States (sometimes the seller or its freight forwarder sends the documents directly to the buyer's bank—this is known as direct collection), and the U.S. bank will collect payment from the buyer prior to the time that the goods arrive. If payment is not made by the buyer, the U.S. bank does not release the bill of lading to the buyer, and the buyer will be unable to take possession of the goods or clear U.S. Customs. Although it can still be a significant problem for the seller if the buyer does not make payment and the shipment has already arrived in the United States, the seller should still be able to control the goods upon arrival, for example, by asking the bank to place them in a warehouse or by requesting that they be shipped to a third country or back to the seller at the seller's expense. Direct collections are often used for air shipments to avoid delays through the seller's bank, and also because air waybills are nonnegotiable.

Sometimes a buyer will begin purchasing from a particular seller under letters of credit, and as the seller becomes more familiar with the buyer (the buyer honors its obligations, increases its purchases, or enters into an ongoing purchase relationship agreement), the seller will be willing to liberalize its payment terms.

In addition, in international transactions, the buyer may be required to use alternative payment methods, such as wire transfers via banking channels, since payment by check will often involve an inordinate length of time if the check is first sent to the seller in the foreign country and then sent back to the United States to be collected from the buyer's bank. Direct telegraphic transfer from bank account to bank account is a highly efficient and useful way to deal with international payments. However, the buyer should resist making a wire transfer until after the goods have arrived and have been inspected, or at least until after the goods are shipped under a non-negotiable (straight) bill of lading. Other methods of payment, such as cash payments made by employees traveling from the buyer to the seller or vice versa, or payments made in third countries, all carry the risk of violating the seller's foreign exchange control and/or tax laws and should be agreed to only after detailed investigation of the possible risks. A chart comparing these various methods of payment is shown in Figure 3–10.

Finally, an additional method of payment that sellers sometimes use is the factoring of export accounts receivable. This may represent an opportunity for a foreign seller to obtain its money immediately on open account sales in return for accepting a lesser amount, or some discount from the sales price. Such factoring arrangements usually involve a disadvantage for the buyer, however, because the buyer may be obligated to pay the factor when the obligation is due even though the buyer may have a dispute, such as a claim for defective goods, with the seller. To guard against that problem, the buyer should try to make sure that the purchase agreement provides that the seller cannot assign its accounts receivable without the buyer's consent.

f. Import Financing

The substantive aspects of import financing were discussed in Chapter 6, Section N. If import financing is going to be utilized, it should be discussed in the international purchase agreement. The seller will thus be clearly aware that the buyer intends to use such financing. The documentation that the seller is required to provide in order for the buyer to obtain such financing should be specified in the agreement, and the buyer's obligation to purchase should be excused if such import financing is not granted.

g. Security Interest

As discussed in subsection e, above, on payment methods, if the buyer intends to purchase on open account or on documents against acceptance, the seller may request a security interest to protect its rights to payment. Under U.S. law, unless the seller has registered its lien or security interest with a government agency, if the buyer goes into bankruptcy or falls into financial difficulties, the seller will be unable to repossess the merchandise it sold, even if the merchandise is still in the possession of the buyer. Also, the seller may be unable to obtain priority over other creditors, and after such creditors are paid, nothing may remain for the seller. Although granting a security interest does reduce the buyer's flexibility in negotiating with creditors in the event that the buyer falls into financial difficulties, in practice, the buyer will have a difficult time objecting to granting such a security interest. However, the buyer should not accept responsibility for preparing or filing such a security interest or notifying other creditors, since, if it does so improperly, the seller may sue the buyer for negligence. If a security interest is granted by the buyer and the buyer does experience financial difficulties, it should make sure that it makes payments in accordance with the priority of the security interests or the directors of the company may become personally liable. Sometimes, the buyer's bank or other creditor will have been granted a security interest in the assets of the buyer. In order for a seller to take priority over the previous creditors, it may try to impose upon the buyer an obligation to obtain subordination agreements from the buyer's other creditors. Generally, the buyer should resist this and insist that the seller obtain such agreements itself.

h. *Passage of Title, Delivery, and Risk of Loss*

Ownership is transferred from the seller to the buyer by the passage of title. Under the Convention on Contracts for the International Sale of Goods (discussed in subsection l), unless otherwise agreed, title and risk of loss will pass to the buyer when the seller delivers the merchandise to the first transportation carrier. The buyer's payment will be due at that time. Under U.S. law, title passes at the time and place agreed to by the parties to the international purchase agreement. It can pass at the seller's plant, at the port of export, upon arrival in the United States after clearance of Customs, upon arrival at the buyer's place of business, or at any other place, time, or manner agreed to by the parties. Usually the risk of loss for any subsequent casualty or damage to the products will pass to the buyer at the same time as the title passes. However, it is possible to specify in the purchase agreement that it will pass at a different time.

i. *Warranties and Product Defects*

From the buyer's point of view, one of the most important provisions in the international purchase agreement is the one that specifies the warranty terms. Under the law of the United States and the Convention on Contracts for the International Sale of Goods (discussed in subsection l), unless the seller limits its warranty expressly in writing in the international purchase agreement, the seller will be responsible and liable for all foreseeable consequential damages that result to the buyer from defective products. Consequently, it is common for the seller to try to eliminate all or most warranties. The purchase agreement should specify exactly what warranty the seller is giving for the products, whether the products are being sold "as is" with no warranty, whether there is a limited warranty such as repair or replacement, whether there is a dollar limit on the warranty, whether there is a time period within which the warranty claim must be made, and/or whether there is any limitation on consequential damages. In the United States, as a matter of public policy, the law prohibits certain types of warranty disclaimers or exclusions. For example, imported products have to comply with the Magnuson-Moss Warranty Act. Consequently, in reviewing the warranty limitation, the buyer may need to consult with an attorney to make sure that the warranty will be effective. If the sales agreement is formed by a mere exchange of preprinted forms, the buyer may find that the seller's terms or conditions control the sale and that no warranty exists. Therefore, the buyer should carefully read the seller's communications, and if the warranty is too limited, the buyer must negotiate a warranty acceptable to both sides before going ahead with the purchase.

j. *Preshipment Inspections*

Even if the buyer has not paid in advance, if the products arrive in the United States and are defective, the buyer may be faced with substantial losses or the necessity of re-exporting the merchandise to the seller. Consequently, the buyer should generally insist upon preshipment inspection in the international purchase agreement. In an international purchase agreement, if the buyer can get the seller to agree that the buyer is entitled to purchase at the lowest price at which it sells to any of its other customers, the inspection company may be able to review more than the quality of the goods. For example, the inspection company may require the seller to produce documentation relating to sales of the same product to other customers to ascertain the prices at which such sales were made. If the buyer getting the preshipment inspection determines that the price it is paying is higher than the prices the seller had charged other customers, the buyer can refuse to go forward with the transaction or renegotiate the price.

The buyer should realize, however, that asking for a preshipment inspection will usually delay the shipment anywhere from twenty to forty days and that it will have to pay for such inspection unless it can get the seller to agree to share the costs.

k. Export Licenses

The importance of an export license has been touched upon in Chapter 6, Section E.1. In an international purchase agreement, the buyer should require the seller to warrant that no export license is required, or the exporter should state that an export license is required and should promise to obtain the license in a timely manner. If the seller fails to obtain the license, the buyer could claim damages. The buyer should be aware that, if the seller is required to obtain an export license, the buyer will usually be required to provide an International Import Certificate issued by the U.S. Department of Commerce. The seller will be unable to apply for its export license until it obtains the certificate, and the buyer should obtain it and send it to the seller as soon as possible to avoid delays in obtaining the export license. (Under the Incoterms, the buyer is responsible for obtaining the export license on "ex-works" sales.)

l. Governing Law

In any international purchase agreement, whether the agreement is formed by a written agreement between the parties or whether it is an oral agreement, the rights and obligations of the parties will be governed either by the law of the country of the seller or by the law of the country of the buyer. The laws of most countries permit the seller and the buyer to specifically agree on which law will apply, and that choice will be binding upon both parties whether or not a lawsuit is brought in either the buyer's or the seller's country. Of course, whenever the subject is raised, the seller will prefer the agreement to be governed by the laws of the seller's country, and the buyer will prefer it to be governed by the laws of the buyer's country. If the bargaining leverage of the parties is approximately equal, it is fair to say that it is more customary for the buyer to agree that the seller's law will govern the agreement. However, if the buyer has more bargaining leverage, the buyer may be able to prevail. Before agreeing to have the foreign seller's law govern the agreement, however, the buyer should check on what differences exist between the foreign law and U.S. law, so that the buyer can fully appreciate the risks it is assuming by agreeing to the application of foreign law. The buyer can also determine whether or not the risk is serious enough to negotiate a specific solution to that particular problem with the seller. Frequently, however, the parties do not raise, negotiate, or expressly agree upon the governing law. This may occur as a result of an exchange of preprinted forms wherein the buyer and the seller each have specified that their own law governs, which results in a clear conflict between these two provisions. It may also occur when the parties have not discussed the governing law, as in a situation where an oral agreement or sale has occurred, or when the facsimile, email, or other purchase or sale documentation does not contain any express specification of the governing law. In such cases, if a dispute arises between the parties, it will be extremely difficult to determine with any confidence which law governs the purchase agreement. Often the buyer believes that the law of the country where the offer is accepted will govern. However, the laws of the two countries may be in conflict on this point, and it may be unclear whether this means an offer to sell or an offer to buy, and whether or not the acceptance must be received by the offeror before the formation of the purchase agreement.

An additional development relating to this issue is the Convention on Contracts for the International Sale of Goods (the Convention). On January 1, 1988, this multinational treaty went into effect among the countries that have ;signed it, including the United States. There are currently 73 countries that are contracting parties as follows:

Parties to the Convention on Contracts for the International Sale of Goods

Argentina
Armenia
Australia
Austria
Belarus
Belgium
Bosnia-Herzegovina
Bulgaria
Burundi
Canada
Chile
China (PRC)
Colombia
Croatia
Cuba
Cyprus
Czech Republic
Denmark
Ecuador
Egypt
El Salvador
Estonia
Finland
France
Gabon
Georgia
Germany
Greece
Guinea
Honduras
Hungary
Iceland
Iraq
Israel
Italy
Japan
South Korea
Kyrgystan
Latvia
Lebanon
Lesotho
Liberia
Lithuania
Luxembourg
Macedonia
Mauritania
Mexico
Moldova
Mongolia
Montenegro
Netherlands
New Zealand
Norway
Paraguay
Peru
Poland
Romania
Russian Federation
Saint Vincent & Grenadines
Serbia
Singapore
Slovakia
Slovenia
Spain
Sweden
Switzerland
Syria
Uganda
Ukraine
United States
Uruguay
Uzbekistan
Zambia

The Convention is a detailed listing of over one hundred articles dealing with the rights and responsibilities of the buyer and the seller in international purchase agreements. It is similar in some respects to Article 2 of the U.S. Uniform Commercial Code. Nevertheless, there are many concepts, such as fundamental breach, avoidance, impediment, and nonconformity, that are not identical to U.S. law.

The Convention permits buyers and sellers located in countries that are parties to the Convention to exclude the application of the Convention (by expressly referring to it) and to choose the law of either the seller or the buyer to apply to the international purchase agreement. However, for companies located in any of the countries that are parties to the Convention (including U.S. companies), if the seller and buyer cannot or do not agree on which law will apply, the provisions of the Convention will automatically apply.

In summary, the buyer should include provisions on governing law in its international purchase agreement, and if the seller disagrees, the buyer should negotiate this provision. The buyer should also determine what differences exist between the Convention and U.S. law in case the parties cannot agree and the Convention thereby becomes applicable.

m. Dispute Resolution

One method of resolving disputes that may arise between the parties is litigation in the courts. For a U.S. importer, the most likely dispute to arise relates to defective goods. In such cases, the importer may be limited to going to the courts of the seller's country in order to institute litigation and seek a judgment to obtain assets of the seller. Even if the parties have agreed that U.S. law will govern the purchase agreement, there is a risk that a foreign court may misapply U.S. law, disregard U.S. law, or otherwise favor and protect the seller located in its own country. Furthermore, there can be significant delays in legal proceedings (from two to five years), court and legal expenses can be high, and the outcome may be questionable. In order to reduce such risks, the importer can specify in the international purchase agreement that all disputes must be resolved in the courts of the importer's country, and that the seller consents to jurisdiction there and to the commencement of any such lawsuit by the simple forwarding of any form of written notice by the importer to the seller. Of course, sellers may resist such provisions, and whether the buyer will be able to finally obtain this agreement will depend upon the negotiating and bargaining strength of the parties.

Another form of dispute resolution that is common in international purchase agreements is arbitration. In many foreign countries, sellers take a less adversarial approach to the resolution of contractual disputes, and they feel more comfortable with a less formal proceeding, such as arbitration. While arbitration can be included in an international purchase agreement, an importer should thoroughly understand the advantages and disadvantages of agreeing to resolve disputes by arbitration. First, arbitration is unlikely to save much in expenses and quite often may not involve a significantly shorter time period to resolve the dispute. In fact, from the point of view of expense, in some cases, if the seller refuses to go forward with the arbitration, the buyer will have to advance the seller's portion of the arbitration fees to the arbitration tribunal, or the arbitrators will not proceed with the dispute. Furthermore, in litigation, of course, the judges or juries involved are paid at the public expense, whereas in arbitration, the parties must pay the expenses of the arbitrators, which can be very substantial, especially if there are three arbitrators.

Second, the administering authority must be selected. The International Chamber of Commerce is commonly designated as the administering authority in arbitration clauses, but the fees that it charges are very high. The American Arbitration Association also handles international disputes, but the foreign seller may be unwilling to agree to arbitration by a U.S. administering authority. Other administering authorities, such as the Inter-American Commercial Arbitration Commission, the London Court of International Arbitration, the Stockholm Chamber of Commerce Arbitration Institute, the British Columbia International Arbitration Centre, or an arbitration authority in the seller's country, may be acceptable.

Third, the number of arbitrators should be specified. Since the parties will be paying for them, the author recommends that one arbitrator be utilized to resolve disputes of a smaller amount (a specified dollar figure) and that three arbitrators be utilized for larger disputes.

Fourth, the place of arbitration must be specified. Again, the seller and the buyer will have a natural conflict on this point, so some third country or intermediate location is probably most likely to be mutually agreeable. Another variation that has developed, although its legal validity has been questioned, is an agreement that if the seller commences the arbitration, arbitration will be conducted in the buyer's country, and if the buyer commences the arbitration, the arbitration will be conducted in the seller's country. This has the effect of discouraging either party from commencing arbitration and forcing the parties to reach amicable solutions to their disputes.

Finally, the buyer should ascertain beforehand whether an arbitral award would be enforced in the courts of the seller's country. Some sixty countries have become parties to a multinational treaty known as the New York Convention, which commits them to enforcing the arbitral awards of member countries. Without this assurance, the entire dispute may have to be relitigated in the seller's country.

n. Termination

Protection against termination of an international purchase agreement or distributor or sales agent agreement may prove to be difficult for the U.S. buyer. No federal law specifically protects U.S. buyers, distributors, or sales agents against unfair terminations, although some states, such as Wisconsin, have enacted protective legislation. Although the U.S. buyer may have invested a great deal of time in purchasing products or building up a market for the resale of such products, the seller may terminate the agreement on short notice or without payment of compensation. In general, the buyer may be able to claim damages if the termination is the result of conspiracy, such as the agreement of two or more suppliers not to sell to the buyer (concerted refusal to deal); if the termination is by a seller with monopoly power (such as a 60 percent or greater market share); or if the termination is for an anticompetitive, rather than a business, reason (such as a refusal of the buyer to adhere to the seller's suggested resale prices). The buyer should try to get some protection by entering into an ongoing purchase agreement (rather than simply dealing on a purchase order by purchase order basis) and inserting a provision that there be a long lead time prior to termination or that the seller will pay the buyer some termination compensation for goodwill created by the buyer's market development. (If the purchaser is selling the goods under its own trademark, the seller will not be able to appoint another distributor to sell under the same brand name unless the seller is willing to buy the trademark from the buyer.) Of course, the buyer should always specify in the purchase agreement that it will have no obligation to continue to purchase from the seller if there is a change in control, bankruptcy, insolvency, or breach of the agreement by the seller.

C. Import Distributor and Sales Agent Agreements

In addition to the foregoing provisions, which arise in all international purchase agreements, there are other specific provisions that arise in import distributor agreements and sales agent agreements.

1. Distinction Between Distributor and Sales Agent

A distributor is a company that buys products from a seller, takes title thereto, and assumes the risk of resale. A distributor will purchase at a specific price and will be compensated by reselling the product at a higher price. Under the antitrust laws of the United States, the seller cannot restrict or require a distributor to resell the product at any specific price, although it may be able to restrict the customers to whom or the territories in which the buyer resells.

A sales agent does not purchase from the seller. The sales agent or representative locates customers and solicits offers to purchase the product from the potential buyers. In order to avoid tax liability for the seller in the United States, the sales agent normally will not have any authority to accept offers to purchase from potential customers. Instead, the offers from the customer are forwarded to the seller for final acceptance, and shipment and billing is direct between the seller and the customer. Furthermore, since the sales agent normally does not take title, it will ordinarily not act as importer of record and will not assume liabilities for customs duties or penalties. For such services, the sales agent is paid a commission or some other type of compensation. Because no sale occurs between the seller and the sales agent, the seller can specify the price at which it will sell to customers, and the sales agent can be restricted to quoting only that price to a potential customer. Likewise, the sales agent can be restricted as to its territory or the types of customers from which it has been given the right to solicit orders. Sometimes the sales agent will guarantee payment by the customers or perform other services, such as after-sales service or invoicing of the customers.

A chart summarizing these differences is shown in Figure 3–11. Another chart analyzing the financial comparison of acting as a distributor or a sales agent is shown in Figure 3–12.

2. Import Distributor Agreements

As previously indicated, when a distributor agreement is utilized, such agreement will act as an umbrella agreement, and specific orders for specific quantities, shipment dates, and possibly prices will be stated in purchase orders, purchase order acceptances, and similar documentation discussed in relation to isolated purchase transactions. A checklist for negotiation issues for a distributor agreement is shown in Figure 3–13.

The important provisions in an import distributor agreement include the following:

a. Territory and Exclusivity

The distributor will normally want to be the exclusive distributor in a territory, whereas the seller would generally prefer to make a nonexclusive appointment so that if the distributor fails to perform, it can appoint other distributors. Also, the seller may simply wish from the outset to appoint a number of distributors in the United States to adequately serve the market. A possible compromise is that the appointment will be exclusive unless certain minimum purchase obligations are not met, in which case the seller has the right to convert the agreement to a nonexclusive agreement.

Usually the entire United States or the part of the United States that is granted to the distributor is specified. The distributor may be required to agree not to solicit sales from outside the territory. The distributor may be prohibited from establishing any warehouse or sales outlet outside of the territory.

b. Pricing

As indicated, normally it is illegal for the seller to specify the price at which the U.S. distributor can resell the merchandise. Of course, ordinarily the distributor would not mark up the product too much, gouging end users and resulting in less sales and market penetration for the products. In addition, because of the gray market problem, the price at which the buyer resells should not be set too high, thereby attracting diversions from other countries. Gray markets can occur as a result of exchange rate fluctuations, where one of the seller's other distributors in another country is able to obtain a product at a lower price in its own currency than is available in the United States.

Currency fluctuations must be monitored, and the right to price reductions is normally necessary to make sure that the buyer is participating fairly in the profits that are being created along the chain of distribution. For example, if a French seller sells a product for $1 at a time when the French exchange rate is 5 euros to $1, the seller will be receiving $1 (or 5 euros) when its cost of production may be 4 euros, or a 1 euro profit. However, if the euro weakens to 10 euros to $1, and the seller still sells the product for $1, now it will receive 10 euros and its profit will increase. Sometimes the seller will continue to ask for price increases from the buyer even though the seller has had a very favorable exchange rate movement. Normally it is in the buyer's interest to have the seller reduce the price whenever the foreign currency weakens (or the dollar strengthens). When the seller does decrease its price to the U.S. distributor, however, normally the seller will also want the U.S. distributor to reduce its price on resale to the end users so that more sales will be made, volume will increase, and the seller can increase its market share.

c. Minimum Purchase Quantities

In most long-term purchase agreements or distributor agreements, the seller will ask for a commitment for purchase of a significant quantity. The buyer should request some price discount for such a commitment. Ordinarily, it is in the buyer's interest to commit only to a target amount or to use its best efforts to make sales. In such cases, if the buyer fails to make the target, there is no breach of the agreement and the seller cannot sue the buyer for damages. If the buyer commits to purchase fixed quantities or dollar amounts, however, and fails to perform, the seller may be able to sue for damages and terminate the distributor agreement.

d. Handling Competing Products

Normally a seller will want a provision wherein the distributor agrees not to handle competing products. If the distributor is already handling any competing products (either manufacturing them or purchasing them from alternative sources), the distributor may not want to agree to this provision, and there is no legal requirement that it do so. In fact, in certain situations, such as where other competing sellers do not have adequate outlets for their products, a violation of the U.S. antitrust laws can result if the buyer is required not to handle competing products. However, the seller will normally be unwilling to give the distributor an exclusive appointment in the territory unless the distributor agrees not to handle competing products.

e. Appointment of Subdistributors

Whether or not the distributor has the right to appoint subdistributors should be expressly stated in the distributor agreement. If this right is not discussed, the distributor may not have the right under U.S. law to appoint subdistributors. This can cause various problems for the distributor. Not only will the distributor possibly be unable to meet its purchase commitments to the seller, which could result in termination of the distributor agreement, but the distributor may lose chances to multiply its sales. In appointing subdistributors, the distributor needs to control the resale territories (but not the prices) to maximize distribution and sales potential. If the right to appoint subdistributors is granted, the distributor should try to avoid responsibility for their activities in the distribution agreement, such as sales outside their territories; otherwise, the distributor may find that its master distribution agreement with the seller is being terminated due to breaches by the independent subdistributors.

f. Use of Trade Names, Trademarks, and Copyrights

As discussed in Chapter 6, Section O, control of intellectual property rights is quite important. Sometimes U.S. distributors can protect their market position by registering their intellectual property rights, such as trademarks, in the United States. This is a particular disadvantage for the foreign seller, because if the seller wishes to terminate the distributor and to appoint a new distributor, the past distributor may own the intellectual property rights to distribute the products in the United States. Until the distributor consents to the assignment of the intellectual property rights to the seller or the new distributor, any sales by the seller into the United States or by the new distributor will be an infringement of the intellectual property rights owned by the former distributor. This puts the former distributor in a very strong bargaining position to negotiate a substantial termination compensation payment. The distributor may do this in a private branding arrangement where the seller, if it is a manufacturer, puts the distributor's own trademark or brand on the product. In the international purchase agreement, the distributor could specify that it has the exclusive rights to that name or brand, and the distributor should register the name with the U.S. Patent and Trademark Office. Upon termination of the distributorship agreement, the seller could not sell the products under that name or appoint another distributor to do so (but the seller could sell identical products under another brand name).

g. Warranties and Product Liability

In addition to the considerations discussed in Section B.2.i, the importer should require the seller to maintain product liability insurance in its own name and to name the importer as an additional insured in amounts deemed satisfactory by the importer. Product liability claims are not as common overseas as they are in the United States, and foreign sellers may not have product liability insurance. Furthermore, the customer will find it easier to sue the importer in the United States. The overseas seller may have no office in the United States, and the importer may be unable to sue the seller in the United States for warranty claims by the importer's customers. The seller should use a U.S. insurance company or a foreign insurance company that is doing business in the United States and is subject to the jurisdiction of the United States. Before modifying or adding to any of the seller's warranties, the buyer should obtain the seller's consent. If the distributor agrees to perform warranty or after-sales service for the seller, it should make sure that it clearly understands its responsibilities and the terms for reimbursement for warranty labor it performs.

3. Import Sales Agent Agreements

Like distributor agreements, sales agent agreements often contain many of the same provisions that are included in an international purchase agreement, but there are certain provisions peculiar to the sales agent agreement that must be considered. A checklist for negotiation issues for a sales agent agreement is shown in Figure 3–14.

a. Commissions

The sales agent is compensated for its efforts by payment of a commission by the seller. The sales agent is appointed to solicit orders, and when such orders are accepted by the seller, the agent is paid a commission. The U.S. sales agent should try to have its commission due upon solicitation or acceptance of the order instead of when the customer actually makes payment to the seller. The sales agent is not normally guaranteeing payment by the customers or making credit decisions, so it should not have to wait for its commission—its work is done when it brings a customer to the seller. Generally, the seller should not bill the agent for the price of the product (less commission) because such practice could result in characterizing the relationship as a distributorship rather than a sales agency.

b. Pricing

Because there is no sale between the seller and the sales agent, the seller can lawfully require the sales agent to quote only prices that the seller has authorized. For sellers who wish to establish uniform pricing on a worldwide basis, eliminate gray markets, and control markups, use of the sales agent appointment can be highly beneficial. However, the trade-off is that the seller will ordinarily assume the credit risk and will have to satisfy itself with regard to the ability of the customer to pay. This sometimes presents difficulties in obtaining sufficient information, although the sales agent can be given the responsibility of gathering such information and forwarding it to the seller prior to acceptance of any orders. In addition, some sales agents are willing to be appointed as *del credere* agents, wherein the sales agent guarantees the payment by any customer from whom it solicits an order. Obviously, a sales agent should require higher commissions for guaranteeing payment.

c. Shipment

Shipment is not made to the sales agent; it is made directly to the customer from whom the sales agent solicited the order. Generally there will be problems associated with trying to maintain an inventory at the agent's place of business in the United States. If the seller maintains an inventory in its own name or through an agent, the seller can become taxable on its own sales profits to customers in the United States. If the customer cannot wait for shipment from the foreign country, or if it is important to maintain an inventory in the United States, the appropriate way to do so while using sales agents must be investigated with a knowledgeable attorney.

Chapter 8

Import Process and Documentation

In addition to the purchase agreement, there are numerous other documents that the importer will commonly encounter in the process of importing merchandise. Since some of these documents may be prepared by the customs broker or others, the importer may not see such documents or realize that they have been prepared. Nevertheless, because the importer is responsible for the actions of its agent, the customs broker, it is imperative that the importer understand what documents are being prepared and filed on each importation. Furthermore, since the documents filed by the customs broker may be based on information provided by the importer, if the importer does not understand the documents or provides incorrect information, the customs broker will disclaim any responsibility therefor. Additionally, U.S. Customs expects that an importer will audit the information filed by the customs broker on its behalf in exercising reasonable care over its import transactions.

An overview of the U.S. Customs import process, which will be described in more detail in this chapter, is shown in Figure 8–1.

A. Importer Security Filing and the 10+2 Program

Increased security since September 11, 2001, has resulted in a number of new measures to collect data on shipments arriving in the United States prior to their departure from the country of exportation. Among these measures is the Importer Security Filing, which was implemented on January 26, 2009, with full compliance required by January 26, 2010. The program requires ten data elements to be transmitted by the importer prior to export. The time frames in which to transmit differ according to the type of transportation. These include:

1. Manufacturer*—consistent with Customs Entry/Immediate Delivery form
2. Seller
3. Buyer
4. Ship to party (if not the buyer)

5. Container stuffing location
6. Consolidator
7. Importer of record
8. Consignee
9. Country of origin*
10. Harmonized Tariff Number*

* Manufacturer, country of origin, and Harmonized Tariff Number must be at the line item level.

The remaining two elements must be supplied by the carrier: (1) the vessel stow plan and (2) container status messages. The information is to be reported at the lowest bill of lading level. The importer may file this information directly with CBP or use an agent with a valid power of attorney.

B. Bills of Lading

The bill of lading or loading is issued by the transportation carrier, either the airline or the steamship company. It evidences receipt of the merchandise for transportation to the destination specified in the bill. In the case of ocean shipments, the original bill of lading will have been obtained by the exporter and will be forwarded by air courier service through banking channels (or directly to the buyer on open account purchases) for arrival in advance of the shipment. Customs requires that the person making entry of the goods into the United States (the importer of record) present a properly endorsed bill of lading with the other customs entry documents in order to establish that that person has the right to make entry of the goods. Where the transportation is under a negotiable bill of lading, the importer will also have to present the bill of lading to the transportation carrier in order to obtain release of the goods. On import transactions, the Uniform Commercial Code requires that the bill of lading be negotiable unless the parties agree to a non-negotiable bill of lading in their purchase agreement. Where a negotiable bill of lading has been lost or the importer cannot present it, the steamship line may permit the importer to obtain the merchandise if it signs a "letter of indemnity" and the importer is determined to be a good credit risk. Sample ocean and air bills of lading are shown in Figures 4–6 and 4–7. Additional information on bills of lading is contained in Chapter 4, Section D.

C. Commercial Invoices

At the same time that the exporter forwards the bill of lading, it will include a commercial invoice (which must be in the English language) itemizing the merchandise sold and the amount due for payment. There must be one invoice for each separate shipment. Under U.S. Customs regulations, these commercial invoices must contain very specific items of information, such as quantities, description, purchase price, country of origin, assists, transportation charges, commissions, installation

Figure 8–1. Import process.

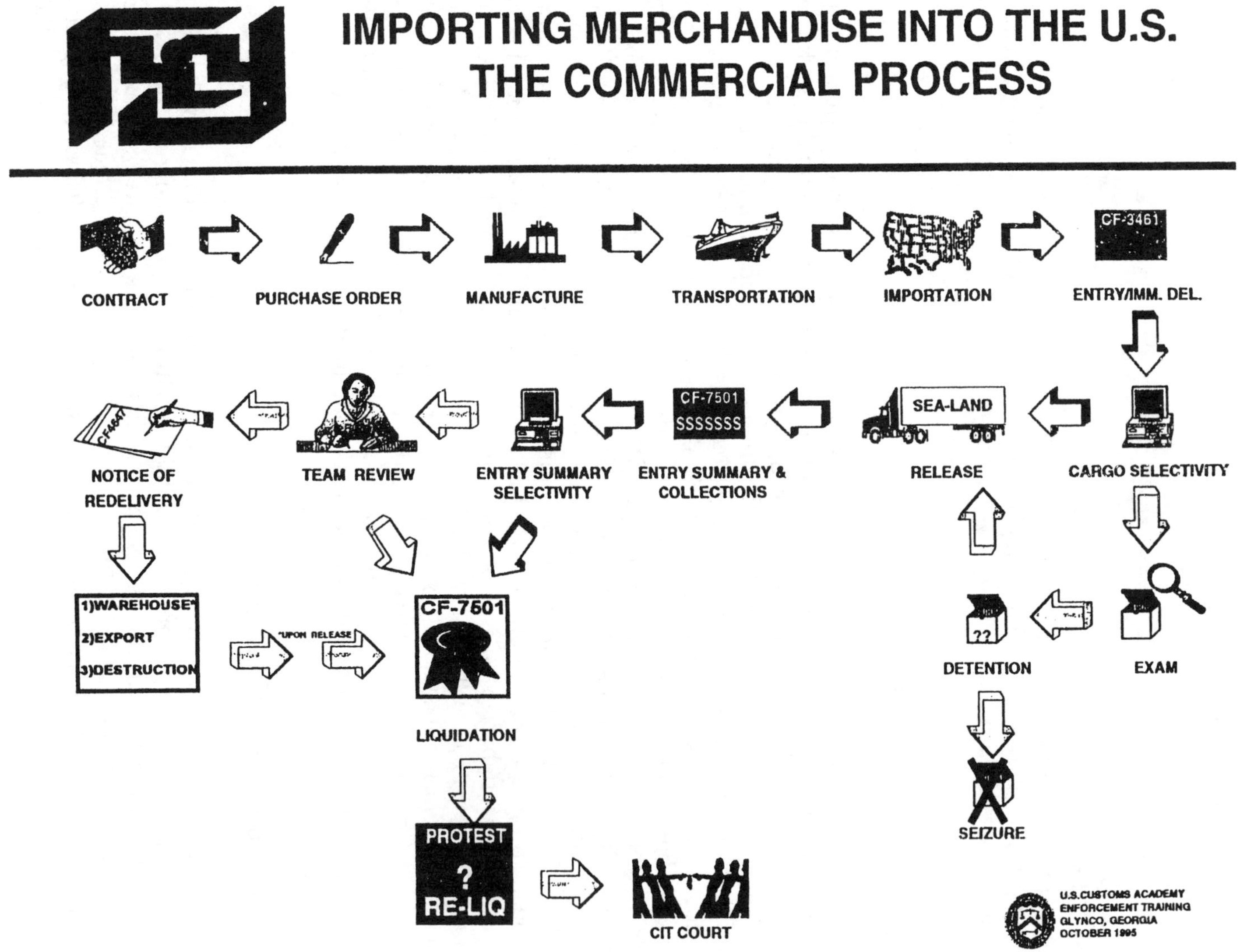
IMPORTING MERCHANDISE INTO THE U.S.
THE COMMERCIAL PROCESS
CONTRACT
PURCHASE ORDER
MANUFACTURE
TRANSPORTATION
IMPORTATION
CF-3461
ENTRY/IMM. DEL.
CARGO SELECTIVITY
SEA-LAND
RELEASE
CF-7501
SSSSSSS
ENTRY SUMMARY & COLLECTIONS
ENTRY SUMMARY SELECTIVITY
TEAM REVIEW
NOTICE OF REDELIVERY
1)WAREHOUSE*
2)EXPORT
3)DESTRUCTION
*UPON RELEASE
CF-7501
LIQUIDATION
PROTEST
?
RE-LIQ
CIT COURT
EXAM
DETENTION
SEIZURE
U.S.CUSTOMS ACADEMY
ENFORCEMENT TRAINING
GLYNCO, GEORGIA
OCTOBER 1995

service, and financing charges. For forty-five classes of products, the commercial invoice must contain certain additional information. Prior to exportation, the importer should identify what specialized information is required by the U.S. Customs regulations and communicate that to the exporter. A summary of the required contents is shown in Figure 4–4. Recently, U.S. Customs and Border Protection has indicated that it will detain and refuse to release shipments where the invoice does not contain all of the necessary information. (A sample invoice is shown in Figure 3–9.) Showing the package numbers and quantities on the commercial invoice facilitates Customs examination of the merchandise. Putting the commercial invoice number on all of the shipping documents helps to tie the documents together. The importer should understand that the invoice amount and the declared value have consequences for the "cost of goods" calculation for U.S. income tax purposes under section 1059A of the Internal Revenue Code.

D. Pro Forma Invoices

When the importer receives a shipment and no commercial invoice is available, it can prepare its own invoice, known as a pro forma invoice, and submit it to Customs for entry of the merchandise, provided it supplies a bond for its production. (A sample pro forma invoice is shown in Figure 8–2.) This is merely the representation by the buyer as to the price that it paid or that is payable for purchase of the goods. The commercial invoice signed by the exporter must be furnished to Customs within fifty days or the bond will be forfeited.

E. Packing Lists

The buyer may request or the seller may include a packing list with the merchandise. Although this is not strictly required by U.S. Customs laws, if one is sent, it must also be filed with U.S. Customs and Border Protection. It is important where different types of merchandise subject to different rates of duty are shipped in one shipment. In the event that there is any shortage, damage, or defects, the packing list is also important for making insurance claims. When the buyer is responsible for obtaining such insurance, the buyer/importer should require the seller to send a packing list (see Figure 4–8).

F. Inspection Certificates

If the buyer requires a preshipment inspection in its purchase agreement, the inspection certificate should be furnished by the third-party company that performed the inspection prior to exportation. This need not be filed with U.S. Customs and Border Protection, but in the event of any discrepancy between the merchandise upon arrival and the inspection certificate, the importer should notify the inspection service (and the courier and the insurance company) immediately.

Figure 8–2. Pro forma invoice.

ProForma Invoice

Exporter

Ultimate Consignee

Intermediate Consignee

Date

Order Number

Commercial Invoice Number

Ultimate Consignee Phone

Exporting Carrier

Origination State

Exporter Contact Name

PO Number

Terms

ProForm Invoice Number

Customer Account Number

Loading Pier/Terminal

Country of Destination

Exporter Contact Phone

Quantity	Product ID	Description	Schedule B Code	Unit Price	Total Price

Ex-Works Value	
Inland Freight Fees	
Handling Fees	
Consular Fees	
Ocean/Air Fees	
Insurance Fees	
Other Charges	

Total: USD

Title:

Authorized Signature:

Page of

This document created using Shipping Solutions Professional export software, www.shipsolutions.com.

G. Drafts for Payment

Where the seller/exporter has made shipment under a letter of credit opened by the buyer/importer, or under an agreement with a bank for documentary collection, the buyer's bank will pay the amount owed on sight drafts to the seller's bank immediately and will present any time drafts to the buyer/importer for acceptance. (Samples are shown in Figures 4–29 and 4–30, respectively.)

H. Arrival Notices

The transportation carrier (steamship company or airline) will send an arrival notice to the customs broker or to the importer (the consignee or notify party in the bill of lading) upon arrival of the merchandise in the port. The party who is notified will be in accordance with the instructions that the transportation carrier received from the seller/exporter or the seller's freight forwarder in the foreign country, which is usually based on the instructions of the buyer to the seller. After receiving an arrival notice, the importer or its customs broker will ordinarily have five days within which to supply the necessary documents to U.S. Customs and Border Protection to make entry and obtain release and delivery of the merchandise.

I. Pickup and Delivery Orders

If the foreign exporter has agreed to deliver the merchandise to the buyer/importer's premises, the foreign exporter or, more usually, its freight forwarder will issue a delivery order to the freight forwarder in the United States upon arrival of the goods in the United States to effect the inland transportation between the U.S. port of arrival and the buyer's premises. Or, if the title has passed to the buyer prior to or upon arrival, the importer will instruct the customs broker to make entry with U.S. Customs and Border Protection. Once entry has been made, the customs broker will instruct the trucking company to pick up the merchandise from the international transportation carrier and deliver it to the importer.

J. Entry/Immediate Delivery

Traditionally, when an importer imports merchandise, it must prepare the necessary customs entry documents and present them to U.S. Customs and Border Protection along with payment of estimated duties before release of the goods to the importer can be authorized by U.S. Customs and Border Protection. However, as a general practice, most importers have provided a customs bond, and so (if the importer is not in default on the payment of its customs bills) the importer can apply for immediate release of the goods by filing an Entry/Immediate Delivery form (Customs Form 3461). (See sample in Figure 8–3.) Customs brokers or importers who have been accepted under the Automated Broker Interface (ABI) or more recently under the Automated Commercial Environment (ACE) may file this form electronically. If entry is made using this form, the importer is required to file an Entry Summary form (CF-7501), with the additional information required by that form and payment of estimated duties, within ten days thereafter or Customs will make a liquidated damages assessment, a form of customs penalty. This form can be filed within five days prior to the arrival of the merchandise if shipped by ocean or as soon as the wheels are up in the exporting country on air shipments. When the Entry/Immediate Delivery form has been submitted electronically, it is processed electronically and audited against predetermined criteria based on the past import records of the importer, the exporter, the classification, and the country of origin to determine whether the merchandise should be examined or not. The computer determines which shipments should undergo a physical examination, which should have their documentation reviewed, and which may bypass an examination entirely and be released "paperless." Local Customs authorities have the ability to alter the instructions from the computer audit, but they are required to provide an explanation for any deviation.

K. Entry Summary

The Entry Summary is the main document used to enter goods into the United States. Either the Entry/Immediate Delivery form or the Entry Summary must be filed with U.S. Customs and Border Protection within five working days after arrival of the shipment at the port of entry (or the port of destination for in-bond shipments). Where no Entry/Immediate Delivery form was filed before the filing of the Entry Summary, the Entry Summary is referred to as a "live entry." Certain commodities require a live entry to be submitted, with all duties and fees paid prior to the release of merchandise, for example, food products that are under a quantitative quota subject to immediate filing on the date of opening. Importers who are on the ACE system may pay the duties on a monthly basis using the Automated Clearing House wire transfer process. The entry may specify that the merchandise is for consumption or is for storage in a warehouse, to be withdrawn for consumption at a later date. If no entry is made, the merchandise will be transferred to a "general order" warehouse. If no entry is made within six months (immediately for perishable goods), the merchandise will be sold. (An Entry Summary and Continuation Sheet are shown in Figure 8–4.) Several items on the Entry Summary are worthy of note.

Box 21 of the Entry Summary requires the importer to show the manufacturer's/shipper's identification. This is a special code that must be constructed from the name and address of the manufacturer/shipper.

Column 32 of the Entry Summary requires the importer to state the entered value. CHGS stands for charges, and means items such as foreign inland freight, ocean transportation, and ocean insurance, which are not dutiable. The "relationship" line is asking whether or not the seller and buyer are affiliated companies. It is important

(*Text continues on page 328.*)

Figure 8–3. Entry/Immediate Delivery form.

DEPARTMENT OF HOMELAND SECURITY
U.S. Customs and Border Protection

Form Approved
OMB No. 1651-0024
Exp. 11-30-2008

ENTRY/IMMEDIATE DELIVERY

19 CFR 142.3, 142.16, 142.22, 142.24

1. ARRIVAL DATE
2. ELECTED ENTRY DATA
3. ENTRY TYPE CODE/NAME
4. ENTRY NUMBER
5. PORT
6. SINGLE TRANS. BOND
7. BROKER/IMPORTER FILE NUMBER
8. CONSIGNEE NUMBER
9. IMPORTER NUMBER
10. ULTIMATE CONSIGNEE NAME
11. IMPORTER OF RECORD NAME
12. CARRIER CODE
13. VOYAGE/FLIGHT/TRIP
14. LOCATION OF GOODS-CODE(S)/NAME(S)
15. VESSEL CODE/NAME
16. U.S. PORT OF UNLADING
17. MANIFEST NUMBER
18. G.O. NUMBER
19. TOTAL VALUE
20. DESCRIPTION OF MERCHANDISE

21. IT/BL/AWB CODE	22. IT/BL/AWB NO.	23. MANIFEST QUANTITY	24. H.S. NUMBER	25. COUNTRY OF ORIGIN	26. MANUFACTURER NO.

27. CERTIFICATION

I hereby make application for entry/immediate delivery. I certify that the above information is accurate, the bond is sufficient, valid, and current, and that all requirements of 19 CFR Part 142 have been met.

SIGNATURE OF APPLICANT

X

PHONE NO.

DATE

29. BROKER OR OTHER GOVT. AGENCY USE

28. CBP USE ONLY

☐ OTHER AGENCY ACTION REQUIRED, NAMELY:

☐ CBP EXAMINATION REQUIRED.

☐ ENTRY REJECTED, BECAUSE:

DELIVERY AUTHORIZED: SIGNATURE DATE

PAPERWORK REDUCTION ACT NOTICE: This information is to determine the admissibility of imports into the United States and to provide the necessary information for the examination of the cargo and to establish the liability for payment of duties and taxes. Your response is necessary. The estimated average burden associated with this collection of information is 15 minutes per respondent depending on individual circumstances. Comments concerning the accuracy of this burden estimate and suggestions for reducing this burden should be directed to U.S. Customs and Border Protection, Information Services Branch, Washington, DC 20229, and to the Office of Management and Budget, Paperwork Reduction Project (1651-0024), Washington, DC 20503.

CBP Form 3461 (01/89)

Figure 8–4. Entry Summary and Continuation Sheet.

Form Approved OMB No. 1651-0022

DEPARTMENT OF HOMELAND SECURITY
U.S. Customs and Border Protection
ENTRY SUMMARY

1. Filer Code/Entry No.		2. Entry Type	3. Summary Date
4. Surety No.	5. Bond Type	6. Port Code	7. Entry Date

8. Importing Carrier		9. Mode of Transport	10. Country of Origin	11. Import Date
12. B/L or AWB No.		13. Manufacturer ID	14. Exporting Country	15. Export Date
16. I.T. No.	17. I.T. Date	18. Missing Docs	19. Foreign Port of Lading	20. U.S. Port of Unlading
21. Location of Goods/G.O. No.	22. Consignee No.		23. Importer No.	24. Reference No.

25. Ultimate Consignee Name and Address City State Zip	26. Importer of Record Name and Address City State Zip

27.	28. Description of Merchandise			32.	33.	34.
Line No.	29. A. HTSUS No. B. ADA/CVD No.	30. A. Grossweight B. Manifest Qty.	31. Net Quantity in HTSUS Units	A. Entered Value B. CHGS C. Relationship	A. HTSUS Rate B. ADA/CVD Rate C. IRC Rate D. Visa No.	Duty and I.R. Tax Dollars Cents

Other Fee Summary for Block 39	35. Total Entered Value $	**CBP USE ONLY**		TOTALS
		A. LIQ CODE	B. Ascertained Duty	37. Duty
	Total Other Fees $	REASON CODE	C. Ascertained Tax	38. Tax
36. DECLARATION OF IMPORTER OF RECORD (OWNER OR PURCHASER) OR AUTHORIZED AGENT			D. Ascertained Other	39. Other
			E. Ascertained Total	40. Total

I declare that I am the ☐ Importer of record and that the actual owner, purchaser, or consignee for CBP purposes is as shown above, **OR** ☐ owner or purchaser or agent thereof. I further declare that the merchandise ☐ was obtained pursuant to a purchase or agreement to purchase and that the prices set forth in the invoices are true, **OR** ☐ was not obtained pursuant to a purchase or agreement to purchase and the statements in the invoices as to value or price are true to the best of my knowledge and belief. I also declare that the statements in the documents herein filed fully disclose to the best of my knowledge and belief the true prices, values, quantities, rebates, drawbacks, fees, commissions, and royalties and are true and correct, and that all goods or services provided to the seller of the merchandise either free or at reduced cost are fully disclosed.
I will immediately furnish to the appropriate CBP officer any information showing a different statement of facts.

41. DECLARANT NAME	TITLE	SIGNATURE	DATE

42. Broker/Filer Information (Name, address, phone number)	43. Broker/Importer File No.

CBP Form 7501 (04/05)

Figure 8–4. *(continued)*

DEPARTMENT OF HOMELAND SECURITY
U.S. Customs and Border Protection

ENTRY SUMMARY CONTINUATION SHEET

OMB No. 1651-0022

1. Filer Code/Entry No.

27.	28. Description of Merchandise			32.	33.	34.	
	29.	30.	31.		A. HTSUS Rate	Duty and I.R. Tax	
Line No.	A. HTSUS No. B. ADA/CVD No.	A. Grossweight B. Manifest Qty.	Net Quantity in HTSUS Units	A. Entered Value B. CHGS C. Relationship	B. ADA/CVD Rate C. IRC Rate D. Visa No.	Dollars	Cents

CBP Form 7501 (04/05)

to ensure that the proper relationship is indicated, as this will affect how Customs determines the proper valuation.

In addition to the customs duties, the importer is required to calculate the merchandise processing fee (currently 0.21 percent) and the harbor maintenance fee (currently 0.125 percent) for shipments using a U.S. harbor and make payment at the times of entry. There is a cap of $485 per entry on merchandise processing fees, but no cap on harbor maintenance fees.

At the bottom of the form, the signer is required to declare that the statements in the Entry Summary fully disclose the true prices, values, quantities, rebates, drawbacks, fees, commissions, and royalties on the purchase, and that all goods or services provided to the seller of the merchandise either free or at reduced costs have been fully disclosed. The signer represents that it will immediately furnish to the appropriate U.S. Customs officer any information showing facts different from those stated in the Entry Summary. This is extremely important, because incorrect and therefore false statements on the Entry Summary can be the basis for both criminal and civil penalties assessed by U.S. Customs and Border Protection against the importer. Such errors need not be intentional, and even accidental errors can be the basis for penalties.

L. Other Entries

In place of the Entry Summary used for consumption, warehouse, and temporary import entries, transportation and exportation entries, immediate transportation entries, and entries for admission to a foreign trade zone are listed on their own forms. (Samples are shown in Figures 8–5 and 8–6. An Application for a Foreign Trade Zone Activity Permit is shown in Figure 8–7.) Transportation and exportation entries are used when the importer knows at the time of import that the product will be exported and the merchandise is merely being transported temporarily through the United States. No manipulation or modification of the merchandise is permitted during the time that it is in the United States, and the merchandise technically remains in Customs' custody. No customs duties are payable, but the importer must have a customs bond to guarantee payment of the customs duties in case the shipment is accidentally diverted into the United States. Immediate transit entries are used to move merchandise from the port of arrival to an inland port of entry nearer to the buyer where the customs entries and formalities are completed and the merchandise is released to the importer. The foreign trade zone entry is used when the goods are to be entered into a foreign trade zone for manipulation or further manufacturing. Finally, when merchandise is to be stored in a public or private customs-bonded warehouse for future consumption, entry is made on the regular Entry/Immediate Delivery or Entry Summary, marked with the type code for warehouse entries, in which case no estimated duties need be paid until the merchandise is later withdrawn for consumption. Depending on the type of warehouse, merchandise in a bonded facility may be manipulated, but only under Customs supervision. The importer must file an Application and Approval to Manipulate, Examine, Sample or Transfer Goods, CBP 3499. (See Figure 8–8.)

(*Text continues on page 333.*)

Figure 8–5. Transportation Entry.

19 CFR 10.60, 10.61, 123.41, 123.42

____ *Entry No.* ______

Port ______

Date ______

TRANSPORTATION ENTRY AND MANIFEST OF GOODS SUBJECT TO CBP INSPECTION AND PERMIT

U.S. Customs and Border Protection

OMB No. 1651-0003 Exp. 12-31-2010

Entry No. ______

Class of Entry ______

(I.T.) (T.E.) (WD.1E) (Drawback, etc.)

PORT CODE NO. ______ FIRST U.S. PORT OF UNLADING ______

PORT OF ______ DATE ______

Entered or imported by ______ Importer/IRS # ______ to be shipped

in bond via ______ (C.H.L number) (Vessel or carrier) (Car number and initial) (Pier or station) consigned to

CBP Port Director ______ Final foreign destination ______ (For exportations only)

Consignee ______ (At CBP port of exit or destination)

Foreign port of lading ______ B/L No. ______ Date of sailing ______

(Above information to be furnished only when merchandise is imported by vessel)

Imported on the ______ (Name of vessel or carrier and motive power) Flag ______ on ______ (Date imported) via ______ (Last foreign port)

Exported from ______ (Country) on ______ (Date) Goods now at ______ (Name of warehouse, station, pier, etc.)

Marks and Numbers of Packages	Description and Quantity of Merchandise Number and Kind of Packages (Describe fully as per shipping papers)	Gross Weight in Pounds	Value (Dollars only)	Rate	Duty

G.O. No. ______ ☐ Check if withdrawn for Vessel supplies (19 U.S.C. 1309)

CERTIFICATE OF LADING FOR TRANSPORTATION IN BOND AND/OR LADING FOR EXPORTATION FOR

______ (Port)

WITH THE EXCEPTIONS NOTED ABOVE, THE WITHIN-DESCRIBED GOODS WERE:

Delivered to the Carrier named above, for delivery to the CBP Port Director at destination sealed with CBP seals Nos. ______ or the packages (were) (were not) labeled, or corded and sealed.

______ (Inspector)

______ (Date)

Laden on the--

______ (Vessel, vehicle, or aircraft)

which cleared for--

______

on ______ (Date)

as verified by export records.

______ (Inspector)

______ (Date)

I truly declare that the statements contained herein are true and correct to the best of my knowledge and belief.

Entered or withdrawn by ______

To the Inspector: The above-described goods shall be disposed of

______ For the Port Director

Received from the Port Director of the above CBP location the merchandise described in this manifest for transportation and delivery into the custody of the CBP officers at the port named above, all packages in apparent good order except as noted hereon.

______

______ Attorney or Agent of Carrier

CBP Form 7512 (03/08)

(continues)

Figure 8–5. *(continued)*

INSTRUCTIONS

Consult CBP officer or Part 18, Customs Regulations, for the appropriate number of copies required for entry, withdrawal, or manifest purposes.

For the purpose of transfer under the cartage or lighterage provisions of a proper bond to the place of shipment from the port of entry, extra copies bearing a stamp, or notation as to their intended use may be required for local administration.

As the form is the same whether used as an entry or withdrawal or manifest, all copies may be prepared at the same time by carbon process, unless more than one vessel or vehicle is used, in which case a separate manifest must be prepared for each such vessel or vehicle.

Whenever this form is used as an entry or withdrawal, care should be taken that the kind of entry is plainly shown in the block in the upper right-hand corner of the face of the entry.

This form may be printed by private parties provided that the supply printed conforms to the official form in size, wording arrangement, and quality and color of paper.

RECORD OF CARTAGE OR LIGHTERAGE

Delivered to Cartman or Lighterman in apparent good condition except as noted on this form

Conveyance	Quantity	Date	Delivered	Received	Received	
			(Inspector)	(Cartman or Lighterman)	(Date)	(Inspector)
			(Inspector)	(Cartman or Lighterman)	(Date)	(Inspector)
			(Inspector)	(Cartman or Lighterman)	(Date)	(Inspector)
Total						

(Warehouse proprietor)

CERTIFICATES OF TRANSFER. (If required)

I certify that within-described goods were transferred by reason of ____________ to ____________ on ____________, at ____________ and sealed with ____________ or seals Nos. ____________, and that goods were in same apparent condition as noted on original lading except ____________

Inspector, Conductor, or Master

I certify that within-described goods were transferred by reason of ____________ to ____________ on ____________, at ____________ and sealed with ____________ or seals Nos. ____________, and that goods were in same apparent condition as noted on original lading except ____________

Inspector, Conductor, or Master

INSPECTED

at ____________

on ____________ (Date)

and seals found ____________

Inspector.

If transfer occurs within city limits of a CBP port or station, CBP officers must be notified to supervise transfer.

INSPECTOR'S REPORT OF DISCHARGE AT DESTINATION

Port ____________ *Station* ____________, ____________ (Date)

TO THE PORT DIRECTOR: Delivering line ____________ Car No. ____________ Initial ____________

Arrived ____________ (Date) Condition of car ____________, of seals ____________, of packages ____________

Date of Delivery to Importer, or Gen. Order	Packages	No. and Kind of Entry or General Order	Bonded Truck or Lighter No.	Conditions, Etc.

I certify above report is correct. ____________, *Inspector.*

PAPERWORK REDUCTION ACT NOTICE: The Paperwork Reduction Act says we must tell you why we are collecting this information, how we will use it, and whether you have to give it to us. We ask for the information in order to carry out the laws and regulations administered by U.S. Customs and Border Protection. These regulations and form apply to carriers and brokers who are transporting merchandise in-bond from a port of importation to another CBP port prior to final release of the merchandise from CBP custody. It is mandatory. The estimated average burden associated with this collection of information is 10 minutes per respondent depending on individual circumstances. Comments concerning the accuracy of this burden estimate and suggestions for reducing this burden should be directed to U.S. Customs and Border Protection, Information Service Branch, Washington, DC 20229, and to the Office of Management and Budget, Paperwork Reduction Project (1651-0003), Washington, DC 20503.

CBP Form 7512 (03/08)(Back)

Figure 8–6. Application for Foreign Trade Zone Admission.

CENSUS USE ONLY	DEPARTMENT OF HOMELAND SECURITY U.S. Customs and Border Protection **APPLICATION FOR FOREIGN-TRADE ZONE ADMISSION AND/OR STATUS DESIGNATION** 19 CFR 146.22, 146.32, 146.35-146.37, 146.39-146.41, 146.44, 146.53, 146.66	OMB No. 1651-0029 Exp. 01-31-2010 1. ZONE NO. AND LOCATION *(Address)* 2. PORT CODE

3. IMPORTING VESSEL (& FLAG)/OTHER CARRIER	4. EXPORT DATE	5. IMPORT DATE	6. ZONE ADMISSION NO.	
7. U.S. PORT OF UNLADING	8. FOREIGN PORT OF LADING	9. BILL OF LADING/AWB NO.	10. INWARD M'FEST NO.	
11. INBOND CARRIER	12. I.T. NO. AND DATE	13. I.T. FROM *(Port)*		

14. STATISTICAL INFORMATION FURNISHED DIRECTLY TO BUREAU OF CENSUS BY APPLICANT? ☐ YES ☐ NO

15. NO. OF PACKAGES AND COUNTRY OF ORIGIN CODE	16. DESCRIPTION OF MERCHANDISE	17. HTSUS NO.	18. QUANTITY (HTSUS)	19. GROSS WEIGHT	20. SEPARATE VALUE & AGGR CHGS.
		21. HARBOR MAINTENANCE FEE (19 CFR 24.24) ➧			

22. I hereby apply for admission of the above merchandise into the Foreign-Trade Zone. I declare to the best of my knowledge and belief that the above merchandise is not prohibited entry in the Foreign-Trade Zone within the meaning of section 3 of the Foreign-Trade Zones Act of 1934, as amended, and section 146.31, Customs Regulations.

23. I hereby apply for the status designation indicated:
☐ NONPRIVILEGED FOREIGN (19 CFR 146.42) ☐ PRIVILEGED FOREIGN (19 CFR 146.41) ☐ ZONE RESTRICTED (19 CFR 146.44) ☐ DOMESTIC (19 CFR 146.43)

24. APPLICANT FIRM NAME		25. BY *(Signature)*	26. TITLE	27. DATE
F.T.Z. AGREES TO RECEIVE MERCHANDISE INTO THE ZONE ➧		28. FOR THE F.T.Z. OPERATOR *(Signature)*	29. TITLE	30. DATE
PERMIT	**Permission is hereby granted to transfer the above merchandise into the Zone.**	31. PORT DIRECTOR OF CBP: BY *(Signature)*	32. TITLE	33. DATE
PERMIT	The above merchandise has been granted the requested status.	34. PORT DIRECTOR OF CBP: BY *(Signature)*	35. TITLE	36. DATE

PERMIT TO TRANSFER	37. The goods described herein are authorized to be transferred: ☐ without exception ☐ except as noted below			
	38. CBP OFFICER AT STATION *(Signature)*	39. TITLE	40. STATION	41. DATE
	42. RECEIVED FOR TRANSFER TO ZONE *(Driver's Signature)*	43. CARTMAN	44. CHL NO.	45. DATE
FTZ OPERATOR'S REPORT OF MERCHANDISE RECEIVED AT ZONE	46. To the Port Director of CBP: The above merchandise was received at the Zone on the date shown except as noted below:			
	47. FOR THE FTZ OPERATOR *(Signature)*	48. TITLE		49. DATE

(See page 2 for Paperwork Reduction Act Notice.) *Previous Editions are Obsolete* CBP Form 214 (02/96)

Figure 8–7. Application for Foreign Trade Zone Activity Permit.

Approved through OMB No. 1651-0029 Exp. 01-31-2010

DEPARTMENT OF HOMELAND SECURITY
U.S.Customs and Border Protection

APPLICATION FOR FOREIGN-TRADE ZONE ACTIVITY PERMIT

19 CFR 146.52, 146.66

1. ZONE NO. AND LOCATION *(Address)*

2. ZONE ADMISSION NO.

3. APPLICATION DATE

4. TYPE OF ACTIVITY FOR WHICH PERMIT REQUESTED
☐ Manipulate ☐ Manufacture ☐ Exhibit ☐ Destroy ☐ Temporary Removal

5. FULL DESCRIPTION OF THE ACTIVITY *(Include designation of the exact place in zone where the operation is to be performed and, in the case of a proposed manipulation or manufacture, a statement as to whether merchandise with one zone status is to be packed, commingled, or combined with merchandise having different zone status. If additional space required, attach separate sheet. If first application for manufacturing of this kind, state whether Foreign-Trade Zones board has occurred in proposed operation.)*

6. ZONE LOT NO. OR UNIQUE IDENTIFIER	7. MARKS AND NUMBERS	8. DESCRIPTION OF MERCHANDISE	9. QUANTITY	10. WEIGHTS, MEASURES	11. ZONE STATUS

If any merchandise is to be manipulated in any way or manufactured, I agree to maintain the records provided for in sections 146.21(a), 146.23, and 146.52(d) of the Customs Regulations and to make them available to CBP officers for inspection.

12. APPLICANT FIRM NAME	13. BY *(Signature)*	14. TITLE
APPROVED BY FOREIGN-TRADE ZONE OPERATOR ➧	15. BY *(Signature)*	16. TITLE

PERMIT

The application made above is hereby approved and permission is granted to manipulate, manufacture, exhibit, destroy, or temporarily removed, as requested, on condition that the applicable regulations are complied with and the records required to be maintained will be available for inspection.

17. PORT DIRECTOR OF CBP: By *(Signature)*	18. TITLE	19. DATE

FTZ OPERATOR'S

20. TO THE PORT DIRECTOR OF CBP:
I certify that the goods described herein have been disposed of as directed except as noted below.

21. FOR THE FTZ OPERATOR: *(Signature)*	22. TITLE	23. DATE

CBP Form 216 (01/01)

M. Reconciliation

Sometimes, the importer may not have the final information necessary to complete and file an Entry Summary at the time of importation. In some cases, such situations may be routine, for example, when the importer is using the constructed value method of calculation or importing under Harmonized Tariff classification 9802 and the costs of manufacture or processing are based on standard costs subject to revision at the end of the accounting period. It can also arise when regional value content calculations are necessary for NAFTA eligibility. Customs has developed a program, first offered in 1998 as a prototype, but now extended indefinitely, for filing the usual Entry Summary at the time of entry with the "best information available," but "flagging" individual entries or all entries during a specified period. The result is that the importer is allowed twenty-one months (twelve months for NAFTA and US–Chile Free Trade Agreement claims) to file a "reconciliation" containing the final information. This process is available for missing information relating to the correct value of the imported merchandise (including value under 9802), classification, and NAFTA and CAFTA-DR eligibility. In order to participate in the program, it is necessary to file an application with U.S. Customs and Border Protection and to provide a rider to the importer's customs bond to cover the open import entries. Once accepted, reconciliation may be filed either with entry-by-entry adjustments or with an aggregate calculation for all the entries covered by the reconciliation (aggregate adjustment is not allowed when the reconciler claims a refund, and refunds may not be netted against duties owed). Failure to file the reconciliation "entry" in a timely fashion will result in penalties.

N. GSP, ATPA, AGOA—Special Programs

There are many specal duty programs available to importers provided the imported goods meet the qualifying criteria. Where the importer is claiming duty-free importation of the merchandise under the terms of the Generalized System of Preferences (GSP) program, it is necessary for the importer to indicate its intention by using the letter "A" next to the tariff number on the Entry Summary. The importer should advise the customs broker that the imported goods qualify under GSP, and the broker will make the proper indication. It is important that the importer issue clear instructions to the broker that it should NOT claim preferential duty treatments unless the importer is confident that the merchandise qualifies. Under audit, the exporter must provide evidence that the merchandise meets the 35 percent origin criteria. In the past a "GSP Declaration" was all that was needed to comply, but recently those documents have been called into question, and so further substantiating documentation will be required. If the auditor is unable to confirm that the imported goods qualify, then the importer will owe past duties plus interest. In addition, the importer could be subject to penalties for making a false statement on the Entry Summary; therefore, it is always advisable that the importer and the exporter are clear on the requirements and that the exporter can and will provide the necessary evidence to support the claim.

(*Text continues on page 336.*)

Figure 8–8. Bonded warehouse manipulation form.

DEPARTMENT OF HOMELAND SECURITY
U.S. Customs and Border Protection

APPLICATION AND APPROVAL
TO MANIPULATE, EXAMINE, SAMPLE OR TRANSFER GOODS
19 CFR 19.8, 19.11, 158.43

Form Approved
OMB No. 1651-0006
Exp. 07-31-2009

1. GOODS CONSIGNED TO *(Name)*	2. GOODS EXPORTED FROM	3. PORT/PORT CODE AND DATE OF APPLICATION
4. LOCATION OF GOODS	5. CARRIER OR SHIP *(Name)*	6. BILL OF LADING OR CBP 7512 NO.
7. IS AREA BONDED? ☐ YES ☐ NO	8. ENTRY INFORMATION ☐ Warehouse ☐ Consumption	Number: Date:

PERMISSION IS REQUESTED TO: (Describe the complete operation to be performed under CBP supervision on the goods listed below):

		FOR CBP USE ONLY
9. MARKS AND NUMBERS	10. DESCRIPTION	11. MANIPULATED VALUE

12. SIGNATURE OF APPLICANT

APPROVED

13. DATE	14. SIGNATURE AND TITLE OF APPROVING CBP OFFICER

See Page 2 of form for Paperwork Reduction Act Notice. Customs and Border Protection Officers Report on Reverse

CBP Form 3499 (10/95)

Figure 8–8. *(continued)*

CUSTOMS AND BORDER PROTECTION OFFICER'S REPORT

Date:

MANIPULATION COMPLETED AS REQUESTED: When goods are repacked the CBP (warehouse) officer will report hereon the marks and numbers of packages repacked and the marks and numbers of packages and the weights or guage of same after repacking.

(CBP Officer and Title)

PAPERWORK REDUCTION ACT NOTICE: The Paperwork Reduction says we must tell you why we are collecting this information, how we will use it, and whether you have to give it to us. We ask for the information in order to carry out U.S. Customs and Border Protection laws of the United States. This form is used by importers as an application to examine, sample, repack or transfer merchandise under CBP supervision; as a request for manipulation of merchandise in a bonded warehouse; and as an application for abandonment or destruction of merchandise in bond. It is required to obtain or retain a benefit. The estimated average burden associated with this collection of information is 6 minutes per respondent depending on individual circumstances. Comments concerning the accuracy of this burden estimate and suggestions for reducing this burden should be directed to U.S. Customs and Border Protection, Information Services Branch, Washington, DC 20229, and to the Office of Management and Budget, Paperwork Reduction Project (1651-0006), Washington, DC 20503.

CBP Form 3499 (10/95)

The same is true with the other preferential duty programs. Any importer wishing to claim the benefits of the Caribbean Basin Economic Recovery Act, the Andean Trade Preference Act, the U.S.–Israel Free Trade Agreement, or the African Growth and Opportunity Act must be able prove similar requirements: 35 percent of the finished goods must originate in the eligible country, and the goods must be shipped directly from the eligible country to the United States. Unlike the GSP program, under these agreements, 15 percent of the 35 percent may come from U.S.-origin components. However, similar to GSP, the importer will also be required to obtain similar evidence from the exporter, even if the exporter provides it directly to U.S. Customs and Border Protection in order to maintain the confidentiality of the information. It is strongly recommended that an importer obtain guarantees from its manufacturer that it will produce any necessary supporting documentation directly to U.S. Customs and Border Protection if requested before making a claim of preferential duty under one of these programs.

O. NAFTA/Other FTA Certificates of Origin

Under the North American Free Trade Agreement, articles from Canada and Mexico may be imported duty-free or at a reduced rate of duty. In order to qualify for the tariff concession, however, the articles must be a product of Canada or Mexico under one of six eligibility rules. The exact method of determining eligibility is specific to each type of merchandise involved and must be checked in the headnotes of the Harmonized Tariff Schedules. The importer must obtain a certificate from the Canadian or Mexican exporter certifying the country of origin. (A sample of the certificate is shown in Figure 4–16.)

Some of the FTAs have forms, while others use general certificates of origin to substantiate the origin of goods eligible for preferential duties. (See Figures 4–17 and 4–18.)

P. Specialized Products Import Entry Forms

Food, drug, cosmetic, and medical device imports are monitored by the Food and Drug Administration (FDA) through U.S. Customs and Border Protection. For shipments subject to the FDA, the customs broker must file information about the shipment through the OASIS (Operational and Administrative System for Import Support) system at the same time it is filing the Customs Form 3461 (Entry/Immediate Delivery). The FDA inspector will then determine whether the product is being imported in compliance with U.S. law. It should also be noted that the FDA requires that all owners or operators in charge of domestic or foreign facilities that manufacturer, process, pack, or hold food for human or animal consumption in the United States be registered with the FDA prior to export. Importers of certain radiation-producing electronic products such as televisions, monitors, microwave ovens, x-ray equipment, laser products, ultrasound equipment, sunlamps, CD-ROM players, and cellular and cordless telephones are required to file FDA Form 2877 (see Figure 8–9), and importers of certain radio-frequency devices such as radios, tape recorders, stereos, televisions, and citizen's band radios are required to file FCC Form 740. Importers of plants are required to file U.S. Department of Agriculture Form 368, Notice of Arrival (see Figure 8–10). A number of agricultural products require import permits, including plants and timber logs, and some products require import licenses, such as dairy products. In addition, the USDA enforces the International Standards for Phytosanitary Measures No. 15 (ISPM-15) and requires export certifications for all wood packaging materials (WPM) to reduce the risk of introducing quarantined pests, such as the Asian long-horned beetle, into the United States. All WPM must be heat-treated or fumigated with methyl bromide and marked with the International Plant Protection Convention Logo.

Originally introduced in 1900, the Lacey Act was enacted to protect wildlife, fish, and plants. A 2008 amendment brought increased focus on illegal logging by banning the import, transport, sale, receipt, acquisition, or purchase of illegally obtained plants from a foreign country or a U.S. state. These include plants that are (1) stolen; (2) taken from officially protected areas, such as parks and reserves; (3) taken without or contrary to required authorization; (4) taken without payment of the applicable taxes, royalties, or fees; or (5) shipped in violation of governing export or transshipment laws, such as log export bans. In addition, the amendment makes it unlawful to falsely identify or label any plant or plant product. The amendment requires that importation of any product containing any form of plant species must—electronically—file a certification, the Plant Protection and Quarantine Form 505, as to the country of harvest by the scientific name of the species. There is a phased-in compliance program beginning in March of 2009. See Appendix L for more information on the form and the requirements.

When importing (or exporting) fish or wildlife, U.S. Fish and Wildlife Service Form 3-177 must be filed (see Figure 8–11). The United States supports the Convention on International Trade of Endangered Species (CITES) to protect endangered species. There are more than 170 countries that are parties to the CITES. In compliance with the CITES, imports of certain species are prohibited and others require import permits (see Figure 8–12). More information is available at www.fws.gov. Note that not all U.S. ports of entry have Fish and Wildlife offices, so imports may be cleared only at the ports of Anchorage, AK; Atlanta, GA; Baltimore, MD; Boston, MA; Chicago, IL; Dallas, TX; Honolulu, HI; Houston, TX; Los Angeles, CA; Louisville, KY, Memphis, TN, Miami, FL; New Orleans, LA; New York, NY; Newark, NJ; Portland, OR; San Francisco, CA; or Seattle, WA.

Importers of textiles composed of cotton, wool, or man-made fibers are required to file certain declarations, a Single Country Declaration if the textiles are products of a single country (Figure 8–13), or a Multiple Country Declaration if they are processed in more than one country (Figure 8–14). Importers of "precursor" and "essential" chemicals that can be used to manufacture illegal drugs are required to file DEA Form 486 (sometimes fifteen days in advance) (see Chapter 4, Section P and Figure 4–27).

The Consumer Products Safety Commission has recently taken a very active role in regulating imports of children's and consumer products. New certifications regarding the lead levels in children's toys and other articles require the importer to provide a certificate (based on test analysis) that the imported goods do not contain over 600 ppm (parts per million) of lead effective February 10, 2009, but these levels will be reduced to no more than 100 ppm by 2011. CPSC also has prohibited the sale of certain children's products containing phthalates. Currently CPSC is requesting that importers provide general certificates of compliance (see Figure 8–15) that imported consumer goods meet the CPSC standards currently in place under the Federal Hazardous Substances Act, the Poison Prevention Packaging Act, the Flammable Fabrics Act, the Refrigerator Safety Act, or the Consumer Products Safety Act. More information is available at www.cpsc.gov.

Q. Examination and Detention

After a customs entry is electronically filed (Entry/Immediate Delivery or Entry Summary, along with any other specialized forms), the computer audits the information against historical data and makes a determination as to whether Customs will examine the merchandise. If Customs elects not to examine the merchandise and is otherwise satisfied from the entry documents that the goods are entitled to entry, it will release the goods by stamping the Entry/Immediate Delivery or Entry Summary form, perforating the form, or issuing an electronic "paperless" release. This releases the merchandise and authorizes the transportation carrier to surrender possession of the goods to the importer and is effective when the importer presents the release to the transportation carrier.

If Customs elects to examine the merchandise, it has a period of five days following presentation for examination to determine whether to detain the merchandise. If it determines to detain the merchandise, it must give a notice to the importer within an additional five days specifying the reason for the detention, the anticipated length of the detention, and additional information being requested. If Customs determines that the merchandise is not eligible for entry, it may pursue the procedures for seizure and forfeiture of the merchandise. If Customs takes no action within thirty days after presentation of the merchandise for examination, the importer may file a protest and seek expedited review in the appropriate court (usually the Court of International Trade).

R. Liquidation Notices

After entry has been made, U.S. Customs and Border Protection will process the entry documentation and liquidate the entry. When the importer makes the original entry, it is required to declare (state its opinion of) the correct classification, value, and duties payable and to tender those duties. After Customs has reviewed the classification, value, and duties payable, if it agrees with the importer's entry, liquidation will occur with no change. Currently, entries are scheduled by Customs for liquidation 314 days after entry. Sometimes, when information is needed by Customs to verify the classification or value (or when the importer requests for good cause), liquidation may be suspended up to a maximum of four years from the date of entry. The official notice of liquidation, known as the Bulletin Notice, is published in the port where entry was made at the Customs office. The official notice is the only one binding upon Customs. However, it is the practice of U.S. Customs and Border Protection to mail to the importer (or its customs broker) a nonbinding courtesy notice

(*Text continues on page 350.*)

Figure 8–9. FDA Form 2877.

DEPARTMENT OF HEALTH AND HUMAN SERVICES
PUBLIC HEALTH SERVICE
FOOD AND DRUG ADMINISTRATION

DECLARATION FOR IMPORTED ELECTRONIC PRODUCTS SUBJECT TO RADIATION CONTROL STANDARDS

Form Approved OMB No. 0910-0025
Expiration Date: December 31, 2006.

INSTRUCTIONS
1. If submitting entries electronically through ACS/ABI, hold FDA-2877 in entry file. Do not submit to FDA unless requested.
2. If submitting paper entry documents, submit the following to FDA:
   a. 2 copies of Customs Entry Form (e.g. CF 3461, CF 3461 Alt, CF 7501, etc.)
   b. 1 copy of FDA 2877
   c. Commercial Invoice(s) in English.

U.S. CUSTOMS PORT OF ENTRY	ENTRY NUMBER	DATE OF ENTRY
NAME & ADDRESS OF MANUFACTURING SITE; COUNTRY OF ORIGIN	NAME & ADDRESS OF IMPORTER & ULTIMATE CONSIGNEE *(if not importer)*	

PRODUCT DESCRIPTION	QUANTITY *(Items/Containers)*	MODEL NUMBER(S) & BRAND NAME(S)

DECLARATION: I / WE DECLARE THAT THE PRODUCTS IDENTIFIED ABOVE: ***(Mark X applicable statements, fill in blanks, & sign)***

☐ **A. ARE NOT SUBJECT TO RADIATION PERFORMANCE STANDARDS BECAUSE THEY:**
- ☐ 1. Were manufactured prior to the effective date of any applicable standard; Date of Manufacture ____________.
- ☐ 2. Are excluded by the applicability clause or definition in the standard or by FDA written guidance. Specify reason for exclusion ____________.
- ☐ 3. Are personal household goods of an individual entering the U.S. or being returned to a U.S. resident. (Limit: 3 of each product type).
- ☐ 4. Are property of a party residing outside the U.S. and will be returned to the owner after repair or servicing.
- ☐ 5. Are components or subassemblies to be used in manufacturing or as replacement parts (NOT APPLICABLE to diagnostic x-ray parts).
- ☐ 6. Are prototypes intended for on going product development by the importing firm, are labeled "FOR TEST/EVALUATION ONLY," and will be exported, destroyed, or held for future testing (i.e., not distributed). (Quantities Limited - see reverse.)
- ☐ 7. Are being reprocessed in accordance with P.L. 104-134 or other FDA guidance, are labeled "FOR EXPORT ONLY," and will not be sold, distributed, or transferred without FDA approval.

☐ **B. COMPLY WITH THE PERFORMANCE STANDARDS** WHICH ARE APPLICABLE AT DATE OF MANUFACTURE AND THAT A CERTIFICATION LABEL OR TAG TO THIS EFFECT IS AFFIXED TO EACH PRODUCT. COMPLIANCE DOCUMENTED IN:
- ☐ 1. Last annual report or Product/Initial report

  ____________ ACCESSION NUMBER of Report ____________ Name of MANUFACTURER OF RECORD *(Filed report with FDA/CDRH)*
- ☐ 2. Unknown manufacturer or report number; State reason: ____________

☐ **C. DO NOT COMPLY WITH PERFORMANCE STANDARDS;** ARE BEING HELD UNDER A TEMPORARY IMPORT BOND; WILL NOT BE INTRODUCED INTO COMMERCE; WILL BE USED UNDER A RADIATION PROTECTION PLAN; AND WILL BE DESTROYED OR EXPORTED UNDER U.S. CUSTOMS SUPERVISION WHEN THE FOLLOWING MISSION IS COMPLETE:
- ☐ 1. Research, Investigations/Studies, or Training (attach Form FDA 766)
- ☐ 2. Trade Show/Demonstration; List dates & use restrictions ____________

☐ **D. DO NOT COMPLY WITH PERFORMANCE STANDARDS;** ARE HELD AND WILL REMAIN UNDER BOND; AND WILL NOT BE INTRODUCED INTO COMMERCE UNTIL NOTIFICATION IS RECEIVED FROM FDA THAT PRODUCTS HAVE BEEN BROUGHT INTO COMPLIANCE IN ACCORDANCE WITH AN FDA APPROVED PETITION. *(See Form FDA 766.)*
- ☐ 1. Approved Petition is attached. ☐ 2. Petition Request is attached. ☐ 3. Request will be submitted within 60 days.

WARNING: Any person who knowingly makes a false declaration may be fined not more than $10,000 or imprisoned not more than 5 years or both, pursuant to Title 18 U.S.C. 1001. Any person importing a non- compliant electronic product may also be subject to civil penalties of $1000 per violation, up to a maximum $300,000 for related violations pursuant to Title 21 U.S.C. 360pp.	SIGNATURE OF IMPORTER OF RECORD NAME AND TITLE OF RESPONSIBLE PERSON

Public reporting burden for this collection of information is estimated to average 0.2 hour per response, including the time for reviewing instructions, searching existing data sources, gathering and maintaining the data needed, and completing reviewing the collection of information. Send comments regarding this burden estimate or any other aspect of this collection of information, including suggestions for reducing this burden to:

Food and Drug Administration
CDRH (HFZ-342)
2094 Gaither Road
Rockville, MD 20850

An agency may not conduct or sponsor, and a person is not required to respond to, a collection of information unless it displays a currently valid OMB control number.

FORM FDA 2877 (12/03) PREVIOUS EDITION IS OBSOLETE. PSC Media Arts (301) 443-2454 PAGE 1 OF 2 PAGES BP

Figure 8–9. *(continued)*

INSTRUCTIONS TO IMPORTERS/BROKERS OF ELECTRONIC PRODUCTS

PURPOSE: The Form FDA 2877 must be completed for electronic products subject to Radiation Control Standards (21 CFR 1010 and 1020-1050) prior to entry into the United States. The local Food and Drug Administration (FDA) district office will review the declaration and notify the importer/agent if the products may be released into U.S. commerce or if they must be held under bond until exported, destroyed, or reconditioned. Until the shipment is released, it may be subject to redelivery for FDA examination.

PAPER OR ELECTRONIC SUBMISSION: Paper entries may be made by submitting the signed original FDA 2877 along with U.S. Customs forms to the local FDA district office; if electronic products are given a MAY PROCEED, a signed copy of CF 3461 will be returned, or if not given a MAY PROCEED, a FDA Notice of Action will be issued. For electronic entries, follow U.S. Customs Service ACS/ABI format and procedures, supported by a signed copy of this form or similar letter. Multiple entries of the same product and model families that are filed electronically may be supported by one form dated not more than 12 months previously.

DECLARATION: Select A, B, C, or D and then select the appropriate number; fill in requested information and sign. For electronic entries, AofC (affirmation of compliance) = RA#, RB#, RC#, or RD# (e.g., Radiation Declaration A5 = RA5). **Transmit model number using AofC code MDL and transmit brand name using FDA line level brand name field. If RA3 or RA6 is selected, you must transmit quantity (number of units) using the Quantity and Unit of Measure Pairs at the FDA line level.**

DECLARATION A: Importers should be prepared to demonstrate compliance to or non-applicability of FDA standards, regulations, or guidance. Components or sub-assemblies must be non-functioning. Products being reprocessed must be exported by the importer, without intermediate transfer of ownership. For RA3 the quantity limit is 3 and for RA6 the limit = 50 units TV products, microwave ovens, and Class 1 laser products limit = 200 units CD-ROM and DVD (digital versatile disc) laser products; see May 14, 1997, notice to industry issued by the Center for Devices and Radiological Health (CDRH).

DECLARATION B: If declaration RB1 is selected, provide the FDA Establishment Identifier (FEI) of the manufacturer who filed the radiation product/abbreviated report to FDA, CDRH, Rockville, Maryland. To transmit the accession number of that report use AofC code ACC. If the manufacturer cannot be determined or located, the importer must be able to provide evidence showing a certification (certifi.) label on each product and state reason: returned to orig exporter or certifi. label evidence. The new AofC codes (RB1, RB2) for this declaration will not be activated until a process is made available to determine the FEI of the responsible firm. Continue to use RAB in electronic transmission until the FEI query is available and industry is notified of its availability.

DECLARATION C: Noncompliant products may be imported only for research, investigations/studies, demonstration or training. They should be used only by trained personnel and under controlled conditions to avoid unnecessary radiation exposure. Product(s) will be detained by the local FDA district office. Since product(s) for which "C" Declarations are made will be under Temporary Import Bond (TIB) or equivalent, ultimate disposition is limited to export or destruction under U.S. Customs supervision when the purpose has been achieved or the length of time stated has expired. For purposes other than demonstration, the Form FDA 766, outlining protections, must be approved by FDA prior to use. The importer/broker must include with the FDA 766:

1. A full description of the subject electronic product(s).
2. The purpose for which the product(s) is being imported.
3. How the product(s) will be used.
4. Where the product(s) will be located.
5. The approximate length of time and dates the product(s) will be in this country.

For product(s) being used for trade shows/demonstrations, list the dates and use restrictions (Form FDA 766 is not required). A sign stating that the product does not comply with FDA performance standards must be displayed and viewable at all times during the use of product(s). All medical products, cabinet x-ray, or Class IIIb and IV lasers may NOT operate (turn on product(s)) at trade shows.

DECLARATION D: Noncompliant products must be brought into compliance with standards under FDA supervision and following a plan approved by FDA. The plan, documented on the Form FDA 766, must address technical requirements, labeling, and reporting. Some plans may need approval by both the CDRH and the local FDA district office. Use of this declaration is limited to occasional shipments; ongoing reconditioning is considered manufacturing that is handled through other means. Product(s) will be detained by the local FDA district office. An FDA 766 must be filed indicating the procedure intended to bring the product into compliance. This procedure will include a satisfactory corrective action plan and/or a product report. The FDA 766 must include all of the information requested under Declaration C. The approximate length of time will be for the amount of time needed to bring product(s) into compliance. Declaration D is also made for failure to provide reports, failure to certify, etc.

If an importer/broker intends to import equipment into the United States for purposes of research, investigation, studies, demonstrations, or training but also wishes to retain the option of bringing the product into compliance with the performance standard, check Declarations C and D on the FDA 2877 and insert the word "or " between the Affirmations. Note: The U.S. Customs Service will treat this entry as a "D" Declaration for purposes of duty. Such requests must be made on the FDA 766; include Items 1, 2, and 3 under Declaration C, a statement of the need to use the option "C" or "D" Declaration, a statement of how the product(s) will be brought into compliance and the approximate length of time necessary to evaluate or demonstrate the product(s) and the time necessary to bring the product(s) into compliance (both actions must be accomplished within the period of time granted by FDA). For electronic entries select Declaration RD3.

Ultimately, product(s) must be brought into compliance with the applicable standard in accordance with a corrective action plan which has been approved by the FDA. If the product(s) are not brought into compliance within the allotted time frame of the approved application and an extension is not requested of, or granted by, the FDA, the local FDA district office shall refuse entry on the shipment and require the product(s) to be either exported or destroyed under U.S. Customs supervision.

If additional guidance is needed, please contact your local FDA district office or consult the following FDA web pages: www.fda.gov/cdrh, www.fda.gov/ora/hier/ora_field_names.txt, and www.fda.gov/ora/compliance_ref/rpm_new2/contens.html.

[Ref: 21 U.S.C. 360mm, 21 CFR 1005, 19 CFR 12.90-12.91.] FDA: CP 7382.007/.007A

FORM FDA 2877 (12/03) PREVIOUS EDITION IS OBSOLETE. PAGE 2 OF 2 PAGES

Figure 8–10. U.S. Department of Agriculture Form 368, Notice of Arrival.

This notice informs the PPQ Office of the arrival of a restricted article at a port of entry.
The information is used to schedule required inspections. (7 CFR 319.321, 322, and 325).

FORM APPROVED
OMB NO: 0579-0049

U.S. DEPARTMENT OF AGRICULTURE
ANIMAL AND PLANT HEALTH INSPECTION SERVICE
PLANT PROTECTION AND QUARANTINE

NOTICE OF ARRIVAL

INSTRUCTIONS: Immediately upon arrival, the permittee or his agent should prepare original and one copy of this form. Submit copies to the Plant Protection and Quarantine office having jurisdiction over the port of arrival.	1. NAME OF CARRIER
3. NAME OF PERMITTEE/CONSIGNEE	2. DATE OF ARRIVAL 4. PORT OF ARRIVAL 5. PERMIT NO.
6. PORT OF DEPARTURE	7. CUSTOMS ENTRY NO.
8. CONSIGNOR/SHIPPER (Name and Address)	9. PRESENT LOCATION 10. COUNTRY AND LOCALITY WHERE GROWN 11. NAME OF PREVIOUS U.S. PORT (In Transit Only) 12. I.T. NO.(In Transit Shipments Only)

13. DESCRIPTION OF PRODUCT

MARKS, BILL OF LADING, AND/OR CONTAINER NO.	QUANTITY AND NET WEIGHT	COMMODITY

14. SIGNATURE OF IMPORTER OR BROKER	15. FULL BUSINESS ADDRESS OF IMPORTER OR BROKER
16. DATE SIGNED	TELEPHONE NUMBER (INCLUDE AREA CODE)

TO BE COMPLETED BY PPQ OFFICAL

17. DISPOSITION OF PRODUCT	
18. SIGNATURE AND TITLE OF PPQ OFFICAL	19. DATE SIGNED

According to the Paperwork Reduction Act of 1995, no persons are required to respond to a collection of information unless it displays a valid OMB control number. The valid OMB control number for this information collection is 0579-0049. The time required to complete this information collection is estimated to average .08 hours per response, including the time for reviewing instructions, searching existing data sources, gathering and maintaining the data needed, and completing and reviewing the collection of information.

PPQ FORM 368
(AUG 2005)

Previous editions are obsolete.

(*continues*)

Figure 8–10. *(continued)*

Instructions for completing PPQ Form 368
Notice of Arrival to import plants or plant products

Please TYPE or PRINT legibly.

1. Name of Carrier: List the name of carrier by identifying the airline with the flight number, ship name with the voyage number, truck and container number used to transport the agricultural product.
2. Date of Arrival: List the date on which the carrier arrives at the port on entry.
3. Name of Permittee/Consignee: List the name and street address of the person responsible for the importation. The applicant must be a United States resident. List the organization or company name, if applicable. A physical address of the facility or business is required. You may include a post office box address **in addition** to the street address for mailing purposes. List your daytime telephone number, including the Area Code. List your facsimile number, including the Area Code. List your email address if applicable.
4. Port of Arrival: List the port on which the carrier arrives.
5. Permit No.: List the USDA-APHIS-PPQ permit if the commodity requires a permit as a condition of entry.
6. Port of Departure: List the name of the port where the carrier originated in the country of origin.
7. Customs Entry No.: List the Customs and Border Protection entry number associated with this shipment.
8. Consignor/Shipper: List the name and street address of the person responsible for the shipping. List the organization or company name, if applicable. A physical address of the facility or business is required. You may include a post office box address **in addition** to the street address for mailing purposes. List your daytime telephone number, including the country code, facsimile number, including the Area Code. List the email address, if applicable.
9. Present Location: List the physical location where the commodity is to be inspected.
10. Country and Locality Where Grown: List Country, Province, State and Location where the commodities where grown.
11. Name of Previous U.S. Port: List If the commodity transited in any country prior to arrival to U.S. port.
12. I.T. No. (In transit shipment only): list the in-bond IT number this shipment is moving under.
13. Description of Product: List the following information in the space provided: Marks, Bill of Lading No., and/or Container No.; Quantity and Net Weight; and the Commodity arriving under this notice of arrival.
14. Signature of Importer or Broker: The person that is responsible for the accuracy of the responses submitted on this form.
15. Full Business Address of Importer or Broker: List the full business address and telephone number of the person whose signatory appears in Block 14.
16. Date Signed: List the date the form is completed and signed, using this format: dd/mm/yyyy.

If attachments are necessary, type or print "PPQ Form 368" along with the Company Name and address of the Importer or Broker, at the top of each page.

Send the completed original signed form to the CBP Agriculture office or PPQ port office where the shipment is arriving and making official entry. In the case of IT shipments, send the form to the port of arrival and port of entry.

For assistance with filling out this form, contact:
USDA-APHIS-PPQ-QPAS-Agriculture Quarantine Inspection
4700 River Road, Unit # 60
Riverdale, MD 20737
Phone number (301) 734-8295; ask for a staff officer.

Figure 8–11. U.S. Fish and Wildlife Service Declaration for Importation and Exportation, Form 3-177.

USFWS Form 3-177
(Revised 12/06)
O.M.B. No. 1018-0012
Expiration Date: 12/31/2009

U.S. FISH AND WILDLIFE SERVICE
DECLARATION FOR IMPORTATION
OR EXPORTATION OF
FISH OR WILDLIFE

Page ____ of ____

1. Date of Import/Export: (mm/dd/yyyy)
2. Import/Export License Number:
3. Indicate One: ☐ Import ☐ Export
4. Port of Clearance: __ __
5. Purpose Code: ______
6. Customs Document Number (s)
7. Name of Carrier:
8. Air Waybill or Bill of Lading Number:
   Master:
   House:
9. Transportation Code: ________
   License # ________ State or Province ________
10. Bonded Location for Inspection:
11. Number of Cartons Containing Wildlife:
12. Markings on Cartons Containing Wildlife:

13a. (Indicate One) (Complete name/U.S. address/telephone number/e-mail address)
☐ U.S. Importer
☐ U.S. Exporter

13b. Identifier Number: ____________ ID Type: ____________

14a. (Indicate One) (Complete name/foreign address/telephone number/e-mail address)
☐ Foreign Importer
☐ Foreign Exporter

14b. Country Code __ __

14c. Identifier Number: ____________ ID Type: ____________

15a. Customs Broker, Shipping Agent or Freight Forwarder:
(Complete business name/address/telephone and fax number/e-mail address)

15b. Identifier Number: ____________ ID Type: ____________

15c. Contact Name: ____________

Species Code (Official Use Only)	16a. Scientific Name / 16b. Common Name	17a. Foreign CITES Permit Number / 17b. U.S. CITES Permit Number	18a. Description Code / 18b. Source Code	19a. Quantity/Unit / 19b. Total Monetary Value	20. Country of Species Origin Code (ISO Code)	21. Venomous Live Wildlife Indicator ☑ (Check if yes)
						☐
						☐
						☐
						☐

Knowingly making a false statement in a Declaration for Importation or Exportation of Fish or Wildlife may subject the declarant to the penalty provided by 18 U.S.C. 1001 and 16 U.S.C. 3372(d)

22. I certify under penalty of perjury that the information furnished is true and correct:

Signature ____________ Date ________

Type or Print Name ____________

For Official Use Only
Action/Comments:

Wildlife Declared: Yes No

Wildlife Inspected:
None / Partial / Full

See Reverse Side of this Form for Privacy Act Notice

Figure 8–12. U.S. Fish and Wildlife Permit Application, Form 3-200-3.

Expires 11/30/2010
OMB No. 1018-0092

Department of the Interior
U.S. Fish and Wildlife Service
Federal Fish and Wildlife Permit Application Form

Return to: Click here for addresses

Type of Activity: Import/Export License

Office of Law Enforcement
U.S. Fish and Wildlife Service

Complete Sections A or B, and C, D, and E of this application. U.S. address may be required in Section C, see instructions for details.
See attached instruction pages for information on how to make your application complete and help avoid unnecessary delays.

A. Complete if applying as an individual			
1.a. Last name	1.b. First name	1.c. Middle name or initial	1.d. Suffix
2. Date of birth (mm/dd/yyyy)	3. Social Security No.	4. Occupation	5. Affiliation/ Doing business as (see instructions)
6.a. Telephone number	6.b. Alternate telephone number	6.c. Fax number	6.d. E-mail address

B. Complete if applying on behalf of a business, corporation, public agency or institution			
1.a. Name of business, agency, or institution	1.b. Doing business as (dba)		
2. Tax identification no.	3. Description of business, agency, or institution		
4.a. Principal officer Last name	4.b. Principal officer First name	4.c. Principal officer Middle name/ initial	4.d. Suffix
5. Principal officer title	6. Primary contact		
7.a. Business telephone number	7.b. Alternate telephone number	7.c. Business fax number	7.d. Business e-mail address

C. All applicants complete address information				
1.a. Physical address (Street address; Apartment #, Suite #, or Room #; no P.O. Boxes)				
1.b. City	1.c. State	1.d. Zip code/Postal code:	1.e. County/Province	1.f. Country
2.a. Mailing Address (include if different than physical address; include name of contact person if applicable)				
2.b. City	2.c. State	2.d. Zip code/Postal code:	2.e. County/Province	2.f. Country

D. **All applicants MUST complete**

1. Attach check or money order payable to the U.S. FISH AND WILDLIFE SERVICE in the amount of $100.00 if you are applying for a new Import/Export license or $50.00 if you are requesting a substantive amendment of your existing valid Import/Export license. Federal, tribal, State, and local government agencies, and those acting on behalf of such agencies, are exempt from the processing fee – ***attach documentation of fee exempt status as outlined in instructions.*** (50 CFR 13.11(d))
2. Do you currently have or have you ever had any Federal Fish and Wildlife permits?
   Yes ☐ If yes, list the number of the most current permit you have held or that you are applying to renew/re-issue: ____________
   No ☐
3. Certification: I hereby certify that I have read and am familiar with the regulations contained in ***Title 50, Part 13 of the Code of Federal Regulations*** and the other ***applicable parts in subchapter B of Chapter I of Title 50,*** and I certify that the information submitted in this application for a permit is complete and accurate to the best of my knowledge and belief. I understand that any false statement herein may subject me to the criminal penalties of 18 U.S.C. 1001.

Signature (in blue ink) of applicant/person responsible for permit (No photocopied or stamped signatures) Date of signature (mm/dd/yyyy)

Form 3-200-3 Rev. November 2007 Page 1 of 4

Figure 8–12. *(continued)*

ALL APPLICANTS COMPLETE SECTION E:

IMPORT/EXPORT LICENSE APPLICATION CONTINUATION SHEET

1. **Name, street address** (not a P.O. Box), **telephone, fax number, and email address** of additional partners and principal officers of the entity applying for this license. If the applicant is the sole owner, or the application is for an individual, indicate "same as page 1."

2. **Street address** (not a P.O. Box), **telephone,** and **fax number** of the location(s) where business records concerning imports or exports of wildlife will be kept. If the location(s) is the same as on the first page, indicate "same as Page 1".

3. **Street address** (not a P.O. Box), **telephone,** and **fax number** of the location(s) wildlife inventories will be kept. If the location(s) is the same as on the first page, indicate "same as page 1".

4. **General description** of the wildlife or wildlife products to be imported / exported.

Form 3-200-3 Rev. November 2007 Page 2 of 4

Figure 8–12. (continued)

PERMIT APPLICATION FORM INSTRUCTIONS

The following instructions pertain to the standard permit form 3-200 that must be completed as an application for a U.S. Fish and Wildlife Service or CITES permit. The General Permit Procedures in 50 CFR 13 address the permitting process. For simplicity, all licenses, permits, registrations, and certificates will be referred to as a permit.

GENERAL INSTRUCTIONS:

- Complete all blocks/lines/questions in Sections A or B, and C and D. Complete all of Section E.
- **An incomplete application may cause delays in processing or may be returned to the applicant. Be sure you are filling in the appropriate application form for the proposed activity.**
- Print clearly or type in the information. Illegible applications may cause delays.
- Sign the application in blue ink. Faxes or copies of the original signature will not be accepted.
- Mail the original application to the address at the top of page one of the application or if applicable on the attached address list.
- **Keep a copy of your completed application.**
- **Please plan ahead. Allow at least 60 days for your application to be processed. Some applications may take longer than 90 days to process. (50 CFR 13.11)**
- Applications are processed in the order they are received.
- Additional forms and instructions are available from http://permits.fws.gov/ .

COMPLETE EITHER SECTION A OR SECTION B:

Section A. **Complete if applying as an individual:**

- Enter the complete name of the responsible individual who will be the permittee if a permit is issued. Enter personal information that identifies the applicant. ***Fax and e-mail are not required if not available.***
- If you are applying on behalf of a client, the personal information must pertain to the client, and a document evidencing power of attorney must be included with the application.
- **Affiliation/ Doing business as (dba)**: business, agency, organizational, or institutional affiliation *directly* related to the activity requested in the application (e.g., a taxidermist is an individual whose business can *directly* relate to the requested activity). The Division of Management Authority (DMA) will **not** accept *doing business as* affiliations for individuals.

Section B. **Complete if applying as a business, corporation, public agency, or institution:**

- Enter the complete name of the business, agency or institution that will be the permittee if a permit is issued. Give a brief description of the type of business the applicant is engaged in. Provide contact phone number(s) of the business.
- **Principal Officer** is the person in charge of the listed business, corporation, public agency, or institution. The principal officer is the person responsible for the application and any permitted activities. Often the principal officer is a Director or President. **Primary Contact** is the person at the business, corporation, public agency, or institution who will be available to answer questions about the application or permitted activities. Often this is the preparer of the application.

ALL APPLICANTS COMPLETE SECTION C:

- For all applications submitted to the Division of Management Authority (DMA) a physical U.S. address is **required**. Province and Country blocks are provided for those USFWS programs which use foreign addresses and are not required by DMA..
- **Mailing address** is address where communications from USFWS should be mailed if different than applicant's physical address.

ALL APPLICANTS COMPLETE SECTION D:

Section D.1 **Application processing fee:**

- An application processing fee is required at the time of application; unless exempted under 50 CFR13.11(d)(3). The application processing fee is assessed to partially cover the cost of processing a request. **The fee does not guarantee the issuance of a permit. Fees will not be refunded for applications that are approved, abandoned, or denied.** We may return fees for withdrawn applications prior to any significant processing occurring.
- **Documentation of fee exempt status is not required for Federal, tribal, State, or local government agencies; but must be supplied by those applicants acting on behalf of such agencies.** Those applicants acting on behalf of such agencies must submit a letter on agency letterhead and signed by the head of the unit of government for which the applicant is acting on behalf, confirming that the applicant will be carrying out the permitted activity for the agency.

Section D.2 **Federal Fish and Wildlife permits:**

- List the number(s) of your most current FWS or CITES permit or the number of the most recent permit if none are currently valid. If applying for re-issuance of a CITES permit, the original permit must be returned with this application.

Section D.3 **CERTIFICATION:**

- **The individual identified in Section A, the principal officer named in Section B, or person with a valid power of attorney (documentation must be included in the application) must sign and date the application in blue ink.** This signature binds the applicant to the statement of certification. This means that you certify that you have read and understand the regulations that apply to the permit. You also certify that everything included in the application is true to the best of your knowledge. Be sure to read the statement and re-read the application and your answers before signing.

Please continue to next page

Form 3-200-3 Rev. November 2007 Page 3 of 4

Figure 8–12. *(continued)*

APPLICATION FOR A FEDERAL FISH AND WILDLIFE PERMIT
Paperwork Reduction Act, Privacy Act, and Freedom of Information Act – Notices

In accordance with the Paperwork Reduction Act of 1995 (44 U.S.C. 3501, *et seq.*) and the Privacy Act of 1974 (5 U.S.C. 552a), please be advised:

1. The gathering of information on fish and wildlife is authorized by:
   (Authorizing statutes can be found at: http://www.gpoaccess.gov/cfr/index.html and http://www.fws.gov/permits/ltr/ltr.shtml.)

   a. Bald and Golden Eagle Protection Act (16 U.S.C. 668), 50 CFR 22;
   b. Endangered Species Act of 1973 (16 U.S.C. 1531-1544), 50CFR 17;
   c. Migratory Bird Treaty Act (16 U.S.C. 703-712), 50 CFR 21;
   d. Marine Mammal Protection Act of 1972 (16 U.S.C. 1361, *et. seq.*), 50 CFR 18;
   e. Wild Bird Conservation Act (16 U.S.C. 4901-4916), 50 CFR 15;
   f. Lacey Act: Injurious Wildlife (18 U.S.C. 42), 50 CFR 16;
   g. Convention on International Trade in Endangered Species of Wild Fauna and Flora (TIAS 8249), http://www.cites.org/, 50 CFR 23;
   h. General Provisions, 50 CFR 10;
   i. General Permit Procedures, 50 CFR 13; and
   j. Wildlife Provisions (Import/export/transport), 50 CFR 14.

2. Information requested in this form is purely voluntary. However, submission of requested information is required in order to process applications for permits authorized under the above laws. Failure to provide all requested information may be sufficient cause for the U.S. Fish and Wildlife Service to deny the request. Response is not required unless a currently valid Office of Management and Budget (OMB) control number is displayed on form.

3. Certain applications for permits authorized under the Endangered Species Act of 1973 (16 U.S.C. 1539) and the Marine Mammal Protection Act of 1972 (16 U.S.C. 1374) will be published in the **Federal Register** as required by the two laws.

4. Disclosures outside the Department of the Interior may be made without the consent of an individual under the routine uses listed below, if the disclosure is compatible with the purposes for which the record was collected. (Ref. 68 FR 52611, September 4, 2003)

   a. Routine disclosure to subject matter experts, and Federal, tribal, State, local, and foreign agencies, for the purpose of obtaining advice relevant to making a decision on an application for a permit or when necessary to accomplish a FWS function related to this system of records.
   b. Routine disclosure to the public as a result of publishing **Federal Register** notices announcing the receipt of permit applications for public comment or notice of the decision on a permit application.
   c. Routine disclosure to Federal, tribal, State, local, or foreign wildlife and plant agencies for the exchange of information on permits granted or denied to assure compliance with all applicable permitting requirements.
   d. Routine disclosure to Captive-bred Wildlife registrants under the Endangered Species Act for the exchange of authorized species, and to share information on the captive breeding of these species.
   e. Routine disclosure to Federal, tribal, State, and local authorities who need to know who is permitted to receive and rehabilitate sick, orphaned, and injured birds under the Migratory Bird Treaty Act and the Bald and Golden Eagle Protection Act; federally permitted rehabilitators; individuals seeking a permitted rehabilitator with whom to place a bird in need of care; and licensed veterinarians who receive, treat, or diagnose sick, orphaned, and injured birds.
   f. Routine disclosure to the Department of Justice, or a court, adjudicative, or other administrative body or to a party in litigation before a court or adjudicative or administrative body, under certain circumstances.
   g. Routine disclosure to the appropriate Federal, tribal, State, local, or foreign governmental agency responsible for investigating, prosecuting, enforcing, or implementing statutes, rules, or licenses, when we become aware of a violation or potential violation of such statutes, rules, or licenses, or when we need to monitor activities associated with a permit or regulated use.
   h. Routine disclosure to a congressional office in response to an inquiry to the office by the individual to whom the record pertains.
   i. Routine disclosure to the General Accounting Office or Congress when the information is required for the evaluation of the permit programs.
   j. Routine disclosure to provide addresses obtained from the Internal Revenue Service to debt collection agencies for purposes of locating a debtor to collect or compromise a Federal claim against the debtor or to consumer reporting agencies to prepare a commercial credit report for use by the FWS.

5. For individuals, personal information such as home address and telephone number, financial data, and personal identifiers (social security number, birth date, etc.) will be removed prior to any release of the application.

6. The public reporting burden on the applicant for information collection varies depending on the activity for which a permit is requested. The relevant burden for an Import/Export license application is 1.25 hours. This burden estimate includes time for reviewing instructions, gathering and maintaining data and completing and reviewing the form. You may direct comments regarding the burden estimate or any other aspect of the form to the Service Information Clearance Officer, U.S. Fish and Wildlife Service, Mail Stop 222, Arlington Square, U.S. Department of the Interior, 1849 C Street, NW, Washington D.C. 20240.

Freedom of Information Act – Notice

For organizations, businesses, or individuals operating as a business (i.e., permittees not covered by the Privacy Act), we request that you identify any information that should be considered privileged and confidential business information to allow the Service to meet its responsibilities under FOIA. Confidential business information must be clearly marked "Business Confidential" at the top of the letter or page and each succeeding page and must be accompanied by a non-confidential summary of the confidential information. The non-confidential summary and remaining documents may be made available to the public under FOIA [43 CFR 2.13(c)(4), 43 CFR 2.15(d)(1)(i)].

Form 3-200-3 Rev. November 2007 Page 4 of 4

Figure 8–13. Textile declaration form—single country.

Single Country Declaration

I,______________________________ , declare that the articles listed below, covered by the invoice or entry to which this declaration relates are, wholly the growth, product, or manufacture of a single foreign territory or country, or insular possession of the U.S., or were assembled in the single foreign territory or country, or insular possession of the U.S. of fabricated components which are in whole the product of the U.S. and/or the single foreign territory or country, or insular possession of the U.S. as identified below. I declare that the information set forth in this declaration is correct and true to the best of my information, knowledge, and belief.

Marks of Identification Articles Numbers	Description of Articles W/Fabric Content %	Origin	Date Shipped

Date:	If Upper Body Knit Detail:
Name:	Stitches/cm:
Signature:	Type Neck:
Title:	Type Bottom:
Company:	Sleeve:
Address	

Country or countries when used in this declaration includes territories and U.S. insular possessions. The country will be identified in the above declaration by the alphabetical designation appearing next to the country name.

Figure 8–14. Textile declaration form—multiple countries.

Multiple Country Declaration

Declaration for textiles and textile products, wholly the growth product or manufacture of a single foreign territory or country or insular possession.

Declaration

I ______________________________ , declare that the articles listed below and covered by the invoice or entry to which this declaration relates are wholly the growth, product, or manufacture of a single foreign territory or country, or insular possession of the U.S., or were assembled in the single foreign territory or country, or insular possession of the U.S., or were assembled in the single foreign territory or country, or insular possession of the U.S. of fabricated components which are in whole the product of the U.S. and/or the single foreign territory or country, or insul ar possession of the U.S. as identified below. I declare, that this information set forth in this declaration is correct and true to the best information, knowledge, and belief.

A.	D.	G.
B.	E.	H.
C.	F.	I.

Marks	Description of article and Quantities & Fabric Content	Manufacturing Procedures	Country of origin of fabric/accessories	Date of Export

Date:	Knit Detail (Upper body Wear):
Name:	Stitches per/cm:
Signature:	Type Neck:
Title:	Type Bottom:
Company:	Type Sleeve:
Address:	

* Country when used in this declaration includes territories and insular possessions on the United States, if the entry or invoice to which the declaration related covers merchandise from more than one country each country will be identified by the alphabetical designation appearing next to the named country. In the case of an assembly operation of U.S. components, both the country of assembly and the U.S. shall be reported (eg. Haiti/US), along with the date of exportation from the country of assembly.

of liquidation (Form 4333A), advising the importer that the entry has been liquidated. (A sample is shown in Figure 8–16.)

S. Notices of Redelivery

Where merchandise has been released to the importer and Customs comes to believe that the merchandise has been entered in violation of the laws of the United States—for example, the goods have not been properly marked with the foreign country of origin—Customs may issue a notice of redelivery (CF-4647; see Figure 8–17) to the importer. This form will be issued electronically through the Automated Commercial System (ACE) beginning in 2009. The form will specify the law that has been violated and will order the redelivery of the merchandise to Customs' custody within a thirty-day period. If no redelivery is made, the customs bond covering the entry of the merchandise will be declared forfeited and the importer will become liable for liquidated damages. For the purpose of determining the country of origin on textiles and apparel, Customs has up to 180 days to issue the notice of redelivery after release of the merchandise.

T. Post Entry Amendment

After the entry summary has been filed and duties paid, if the importer determines that an error has been made, the importer may file a Post Entry Amendment (PEA) (see Figure 8–18) to amend the information that is incorrect. This may be done prior to liquidation. If Customs agrees with the information provided on the PEA, it will liquidate the entry as suggested. If Customs disagrees with the information on the PEA, it will liquidate as entered and the importer will be required to file a protest.

U. Requests for Information

Sometimes, after the importer has made entry of merchandise, Customs will decide that it needs additional information in order to decide whether or not it agrees with the classification, value, and duties payable declared by the importer at the time of entry. Ordinarily, in such cases, Customs will send the importer a Request for Information (see Figure 8–19). A common request by Customs is for more information relating to the relationship between the seller and the buyer (Field 12A.). Other standard items requested include brochures or catalogs describing the merchandise in order to determine if the classification is correct, or information about the dutiable and nondutiable charges or assists and royalties to determine if the value has been properly declared. Customs may request any information, however, that it believes is necessary in order to confirm that the merchandise is being entered in accordance with the customs laws of the United States. Customs intends to issue this document to importers electronically through the ACE system beginning in 2009.

(*Text continues on page 354.*)

Figure 8–15. General certificate of compliance.

SAMPLE GENERAL CERTIFICATION OF CONFORMITY

CERTIFICATION OF COMPLIANCE

1. Identification of the product covered by this certificate:

2. Citation to each CPSC product safety regulation to which this product is being certified:

3. Identification of the U.S. importer or domestic manufacturer certifying compliance of the product:

4. Contact information for the individual maintaining records of test results:

5. Date and place where this product was manufactured:

6. Date and place where this product was tested for compliance with the regulation(s) cited above:

7. Identification of any third-party laboratory on whose testing the certificate depends:

This form of certificate and instructions are staff interpretations and do not replace or supersede the statutory requirements of the new legislation. They were prepared by CPSC staff, have not been reviewed or approved by, and may not necessarily reflect the views of, the Commission. They may be subject to change based on Commission action.

Figure 8–15. *(continued)*

Instructions for completing the General Certification of Conformity

General Instructions. This sample shows the information that is required for an acceptable certification required by section 14(g) of the Consumer Product Safety Act, 15 U.S.C. § 2063(g).

The required information must be provided in English.

Item 1: Describe the product covered by this certification in enough detail to match the certificate to each product it covers and no others.

Item 2: The certificate must identify separately each rule, ban, standard or regulation under the Acts administered by the Commission that is applicable to the product.

Item 3: Provide the name, full mailing address, and telephone number of the importer or U.S. domestic manufacturer certifying the product.

Item 4: Provide the name, full mailing address, e-mail address and telephone number of the person maintaining test records in support of the certification.

Item 5: Provide the date(s) when the product was manufactured by at least month and year. For the place of manufacture provide at least the city and country or administrative region of the place where the product was finally manufactured or assembled. If the same manufacturer operates more than one location in the same city, provide the street address of the factory.

Item 6: Give the date of the tests or test report(s) on which certification is being based and the location(s) of the testing.

Item 7: If a third-party laboratory tested the product or conducted a testing program on which the certification is based, give the name, full mailing address and telephone number of the laboratory.

This form of certificate and instructions are staff interpretations and do not replace or supersede the statutory requirements of the new legislation. They were prepared by CPSC staff, have not been reviewed or approved by, and may not necessarily reflect the views of, the Commission. They may be subject to change based on Commission action.

Figure 8–15. *(continued)*

Q. Can electronic certificates be used to meet the requirements of Section 102 rather than paper?

A. The Commission has issued a rule specifically allowing use of an electronic certificate provided the Commission has reasonable access to it, it contains all of the information required by section 102 of the CPSIA, and it complies with the other requirements of the rule. The rule is available on the CPSC World Wide Web site at http://www.cpsc.gov/businfo/frnotices/fr09/certification.pdf

Q. Who must issue the certificate?

A. Under the Commission's rule at http://www.cpsc.gov/businfo/frnotices/fr09/certification.pdf, for products manufactured overseas, the certificate must be issued by the importer. For products produced domestically, the certificate must be issued by the U.S. manufacturer.
Neither a foreign manufacturer nor a private labeler is required to issue a certificate. Neither need be identified on the certificate issued by the importer or domestic manufacturer.

Q. Must each shipment be "accompanied" by a certificate?

A. Yes, the law requires that each import (and domestic manufacturer) shipment be "accompanied" by the required certificate. The requirement applies to imports and products manufactured domestically. Under the rule issued by the Commission an electronic certificate is "accompanying" a shipment if the certificate is identified by a unique identifier and can be accessed via a World Wide Web URL or other electronic means, provided the URL or other electronic means and the unique identifier are created in advance and available with the shipment. Certificates can also be transmitted electronically to a broker with other customs entry documents before a shipment arrives so long as they are available to the Commission or Customs and Border Protection staff if the product or shipment is inspected.

Q. Is the importer or U.S. manufacturer required to supply the certificate to its distributors and retailers?

A. Yes. The importer or U.S. manufacturer is required to "furnish" the certificate to its distributors and retailers. The Commission's rule states that this requirement is satisfied if the importer or U.S. manufacturer provides its distributors and retailers a reasonable means to access the certificate.

Q. Must the certifier sign the certificate?

A. No. Issuing the certificate satisfies the new law. It does not have to be signed by the issuer.

(*continues*)

Figure 8–15. *(continued)*

Q. On what does my certification have to be based?

A. The general conformity certification must be based on a test of each product or a reasonable testing program.

Q. Where must these certificates be filed?

A. A certificate does not have to be filed with the government. As noted above, the certificate must "accompany" the product shipment, and be "furnished" to distributors and retailers, and be furnished to CPSC upon request.

These FAQs are unofficial descriptions and interpretations of various features of CPSIA and do not replace or supersede the statutory requirements of the new legislation. These FAQs were prepared by CPSC staff, have not been reviewed or approved by, and may not necessarily reflect the views of, the Commission. Some FAQs may be subject to change based on Commission action.

V. Notices of Action

When Customs determines that it disagrees with the way in which the importer originally entered the merchandise, either prior to sending a Request for Information or after receiving a response to a Request for Information, it will send a Notice of Action to the importer (see Figure 8–20). A Notice of Action may indicate that Customs proposes to take certain action and may invite the importer to give its reasons as to why that action should not be taken within twenty days, or the notice may specify that Customs has already taken that action. Often, the action taken is an advance in value, where Customs has determined that the value declared by the importer at the time of entry was too low, and therefore, additional customs duties are being assessed. Other actions, such as reclassification of the merchandise, can also be taken. If Customs receives no response from the importer, the entry will be liquidated in accordance with Customs' notice. This means that additional customs duties will be payable, and a bill for such duties will be sent to the importer. The Notice of Action is another form that Customs intends to issue electronically through the ACE system beginning in 2009.

W. Protests

Where the entry is liquidated with an increase in duty or merchandise is excluded from entry, the importer may request a written explanation from Customs for the duty increase. The importer also may protest such action by filing Customs Form 19. (A sample protest and instructions form is shown in Figure 8–21.) This form must be filed within 180 days of the bulletin notice of liquidation or date of exclusion. Consequently, if the importer does not receive the courtesy notice of liquidation and the entry is liquidated by posting the bulletin at the customs house, the importer may

(*Text continues on page 359.*)

Figure 8–16. Courtesy notice of liquidation.

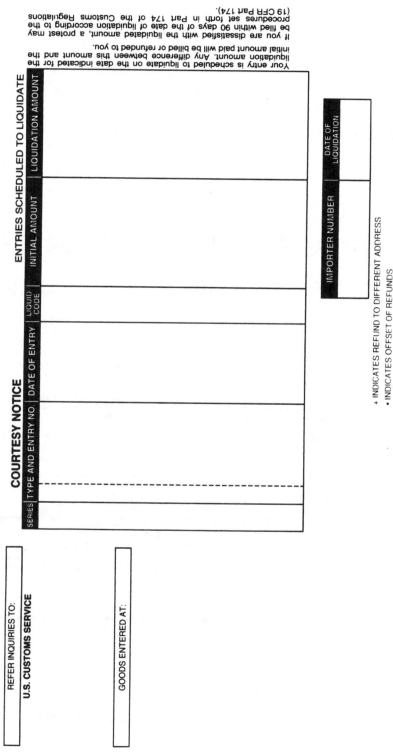

REFER INQUIRIES TO:

U.S. CUSTOMS SERVICE

GOODS ENTERED AT:

COURTESY NOTICE

ENTRIES SCHEDULED TO LIQUIDATE

SERIES	TYPE AND ENTRY NO.	DATE OF ENTRY	LIQUID CODE	INITIAL AMOUNT	LIQUIDATION AMOUNT

Your entry is scheduled to liquidate on the date indicated for the liquidation amount. Any difference between this amount and the initial amount paid will be billed or refunded to you.

If you are dissatisfied with the liquidated amount, a protest may be filed within 90 days of the date of liquidation according to the procedures set forth in Part 174 of the Customs Regulations (19 CFR Part 174).

IMPORTER NUMBER	DATE OF LIQUIDATION

+ INDICATES REFUND TO DIFFERENT ADDRESS

• INDICATES OFFSET OF REFUNDS

DEPARTMENT OF THE TREASURY
U.S. CUSTOMS SERVICE
Customs Form 4333A (041593)

Figure 8–17. Notice of redelivery.

DEPARTMENT OF THE TREASURY
UNITED STATES CUSTOMS SERVICE

NOTICE TO MARK
AND/OR
NOTICE TO REDELIVER

19 CFR 134.51, 134.52, 141.113

SECTION I (To Be Completed By Customs)

1. FROM

2. NAME OF CONTACT PERSON

3. TELEPHONE NO.

4. TO (Importer of Record Name and Address):

ENTRY DATA

5. PORT OF ENTRY

6. ENTRY NO.

7. DATE OF ENTRY

8. BROKER OR IMPORTER FILE NO.

The merchandise described below is in violation of statutes(s)/regulation(s) as indicated, and cannot be entered into the commerce of the U.S. until brought into conformity as noted below in Section II. If it is not brought into conformity, redelivered, exported, or destroyed under Customs supervision within 30 days from the date of this Notice or the time specified by another Government agency having jurisdiction over the importation, **liquidated damages and/or criminal/civil penalties shall apply.**

9. STATUTE(S)/REGULATION(S) VIOLATED

☐ 19 U.S.C. 1304 (Section 304, Tariff Act of 1930) (Country of Origin Marking Violation) ☐ Other, Namely:

10. DESCRIPTION OF MERCHANDISE	11. QUANTITY	12. IDENTIFYING MARKS AND NUMBERS	13. SHIPPER/MANUFACTURER

SECTION II (To Be Completed By Customs)

14. ACTION REQUIRED OF IMPORTER

☐ Merchandise must be brought into compliance as specified below or returned to Customs custody within 30 days of this Notice or other time specified.

☐ Marking or other corrective action must be done under Customs supervision.

☐ Customs supervision of marking or other corrective action not required. After all merchandise has been brought into conformity with cited statute(s)/regulation(s), complete the certification below and return copy to Customs ☐ with ☐ without a sample.
WARNING: All merchandise must be retained until you are notified by Customs that corrective action is acceptable.

☐ Merchandise must be redelivered to Customs within 30 days from date of this notice or other time specified.

15. REMARKS/INSTRUCTIONS/OTHER ACTION REQUIRED OF IMPORTER

16. SIGNATURE OF CUSTOMS OFFICER

17. DATE

SECTION III – IMPORTER CERTIFICATION (To Be Completed By Importer/Authorized Agent)
IMPORTER:— APPROPRIATE ITEMS MUST BE COMPLETED, SIGNED, AND DATED BEFORE ACCEPTANCE BY CUSTOMS.

☐ Merchandise to be ☐ exported. ☐ destroyed under Customs supervision in lieu of marking or other required corrective measures.

☐ I certify that all merchandise has been marked to indicate the country of origin as required by 19 U.S.C. 1304, or otherwise brought into compliance with cited statute(s) or regulation(s). Sample ☐ is ☐ is not submitted herein. Merchandise and original containers being held intact and available for Customs inspection at: (Indicate Place and Phone No.)

PLACE | DATE | TIME

I (We) guarantee the payment of all expenses incident to the above action.

SIGNATURE OF IMPORTER OR AUTHORIZED AGENT
X
TITLE | TELEPHONE | DATE

SECTION IV (To Be Completed By Customs)

☐ Merchandise excepted from marking under

☐ Merchandise has been legally marked or otherwise brought into conformity with cited statute(s)/regulation(s): ☐ under Customs supervision ☐ certification accepted.

☐ Merchandise was ☐ exported ☐ destroyed under Customs supervision. ☐ Other, namely:

SIGNATURE OF CUSTOMS OFFICER | DATE

Customs Form 4647 (121592)

PART 1 - IMPORTER - RETURN TO CUSTOMS

Figure 8–17. *(continued)*

CUSTOMS FORM 4647 INFORMATION AND INSTRUCTIONS

This form is notification that the imported merchandise is not in conformity with statutory or regulatory requirements and must be marked, labeled, or otherwise brought into conformity with the applicable requirements within 30 days of this notice. The form also serves as a redelivery notice and requires redelivery to Customs custody within the specified time.

The following instructions are provided to assist importers in fulfilling the statutory and regulatory obligations.

SECTIONS I AND II: COMPLETED BY THE CUSTOMS SERVICE.

SECTION III: COMPLETED BY THE IMPORTER OF RECORD OR AUTHORIZED AGENT.

1. Retain control of all merchandise described on the Customs Form 4647. The merchandise must be held intact; it cannot be moved or distributed until authorized by the Customs Service.

2. Marking and/or additional instructions are provided in SECTION II.

3. Upon completion of marking, complete the appropriate item(s). **SIGNATURE MUST BE THAT OF THE IMPORTER OR AUTHORIZED AGENT.**

4. Identify the location where the merchandise will be available for Customs verification and provide a contact telephone number.

5. Upon completion of SECTION III, submit the "Return to Customs" copy of the form with a sample, if requested, to the office specified in SECTION I of this form. NOTE: Appropriate items must be completed, signed, and dated before acceptance by Customs.

SECTION IV: COMPLETED BY THE CUSTOMS SERVICE.

Upon return of the Customs Form 4647, Customs will review the form to ensure that SECTION III has been completed, signed, and dated by the IMPORTER OF RECORD OR AUTHORIZED AGENT, and take one of the following actions:

1. A Customs officer will visit your premises to verify your certification of marking and to notify you whether or not it is acceptable.

2. Notify you (in writing) that (a) the marking or corrective action is acceptable and the merchandise is officially released by Customs; or (b) the marking or corrective action is not acceptable and that the merchandise must be redelivered to Customs custody within the prescribed time.

If you have any questions or find that the marking procedure or other corrective action requires more than 30 days, contact the office indicated in SECTION I.

Customs Form 4647 (121592)(Back)

Figure 8–18. Post Entry Amendment

POST ENTRY AMENDMENT
(CORRECTION TO AN ENTRY SUMMARY)

FILER

DATE

LIQUIDATION DATE[1]
[1]IF AVAILABLE.

ENTRY NUMBER

PORT

IMPORTER NUMBER

REASON CODE

IMPORTER NAME

NARRATIVE DESCRIPTION

CORRECTED DUTY AMOUNT: TOTAL ASCERTAINED AMOUNT SHOWN ON CORRECTED 7501

DUTY

HMF

MPF

TAX

ADD

CVD

TOTAL

PAYMENT

REFUND

BILL

NON-REVENUE[2]

[2]STATISTICAL INFORMATION ERRORS THAT MEET OR EXCEED CENSUS BUREAU REPORTING LEVELS. REFERENCE FEDERAL REGISTER NOTICE DATED NOVEMBER 28, 2000.

TOTAL PAID, REFUND OR BILL AMOUNT

FILER POINT OF CONTACT NAME/PHONE

CUSTOMS & BORDER PROTECTION ONLY

INTEREST

TOTAL LIQUIDATION AMOUNT

Figure 8–18. *(continued)*

REASON CODES

11- VALUATION
12- CLASSIFICATION
13- QUANTITY
14- ANTI-DUMPING DUTY
15-COUNTERVAILING DUTY
16- SPECIAL TRADE PROGRAMS
17- INTEREST ONLY
18- NON-REVENUE
19- OTHER

AMOUNTS ON THE WORKSHEET SHOULD BE THE CORRECTED DUTY AMOUNT - NOT THE DIFFERENCE

WORKSHEET SHOULD HAVE THE SAME ASCERTAINED AMOUNTS AS THE CORRECTED CBP FORM 7501

miss the protest deadline. For this reason, it is important for the importer to establish a procedure whereby the status of entries is checked from time to time.

Similarly, sometimes liquidation will be suspended. In general, entries will be automatically liquidated 314 days from the date of entry. If an entry is not liquidated, the importer should investigate why it is being suspended to avoid a future liquidation with a duty increase long after the time of importation. A protest gives the importer an additional opportunity to present its reasons why the entry should be liquidated as originally entered with no increase in duties. Customs must grant or deny a protest within two years of filing (thirty days for excluded merchandise). In order to obtain a decision more quickly, a request for accelerated disposition may be filed, which Customs must act upon within an additional thirty days. In certain circumstances, an importer may request that its protest be reviewed by Customs Headquarters as an Application for Further Review.

X. Administrative Summons

If Customs suspects that a violation of the customs laws has occurred, it may issue a summons to an importer or to third-party record-keepers, such as customs brokers, accountants, and attorneys, requesting them to produce documents or to give testimony relating to the importations. (A sample summons is shown in Figure 8–22.) When a summons is being issued to a third-party record-keeper, Customs sends a copy of the notice to the importer of record (see Figure 8–23). If the recipient does not comply with the summons, U.S. Customs and Border Protection can seek an order from the U.S. district court compelling the importer to produce the documents or provide the testimony requested. Upon receipt of a summons and before providing any documents or answering any questions from a Customs agent, the importer should consult with its attorney.

(*Text continues on page 367.*)

Figure 8–19. Request for Information.

OMB No. 1651-0023
Exp. 05-31-2011

DEPARTMENT OF HOMELAND SECURITY
U.S. Customs and Border Protection

REQUEST FOR INFORMATION

19 CFR 151.11

			1. Date of Request
			2. Date of Entry and Importation
3. Manufacturer/Seller/Shipper	4. Carrier		5. Entry No.
5a. Invoice Description of Merchandise		5b. Invoice No.	6. HTSUS Item No.
7. Country of Origin/Exportation		8. CBP Broker and Reference or File No.	
9. TO:		10. FROM:	
Production of Documents and/or Information Required by Law: If you have provided the information requested on this form to U.S. Customs and Border Protection at other ports, please indicate the port of entry to which it was supplied, and furnish a copy of your reply to this office, if possible.		11a. Port	11b. Date Information Furnished

General Information and Instructions on Reverse

12. Please Answer Indicated Question(s)		13. Please Furnish Indicated Item(s)	
☐ A.	Are you related (see reverse) in any way to the seller of this merchandise? If you are related, please describe the relationship, and explain how this relationship affects the price paid or payable for the merchandise.	☐ A.	Copy of contract (or purchase order and seller's confirmation thereof) covering this transaction, and any revisions thereto.
		☐ B.	Descriptive or illustrative literature or information explaining what the merchandise is, where and how it is used, and exactly how it operates.
		☐ C.	Breakdown of components, materials, or ingredients by weight and the actual cost of the components at the time of assembly into the finished article.
☐ B.	Identify and give details of any additional costs/ expenses incurred in this transaction, such as: ☐ (1) packing ☐ (2) commissions ☐ (3) proceeds that accrue to the seller ☐ (4) assists ☐ (5) royalties and/or license fees	☐ D.	Submit samples: Article number and description ____________ ____________ from container ____________ mark(s)and number ____________ Samples consumed in analysis, and other samples whose return is not specifically requested, will not normally be returned.
		☐ E.	See item 14 below.

14. CBP Officer Message

15. Reply Message (Use additional sheets if more space is needed.)

16. CERTIFICATION	It is required that an appropriate corporate/company official execute this certificate and/or endorse all correspondence in response to the information requested. (**NOTE**: NOT REQUIRED IF FOREIGN FIRM COMPLETES THIS FORM.)		
I hereby certify that the information furnished herewith or upon this form in response to this inquiry is true and correct, and that any samples provided were taken from the shipment covered by this entry.	16a. Name and Title/Position of Signer (Owner, Importer, or Corporate/Company Official)	16b. Signature	
		16c. Telephone No.	16d. Date
17. CBP Officer	18. Team Designation	19. Telephone No.	

CBP Form 28 (02/02)

Figure 8–19. *(continued)*

GENERAL INFORMATION AND INSTRUCTIONS

1. The requested information is necessary for proper classification and/or appraisement of your merchandise and/or for insuring import compliance of such merchandise. Your reply is required in accordance with section 509(a), Tariff Action of 1930, as amended (19 U.S.C. 1509).
2. All information, documents, and samples requested must relate to the shipment of merchandise described on the front of this form.
3. Please answer all indicated questions to the best of your knowledge.
4. All information submitted will be treated confidentially.
5. If a reply cannot be made within 30 days from the date of this request or if you wish to discuss any of the questions designated for your reply, please contact the CBP officer whose name appears on the front of this form.
6. Return a copy of this form with your reply.

DEFINITIONS OF KEY WORDS IN BLOCK 12

Question A: RELATED - The persons specified below shall be treated as persons who are related:

(A) Members of the same family, including brothers and sisters (whether by whole or half blood), spouse, ancestors, and lineal descendants.

(B) Any officer or director of an organization and such organization.

(C) An officer or director of an organization and an officer or director of another organization, if each such individual is also an officer or director in the other organization.

(D) Partners.

(E) Employer and employee.

(F) Any person directly or indirectly owning, controlling, or holding with power to vote, 5 percent or more of the outstanding voting stock or shares of any organization and such organization.

(G) Two or more persons directly or indirectly controlling, controlled by or under common control with, any person.

PRICE PAID OR PAYABLE - This term is defined as the total payment (whether direct or indirect and exclusive of any costs, charges, or expenses incurred for transportation, insurance, and other C.I.F. charges) made, or to be made, for imported merchandise by the buyer to, or for the benefit of, the seller.

Question B: ASSISTS - The term "assist" means any of the following if supplied directly or indirectly, and free of charge or at reduced cost, by the buyer of the imported merchandise for use in connection with the production or the sale for export to the United States of the merchandise:

(1) Materials, components, parts, and similar items incorporated in the imported merchandise.

(2) Tools, dies, molds, and similar items used in the production of the imported merchandise.

(3) Merchandise consumed in the production of the imported merchandise.

(4) Engineering, development, artwork, design work, and plans and sketches that are undertaken elsewhere than in the United States and are necessary for the production of the imported merchandise.

PROCEEDS THAT ACCRUE TO THE SELLER - This term is defined as the amount of any subsequent resale, disposal, or use of the imported merchandise that accrues, directly or indirectly, to the seller.

ROYALTIES AND/OR LICENSE FEES - This term relates to those amounts that the buyer is required to pay, directly or indirectly, as a condition of the sale of the imported merchandised for exportation to the United States.

PAPERWORK REDUCTION ACT NOTICE: This request is in accordance with the Paperwork Reduction Act. We ask for the information to carry out the laws of the United States. We need it to ensure importers/brokers are complying with these laws and to allow us to properly appraise and classify imported merchandise or correct duties and determine import admissibility, where appropriate. Your response is mandatory. The estimated average burden associated with this collection of information is 60 minutes per respondent or recordkeeper depending on individual circumstances. Comments concerning the accuracy of this burden estimate and suggestions for reducing this burden should be directed to U.S. Customs and Border Protection, Information Services Branch, Washington, DC 20229, and to the Office of Management and Budget, Paperwork Reduction Project (1651-0023), Washington, DC 20503.

CBP Form 28 (02/02)(Back)

Figure 8–20. Notice of Action.

DEPARTMENT OF THE TREASURY
UNITED STATES CUSTOMS SERVICE
19 CFR 152.2

NOTICE OF ACTION
This is NOT a Notice of Liquidation

			1. DATE OF THIS NOTICE
2. CARRIER	3. DATE OF IMPORTATION	4. DATE OF ENTRY	5. ENTRY NO.
6. MFR/SELLER/SHIPPER	7. COUNTRY	8. CUSTOMS BROKER AND FILE NO.	
9. DESCRIPTION OF MERCHANDISE			
10. TO ▶		11. FROM	

12. THE FOLLOWING ACTION, WHICH WILL RESULT IN AN INCREASE IN DUTIES,—

☐ IS **PROPOSED** — IF YOU DISAGREE WITH THIS PROPOSED ACTION, PLEASE FURNISH YOUR REASONS IN WRITING TO THIS OFFICE WITHIN 20 DAYS FROM THE DATE OF THIS NOTICE. AFTER 20 DAYS THE ENTRY WILL BE LIQUIDATED AS PROPOSED.

☐ HAS BEEN **TAKEN** — THE ENTRY IS IN THE LIQUIDATION PROCESS AND IS NOT AVAILABLE FOR REVIEW IN THIS OFFICE.

TYPE OF ACTION

A. ☐ RATE ADVANCE

B. ☐ VALUE ADVANCE

C. ☐ EXCESS ☐ WEIGHT ☐ QUANTITY

D. ☐ OTHER *(See below)*

13. EXPLANATION *(Refer to Action letter designations above)*

14. CUSTOMS OFFICER *(Print or Type)*	15. TEAM DESIGNATION	16. TELEPHONE

Customs Form 29 (031795)

ORIGINAL (WHITE) - IMPORTER

Figure 8–21. Protest and instructions.

DEPARTMENT OF HOMELAND SECURITY
U.S. Customs and Border Protection

PROTEST

Pursuant to Sections 514 & 514(a), Tariff Act of 1930 as amended, 19 CFR Part 174 et. seq.

Approved OMB No. 1651-0017
Exp. 09-30-2009

1. PROTEST NO. *(Supplied by CBP)*

2. DATE RECEIVED *(CBP Use Only)*

NOTE: If your protest is denied, in whole or in part, and you wish to CONTEST the denial, you may do so by bringing a civil action in the U.S. Court of International Trade within 180 days after the date of mailing of Notice of Denial. You may obtain further information concerning the institution of an action by writing the Clerk of U.S. Court of International Trade, One Federal Plaza, New York NY 10007 (212-264-2800).

SECTION I - IMPORTER AND ENTRY IDENTIFICATION

3. PORT

4. IMPORTER NO.

5. ENTRY DETAILS

PORT CODE	FILER CODE	ENTRY NO.	CHECK DIGIT	DATE OF ENTRY	DATE OF LIQUIDATION

6. NAME AND ADDRESS OF IMPORTER OR OTHER PROTESTING PARTY

7. Is Accelerated Disposition being requested (19 CFR 174.22)?
☐ Yes ☐ No

SECTION II - DETAILED REASONS FOR PROTEST

8. With respect to each category of merchandise, set forth, separately, (1) each decision protested, (2) the claim of the protesting party, and (3) the factual material and legal arguments which are believed to support the protest. All such material and arguments should be specific. General statements of conclusions are not sufficient.

(Attach Additional Sheets if necessary.)

SECTION III - REQUEST FOR DISPOSITION IN ACCORDANCE WITH ACTION ON PREVIOUSLY FILED PROTEST

Protesting party may request disposition in accordance with the action taken on a previously filed protest that is the subject of a pending application for further review and is alleged to involve the same merchandise and the same issues. (See 19 CFR 174.13(a)(7).) To request such disposition, enter in Blocks 8 and 9 the protest number and date of receipt of such previously filed protest. ▶

9. PROTEST NO. OF PREVIOUSLY FILED PROTEST

10. DATE OF RECEIPT

SECTION IV - SIGNATURE AND MAILING INSTRUCTIONS

11. NAME AND ADDRESS OF PERSON TO WHOM ANY NOTICE OF APPROVAL OR DENIAL SHOULD BE SENT

12. NAME, ADDRESS, AND CBP IDENTIFICATION NUMBER TO WHICH REFUND SHOULD BE SENT

13. IF FILING AS ATTORNEY OR AGENT, TYPE OR PRINT YOUR NAME, ADDRESS AND IMPORTER NUMBER, IF ANY

14. SIGNATURE
X

DATE

(Optional) **SECTION V - APPLICATION FOR FURTHER REVIEW** *(Fill in Item 1 above if this is a separate Application for Further Review.)*

15. MARK BOX CORRESPONDING TO YOUR ANSWER TO EACH OF THE FOLLOWING QUESTIONS

YES	NO	
☐	☐	(A) Have you made prior request of a port director for a further review of the same claim with respect to the same substantially similar merchandise?
☐	☐	(B) Have you received a final adverse decision from the U.S. Court of International Trade on the same claim with respect to the same category of merchandise or do you have action involving such a claim pending before the U.S. Court of International Trade?
☐	☐	(C) Have you previously received an adverse administrative decision from the Commissioner of CBP or his designee or have you presently pending an application for an administrative decision on the same claim with respect to the same category of merchandise?

16. JUSTIFICATION FOR FURTHER REVIEW UNDER THE CRITERIA IN 19 CFR 174.24 AND 174.25 (Include Applicable Rulings)

(Attach Additional Sheets If Necessary.)

SECTION VI - DECISION *(CBP USE ONLY)*

17. APPLICATION FOR FURTHER REVIEW EXPLANATION: ☐ Approved* ☐ Denied for the reason checked: ☐ Untimely filed ☐ Does not meet criteria ☐ Other, namely

*When further review only is approved the decision on the protest is suspended, pending issuance of a protest review decision.

18. PROTEST EXPLANATION: ☐ Approved ☐ Rejected as non-protestable ☐ Denied in full for the reason checked: ☐ Denied in part for the reason checked: ☐ Untimely filed ☐ See attached protest review decision ☐ Other, namely

19. TITLE OF CBP OFFICER

20. SIGNATURE AND DATE

Previous Editions are Obsolete

CBP Form 19 (12/95)

(continues)

Figure 8–21. *(continued)*

Paperwork Reduction Act Notice: The Paperwork Reduction Act says we must tell you why we aare collecting this information, how we will use it, and whether you have to give it to us. We ask for this information to carry out the Customs laws and regulations of the United States. The CBP requires the information in this form to ensure compliance with Customs laws, to identify documents and statements in order to allow or deny the protest, and to advise protestant. Your response is required to obtain a benefit. The estimated average burden associated with this collection of information is 1 hour and 3 minutes per respondent or recordkeeper depending on individual circumstances. Comments concerning the accuracy of this burden estimate and suggestions for reducing this burden should be directed to U.S. Customs and Border Protection, Information Services Branch, Washington, DC 20229 and to the Office of Management and Budget, Paperwork Reduction Project (1651-0017) Washington, DC 20503.

INSTRUCTIONS

PLEASE REFER TO: Part 174, Customs Regulations

Definitions*

"Liquidation" means the final computation or ascertainment of the duties or drawback accruing on an entry.

"Protest" means the seeking of review of a decision of an appropriate CBP officer. Such a review may be conducted by CBP officers who participated directly in the underlying decision.

"Further Review" means a request for review of the protest to be performed by a CBP officer who did not participate directly in the protested decision, or by the Commissioner, or his designee as provided in the CBP Regulations. This request will only be acted upon in the event that the protest would have been denied at the initial level of review. If you are filing for further review, you must answer each question in Item 15 on CBP Form 19 and provide justification for further review in Item 16.

What matters may be protested?

1. The appraised value of merchandise;
2. The classification and rate and amount of duties chargeable;
3. All charges within the jurisdiction of the U.S. Department of Homeland Security;
4. Exclusion of merchandise from entry or delivery, or demand for redelivery;
5. The liquidation or reliquidation of an entry;
6. The refusal to pay a claim for drawback; and

Who may file a protest or application for further review?

1. The importer or consignee shown on the entry papers, or their sureties;
2. Any person paying any charge or exaction;
3. Any person seeking entry or delivery, or upon whom a demand for redelivery has been made;
4. Any person filing a claim for drawback; or
5. Any authorized agent of any of the persons described above.

Where to file protest:

With the port director whose decision is protested (at the port where entry was made).

When to file a protest:

Within 180 days after either: 1) the date of notice of liquidation or reliquidation; or 2) the date of the decision, involving neither a liquidation nor reliquidation, as to which the protest is made (e.g., the date of an exaction, the date of written notice excluding merchandise from entry or delivery or demand for redelivery); or 3) a surety may file within 180 days after the date of mailing of notice of demand for payment against its bond.

Contents of protest:

1. Name and address of the protestant;
2. The importer number of the protestant;
3. The number and date(s) of the entry(s);
4. The date of liquidation of the entry (or the date of a decision);
5. A specific description of the merchandise;
6. The nature of and justification for the objection set forth distinctly and specifically with respect to each category, claim, decision, or refusal;
7. The date of receipt and protest number of any protest previously filed that is the subject of a pending application for further review; and
8. If another party has not filed a timely protest, the surety's protest shall certify that the protest is not being filed collusively to extend another authorized person's time to protest.
9. Whether accelerated disposition is being requested.

NOTE: Under Item 5, Entry Details, "Check Digit" information is optional; however, CBP would appreciate receiving the information if you can provide it. All attachments to a protest (other than samples or similar exhibits) must be filed in triplicate.

CBP Form 19 (Back)(12/95)

Figure 8–22. Administrative summons.

1 TO (Name, Address, City, State, ZIP)	**DEPARTMENT OF THE TREASURY** UNITED STATES CUSTOMS SERVICE **SUMMONS** **TO APPEAR AND/OR PRODUCE RECORDS**

By the service of of this summons upon you, YOU ARE HEREBY SUMMONED AND REQUIRED TO:

(A) ☐ APPEAR before the Customs officer named in Block 2 below at the place, date, and time indicated, to testify and give information.

(B) ☐ PRODUCE the records (including statements, declarations, and other documents) indicated in Block 3 below, before the Customs officer named in Block 2 at the place, date, and time indicated.

Your testimony and/or the production of the indicated records is required in connection with an investigation or inquiry to ascertain the correctness of entries, to determine the liability for duties, taxes, fines, penalties or forfeitures, and/or to insure compliance with the laws or regulations administered by the U.S. Customs Service.

Failure to comply with this summons will render you liable to proceedings in a U.S. District Court to enforce compliance with this summons as well as other sanctions

2 (A) NAME, TITLE, ADDRESS, AND TELEPHONE NUMBER OF CUSTOMS OFFICER BEFORE WHOM YOU ARE TO APPEAR	(B) DATE (C) TIME

3 RECORDS REQUIRED TO BE PRODUCED FOR INSPECTION

Issued under authority of section 509, Tariff Act of 1930, as amended by Public Law 95-410 (19 U.S.C. 1509); Customs Delegation Order No. 55 (44 F.R. 2217).

4 NAME OF PERSON AUTHORIZED TO SERVE SUMMONS: or any other Customs officer.	5 DATE OF ISSUE COMMISSIONER OF CUSTOMS BY (Signature):
If you have any questions regarding this summons, contact the Customs officer identified in Block 2.	6 NAME, TITLE, ADDRESS, AND TELEPHONE NUMBER OF PERSON ISSUING THIS SUMMONS

TREASURY · U.S. CUSTOMS SERVICE

Customs Form 3115 (101091)

*U.S. GPO: 1991-312-754/50236

Figure 8–23. Summons notice to importer of record.

TO

DEPARTMENT OF THE TREASURY
UNITED STATES CUSTOMS SERVICE

SUMMONS NOTICE

section 509(c)(2), Tariff Act of 1930, as amended

REFERENCE

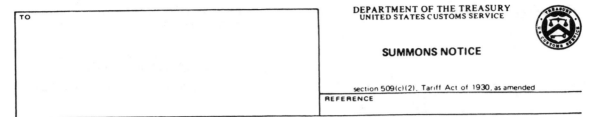

Enclosed is a copy of a Summons served by the United States Customs Service to examine records or to request testimony relating to records of your business transactions or affairs which have been made or kept by the person named in Block 1 of the Summons. If you object to the examination of these records, you may stay (prevent) examination of the records until a summons enforcement proceeding is commenced in court. Compliance with the Summons will be stayed if, not later than the day before the date indicated in Block 2 of the Summons, you advise the person summoned (the person named in Block 1), in writing, not to comply with the Summons, and you send a copy of that notice by registered or certified mail to the officer who issued the Summons at the address shown in Block 6 of the Summons.

The United States Customs Service may begin an action to enforce the Summons in the appropriate United States District Court. In such cases, you will be notified and you will have the right to intervene and present your objections before the court. The court will decide whether the person summoned should be required to comply with the Summons.

If the court issues an order to comply with the Summons and the person summoned fails to comply, the court may punish such failure as a contempt of court. Other sanctions may be provided by law.

If you have any questions regarding this matter, please contact the Customs officer before whom the summoned person is required to appear. The officer's name and telephone number are given in Block 2 of the Summons.

Customs Form 3115-B (1-19-79)

Y. Search Warrants

When Customs believes that a criminal or intentional violation of the customs laws has occurred, it may apply to the appropriate U.S. district court for a search warrant to inspect the premises or seize records of an importer. A sample affidavit, which must be filed with the court, and a search warrant are shown in Figures 8–24 and 8–25, respectively. When Customs agents approach an importer with a search warrant, the importer should realize that the case is a criminal case and that individuals as well as the company may be subject to fines or imprisonment. The importer should not discuss the case with the Customs agent without consulting its attorney.

Z. Grand Jury Subpoenas

When Customs investigates a criminal violation of the customs laws, the U.S. attorney may convene a grand jury. The grand jury may subpoena persons employed by the importer or other persons to testify before the grand jury. Obviously, these are extremely serious proceedings, and before any person testifies before a grand jury, he should be advised by legal counsel. (A sample subpoena is shown in Figure 8–26.)

AA. Seizure Notices

When Customs believes that goods have been imported into the United States in violation of the customs laws, it may issue a seizure notice and information for claimants (see Figure 8–27). Once a seizure notice has been issued, the importer must proceed by means of the procedures specified in the Customs regulations to try to repossess the merchandise. Sometimes, in order to avoid additional assessments of customs penalties or the expenses of further proceedings, the importer may agree or consent to abandon the merchandise that has been seized. (A form of consent is shown in Figure 8–28.) However, the importer should not be pressured into abandoning the merchandise by threats that Customs will pursue further penalties against the importer unless it abandons the merchandise. Although no particular form is required, a sample form of a petition for remission or mitigation is shown in Figure 8–29, which is filed to try to obtain release of the seized merchandise.

BB. Prepenalty Notices

When Customs determines that a civil violation of the customs laws has occurred, it issues a prepenalty notice (see Figure 8–30). The prepenalty notice states the customs law or regulation that has been violated. This notice is also used where Customs claims liquidated damages, for example, because merchandise was released to the importer under an Entry/Immediate Delivery and the importer failed to file the Entry Summary

(*Text continues on page 370.*)

Figure 8–24. Affidavit.

Form A. O. 106

Affidavit for Search Warrant

United States District Court

FOR THE

Commissioner's Docket No.

Case No.

UNITED STATES OF AMERICA

vs.

AFFIDAVIT FOR SEARCH WARRANT

BEFORE — Name of Commissioner — Address of Commissioner

The undersigned being duly sworn deposes and says:

That he (has reason to believe) (is positive)[1] that (on the person of) (on the premises known as)

in the District of

there is now being concealed certain property, namely — here describe property

which are — here give alleged grounds for search and seizure

And that the facts tending to establish the foregoing grounds for issuance of a Search Warrant are as follows:

Signature of Affiant.

Official Title, if any.

Sworn to before me, and subscribed in my presence, , 19

United States Commissioner.

[1] The Federal Rules of Criminal Procedure provide: "The warrant shall direct that it be served in the daytime, but if the affidavits are positive that the property is on the person or in the place to be searched, the warrant may direct that it be served at any time." (Rule 41C)

Figure 8–25. Search warrant.

Form A. O. 93 (Revised June 1964) **Search Warrant**

United States District Court

FOR THE

UNITED STATES OF AMERICA	Commissioner's Docket No.
vs.	Case No.
	SEARCH WARRANT

To

Affidavit having been made before me by

that he { has reason to believe / is positive[1] } that { on the person of / on the premises known as }

in the District of

there is now being concealed certain property, namely

here describe property

which are

here give alleged grounds for search and seizure

and as I am satisfied that there is probable cause to believe that the property so described is being concealed on the { person / premises } above described and that the foregoing grounds for application for issuance of the search warrant exist.

You are hereby commanded to search forthwith the { person / place } named for the property specified, serving this warrant and making the search { in the daytime / at any time in the day or night[1] } and if the property be found there to seize it, leaving a copy of this warrant and a receipt for the property taken, and prepare a written inventory of the property seized and return this warrant and bring the property before me within ten days of this date, as required by law.

Dated this day of , 19

_______________________,
U. S. Commissioner.

[1] The Federal Rules of Criminal Procedure provide: "The warrant shall direct that it be served in the daytime, but if the affidavits are positive that the property is on the person or in the place to be searched, the warrant may direct that it be served at any time." (Rule 41C)

(*continues*)

Figure 8–25. *(continued)*

[*reverse*]

RETURN

I received the attached search warrant , 19 , and have executed it as follows:

On , 19 at o'clock M, I searched { the person / the premises } described in the warrant and

I left a copy of the warrant with ....
name of person searched or owner or "at the place of search"

together with a receipt for the items seized.

The following is an inventory of property taken pursuant to the warrant:

This inventory was made in the presence of

and

I swear that this Inventory is a true and detailed account of all the property taken by me on the warrant.

....

Subscribed and sworn to and returned before me this day of , 19

....,
U. S. Commissioner.

and other necessary customs entry documents within the allotted time period. The importer will normally be given thirty days to present reasons explaining why the penalty should be reduced or forgiven.

CC. Penalty Notices

After U.S. Customs and Border Protection receives and rejects the importer's explanation or if the importer files no explanation, Customs will issue a penalty notice. This is the formal assessment of penalty (see Figure 8–31). A petition for remission or mitigation may be filed within the time period specified on the penalty notice. Thereafter, if the importer fails to pay, collection will be referred to the U.S. Department of Justice Civil Division, for the filing of a civil collection action in the Court of International Trade.

(*Text continues on page 382.*)

Figure 8–26. Grand jury subpoena.

United States District Court

__________ DISTRICT OF __________

TO: SAMPLE ONLY

SUBPOENA TO TESTIFY BEFORE GRAND JURY

SUBPOENA FOR:
☐ PERSON ☐ DOCUMENTS OR OBJECT(S)

YOU ARE HEREBY COMMANDED to appear and testify before the Grand Jury of the United States District Court at the place, date, and time specified below.

PLACE	ROOM
	DATE AND TIME

YOU ARE ALSO COMMANDED to bring with you the following document(s) or object(s):*

VOID SAMPLE ONLY

☐ *Please see additional information on reverse*

This subpoena shall remain in effect until you are granted leave to depart by the court or by an officer acting on behalf of the court.

CLERK	DATE
VOID SAMPLE ONLY	
(BY) DEPUTY CLERK	SAMPLE
VOID SAMPLE ONLY	

This subpoena is issued upon application of the United States of America	NAME, ADDRESS AND PHONE NUMBER OF ASSISTANT U.S. ATTORNEY

*If not applicable, enter "none." To be used in lieu of AO110 FORM OBD-227 JAN. 86

(continues)

Figure 8–26. *(continued)*

[*reverse*]

RETURN OF SERVICE(1)		
RECEIVED BY SERVER	DATE	PLACE
SERVED	DATE	PLACE
SERVED ON (NAME)		
SERVED BY	TITLE	

STATEMENT OF SERVICE FEES		
TRAVEL	SERVICES	TOTAL

DECLARATION OF SERVER(2)

I declare under penalty of perjury under the laws of the United States of America that the foregoing information contained in the Return of Service and Statement of Service Fees is true and correct.

Executed on ____________________ ____
Date *Signature of Server*

____
Address of Server

ADDITIONAL INFORMATION

(1) As to who may serve a subpoena and the manner of its service see Rule 17(d), Federal Rules of Criminal Procedure, or Rule 45(c), Federal Rules of Civil Procedure.

(2) "Fees and mileage need not be tendered to the witness upon service of a subpoena issued on behalf of the United States or an officer or agency thereof (Rule 45(c), Federal Rules of Civil Procedure; Rule 17(d), Federal Rules of Criminal Procedure) or on behalf of certain indigent parties and criminal defendants who are unable to pay such costs (28 USC 1825, Rule 17(b) Federal Rules of Criminal Procedure)".

Figure 8–27. Notice of seizure.

U.S. Customs Service
610 S. Canal Street
Chicago, IL 60607-4523

FILE: ENF-4-02 PD:P
CASE NO:

Dear :

The records of this office indicate that you might have an interest in certain property seized by U. S. Customs in (location)______________ on (date)_______________. The property was seized under the provisions of Title 19, United States Code, Section 1595a(c). Specifically, it violates (citation of law)._______________. The property consists of the following items:

(DESCRIPTION OF SEIZED MERCHANDISE)

The value of the merchandise is ________________ .

Under the provisions of Title 19, United States Code, Section 1618, you may petition for relief from the above liability(ies). The enclosed Notice of Seizure and Information for Claimants explains your options with regard to the remission of the forfeiture and possible return to you of the seized property. If you decide to petition for relief, you must check the first box on the enclosed Election of Proceeding/Waiver form indicating that you wish this office to consider your petition administratively. By checking this box you are providing an express agreement to defer judicial or administrative forfeiture proceedings until completion of the administrative process. Checking the second or third box indicates that you desire Customs to begin appropriate forfeiture proceedings. No matter which box you check, you must also sign and return the form.

All petitions should be filed, in triplicate, at the following address: Port Director, U. S. Customs Service, (address), _____________, Attn: FP&F Section. If a petition is not received within 30 days from the date of this letter, appropriate forfeiture action will be initiated.

Sincerely,

Fines, Penalties & Forfeitures Officer

Enclosure

TRADITION ★ SERVICE ★ HONOR

(*continues*)

Figure 8–27. *(continued)*

NOTICE OF SEIZURE AND INFORMATION FOR CLAIMANTS
FORM AF

PORT DIRECTOR OF CUSTOMS
610 SOUTH CANAL ST, FP&F
CHICAGO, IL 60607

PLEASE TAKE PARTICULAR
NOTE OF INFORMATION
FOLLOWING CHECKED BOXES

(312) 983-1324

To The Party Named in The Attached Letter:

You are hereby notified that the merchandise, conveyances, monetary instruments, or other property shown on the attached document(s), or other property shown on the attached document(s) were seized for violation of the Customs laws or the other laws enforced or administered by the U. S. Customs Service, as indicated on the attachment.

The facts available to the U. S. Customs Service indicate that you have an interest in the seized property. The purpose of this letter is to advise you of the options available to you concerning this seizure:

1. You may choose to take no action. If you take no action, the Customs Service will seek to forfeit the property by administrative action in accordance with section 607, Tariff Act of 1930, as amended (19 U.S.C. 1607) and section 162.45, Title 19, Code of Federal Regulations. In order to obtain forfeiture, the Customs Service must publish a notice of seizure and intent to forfeit in a newspaper for three successive weeks. After that time, the Government acquires full title to the seized property. The first notice will be published on or about 30 days in the Chicago Sun Times.

2. You may request the Port (or Area) Director of Customs to publish the first notice sooner than the scheduled date which appears above.

In either case (#1 or #2 above), once the first notice is published, and within 20 days of the publication, you may appear before the Port (or Area) Director of Customs and file a claim and a bond in the amount of $5,000.00 or 10 percent of the value of the claimed property, whichever is lower, but not less than $250. If you file the claim and bond, the matter will immediately be referred to the appropriate United States Attorney for the institution of judicial proceedings in Federal court to forfeit the seized property, in accordance with section 608, Tariff Act of 1930, as amended (19 U.S.C. 1608) and section 162.47, Title 19, Code of Federal Regulations. If you wish the Government to seek judicial forfeiture proceedings but cannot afford to post the bond, you should contact the Port (or Area) Director of Customs. Upon satisfactory proof of financial inability to pay the bond, it will be waived; or

Figure 8–27. *(continued)*

FORM AF
-2-

3. If you wish to seek administrative relief, you must, within 30 days from the date of the attached letter (unless some other period is stated in the letter), file a completed copy of the attached form waiving your right to prompt commencement of administrative forfeiture proceedings in accordance with section 609, Tariff Act of 1930, as amended (19 U.S.C. 1609) and request administrative action, and:

(a) File a petition for administrative relief with the Port (Area) Director of Customs in accordance with section 618, Tariff Act of 1930, as amended (19 U.S.C. 1618) and section 171.11, Title 19, Code of Federal Regulations; or

(b) Submit an offer in compromise to the Port (or Area) Director of Customs in accordance with section 617, Tariff Act of 1930, as amended (19 U.S.C. 1617) and section 161.5, Title 19, Code of Federal Regulations; or

(c) Unless the seized property is prohibited entry into the United States, submit an offer to pay the appraised domestic value of the seized property accompanied by payment or an irrevocable letter of credit with the Port (or Area) Director of Customs in accordance with section 614, Tariff Act of 1930, as amended (19 U.S.C. 1614) and section 162.44, Title 19, Code of Federal Regulations. If Customs accepts your offer, the property will be immediately released, the security will be substituted for the seized property, and you may still petition for relief [see 3(a) above] or submit an offer in compromise [see 3(b) above].

If you complete and submit the attached waiver requesting administrative proceedings, together with any of the options in 3(a), (b), or (c) above, you will be requesting the Customs Service NOT to begin administrative forfeiture proceedings by publication of the notice of seizure and intent to forfeit while your petition or offer is pending administratively, or to halt proceedings if they have already commenced. However, if the matter has been referred to the United States attorney for the institution of judicial forfeiture proceedings because a claim and bond were filed with Customs, your petition or offer will be forwarded to the United States Attorney for consideration under Department of Justice Regulations.

If your petition or offer is NOT accompanied by the attached waiver, or you request immediate commencement of administrative forfeiture proceedings on that form, publication of the notice of seizure and intent to forfeit will begin promptly, unless the matter has been referred to the United States Attorney because a claim and cost bond were filed by another party. If a claim and cost bond have been filed, your petition or offer will be forwarded to the United States Attorney for consideration.

(continues)

Figure 8–27. *(continued)*

FORM AF
- 3 -

If you decide to file a petition for relief, an offer in compromise, or an offer to pay the value to obtain release, with the Customs Service, you should address it to the Commissioner of Customs and submit it in triplicate (3 copies) to the Port (or Area) Director of Customs at the address shown in the attached letter.

If you follow any of the options in #3 above and you do not believe that the Customs Service is acting expeditiously on your request, you may notify the Port (or Area) Director of Customs in writing that you are withdrawing your request and the Customs Service will, within 14 days from receipt of your notice, begin to publish the notice of seizure and intent to forfeit in a newspaper (see #1 and #2 above).

If you have any questions concerning the reasons for, or the circumstances surrounding the seizure, or the procedures to be followed in connection with this matter, or if you require additional information, you may request an informal conference with the Port (or Area) Director of Customs or one of his designated employees.

[ ] SPECIAL NOTICE TO MULTIPLE CLAIMANTS AND HOLDERS OF LIENS OR SECURITY INTERESTS

The information available to Customs indicates that another party has an ownership interest in the seized property identified on the attachment. Although you may avail yourself of the options listed above, no relief will be granted to you until AFTER forfeiture unless your petition, offer, or request is accompanied by an agreement to hold the United States, its officers and employees harmless, and a release from the registered owner, and/or the person from whom the property was seized [contact the Port (or Area) Director of Customs for details]. If you do not submit the hold harmless agreement and release(s), the administrative forfeiture proceedings will proceed, unless you file a claim and a bond in the amount of $5,000 or 10 percent of the value of the claimed property, whichever is lower, but not less than $250, in which case the matter will be referred to the United States Attorney for the institution of judicial forfeiture proceedings.

[ ] PENALTY INFORMATION

In addition to the seizure(s) and forfeiture liability, a civil penalty has been or will be assessed in this matter. Details on the civil penalty are:

[ ] in the attached letter; or

[ ] being prepared and will be mailed shortly.

Figure 8–27. *(continued)*

ELECTION OF PROCEEDINGS
FORM AF- PUBLISH

NOTE: READ THE ATTACHED "NOTICE OF SEIZURE AND INFORMATION FOR CLAIMANTS" BEFORE YOU FILL OUT THIS FORM. THIS FORM MUST BE COMPLETED AND RETURNED WITH YOUR PETITION OR OFFER. IF YOU DO NOT COMPLETE AND RETURN THIS FORM, WE SHALL PROCEED TO FORFEIT THE PROPERTY ADMINISTRATIVELY, REGARDLESS OF WHETHER YOU FILE A PETITION OR OFFER.

TO: CUSTOMS FINES, PENALTIES AND FORFEITURE OFFICER:

I understand that property in which I have an interest has been seized by the U.S. Customs Service, under Case Number: ______________________________.

Check ONLY ONE (1) of the following choices:

[ ] I REQUEST THAT THE CUSTOMS SERVICE CONSIDER MY PETITION OR OFFER ADMINISTRATIVELY. That document is attached. By making this request, I understand that I am giving up my right to (1) begin administrative forfeiture proceedings immediately, as provided under title19, United States Code (U.S.C.), section 1607 and title 19, Code of Federal Regulations (CFR), section 162.45, or (2) immediate referral to the U.S. Attorney for court action, as provided by 19 U.S.C. 1608 and 19 CFR 162.47. If administrative forfeiture has begun, it will be stopped until my petition or offer is considered. However, I understand that *at any time* I can request, in writing, that you begin adminstrative proceedings, and you will continue to consider my petition or offer. I also understand that *at any time* I can file a claim and cost bond with you, and Customs consideration of my petition or offer will stop and the case will be sent to the U.S. Attorney for court action.

[ ] I REQUEST THAT THE CUSTOMS SERVICE BEGIN ADMINISTRATIVE PROCEEDINGS TO FORFEIT THE PROPERTY. Please immediately begin publication of the notice of seizure and intent to forfeit, and consider my petition or offer, if any. I understand that within 20 days of the first publication of the notice, I can request that you send the case to the U.S. Attorney for court action.

( ) I REQUEST THAT THE CUSTOMS SERVICE SEND MY CASE FOR COURT ACTION. Please immediately send the case to the U.S. Attorney for a court decision. I am filing /will file a claim and cost bond with you.

______________________________ ______________________________

Signature Date

Figure 8–28. Consent to forfeiture.

DEPARTMENT OF THE TREASURY
UNITED STATES CUSTOMS SERVICE

NOTICE OF ABANDONMENT AND ASSENT TO FORFEITURE OF PROHIBITED OR SEIZED MERCHANDISE AND CERTIFICATE OF DESTRUCTION

19 CFR Part 162

1. PORT	2. DATE	3. SEIZURE NO.

4. DESCRIPTION OF MERCHANDISE

PLEASE PRINT:

5. NAME	6. ADDRESS

I hereby abandon all claim to the above-described articles, and waive any further rights or proceedings relative to these articles, other than my right to file a petition for administrative relief.

7. SIGNATURE OF IMPORTER	8.DATE	9. WITNESS (CUSTOMS OFFICER)	10.DATE

CUSTOMS USE ONLY — CERTIFICATE OF DESTRUCTION

11. LOCATION	12. DATE	13. METHOD OF DESTRUCTION

14. SIGNATURE OF CUSTOMS OFFICER	15. WITNESS

Customs Form 4607 (09/00)

Figure 8–29. Petition for remission or mitigation.

OMB No. 1651-0100
Expires 10/2008

DEPARTMENT OF HOMELAND SECURITY
U.S. Customs and Border Protection

PETITION FOR RELIEF FROM FORFEITURE

Notice : Use this form if you want U.S. Customs and Border Protection to decide your request for the release of property.
Instructions : This form (Parts I - IV) must be completed *in English, signed and notarized.*

In accordance with Title 8, Code of Federal Regulations, Part 274, I request U.S. Customs and Border Protection consider my petition for relief from forfeiture administratively in order to obtain the release of my property.	
PART I	
Seizure Case Number:	
Date of Seizure:	Place of Seizure:
Full Name (First, Middle, Last)	
Date of Birth (mm/dd/yyyy):	
City, State, and County of Birth:	
PART II	
Instructions: Provide certified copies (or originals) of all bills of sale, purchase contracts, receipts, or any other documentary evidence to establish your interest in the seized property. Failure to do so may result in denial of your petition.	
A. Describe the property that was seized, to include the year, make, model, and serial number or Vehicle Identification Number. Use continuation sheets if more space is needed.	
B. State your interest in the seized property listed above. Are you the owner, lien holder, or otherwise? Use continuation sheets if more space is needed.	
C. State the facts and circumstances, with satisfactory proof thereof, relied upon to justify relief from forfeiture. If the property was in someone else's possession at the time of seizure, please provide an explanation how it came into their possession. Use continuation sheets if more space is needed.	
PART III	
I swear under penalty of perjury that all of the information provided is true and correct to the best of my knowledge and belief.	
Signature	Date
PART IV *(Notary Public)*	
STATE OF	
COUNTY OF	
SIGNED AND SWORN TO BEFORE ME ON THIS	DAY OF
	NOTARY PUBLIC
	COUNTY
MY COMMISSION EXPIRES:	
Paperwork Reduction Act Statement: An agency may not conduct or sponsor an information collection and a person is not required to respond to this information unless it displays a current valid OMB control number and an expiration date. The control number for this collection is 1651-0100. The estimated average time to complete this application is 13 minutes per respondent. If you have any comments regarding the burden estimate you can write to U.S. Customs and Border Protection, Information Services Branch,1300 Pennsylvania Avenue, NW, Washington DC 20229	

CBP Form 4630 (07/07)

(*continues*)

Figure 8–29. *(continued)*

CONTINUATION SHEET

Seizure Case Number:	Full Name (First, Middle, Last)

A.

B.

C.

CBP Form 4630 (07/07)

Figure 8–30. Prepenalty notice.

U.S. Customs Service
610 S. Canal Street
Chicago, IL 60607-4523

ENF 4-02 PD:P
Port Case

Gentlemen:

This is to inform you that pursuant to Title 19, Code of Federal Regulations, Section 162, notice is hereby given that the United States Customs Service is contemplating assessing a penalty against you in the amount of $_________. This amount represents the maximum penalty for (culpability) for your introduction of merchandise into the United States in violation of Title 19, United States Code, Section 1592.

Prior to the issuance of a notice of penalty, you have the right to make an oral and written presentation as to why the claim for monetary penalty should not be issued in the amount proposed. The written presentation must be made within thirty (30) business days from the date of the mailing of the pre-penalty notice as provided for in sections 162.77/78 of the Customs Regulations. Should you wish to make an oral presentation, please contact ___________ of my staff at the above telephone number to arrange a mutually convenient time and date for the presentation. Please be advised that we prefer the oral presentation be arranged after submission of the written response. The penalty notice will be issued automatically should you fail to respond to the pre-penalty notice within the effective period.

Exhibit A contains relevant information concerning the penalty action, i.e. specific details of the violation. Exhibit B represents the consumption entries involved in the penalty action.

If we do not hear from you within the time frame stipulated above the matter will be referred to the Court of International Trade for the institution of judicial proceedings.

Sincerely,

Fines, Penalties & Forfeitures Officer

TRADITION
★
SERVICE
★
HONOR

(*continues*)

Figure 8–30. *(continued)*

EXHIBIT A

1. **Description of Merchandise:**
2. **Shipper/Manufacturer:**
3. **Broker:**
4. **Consignee:**
5. **Details of Entry Introduction:**
6. **Loss of Revenue:**
7. **Law(s) Violated:**
8. **Facts Establishing Violation:**
9. **Culpability**
10. **Penalty Amount:**

DD. Customs Audits

U.S. Customs and Border Protection has always had the authority to conduct audits in which it reviews an importer's records to determine compliance with the customs laws, but such audits have assumed a new significance following enactment of the Customs Modernization Act. The Act enables importers to file customs entries electronically. Since additional documents that were traditionally attached to the customs entries, such as hard copies of the exporter's commercial invoice and bills of lading, are not available to the Customs officers at the time of electronic filing, post-importation audits become much more critical in Customs' ability to ensure compliance and detect fraud.

Under the Customs Modernization Act, Customs is required to follow certain procedures in conducting audits. It must give the importer an estimate of the duration of the audit, explain the purpose of the audit at the entry conference, explain the preliminary results of the audit at the closing conference, and, subject to certain exceptions, provide a copy of the final audit report to the importer within 120 days of the closing conference.

Customs has issued certain documents to the trade community to inform them of the compliance issues that Customs will review, called "Focused Assessments." Appendix I contains sample Internal Control and Electronic Data Processing

(*Text continues on page 385.*)

Figure 8–31. Notice of penalty.

U.S. Customs Service
610 S. Canal Street
Chicago, IL 60607-4523

FILE: ENF-4-02 PD:P
CASE NO:

Dear :

Consideration has been given to the prepenalty response submitted in the above referenced case number. The letter was submitted in response to a prepenalty notice issued to on , informing them that U. S. Customs was contemplating issuing a penalty for (level of culpability). The claim arose due to (facts of violation).

Based upon information in your prepenalty response, it has been determined that the facts indicate a finding that the violation occurred as a result of (culpability) on the part of __________. Exhibit A contains relevant information concerning the penalty action, i.e., specific details of the violation. Exhibit B represents the entries involved in this penalty action.

Pursuant to Section 171.12 of the Customs Regulations, your client has the right to submit a petition. The petition must be submitted within 30 days from the date of this letter. If payment or a petition is not submitted within the effective period, the matter will be referred to the Court of International Trade for the institution of judicial proceedings. If you have any questions in this matter, please contact ____________ of my staff at the above listed telephone number.

Sincerely,

Fines, Penalties & Forfeitures Officer

Enclosures

TRADITION ★ SERVICE ★ HONOR

(*continues*)

Figure 8–31. *(continued)*

DEPARTMENT OF THE TREASURY
UNITED STATES CUSTOMS SERVICE

NOTICE OF PENALTY OR LIQUIDATED DAMAGES INCURRED AND DEMAND FOR PAYMENT

19 USC 1618, 19 USC 1623

Case Number	
Port Name and Code	
Investigation File No.	

TO:

DEMAND IS HEREBY MADE FOR PAYMENT OF $ ____________, representing ☐ Penalties or ☐ Liquidated Damages assessed against you for violation or law or regulation, or breach of bond, as set forth below:

LAW OR REGULATION VIOLATED	BOND BREACHED

DESCRIPTION OF BOND (if any)	Form Number	Amount $	Date
Name and Address of Principal on Bond			
Name and Address of Surety on Bond			Surety Identification No.

If you feel there are extenuating circumstances, you have the right to object to the above action. Your petition should explain why you should not be penalized for the cited violation. Write the petition as a letter or in legal form; submit in (duplicate) (triplicate), addressed to the Commissioner of Customs, and forward to the FP&F Officer at

Unless the amount herein demanded is paid or a petition for relief is filed with the FP&F Officer within the indicated time limit, further action will be taken in connection with your bond or the matter will be referred to the United States Attorney.

TIME LIMIT FOR PAYMENT OR FILING PETITION FOR RELIEF (Days from the date of this Notice)

Signature	Title	Date
By		

Customs Form 5955A (08/00)

Questionnaires. Reviewing these documents will assist an importer in establishing proper importing procedures and compliance.

If, as a result of an audit, Customs assesses additional duties and penalties, the importer may file a protest and/or a petition for remission or mitigation.

EE. Prior Disclosure

An importer who has become aware that it has accidentally violated the customs laws or who determines that one of its employees intentionally violated the customs laws can utilize a procedure called "prior disclosure," which permits an importer to voluntarily tender the customs duties that were avoided and reduce the penalties it would otherwise have to pay if the Customs authorities discovered the violation themselves. If the violation was accidental, the only penalty is payment of interest in addition to the duties; if it was fraudulent, a penalty equal to the amount of the duties is payable. Nevertheless, these penalties are far lower than the ordinary penalties that can be assessed, including the full domestic value of the goods in the event of fraud.

In order to make a prior disclosure, information detailing the nature of the error, the entries affected by the error, the ports of entry, and the merchandise affected must be furnished to Customs before Customs commences any investigation. The duties must be paid in order to qualify for the reduced penalty.

FF. Court of International Trade

If the importer's protest is denied, the importer may appeal the decision of U.S. Customs and Border Protection to the Court of International Trade. It must file its "summons" and Information Statement with the Court of International Trade within 180 days following the denial of the protest (see Figures 8–32 and 8–33). All additional duties must also be paid. Within thirty days thereafter, the importer must file its complaint with the court. In the meantime, U.S. Customs and Border Protection will transmit all of the documents relating to the case to the Court of International Trade (see Figure 8–34). Electronic filing of documentation is required at the Court of International Trade today through the Case Management/Electronic Case Filing system.

GG. Appeals

Following the decision of the Court of International Trade, the importer may appeal to the U.S. Court of Appeals for the Federal Circuit in Washington, D.C. No special form is used to docket an appeal on a customs matter. The Notice of Appeal form must be filed within thirty days following the decision of the Court of International Trade. If the decision of the Court of Appeals is adverse to the importer, the importer may seek review by the U.S. Supreme Court via a petition for certiorari, but such petitions are not granted frequently.

(*Text continues on page 392.*)

Figure 8–32. Court of International Trade summons.

Form 1-1

UNITED STATES COURT OF INTERNATIONAL TRADE **FORM 1**

Plaintiff,
v.
UNITED STATES, **Defendant.**

SUMMONS
In Actions Under
28 U.S.C. § 1581 (a)

TO: The Attorney General and the Secretary of the Treasury:

PLEASE TAKE NOTICE that a civil action has been commenced pursuant to 28 U.S.C. § 1581(a) to contest denial of the protest specified below (and the protests listed in the attached schedule).

L. S.

Clerk of the Court

PROTEST

Port of Entry:	Date Protest Filed:
Protest Number:	Date Protest Denied:
Importer:	
Category of Merchandise:	

ENTRIES INVOLVED IN ABOVE PROTEST

Entry Number	Date of Entry	Date of Liquidation	Entry Number	Date of Entry	Date of Liquidation

District Director,

Address of Customs District in Which Protest was Denied

Name, Address and Telephone Number of Plaintiff's Attorney

Figure 8–32. *(continued)*

Form 1-2

CONTESTED ADMINISTRATIVE DECISION

Appraised Value of Merchandise		
	Statutory Basis	Statement of Value
Appraised:		
Protest Claim:		

Classification, Rate or Amount				
	Assessed		Protest Claim	
Merchandise	Paragraph or Item Number	Rate	Paragraph or Item Number	Rate

Other
State Specifically the Decision [as Described in 19 U.S.C. § 1514(a)] and the Protest Claim:

The issue which was common to all such denied protests:

Every denied protest included in this civil action was filed by the same above-named importer, or by an authorized person in the importer's behalf. The category of merchandise specified above was involved in each entry of merchandise included in every such denied protest. The issue or issues stated above were common to all such denied protests. All such protests were filed and denied as prescribed by law. All liquidated duties, charges or exactions have been paid, and were paid at the port of entry unless otherwise shown.

____
Signature of Plaintiff's Attorney

____
Date

Figure 8–32. *(continued)*

Form 1-3

SCHEDULE OF PROTESTS

____
Port of Entry

Protest Number	Date Protest Filed	Date Protest Denied	Entry Number	Date of Entry	Date of Liquidation

District Director of Customs,

If the port of entry shown above is different from the port of entry shown on the first page of the summons, the address of the District Director for such different port of entry must be given in the space provided.

Figure 8–33. Information Statement.

Form 5-1

FORM 5

UNITED STATES COURT OF INTERNATIONAL TRADE

INFORMATION STATEMENT

(Place an "X" in applicable [ ])

PLAINTIFF: ____________ **ATTORNEY** *(Name, Address, Telephone No.)*:	**PRECEDENCE** If the action is to be given precedence under Rule 3(g), indicate the applicable paragraph of that section: [ ] (1) [ ] (3) [ ] (5) [ ] (2) [ ] (4)

J U R I S D I C T I O N

28 U.S.C. § 1581(a) - Tariff Act of 1930, Section 515 - 19 U.S.C. § 1515

[ ] Appraisal [ ] Classification [ ] Charges or Exactions

[ ] Exclusion [ ] Liquidation [ ] Drawback

[ ] Refusal to Reliquidate [ ] Rate of Duty [ ] Redelivery

28 U.S.C. § 1581(b) - Tariff Act of 1930, Section 516 - 19 U.S.C. § 1516

[ ] Appraisal [ ] Classification [ ] Rate of Duty

28 U.S.C. § 1581(c) - Tariff Act of 1930, Section 516A(a)(1), (a)(2) or (a)(3) - 19 U.S.C. § 1516a *(Provide a brief description of the administrative determination you are contesting, including the relevant* ***Federal Register*** *citation(s) and the product(s) involved in the determination. For Section 516A(a)(1) or (a)(2), cite the specific subparagraph and clause of the section.)*

Subparagraph and Clause ____________ Agency____________

Federal Register Cite(s)____________

Product(s) ____________

28 U.S.C. § 1581(d) - Trade Act of 1974 - 19 U.S.C. §§ 2273, 2341, 2371

[ ] U.S. Secretary of Labor [ ] U.S. Secretary of Commerce

28 U.S.C. § 1581(e) - Trade Agreements Act of 1979, Section 305(b)(1) - 19 U.S.C. § 2515
(Provide a brief statement of the final determination to be reviewed.)

28 U.S.C. § 1581(f) - Tariff Act of 1930, Section 777(c)(2) - 19 U.S.C. § 1677f(c)(2)

Agency: [ ] U.S. International Trade Commission [ ] Administering Authority

28 U.S.C. § 1581(g) - Tariff Act of 1930, Section 641 - 19 U.S.C. § 1641 - or Section 499 - 19 U.S.C. § 1499

[ ] Sec. 641(b)(2) [ ] Sec. 641(b)(3) [ ] Sec. 641(c)(1) [ ] Sec. 641(b)(5)

[ ] Sec. 641(c)(2) [ ] Sec. 641(d)(2)(B) [ ] Sec. 499(b)

(Continued on reverse side)

(continues)

Figure 8–33. *(continued)*

Form 5-2

J U R I S D I C T I O N
(Continued)

28 U.S.C. § 1581(h) - Ruling relating to:

[ ] Classification	[ ] Valuation	[ ] Restricted Merchandise
[ ] Rate of Duty	[ ] Marking	[ ] Entry Requirements
[ ] Drawbacks	[ ] Vessel Repairs	[ ] Other: ________________

28 U.S.C. § 1581(i) - *(Cite any applicable statute and provide a brief statement describing jurisdictional basis.)*

28 U.S.C. § 1582 - Actions Commenced by the United States

[ ] (1) Recover civil penalty under Tariff Act of 1930:

[ ] Sec. 592	[ ] Sec. 593A	[ ] Sec. 641(b)(6)
[ ] Sec. 641(d)(2)(A)	[ ] Sec. 704(i)(2)	[ ] Sec. 734(i)(2)

[ ] (2) Recover upon a bond

[ ] (3) Recover customs duties

R E L A T E D   C A S E (S)

To your knowledge, does this action involve a common question of law or fact with any other action(s) previously decided or now pending?

	PLAINTIFF	COURT NUMBER	JUDGE
[ ] Decided:			
[ ] Pending:			

(Attach additional sheets, if necessary.)

(As amended, eff. Jan. 1, 1985; Jan. 25, 2000, eff. May 1, 2000.)

Figure 8–34. Transmittal to the Court of International Trade.

DEPARTMENT OF THE TREASURY
UNITED STATES CUSTOMS SERVICE

DISTRICT	
DATE	

Clerk of the Court
U.S. Court of International Trade
1 Federal Plaza
New York, NY 10007

Re: U.S. Court of International Trade (Summons)
No.

In compliance with Section 2635 of Title 28, United States Code, there are transmitted herewith a copy of the Protest(s) and Denial of Protest(s) required in connection with the above summons. There are also transmitted all the additional items required by that section, which have been found to exist for the above civil action, subject to the exceptions noted below. Any of the required items which are not herewith submitted or noted below do not exist for this civil action.

EXCEPTION(S)

PROTEST NUMBER	ENTRY NUMBER	EXPLANATION

DISTRICT DIRECTOR

cc: Assistant Chief Counsel

SUMMONS DOCUMENTATION TRANSMITTAL

Customs Form 322 (031684)

HH. Offers of Compromise

If Customs has assessed a penalty, the importer may make an offer of compromise addressed to the secretary of the treasury in Washington, D.C. While there is no guarantee that such an offer will be accepted, this is one avenue to resolve a customs penalty without the necessity of court proceedings or admission of guilt. Normally, such an offer would not be made until some later stage in the administrative process, for example, after denial of a protest, request for reliquidation, or the initiation of court proceedings.

II. ITC and Commerce Questionnaires

Another type of document that importers may see in the course of importation is a questionnaire sent to the importer by the International Trade Commission (ITC). The ITC has an investigatory or adjudicatory role under a number of different trade laws relating to the importation of merchandise. Sections 201 and 406 of the Trade Act of 1974 permit the ITC, with presidential approval, to assess additional customs duties or impose quotas when importation of merchandise has increased substantially and is injuring U.S. producers. Under Section 301 of the Trade Act of 1974, the ITC can impose similar sanctions when a foreign government is unjustifiably or unreasonably burdening U.S. export commerce. Under the antidumping and countervailing duty laws, the ITC seeks to determine the quantity of imports, prices, and whether U.S. manufacturers have been injured by imported products. Under Section 337 of the Tariff Act, the ITC may impose restrictions on the import of merchandise if it determines that there have been unfair practices in the import trade, such as patent infringement. Under Section 332, the ITC may conduct general investigations simply to determine the quantity of imports, and changes in import trends, and to advise Congress on appropriate legislation to regulate international trade. In all of these investigations, the ITC normally issues lengthy (sometimes fifty- or sixty-page) questionnaires to importers. Under these laws, the importers are required to respond to the questionnaires; however, the ITC will normally grant an extension of time if the importer needs it.

The Department of Commerce conducts national security investigations under Section 232 of the Trade Act of 1974 to determine whether U.S. national security is being endangered by overdependence on foreign products.

Part IV

Specialized Exporting and Importing

Chapter 9

Specialized Exporting and Importing

The transactions described in this part are distinguished by the fact that they involve a combination of both exporting and importing. Several such transactions are described in this chapter.

A. Drawback

Drawback is a program administered by U.S. Customs and Border Protection that permits a refund of 99 percent of the U.S. customs duties paid on merchandise that has been imported into the United States and is thereafter exported (certain duties, such as antidumping duties, are not eligible for drawback). In order to claim the refund, Customs must be able to trace that the merchandise was actually imported and then exported. Several types of drawback programs exist.

The first is called manufacturing drawback. Under this program, merchandise may be imported by a manufacturer and used as a raw material or component in manufacturing a finished product, which is then exported. This is known as direct identification manufacturing drawback. In order to encourage U.S. manufacturers to use U.S.-origin raw materials and components, Congress has provided for substitution drawback. In this type of drawback, the U.S. manufacturer that imports a foreign-origin raw material or component and then decides instead to substitute a U.S.-origin raw material or component of the *same kind and quality* in the manufacturing process can also claim a refund of duties on the imported raw materials or components that were not used. Under the North American Free Trade Agreement, beginning January 1, 1996, on exports to Canada and January 1, 2001, on exports to Mexico, the amount of direct identification drawback will be limited to the lower of the amount of duties paid at the time of importation to the United States or the amount of duties paid on the exported goods when imported into Canada or Mexico. Substitution drawback on such exports was eliminated as of January 1, 1994. In both types of manufacturing drawback, the manufacturer must maintain records showing the amount of waste in the manufacturing process. The manufacturer must also maintain records from which the utilization of raw materials or components in the manufacture of the finished product can be verified for a period of three years from the date of payment of the drawback claim or five years from the date of importation, whichever is longer. The manufacturer must have applied for and obtained an importer's identification number and must apply for a drawback contract. In order to meet the needs of most manufacturers, Customs has issued general drawback offers, specifying the terms and conditions under which the manufacturing must take place. The manufacturer must file an acceptance of the offer that contains certain information and undertakings. Where the manufacturer's case is unusual or does not fit the general drawback offer, the manufacturer must apply for and enter into a specific drawback contract with U.S. Customs and Border Protection.

Anytime within three years after exportation, the exporter can file its Drawback Entry (see Figure 9–1), along with evidence of exportation, which is a claim for the refund. The merchandise for which a refund is being sought must have been imported within five years prior to the filing of the claim (for substitution manufacturing drawback, the exported merchandise also must have been produced within three years from the time the manufacturer received the imported merchandise). Where the manufacturer is the exporter of the imported articles, the manufacturer files the Drawback Entry. However, where the exporter is not the manufacturer, the exporter must obtain a Delivery Certificate (see Figure 9–2) from the importer and each intermediate transferee and file it with the Drawback Entry. It should be noted that the exporter is the one who is entitled to the refund of the duties, not the importer (unless the exporter has expressly assigned its right to the importer). Congress assumes that the exporter paid the customs duties as part of the price when it purchased the merchandise from the importer.

The second type of drawback is the same condition drawback. Essentially, there are two types of same condition drawback: merchandise that is unused and merchandise that has been rejected by the importer. Unused drawback arises when an article has been imported into the United States but is exported without being "used"; that is, the imported article has not been processed into a new and different article having a distinctive name, character, or use and has not been processed in a manner that has made it fit for a particular use (direct unused merchandise drawback), such as when a U.S. importer sells the articles to another country. Alternatively, the importer can substitute commercially interchangeable merchandise and export that merchandise (substitution unused merchandise drawback). If the exporter is not the importer, the exporter must file Delivery Certificates with its Drawback Entry. At least two days prior to export (seven days if the exporter intends to destroy the merchandise under Customs' supervision), the exporter must file the Notice of Intent to Export with Customs (see Figure 9–3). Customs will either examine the merchandise prior to export or waive examination. Exportation must occur within three years after importation.

The second kind of same condition drawback is rejected merchandise. This arises when the buyer/importer receives merchandise from a foreign supplier that does not conform to sample or specifications, is defective at the time of import, or was shipped without the consent of the consignee. Rejected merchandise must be returned to Customs' custody within three years of import. If the exporter was not the importer, the exporter must submit a statement signed by the importer and every

(*Text continues on page 402.*)

Figure 9–1. Drawback Entry.

DEPARTMENT OF HOMELAND SECURITY
U.S. Customs and Border Protection

DRAWBACK ENTRY
19 CFR 191

PAPERWORK REDUCTION ACT NOTICE: This request is in accordance with the Paperwork Reduction Act. We ask for the information in order to carry out U.S. Department of Homeland Security laws and regulations, to determine the eligibility for refund of taxes on domestic alcohol (if applicable), and to determine the proper amount of drawback. Your response is required to obtain or retain a benefit. The estimated average burden associated with this collection of information is 35 minutes per respondent depending on individual circumstances. Comments concerning the accuracy of this burden estimates and suggestions for reducing this burden should be directed to U.S. Customs and Border Protection, Asset Management, Washington, DC 20229, and to the Office of Management and Budget, Paperwork Reduction Project (1651-0075) Washington, DC 20503.

Section I - Claim Header — OMB No. 1651-0075 Expires 10/31/2011

1. Drawback Entry Number	2. Entry Type Code	3. Port Code	4. Surety Code	5. Bond Type
6. Claimant ID Number	7. Broker ID Number (CBP 4811)	8. DBK Ruling Number	9. Duty Claimed	

10. Puerto Rico Claimed	11. HMF Claimed	12. MPF Claimed	13. Other Taxes/Fees Claimed	14. Total Drawback Claimed	15. Total I.R. Tax Claimed

16. Method of Filing ☐ ABI ☐ Manual ☐ Disk
17. NAFTA DBK ☐ Yes ☐ No
18. Privilege Authorized ☐ Accelerated Payment ☐ WPN
19. Drawback Statutory Provision
20. Name and Address of Claimant
21. Contact Name, Address, E-mail, Phone & Fax Numbers of Preparer

Section II - Imported Duty Paid, Designated Merchandise or Drawback Product

22. Import Entry Or CM&D Numbers (List Once in Chronological Order)	23. Port Code	24. Import Date	25. CD	26. (If using 1313(b)) A. Date(s) Received	B. Date(s) Used	27. HTSUS No.	28. Description of Merchandise (Include Part/Style/Serial Numbers)	29. Quantity & Unit of Measure	30. Entered Value Per Unit	31. Duty Rate	32. 99% Duty
										33. Total	

34. STATUS - The Import entries as listed on this form are subject to:
(Must be identified on claim or coding sheet)

☐ Reconciliation ☐ 19 USC 1514, Protest
☐ 19 USC 1520 (c)(1) ☐ 19 USC 1520 (d)

DATE RECEIVED

CBP USE ONLY

Class Code	Accelerated	Liquidated	Bill/Refund
364 Duty			
365 Excise Tax			
369 Puerto Rico			
398 HMF			
399 MPF			
____ Other Tax or Fee			
Total Drawback Claimed			

INTERNAL CONTROL REVIEW
Date ________ DS Number ________ ☐ IC OK
Reason ☐ 21 ☐ 23 ☐ 24 ☐ 25 ☐ 26 | Specialist Code

CBP Form 7551 (07/08)

Figure 9–1. *(continued)*

Section III - Manufactured Articles

35. Quantity & Description of Merchandise Used	36. Date(s) of Manufacture or Production	37. Description of Articles Manufactured or Produced	38. Quantity and Unit of Measure	39. Factory Location

Section IV - Information on Exported or Destroyed Merchandise

PERIOD COVERED ________ TO ________

40. Exhibits to be attached for the following:

☐ Relative Value ☐ Petroleum ☐ Domestic Tax Paid Alcohol ☐ Piece Goods ☐ Waste Calculation ☐ Recycled ☐ Harbor Maintenance Fee ☐ Merchandise Processing Fee ☐ Other Taxes/Fees

41. Date (MM/DD/YYYY)	42. Action Code	43. Unique Indentifier No.	44. Name of Exporter/Destroyer	45. Description of Articles (Include Part/Style/Serial Numbers)	46. Quantity and Unit of Measure	47. Export Destination	48. HTSUS No.

Section V - Declarations

☐ Same condition to NAFTA countries - The undersigned herein certifies that the merchandise herein described is in the same condition as when it was imported under above import entry(ies) and further certifies that this merchandise was not subjected to any process of manufacturer or other operation except the following allowable operations: ________

☐ The undersigned hereby certifies that the merchandise herein described is unused in the United States and further certifies that this merchandise was not subjected to any process of manufacture or other operation except the following allowable operations: ________

☐ The undersigned hereby certifies that the merchandise herein described is commercially interchangeable with the designated imported merchandise and further certifies that the substituted merchandise is unused in the United States and that the substituted merchandise was in our possession prior to exportation or destruction.

☐ Merchandise does not conform to sample or specifications. ☐ Merchandise was defective at time of importation. ☐ Merchandise was shipped without consent of the consignee.

☐ The undersigned hereby certifies that the merchandise herein described is the same kind and quality as defined in 19 U.S.C. 1313(p)(3)(B), with the designated imported merchandise or the article manufactured or produced under 1313(a) or (b), as appropriate.

☐ The article(s) described above were manufactured or produced and disposed of as stated herein in accordance with the drawback ruling on file with CBP and in compliance with applicable laws and regulations.

The undersigned acknowledges statutory requirements that all records supporting the information on this document are to be retained by the issuing party for a period of three years from the date of payment of the drawback claim. The undersigned is fully aware of the sanctions provided in 18 U.S.C. 1001 and 18 U.S.C. 550 and 19 U.S.C. 1593a.

I declare that according to the best of my knowledge and belief, all of the statements in this document are correct and that the exported article is not to be relanded in the United States or any of its possessions without paying duty.

☐ Member of Firm with Power of Attorney ☐ Officer of Corporation ☐ Broker with Power of Attorney

Printed Name and Title	Signature and Date

CBP Form 7551 (07/08)

Figure 9–2. Delivery Certificate.

OMB 1651-0075 Exp. 10/31/2011

DEPARTMENT OF HOMELAND SECURITY
U.S. Customs and Border Protection

DELIVERY CERTIFICATE FOR PURPOSES OF DRAWBACK

19 CFR 191

PAPERWORK REDUCTION ACT NOTICE: This request is in accordance with the Paperwork Reduction Act. We ask for the information in order to carry out U.S. Department of Homeland Security laws and regulations, to determine the eligibility for refund of taxes on domestic alcohol (if applicable), and to determine the proper amount of drawback. Your response is required to obtain or retain a benefit. The estimated average burden associated with this collection of information is 33 minutes per respondent depending on individual circumstances. Comments concerning the accuracy of this burden estimate and suggestions for reducing this burden should be directed to U.S. Customs and Border Protection, Asset Management, Washington, DC 20229, and to the Office of Management and Budget, Paperwork Reduction Project (1651-0075) Washington, DC 20503.

☐ Certificate of Delivery

☐ Certificate of Manufacture and Delivery

1. CM&D No.	2. Port Code	3. DBK Ruling No.
4. Type Code	5. ID No. of Transferor	

6. FROM TRANSFEROR: Company Name and Complete Address	7. TO TRANSFEREE: Company Name and Complete Address	RECEIVED DATE

IMPORTED DUTY PAID, DESIGNATED MERCHANDISE OR DRAWBACK PRODUCT

8. Use	9. Import Entry or CM&D Number	10. Port Code	11. Import Date (MM/DD/YYYY)	12. CD	13. (If using 1313(b)) A. Date(s) Received	13. B. Date(s) Used	14. Date Delivered	15. HTSUS No.	16. Description of Merchandise (Include Part/Style/Serial Numbers)	17. Quantity & Unit of Measure	18. Entered Value Per Unit	19. 100% Duty

21. Contact Name and Address	PREPARER Phone Number ______ Ext. ______ FAX Number ______		20. **Total**

CBP Form 7552 (07/08)

Figure 9–2. *(continued)*

22. Quantity & Description of Merchandise Used	23. Date(s) of Manufacture (MM/DD/YYYY)	24. Description of Articles Manufactured or Produced (Include Part/Style/Serial Numbers)	25. Quantity & Unit of Measure	26. Date Delivered

27. Duty Available on Manufacture Articles (Total of Duties in Block 20)	28. Drawback Available Per Unit of Measure on Manufactured Article	29. Factory Location

30. Exhibits to be attached for the following:
☐ Relative Value ☐ Petroleum ☐ Domestic Tax Paid Alcohol ☐ Piece Goods ☐ Waste Calculation ☐ Recycled ☐ Harbor Maintenance Fee ☐ Merchandise Processing Fee ☐ Other Taxes/Fees

31. STATUS - Import Entries listed on this form are subject to (If CD, identify on this form; if CM&D, identify on coding sheet):
☐ Reconciliation ☐ 19 USC 1514, Protest ☐ 19 USC 1520 (c)(1) ☐ 19 USC 1520 (d)

DECLARATIONS

☐ The merchandise transferred on this CD is the imported merchandise.

☐ The merchandise transferred on this CD is pursuant to 19 U.S.C. 1313(j)(2) and will not be designated for any other Drawback purposes.

☐ The article(s) described above were manufactured or produced and delivered as stated herein in accordance with the Drawback ruling on file with CBP and in compliance with applicable laws and regulations.

☐ This Certificate of Delivery is a subsequent transfer and the merchandise is the same as received.

The undersigned acknowledges statutory requirements that all records supporting the information on this document are to be retained by the issuing party for a period of three years from the date of payment of the related drawback entry.

Assignment of Rights is transferred when this form is prepared as a CD or CM&D.

I declare that according to the best of my knowledge and belief, all of the statements in this document are correct and I am fully aware of the sanctions provided in18 U.S.C.1001 and 18 U.S.C. 550 and 19 U.S.C. 1593a.

☐ Member of Firm with Power of Attorney ☐ Officer of Corporation ☐ Broker with Power of Attorney

Printed Name and Title	Signature and Date

CBP Form 7552 (07/08)

Figure 9–3. Notice of Intent to Export.

OMB No. 1651-0075 Exp. 10/31/2011

DEPARTMENT OF HOMELAND SECURITY
U.S. Customs and Border Protection

NOTICE OF INTENT TO EXPORT, DESTROY OR RETURN MERCHANDISE FOR PURPOSES OF DRAWBACK
19 CFR 191

PAPERWORK REDUCTION ACT NOTICE: This request is in accordance with the Paperwork Reduction Act. We ask for the information in order to enforce the laws of the United States, to fulfill the U.S. Customs Regulations, to ensure that the claimant is entitled to drawback, and to have the necessary information which permits CBP to calculate and refund (or increase) the correct amount of duty and/or tax. Your response is required to obtain a benefit. The estimated average burden associated with this collection of information is 33 minutes per respondent depending on individual circumstances. Comments concerning the accuracy of this burden estimate and suggestions for reducing this burden should be directed to U.S. Customs and Border Protection, Asset Management, Washington, DC 20229, and to the Office of Management and Budget, Paperwork Reduction Project (1651-0075) Washington, DC 20503.

1. Exporter or Destroyer
Name ____
Address ____
____
I.D. Number ____

2. Drawback Entry No.

3. Intended Action ☐ Export ☐ Destroy

4. Intended Date of Action (MM/DD/YYYY)

5. Drawback Center

6. Contact Name ____
Address ____
____
Phone ____ Ext. ____
FAX ____

DATE RECEIVED

7. Location of Merchandise	8. Method of Destruction	9. Location of Destruction	10. Exporting Carrier Name (if known)	11. Intended Port of Export	12. Unique Identifier No.
				13. T & E No.	14. Country of Ultimate Destination

15. Import Entry No.	16. Description of Merchandise (Include Part/Style/Serial Numbers)	17. Drawback Amount	18. Quantity & Unit of Measure
			19. HTSUS No./Schedule B

20. Drawback to be filled as:

☐ Unused Merchandise Drawback ☐ J1 ☐ J2
☐ Manufacturing Drawback
☐ Same Condition Drawback under NAFTA
☐ Distilled Spirits, Wine or Beer under 26 U.S.C. 5062 (c)
☐ Rejected Merchandise
☐ Shipped without Consent
☐ Defective at Time of Importation
☐ Not Conforming to Sample or Specifications

21. Preparer
____ Printed Name X ____ Signature ____ Title ____ Date

THIS FORM MUST BE SUBMITTED WITH THE DRAWBACK CLAIM

CBP USE ONLY

22. Examination ☐ Required **or** ☐ Waived (Additional information may be required if exam requested, T & E may be required)

23. Present Merchandise to CBP at:

24. Destruction to be Witnessed by Customs ☐ Yes ☐ No

25. Printed Name ____
Phone Number ____

26. Signature & Badge No.
X

27. Date

28. Port

29. Comments/Results of Examination or Witnessing of Destruction. (Merchandise matches invoice description)

30. Date Destroyed or Exam Conducted

31. Printed Name of Examining Officer ____
Phone Number ____ Ext ____

32. Signature & Badge No.
X ____ Date

CBP Form 7553 (07/08)

other intermediate owner that no other claim for drawback was made on the goods. The Notice of Intent to Export must be submitted to U.S. Customs at least five working days prior to the intended return to Customs' custody (seven days if the exporter intends to destroy the merchandise). Customs will examine the merchandise or waive examination. In some situations, rejected merchandise may also qualify for an unused merchandise drawback claim. When an importer has established some history of drawback claims, the importer may apply for the accelerated drawback payment program. The importer must file the application with the information required by the regulations, including a description of the claimant's drawback compliance program, procedures, and controls. The exporter must post a customs bond to guarantee a refund of any overpayments made by Customs to the exporter in an amount equal to the estimated amount of the drawback to be claimed during the term of the bond (usually twelve months). When the exporter has qualified for the accelerated program, it may obtain payment of drawback claims as soon as three weeks after filing the claim electronically or three months if filed manually. The exporter may also obtain a Waiver of Prior Notice agreement with U.S. Customs and Border Protection to allow it to export without the prior notice requirement. There are drawback penalties for failure to follow the guidelines of the contract between Customs and the drawback claimant and for failing to maintain records.

B. Foreign Processing and Assembly Operations

In some circumstances, U.S. companies may wish to export U.S.-origin products to foreign countries, such as Mexico, for further manufacture, processing, or assembly, and then re-import the resulting products into the United States. Ordinarily, the products when imported to the United States would be subject to U.S. Customs duties on the full value of the product, notwithstanding the fact that part of the value of the product was originally U.S.-origin products exported to that country. There are three exceptions to the general rule.

First, when goods that were originally the product of the United States (not imported) are exported, and then re-imported without having been advanced in value or improved in condition by any process of manufacture or other means while abroad, and the U.S. importer certifies that no drawback was claimed when the goods were exported, then the goods can be imported into the United States without payment of duty (under classification 9801.00.10 of the HTS). (A sample Foreign Shipper's Declaration and Importer's Endorsement is shown in Figure 9–4.)

Second, when the exporter exported merchandise for alteration, repair, use abroad, replacement, or processing, thereafter, when the goods are imported (under 9802.00.40 or 9802.00.50 of the HTS), they will not be subject to U.S. Customs duties except that duties will be assessed on the cost or value of the alterations, repairs, or processing. (A sample declaration is shown in Figure 9–5.)

Finally, an exporter who intends to export U.S.-origin commodities, assemble them abroad, and import the finished product may qualify for reduced duty under classification 9802.00.80 of the HTS. This provision, previously known as classification 807 of

(*Text continues on page 405.*)

Figure 9–4. Foreign Shipper's Declaration and Importer's Endorsement.

FOREIGN SHIPPER'S DECLARATION AND IMPORTER'S ENDORSEMENT
(U.S. Goods Returned - HS 9801.00.10)

I, ________________, declare that to the best of my knowledge and belief the articles herein specified were exported from the United States, from the port of _____________ on or about __________, 19__, and that they are returned without having been advanced in value or improved in condition by any process of manufacture or other means.

Marks	Number	Quantity	Description	Value, in U.S. coin
	________	________	____________	____________
	________	________	____________	____________
	________	________	____________	____________
	________	________	____________	____________

______________________ (Date)

______________________ (Address)

______________________ (Signature)

______________________ (Capacity)

I, ______________, declare that the above declaration by the foreign shipper is true and correct to the best of my knowledge and belief, that the articles were manufactured by ______ ________ (name of manufacturer) located in _______________ (city and state), that the articles were not manufactured or produced in the United States under subheading 9813.00.05, HTSUS, and that the articles were exported from the United States without benefit of drawback.

______________________ (Date)

______________________ (Address)

______________________ (Signature)

______________________ (Capacity)

Figure 9–5. Foreign Repairer's Declaration and Importer's Endorsement.

FOREIGN REPAIRER'S DECLARATION AND IMPORTER'S ENDORSEMENT
(Repairs and Alterations - HS 9802.00.40 and 9802.00.50)

I, __________________, declare that the articles herein specified are the articles which, in the condition in which they were exported from the United States, were received by me (us) on __________, 19____, from ______________ (name and address of owner or exporter in the United States); that they were received by me (us) for the sole purpose of being repaired or altered; that only the repairs or alterations described below were performed by me (us); that the full cost or (when no charge is made) value of such repairs or alterations are correctly stated below; and that no substitution whatever has been made to replace any of the articles originally received by me (us) from the owner or exporter thereof mentioned above.

Marks and numbers	Description of articles and of repairs or alterations	Full cost or (when no charge is made) value of repairs or alterations (see subchapter II, chapter 98, HTSUS)	Total value of articles after repairs or alterations

_______________ (Date)

_______________ (Signature)

_______________ (Address)

_______________ (Capacity)

I, ______________, declare that the (above) (attached) declaration by the person who performed the repairs or alterations abroad is true and correct to the best of my knowledge and belief; that the articles were not manufactured or produced in the United States under subheading 9813.00.05 HTSUS; that such articles were exported from the United States for repairs or alterations and without benefit of drawback from ______________________ (port) on _______, 19___; and that the articles entered in their repaired or altered condition are the same articles that were exported on the above date and that are identified in the (above) (attached) declaration.

_______________ (Date)

_______________ (Signature)

_______________ (Address)

_______________ (Capacity)

the Tariff Schedules of the United States, permits only assembly operations; manufacturing operations are prohibited. Since this is a point of importance, 807 operations should be discussed with and approved by Customs in advance. Sometimes Customs rulings are necessary. If the operation qualifies as an assembly operation, the imported finished article is dutiable on the full value of the article reduced by the value of the U.S.-origin parts or components. The person or entity performing the assembly operations must file a Foreign Assembler's Declaration, and any unreported change in the operation or a false declaration can lead to serious customs penalties. A sample Foreign Assembler's Declaration is shown in Figure 9–6. Customs must be notified of any variation in the assembly operation of more than 5 percent of the total cost or value. Where cost data is estimated or standard costs are being used at the time of entry, that must be stated on the entry; liquidation of the entry must be suspended, and actual cost data must be submitted as soon as accounting procedures permit. This is submitted via the "reconciliation" procedure (see Chapter 8, Section M). 807 treatment is not available on foreign-origin components imported into the United States and then exported for assembly, unless the foreign components were subjected to additional processing in the United States, resulting in a substantial transformation into a new and different article of commerce, and the imported components were not imported under a temporary importation bond. Foreign-origin components can be used in the assembly process; however, no reduction of U.S. duties is allowed for their value. Articles assembled abroad are considered to be a product of the country of assembly for country of origin marking requirements.

When U.S.-origin commodities are exported to foreign countries and further processed, if the country of processing is a beneficiary country under the Generalized System of Preferences (or the Caribbean Basin Initiative) and at least 35 percent of the value is added in the foreign country, the foreign country becomes the new country of origin, and importation of the articles to the United States may be made duty-free.

Due to the low labor rates and the close proximity to the U.S. market, many U.S. and foreign companies have established assembly or processing operations under Mexican law. Mexican law provides for the equivalent of temporary importations under bond that permit the U.S.-origin raw materials or components to be brought into Mexico, assembled or further processed, and then exported to the United States without payment of Mexican customs duties. In order to establish a successful *maquiladora* operation, it is necessary to comply with both Mexican and U.S. Customs requirements. Otherwise, the full value of the articles can be dutiable both in Mexico and in the United States. Under the North American Free Trade Agreement, beginning January 1, 2001, the duty-free treatment of raw materials or components was eliminated and they became dutiable at the regular duty rate or the lower duty rate applicable to products meeting the eligibility rules of NAFTA.

The original *maquila* program required all manufactured goods to be exported to the United States. Later the PITEX program was developed to allow for the same benefits of the *maquiladora* for the manufacturers making sales into the Mexican market as well. In 2006, the "Decree on the Promotion of the Manufacturing and In-Bond Assembly Industry and Export Services" (IMMEX) was published by the Mexican government in its efforts to introduce efficiency into the *maquila* and PITEX programs by combining the two. There is still a requirement of exports at least US$500,000

Figure 9–6. Foreign Assembler's Declaration.

FOREIGN ASSEMBLER'S DECLARATION

I, ______________________________, declare that to the best of my knowledge and belief the ____________________________ were assembled in whole or in part from fabricated components listed and described below, which are products in the United States:

Marks of identification, numbers	Description of component	Quality	Unit value at time and place of export from United States	Port and date of export from United States	Name and address of manufacturer

____

Date Signature

____

Address Capacity

U.S. IMPORTER'S ENDORSEMENT

I declare that to the best of my knowledge and belief the (above), (attached) declaration, and any other information submitted herewith, or otherwise supplied or referred to, is correct in every respect and there has been compliance with all pertinent legal notes to the Harmonized Tariff Schedule of the United States (19 U.S.C. 1202).

____

Date Signature

____

Address Capacity

or 10 percent of the total sales, although this requirement is a violation of NAFTA. Companies wishing to use the services of an IMMEX should discuss the full ramifications under both Mexican and U.S. regulations before beginning operations.

C. Plant Construction Contracts

Sometimes an exporter will be a person who has contracted with a foreign purchaser to build an entire plant, sometimes pursuant to a turnkey contract. In such cases, thousands of items may be exported, and all of the many considerations discussed in Part II on exporting will be applicable. However, one significant provision in the export control laws is the availability of a special project license from the U.S. Department of Commerce, Office of Export Licensing, where some of the items being exported require individual validated licenses for export. By applying for a project license, the exporter can obtain a blanket license covering all of the items, thereby substantially reducing the effort required to obtain individual validated licenses for each product exported.

D. Barter and Countertrade Transactions

Presently in international trade, an exporter may be asked to accept payment in merchandise rather than cash (barter). Moreover, in other situations, such as compensation arrangements or switch transactions, both export and import transactions may be involved. Such transactions give rise to unique documentation and procedural problems. First, the U.S. company having a role in such a transaction should not try to use its standard-form sales or purchase documents. These transactions require special terms and conditions to protect the participant and should be specifically tailored to the transaction. Second, even though no money will change hands, the parties should value the merchandise or services that will be exchanged. This will be necessary for tax, customs, and foreign exchange control purposes. U.S. Customs and Border Protection recommends that the parties seek an advance ruling. In most countries, attempts to engage in barter transactions for the purpose of avoiding these laws will subject the participants to prosecution for evasion. Correlatively, the participant should satisfy itself that all necessary government notifications and forms are filed, just as if it were a cash transaction, and that all values stated are accurate, consistent, and supportable.

Appendix A
Exporter Assistance

EXPORT.GOV

Helping U.S. Companies Export

Export Basics Home

Are you ready to make international sales? *Export Basics* helps you assess your export readiness, understand what you need to know and consider before pursuing an international sales strategy, and, when you are ready, develop and implement your export strategy.

The subsequent sections of *Export Basics* (see navigation to the right) — starting with *Develop Your Export Plan* — will help you develop and implement your export plan. Each section corresponds to the key components of an effective export plan — posing questions you should answer to complete your plan and providing resources to help you answer those questions.

Export University 101

Export University 101 is a webinar that presents basic information on exporting, including:

- organizational and product readiness,
- market research,
- guidance for developing your strategy and marketing plan,
- promoting your products in target market, and
- complying with US and foreign regulations.

It presents useful methods and strategies to help you export your products successfully abroad.

Start here!

- Agricultural Exporters Click Here
- Take our Are you Export Ready? online readiness assessment to find out if you're ready to pursue international sales.
- Need an introduction to exporting? Browse our step-by-step Basic Guide to Exporting.
- Watch our Are You Ready? and Going Beyond Borders videos to hear a U.S. Commercial Officer talk about issues you should consider before going global and to hear from companies that have worked with the U.S. Commercial Service to make international sales.
- Think export success is out of your reach? Read success stories about how companies like yours are succeeding in the international marketplace.

Stuck? Speak with a trade specialist at 1-800-USA-TRADE.

Frequently Asked Questions

Go! If you are ready to begin developing your export plan, please proceed onto the next section, Develop Your Export Plan

EXPORT.GOV

Helping U.S. Companies Export

FREQUENTLY ASKED QUESTIONS AND ANSWERS

I. Getting Started

- What is the Trade Information Center (TIC)? How do I get export assistance?
- What should I consider when making the decision to begin exporting and how do I begin?
- Are there sources of legal assistance for people who are new to exporting?
- How can I find export financing?

II. Market Research

- How do I obtain market research for a specific country or product?
- Where can I obtain information on foreign markets and trade opportunities for fish and agricultural products?
- Does the U.S. Federal Government have any programs to help advertise my products overseas?
- Where can I find trade statistics?
- How can I find out about investment practices in a certain country?

III. Trade Leads / Company Information

- Does the Trade Information Center have lists of company-specific information?
- How do I locate trade leads for my exporting business? How do I locate potential distributors in overseas markets?
- Where can I find a list of foreign companies in a particular industry or sector?
- How do I find information about a particular overseas company?

IV. Documentation / Regulations / Standards

- How can I receive information on foreign regulations, standards, or certification requirements for my product?
- Is there a tariff (duty) that applies to my product in a foreign country?
- What is a Harmonized System (HS) classification number, the Schedule B number, and is there a difference between the two numbers?
- Do I need an export license to ship my product to a particular market? How do I obtain a license?
- Where can I find information on trade sanctions?
- Is the NAFTA Certificate of Origin required for shipments to Mexico and Canada?

V. Other

- How can I obtain information about importing products into the United States?

For More Information:

The Trade Information Center

International Trade Administration

U.S. Department of Commerce

1401 Constitution Ave., NW

Mail Stop R-TIC

Washington, DC 20230

Tel: 1-800-USA-TRAD(E) (1-800-872-8723)

Fax: (202) 482-4473

EXPORT.GOV

Helping U.S. Companies Export

Market Research

Plan your market entry the right way – use market research to learn your product's potential in a given market, the best prospects for success, and the market's business practices before you first export.

If you're just beginning to sell internationally, narrow your focus by concentrating on no more than *two* or *three* best-prospect markets. Use our Step-by-Step research guidelines to get started.

Market Research

Access the U.S. Commercial Service Market Research Library containing more than 100,000 industry and country-specific market reports, authored by our specialists working in overseas posts.

The Library Includes:

- Country Commercial Guides
- Industry Overviews*
- Market Updates*
- Multilateral Development Bank Reports*
- Best Markets*
- Industry/Regional Reports*

Agricultural Goods Market Research Reports

Market research, crop reports, export statistics, and the National Agricultural Library -- all focusing on exporters of agricultural goods and commodities. Market reports on processed and finished agricultural products can also be found in the "Country and Industry Market Reports" above.

** These market research reports are available only to U.S. companies that are registered with Export.gov. Register above to get access.*

EXPORT.GOV

Helping U.S. Companies Export

International Sales & Marketing

"Your international business partner"

Leverage the knowledge and influence of the U.S. government and our vast global network of international business experts, contacts and partners.

With offices in more than 100 U.S. cities and 80 countries across the globe, the U.S. government offers U.S. companies exporting information, advice and cost-effective end-to-end international business solutions.

Whether you are new to international sales, trying to enter a new market or looking to expand your business in a specific market here is how we can help you:

For U.S. Companies:

- Information and Counseling - access online resources and get personalized counseling
- Strategy and Planning - develop and improve your international business strategy
- Market Research and Due Diligence - target the best international markets and evaluate potential overseas business partners
- Advertising and Promotional Events - increase your brand awareness and market exposure in countries around the world
- Market Entry and Expansion - find and establish relationships with potential overseas business partners
- Advocacy and Dispute Resolution - get help competing for foreign government contracts and settling payment disputes

For U.S. Trade Show Organizers:

- Attract foreign buyers to your trade show
- Get U.S. Government support and certification for your trade show

EXPORT.GOV

Helping U.S. Companies Export

International Finance

Become familiar with the various government programs designed to help your company finance its export transactions, and give it the capital to carry out its export operations.

We recommend that you review this information and then contact your local Commercial Service Trade Specialists to discuss how these programs can help you achieve your international sales goals.

Financing

Do you need working capital loans? Does your foreign buyer need financing to buy your products? Do they prefer lease financing? Check out the U.S. Government International Financing Programs.

Insurance

The U.S. Government offers U.S. companies Insurance and Risk Mitigation policies that cover export transactions and for overseas investments. Coverage includes losses for non-payment, currency inconvertibility, asset expropriation and political violence.

Grants

The U.S. Government provides grants to U.S. firms to conduct feasibility studies on infrastructure projects and to train the foreign business community and government officials on U.S. business practices, regulatory reform and other economic development activities.

Appendix B
International Sales Agreement (Export)

FORM

AGREEMENT made January 4, 1982, between Panoramic Export Company, Inc., a New York corporation having its principal place of business at 71 West 42d Street, New York, New York (the "Seller"), and Miguel Vellos, of 31 Avenida de Cortez, Lima, Peru (the "Purchaser").

1. *Sale.* The Seller shall cause to be manufactured, and shall sell and deliver to the Purchaser certain machinery and equipment (the "goods"), to be manufactured specially for the Purchaser by Rollo Manufacturing Company (the "Manufacturer"), at the Manufacturer's plant in Detroit, Michigan, according to the specifications appearing in Exhibit A annexed.

2. *Price.* The purchase price shall be $1,857.60 F.O.B. mill, freight prepaid to New Orleans, Louisiana, payable in currency of the United States of America. The term "F.O.B. mill" means delivery free on board cars at the Manufacturer's works.

3. *Payment.* The terms are net cash on presentation of invoice and inland bill of lading to bankers approved by the Seller, with whom credit in favor of the Seller for the full amount of the purchase price is to be established forthwith. This credit shall be confirmed to the Seller by the bankers, and shall remain in full force until this contract shall have been completely performed. Delay by the Purchaser in establishing this credit shall extend the time for the performance of this contract by the Seller to such extent as may be necessary to enable it to make delivery in the exercise of reasonable diligence after such credit has been established; or, at the Seller's option, such delay may be treated by the Seller as a wrongful termination of this contract on the part of the Purchaser.

4. *Delivery.* The Seller shall notify the Purchaser when the goods are ready for shipment. Thereupon the Purchaser shall furnish shipping instructions to the Seller, stating the date of shipment, the carrier, and the routing. The

Purchaser shall be entitled to select any routing officially authorized and published by the transportation companies, provided that the Seller may change the routing if inability to secure cars promptly, or other reasons, would involve delay in forwarding the goods over the route selected by the Purchaser. The Seller shall not be required to ship the goods until it has received shipping instructions from the Purchaser. If the Purchaser fails to furnish shipping instructions promptly, so as to enable the Seller to perform this contract in accordance with its terms, the Seller may, at its option, and in addition to all other rights it may possess, cancel such portion of this contract as may remain unexecuted, or make shipment in accordance with any routing of its own selection.

5. *Freight charges.* Any prepayment by the Seller of freight charges shall be for the account of the Purchaser, and shall be included in the amount of the invoice and repaid by the Purchaser on presentation thereof, and shall not affect the obligations of the Seller with respect to delivery. Insofar as the purchase price includes freight charges, such price is based upon the lowest official freight rate in effect at the date of this contract. Any difference between such rate and the rate actually paid, when the goods are shipped from the Manufacturer's plant, shall be for the Purchaser's account, and shall be reflected in the invoice, whether such difference results from a change in rate or a change in route.

6. *Insurance.* In no case does the purchase price, even though inclusive of freight, cover the cost of any insurance; but if the route selected involves movement of the goods by water, or by rail and water, for which the freight rate does not include insurance, the Seller shall effect marine insurance for the account of the Purchaser, and the Purchaser shall repay to the Seller the cost of such insurance.

7. *Partial delivery.* The Seller may ship any portion of the goods as soon as completed at the Manufacturer's plant, upon compliance with the terms of paragraph 4; and payment for any portion of the goods as shipped shall become

due in accordance with the terms of payment stated in paragraph 3.

8. *Contingencies.* The Seller shall not be liable for any delay in manufacture or delivery due to fires, strikes, labor disputes, war, civil commotion, delays in transportation, shortages of labor or material, or other causes beyond the control of the Seller. The existence of such causes of delay shall justify the suspension of manufacture, and shall extend the time of performance on the part of the Seller to the extent necessary to enable it to make delivery in the exercise of reasonable diligence after the causes of delay have been removed. However, that in the event of the existence of any such causes of delay, the Purchaser may cancel the purchase of such portion of the goods as may have been subjected to such delay, provided such portion of the goods has not been manufactured nor is in process of manufacture at the time the Purchaser's notice of cancellation arrives at the Manufacturer's plant.

9. *Warranty.* The Seller guarantees that the goods will generate or utilize electrical energy to their rated capacities without undue heating, and will do their work in a successful manner, provided that they are kept in proper condition and operated under normal conditions, and that their operation is properly supervised. THE WARRANTIES SPECIFIED IN THIS CONTRACT ARE IN LIEU OF ANY AND ALL OTHER WARRANTIES, EXPRESS OR IMPLIED, INCLUDING ANY WARRANTY OF MERCHANTABILITY OR FITNESS FOR A PARTICULAR PURPOSE.

10. *Inspection.* The Purchaser may inspect the goods at the Manufacturer's plant, and such inspection and acceptance shall be final. Reasonable facilities shall be afforded to inspectors representing the Purchaser to make the inspection, and to apply, before shipment from the Manufacturer's plant, tests in accordance with the specifications contained in paragraph 1. If the Purchaser fails to inspect

the goods, the failure shall be deemed an acceptance of the goods, and any acceptance shall be deemed a waiver of any right to revoke acceptance at some future date with respect to any defect that a proper inspection would have revealed.

11. *Claims.* The Seller shall not be liable for any claims unless they are made promptly after receipt of the goods and due opportunity has been given for investigation by the Seller's representatives. Goods shall not be returned except with the Seller's permission.

12. *Country of importation.* The Purchaser represents that the goods are purchased for the purpose of exportation to Peru, and the Purchaser covenants that the goods will be shipped to that destination, and shall furnish, if required by the Seller, a landing certificate duly executed by the customs authorities at the port of importation, certifying that the goods have been landed and entered at that port.

13. *Duties.* All drawbacks of duties paid on materials entering into the manufacture of the goods shall accrue to the Seller, and the Purchaser shall furnish the Seller with all documents necessary to obtain payment of such drawbacks, and to cooperate with the Seller in obtaining such payment.

14. *Cancellation by purchaser.* The Purchaser may cancel this contract, as to any goods not manufactured or in process of manufacture at the time the Purchaser's notice of cancellation arrives at the Manufacturer's plant, in any of the following events:

(a) if the country of importation becomes involved in civil or foreign war, insurrection, or riot, or is invaded by armed forces; or if, as a result of war, treaty, or otherwise, it is added to or becomes a part of the domain of any other sovereignty; or

(b) if a countervailing duty is declared or imposed on the goods by the country of importation; or

(c) if by reason of an embargo the goods cannot be exported from the United States; or

(d) if the Purchaser is unable to obtain an export shipping license for the purpose of exporting the goods to Peru.

15. *Benefit.* This agreement shall be binding upon and shall inure to the benefit of the parties, their legal representatives, successors, and assigns, provided that the Purchaser shall not assign this contract without the prior written consent of the Seller.

16. *Construction.* This contract shall be construed under the laws of New York.

In witness whereof the parties have executed this contract.

Corporate Seal Attest:	Panoramic Export Company, Inc. by . . . . President
. . . . Secretary	. . . . (L.S.) Miguel Vellos

Appendix C

Federal Register Notice: Mandatory AES

Federal Register

Monday,
June 2, 2008

Part II

Department of Commerce

Bureau of the Census

15 CFR Part 30

Foreign Trade Regulations: Mandatory Automated Export System Filing for All Shipments Requiring Shipper's Export Declaration Information; Final Rule

Federal Register Notice: Mandatory AES

31548 Federal Register / Vol. 73, No. 106 / Monday, June 2, 2008 / Rules and Regulations

DEPARTMENT OF COMMERCE

Bureau of the Census

15 CFR Part 30

[Docket Number: 031009254–6014–03]

RIN 0607–AA38

Foreign Trade Regulations: Mandatory Automated Export System Filing for All Shipments Requiring Shipper's Export Declaration Information

AGENCY: Bureau of the Census, Commerce Department.

ACTION: Final rule.

SUMMARY: The U.S. Census Bureau (Census Bureau) issues this final rule to amend its regulations to implement provisions in the Foreign Relations Authorization Act. Specifically, the Census Bureau is requiring mandatory filing of export information through the Automated Export System (AES) or through AES*Direct* for all shipments where a Shipper's Export Declaration (SED) is required.

DATES: *Effective Date:* This rule is effective July 2, 2008.

Implementation Date: The Census Bureau will implement provisions of this rule on September 30, 2008. This will allow all affected entities sufficient time to come into compliance with this rule.

FOR FURTHER INFORMATION CONTACT: C. Harvey Monk, Jr., Assistant Director for Economic Programs, U.S. Census Bureau, Room 8K108, Washington, DC 20233–6010, by phone (301) 763–2932, by fax (301) 457–3767, or by e-mail *c.harvey.monk.jr@census.gov.*

SUPPLEMENTARY INFORMATION:

Background

The Census Bureau is responsible for collecting, compiling, and publishing export trade statistics for the United States under the provisions of Title 13, United States Code (U.S.C.), Chapter 9, Section 301. The paper SED and the AES are the primary media used for collecting export trade data, and such data is used by the Census Bureau for statistical purposes only. The export trade data reported pursuant to this Part is referred to as Electronic Export Information (EEI). The SED and the EEI also are used for export control purposes under Title 50, U.S.C., Export Administration Act, to detect and prevent the export of certain items by unauthorized parties or to unauthorized destinations or end users. This information is exempt from public disclosure unless the Secretary of Commerce determines under the provisions of Title 13, U.S.C., Chapter 9, Section 301(g), that such exemption would be contrary to the national interest.

This rule provides that all export information for which an SED is required be filed through the AES. The AES is an electronic method for filing the paper SED information directly with the U.S. Customs and Border Protection (CBP) and the Census Bureau. The AES*Direct* is the Census Bureau's free Internet-based system for filing SED information through the AES. Future references to the AES also shall apply to AES*Direct* unless otherwise specified. In addition, with regards to postdeparture filing, the Census Bureau and CBP have agreed that the moratorium placed on Option 4 (postdeparture filing) in August 2003, will remain in effect pending further review of the postdeparture filing program.

Electronic filing strengthens the U.S. government's ability to prevent the export of certain items by unauthorized parties to unauthorized destinations and end users, because the AES aids in targeting and identifying suspicious shipments prior to export and affords the government the ability to significantly improve the quality, timeliness, and coverage of export statistics. Since July 1995, the AES has served as an information gateway for the Census Bureau and CBP to improve the reporting of export trade information, customer service, compliance with and enforcement of export laws, and to provide paperless reports of export information.

On November 29, 1999, the President signed into law the Proliferation Prevention Enhancement Act of 1999, which authorized the Secretary of Commerce to require the mandatory filing of items on the Commerce Control List (CCL) and the U.S. Munitions List (USML). Regulations implementing this requirement were effective October 2003 (see 68 FR 42533–42543). On September 30, 2002, the President signed into law the Foreign Relations Authorization Act, Public Law 107–228. This law authorized the Secretary of Commerce, with the concurrence of the Secretary of State and the Secretary of Homeland Security, to publish regulations in the **Federal Register** mandating that all persons who are required to file export information via the SED under Chapter 9 of Title 13, U.S.C., file such information through the AES.

The Foreign Relations Authorization Act further authorized the Secretary of Commerce to issue regulations regarding imposition of penalties, both civil and criminal, for the delayed filing, failure to file, false filing of export information, and/or using the AES to further any illegal activity. The Act provided for administrative proceedings for imposition of a civil penalty for violation(s) of Public Law 107–228. Finally, the Act authorized the Secretary of Commerce to designate employees of the Office of Export Enforcement of the Department of Commerce (DOC) to conduct investigations and perform the enforcement functions in Title 13, U.S.C., Chapter 9, and the Commissioner of Customs to designate employees of the Customs Service to enforce and conduct investigations under the same provisions. The latter authority is now exercised by the U.S. Immigration and Customs Enforcement (ICE) and CBP officials in the U.S. Department of Homeland Security (DHS). In addition, by Memorandum of Understanding dated September 25, 2005, the Secretary delegated the authority to enforce sections 304 and 305 of Title 13, U.S.C., and 15 CFR, part 30 to the Secretary of Homeland Security. Nothing in this rule is intended to restrict the authority of DHS under Section 343 of the Trade Act of 2002.

In the February 17, 2005, **Federal Register** (70 FR 8200), the Census Bureau published a Notice of Proposed Rulemaking (NPR) and request for comments on the regulations implementing the mandatory requirement to file export information through the AES or AES*Direct* for all shipments where SED information is required. Public comments were requested through April 18, 2005. A summary of comments received from the export trade community and the Census Bureau's response to those comments are presented in this rule.

Response to Comments

The Census Bureau received 45 letters and/or e-mails commenting on the NPR published in the **Federal Register** on February 17, 2005, (70 FR 8200). All the letters and/or e-mails contained comments on two or more issues. A summary of the comments and the Census Bureau's responses are provided below.

The major concerns were as follows:

1. *Clarify the filing requirement for Electronic Export Information (EEI).* Several commentors questioned whether the filing requirements had changed under the mandatory AES versus filing the paper SED. In addition, the commentors wanted clarification regarding the filing of EEI for Puerto Rico and U.S. territories. The requirements for filing EEI have not changed. All persons currently required

to file the SED will be required to file the same information through the AES. The requirements to file EEI for goods shipped to the United States from Puerto Rico, goods shipped to Puerto Rico from the United States, and goods shipped to the U.S. Virgin Islands from the United States or Puerto Rico, remain unchanged.

2. *Status of the use of the External Transaction Number (XTN) and the Internal Transaction Number (ITN).* Commentors wanted clarification on when the XTN and the ITN could be used under the new regulations. Under the Final Rule, only the ITN is acceptable as the proof of filing citation. The ITN confirms that the shipment information has been accepted in the AES. The XTN will no longer be accepted as a proof of filing.

3. *Clarify the time frame for filing EEI.* Commentors indicated they were unclear about the time frames for filing in the AES. The time frame varies according to method of transportation for predeparture filing. For State Department USML shipments, refer to the International Traffic in Arms Regulations (ITAR) (22 CFR 120–130), § 123.22, for the specific requirements concerning filing time frames. For non-USML shipments, file the EEI as follows: (1) For vessel cargo, the U.S. Principal Party in Interest (USPPI) or authorized agent shall file the EEI as required by § 30.6 and provide the filing citation or exemption legend to the exporting carrier 24 hours prior to loading cargo on the vessel at the U.S. port where the cargo is laden; (2) for air cargo, the USPPI or authorized agent shall file the EEI as required by § 30.6 and provide the filing citation or exemption legend to the exporting carrier, including air express couriers, no later than two hours prior to the scheduled departure time of the aircraft; (3) for truck cargo, the USPPI or authorized agent shall file the EEI as required by § 30.6 and provide the filing citation or exemption legend to the exporting carrier no later than one hour prior to the arrival of the truck at the U.S. border to go foreign; (4) for rail cargo, the USPPI or authorized agent shall file the EEI as required by § 30.6 and provide the filing citation or exemption legend to the exporting carrier no later then two hours prior to the time the cargo arrives at the U.S. border to go foreign; (5) for mail and cargo shipped by other methods, except pipeline exports, the USPPI or authorized agent shall file the EEI as required by § 30.6 and provide the filing citation or exemption legend to the exporting carrier no later than two hours prior to exportation; (6) for pipeline exports, the USPPI or authorized agent shall file the EEI as required by § 30.6 and provide the filing citation or exemption legend to the operator of the pipeline within four days following the end of each calendar month; and, (7) for postdeparture filing, by approved USPPIs, in accordance with § 30.5(c), the USPPI or authorized agent shall file the EEI as required by § 30.6 and provide the filing citation or exemption legend to the exporting carrier no later than ten calendar days from the date of export.

4. *Clarify Option 4 (Postdeparture) filing requirements.* Commentors wanted clarification regarding parties that would be approved for postdeparture filing. In agreement with the Census Bureau and CBP, the moratorium placed on Option 4 (postdeparture filing) on August 15, 2003 (see notice at *http://www.census.gov/aes*) will remain in effect pending further review of the postdeparture filing program.

5. *Amend the regulations to reduce or eliminate the $2,500 exemption level.* Several commentors proposed that the Census Bureau remove or reduce the current $2,500 exemption level. The Census Bureau believes that removing the $2,500 exemption level for reporting would substantially increase the reporting burden on the exporting community, especially on small businesses. This change would increase the number of shipments reported each month by approximately 4,000,000. In addition, the Census Bureau and CBP do not have the resources to process the additional workload.

6. *Amend the downtime requirements.* Commentors were concerned that export shipments would be delayed if the AES became unavailable. The Census Bureau has found that during its 12 years in operation, the AES has demonstrated a high level of reliability in performance. The system has been available to users 99 percent of the time. For this reason, the Census Bureau has determined that mandatory filing through the AES would not cause a substantial delay in export shipments. In the unlikely event that the AES is unavailable, the filer of a USML shipment shall not be allowed to export until the AES is operational and the filer is able to acquire an ITN. See § 30.4(b)(1) for more information. For non-USML shipments, the regulation provides for a downtime filing citation to allow goods to be exported. See § 30.4(b)(2) for more information.

7. *Clarify the requirements for power of attorney or written authorization.* Commentors were concerned that the language regarding the requirement for power of attorney or written authorization was drafted incorrectly. The Census Bureau reviewed the NPR regarding the requirement and found an instance where it stated "power of attorney and written authorization," and it should read "power of attorney or written authorization." This language has been changed in the Final Rule. In addition, a commentor questioned whether the language had been changed regarding the power of attorney or written authorization requirement. The Census Bureau did not change the language or the requirement for power of attorney or the need for written authorization that currently exists in the regulations.

8. *Clarify manner in which fines and penalties will be enforced and how a filer submits a voluntary self-disclosure.* Several commentors were concerned about which agency would enforce the penalty provisions of the Foreign Trade Regulations (FTR). Pursuant to the authority in Public Law 107–228, the Secretary of Commerce has delegated authority for enforcement to the Bureau of Industry and Security's (BIS) Office of Export Enforcement (OEE) and the DHS. The Census Bureau has worked with CBP and the BIS to develop regulations implementing the process and requirements for submitting a notification disclosing a violation or suspected violation of the FTR. These regulations are found in Subpart H, § 30.74 Voluntary Self-Disclosure.

9. *Amend a number of definitions in the definition section of the proposed rule.* Several commentors proposed changes to definitions contained in the NPR. The Census Bureau revised the following definitions in § 30.1:

Booking. The Census Bureau revised this definition to add "truck and train" as methods of transportation. The Census Bureau made this revision as a result of public comments.

Carrier. The Census Bureau deleted "non-vessel operating common carriers" because a commentor felt that the term could cause confusion and the Census Bureau agreed.

Commerce Control List (CCL). The Census Bureau revised the definition to provide the location of CCL items in the Export Administration Regulations (EAR).

Commodity. The Census Bureau deleted this term and the corresponding definition because commentors indicated that it was too general.

Domicile. The Census Bureau deleted this term because it is no longer used in the FTR.

Exceptions. This term was changed to "license exception" and moved accordingly.

Exclusions. The Census Bureau added this definition as a result of comments that requested clarification of this term.

Export Control Classification Number (ECCN). This definition was revised to clarify the description and purpose of this number.

Filers. The Census Bureau added this definition as a result of comments that requested clarification of this term.

Filing Electronic Export Information. The Census Bureau added this definition as a result of comments that requested clarification of this term.

Foreign Entity. The Census Bureau added this definition as a result of comments that requested clarification of this term.

Foreign Principal Party in Interest (FPPI). The Census Bureau revised this definition because it was inconsistent with the regulations defining the responsibilities of the parties to an export transaction. Therefore the Census Bureau revised this definition to ensure clarity.

Merchandise. The Census Bureau revised this term and corresponding definition in accordance with industry standards as commentors indicated that it was too general.

Service Center. The Census Bureau added this definition as a result of comments that requested clarification of this term.

Transmitting Electronic Export Information. The Census Bureau added this definition as a result of comments that requested clarification of this term.

Ultimate Consignee. The Census Bureau revised this definition to expand the definition of ultimate consignee to also include a party or designee that is located abroad and actually receives the export shipment. The definition was also revised to provide examples of the ultimate consignee. The Census Bureau revised the definition as a result of comments that indicated that the definition was inaccurate.

Violation of the FTR. The Census Bureau added this definition to clarify what constitutes a violation.

10. *Amend the proposed rule to make it a requirement that the agent of FPPI provides the USPPI with a copy of the power of attorney or written authorization from the FPPI.* Commentors were concerned about the requirement to provide information to an agent of the FPPI in a routed export transaction. The Census Bureau has revised § 30.3(e)(2) of the FTR to require the agent of the FPPI, upon request, to provide the USPPI with a copy of power of attorney or the written authorization giving the agent the authority to file the EEI on behalf of the FPPI before the USPPI provides the required information necessary to complete the EEI filings.

11. *Clarify whether an export license or license exemption is required for exports from U.S. territories. Also clarify whether paper SEDs are required by CBP for items that are controlled by the Department of State or the BIS.* The commentor's request for clarification on whether an export license or license exemption or items that are controlled by the Department of State or the BIS is required for export from U.S. territories is outside the scope of the Foreign Trade Regulations. The commentor's question should be addressed to the Department of State and the BIS. Neither the Census Bureau nor CBP requires EEI or a paper SED for goods shipped from U.S. territories including, Guam Island, American Samoa, Wake Island, Midway Island, and the Northern Mariana Islands to foreign countries or areas and goods shipped between the United States and these territories.

12. *Amend the proposed rule to address the treatment of split shipments by air.* Several commentors were concerned about having to identify the piece count details of shipments that are split among multiple flights. The commentors indicated that the regulations regarding the treatment of split shipments by air would have a substantial impact on air carriers. Commentors provided no further information. The Census Bureau reviewed this section of the NPR and found that the requirement was not changed from the previous regulations and remains appropriate. This requirement has existed for more than 20 years.

13. *Amend the proposed rule to relax the security requirements regarding reporting computer viruses and the requirement that the AES Administrator change administrator codes or passwords for security purposes when employees leave the company.* Several commentors were concerned that these requirements would be a burden to the AES filers. The requirement to notify the Census Bureau Foreign Trade Division's Security Officer when a virus infection occurs only applies to systems connected to the AES*Direct*. This procedure is a security requirement for the purpose of maintaining the federal government's system certification for AES*Direct*. The requirement to change the password when an employee leaves the company only applies to employees leaving the company who had direct access to the AES § 30.5(d)(2). This is not a new requirement and remains appropriate.

14. *Amend the regulations by dropping Subpart F—Import Requirements.* One commentor believes that having import regulations in 15 CFR 30, and also in 19 CFR is confusing to the trade. More than one federal agency has jurisdiction over imports, therefore, it is appropriate for regulations to exist in more than one place. While CBP regulations (19 CFR) cover most of the requirements for filing import information, there are additional statistical requirements specific to the Census Bureau that are found in the FTR (15 CFR) and that are not the subject of CBP regulations.

15. *Amend the proposed rule § 30.52—Foreign Trade Zones (FTZ).* Commentors are concerned that language in § 30.52 did not describe some of the activities of FTZs. The Census Bureau reviewed the proposed language changes and replaced the word "enter" with "are admitted into" in the introductory paragraph and the word "mode" with "method" in § 30.52(h) to more accurately reflect the activities of the zones.

16. *Create a registration number to be used in place of the Employer Identification Number (EIN) or Social Security Number (SSN).* A commentor was concerned about providing the EIN or SSN to a FPPI's agent or placing the EIN or SSN on the proof of filing citation. The Census Bureau agrees that a registration number should be created so that filers', USPPI's, or agents' EIN or SSN can be kept confidential. The Census Bureau is currently working with CBP to develop a system that allows the reporting of registration numbers, and will address this issue in a future rulemaking.

17. *Clarify the filing of foreign waterborne in-transit shipments by the U.S. Army Corps of Engineers.* A commentor believes that the U.S. Army Corps of Engineers should not be responsible for reporting EEI on export of in-transit shipments. Previously, the Census Bureau, the U.S. Army Corps of Engineers, and the Maritime Administration jointly collected in-transit information for vessel shipments. This joint collection activity dates back to 1948, with the Census Bureau designated as the primary collection agency. In 1996, under joint agreement among the Census Bureau, U.S. Army Corps of Engineers, the Maritime Administration, and the Office of Management and Budget (OMB), the U.S. Army Corps of Engineers was designated the primary data collection agency for vessel in-transit data. Thus, it is the responsibility of the U.S. Army Corps of Engineers to collect data regarding vessel in-transit shipments leaving the United States. This does not, however, affect or alter the

responsibility of USPPIs and others to comply with other agency in-transit requirements such as those required by CBP. (See *e.g.*, 19 CFR 18)

18. *Redesign the Vessel Transportation Module (VTM) of the AES to allow paperless submissions of proof of filing citations and exemption legends and revise the FTR to require the paperless submission of the proof of filing citation and exemption legends.* Several commentors from the vessel shipping lines wanted to submit electronic manifests and wanted to receive the proof of filing citation and exemption legends from the filers electronically. The Census Bureau determined that this proposal would require a significant redesign of the AES, VTM, and the AES Commodity Module, and would likely need to be developed as a part of CBP's Automated Commercial Environment development. At this time, neither CBP nor the Census Bureau has the resources available to implement this proposal. Until the implementation of a system that has the capability described by the commentor, the AES will continue to require the filer to provide the vessel carriers with the proof of filing citations or the exemption legends.

19. *Clarify the retention of export information and the authority to require proof of documentation of EEI.* Several commentors indicated that the requirements of § 30.10 were unclear. The Census Bureau agreed, and the section was completely revised to clarify the requirements for retaining export information and to eliminate the requirement to retain paper certification notices. In the course of clarifying this section, the Census Bureau determined that it was not necessary for filers to retain paper copies of certain documents. In order to reduce the recordkeeping burdens on filers, the Census Bureau eliminated the requirement that AES filers retain a paper copy of the Letter of Intent to participate in the AES and the requirement that AESDirect and/or AESPcLink filers print and maintain a copy of their electronic certification notice. In addition, the Census Bureau modified this section to add a note describing its responsibilities with respect to the retention and maintenance of EEI.

20. *Amend the rule to provide exemption from filing EEI for temporary exports including carnets.* Several commentors believe that the regulation should state that temporary exports are exempt from filing. The Census Bureau's regulations have always exempted temporary exports, such as carnets, from filing requirements. However, the Census Bureau agrees that carnets should be expressly stated in regulations and thus it has been added to that exemption in § 30.37. However, temporary exports that require an export license, temporary exports destined for a country listed in Country Group E:1 as set forth in Supplement 1 to 15 CFR 740, or an ITAR licensing exemption are not exempt.

21. *Amend the filing citation and exemption legend requirements.* Several commentors requested changes in language with respect to the filing citations and exemption legends requirement because it was inconsistent with industry practice. The Census Bureau made several changes to the language to reflect industry practice with respect to who must provide exemption legends (see § 30.7).

22. *Clarify the procedures for responding to fatal error messages when filing postdeparture.* A commentor stated that § 30.9(b) did not take postdeparture filing into account. The Census Bureau has reviewed the section and has revised the Final Rule to address postdeparture filings. If a filer encounters a fatal error when filing a postdeparture shipment, the filer must resubmit the EEI no later than ten calendar days after export.

23. *Clarify that estimated date of departure can be used if the actual date of departure is not known.* A commentor was concerned that sometimes the filer may not know the actual date of departure. The Census Bureau acknowledges that there are times when the filer may not know the actual date of departure. In these instances, the filer may provide an estimated departure date. However, it is the USPPI's or the authorized filing agent's responsibility to transmit accurate export information as known at the time of filing in the AES and transmit any changes to that information as soon as they are known.

24. *Clarify whether export shipments to Mexico and Canada must be filed in AES.* A commentor questioned whether SEDs are required to be filed for shipments destined to Canada and Mexico. All export shipments to Mexico valued over $2,500 or shipments that require an export license, a license exemption, or a Kimberley Process Certificate for rough diamonds classified under the 6-digit Harmonized Schedule subheadings 7102.10, 7102.21, and 7102.31, are required to be reported in the AES. Export shipments to Canada are not required to be filed through the AES, unless they require an export license, a license exemption, or a Kimberley Process Certificate for rough diamonds classified under the 6-digit Harmonized Schedule subheadings 7102.10, 7102.21, and 7102.31. See §§ 30.2(a) and 30.36.

25. *Amend the proposed rule regarding the annotation of proof of filing citations, 15 CFR § 30.7.* A commentor requested that the Census Bureau limit the length of the AES downtime filing citation to no more than 32 characters. The Census Bureau acknowledges that the filing citation may be lengthy, and thus may result in mistakes. Therefore, the Census Bureau has removed the "shipment reference number" from the downtime citation to make the AES downtime filing citation less than 32 characters.

26. *Amend § 30.7 Annotating Proof of Filing Citation.* The commentor requested that the Census Bureau amend the regulations to define the difference between an authorized agent and an exporting carrier when both roles are fulfilled by the same, affiliated, or controlled subsidiary legal entity. The Census Bureau reviewed the request and § 30.7 was revised to define the different roles of authorized agents and carriers.

27. *Clarify that intangible exports of software and technology are exempt from the EEI requirements.* A commentor requested that the Census Bureau confirm that EEI is not required for intangible exports of software and technology. The Census Bureau's FTR does not require the reporting of intangible exports of software and technology. However, the Department of State, and/or the DOC may require separate filings for intangible exports of software and technology and technical data that require a license. The Census Bureau recommends that the Department of State and DOC be contacted regarding their specific licensing requirements.

28. *Amend the proposed rule by removing the carrier name and Standard Carrier Alpha Code (SCAC) as data elements.* One commentor requested that carrier name and SCAC be removed as data elements. The Census Bureau is unable to discontinue collection of these data elements because each remains a statistical and enforcement requirement.

29. *Amend the proposed rule regarding responsibilities in a routed export transaction.* A commentor requested language be added to § 30.3(e), "Parties are free to structure transactions as they wish and to delegate functions and tasks as they deem necessary, as long as the transactions comply with the FTR." The Census Bureau considered the proposal and decided that the addition of the proposed language would create confusion rather than clarity. In a routed

export transaction the authorized agent of the FPPI shall be responsible for filing the EEI accurately and timely in accordance with the FTR.

30. *Amend the rule by adding a note to § 30.3.* A commentor requested that the Census Bureau revise the FTR to be consistent with the EAR. The Census Bureau added a note to § 30.3 to alert filers that the definition used for exporter in the EAR is different from the definition used for the USPPI in the FTR because of each agency's distinct obligations and requirements. Therefore, due to the different mission of each agency, conformity of documentation is not required in the FTR.

31. *Amend the proposed rule, § 30.37(a)—Miscellaneous Exemptions.* A commentor requested that the Census Bureau confirm if the miscellaneous exemption for goods valued $2,500 or less can be used if the domestic value and the foreign value are each under $2,500, even if their total value exceeds $2,500. The Census Bureau's FTR requires that items of domestic or foreign origin under the same commodity classification number should always be reported separately and listed only if either is valued over $2,500.

Changes to the Proposed Rule Made by This Final Rule

After consideration of the comments received, the Census Bureau revised certain provisions and added several provisions in the Final Rule to address the concerns of the commentors and to clarify the requirements of the rule. The changes made in this Final Rule are as follows:

1. Section 30.2(a)(ii) is amended to clarify that goods previously admitted to customs warehouses or FTZs moving under CBP bond between Puerto Rico and United States and to the U.S. Virgin Islands from the United States or Puerto Rico shall require filing EEI. This change is in response to concerns addressed in item 15 in the "Response to Comments" section.

2. Section 30.2(a)(iv) is amended to clarify exemptions in Subpart D by deleting (A), specific references to Office of Foreign Assets Control regulations, renumbering existing (B) through (E) to (A) through (D), and adding a new (E) to clarify a BIS requirement. This change was made to provide clarity and consistency.

3. Section 30.2(d)(2) is amended by deleting "* * * when an export license or license exemption is not required," because currently no export license is required for the following U.S. territories: Guam Island, American Samoa, Wake Island, Midway Island, and the Northern Mariana Islands. This change was in response to concerns addressed in item 11 in the "Response to Comments" section.

4. In response to item 20 in the "Response to Comments" section, § 30.3(b)(2)(iv) is deleted because it relates to an exemption for reexports that is addressed in § 30.37. Section 30.3(b)(2)(v) is renumbered § 30.3(b)(2)(iv). A new § 30.3(b)(2)(v) has been added to provide clarification on who shall be the USPPI when goods are imported for consumption and reexported without being changed or enhanced. This change was made during internal agency review.

5. Section 30.3(e)(1) is amended to clarify the language describing the treatment of a routed export transaction if the FPPI agrees to allow the USPPI to file EEI. This change is in response to concerns addressed in item 10 in the "Response to Comments" section. Also, § 30.3(e)(1) is amended by adding a note to paragraph (e)(1) that was inadvertently dropped in the proposed rule.

6. Section 30.3(e)(2) is amended to clarify the authorized agents responsibilities in a routed export transaction. This change is in response to concerns addressed in item 10 in the "Response to Comments" section.

7. Section 30.3(e)(2)(xiii) and (xiv) is amended by adding a clarifying note to this paragraph that was inadvertently dropped in the proposed rule. This change was made to provide clarity and consistency.

8. Section 30.3(e)(1) is amended by adding a clarifying note to this section that was inadvertently dropped in the proposed rule. This change is in response to concerns addressed in item 29 in the "Response to Comments" section.

9. Section 30.3(f) is amended to clarify that in a routed export transaction the USPPI is not required to provide the agent of the FPPI with a power of attorney or written authorization. This change is in response to concerns addressed in item 10 in the "Response to Comments" section.

10. Section 30.6(a)(18) is amended by deleting shipments under carnet from the list of export codes. This listing of carnets in the export codes was in error. This change is made to ensure consistency with the response to concerns addressed in item 20 in the "Response to Comments" section.

11. Section 30.6(b)(13) is amended to specify that an entry number is required for goods withdrawn from a FTZ and exported. This change is in response to concerns addressed in item 15 in the "Response to Comments" section.

12. Section 30.10 is amended to clarify the requirements for the retention of EEI and the authority to require production of documentation of EEI. This change is in response to concerns addressed in item 19 in the "Response to Comments" section.

13. Section 30.37 is amended by adding exemptions (q), (r), (s), and (t) that were not included in the proposed rule. This change was made to provide clarity and consistency.

14. Section 30.4(b)(2)(i) is amended to read: "(i) For vessel cargo, the USPPI or authorized agent shall file the EEI required by § 30.6 and provide the filing citation or exemption legend to the exporting carrier 24 hours prior to the cargo being loaded on the vessel at the U.S. port where the cargo is laden." This change is in response to concerns addressed in item 21 in the "Response to Comments" section.

15. Section 30.4(b)(2)(iv) is amended to read: "(iv) For rail cargo, the USPPI or the authorized agent shall file the EEI, required by § 30.6, and provide the filing citation or exemption legend to the exporting carrier no later than two hours prior to the time train arrives at the U.S. border to go foreign." This change is in response to concerns addressed in item 21 in the "Response to Comments" section.

16. Section 30.45(a) is amended by deleting "* * * U.S. possessions" and replacing it with "the U.S. Virgin Islands." The reference to U.S. territories was too broad. Also language was added to clarify that CBP may require a variety of documents, depending upon the method of transportation, to contain the proof of filing citation or exemption legend. This change is in response to concerns addressed in item 21 in the "Response to Comments" section.

17. Section 30.45(f) is amended to clarify by method of transportation when the carrier must obtain the filing citations or exemption legends. This change is in response to concerns addressed in item 21 in the "Response to Comments" section.

18. Section 30.37 is amended to include carnets as temporary exports that should have been included in the proposed rule. This change is in response to concerns addressed in item 20 in the "Response to Comments" section.

19. Section 30.71(b)(1) is amended by adding a note to paragraph (b)(1), which notes an inflation adjustment to penalty provision of Subpart H. This change was made as a result of the Adjustment for Inflation Final Rule effective December

14, 2004, and provided for by the Debt Collection Improvement Act of 1996, Public Law 104–134.

20. Subpart H is amended by adding § 30.74, Voluntary Self-Disclosure, to specify how to disclose violations or suspected violations of the FTR. This change is in response to concerns addressed in item 8 in the "Response to Comments" section.

21. Sections 30.2(c)(1), 30.5(a), and 30.5(c) are amended to clarify that the letter of intent to participate in AES must be filed electronically at *www.aesdirect.gov*. This change was made to eliminate the requirement to submit the paper letter of intent and to be consistent with a pure electronic environment because filing the information electronically reduces the burden on both trade and the government.

22. Section 30.1 is amended to clarify a number of definitions. These changes are in response to concerns addressed in item 9 in the "Response to Comments" section.

23. Section 30.5(d)(1) is amended to clarify that the requirement to change password only applies to employees leaving the company that had direct access to the AES. This change is in response to concerns addressed in item 13 in the "Response to Comments" section.

24. Section 30.9(b) is amended to clarify that fatal errors for EEI filed postdeparture must be corrected as soon as possible, but no later than ten days after departure if filed postdeparture. This change is in response to concerns addressed in item 22 in the "Response to Comments" section.

25. Section 30.7 is amended by deleting the filing citation from the section and adding an Appendix D to Part 30 AES Filing Citation, Exemption and Exclusion Legends. In addition, the Census Bureau limited the length of the AES downtime filing citation to no more than 32 characters. These changes were in response to concerns addressed in item 25 of the "Response to Comments" section and to provide clarity and consistency.

26. Appendix A to Part 30—Format for Letter of Intent has been removed. The Appendix B sample of Power of Attorney and written authorization has been renamed A.

27. Appendix B to Part 30—AES Filing Codes have been added to provide one reference for all the filing codes.

28. Appendix C to Part 30—Summary of Exemptions and Exclusions from EEI filing is being added to provide a summary of all FTR exemptions and exclusions.

29. Appendix D to Part 30—AES Filing Citation, Exemption and Exclusion Legends are being added to provide a summary of all citations and legends.

30. Appendix E to Part 30—FTSR to FTR Concordances are being added to provide a crosswalk between the FTSR and FTR.

31. Appendix F to Part 30—FTR to FTSR Concordances are being added to provide a crosswalk between the FTR and FTSR.

Program Requirements

To comply with the requirements of Public Law 107–228, the Census Bureau is amending in its entirety the FTSR to specify the requirements for the mandatory reporting of all export information through the AES when a SED was required. All future references to the SED shall be referred to as AES EEI.

The Census Bureau is making the following changes to Title 15, Code of Federal Regulations (CFR), part 30:

- Rename the FTSR to "Part 30—Foreign Trade Regulations" to more accurately reflect the scope of the revised regulations implementing full mandatory AES filing, such as the inclusion of Department of State requirements and the advanced filing requirement implemented by CBP.
- Remove requirements for filing a paper SED (Option 1), Commerce Form 7525–V, from Title 15 CFR 30, so that the AES will be the only mode for filing information previously required by the SED.
- Remove requirements for filing the in-transit SED, ENG Form 7513, from 15 CFR 30. Responsibility for ENG Form 7513 was transferred to the U.S. Department of the Army, U.S. Army Corps of Engineers.
- In § 30.2(a)(2), language was included to specify the four optional means for filing EEI. Two of those methods require the development of AES software using the Automated Export System Trade Interface Requirements (AESTIR).
- Section 30.2(d), lists types of export transactions outside the scope of the FTR. The list of out-of-scope transactions included in § 30.2(d) is not all-inclusive, but includes those types of shipments about which the Census Bureau receives frequent inquiries. These types of shipments are to be excluded from EEI filing.
- In § 30.3, language was included to specify that in a "routed" transaction, the USPPI can compile and transmit export information on behalf of the FPPI when agreed upon by the FPPI. This language is consistent with the language of § 758.3 of the EAR and permits the USPPI to act as an agent of the FPPI upon the written authorization by the FPPI.
- In § 30.4, the time and place-of-filing requirements for presenting proof of filing citations, postdeparture filing citations, and/or exemption legends are specified. Specific time and place-of-filing requirements are included in the FTR in accordance with provisions of § 341(a) of Public Law 107–210, the Trade Act of 2002. With the exception of the State Department, USML shipments under the control of the ITAR and shipments approved for postdeparture filing, the appropriate proof of filing citations and/or exemption legends are required to be provided to the exporting carrier within specified time frames depending on the mode of transportation used. For example, proof of filing citations for vessel cargo shall be provided to the exporting carrier no later than 24 hours prior to departure of the vessel from the U.S. port where the cargo is laden. Time and place-of-filing requirements for other modes of transportation also are presented in § 30.4 of the FTR.
- In § 30.4(b)(1) and § 30.4(b)(3) specify how to file EEI and acquire an ITN when AES, AES*Direct* or the participant's AES is unavailable for filing.
- In § 30.5(c), the postdeparture (formerly Option 4) approval procedures were removed. Certification and approval requirements for postdeparture filing of EEI were strengthened to address U.S. national security concerns and interests. Applications submitted by USPPIs for postdeparture filing will be subjected to closer scrutiny by the Census Bureau and other federal government partnership agencies participating in the AES postdeparture filing review process. Under the revised postdeparture filing requirements: (1) Authorized agents may no longer apply for postdeparture filing status on behalf of individual USPPIs. Only USPPIs may apply; (2) USPPIs must demonstrate the ability to meet the AES predeparture filing requirements by filing EEI through the AES before being approved for the postdeparture filing privilege; (3) USPPIs must meet a minimum number of shipments requirement before being authorized to file postdeparture; and (4) partnership agencies of the U.S. government shall determine whether or not a USPPI poses a significant threat to U.S. national security before granting the applicant postdeparture filing status.
- In § 30.6, language was added delineating the specific procedure for reporting the value of goods to the AES when inland freight and insurance

31554 **Federal Register** / Vol. 73, No. 106 / Monday, June 2, 2008 / Rules and Regulations

charges are not known at the time of exportation. When goods are sold at a point other than the port of export, freight, insurance, and other charges required to move the goods from their U.S. point of origin to the carrier at the port of export must be added to the selling price (or cost, if not sold) of the goods. Where the actual amount of freight, insurance, and other domestic charges are not available, an estimate of the domestic cost must be made and added to the cost or selling price of the goods to obtain the value to be reported to the AES.

- In § 30.6, a Routed Export Transaction Indicator and a Vehicle Identification Qualifier were added to the list of data elements to be reported through the AES. Both the Routed Export Transaction Indicator and the Vehicle Identification Qualifier indicate the conditions of other data elements reported to the AES. The Routed Export Transaction Indicator gives an indication of whether or not the EEI reported represents a routed export transaction. The Vehicle Identification Qualifier, when reported, identifies the type of vehicle number reported.
- In § 30.6, the Date of Arrival and the Waiver of Prior Notice Indicator were removed from the list of data elements that should be reported through the AES. These data elements were previously required to overcome disparities in reporting requirements for certain export shipments sent between the United States and Puerto Rico. With mandatory AES reporting, the Date of Arrival and Waiver of Prior Notice Indicator are no longer required, since shipments sent between the United States and Puerto Rico will no longer be reported differently from other export shipments.
- Subpart B sets forth export control and export licensing issues relevant to 15 CFR 30. This subpart adds references to export control and licensing requirements of the Department of State and other federal agencies. General guidelines for obtaining export control and licensing information also are presented for use by preparers and filers of EEI. The purpose of this subpart is to consolidate references to export control issues. No new requirements are introduced.
- In § 30.29, the language that describes the proper manner for reporting cost of repairs and/or alterations to goods, and the reporting of the value of replacement parts exported was revised. The FTSR did not specifically describe the manner in which these export transactions should be reported. Goods previously imported for repair and alteration only, and reexported, shall only include the value for parts and labor. Goods exported as replacement parts shall only include the value of the replacement part. No new requirements are specified in § 30.29.
- Subpart E sets forth carrier and manifest issues pertaining to provisions relevant to 15 CFR 30. Carrier and manifest issues are consolidated in Subpart E. Requirements for SEDs being attached to the manifest are replaced with requirements for proof of filing citations and/or exemption legends to be shown on the bill of lading, air waybill, or other commercial loading documents attached to the manifest. Specific requirements for annotating the bill of lading, air waybill, or other commercial loading documents are included in § 30.7, Subpart A of Part 30.
- Subpart F sets forth requirements for import shipments relevant to 15 CFR 30, including requirements for the electronic filing of statistical data for shipments imported into FTZs. Currently, requirements for electronically reporting FTZ admissions are included in the Census Bureau's "Automated Foreign Trade Zone Reporting Program" manual. Instructions to import filers on where to obtain information on reporting import data are added to Subpart F. Requirements for information on imports of goods into Guam are excluded from the FTR since Guam collects its own information on goods entering and leaving the area.
- A new Subpart H was created to cover the FTR penalty provisions formerly addressed in § 30.95 of the FTSR. New penalty provisions addressed in Subpart H of this part describe the increase in penalties imposed for violations from $100 to $1,000 for each day of delinquency, to a maximum from $1,100 to $10,000 per violation. In addition, the penalty provisions provide for situations when the filer knowingly fails to file, files false and/or misleading information and other violations of the FTR where a civil penalty shall not exceed $10,000 per violation and a criminal penalty shall not exceed $10,000 or imprisonment for no more than five years, or both, per violation. Finally, Subpart H provides for the enforcement of these penalty provisions by the BIS' Office of Export Enforcement (OEE) and the DHS's CBP, and ICE.
- Other nonsubstantive revisions were made to include language incorporated from the FTSR to clarify the intent of the provisions in the FTR.

The Department of State and DHS concur with the provisions contained in this Final Rule.

Rulemaking Requirements

Regulatory Flexibility Act

The Chief Counsel for Regulation of the DOC certified to the Chief Counsel for Advocacy of the Small Business Administration (SBA) that this rule will not have a significant impact on a substantial number of small entities. The factual basis for this certification was published in the proposed rule and is not repeated here. No comments were received regarding the economic impact of this rule. As a result, a final regulatory flexibility analysis is not required and none was prepared.

Executive Orders

This rule has been determined to be not significant for purposes of Executive Order 12866. It has been determined that this rule does not contain policies with Federalism implications as that term is defined under Executive Order 13132.

Paperwork Reduction Act

Notwithstanding any other provision of law, no person is required to respond to, nor shall a person be subject to a penalty for failure to comply with, a collection of information subject to the requirements of the Paperwork Reduction Act (PRA), unless that collection of information displays a current, valid OMB control number. This rule contains a collection-of-information subject to the requirements of the PRA (44 U.S.C. 3501 *et seq.*) and that has been approved under OMB control number 0607–0152. The estimated burden hours for filing the SED information through the AES and related documents (*e.g.*, the AES Participant Application (APA) and AES*Direct*) are 752,000. In addition, this rule contains a collection of information that has been approved under OMB control numbers: OMB No. 1651–0022 (Entry Summary—CBP–7501), OMB No. 1651–0027 (Record of Vessel, Foreign Repair, or Equipment—CBP–226), and OMB No. 1651–0029 (Application for Foreign Trade Zone Admission and Status Designation—CBP–214). The public's reporting burden for the collection-of-information requirements includes the time for reviewing instructions, searching existing data sources, gathering and maintaining the data needed, and completing and reviewing the collection-of-information requirements.

List of Subjects in 15 CFR Part 30

Economic statistics, Exports, Foreign trade, Reporting and recordkeeping requirements.

■ For the reason stated in the preamble, the Census Bureau revises 15 CFR part 30 to read as follows:

PART 30—FOREIGN TRADE REGULATIONS

Subpart A—General Requirements

Authority: 5 U.S.C. 301; 13 U.S.C. 301–307; Reorganization plan No. 5 of 1990 (3 CFR 1949–1953 Comp., p.1004); Department of Commerce Organization Order No. 35–2A, July 22, 1987, as amended and No. 35–2B, December 20, 1996, as amended; Public Law 107–228, 116 Stat. 1350.

Subpart A—General Requirements

§ 30.1 Purpose and definitions.

(a) This part sets forth the Foreign Trade Regulations (FTR) as required under the provisions of Title 13, United States Code (U.S.C.), Chapter 9, section 301. These regulations are revised pursuant to provisions of the Foreign Relations Authorization Act, Public Law 107–228 (the Act). This Act authorizes the Secretary of Commerce, with the concurrence of the Secretary of State and the Secretary of Homeland Security, to publish regulations mandating that all persons who are required to file export information under Chapter 9 of 13 U.S.C., file such information through the Automated Export System (AES) for all shipments where a Shipper's Export Declaration (SED) was previously required. The law further authorizes the Secretary of Commerce to issue regulations regarding imposition of civil and criminal penalties for violations of the provisions of the Act and these regulations.

(b) Electronic filing through the AES strengthens the U.S. government's ability to prevent the export of certain items to unauthorized destinations and/or end users because the AES aids in targeting, identifying, and when necessary confiscating suspicious or illegal shipments prior to exportation.

(c) Definitions used in the FTR. As used in this part, the following definitions apply:

AES applicant. The USPPI or authorized agent who applies to the Census Bureau for authorization to report export information electronically to the AES, or through AES*Direct* or its related applications.

AES*Direct.* A free Internet application supported by the Census Bureau that allows USPPIs, their authorized agent, or the authorized agent of the FPPI to transmit EEI through the AES via the Internet at *http://www.aesdirect.gov.*

AES downtime filing citation. A statement used in place of a proof of filing citation when the AES or AES*Direct* computer systems experiences a major failure. The downtime filing citation must appear on the bill of lading, air waybill, export shipping instructions, or other commercial loading documents.

AES participant application (APA). An electronic submission of an individual or a company's desire to participate in the AES. It sets forth a commitment to develop, maintain, and adhere to CBP and Census Bureau performance requirements and operational standards.

Air waybill. The shipping document used for the transportation of air freight includes conditions, limitations of liability, shipping instructions, description of commodity, and applicable transportation charges. It is generally similar to a straight non-negotiable bill of lading and is used for similar purposes.

Annotation. An explanatory note (*e.g.*, proof of filing citation, postdeparture filing citation, AES downtime filing citation, exemption, or exclusion legend) placed on the bill of lading, air waybill, export shipping instructions, or other loading document.

Authorized agent. An individual or legal entity physically located in or otherwise under the jurisdiction of the United States that has obtained power of attorney or written authorization from a USPPI or FPPI to act on its behalf, and for purposes of this part, to complete and file the EEI.

Automated Broker Interface (ABI). A CBP system through which an importer or licensed customs broker can electronically file entry and entry summary data on goods imported into the United States.

Automated Export System (AES). The system, including AESDirect, for collecting EEI information (or any successor document) from persons exporting goods from the United States, Puerto Rico, or the U.S. Virgin Islands; between Puerto Rico and the United States; and to the U.S. Virgin Islands from the United States or Puerto Rico.

Automated Export System Trade Interface Requirements (AESTIR). The document that describes the operational requirements of the AES. The AESTIR presents record formats and other reference information used in the AES.

Automated Foreign Trade Zone Reporting Program (AFTZRP). The electronic reporting program used to transmit statistical data on goods admitted into a FTZ directly to the Census Bureau.

Bill of lading (BL). A document that establishes the terms of a contract between a shipper and a transportation company under which freight is to be moved between specified points for a specified charge. Usually prepared by the authorized agent on forms issued by the carrier, it serves as a document of title, a contract of carriage, and a receipt for goods.

Bond. An instrument used by CBP as security to ensure the payment of duties, taxes and fees and/or compliance with certain requirements such as the submission of manifest information.

Bonded warehouse. An approved private warehouse used for the storage of goods until duties or taxes are paid and the goods are properly released by CBP. Bonds must be posted by the warehouse proprietor and by the importer to indemnify the government if the goods are released improperly.

Booking. A reservation made with a carrier for a shipment of goods on a specific voyage, flight, truck or train.

Bureau of Industry and Security (BIS). This bureau within the U.S. Department of Commerce is concerned with the advancement of U.S. national security, foreign policy, and economic interests. The BIS is responsible for regulating the export of sensitive goods and technologies; enforcing export control, antiboycott, and public safety laws; cooperating with and assisting other countries on export control and strategic trade issues; and assisting U.S. industry to comply with international arms control agreements.

Buyer. The principal in the export transaction that purchases the commodities for delivery to the ultimate consignee. The buyer and ultimate consignee may be the same.

Cargo. Goods being transported.

Carnet. An international customs document that allows the carnet holder to import into the United States or export to foreign countries certain goods on a temporary basis without the payment of duties.

Carrier. An individual or legal entity in the business of transporting passengers or goods. Airlines, trucking companies, railroad companies, shipping lines, pipeline companies, and slot charterers are all examples of carriers.

Civil penalty. A monetary penalty imposed on a USPPI, authorized agent, FPPI, carrier, or other party to the transaction for violating the FTR, including failing to file export information, filing false or misleading information, filing information late, and/or using the AES to further any illegal activity, and/or violating any other regulations of this part.

Commerce Control List (CCL). A list of items found in Supplement No. 1 to Part 774 of the EAR. Supplement No. 2 to Part 774 of the EAR contains the General Technology and Software Notes relevant to entries contained in the CCL.

Compliance alert. An electronic response sent to the filer by the AES when the shipment was not reported in accordance with this part (*e.g.*, late filing). The filer is required to review their filing practices and take steps to conform with export reporting requirements.

Consignee. The person or entity named in a freight contract, a contract of carriage that designates to whom goods have been consigned, and that has the legal right to claim the goods at the destination.

Consignment. Delivery of goods from a USPPI (the consignor) to an agent (consignee) under agreement that the agent sells the goods for the account of the USPPI.

Container. A uniform, reusable metal "box" in which goods are shipped by vessel, truck, or rail as defined in the International Convention for Safe Containers, as amended (TIAS 9037; 29 U.S.T. 3709).

Controlling agency. The agency responsible for the license determination on specified goods exported from the United States.

Cost of goods sold. Cost of goods is the sum of expenses incurred in the USPPI acquisition or production of the goods.

Country of origin. The country where the goods were mined, grown, or manufactured or where each foreign material used or incorporated in a good underwent a change in tariff classification indicating a substantial transformation under the applicable rule of origin for the good. The country of origin for U.S. imports are reported in terms of the International Standards Organization (ISO) codes designated in the Schedule C, Classification of Country and Territory Designations.

Country of ultimate destination. The country where the goods are to be consumed, further processed, stored, or manufactured, as known to the USPPI at the time of export.

Criminal penalty. For the purpose of this part, a penalty imposed for knowingly or willfully violating the FTR, including failing to file export information, filing false or misleading information, filing information late, and/or using the AES to further illegal activity. The criminal penalty includes fines, imprisonment, and/or forfeiture.

Customs broker. An individual or entity licensed to enter and clear imported goods through CBP for another individual or entity.

Destination. The foreign location to which a shipment is consigned.

Distributor. An agent who sells directly for a supplier and maintains an inventory of the supplier's products.

Domestic exports. Goods that are grown, produced, or manufactured in the United States, and commodities of foreign origin that have been changed in the United States, including changes made in a U.S. FTZ, from the form in which they were imported, or that have been enhanced in value or improved in condition by further processing or manufacturing in the United States.

Drayage. The charge made for hauling freight, carts, drays, or trucks.

Dun & Bradstreet Number (DUNS). The DUNS Number is a unique 9-digit identification sequence that provides identifiers to single business entities

Appendix C

while linking corporate family structures together.

Dunnage. Materials placed around cargo to prevent shifting or damage while in transit.

Duty. A charge imposed on the import of goods. Duties are generally based on the value of the goods (ad valorem duties), some other factor, such as weight or quantity (specific duties), or a combination of value and other factors (compound duties).

Electronic export information (EEI). The electronic export data as filed in the AES. This is the electronic equivalent of the export data formerly collected as Shipper's Export Declaration (SED) information and now mandated to be filed through the AES or AESDirect.

Employer identification number (EIN). The USPPI's Internal Revenue Service (IRS) EIN is the 9-digit numerical code as reported on the Employer's Quarterly Federal Tax Return, Treasury Form 941.

End user. The person abroad that receives and ultimately uses the exported or reexported items. The end user is not an authorized agent or intermediary, but may be the FPPI or ultimate consignee.

Enhancement. A change or modification to goods that increases their value or improves their condition.

Entry number. Consists of a three-position entry filer code and a seven-position transaction code, plus a check digit assigned by the entry filer as a tracking number for goods entered into the United States.

Equipment number. The identification number for shipping equipment, such as container or igloo (Unit Load Device (ULD)) number, truck license number, or rail car number.

Exclusions. Transactions outside of the scope of the FTR that are excluded from the requirement of filing EEI.

Exemption. A specific reason as cited within this part that eliminates the requirement for filing EEI.

Exemption legend. A notation placed on the bill of lading, air waybill, export shipping instructions, or other commercial loading document that describes the basis for not filing EEI for an export transaction. The exemption legend shall reference the number of the section or provision in the FTR where the particular exemption is provided (See Appendix D to this part).

Export. To send or transport goods out of a country.

Export Administration Regulations (EAR). Regulations administered by the BIS that, among other things, provide specific instructions on the use and types of export licenses required for certain commodities, software, and technology. These regulations are located in 15 CFR parts 730 through 774.

Export control. Governmental control of exports for statistical or strategic and short supply or national security purposes, and/or for foreign policy purposes.

Export Control Classification Number (ECCN). The number used to identify items on the CCL, Supplement No. 1 to Part 774 of the EAR. The ECCN consists of a set of digits and a letter. Items that are not classified under an ECCN are designated "EAR99." Section 738.2 of the EAR describes the ECCN format.

Export license. A controlling agency's document authorizing export of particular goods in specific quantities or values to a particular destination. Issuing agencies include, but are not limited to, the U.S. State Department; the BIS; the Bureau of Alcohol, Tobacco, and Firearms; and the Drug Enforcement Administration permit to export.

Export statistics. The measure of quantity and value of goods (except for shipments to U.S. military forces overseas) moving out of the United States to foreign countries, whether such goods are exported from within the Customs territory of the United States, a CBP bonded warehouse, or a U.S. Foreign Trade Zone (FTZ).

Export value. The value of the goods at the U.S. port of export. The value shall be the selling price (or the cost if the goods are not sold), including inland or domestic freight, insurance, and other charges to the U.S. seaport, airport, or land border port of export. Cost of goods is the sum of expenses incurred in the USPPI's acquisition or production of the goods. (See § 30.6(a)(17)).

Fatal error message. An electronic response sent to the filer by the AES when invalid or missing data has been encountered, the EEI has been rejected, and the information is not on file in the AES. The filer is required to immediately correct the problem, correct the data, and retransmit the EEI.

Filers. Those USPPIs or authorized agents (of either the USPPI or the FPPI) who have been approved to file EEI directly in the AES system or AES*Direct* Internet application.

Filing electronic export information. The act of entering the EEI in the AES.

Foreign entity. A person that temporarily enters into the United States and purchases or obtains goods for export. This person does not physically maintain an office or residence in the United States. This is a special class of USPPI.

Foreign exports. Commodities of foreign origin that have entered the United States for consumption, for entry into a CBP bonded warehouse or U.S. FTZ, and which, at the time of exportation, are in substantially the same condition as when imported.

Foreign principal party in interest (FPPI). The party shown on the transportation document to whom final delivery or end-use of the goods will be made. This party may be the ultimate consignee.

Foreign Trade Zone (FTZ). Specially licensed commercial and industrial areas in or near ports of entry where foreign and domestic goods, including raw materials, components, and finished goods, may be brought in without being subject to payment of customs duties. Goods brought into these zones may be stored, sold, exhibited, repacked, assembled, sorted, graded, cleaned, or otherwise manipulated prior to reexport or entry into the country's customs territory.

Forwarding agent. The person in the United States who is authorized by the principal party in interest to facilitate the movement of the cargo from the United States to the foreign destination and/or prepare and file the required documentation.

Goods. Merchandise, supplies, raw materials, and products or any other item identified by a Harmonized Tariff System (HTS) code.

Harmonized system. A method of classifying goods for international trade developed by the Customs Cooperation Council (now the World Customs Organization).

Harmonized Tariff Schedule of the United States (HTSUS). An organized listing of goods and their duty rates, developed by the U.S. International Trade Commission, which is used by CBP as the basis for classifying imported products, including establishing the duty to be charged and providing statistical information about imports and exports.

Imports. All goods physically brought into the United States, including:

(1) Goods of foreign origin, and

(2) Goods of domestic origin returned to the United States without substantial transformation affecting a change in tariff classification under an applicable rule of origin.

Inbond. A procedure administered by CBP under which goods are transported or warehoused under CBP supervision until the goods are either formally entered into the customs territory of the United States and duties are paid, or until they are exported from the United States. The procedure is so named because the cargo moves under a bond (financial liability assured by the principal on the bond) from the gateway seaport, airport, or land border port and remains "inbond" until CBP releases the

31558 Federal Register / Vol. 73, No. 106 / Monday, June 2, 2008 / Rules and Regulations

cargo at the inland Customs point or at the port of export.

Inland freight. The cost to ship goods between points inland and the seaport, airport, or land border port of exportation, other than baggage, express mail, or regular mail.

Intermediate consignee. The person or entity in the foreign country who acts as an agent for the principal party in interest with the purpose of effecting delivery of items to the ultimate consignee. The intermediate consignee may be a bank, forwarding agent, or other person who acts as an agent for a principal party in interest.

Internal Transaction Number (ITN). The AES generated number assigned to a shipment confirming that an EEI transaction was accepted and is on file in the AES.

International Standards Organization (ISO) Country Codes. The 2-position alphabetic ISO code for countries used to identify countries for which shipments are reportable.

International Traffic in Arms Regulations (ITAR). Regulations administered by the Directorate of Defense Trade Controls within the U.S. State Department that provide for the control of the export and temporary import of defense articles and defense services. These regulations are located in 22 CFR 120–130.

Interplant correspondence. Records or documents from a U.S. firm to its subsidiary or affiliate, whether in the United States or overseas.

In-transit. Goods shipped through the United States, Puerto Rico, or the U.S. Virgin Islands from one foreign country or area to another foreign country or area without entering the consumption channels of the United States.

License applicant. The person who applies for an export or reexport license. (For example, obtaining a license for commodities, software, or technology that are listed on the CCL.)

License exception. An authorization that allows a USPPI or other appropriate party to export or reexport under stated conditions, items subject to the EAR that would otherwise require a license under the EAR. The BIS License Exceptions are currently contained in Part 740 of the EAR (15 CFR part 740).

Loading document. A document that establishes the terms of a contract between a shipper and a transportation company under which freight is to be moved between points for a specific charge. It is usually prepared by the shipper and actuated by the carrier and serves as a document of title, a contract of carriage, and a receipt for goods. Examples of loading documents include the air waybill, inland bill of lading, ocean bill of lading, and through bill of lading.

Manifest. A collection of documents, including forms, such as the cargo declaration and annotated bills of lading, that lists and describes the cargo contents of a carrier, container, or warehouse. Carriers required to file manifests with CBP Port Director must include an AES filing citation, or exemption or exclusion legend for all cargo being transported.

Merchandise. Goods, wares, and chattels of every description, and includes merchandise the exportation of which is prohibited, and monetary instruments as defined in 31 U.S.C. 5312.

Method of transportation. The method by which goods arrive in or are exported from the United States by way of seaports, airports, or land border crossing points. Methods of transportation include vessel, air, truck, rail, or other.

North American Free Trade Agreement (NAFTA). The formal agreement, or treaty, among Canada, Mexico, and the United States to promote trade amongst the three countries. It includes measures for the elimination of tariffs and nontariff barriers to trade, as well as numerous specific provisions concerning the conduct of trade and investment.

Office of Foreign Assets Control (OFAC). An agency within the U.S. Department of the Treasury that administers and enforces economic and trade sanctions based on U.S. foreign policy and national security goals against targeted foreign countries, terrorists, international narcotics traffickers, and those engaged in activities related to the proliferation of weapons of mass destruction. The OFAC acts under Presidential wartime and national emergency powers, as well as authority granted by specific legislation, to impose controls on transactions and freeze foreign assets under U.S. jurisdiction.

Order party. The person in the United States that conducts the direct negotiations or correspondence with the foreign purchaser or ultimate consignee and who, as a result of these negotiations, receives the order from the FPPI. If a U.S. order party directly arranges for the sale and export of goods to the FPPI, the U.S. order party shall be listed as the USPPI in the EEI.

Packing list. A list showing the number and kinds of items being shipped, as well as other information needed for transportation purposes.

Partnership agencies. U.S. government agencies that have statistical and analytical reporting and/or monitoring and enforcement responsibilities related to AES postdeparture filing privileges.

Party ID type. Identifies whether the Party ID is an EIN, SSN, DUNS, or Foreign Entity reported to the AES, *i.e.*, E=EIN, S=SSN, D=DUNS, T=Foreign Entity.

Person. Any natural person, corporation partnership or other legal entity of any kind, domestic or foreign.

Port of export. The seaport or airport where the goods are loaded on the exporting carrier that is taking the goods out of the United States, or the port where exports by overland transportation cross the U.S. border into a foreign country. In the case of an export by mail, use port code 8000.

Postdeparture filing. The privilege granted to approved USPPIs for their EEI to be filed up to 10 calendar days after the date of export, *i.e.*, the date the goods are scheduled to cross the U.S. border.

Postdeparture filing citation. A notation placed on the bill of lading, air waybill, export shipping instructions, or other commercial loading documents that states that the EEI will be filed after departure of the carrier. (See Appendix D of this part.)

Power of attorney. A legal authorization, in writing, from a USPPI or FPPI stating that the agent has authority to act as the principal party's true and lawful agent for purposes of preparing and filing the EEI in accordance with the laws and regulations of the United States.

Primary benefit. Receiving the majority payment or exchange of item of value or other legal consideration resulting from an export trade transaction; usually monetary.

Principal parties in interest. Those persons in a transaction that receive the primary benefit, monetary or otherwise, from the transaction. Generally, the principals in a transaction are the seller and the buyer. In most cases, the forwarding or other agent is not a principal party in interest.

Proof of filing citation. A notation placed on the bill of lading, air waybill, export shipping instructions, or other commercial loading document, usually for carrier use, that provides evidence that the EEI has been filed and accepted in the AES.

Reexport. For statistical purposes: These are exports of foreign-origin goods that have previously entered the United States, Puerto Rico, or the U.S. Virgin Islands for consumption, entry into a CBP bonded warehouse, or a U.S. FTZ, and at the time of exportation, have undergone no change in form or condition or enhancement in value by further manufacturing in the United States, Puerto Rico, the U.S. Virgin Islands, or U.S. FTZs. For the purpose of goods subject to export controls (*e.g.*, U.S. Munitions List (USML) articles) these are shipments of U.S.-origin products from one foreign destination to another.

Related party transaction. A transaction involving trade between a USPPI and an ultimate consignee where either party owns directly or indirectly 10 percent or more of the other party.

Remission. The cancellation or release from a penalty, including fines, and/or forfeiture, under this part.

Retention. The necessary act of keeping all documentation pertaining to an export transaction for a period of at least five years for an EEI filing, or a time frame designated by the controlling agency for licensed shipments, whichever is longer.

Routed export transaction. A transaction in which the FPPI authorizes a U.S. agent to facilitate export of items from the United States on its behalf and prepare and file the EEI.

Schedule B. The Statistical Classification of Domestic and Foreign Commodities Exported from the United States. These 10-digit commodity classification numbers are administered by the Census Bureau and cover everything from live animals and food products to computers and airplanes. It should also be noted that all import and export codes used by the United States are based on the Harmonized Tariff System.

Schedule C. The Classification of Country and Territory Designations. The Schedule C provides a list of country of origin codes. The country of origin is reported in terms of the International Standards Organization codes.

Schedule D. The Classification of CBP districts and ports. The Schedule D provides a list of CBP districts and ports and the corresponding numeric codes used in compiling U.S. foreign trade statistics.

Schedule K. The Classification of Foreign Ports by Geographic Trade Area and Country. The Schedule K lists the major seaports of the world that directly handle waterborne shipments in the foreign trade of the United States, and includes numeric codes to identify these ports. This schedule is maintained by the U.S. Army Corps of Engineers.

Seller. A principal in the transaction, usually the manufacturer, producer, wholesaler, or distributor of the goods, that receives the monetary benefit or other consideration for the exported goods.

Service center. A company, entity, or organization which has been certified and approved to only transmit complete EEI to the AES.

Shipment. Unless as otherwise provided, all goods being sent from one USPPI to one consignee to a single country of destination on a single conveyance and on the same day.

Shipment reference number. A unique identification number assigned to the shipment by the filer for reference purposes. This number must remain unique for a period of five years.

Shipper's Export Declaration. The DOC paper form used under the FTSR to collect information from a person exporting from the United States. This form was used for compiling the official U.S. export statistics for the United States and for export control purposes.

Shipping weight. The total weight of a shipment in kilograms including goods and packaging.

Split shipment. A shipment booked for export on one aircraft, but split by the carrier and sent on two or more aircrafts of the same carrier.

Subzone. A special purpose foreign trade zone established as part of a foreign trade zone project with a limited purpose that cannot be accommodated within an existing zone. Subzones are often established to serve the needs of a specific company and may be located within an existing facility of the company.

Tariff schedule. A comprehensive list or schedule of goods with applicable duty rates to be paid or charged for each listed article as it enters or leaves a country.

Transmitting electronic export information. The act of sending the completed EEI to the AES.

Transportation reference number. A reservation number assigned by the carrier to hold space on the carrier for cargo being shipped. It is the booking number for vessel shipments and the master air waybill number for air shipments, the bill of lading number for rail shipments, and the freight or pro bill for truck shipments.

Ultimate consignee. The person, party, or designee that is located abroad and actually receives the export shipment. This party may be the end user or the FPPI.

United States Munitions List (USML). Articles and services designated for defense purposes under the ITAR and specified in 22 CFR 121.

Unlading. The physical removal of cargo from an aircraft, truck, rail, or vessel.

U.S. Customs and Border Protection (CBP). CBP is the unified border agency within the DHS charged with the management, control, and protection of our Nation's borders at and between the official ports of entry to the United States. CBP is charged with keeping terrorist and terrorist weapons from entering the country and enforcing customs, immigration, agricultural and countless other laws of the United States.

U.S. Immigration and Customs Enforcement (ICE). An agency within the DHS that is responsible for enforcing customs, immigration and related laws and investigating violations of laws to secure the Nation's borders.

U.S. principal party in interest (USPPI). The person or legal entity in the United States that receives the primary benefit, monetary or otherwise, from the export transaction. Generally, that person or entity is the U.S. seller, manufacturer, or order party, or the foreign entity while in the United States when purchasing or obtaining the goods for export.

Vehicle Identification Number (VIN). A number issued by the manufacturer and used for the identification of a self-propelled vehicle.

Verify message. An electronic response sent to the filer by the AES when an unlikely condition is found.

Violation of the FTR. Failure of the USPPI, FPPI, authorized agent of the USPPI, FPPI, carrier, or other party to the transaction to comply with the requirements set forth in 15 CFR 30, for each export shipment.

Warning message. An electronic response sent to the filer by the AES when certain incomplete and conflicting data reporting conditions are encountered.

Wholesaler/distributor. An agent who sells directly for a supplier and maintains an inventory of the supplier's products.

Written authorization. A legal authorization, in writing, by the USPPI or FPPI stating that the agent has authority to act as the USPPI's or FPPI's true and lawful agent for purposes of preparing and filing the EEI in accordance with the laws and regulations of the United States.

Zone admission number. A unique and sequential number assigned by a FTZ operator or user for shipments admitted to a zone.

§ 30.2 General requirements for filing Electronic Export Information (EEI).

(a) *Filing requirements*—(1) The EEI shall be filed through the AES by the United States Principal Party In Interest (USPPI), the USPPI's authorized agent, or the authorized U.S. agent of the Foreign Principal Party In Interest (FPPI) for all exports of physical goods,

31560 **Federal Register** / Vol. 73, No. 106 / Monday, June 2, 2008 / Rules and Regulations

including shipments moving pursuant to orders received over the Internet. The Automated Export System (AES) is the electronic system for collecting Shipper's Export Declaration (SED) (or any successor document) information from persons exporting goods from the United States, Puerto Rico, Foreign Trade Zones (FTZs) located in the United States or Puerto Rico, the U.S. Virgin Islands, between Puerto Rico and the United States, and to the U.S. Virgin Islands from the United States or Puerto Rico. Exceptions, exclusions, and exemptions to this requirement are provided for in paragraph (d) of this section and Subpart D of this part. References to the AES also shall apply to AES*Direct* unless otherwise specified. For purposes of the regulations in this part, the SED information shall be referred to as EEI. Filing through the AES shall be done in accordance with the definitions, specifications, and requirements of the regulations in this part for all export shipments, except as specifically excluded in § 30.2(d) or exempted in Subpart D of this part, when shipped as follows:

(i) To foreign countries or areas, including free (foreign trade) zones located therein (see § 30.36 for exemptions for shipments from the United States to Canada) from any of the following:

(A) The United States, including the 50 states and the District of Columbia.

(B) Puerto Rico.

(C) FTZs located in the United States or Puerto Rico.

(D) The U.S. Virgin Islands.

(ii) Between any of the following nonforeign areas including goods previously admitted to customs warehouses or FTZs and moving under a U.S. Customs and Border Protection (CBP) bond:

(A) To Puerto Rico from the United States.

(B) To the United States from Puerto Rico.

(C) To the U.S. Virgin Islands from the United States or Puerto Rico.

(iii) The EEI shall be filed for goods moving as described in paragraphs (a)(1)(i) and (ii) of this section by any mode of transportation. (Instructions for filing EEI for vessels, aircraft, railway cars, and other carriers when sold while outside the areas described in paragraphs (a)(1)(i) and (ii) are covered in § 30.26.)

(iv) Notwithstanding exemptions in Subpart D, EEI shall be filed for the following types of export shipments, regardless of value:

(A) Requiring a Department of Commerce, Bureau of Industry and Security (BIS) license (15 CFR 730–774).

(B) Requiring a Department of State, Directorate of Defense Trade Controls (DDTC) license under the International Traffic in Arms Regulations (ITAR) (22 CFR Parts 120 through 130).

(C) Subject to the ITAR, but exempt from license requirements.

(D) Requiring a Department of Justice, Drug Enforcement Administration (DEA) export permit (21 CFR 1312).

(E) Destined for a country listed in Country Group E:1 as set forth in Supplement 1 to 15 CFR 740.

(F) Requiring an export license issued by any other federal government agency.

(G) Classified as rough diamonds under 6-digit HS subheadings 7102.10, 7102.21, and 7102.31.

(2) *Filing methods.* The USPPI has four means for filing EEI: use AES*Direct*; develop AES software using the AESTIR (see *http://www.cbp.gov/xp/cgov/export/aes/*); purchase software developed by certified vendors using the AESTIR; or use an authorized agent. An FPPI can only use an authorized agent in a routed export transaction.

(b) *General requirements*—(1) The EEI shall be filed prior to exportation (see § 30.4) unless the USPPI has been approved to submit export data on a postdeparture basis (see § 30.5(c)). Shipments requiring a license or license exemption may be filed postdeparture only when the appropriate licensing agency has granted the USPPI authorization. See Subpart B of this part.

(2) Specific data elements required for EEI filing are contained in § 30.6.

(3) The AES downtime procedures provide uniform instructions for processing export transactions when the AES or AES*Direct* or the computer system of an AES participant is unavailable for transmission. (See § 30.4(b)(1) and § 30.4(b)(3).)

(4) Instructions for particular types of transactions and exemptions from these requirements are found in Subparts C and D of this part.

(5) The EEI is required to be filed in the AES prior to export for shipments by vessel going directly to the countries identified in U.S. Customs and Border Protection regulations 19 CFR 4.75(c) and by aircraft going directly or indirectly to those countries. (See U.S. Customs and Border Protection regulations 19 CFR 122.74(b)(2).)

(c) *Certification and filing requirements.* Filers of EEI shall be required to meet application, certification, and filing requirements before being approved to submit EEI. Steps leading toward approval for the AES or the AES*Direct* filing include the following processes: (See § 30.5 for specific application, certification, and filing standards applicable to AES and AES*Direct* submissions.)

(1) Submission of an electronic AES Participant Application (APA) for AES filing or submission of an online registration for filing through *http://www.census.gov/aes.*

(2) Successful completion of certification testing for AES or for AES*Direct* filing.

(d) *Exclusions from filing EEI.* The following types of transactions are outside the scope of this part and shall be excluded from EEI filing:

(1) Goods shipped under CBP bond through the United States, Puerto Rico, or the U.S. Virgin Islands from one foreign country or area to another where such goods do not enter the consumption channels of the United States.

(2) Goods shipped from the U.S. territories and goods shipped between the United States and these territories do not require EEI filing. However, goods transiting U.S. territories to foreign destinations require EEI filing.

(3) Electronic transmissions and intangible transfers. (See Subpart B of this part for export control requirements for these types of transactions.)

(4) Goods shipped to Guantanamo Bay Naval Base in Cuba from the United States, Puerto Rico, or the U.S. Virgin Islands and from Guantanamo Bay Naval Base to the United States, Puerto Rico, or the U.S. Virgin Islands. (See § 30.39 for filing requirements for shipments exported by the U.S. Armed Services.)

(e) *Penalties.* Failure of the USPPI, the authorized agent of either the USPPI or the FPPI, the exporting carrier, or any other person subject thereto to comply with any of the requirements of the regulations in this part renders such persons subject to the penalties provided for in Subpart H of this part.

§ 30.3 Electronic Export Information filer requirements, parties to export transactions, and responsibilities of parties to export transactions.

(a) *General requirements.* The filer of EEI for export transactions is either the USPPI, the authorized agent, or the authorized U.S. agent of the FPPI. All EEI submitted to the AES shall be complete, correct, and based on personal knowledge of the facts stated or on information furnished by the parties to the export transaction. The filer shall be physically located in the United States at the time of filing, have an EIN or SSN, or DUNS number and be certified to report in the AES. The filer is responsible for the truth, accuracy, and completeness of the EEI, except insofar as that party can demonstrate

Appendix C

that he or she reasonably relied on information furnished by other responsible persons participating in the transaction. All parties involved in export transactions, including U.S. authorized agents, should be aware that invoices and other commercial documents may not necessarily contain all the information needed to prepare the EEI. The parties shall ensure that all information needed for reporting to the AES, including correct export licensing information, is provided to the authorized agent for the purpose of correctly preparing the EEI.

(b) *Parties to the export transaction*—(1) *Principal parties in interest.* Those persons in a transaction that receive the primary benefit, monetary or otherwise, are considered principal parties to the transaction. Generally, the principal parties in interest in a transaction are the seller and buyer. In most cases, the forwarding or other agent is not a principal party in interest.

(2) *USPPI.* For purposes of filing EEI, the USPPI is the person or legal entity in the United States that receives the primary benefit, monetary or otherwise, from the transaction. Generally, that person or entity is the U.S. seller, manufacturer, order party, or foreign entity purchasing or obtaining goods for export. The foreign entity shall be listed as the USPPI if it is in the United States when the items are purchased or obtained for export. The foreign entity shall then follow the provisions for filing the EEI specified in § 30.3 and § 30.6 pertaining to the USPPI.

(i) If a U.S. manufacturer sells goods directly to an entity in a foreign area, the U.S. manufacturer shall be listed as the USPPI in the EEI.

(ii) If a U.S. manufacturer sells goods, as a domestic sale, to a U.S. buyer (wholesaler/distributor) and that U.S. buyer sells the goods for export to a FPPI, the U.S. buyer (wholesaler/distributor) shall be listed as the USPPI in the EEI.

(iii) If a U.S. order party directly arranges for the sale and export of goods to a foreign entity, the U.S. order party shall be listed as the USPPI in the EEI.

(iv) If a customs broker is listed as the importer of record when entering goods into the United States for immediate consumption or warehousing entry, the customs broker may be listed as the USPPI in the EEI if the goods are subsequently exported without change or enhancement.

(v) If a foreign person is listed as the importer of record when entering goods into the United States for immediate consumption or warehousing entry, the customs broker who entered the goods, may be listed as the USPPI in the EEI if the goods are subsequently exported without change or enhancement.

(3) *Authorized agent.* The agent shall be authorized by the USPPI or, in the case of a routed export transaction, the agent shall be authorized by the FPPI to prepare and file the EEI. In a routed export transaction, the authorized agent can be the "exporter" for export control purposes as defined in 15 CFR 772.1 of the U.S. Department of Commerce EAR. However, the authorized agent shall not be shown as the USPPI in the EEI unless the agent acts as a USPPI in the export transaction as defined in paragraphs (b)(2)(iii), (iv), and (v) of this section.

(c) *General responsibilities of parties in export transactions*—(1) *USPPI responsibilities.*

(i) The USPPI can prepare and file the EEI itself, or it can authorize an agent to prepare and file the EEI on its behalf. If the USPPI prepares the EEI itself, the USPPI is responsible for the accuracy and timely transmission of all the export information reported to the AES.

(ii) When the USPPI authorizes an agent to file the EEI on its behalf, the USPPI is responsible for:

(A) Providing the authorized agent with accurate and timely export information necessary to file the EEI.

(B) Providing the authorized agent with a power of attorney or written authorization to file the EEI (see paragraph (f) of this section for written authorization requirements for agents).

(C) Retaining documentation to support the information provided to the authorized agent for filing the EEI, as specified in § 30.10.

(2) *Authorized agent responsibilities.* The agent, when authorized by a USPPI to prepare and file the EEI for an export transaction, is responsible for performing the following activities:

(i) Accurate preparation and timely filing of the EEI based on information received from the USPPI and other parties involved in the transaction.

(ii) Obtaining a power of attorney or written authorization to file the EEI.

(iii) Retaining documentation to support the information reported to the AES, as specified in § 30.10.

(iv) Upon request, providing the USPPI with a copy of the export information filed in a mutually agreed upon format.

(d) *Filer responsibilities.* Responsibilities of USPPIs and authorized agents filing EEI are as follows:

(1) Filing complete and accurate information (see § 30.4 for a delineation of filing responsibilities of USPPIs and authorized agents).

(2) Filing information in a timely manner in accordance with the provisions and requirements contained in this part.

(3) Responding to fatal errors, warning, verify and reminder messages, and compliance alerts generated by the AES in accordance with provisions and requirements contained in this part.

(4) Providing the exporting carrier with the required proof of filing citations or exemption legends in accordance with provisions contained in this part.

(5) Promptly filing corrections or cancellations to EEI in accordance with provisions contained in § 30.9.

(6) Retaining all necessary and proper documentation related to EEI transactions in accordance with provisions contained in this part (see § 30.10 for specific requirements for retaining and producing documentation for export shipments).

(e) *Responsibilities of parties in a routed export transaction.* The Census Bureau recognizes "routed export transactions" as a subset of export transactions. A routed export transaction is a transaction in which the FPPI authorizes a U.S. agent to facilitate the export of items from the United States and to prepare and file EEI.

(1) *USPPI responsibilities.* In a routed export transaction, the FPPI may authorize or agree to allow the USPPI to prepare and file the EEI. If the FPPI agrees to allow the USPPI to file the EEI, the FPPI must provide a written authorization to the USPPI assuming the responsibility for filing. The USPPI may authorize an agent to file the EEI on its behalf. If the USPPI or its agent prepares and files the EEI, it shall retain documentation to support the EEI filed. If the FPPI agrees to allow the USPPI to file EEI, the filing of the export transaction shall be treated as a routed export transaction. If the FPPI authorizes an agent to prepare and file the EEI, the USPPI shall retain documentation to support the information provided to the agent for preparing the EEI as specified in § 30.10 and provide the agent with the following information to assist in preparing the EEI:

(i) Name and address of the USPPI.

(ii) USPPI's EIN or SSN.

(iii) State of origin (State).

(iv) FTZ if applicable.

(v) Commercial description of commodities.

(vi) Origin of goods indicator: Domestic (D) or Foreign (F).

(vii) Schedule B or HTSUSA, Classification Commodity Code.

(viii) Quantities/units of measure.

(ix) Value.

(x) Export Control Classification Number (ECCN) or sufficient technical information to determine the ECCN.

(xi) All licensing information necessary to file the EEI for commodities where the Department of State, the Department of Commerce, or other U.S. government agency issues a license for the commodities being exported, or the merchandise is being exported under a license exemption or license exception.

(xii) Any information that it knows will affect the determination of license authorization (see Subpart B of this part for additional information on licensing requirements).

Note to Paragraph (e)(1) of this section: For items in paragraph (e) (1) (ix), (x),(xi) and (xii) of this section, where the FPPI has assumed responsibility for determining and obtaining license authority see requirements set forth in 15 CFR 758.3 of the EAR.

(2) *Authorized agent responsibilities.* In a routed export transaction, if an authorized agent is preparing and filing the EEI on behalf of the FPPI, the authorized agent must obtain a power of attorney or written authorization from the FPPI and prepare and file the EEI based on information obtained from the USPPI or other parties involved in the transaction. The authorized agent shall be responsible for filing the EEI accurately and timely in accordance with the FTR. Upon request, the authorized agent will provide the USPPI with a copy of the power of attorney or written authorization from the FPPI. The authorized agent shall also retain documentation to support the EEI reported through the AES. The agents shall upon request, provide the USPPI with the data elements in paragraphs (e)(1)(i) through (xii) of this section as submitted through the AES. The authorized agent shall provide the following export information through the AES:

(i) Date of export.

(ii) Transportation Reference Number.

(iii) Ultimate consignee.

(iv) Intermediate consignee, if applicable.

(v) Authorized agent name and address.

(vi) EIN, SSN, or DUNS number of the authorized agent.

(vii) Country of ultimate destination.

(viii) Method of transportation.

(ix) Carrier identification and conveyance name.

(x) Port of export.

(xi) Foreign port of unloading.

(xii) Shipping weight.

(xiii) ECCN.

(xiv) License or license exemption information.

Note to Paragraph (e)(2) of this section: For items in paragraphs (e)(2)(xiii) and (xiv) of this section, where the FPPI has assumed responsibility for determining and obtaining license authority, see requirements set forth in 15 CFR 758.3 of the EAR.

(f) *Authorizing an agent.* In a power of attorney or other written authorization, authority is conferred upon an agent to perform certain specified acts or kinds of acts on behalf of a principal (see 15 CFR 758.1(h) of the EAR). In cases where an authorized agent is filing EEI to the AES, the agent shall obtain a power of attorney or written authorization from a principal party in interest to file the information on its behalf. A power of attorney or written authorization should specify the responsibilities of the parties with particularity and should state that the agent has authority to act on behalf of a principal party in interest as its true and lawful agent for purposes of creating and filing EEI in accordance with the laws and regulations of the United States. In routed export transactions the USPPI is not required to provide an agent of the FPPI with a power of attorney or written authorization.

Note to § 30.3: The EAR defines the "exporter" as the person in the United States who has the authority of a principal party in interest to determine and control the sending of items out of the United States (see 15 CFR 772 of the EAR). For statistical purposes "exporter" is not defined in the FTR. Instead, however, the USPPI is defined in the FTR.

For purposes of licensing responsibility under the EAR, the U.S. agent of the FPPI may be the "exporter" or applicant on the license in certain routed export transactions (see 15 CFR 758.3 of the EAR). Therefore, due to the differences in export reporting requirements among Federal agencies, conformity of documentation is not required in the FTR.

§ 30.4 Electronic Export Information filing procedures, deadlines, and certification statements.

Two electronic filing options (predeparture and postdeparture) for transmitting EEI are available to the USPPI or authorized agent. The electronic postdeparture filing takes into account that complete information concerning export shipments may not always be available prior to exportation and accommodates these circumstances by providing, when authorized, for filing of EEI after departure. For example, for exports of seasonal and agricultural commodities, only estimated quantities, values, and consignees may be known prior to exportation. The procedures for obtaining certification as an AES filer and for applying for authorization to file on a postdeparture basis are described in § 30.5.

(a) *EEI transmitted predeparture.* The EEI shall always be transmitted prior to departure for the following types of shipments:

(1) Used self-propelled vehicles as defined in 19 CFR 192.1 of U.S. Customs and Border Protection regulations.

(2) Essential and precursor chemicals requiring a permit from the DEA;

(3) Shipments defined as "sensitive" by Executive Order;

(4) Shipments where a U.S. government agency requires predeparture filing;

(5) Shipments defined as "routed export transactions" (see § 30.3(e));

(6) Shipments to countries where complete outbound manifests are required prior to clearing vessels or aircraft for export (see U.S. Customs and Border Protection regulations 19 CFR 4.75(c) and 122.74(b)(2) for a listing of these countries);

(7) Items identified on the USML of the ITAR (22 CFR 121);

(8) Exports that require a license from the BIS, unless the BIS has approved postdeparture filing privileges for the USPPI;

(9) Shipments of rough diamonds classified under HS subheadings 7102.10, 7102.21, and 7102.31 and exported (reexported) in accordance with the Kimberley Process; and

(10) Shipments for which the USPPI has not been approved for postdeparture filing.

(b) *Filing deadlines for EEI transmitted predeparture.* The USPPI or the authorized agent shall file the required EEI and have received the AES ITN no later than the time period specified as follows:

(1) For USML shipments, refer to the ITAR (22 CFR 120 through 130) for specific requirements concerning predeparture filing time frames. In addition, if a filer is unable to acquire an ITN because the AES is not operating, the filer shall not export until the AES is operating and an ITN is acquired.

(2) For non-USML shipments, file the EEI and provide the ITN as follows:

(i) For vessel cargo, the USPPI or the authorized agent shall file the EEI required by § 30.6 and provide the filing citation or exemption legend to the exporting carrier twenty-four hours prior to loading cargo on the vessel at the U.S. port where the cargo is laden.

(ii) For air cargo, including cargo being transported by Air Express Couriers, the USPPI or the authorized agent shall file the EEI required by § 30.6 and provide the filing citation or exemption legend to the exporting carrier no later than two (2) hours prior to the scheduled departure time of the aircraft.

(iii) For truck cargo, including cargo departing by Express Consignment Couriers, the USPPI or the authorized agent shall file the EEI required by § 30.6 and provide the filing citation or exemption legend to the exporting carrier no later than one (1) hour prior to the arrival of the truck at the United States border to go foreign.

(iv) For rail cargo, the USPPI or the authorized agent shall file the EEI required by § 30.6 and provide the filing citation or exemption legend to the exporting carrier no later than two (2) hours prior to the time the train arrives at the U.S. border to go foreign.

(v) For mail and cargo shipped by other methods, except pipeline, the USPPI or the authorized agent shall file the EEI required by § 30.6 and provide the filing citation or exemption legend to the exporting carrier no later than two (2) hours prior to exportation. (See § 30.46 for filing deadlines for shipments sent by pipeline.)

(vi) For all other modes, the USPPI or the authorized agent shall file the required EEI no later than two (2) hours prior to exportation.

(3) For non-USML shipments when the AES is unavailable, use the following instructions:

(i) If the participant's AES is unavailable, the filer must delay the export of the goods or find an alternative filing method;

(ii) If AES or AES*Direct* is unavailable, the goods may be exported and the filer must:

(A) Provide the appropriate downtime filing citation as described in § 30.7(b) and Appendix D; and

(B) Report the EEI at the first opportunity AES is available.

(c) *EEI transmitted postdeparture.* Postdeparture filing is only available for approved USPPIs and provides for the electronic filing of the data elements required by § 30.6 no later than ten calendar days from the date of exportation. For USPPIs approved for postdeparture filing, all shipments (other than those for which predeparture filing is specifically required), by all methods of transportation, may be exported with the filing of EEI made postdeparture. Certified AES authorized agents or service centers may transmit information postdeparture on behalf of USPPIs approved for postdeparture filing, or the approved USPPI may transmit the data postdeparture itself. However, authorized agents or service centers will not be approved for postdeparture filing.

(d) *Proof of filing citation and exemption and exclusion legends.* The USPPI or the authorized agent shall provide the exporting carrier with the proof of filing citation and exemption and exclusion legends as described in § 30.7.

§ 30.5 Electronic Export Information filing application and certification processes and standards.

Prior to filing EEI, the USPPI or the authorized agent must be certified to file through the AES. A service center shall be certified to transmit electronically to the AES. The USPPI, authorized agent, or service center may use a software package designed by a certified vendor to file EEI through the AES. Once an authorized agent has successfully completed the certification process, any USPPI using that agent does not have to be certified. The certified authorized agent shall have a properly executed power of attorney or written authorization from the USPPI or FPPI, and be physically located in the United States to file EEI through the AES. The USPPI or authorized agent that utilizes a certified software vendor or service center shall complete certification testing. Service centers may only transmit export information; they may not prepare and file export information unless they have authorization from the USPPI in the form of a power of attorney or written authorization, thus making them authorized agents. The USPPI seeking approval for postdeparture filing privileges shall be approved before they or their authorized agent may file on a postdeparture basis.

(a) *AES application process*—(1) *AES Participation Application.* The USPPI or authorized agent who chooses to file through the AES and seek approval for postdeparture filing privileges, must submit a complete on-line LOI at *http://www.census.gov/aes.*

(2) *AESDirect registration.* The USPPI or authorized agent who chooses to file through AES*Direct* shall also complete the online AES*Direct* registration form at *http://www.aesdirect.gov.* After submitting the registration, an AES*Direct* filing account is created for the filing company. The person designated as the account administrator is responsible for activating the account and completing the certification process as discussed in paragraph (b)(2) of this section.

(b) *Certification process*—(1) *AES certification process.* The USPPI or authorized agent shall perform an initial two-part communication test to ascertain whether its system is capable of both transmitting data to, and receiving data from, the AES. The USPPI or authorized agent shall demonstrate specific system application capabilities. The capability to correctly handle these system applications is the prerequisite to certification for participation in the AES. The USPPI or authorized agent shall successfully transmit the AES certification test. CBP's and/or Census Bureau's client representatives provide assistance during certification testing. These representatives make the sole determination as to whether or not the USPPI or authorized agent qualifies for certification. Upon successful completion of certification testing, the USPPI's or authorized agent's status is moved from testing mode to operational status. The AES filers may be required to repeat the certification testing process at any time. The Census Bureau will provide the AES filer with a certification notice after the USPPI or authorized agent has been approved for operational status. The certification notice will include:

(i) The date that filers may begin transmitting data;

(ii) Reporting instructions; and

(iii) Examples of the required AES proof of filing citations, postdeparture filing citations, AES downtime filing citation, and exemption legends.

(2) AES*Direct certification process.* To become certified for AES*Direct*, filers shall demonstrate knowledge of this part and the ability to successfully transmit EEI. Upon successful completion of the certification testing, notification by e-mail will be sent to the account administrator when an account is fully activated for filing via AES*Direct.* Certified filers should print and retain the page congratulating the filer on passing the test.

(c) *Postdeparture filing approval process.* The USPPI may apply for postdeparture filing privileges by submitting a postdeparture filing application at *http://www.census.gov/aes.* An authorized agent may not apply on behalf of a USPPI. The Census Bureau will distribute the LOI to CBP and the other federal government partnership agencies participating in the AES postdeparture filing review process. Failure to meet the standards of the Census Bureau, CBP or any of the partnership agencies is reason for denial of the AES applicant for postdeparture filing privileges. Each partnership agency will develop its own internal postdeparture filing acceptance standards, and each agency will notify the Census Bureau of the USPPI's success or failure to meet that agency's acceptance standards. Any partnership agency may require additional information from USPPIs that are applying for postdeparture filing. The Census Bureau will notify the USPPI of the decision to either deny or approve their application for postdeparture filing privileges within thirty (30) calendar days of receipt of the postdeparture filing application by the Census Bureau, or if a decision cannot be reached at that time, the USPPI will be notified of an extension for a final decision as soon as possible after the thirty (30) calendar days.

(1) *Grounds for denial of postdeparture filing status.* The Census Bureau may deny a USPPI's application for postdeparture filing privileges for any of the following reasons:

(i) There is no history of filing for the USPPI through the AES.

(ii) The USPPI's volume of EEI reported through the AES does not warrant participation in postdeparture filing.

(iii) The USPPI or its authorized agent has failed to submit EEI through the AES in a timely and accurate manner.

(iv) The USPPI has a history of noncompliance with the Census Bureau export regulations contained in this part.

(v) The USPPI has been indicted, convicted, or is currently under investigation for a felony involving a violation of federal export laws or regulations and the Census Bureau has evidence of probable cause supporting such violation, or the USPPI is in violation of Census Bureau export regulations contained in this part.

(vi) The USPPI has made or caused to be made in the LOI a false or misleading statement or omission with respect to any material fact.

(vii) The USPPI would pose a significant threat to national security interests such that its participation in postdeparture filing should be denied.

(viii) The USPPI has multiple violations of either the EAR (15 CFR 730 through 774) or the ITAR (22 CFR 120 through 130) within the last three (3) years.

(2) *Notice of denial.* A USPPI denied postdeparture filing privileges by other agencies shall contact those agencies regarding the specific reason(s) for nonselection and for their appeal procedures. A USPPI denied postdeparture filing status by the Census Bureau will be provided with a specific reason for nonselection and a Census Bureau point of contact in an electronic notification letter. A USPPI may appeal the Census Bureau's nonselection decision by following the appeal procedure and reapplication procedure provided in paragraph (c)(5) of this section.

(3) *Revocation of postdeparture filing privileges*—(i) *Revocation by the Census Bureau.* The Census Bureau may revoke postdeparture filing privileges of an approved USPPI for the following reasons:

(A) The USPPI's volume of EEI reported in the AES does not warrant continued participation in postdeparture filing;

(B) The USPPI or its authorized agent has failed to submit EEI through the AES in a timely and accurate manner;

(C) The USPPI has made or caused to be made in the LOI a false or misleading statement or omission with respect to material fact;

(D) The USPPI submitting the LOI has been indicted, convicted, or is currently under investigation for a felony involving a violation of federal export laws or regulations and the Census Bureau has evidence of probable cause supporting such violation, or the AES applicant is in violation of export rules and regulations contained in this part;

(E) The USPPI has failed to comply with existing export regulations or has failed to pay any outstanding penalties assessed in connection with such noncompliance; or

(F) The USPPI would pose a significant threat to national security interests such that its continued participation in postdeparture filing should be terminated.

(ii) *Revocation by other agencies.* Any of the other agencies may revoke a USPPI's postdeparture filing privileges with respect to transactions subject to the jurisdiction of that agency. When doing so, the agency shall notify both the Census Bureau and the USPPI whose authorization is being revoked.

(4) *Notice of revocation.* Approved postdeparture filing USPPIs whose postdeparture filing privileges have been revoked by other agencies shall contact those agencies for their specific revocation and appeal procedures. When the Census Bureau makes a determination to revoke an approved USPPI's postdeparture filing privileges, the USPPI will be notified electronically of the reason(s) for the decision. In most cases, the revocation shall become effective when the USPPI has either exhausted all appeal procedures, or thirty (30) calendar days after receipt of the notice of revocation, if no appeal is filed. However, in cases judged to affect national security, revocations shall become effective immediately upon notification.

(5) *Appeal procedure.* Any USPPI whose request for postdeparture filing privileges has been denied by the Census Bureau or whose postdeparture filing privileges have been revoked by the Census Bureau may appeal the decision by filing an appeal within thirty (30) calendar days of receipt of the notice of decision. Appeals should be addressed to the Chief, Foreign Trade Division, U.S. Census Bureau, Washington, DC 20233–6700. The Census Bureau will issue a written decision to the USPPI within thirty (30) calendar days from the date of receipt of the appeal by the Census Bureau. If a written decision is not issued within thirty (30) calendar days, the Census Bureau will forward to the USPPI a notice of extension within that time period. The USPPI will be provided with the reasons for the extension of this time period and an expected date of decision. The USPPIs who have had their postdeparture filing status denied or revoked may not reapply for this privilege for one year following written notification of the denial or revocation.

(d) *Electronic Export Information filing standards.* The data elements required for filing EEI are contained in § 30.6. When filing EEI, the USPPI or authorized agent shall comply with the data transmission procedures determined by CBP and the Census Bureau and shall agree to stay in complete compliance with all export rules and regulations in this part. Failure of the USPPI or the authorized agent of either the USPPI or FPPI to comply with these requirements constitutes a violation of the regulations in this part, and renders such principal party or the authorized agent subject to the penalties provided for in Subpart H of this part. In the case of AES*Direct*, when submitting a registration form to AES*Direct*, the registering company is certifying that it will be in compliance with all applicable export rules and regulations. This includes complying with the following security requirements:

(1) AES*Direct* user names, administrator codes, and passwords are to be kept secure by the account administrator and not disclosed to any unauthorized user or any persons outside the registered company.

(2) Registered companies are responsible for those persons having access to the user name, administrator code, and password. If an employee with direct access to the user name, administrator code, and password leaves the company or otherwise is no longer an authorized user, the company shall immediately change the password and administrator code in the system to ensure the integrity and confidentiality of Title 13 data.

Federal Register / Vol. 73, No. 106 / Monday, June 2, 2008 / Rules and Regulations **31565**

(3) Antivirus software shall be installed and set to run automatically on all computers that access AES*Direct*. All AES*Direct* registered companies will maintain subscriptions with their antivirus software vendor to keep antivirus lists current. Registered companies are responsible for performing full scans of these systems on a regular basis, but not less than every thirty (30) days, to ensure the elimination of any virus contamination. If the registered company's computer system is infected with a virus, the company shall contact the Census Bureau's Foreign Trade Division Computer Security Officer and refrain from using AES*Direct* until it is virus free. Failure to comply with these requirements will result in immediate loss of privilege to use AES*Direct* until the registered company can establish to the satisfaction of the Census Bureau's Foreign Trade Division Computer Security Officer that the company's computer systems accessing AES*Direct* are virus free.

(e) *Monitoring the filing of EEI.* The USPPI's or the authorized agent's AES filings will be monitored and reviewed for quality, timeliness, and coverage. The Census Bureau will provide performance reports to USPPIs and authorized agents who file EEI. The Census Bureau will take appropriate action to correct specific situations where the USPPI or authorized agent fails to maintain acceptable levels of data quality, timeliness, or coverage.

(f) *Support.* The Census Bureau provides online services that allow the USPPI and the authorized agent to seek assistance pertaining to AES and this part. For AES assistance, filers may send an e-mail to *ASKAES@census.gov* and for FTR assistance, filers may send an e-mail to *FTDREGS@census.gov.* AES*Direct* is supported by a help desk available twelve (12) hours a day from 7 a.m. to 7 p.m. EST, seven (7) days a week. Filers can obtain contact information from the Web site *http://www.aesdirect.gov.*

§ 30.6 Electronic Export Information data elements.

The information specified in this section is required for shipments transmitted to the AES. The data elements identified as "mandatory" shall be reported for each transaction. The data elements identified as "conditional" shall be reported if they are required for or apply to the specific shipment. The data elements identified as "optional" may be reported at the discretion of the USPPI or the authorized agent.

(a) *Mandatory data elements are as follows:*

(1) *USPPI and USPPI identification.* The name, address, identification, and contact information of the USPPI shall be reported to the AES as follows:

(i) *Name of the USPPI.* In all export transactions, the name listed in the USPPI field in the EEI shall be the USPPI in the transaction. (See § 30.1 for the definition of the USPPI and § 30.3 for details on the USPPI's reporting responsibilities.)

(ii) *Address of the USPPI.* In all EEI filings, the USPPI shall report the address or location (no post office box number) from which the goods actually begin the journey to the port of export. For example, the EEI covering goods laden aboard a truck at a warehouse in Georgia for transport to Florida for loading onto a vessel for export to a foreign country shall show the address of the warehouse in Georgia. For shipments with multiple origins, report the address from which the commodity with the greatest value begins its export journey. If such information is not known, report the address in state in which the commodities are consolidated for export.

(iii) *USPPI identification number.* The USPPI's EIN or SSN. The USPPI shall report its own IRS EIN in the USPPI field of the EEI. If the USPPI has only one EIN report that EIN. If the USPPI has more than one EIN, report an EIN that the USPPI also uses to report employee wages and withholdings, not an EIN used to report only company earnings or receipts. If, and only if, no IRS EIN has been assigned to the USPPI, the USPPI's own SSN shall be reported to the AES. Use of another company's EIN or another individual's SSN is prohibited. The appropriate Party Type code shall be reported through the AES. When a foreign entity is in the United States when the items are purchased or obtained for export, the foreign entity is the USPPI for filing purposes. In such situations, when the foreign entity does not have an EIN or SSN, it shall report in the EEI a DUNS number, border crossing number, passport number, or any number assigned by CBP.

(iv) *Contact information.* Show contact name and telephone number.

(2) *Date of export.* The date of export is the date when goods are scheduled to leave the port of export on the exporting carrier that is taking the goods out of the United States.

(3) *Ultimate consignee.* The ultimate consignee is the person, party, or designee that is located abroad and actually receives the export shipment. The name and address of the ultimate consignee, whether by sale in the United States or abroad or by consignment, shall be reported in the EEI. The ultimate consignee as known at the time of export shall be reported. For shipments requiring an export license, the ultimate consignee shall be the person so designated on the export license or authorized to be the ultimate consignee under the applicable license exemption in conformance with the EAR or ITAR, as applicable. For goods sold en route, report the appropriate "To be Sold En Route" indicator in the EEI, and report corrected information as soon as it is known (see § 30.9 for procedures on correcting AES information).

(4) *U.S. state of origin.* The U.S. state of origin is the 2-character postal code for the state in which the goods begin their journey to the port of export. For example, a shipment covering goods laden aboard a truck at a warehouse in Georgia for transport to Florida for loading onto a vessel for export to a foreign country shall show Georgia as the state of origin. The U.S. state of origin may be different from the U.S. state where the goods were produced, mined, or grown. For shipments of multi-state origin, reported as a single shipment, report the U.S. state of the commodity with the greatest value. If such information is not known, report the state in which the commodities are consolidated for export.

(5) *Country of ultimate destination.* The country of ultimate destination is the country in which the goods are to be consumed or further processed or manufactured. The country of ultimate destination is the code issued by the ISO.

(i) *Shipments under an export license or license exemption.* For shipments under an export license or license exemption issued by the Department of State, DDTC, or the Department of Commerce, BIS, the country of ultimate destination shall conform to the country of ultimate destination as shown on the license. In the case of a Department of State license, the country of ultimate destination is the country specified with respect to the end user. For goods licensed by other government agencies refer to their specific requirements concerning providing country of destination information.

(ii) *Shipments not moving under an export license.* The country of ultimate destination is the country known to the USPPI at the time of exportation. The country to which the goods are being shipped is not the country of ultimate destination if the USPPI has knowledge at the time the goods leave the United States that they are intended for reexport or transshipment in their present form to another known country. For goods shipped to Canada, Mexico, Panama, Hong Kong, Belgium, United Arab Emirates, The Netherlands, or Singapore, for example, special care should be exercised before reporting these countries as the ultimate destination, since these are countries through which goods from the United States are frequently transshipped. If the USPPI does not know the ultimate destination of the goods, the country of destination to be shown is the last country, as known to the USPPI at the time of shipment from the United States, to which the goods are to be shipped in their present form. (For instructions as to the reporting of country of destination for vessels sold or transferred from the United States to foreign ownership, see § 30.26.)

(iii) For goods to be sold en route, report the country of the first port of call and then report corrected information as soon as it is known.

(6) *Method of transportation.* The method of transportation is the means by which the goods are exported from the United States.

(i) *Conveyances exported under their own power.* The mode of transportation for aircraft, vessels, or locomotives (railroad stock) transferring ownership or title and moving out of the United States under its own power is the mode of transportation by which the conveyance moves out of the United States.

(ii) *Exports through Canada, Mexico, or other foreign countries for transshipment to another destination.* For transshipments through Canada, Mexico, or another foreign country, the mode of transportation is the mode of the carrier transporting the goods out of the United States.

(7) *Conveyance name/carrier name.* The conveyance name/carrier name is the name of the conveyance/carrier transporting the goods out of the United States as known at the time of exportation. For exports by sea, the conveyance name is the vessel name. For exports by air, rail, or truck, the carrier name is that which corresponds to the carrier identification as specified in paragraph (a)(8) of this section. Terms, such as airplane, train, rail, truck, vessel, barge, or international footbridge are not acceptable. For shipments by other methods of transportation, including mail, fixed methods (pipeline), the conveyance/carrier name is not required.

(8) *Carrier identification.* The carrier identification specifies the carrier that transports the goods out of the United States. The carrier transporting the goods to the port of export and the carrier transporting the goods out of the United States may be different. For transshipments through Canada, Mexico, or another foreign country, the carrier identification is that of the carrier that transports the goods out of the United States. The carrier identification is the Standard Carrier Alpha Code (SCAC) for vessel, rail, and truck shipments or the International Air Transport Association (IATA) code for air shipments. For other valid method of transportation, including mail, fixed modes (pipeline), and passenger, hand carried the carrier identification is not required. The National Motor Freight Traffic Association (NMFTA) issues and maintains the SCAC. (See *http://www.nmfta.org.*) The IATA issues and maintains the IATA codes. (See *http://www.census.gov/trade* for a list of IATA codes.)

(9) *Port of export.* The port of export is the seaport or airport where the goods are loaded on the exporting carrier that is taking the goods out of the United States, or the port where exports by overland transportation cross the U.S. border into a foreign country. The port of export shall be reported in terms of Schedule D, "Classification of CBP Districts and Ports." Use port code 8000 for shipments by mail.

(i) *Vessel and air exports involving several ports of exportation.* For goods loaded aboard a carrier in a port of lading, where the carrier stops at several ports before clearing to the foreign country, the port of export is the first port where the goods were loaded on the exporting carrier. For goods off-loaded from the original conveyance to another conveyance (even if the aircraft or vessel belongs to the same carrier) at any of the ports, the port where the goods were loaded on the last conveyance before going foreign is the port of export.

(ii) *Exports through Canada, Mexico, or other foreign countries for transshipment to another destination.* For transshipments through Canada, Mexico, or another foreign country to a third country, the port of export is the location where the goods are loaded on the carrier that is taking the goods out of the United States.

(10) *Related party indicator.* Used to indicate when a transaction involving trade between a USPPI and an ultimate consignee where either party owns directly or indirectly 10 percent or more of the other party.

(11) *Domestic or foreign indicator.* Indicates if the goods exported are of domestic or foreign origin. Report foreign goods separately from goods of domestic production even if the commodity classification number is the same.

(i) *Domestic.* Exports of domestic goods include: Those commodities that are grown, produced, or manufactured (including commodities incorporating foreign components) in the United States, including goods exported from U.S. FTZs, Puerto Rico, or the U.S. Virgin Islands; and those articles of foreign origin that have been enhanced in value or changed from the form in which they were originally imported by further manufacture or processing in the United States, including goods exported from U.S. FTZs, Puerto Rico, or the U.S. Virgin Islands.

(ii) *Foreign.* Exports of foreign goods include those commodities that are grown, produced, or manufactured in foreign countries that entered the United States including goods admitted to U.S. FTZs as imports and that, at the time of exportation, have undergone no change in form or condition or enhancement in value by further manufacture in the United States, in U.S. FTZs, in Puerto Rico, or in the U.S. Virgin Islands.

(12) *Commodity classification number.* Report the 10-digit commodity classification number as provided in Schedule B, *Statistical Classification of Domestic and Foreign Commodities Exported from the United States* in the EEI. The 10-digit commodity classification number provided in the Harmonized Tariff Schedule of the United States (HTSUSA) may be reported in lieu of the Schedule B commodity classification number except as noted in the headnotes of the HTSUSA. The HTSUSA is a global classification system used to describe most world trade in goods. Furnishing the correct Schedule B or HTSUSA number does not relieve the USPPI or the authorized agent of furnishing a complete and accurate commodity description. When reporting the Schedule B number or HTSUSA number, the decimals shall be omitted. (See *http://www.census.gov/trade* for a list of Schedule B classification numbers.)

(13) *Commodity description.* Report the description of the goods shipped in English in sufficient detail to permit verification of the Schedule B or HTSUSA number. Clearly and fully state the name of the commodity in terms that can be identified or associated with the language used in Schedule B or HTSUSA (usually the commercial name of the commodity), and any and all characteristics of the commodity that distinguish it from commodities of the same name covered by other Schedule B or HTSUSA

classifications. If the shipment requires a license, the description reported in the EEI shall conform with that shown on the license. If the shipment qualifies for a license exemption, the description shall be sufficient to ensure compliance with that license exemption. However, where the description on the license does not state all of the characteristics of the commodity that are needed to completely verify the commodity classification number, as described in this paragraph, report the missing characteristics, as well as the description shown on the license, in the commodity description field of the EEI.

(14) *Primary unit of measure.* The unit of measure shall correspond to the primary quantity as prescribed in the Schedule B or HTSUSA. If neither Schedule B nor HTSUSA specifies a unit of measure for the item, an "X" is required in the unit of measure field.

(15) *Primary quantity.* The quantity is the total number of units that correspond to the first unit of measure specified in the Schedule B or HTSUSA. Where the unit of measure is in terms of weight (grams, kilograms, metric tons, etc.), the quantity reflects the net weight, not including the weight of barrels, boxes, or other bulky coverings, and not including salt or pickle in the case of salted or pickled fish or meats. For a few commodities where "content grams" or "content kilograms" or some similar weight unit is specified in Schedule B or HTSUSA, the quantity may be less than the net weight. The quantity is reported as a whole unit only, without commas or decimals. If the quantity contains a fraction of a whole unit, round fractions of one-half unit or more up and fractions of less than one-half unit down to the nearest whole unit. (For example, where the unit for a given commodity is in terms of "tons," a net quantity of 8.4 tons would be reported as 8 for the quantity. If the quantity is less than one unit, the quantity is 1.)

(16) *Shipping weight.* The shipping weight is the weight in kilograms, which includes the weight of the commodity, as well as the weight of normal packaging, such as boxes, crates, barrels, etc. The shipping weight is required for exports by air, vessel, rail, and truck, and required for exports of household goods transported by all methods. For exports (except household goods) by mail, fixed transport (pipeline), or other valid methods, the shipping weight is not required and shall be reported as zero. For containerized cargo in lift vans, cargo vans, or similar substantial outer containers, the weight of such containers is not included in the shipping weight. If the shipping weight is not available for each Schedule B or HTSUSA item included in one or more containers, the approximate shipping weight for each item is estimated and reported. The total of these estimated weights equals the actual shipping weight of the entire container or containers.

(17) *Value.* In general, the value to be reported in the EEI shall be the value of the goods at the U.S. port of export. The value shall be the selling price as defined in this paragraph (or the cost if the goods are not sold), including inland or domestic freight, insurance, and other charges to the U.S. seaport, airport, or land border port of export. Cost of goods is the sum of expenses incurred in the USPPI acquisition or production of the goods. Report the value to the nearest dollar; omit cents. Fractions of a dollar less than 50 cents should be ignored, and fractions of 50 cents or more should be rounded up to the next dollar.

(i) *Selling price.* The selling price for goods exported pursuant to sale, and the value to be reported in the EEI, is the USPPI's price to the FPPI (the foreign buyer). Deduct from the selling price any unconditional discounts, but do not deduct discounts that are conditional upon a particular act or performance on the part of the foreign buyer. For goods shipped on consignment without a sale actually having been made at the time of export, the selling price to be reported in the EEI is the market value at the time of export at the U.S. port.

(ii) *Adjustments.* When necessary, make the following adjustments to obtain the value.

(A) Where goods are sold at a point other than the port of export, freight, insurance, and other charges required in moving the goods from their U.S. point of origin to the exporting carrier at the port of export or border crossing point shall be added to the selling price (as defined in paragraph (a)(17)(i) of this section) for purposes of reporting the value in the EEI.

(B) Where the actual amount of freight, insurance, and other domestic costs is not available, an estimate of the domestic costs shall be made and added to the cost of the goods or selling price to derive the value to be reported in the EEI. Add the estimated domestic costs to the cost or selling price of the goods to obtain the value to be reported in the EEI.

(C) Where goods are sold at a "delivered" price to the foreign destination, the cost of loading the goods on the exporting carrier, if any, and freight, insurance, and other costs beyond the port of export shall be subtracted from the selling price for purposes of reporting value in the EEI. If the actual amount of such costs is not available, an estimate of the costs should be subtracted from the selling price.

(D) Costs added to or subtracted from the selling price in accordance with the instructions in this paragraph (a)(17)(ii) should not be shown separately in the EEI, but the value reported should be the value after making such adjustments, where required, to arrive at the value of the goods at the U.S. port of export.

(iii) *Exclusions.* Exclude the following from the selling price of goods exported.

(A) Commissions to be paid by the USPPI to its agent abroad or commissions to be deducted from the selling price by the USPPI's agent abroad.

(B) The cost of loading goods on the exporting carrier at the port of export.

(C) Freight, insurance, and any other charges or transportation costs beyond the port of export.

(D) Any duties, taxes, or other assessments imposed by foreign countries.

(iv) For definitions of the value to be reported in the EEI for special types of transactions where goods are not being exported pursuant to commercial sales, or where subsidies, government financing or participation, or other unusual conditions are involved, see Subpart C of this part.

(18) *Export information code.* A code that identifies the type of export shipment or condition of the exported items (*e.g.*, goods donated for relief or charity, impelled shipments, shipments under the Foreign Military Sales program, household goods, and all other shipments). (For the list of the codes see Appendix B.)

(19) *Shipment reference number.* A unique identification number assigned by the filer that allows for the identification of the shipment in the filer's system. The number must be unique for five years.

(20) *Line number.* A number that identifies the specific commodity line item within a shipment.

(21) *Hazardous material indicator.* An indicator that identifies whether the shipment is hazardous as defined by the Department of Transportation.

(22) *Inbond code.* The code indicating whether the shipment is being transported under bond.

(23) *License code/license exemption code.* The code that identifies the commodity as having a federal government agency requirement for a license, permit, license exception or exemption or that no license is required.

(24) *Routed export transaction indicator.* An indicator that identifies that the shipment is a routed export transaction as defined in § 30.3.

(25) *Shipment filing action request indicator.* An indicator that allows the filer to add, change, replace, or cancel an export shipment transaction.

(26) *Line item filing action request indicator.* An indicator that allows the filer to add, change, or delete a commodity line within an export shipment transaction.

(27) *Filing option indicator.* An indicator of whether the filer is reporting export information predeparture or postdeparture. See § 30.4 for more information on EEI filing options.

(b) *Conditional data elements are as follows:*

(1) *Authorized agent and authorized agent identification.* If an authorized agent is used to prepare and file the EEI, the following information shall be provided to the AES.

(i) *Authorized agent's identification number.* Report the authorized agent's own EIN, SSN, or DUNS in the EEI for the first shipment and for each subsequent shipment. Use of another company's or individual's EIN or other identification number is prohibited. The party ID type (E=EIN, S=SSN, etc.) shall be identified.

(ii) *Name of the authorized agent.* Report the name of the authorized agent. The authorized agent is that person or entity in the United States that is authorized by the USPPI or the FPPI to prepare and file the EEI or the person or entity, if any, named on the export license. (See § 30.3 for details on the specific reporting responsibilities of authorized agents and Subpart B of this part for export control licensing requirements for authorized agents.)

(iii) *Address of the authorized agent.* Report the address or location (no post office box number) of the authorized agent. The authorized agent's address shall be reported with the initial shipment. Subsequent shipments may be identified by the agent's identification number.

(iv) *Contact information.* Report the contact name and telephone number.

(2) *Intermediate consignee.* The name and address of the intermediate consignee (if any) shall be reported. The intermediate consignee acts in a foreign country as an agent for the principal party in interest or the ultimate consignee for the purpose of effecting delivery of the export shipment to the ultimate consignee. The intermediate consignee is the person named as such on the export license or authorized to act as such under the applicable general license and in conformity with the EAR.

(3) *FTZ identifier.* If goods are removed from the FTZ and not entered for consumption, report the FTZ identifier. This is the unique identifier assigned by the Foreign Trade Zone Board that identifies the FTZ, subzone or site from which goods are withdrawn for export.

(4) *Foreign port of unlading.* The foreign port of unlading is the foreign port in the country where the goods are removed from the exporting carrier. The foreign port does not have to be located in the country of destination. For exports by sea to foreign countries, not including Puerto Rico, the foreign port of unlading is the code in terms of Schedule K, *Classification of Foreign Ports by Geographic Trade Area and Country.* For exports by sea or air between the United States and Puerto Rico, the foreign port of unlading is the code in terms of Schedule D, *Classification of CBP Districts and Ports.* The foreign port of unlading is not required for exports by other modes of transportation, including rail, truck, mail, fixed (pipeline), or air (unless between the U.S. and Puerto Rico).

(5) *Export license number/CFR citation/KPC number.* License number, permit number, citation, or authorization number assigned by the Department of Commerce, BIS; Department of State, DDTC; Department of the Treasury, OFAC; Department of Justice, DEA; Nuclear Regulatory Commission; or any other federal government agency.

(6) *Export Control Classification Number (ECCN).* The number used to identify items on the CCL, Supplement No. 1 to Part 774 of the EAR. The ECCN consists of a set of digits and a letter. Items that are not classified under an ECCN are designated "EAR99".

(7) *Secondary unit of measure.* The unit of measure that corresponds to the secondary quantity as prescribed in the Schedule B or HTSUSA. If neither Schedule B nor HTSUSA specifies a secondary unit of measure for the item, the unit of measure is not required.

(8) *Secondary quantity.* The total number of units that correspond to the secondary unit of measure, if any, specified in the Schedule B or HTSUSA. See the definition of primary quantity for specific instructions on reporting the quantity as a weight and whole unit, rounding fractions.

(9) *Vehicle Identification Number (VIN)/Product ID.* The identification number found on the reported used vehicle. For used self-propelled vehicles that do not have a VIN, the Product ID is reported. "Used" vehicle refers to any self-propelled vehicle where the equitable or legal title to which has been transferred by a manufacturer, distributor, or dealer to an ultimate purchaser. See U.S. Customs and Border Protection regulations 19 CFR 192.1 for more information on exports of used vehicles.

(10) *Vehicle ID qualifier.* The qualifier that identifies the type of used vehicle number reported. The valid codes are V for VIN and P for Product ID.

(11) *Vehicle title number.* The number issued by the Motor Vehicle Administration.

(12) *Vehicle title state code.* The 2-character postal code for the state or territory that issued the vehicle title.

(13) *Entry number.* The entry number must be reported for goods that are entered in lieu of being transported under bond for which the importer of record is a foreign entity or, for reexports of goods withdrawn from a FTZ for which a NAFTA deferred duty claim (entry type 08) could have been made, but that the importer elected to enter for consumption under CBP entry type 06. For goods imported into the United States for export to a third country of ultimate destination, where the importer of record on the entry is a foreign entity, the USPPI will be the authorized agent designated by the foreign importer for service of process. The USPPI, in this circumstance, is required to report the import entry number.

(14) *Transportation reference number (TRN).* The TRN is as follows:

(i) *Vessel shipments.* Report the booking number for vessel shipments. The booking number is the reservation number assigned by the carrier to hold space on the vessel for cargo being exported. The TRN is required for all vessel shipments.

(ii) *Air shipments.* Report the master air waybill number for air shipments. The air waybill number is the reservation number assigned by the carrier to hold space on the aircraft for cargo being exported. The TRN is optional for air shipments.

(iii) *Rail shipments.* Report the bill of lading (BL) number for rail shipments. The BL number is the reservation number assigned by the carrier to hold space on the rail car for cargo being exported. The TRN is optional for rail shipments.

(iv) *Truck shipments.* Report the freight or pro bill number for truck shipments. The freight or pro bill number is the number assigned by the carrier to hold space on the truck for cargo being exported. The freight or pro bill number correlates to a bill of lading number, air waybill number or trip

Federal Register / Vol. 73, No. 106 / Monday, June 2, 2008 / Rules and Regulations 31569

number for multimodal shipments. The TRN is optional for truck shipments.

(15) *Department of State Requirements.*

(i) *DDTC registration number.* The number assigned by the DDTC to persons who are required to register per Part 122 of the ITAR (22 CFR 120 through 130), and have an authorization (license or exemption) from DDTC to export the article.

(ii) *DDTC Significant Military Equipment (SME) indicator.* A term used to designate articles on the USML (22 CFR 121) for which special export controls are warranted because of their capacity for substantial military utility or capability. See § 120.7 of the ITAR 22 CFR 120 through 130 for a definition of SME and § 121.1 for items designated as SME articles.

(iii) *DDTC eligible party certification indicator.* Certification by the U.S. exporter that the exporter is an eligible party to participate in defense trade. See 22 CFR 120.1(c). This certification is required only when an exemption is claimed.

(iv) *DDTC USML category code.* The USML category of the article being exported (22 CFR 121).

(v) *DDTC Unit of Measure (UOM).* This unit of measure is the UOM covering the article being shipped as described on the export authorization or declared under an ITAR exemption.

(vi) *DDTC quantity.* This quantity is for the article being shipped. The quantity is the total number of units that corresponds to the DDTC UOM code.

(vii) *DDTC exemption number.* The exemption number is the specific citation from the ITAR (22 CFR 120 through 130) that exempts the shipment from the requirements for a license or other written authorization from DDTC.

(viii) *DDTC export license line number.* The line number of the State Department export license that corresponds to the article being exported.

(16) *Kimberley Process Certificate (KPC) number.* The unique identifying number on the KPC issued by the United States KPC authority that must accompany any export shipment of rough diamonds. Rough diamonds are classified under 6-digit HS subheadings 7102.10, 7102.21, and 7102.31. Enter the KPC number in the license number field excluding the 2-digit U.S. ISO country code.

(c) *Optional data elements:*

(1) *Seal number.* The security seal number placed on the equipment or container.

(2) *Equipment number.* Report the identification number for the shipping equipment, such as container or igloo number (Unit Load Device (ULD)), truck license number, or rail car number.

§ 30.7 Annotating the bill of lading, air waybill, or other commercial loading documents with proof of filing citations, and exemption legends.

(a) Items identified on the USML shall meet the predeparture reporting requirements identified in the ITAR (22 CFR 120 through 130) for the U.S. State Department requirements concerning the time and place of filing. For USML shipments, the proof of filing citations shall include the statement in "AES," followed by the returned confirmation number provided by the AES when the transmission is accepted, referred to as the ITN.

(b) For shipments other than USML, the USPPI or the authorized agent is responsible for annotating the proper proof of filing citation or exemption legend on the first page of the bill of lading, air waybill, export shipping instructions or other commercial loading documents. The USPPI or the authorized agent must provide the proof of filing citation or exemption legend to the exporting carrier. The carrier must annotate the proof of filing citation, exemption or exclusion legends on the carrier's outbound manifest when required. The carrier is responsible for presenting the appropriate proof of filing citation or exemption legend to CBP Port Director at the port of export as stated in Subpart E of this part. Such presentation shall be without material change or amendment of the proof of filing citation, postdeparture filing citation, AES downtime filing citation, or exemption legend as provided to the carrier by the USPPI or the authorized agent. The proof of filing citation will identify that the export information has been accepted as transmitted. The postdeparture filing citation, AES downtime filing citation, or exemption legend will identify that no filing is required prior to export. The proof of filing citations, postdeparture filing citations, or exemption legends shall appear on the bill of lading, air waybill or other commercial loading documentation and shall be clearly visible. The AES filing citation, exemption or exclusion legends are provided for in Appendix D. The exporting carrier shall annotate the manifest or other carrier documentation with the AES filing citations, exemption or exclusions legends.

(c) Exports of rough diamonds classified under HS subheadings 7102.10, 7102.21, and 7102.31, in accordance with the Clean Diamond Trade Act, will require the proof of filing citation, as stated in paragraph (b) of this section, and report the proof of filing citation on the KPC.

§ 30.8 Time and place for presenting proof of filing citations, and exemption and exclusions legends.

The following conditions govern the time and place to present proof of filing citations, postdeparture filing citations, AES downtime filing citation, exemption or exclusion legends. The USPPI or the authorized agent is required to deliver the proof of filing citations, postdeparture filing citations, AES downtime filing citation, exemption or exclusion legends required in § 30.4(e) to the exporting carrier. See Appendix D of this part for the properly formatted proof of filing citations, exemption or exclusion legends. Failure of the USPPI or the authorized agent of either the USPPI or FPPI to comply with these requirements constitutes a violation of the regulations in this part and renders such principal party or the authorized agent subject to the penalties provided for in Subpart H of this part.

(a) *Postal exports.* The proof of filing citations, postdeparture filing citations, AES downtime filing citation, and/or exemption and exclusions legends for items being sent by mail, as required in § 30.2, shall be presented to the postmaster with the packages at the time of mailing. The postmaster is required to deliver the proof of filing citations and/or exemption legends prior to export.

(b) *Pipeline exports.* The proof of filing citations or exemption and exclusion legends for items being sent by pipeline shall be presented to the operator of a pipeline no later than four calendar days after the close of the month.

(c) *Exports by other methods of transportation.* For exports sent other than by mail or pipeline, the USPPI or the authorized agent is required to deliver the proof of filing citations, and/or exemption and exclusion legends to the exporting carrier in accord with the time periods set forth in § 30.4(b).

§ 30.9 Transmitting and correcting Electronic Export Information.

(a) The USPPI or the authorized filing agent is responsible for electronically transmitting accurate EEI as known at the time of filing in the AES and transmitting any changes to that information as soon as they are known. Corrections, cancellations, or amendments to that information shall be electronically identified and transmitted to the AES for all required fields as soon as possible. The provisions of this paragraph relating to the reporting of corrections, cancellations, or amendments to EEI, shall not be construed as a relaxation of the requirements of the rules and regulations pertaining to the preparation and filing of EEI. Failure to correct the EEI is a violation of the provisions of this part.

(b) For shipments where the USPPI or the authorized agent has received an error message from AES, the corrections shall take place as required. Fatal error messages are sent to filers when EEI is not accepted in the AES. These errors must be corrected and EEI resubmitted prior to export for shipments filed predeparture and as soon as possible for shipments filed postdeparture but not later than ten calendar days after departure. Failure to respond to fatal error messages or otherwise transmit corrections to the AES constitutes a violation of the regulations in this part and renders such principal party or authorized agent subject to the penalties provided for in Subpart H of this part. For EEI that generates a warning message, the correction shall be made within four (4) calendar days of receipt of the original transmission. For EEI that generates a verify message, the correction, when warranted, shall be made within four calendar days of receipt of the message. A compliance alert indicates that the shipment was not reported in accordance with regulation. The USPPI or the authorized agent is required to review filing practices and take whatever corrective actions are required to conform with export reporting requirements.

§ 30.10 Retention of export information and the authority to require production of documents.

(a) *Retention of export information.* All parties to the export transaction (owners and operators of export carriers, USPPIs, FPPIs and/or authorized agents) shall retain documents pertaining to the export shipment for five years from the date of export. If the Department of State or other regulatory agency has recordkeeping requirements for exports that exceed the retention period specified in this part, then those requirements prevail. The USPPI or the authorized agent of the USPPI or FPPI may request a copy of the electronic record or submission from the Census Bureau as provided for in Subpart G of this part. The Census Bureau's retention and maintenance of AES records does not relieve filers from requirements in § 30.10.

(1) AES filers shall retain a copy of the electronic certification notice from the Census Bureau showing the filer's approved operational status. The electronic certification notice shall be retained for as long as the filer submits EEI through the AES.

(2) AES*Direct* filers shall retain a copy of the electronic certification notice obtained during the AES*Direct* certification. The electronic certification notice shall be retained for as long as the filer submits EEI through AES*Direct*.

(b) *Authority to require production of documents.* For purposes of verifying the completeness and accuracy of information reported as required under § 30.6, and for other purposes under the regulations in this part, all parties to the export transaction (owners and operators of the exporting carriers, USPPIs, FPPIs, and/or authorized agents) shall provide upon request to the Census Bureau, CBP, ICE, BIS and other participating agencies EEI, shipping documents, invoices, orders, packing lists, and correspondence as well as any other relevant information bearing upon a specific export transaction at anytime within the five year time period.

Note to § 30.10: Section 1252(b)(2) of Public Law 106–113, Proliferation Prevention Enhancement Act of 1999, required the Department of Commerce to print and maintain on file a paper copy or other acceptable back-up record of the individual's submission at a location selected by the Secretary of Commerce. The Census Bureau will maintain a data base of EEI filed in AES to ensure that requirements of Public Law 106–113 are met and that all filers can obtain a validated record of their submissions.

§§ 30.11–30.14 [Reserved]

Subpart B—Export Control and Licensing Requirements

§ 30.15 Introduction.

(a) For export shipments to foreign countries, the EEI is used both for statistical and for export control purposes. All parties to an export transaction must comply with all relevant export control regulations, as well as the requirements of the statistical regulations of this part. For convenience, references to provisions of the EAR, ITAR, CBP, and OFAC regulations that affect the statistical reporting requirements of this part have been incorporated into this part. For regulations and information concerning other agencies that exercise export control and licensing authority for particular types of commodity shipments, a USPPI, its authorized agent, or other party to the transaction shall consult the appropriate agency regulations.

(b) In addition to the reporting requirements set forth in § 30.6, further information may be required for export control purposes by the regulations of CBP, BIS, State Department, or the U.S. Postal Service under particular circumstances.

(c) This part requires the retention of documents or records pertaining to a shipment for five years from the date of export. All records concerning license exceptions or license exemptions shall be retained in the format (including electronic or hard copy) required by the controlling agency's regulations. For information on recordkeeping retention requirements exceeding the requirements of this part, refer to the regulations of the agency exercising export control authority for the specific shipment.

(d) In accordance with the provisions of Subpart G of this part, information from the EEI is used solely for official purposes, as authorized by the Secretary of Commerce, and any unauthorized use is not permitted.

§ 30.16 Export Administration Regulations.

The EAR issued by the U.S. Department of Commerce, BIS, also contain some additional reporting requirements pertaining to EEI (see 15 CFR 730–774).

(a) The EAR requires that export information be filed for shipments from U.S. Possessions to foreign countries or areas. (see 15 CFR 758.1(b) and 772.1, definition of the United States.)

(b) Requirements to place certain export control information in the EEI are found in the EAR.

§ 30.17 Customs and Border Protection regulations.

Refer to the DHS's CBP regulations, 19 CFR 192, for information referencing the advanced electronic submission of cargo information on exports for screening and targeting purposes pursuant to the Trade Act of 2002. The regulations also prohibit postdeparture filing of export information for certain shipments, and contain other regulatory provisions affecting the reporting of EEI. CBP's regulations can be obtained from the U.S. Government Printing Office's Web site at *www.gpoaccess.gov.*

§ 30.18 Department of State regulations.

(a) The USPPI or the authorized agent shall file export information, when required, for items on the USML of the ITAR (22 CFR 121). Information for items identified on the USML, including those exported under an export license exemption, shall be filed prior to export.

(b) Refer to the ITAR 22 CFR 120–130 for requirements regarding information required for electronically reporting export information for USML shipments and filing time requirements.

(c) Department of State regulations can be found at *http://www.state.gov.*

§ 30.19 Other Federal agency regulations.

Other Federal agencies have requirements regarding the reporting of certain types of export transactions. The USPPIs and/or authorized agents are responsible for adhering to these requirements.

§§ 30.20–30.24 [Reserved]

Subpart C—Special Provisions and Specific-Type Transactions

§ 30.25 Values for certain types of transactions.

Special procedures govern the values to be reported for shipments of the following unusual types:

(a) *Subsidized exports of agricultural products.* Where provision is made for the payment to the USPPI for the exportation of agricultural commodities under a program of the Department of Agriculture, the value required to be reported for EEI is the selling price paid by the foreign buyer minus the subsidy.

(b) *General Services Administration (GSA) exports of excess personal property.* For exports of GSA excess personal property, the value to be shown in the EEI will be "fair market value," plus charges when applicable, at which the property was transferred to GSA by the holding agency. These charges include packing, rehabilitation, inland freight, or drayage. The estimated "fair market value" may be zero, or it may be a percentage of the original or estimated acquisition costs. (Bill of lading, air waybill, and other commercial loading documents for such shipments will bear the notation "Excess Personal Property, GSA Regulations 1–III, 303.03.")

§ 30.26 Reporting of vessels, aircraft, cargo vans, and other carriers and containers.

(a) Vessels, locomotives, aircraft, rail cars, trucks, other vehicles, trailers, pallets, cargo vans, lift vans, or similar shipping containers are not considered "shipped" in terms of the regulations in this part, when they are moving, either loaded or empty, without transfer of ownership or title, in their capacity as carriers of goods or as instruments of such carriers, and EEI is not required.

(b) However, EEI shall be filed for such items, when moving as goods pursuant to sale or other transfer from ownership in the United States to ownership abroad. If a vessel, car, aircraft, locomotive, rail car, vehicle, or container, whether in service or newly built or manufactured, is sold or transferred to foreign ownership while in the Customs territory of the United States or at a port in such area, EEI shall be reported in accordance with the general requirements of the regulations in this part, identifying the port through or from which the vessel, aircraft, locomotive, rail car, car, vehicle, or container first leaves the United States after sale or transfer. If the vessel, aircraft, locomotive, rail car, car, vehicle, or shipping container is outside the Customs territory of the United States at the time of sale or transfer to foreign ownership, EEI shall be reported identifying the last port of clearance or departure from the United States prior to sale or transfer. The country of destination to be shown in the EEI for vessels sold foreign is the country of new ownership. The country for which the vessel clears, or the country of registry of the vessel, should not be reported as the country of destination in the EEI unless such country is the country of new ownership.

§ 30.27 Return of exported cargo to the United States prior to reaching its final destination.

When goods reported as exported from the United States are not exported or are returned without having been entered into a foreign destination, the filer shall cancel the EEI.

§ 30.28 "Split shipments" by air.

When a shipment by air covered by a single EEI submission is divided by the exporting carrier at the port of export where the manifest is filed, and part of the shipment is exported on one aircraft and part on another aircraft of the same carrier, the following procedures shall apply:

(a) The carrier shall deliver the manifest to CBP Port Director with the manifest covering the flight on which the first part of the split shipment is exported and shall make no changes to the EEI. However, the manifest shall show in the "number of packages" column the actual portion of the declared total quantity being carried and shall carry a notation to indicate "Split Shipment." All manifests with the notation "Split Shipment" will have identical ITNs.

(b) On each subsequent manifest covering a flight on which any part of a split shipment is exported, a prominent notation "SPLIT SHIPMENT" shall be made on the manifest for identification. On the last shipment, the notation shall read "SPLIT SHIPMENT, FINAL." Each subsequent manifest covering a part of a split shipment shall also show in the "number of packages" column only the goods carried on that particular flight and a reference to the total amount originally declared for export (for example, 5 of 11, or 5/11). Immediately following the line showing the portion of the split shipment carried on that flight, a notation will be made showing the air waybill number shown in the original EEI and the portions of the originally declared total carried on each previous flight, together with the number and date of each such previous flight (for example, air waybill 123; 1 of 2, flight 36A, June 6 SPLIT SHIPMENT; 2 of 2, flight 40X, June 6 SPLIT SHIPMENT, FINAL).

(c) Since the complete EEI was filed for the entire shipment initially, additional electronic reporting will not be required for these subsequent shipments.

§ 30.29 Reporting of repairs and replacements.

These guidelines will govern the reporting of the following:

(a) The return of goods previously imported for repair and alteration only and other returns to the foreign shipper of temporary imported goods (declared as such on importation) shall have Schedule B or HTSUSA classification commodity number 9801.10.0000. The value reported in the EEI shall include parts and labor. The value of the original product shall not be included.

(b) Goods that are covered under warranty.

(1) Goods that are reexported after repair under warranty shall follow the procedures in paragraph (a) of this section. It is recommended that the bill of lading, air waybill, or other loading documents include the statement, "This product was repaired under warranty."

(2) Goods that are replaced under warranty at no charge to the customer shall include the statement, "Product replaced under warranty, value for EEI purposes" on the bill of lading, air waybill, or other commercial-loading documents. Place the notation below the proof of filing citation or exemption legend on the commercial document. Report the value of the replacement parts only.

§§ 30.30–30.34 [Reserved]

Subpart D—Exemptions From the Requirements for the Filing of Electronic Export Information

§ 30.35 Procedure for shipments exempt from filing requirements.

Where an exemption from the filing requirement is provided in this subpart of this part, a legend describing the basis for the exemption shall be made on the first page of the bill of lading, air waybill, or other commercial loading document for carrier use, or on the carrier's outbound manifest. The exemption legend shall reference the

31572 Federal Register / Vol. 73, No. 106 / Monday, June 2, 2008 / Rules and Regulations

number of the section or provision in this part where the particular exemption is provided (see Appendix D of this part).

§ 30.36 Exemption for shipments destined to Canada.

(a) Except as noted in § 30.2(a)(1)(iv), and in paragraph (b) of this section, shipments originating in the United States where the country of ultimate destination is Canada are exempt from the EEI reporting requirements of this part.

(b) This exemption does not apply to the following types of export shipments:

(1) Sent for storage in Canada, but ultimately destined for third countries.

(2) Exports moving from the United States through Canada to a third destination shall be reported in the same manner as for all other exports. The USPPI or authorized agent shall follow the instructions as contained in this part for preparing and filing the EEI.

(3) Requiring a Department of State, DDTC, export license under the ITAR (22 CFR 120–130).

(4) Requiring a Department of Commerce, BIS, export license under the EAR (15 CFR 730–774).

(5) Subject to the ITAR, but exempt from license requirements.

(6) Classified as rough diamonds under the 6-digit HS subheadings (7102.10, 7102.21, or 7102.31).

§ 30.37 Miscellaneous exemptions.

Filing EEI is not required for the following kinds of shipments. However, the Census Bureau has the authority to periodically require the reporting of shipments that are normally exempt from filing.

(a) Except as noted in § 30.2(a)(1)(iv), exports of commodities where the value of the commodities shipped from one USPPI to one consignee on a single exporting carrier, classified under an individual Schedule B or HTSUSA commodity classification code, is $2,500 or less. This exemption applies to individual Schedule B or HTSUSA commodity classification codes regardless of the total shipment value. In instances where a shipment contains a mixture of individual Schedule B or HTSUSA commodity codes valued $2,500 or less and individual Schedule B or HTSUSA commodity classification codes valued over $2,500, only those commodity classification codes valued over $2,500 need to be reported. If the filer reports multiple items of the same Schedule B or HTSUSA code, this exemption only applies if the total value of exports for the Schedule B or HTSUSA code is $2,500 or less.

(b) Tools of trade and their containers that are usual and reasonable kinds and quantities of commodities and software intended for use by individual USPPIs or by employees or representatives of the exporting company in furthering the enterprises and undertakings of the USPPI abroad. Commodities and software eligible for this exemption are those that do not require an export license or that are exported as tools of the trade under a license exception of the EAR (15 CFR 740.9), and are subject to the following provisions:

(1) Are owned by the individual USPPI or exporting company.

(2) Accompany the individual USPPI, employee, or representative of the exporting company.

(3) Are necessary and appropriate and intended for the personal and/or business use of the individual USPPI, employee, or representative of the company or business.

(4) Are not for sale.

(5) Are returned to the United States no later than one (1) year from the date of export.

(6) Are not shipped under a bill of lading or an air waybill.

(c) Shipments from one point in the United States to another point in the United States by routes passing through Canada or Mexico.

(d) Shipments from one point in Canada or Mexico to another point in the same country by routes through the United States.

(e) Shipments transported inbond through the United States and exported from another U.S. port or transshipped and exported directly from the port of arrival. (When goods are shipped through the United States for export to a third country of ultimate destination, but are first entered for consumption or for warehousing in the United States, the EEI shall be filed when the goods are exported from the United States.) Shipments transported inbond through the United States by vessel are subject to the filing requirements of the U.S. Army Corps of Engineers. Shipments transported inbond through the United States which require an export license are subject to the filing requirements of the licensing Federal agency.

(f) Exports of technology and software as defined in 15 CFR 772 of the EAR that do not require an export license are exempt from filing requirements. However, EEI is required for mass-market software. For purposes of this part, mass-market software is defined as software that is generally available to the public by being sold at retail selling points, or directly from the software developer or supplier, by means of over-the-counter transactions, mail-order transactions, telephone transactions, or electronic mail-order transactions, and designed for installation by the user without further substantial technical support by the developer or supplier.

(g) Shipments to foreign libraries, government establishments, or similar institutions, as provided in § 30.40(d).

(h) Shipments as authorized under License Exception GFT for gift parcels and humanitarian donations (see 15 CFR 740.12 of the EAR).

(i) Diplomatic pouches and their contents.

(j) Human remains and accompanying appropriate receptacles and flowers.

(k) Shipments of interplant correspondence, executed invoices and other documents, and other shipments of company business records from a U.S. firm to its subsidiary or affiliate. This excludes highly technical plans, correspondence, etc. that could be licensed.

(l) Shipments of pets as baggage, accompanied or unaccompanied, of persons leaving the United States, including members of crews on vessels and aircraft.

(m) Carriers' stores, not shipped under a bill of lading or an air waybill (including goods carried in ships aboard carriers for sale to passengers), supplies, and equipment for departing vessels, planes, or other carriers, including usual and reasonable kinds and quantities of bunker fuel, deck engine and steward department stores, provisions and supplies, medicinal and surgical supplies, food stores, slop chest articles, and saloon stores or supplies for use or consumption on board and not intended for unlading in a foreign country, and including usual and reasonable kinds and quantities of equipment and spare parts for permanent use on the carrier when necessary for proper operation of such carrier and not intended for unlading in a foreign country. Hay, straw, feed, and other appurtenances necessary to the care and feeding of livestock while en route to a foreign destination are considered part of carriers' stores of carrying vessels, trains, planes, etc.

(n) Dunnage, not shipped under a bill of lading or an air waybill, of usual and reasonable kinds and quantities necessary and appropriate to stow or secure cargo on the outgoing or any immediate return voyage of an exporting carrier, when exported solely for use as dunnage and not intended for unlading in a foreign country.

(o) Shipments of aircraft parts and equipment; food, saloon, slop chest, and related stores; and provisions and supplies for use on aircraft by a U.S. airline to its own installations, aircraft, and agents abroad, under EAR License

Exception AVS for aircraft and vessels (see 15 CFR 740.15(c)).

(p) Filing EEI is not required for the following types of commodities when they are not shipped as cargo under a bill of lading or an air waybill and do not require an export license, but the USPPI shall be prepared to make an oral declaration to CBP Port Director, when required: baggage and personal effects, accompanied or unaccompanied, of persons leaving the United States, including members of crews on vessels and aircraft.

(q) Temporary exports, except those that require licensing, whether shipped or hand carried, (*e.g.*, carnet) that are exported from and returned to the United States in less than one year (12 months) from the date of export.

(r) Goods previously imported under a Temporary Import Bond for return in the same condition as when imported including: goods for testing, experimentation, or demonstration; goods imported for exhibition; samples and models imported for review or for taking orders; goods imported for participation in races or contests, and animals imported for breeding or exhibition and goods imported for use by representatives of foreign governments or international organizations or by members of the armed forces of a foreign country. Goods that were imported under bond for processing and reexportation are not covered by this exemption.

(s) Issued banknotes and securities, and coins in circulation exported as evidence of financial claims. The EEI must be filed for unissued bank notes and securities and coins not in circulation (such as banknotes printed in the United States and exported in fulfillment of the printing contract, or as parts of collections), which should be reported at their commercial or current value.

(t) Documents used in international transactions, documents moving out of the United States to facilitate international transactions including airline tickets, internal revenue stamps, liquor stamps, and advertising literature. Exports of such documents in fulfillment of a contract for their production, however, are not exempt and must be reported at the transaction value for their production.

§ 30.38 Exemption from the requirements for reporting complete commodity information.

The following type of shipments will require limited reporting of EEI when goods are shipped under a bill of lading or an air waybill. In such cases, Schedule B or HTSUSA commodity classification codes and domestic/foreign indicator shall not be required.

(a) Usual and reasonable kinds and quantities of wearing apparel, articles of personal adornment, toilet articles, medicinal supplies, food, souvenirs, games, and similar personal effects and their containers.

(b) Usual and reasonable kinds and quantities of furniture, household effects, household furnishings, and their containers.

(c) Usual and reasonable kinds and quantities of vehicles, such as passenger cars, station wagons, trucks, trailers, motorcycles, bicycles, tricycles, baby carriages, strollers, and their containers provided that the above-indicated baggage, personal effects, and vehicular property: (See U.S. Customs and Border Protection regulations 19 CFR 192 for separate CBP requirements for the exportation of used self-propelled vehicles.)

(1) Shall include only such articles as are owned by such person or members of his/her immediate family;

(2) Shall be in his/her possession at the time of or prior to his/her departure from the United States for the foreign country;

(3) Are necessary and appropriate for the use of such person or his/her immediate family;

(4) Are intended for his/her use or the use of his/her immediate family; and

(5) Are not intended for sale.

§ 30.39 Special exemptions for shipments to the U.S. Armed Services.

Filing of EEI is not required for any and all commodities, whether shipped commercially or through government channels, consigned to the U.S. Armed Services for their exclusive use, including shipments to armed services exchange systems. This exemption does not apply to articles that are on the USML and thus controlled by the ITAR and shipments that are not consigned to the U.S. Armed Services, regardless of whether they may be for their ultimate and exclusive use.

§ 30.40 Special exemptions for certain shipments to U.S. government agencies and employees.

Filing EEI is not required for the following types of shipments to U.S. government agencies and employees:

(a) Office furniture, office equipment, and office supplies shipped to and for the exclusive use of U.S. government offices.

(b) Household goods and personal property shipped to and for the exclusive and personal use of U.S. government employees.

(c) Food, medicines, and related items and other commissary supplies shipped to U.S. government offices or employees for the exclusive use of such employees, or to U.S. government employee cooperatives or other associations for subsequent sale or other distribution to such employees.

(d) Books, maps, charts, pamphlets, and similar articles shipped by U.S. government offices to U.S. or foreign libraries, government establishments, or similar institutions.

§§ 30.41–30.44 [Reserved]

Subpart E—General Carrier and Manifest Requirements

§ 30.45 General statement of requirements for the filing of carrier manifests with proof of filing citations for the electronic submission of export information or exemption legends when Electronic Export Information filing is not required.

(a) *Requirement for filing carrier manifest.* Carriers transporting goods from the United States, Puerto Rico, or the U.S. Virgin Islands to foreign countries; from the United States or Puerto Rico to the U.S. Virgin Islands; or between the United States and Puerto Rico; shall not be granted clearance and shall not depart until complete manifests or other required documentation (for ocean, air, and rail carriers) have been delivered to CBP Port Director in accordance with all applicable requirements under CBP regulations. CBP may require any of the following: bill of lading, air waybill, export shipping instructions, manifest, train consist, or other commercial loading document. The required document shall contain the appropriate AES proof of filing citations, covering all cargo for which the EEI is required, or exemption legends, covering cargo for which EEI need not be filed by the regulations of this part. Such annotation shall be without material change or amendment of proof of filing citations or exemption and exclusion legends as provided to the carrier by the USPPI or its authorized agent.

(1) *Vessels.* Vessels transporting goods as specified (except vessels exempted by paragraph (a)(4) of this section) shall file a complete manifest. Manifests may be filed via paper or electronically through the AES Vessel Transportation Module as provided in CBP Regulations, 19 CFR 4.63 and 4.76.

(i) *Bunker fuel.* The manifest (including vessels taking bunker fuel to be laden aboard vessels on the high seas) clearing for foreign countries shall show the quantities and values of bunker fuel taken aboard at that port for fueling use of the vessel, apart from such quantities as may have been laden on vessels as cargo.

(ii) *Coal and fuel oil.* The quantity of coal shall be reported in metric tons (1000 kgs or 2240 pounds), and the quantity of fuel oil shall be reported in barrels of 158.98 liters (42 gallons). Fuel oil shall be described in such manner as to identify diesel oil as distinguished from other types of fuel oil.

(2) *Aircraft.* Aircraft transporting goods shall file a complete manifest as required in CBP Regulations 19 CFR 122.72–122.76. The manifest shall be filed with CBP Port Director at the port where the goods are laden. For shipments from the United States to Puerto Rico, the manifests shall be filed with CBP Port Director at the port where the goods are unladed in Puerto Rico.

(3) *Rail carriers.* Rail carriers transporting goods shall file a car manifest or train consist with CBP Port Director at the border port of export in accordance with 19 CFR 123.

(4) *Carriers not required to file manifests.* Carriers exempted from filing manifests under applicable CBP regulations are required, upon request, to present to CBP Port Director, the proof of filing citation or exemption and exclusion legends for each shipment.

(5) *Penalties.* Failure of the carrier to file a manifest as required constitutes a violation of the regulations in this part and renders such carrier subject to the penalties provided for in Subpart H of this part.

(b) *Partially exported shipments.* Except as provided in paragraph (c) of this section, when a carrier identifies, prior to filing the manifest, that a portion of the goods covered by a single EEI transaction has not been exported on the intended carrier, it shall be noted on the manifest submitted to CBP. The carrier shall notify the USPPI or the authorized agent of changes to the commodity data, and the USPPI or the authorized agent shall electronically transmit the corrections, cancellations, or amendments as soon as they are known in accordance with § 30.9. Failure by the carrier to correct the manifest constitutes a violation of the provisions of the regulations in this part and renders the carrier subject to the penalties provided for in Subpart H of this part.

(c) *"Split shipments" by air.* When a shipment by air covered by a single EEI transmission is exported in more than one aircraft of the carrier, the "split shipment" procedure provided in § 30.28 shall be followed by the carrier in delivering manifests with the proof of filing citation or exemption legend to CBP Port Director.

(d) *Attachment of commercial documents.* The manifest shall carry a notation that values stated are as presented on the bills of lading, cargo lists, export shipping documents or other commercial documents. The bills of lading, cargo lists, export shipping documents or other commercial documents shall be securely attached to the manifest in such a manner as to constitute one document. The manifest shall reference the statement "Cargo as per bills of lading attached" or "Cargo as per commercial forms attached." Also required on the face of each bill of lading shall be the information required by the manifest for cargo covered by that document.

(e) *Exempt items.* For any item for which EEI is not required by the regulations in this part, a notation on the manifest shall be made by the carrier as to the basis for the exemption. In cases where a manifest is not required and EEI is not required, an oral declaration to CBP Port Director shall be made as to the basis for the exemption.

(f) *Proof of filing citations and exemption legends.*

(1) Ocean and air exporting carriers shall not accept paper SEDs under any circumstances nor load cargo that does not have all proof of filing citations, exemption or exclusion legends as provided for in Appendix D.

(2) Ocean and air exporting carriers are subject to the penalties provided for in Subpart H of this part if the exporting carrier;

(i) Accepts paper SEDs for cargo or,

(ii) Loads cargo without all proof of filing citations, exemption or exclusion legends as provided for in Appendix D.

(3) Truck exporting carriers shall not accept paper SEDs under any circumstances nor cross the border into a foreign country without a proof of filing citations, exemption or exclusion legends for cargo being exported as provided for in Appendix D. Truck exporting carriers accepting paper SEDs for cargo being exported into foreign countries, or carrying cargo into foreign countries without a proof of filing citation, exemption or exclusion legends in their possession are subject to the penalties provided for in Subpart H of this part.

(4) Rail exporting carriers shall not accept paper SEDs under any circumstance nor cross the border into a foreign country without a proof of filing citations, exemption or exclusion legends for cargo being exported as provided in Appendix D. Rail exporting carriers accepting paper SEDs for cargo being exported into foreign countries, or carrying cargo into foreign countries without required proof of filing citations, exemption or exclusion legends in their possession are subject to the penalties provided for in Subpart H of this part.

§ 30.46 Requirements for the filing of export information by pipeline carriers.

The operator of a pipeline may transport goods to a foreign country without the prior filing of the proof of filing citations, exemption or exclusion legends, on the condition that within four calendar days following the end of each calendar month the operator will deliver to CBP Port Director the proof of filing citations, exemption or exclusion legends covering all exports through the pipeline to each consignee during the month.

§ 30.47 Clearance or departure of carriers under bond on incomplete manifest.

(a) For purposes of the regulations in this part, except when carriers are transporting merchandise from the United States to Puerto Rico, clearance (where clearance is required) or permission to depart (where clearance is not required) may be granted to any carrier by CBP Port Director prior to filing of a complete manifest as required under the regulations of this part or prior to filing by the carrier of all filing U.S. Customs and Border Protection regulations citations, exclusion, and/or exemption legends, provided there is a bond as specified in 19 CFR 4.75, 4.76, and 122.74. The conditions of the bond shall be that a complete manifest, where a manifest is required by the regulations in this part and all required filing citations, exclusion, and/or exemption legends shall be filed by the carrier no later than the fourth business day after clearance (where clearance is required) or departure (where clearance is not required) of the carrier except as otherwise specifically provided in paragraph (a)(1), (2), and (3) of this section.

(1) For manifests submitted electronically through AES, the condition of the bond shall be that the manifest and all required filing citations, exclusion, and/or exemption legends shall be completed not later than the tenth business day after departure from each port.

(2) For rail carriers to Canada, the conditions of the bond shall be that manifest and all filing citations, exclusion, and/or exemption legends shall be filed not later than the fifteenth business day after departure.

(3) For carriers under bond on incomplete manifest, the carrier must file prior to departure a list of filing citations, exclusion, and/or exemption legends for export shipments aboard the conveyance. The list of filing citations, exclusion and/or exemption legends

shall be presented to a CBP Export Control Officer at the port of exit prior to departure.

(b) In the event that any required manifest and all required filing citations, exclusion and/or exemption legends are not filed by the carrier within the period provided by the bond, then a penalty of $1,100 shall be exacted for each day's delinquency beyond the prescribed period, but not more than $10,000 per violation.

(c) Remission or mitigation of the penalties for manifest violations provided herein may be granted by CBP as the Administering Authority. Prior disclosure of a manifest violation of this section shall be made in writing to CBP Port Director in the port of export as the Administering Authority.

§§ 30.48–30.49 [Reserved]

Subpart F—Import Requirements

§ 30.50 General requirements for filing import entries.

Electronic entry summary filing through the ABI, paper import entry summaries (CBP–7501), or paper record of vessel foreign repair or equipment purchase (CBP–226) shall be completed by the importer or its licensed import broker and filed directly with CBP in accordance with 19 CFR. Information on all mail and informal entries required for statistical and CBP purposes shall be reported, including value not subject to duty. Upon request, the importer or import broker shall provide the Census Bureau with information or documentation necessary to verify the accuracy of the reported information, or to resolve problems regarding the reported import transaction received by the Census Bureau.

(a) Import information for statistical purposes shall be filed for goods shipped as follows:

(1) Entering the United States from foreign countries.

(2) Admitted to U.S. FTZs.

(3) From the U.S. Virgin Islands.

(4) From other nonforeign areas (except Puerto Rico).

(b) Sources for collecting import statistics include the following:

(1) CBP's ABI Program (see 19 CFR Subpart A, Part 143).

(2) CBP–7501 paper entry summaries required for individual transactions (see 19 CFR Subpart B, Part 142).

(3) CBP–226, Record of Vessel Foreign Repair or Equipment Purchase (see 19 CFR 4.7 and 4.14).

(4) CBP–214, Application for Foreign Trade Zone Admission and/or Status Designation (Statistical copy).

(5) Automated Foreign Trade Zone Reporting Program (AFTZRP).

§ 30.51 Statistical information required for import entries.

The information required for statistical purposes is, in most cases, also required by CBP regulations for other purposes. Refer to CBP Web site at *http://www.cbp.gov* to download "Instructions for Preparation of CBP–7501," for completing the paper entry summary documentation (CBP–7501). Refer to the Customs and Trade Automated Interface Requirements for instructions on submitting an ABI electronic record, or instructions for completing CBP–226 for declaring any equipment, repair parts, materials purchased, or expense for repairs incurred outside of the United States.

§ 30.52 Foreign Trade Zones.

Foreign goods admitted into FTZs shall be reported as a general import. When goods are withdrawn from a FTZ for export to a foreign country, the export shall be reported in accordance with § 30.2. When goods are withdrawn for domestic consumption or entry into a bonded warehouse, the withdrawal shall be reported on CBP–7501 or through the ABI in accordance with CBP regulations. (This section emphasizes the reporting requirements contained in CBP regulations 19 CFR 146, "Foreign Trade Zones.") When foreign goods are admitted into a FTZ, the zone operator is required to file CBP–214, "Application for Foreign Trade Zone Admission and/or Status Designation." Refer to CBP Web site for instructions on completing CBP–214. Per 19 CFR 146.32(a), the applicant for admission shall present CBP–214 to the Port Director and shall include the statistical (pink) copy, CBP–214(A), for transmittal to the Census Bureau, unless the applicant makes arrangements for the electronic transmission of statistical information to the Census Bureau through the AFTZRP. Companies operating in FTZs interested in reporting CBP–214 statistical information electronically on a monthly basis shall apply directly to the Census Bureau. Monthly electronic reports shall be filed with the Census Bureau no later than the tenth (10) calendar day of the month following the report month. Participation in the Census Bureau program does not relieve companies of the responsibility to file CBP–214 with CBP. The following data items are required to be filed, in the AFTZRP, for statistical purposes. (Use the instructions and definitions provided in 19 CFR 146 for completing these fields.):

(a) HTSUSA Classification Code.
(b) Country of Origin.
(c) Country Sub-code.
(d) U.S. Port of Entry.
(e) U.S. Port of Unlading.
(f) Transaction Type.
(g) Statistical Month.
(h) Method of Transportation.
(i) Company Authorization Symbol.
(j) Carrier Code.
(k) Foreign Port of Lading.
(l) Date of Exportation.
(m) Date of Importation.
(n) Special Program Indicator Field.
(o) Unit of Quantity.
(p) CBP (dutiable) Value.
(q) Gross (shipping) Weight.
(r) Charges.
(s) U.S. Value.
(t) FTZ/Subzone Number.
(u) Zone Admission Number.
(v) Vessel Name.
(w) Serial Number.
(x) Trade Identification.
(y) Admission Date.

§ 30.53 Import of goods returned for repair.

Import entries covering U.S. goods imported temporarily for repair or alteration and reexport are required to show the following statement: "Imported for Repair and Reexport" on CBP–7501 or in the ABI entry. Whenever goods are returned to the United States after undergoing either repair, alteration, or assembly under HTS heading 9802, the country of origin shall be shown as the country in which the repair, alteration, or assembly is performed. When the goods are for reexport and meet all of the requirements for filing the EEI, file according to the instructions provided in § 30.2, except for the following data items:

(a) *Value*. Report the value of the repairs, including parts and labor. Do not report the value of the original product. If goods are repaired under warranty, at no charge to the customer, report the cost to repair as if the customer were being charged.

(b) *Schedule B Classification Code*. Report Schedule B commodity classification code 9801.10.0000 for goods reexported after repair.

§ 30.54 Special provisions for imports from Canada.

(a) When certain softwood lumber products described under HTSUSA subheadings 4407.1001, 4409.1010, 4409.1090, and 4409.1020 are imported from Canada, import entry records are required to show a valid Canadian region of manufacture code. The Canadian region of manufacture is determined on a first mill basis (the point at which the item was first manufactured into a covered lumber product). Canadian region of manufacture is the first region where the subject goods underwent a change in tariff classification to the tariff classes cited in this paragraph. The Canadian region code should be transmitted in the electronic ABI summaries. The Canadian region of manufacture code should replace the region of origin code on CBP–7501, entry summary form. These requirements apply only for imports of certain softwood lumber products for which the region of origin is Canada.

(b) All other imports from Canada, including certain softwood lumber products not covered in paragraph (a) of this section, will require the twoletter designation of the Canadian region of origin to be reported on U.S. entry summary records. This information is required only for U.S. imports that under applicable CBP rules of origin are determined to originate in Canada. For nonmanufactured goods determined to be of Canadian origin, the region of origin is defined as the region where the exported goods were originally grown, mined, or otherwise produced. For goods of Canadian origin that are manufactured or assembled in Canada, with the exception of the certain softwood lumber products described in paragraph (a) of this section, the region of origin is that in which the final manufacture or assembly is performed prior to exporting that good to the United States. In cases where the region in which the goods were manufactured, assembled, grown, mined, or otherwise produced is unknown, the region in which the Canadian vendor is located can be reported. For those reporting on paper forms the region of origin code replaces the region of origin code on the CBP–7501, entry summary form.

(c) All electronic ABI entry summaries for imports originating in Canada also require the Canadian region of origin code to be transmitted for each entry summary line item.

(d) The region of origin code replaces the region of origin code only for imports that have been determined, under applicable CBP rules, to originate in Canada. Valid Canadian region/ territory codes are:

XA—Alberta
XB—New Brunswick
XD—British Columbia Coastal
XE—British Columbia Interior
XM—Manitoba
XN—Nova Scotia
XO—Ontario
XP—Prince Edward Island
XQ—Quebec
XS—Saskatchewan
XT—Northwest Territories
XV—Nunavut
XW—Newfoundland
XY—Yukon

§ 30.55 Confidential information, import entries, and withdrawals.

The contents of the statistical copies of import entries and withdrawals on file with the Census Bureau are treated as confidential and will not be released without authorization by CBP, in accordance with 19 CFR 103.5 relating to the copies on file in CBP offices. The importer or import broker must provide the Census Bureau with information or documentation necessary to verify the accuracy or resolve problems regarding the reported import transaction.

(a) The basic responsibility for obtaining and providing the information required by the general statistical headnotes of the HTSUSA rests with the person filing the import entry. This is provided for in section 484(a) of the Tariff Act, 19 CFR 141.61(e) of CBP regulations, and § 30.50 of this subpart. CBP Regulations 19 CFR 141.61(a) specify that the entry summary data clearly set forth all information required.

(b) 19 CFR 141.61(e) of CBP regulations provides that penalty procedures relating to erroneous statistical information shall not be invoked against any person who attempts to comply with the statistical requirements of the General Statistical Notes of the HTSUSA. However, in those instances where there is evidence that statistical suffixes are misstated to avoid quota action, or a misstatement of facts is made to avoid import controls or restrictions related to specific commodities, the importer or its licensed broker should be aware that the appropriate actions will be taken under 19 U.S.C. 1592, as amended.

§§ 30.56–30.59 [Reserved]

Subpart G—General Administrative Provisions

§ 30.60 Confidentiality of Electronic Export Information.

(a) *Confidential status.* The EEI collected pursuant to this Part is confidential, to be used solely for official purposes as authorized by the Secretary of Commerce. The collection of EEI by the Department of Commerce has been approved by the Office of Management and Budget (OMB). The information collected is used by the Census Bureau for statistical purposes only and by the BIS for export control purposes. In addition, EEI is used by other federal government agencies, such as the Department of State, CBP, and ICE for export control and other federal government agencies such as the Bureau of Economic Analysis, Bureau of Labor Statistics, and Bureau of Transportation Statistics for statistical purposes. Except as provided for in paragraph (e) of this section, information collected pursuant to this Part shall not be disclosed to anyone by any officer, employee, contractor, agent of the federal government or other parties with access to the EEI other than to the USPPI, or the authorized agent of the USPPI or the transporting carrier. Such disclosure shall be limited to that information provided by each party pursuant to this Part.

(b) *Supplying EEI for official purposes.*

(1) The EEI may be supplied to federal agencies for official purposes, defined to include, but not limited to:

(i) Verification and investigation of export shipments, including penalty assessments, for export control and compliance purposes,

(ii) Providing proof of export; and

(iii) Statistical purposes;

(iv) Circumstances to be determined in the national interest pursuant to 13 U.S.C., § 301(g) and paragraph (e) of this section.

(2) The EEI may be supplied to the USPPI, or authorized agents of USPPI and carriers for compliance and audit purposes. Such disclosure shall be limited to that information provided to the AES by each party.

(c) *Supplying EEI for nonofficial purposes.* The official report of the EEI submitted to the United States Government shall not be disclosed by the USPPI, or the authorized agent, or representative of the USPPI for "nonofficial purposes," either in whole or in part, or in any form including but not limited to electronic transmission, paper printout, or certified reproduction. "Nonofficial purposes" are defined to include but not limited to use of the official EEI:

(1) In support of claims by the USPPI or its authorized agent for exemption from Federal or state taxation;

(2) By the U.S. Internal Revenue Service for purposes not related to export control or compliance;

(3) By state and local government agencies, and nongovernmental entities or individuals for any purpose; and

(4) By foreign governments for any purposes.

(d) *Copying of information to manifests.* Because the ocean manifest can be made public under provision of CBP regulations, no information from the EEI, except the ITN, filing citation, exemptions or exclusion legends, shall be copied to the outward manifest of ocean carriers.

(e) *Determination by the Secretary of Commerce.* Under 13 U.S.C. 301(g), the

Federal Register / Vol. 73, No. 106 / Monday, June 2, 2008 / Rules and Regulations **31577**

EEI is exempt from public disclosure unless the Secretary or delegate determines that such exemption would be contrary to the national interest. The Secretary or his or her delegate may make such information available, if he or she determines it is in the national interest, taking such safeguards and precautions to limit dissemination as deemed appropriate under the circumstances. In recommendations or decisions regarding such actions, it shall be presumed to be contrary to the national interest to provide EEI for purposes set forth in paragraph (c) of this section. In determining whether, under a particular set of circumstances, it is contrary to the national interest to apply the exemption, the maintenance of confidentiality and national security shall be considered as important elements of national interest. The unauthorized disclosure of confidential EEI granted under National Interest Determination renders such persons subject to the civil penalties provided for in Subpart H of this part.

(f) *Penalties.* Disclosure of confidential EEI by any officer, employee, contractor, or agent of the federal government, except as provided for in paragraphs (a) and (e) of this section renders such persons subject to the civil penalties provided for in Subpart H of this part.

§ 30.61 Statistical classification schedules.

The following statistical classification schedules are referenced in this part. These schedules, may be accessed through the Census Bureau's Web site at *http://www.census.gov/trade.*

(a) *Schedule B—Statistical Classification for Domestic and Foreign Commodities Exported from the United States,* shows the detailed commodity classification requirements and 10-digit statistical reporting numbers to be used in preparing EEI, as required by these regulations.

(b) *Harmonized Tariff Schedules of the United States Annotated for Statistical Reporting,* shows the 10-digit statistical reporting number to be used in preparing import entries and withdrawal forms.

(c) *Schedule C*—Classification of Country and Territory Designations for U.S. Foreign Trade Statistics.

(d) *Schedule D*—Classification of CBP Districts and Ports.

(e) *Schedule K*—Classification of Foreign Ports by Geographic Trade Area and Country.

(f) *International Air Transport Association (IATA)*—Code of the carrier for air shipments. These are the air carrier codes to be used in reporting EEI, as required by the regulations in this part.

(g) *Standard Carrier Alpha Code (SCAC)*—Classification of the carrier for vessel, rail and truck shipments, showing the carrier codes necessary to prepare EEI, as required by the regulations in this part.

§ 30.62 Emergency exceptions.

The Census Bureau and CBP may jointly authorize the postponement of or exception to the requirements of the regulations in this Part as warranted by the circumstances in individual cases of emergency where strict enforcement of the regulations would create a hardship. In cases where export control requirements also are involved, the concurrence of the regulatory agency and CBP also will be obtained.

§ 30.63 Office of Management and Budget control numbers assigned pursuant to the Paperwork Reduction Act.

(a) *Purpose.* This subpart will comply with the requirements of the Paperwork Reduction Act (PRA), 44 U.S.C. 3507(f), which requires that agencies display a current control number assigned by the Director of OMB for each agency information collection requirement.

(b) *Display.*

15 CFR section where identified and described	Current OMB control No.
§§ 30.1 through 30.99	0607–0152

§§ 30.64–30.69 [Reserved]

Subpart H—Penalties

§ 30.70 Violation of the Clean Diamond Trade Act.

Public Law 108–19, the Clean Diamond Trade Act (the Act), section 8(c), authorizes CBP and ICE, as appropriate, to enforce the laws and regulations governing exports of rough diamonds, including those with respect to the validation of the Kimberley Process Certificate by the exporting authority. The Treasury Department's OFAC also has enforcement authority pursuant to section 5(a) of the Act, Executive Order 13312, and Rough Diamonds Control Regulations (31 CFR 592). CBP, ICE, and the OFAC, pursuant to section 5(a) of the Act, are further authorized to enforce provisions of section 8(a) of the Act, that provide for the following civil and criminal penalties:

(a) *Civil penalties.* A civil penalty not to exceed $10,000 may be imposed on any person who violates, or attempts to violate, any order or regulation issued under the Act.

(b) *Criminal penalties.* For the willful violation or attempted violation of any license, order, or regulation issued under the Act, a fine not to exceed $50,000, shall be imposed upon conviction or:

(1) If a natural person, imprisoned for not more than ten years, or both;

(2) If an officer, director, or agent of any corporation, who willfully participates in such violation, imprisoned for not more than ten years, or both.

§ 30.71 False or fraudulent reporting on or misuse of the Automated Export System.

(a) *Criminal penalties*—(1) *Failure to file; submission of false or misleading information.* Any person, including USPPIs, authorized agents or carriers, who knowingly fails to file or knowingly submits, directly or indirectly, to the U.S. Government, false or misleading export information through the AES, shall be subject to a fine not to exceed $10,000 or imprisonment for not more than five years, or both, for each violation.

(2) *Furtherance of illegal activities.* Any person, including USPPIs, authorized agents or carriers, who knowingly reports, directly or indirectly, to the U.S. Government any information through or otherwise uses the AES to further any illegal activity shall be subject to a fine not to exceed $10,000 or imprisonment for not more than five years, or both, for each violation.

(3) *Forfeiture penalties.* Any person who is convicted under this subpart shall, in addition to any other penalty, be subject to forfeiting to the United States:

(i) Any of that person's interest in, security of, claim against, or property or contractual rights of any kind in the goods or tangible items that were the subject of the violation.

(ii) Any of that person's interest in, security of, claim against, or property or contractual rights of any kind in tangible property that was used in the export or attempt to export that was the subject of the violation.

(iii) Any of that person's property constituting, or derived from, any proceeds obtained directly or indirectly as a result of this violation.

(4) *Exemption.* The criminal fines provided for in this subpart are exempt from the provisions of 18 U.S.C. 3571.

(b) *Civil penalties*—(1) *Failure to file or delayed filing violations.* A civil penalty not to exceed $1,100 for each day of delinquency beyond the applicable period prescribed in § 30.4, but not more than $10,000 per violation, may be imposed for failure to

information or reports in connection with the exportation or transportation of cargo.

(2) *Filing false/misleading information, furtherance of illegal activities and penalties for other violations.* A civil penalty not to exceed $10,000 per violation may be imposed for each violation of provisions of this part other than any violation encompassed by paragraph (b)(1) of this section. Such penalty may be in addition to any other penalty imposed by law.

(3) *Forfeiture penalties.* In addition to any other civil penalties specified in this section, any property involved in a violation may be subject to forfeiture under applicable law.

Note to Paragraph (b): The Civil Monetary Penalties; Adjustment for Inflation Final Rule effective December 14, 2004, adjusted the penalty in Title 13, Chapter 9, Section 304, United States Code from $1,000 to $10,000 to $1,100 to $10,000.

§ 30.72 Civil penalty procedures.

(a) *General.* Whenever a civil penalty is sought for a violation of this part, the charged party is entitled to receive a formal complaint specifying the charges and, at his or her request, to contest the charges in a hearing before an administrative law judge. Any such hearing shall be conducted in accordance with 5 U.S.C. 556 and 557.

(b) *Applicable law for delegated function.* If, pursuant to 13 U.S.C. 306, the Secretary delegates functions addressed in this part to another agency, the provisions of law of that agency relating to penalty assessment, remission or mitigation of such penalties, collection of such penalties, and limitations of action and compromise of claims shall apply.

(c) *Commencement of civil actions.* If any person fails to pay a civil penalty imposed under this subpart, the Secretary may request the Attorney General to commence a civil action in an appropriate district court of the United States to recover the amount imposed (plus interest at currently prevailing rates from the date of the final order). No such action may be commenced more than five years after the date the order imposing the civil penalty becomes final. In such action, the validity, amount, and appropriateness of such penalty shall not be subject to review.

(d) *Remission and mitigation.* Any penalties imposed under § 30.71(b)(1) and (b)(2) may be remitted or mitigated, if:

(1) The penalties were incurred without willful negligence or fraud; or

(2) Other circumstances exist that justify a remission or mitigation.

(e) *Deposit of payments in General Fund of the Treasury.* Any amount paid in satisfaction of a civil penalty imposed under this subpart shall be deposited into the general fund of the Treasury and credited as miscellaneous receipts, other than a payment to remit a forfeiture which shall be deposited into the Treasury Forfeiture fund.

§ 30.73 Enforcement.

(a) *Department of Commerce.* The BIS's OEE may conduct investigations pursuant to this part. In conducting investigations, BIS may, to the extent necessary or appropriate to the enforcement of this part, exercise such authorities as are conferred upon BIS by other laws of the United States, subject, as appropriate, to policies and procedures approved by the Attorney General.

(b) *Department of Homeland Security (DHS).* ICE and CBP may enforce the provisions of this part and ICE, as assisted by CBP may conduct investigations under this part.

§ 30.74 Voluntary self-disclosure.

(a) *General policy.* The Census Bureau strongly encourages disclosure of any violation or suspected violation of the FTR. Voluntary self-disclosure is a mitigating factor in determining what administrative sanctions, if any, will be sought. The Secretary of Commerce has delegated all enforcement authority under 13 U.S.C. Chapter 9, to the BIS and the DHS.

(b) *Limitations.*

(1) The provisions of this section apply only when information is provided to the Census Bureau for its review in determining whether to seek administrative action for violations of the FTR.

(2) The provisions of this section apply only when information is received by the Census Bureau for review prior to the time that the Census Bureau, or any other agency of the United States Government, has learned the same or substantially similar information from another source and has commenced an investigation or inquiry in connection with that information.

(3) While voluntary self-disclosure is a mitigating factor in determining what corrective actions will be required by the Census Bureau and/or whether the violation will be referred to the BIS to determine what administrative sanctions, if any, will be sought, it is a factor that is considered together with all other factors in a case. The weight given to voluntary self-disclosure is within the discretion of the Census Bureau and the BIS, and the mitigating effect of voluntary self-disclosure may be outweighed by aggravating factors. Voluntary self-disclosure does not prevent transactions from being referred to the Department of Justice (DOJ) for criminal prosecution. In such a case, the BIS or the DHS would notify the DOJ of the voluntary self-disclosure, but the consideration of that factor is within the discretion of the DOJ.

(4) Any person, including USPPIs, authorized agents, or carriers, will not be deemed to have made a voluntary self-disclosure under this section unless the individual making the disclosure did so with the full knowledge and authorization of senior management.

(5) The provisions of this section do not, nor should they be relied on to, create, confer, or grant any rights, benefits, privileges, or protection enforceable at law or in equity by any person, business, or entity in any civil, criminal, administrative, or other matter.

(c) *Information to be provided*—(1) *General.* Any person disclosing information that constitutes a voluntary self-disclosure should, in the manner outlined below, if a violation is suspected or a violation is discovered, conduct a thorough review of all export transactions for the past five years where violations of the FTR are suspected and notify the Census Bureau as soon as possible.

(2) *Initial notification.*

(i) The initial notification must be in writing and be sent to the address in paragraph (c)(5) of this section. The notification must include the name of the person making the disclosure and a brief description of the suspected violations. The notification should describe the general nature, circumstances, and extent of the violations. If the person making the disclosure subsequently completes the narrative account required by paragraph (c)(3) of this section, the disclosure will be deemed to have been made on the date of the initial notification for purposes of paragraph (b)(2) of this section.

(ii) Disclosure of suspected violations that involve export of items controlled, licensed, or otherwise subject to the jurisdiction by a department or agency of the federal government should be made to the appropriate federal department or agency.

(3) *Narrative account.* After the initial notification, a thorough review should be conducted of all export transactions where possible violations of the FTR are suspected. The Census Bureau recommends that the review cover a

Federal Register / Vol. 73, No. 106 / Monday, June 2, 2008 / Rules and Regulations 31579

period of five years prior to the date of the initial notification. If the review goes back less than five years, there is a risk that violations may not be discovered that later could become the subject of an investigation. Any violations not voluntarily disclosed do not receive consideration under this section. However, the failure to make such disclosures will not be treated as a separate violation unless some other section of the FTR or other provision of law requires disclosure. Upon completion of the review, the Census Bureau should be furnished with a narrative account that sufficiently describes the suspected violations so that their nature and gravity can be assessed. The narrative account should also describe the nature of the review conducted and measures that may have been taken to minimize the likelihood that violations will occur in the future. The narrative account should include:

(i) The kind of violation involved, for example, failure to file EEI, failure to correct fatal errors, failure to file timely corrections;

(ii) Describe all data required to be reported under the FTR that was either not reported or reported incorrectly;

(iii) An explanation of when and how the violations occurred;

(iv) The complete identities and addresses of all individuals and organizations, whether foreign or domestic, involved in the activities giving rise to the violations; and

(v) A description of any mitigating circumstances.

(4) *Electronic Export Information.* Report all data required under the FTR that was not reported. Report corrections for all data reported incorrectly. All reporting of unreported data or corrections to previously reported data shall be made through the AES.

(5) *Where to make voluntary self-disclosures.* With the exception of voluntary disclosures of manifest violations under § 30.47 (c), the information constituting a voluntary self-disclosure or any other correspondence pertaining to a voluntary self-disclosure may be submitted to: Chief, Foreign Trade Division, U.S. Census Bureau, Room 6K032, Washington, DC 20233–6700, by phone 1–800–549–0595, by fax (301) 763–8835, or by e-mail *FTDRegs@census.gov.*

(d) *Action by the Census Bureau.* After the Census Bureau has been provided with the required narrative, it will promptly notify CBP, ICE, and the OEE of the voluntary disclosure, acknowledge the disclosure by letter, provide the person making the disclosure with a point of contact, and take whatever additional action, including further investigation, it deems appropriate. As quickly as the facts and circumstances of a given case permit, the Census Bureau may take any of the following actions:

(1) Inform the person or company making the voluntary self-disclosure of the action to be taken.

(2) Issue a warning letter or letter setting forth corrective measures required.

(3) Refer the matter, if necessary, to the OEE for the appropriate action.

§§ 30.75–30.99 [Reserved]

BILLING CODE 3510–07–P

31580 Federal Register / Vol. 73, No. 106 / Monday, June 2, 2008 / Rules and Regulations

Appendix A to Part 30–Sample for Power of Attorney and Written Authorization
SAMPLE FORMAT: Power of Attorney

POWER OF ATTORNEY
U.S. PRINCIPAL PARTY IN INTEREST/AUTHORIZED AGENT

Know all men by these presents, that________________________________, the
(Name of U.S. Principal Party in Interest (USPPI))
USPPI organized and doing business under the laws of the State or Country of
______________________ and having an office and place of business
at_____________________________hereby
(Address of USPPI)
authorizes__________________________, (Authorized Agent)
(Name of Authorized Agent)
of____
(Address of Authorized Agent)
to act for and on its behalf as a true and lawful agent and attorney of the U.S. Principal Party in Interest (USPPI) for, and in the name, place, and stead of the USPPI, from this date, in the United States either in writing, electronically, or by other authorized means to: act as authorized agent for export control, U.S. Census Bureau (Census Bureau) reporting, and U.S. Customs and Border Protection (CBP) purposes. Also, to prepare and transmit any Electronic Export Information (EEI) or other documents or records required to be filed by the Census Bureau, CBP, the Bureau of Industry and Security, or any other U.S. Government agency, and perform any other act that may be required by law or regulation in connection with the exportation or transportation of any goods shipped or consigned by or to the USPPI, and to receive or ship any goods on behalf of the USPPI.

The USPPI hereby certifies that all statements and information contained in the documentation provided to the authorized agent and relating to exportation will be true and correct. Furthermore, the USPPI understands that civil and criminal penalties may be imposed for making false or fraudulent statements or for the violation of any United States laws or regulations on exportation.

This power of attorney is to remain in full force and effect until revocation in writing is duly given by the U.S. Principal Party in Interest and received by the Authorized Agent.

IN WITNESS WHEREOF, ______________________________ caused these
(Full Name of USPPI/USPPI Company)
presents to be sealed and signed:

Witness: ________________________ Signature:_________________
Capacity: _________________
Date:____________________

Appendix C

Sample Written Authorization
SAMPLE FORMAT: Written Authorization

WRITTEN AUTHORIZATION TO PREPARE OR TRANSMIT ELECTRONIC EXPORT INFORMATION

I, ______________________________, authorize
(Name of U.S. Principal Party in Interest)

______________________________ to act as authorized agent for
(Name of Authorized Agent)

export control, U.S. Customs, and Census Bureau purposes to transmit such export information electronically that may be required by law or regulation in connection with the exportation or transportation of any goods on behalf of said U.S. Principal Party in Interest. The U.S. Principal Party in Interest certifies that necessary and proper documentation to accurately transmit the information electronically is and will be provided to the said Authorized Agent. The U.S. Principal Party in Interest further understands that civil and criminal penalties may be imposed for making false or fraudulent statements or for the violation of any U.S. laws or regulations on exportation and agrees to be bound by all statements of said authorized agent based upon information or documentation provided by the U.S. Principal Party in Interest to said authorized agent.

Signature: ______________________________
(U.S. Principal Party in Interest)

Capacity: ______________________________

Date: ____________________

BILLING CODE 3510–07–C

Appendix B to Part 30—AES Filing Codes

Part I—Method of Transportation Codes

10 Vessel
11 Vessel Containerized
12 Vessel (Barge)
20 Rail
21 Rail Containerized
30 Truck
31 Truck Containerized
32 Auto
33 Pedestrian
34 Road, Other
40 Air
41 Air Containerized
50 Mail
60 Passenger, Hand Carried
70 Fixed Transport (Pipeline and Powerhouse)

Part II—Export Information Codes

TP Temporary exports of domestic merchandise
IP Shipments of merchandise imported under a Temporary Import Bond for further manufacturing or processing
IR Shipments of merchandise imported under a Temporary Import Bond for repair
CH Shipments of goods donated for charity
FS Foreign Military Sales
OS All other exports
HV Shipments of personally owned vehicles
HH Household and personal effects
TE Temporary exports to be returned to the United States
TL Merchandise leased for less than a year
IS Shipments of merchandise imported under a Temporary Import Bond for return in the same condition
CR Shipments moving under a carnet
GP U.S. Government shipments
MS Shipments consigned to the U.S. Armed Forces
GS Shipments to U.S. Government agencies for their use
UG Gift parcels under Bureau of Industry and Security License Exception GFT
DD Other exemptions:
  Currency
  Airline tickets
  Bank notes
  Internal revenue stamps
  State liquor stamps
  Advertising literature
  Shipments of temporary imports by foreign entities for their use
RJ Inadmissible merchandise
(For Manifest Use Only by AES Carriers)
AE Shipment information filed through AES
(See §§ 30.50 through 30.58 for information on filing exemptions.)

Part III—License Codes

Department of Commerce, Bureau of Industry and Security (BIS), Licenses

C30 Licenses issued by BIS authorizing an export, reexport, or other regulated activity.
C31 SCL—Special Comprehensive License
C32 NLR—No License Required (controlled for other than or in addition to Anti-Terrorism)
C33 NLR—No License Required (All others, including Anti-Terrorism controls ONLY)
C35 LVS—Limited Value Shipments
C36 GBS—Shipments to B Countries
C37 CIV—Civil End Users
C38 TSR—Restricted Technology and Software
C40 TMP—Temporary Imports, Exports, and Re-exports
C41 RPL—Servicing and Replacement of Parts and Equipment
C42 GOV—Government and International Organizations
C43 GFT—Gift Parcels and Humanitarian Donations
C44 TSU—Technology and Software—Unrestricted
C45 BAG—Baggage
C46 AVS—Aircraft and Vessels (AES not required)
C47 APR—Additional Permissive Re-exports
C48 KMI—Key Management Intrastructure
C49 TAPS—Trans-Alaska Pipeline Authorization Act
C50 ENC—Encryption Commodities and Software
C51 AGR—License Exception Agricultural Commodities
C53 APP—Adjusted Peak Performance (Computers)
C54 SS–WRC—Western Red Cedar
C55 SS–Sample—Crude Oil Samples
C56 SS–SPR—Strategic Petroleum Reserves

C57 VEU—Validated End User Authorization

Nuclear Regulatory Commission (NRC) Codes

N01 NRC Form 250/250A—NRC Form 250/250A
N02 NRC General License—NRC 'General' Export License

Department of State, Directorate of Defense Trade Controls (DDTC) Codes

SAG—Agreements
SCA—Canadian ITAR Exemption
S00—License Exemption Citation
S05—DSP–5—Permanent export of unclassified defense articles and services
S61—DSP–61—Temporary import of unclassified articles
S73—DSP–73—Temporary export of unclassified articles
S85—DSP–85—Temporary or permanent import or export of classified articles
S94—DSP–94—Foreign Military Sales

Department of Treasury, Office of Foreign Assets Control (OFAC) Codes

T10—OFAC Specific License
T11—OFAC General License
T12—Kimberley Process Certificate Number

Other License Types

OPA—Other Partnership Agency License

For export license exemptions under International Traffic in Arms Regulations, refer to 22 CFR 120–130 of the ITAR for the list of export license exemptions.

Part IV—In-Bond Codes

70 Not In Bond
36 Warehouse Withdrawal for Immediate Exportation
37 Warehouse Withdrawal for Transportation and Exportation
67 Immediate Exportation from a Foreign Trade Zone
68 Transportation and Exportation from a Foreign Trade Zone

Appendix C to Part 30—Summary of Exemptions and Exclusions from EEI Filing

A. EEI is not required for the following types of shipments:[1]

1. Exemption for shipments destined to Canada (§ 30.36).

2. Valued $2,500 or less per Schedule B/HTSUSA classification for commodities shipped from one USPPI to one consignee on a single carrier (§ 30.37(a)).

3. Tools of the trade and their containers that are usual and reasonable kinds and quantities of commodities and software intended for use by individual USPPIs or by employees or representatives of the exporting company in furthering the enterprises and undertakings of the USPPI abroad (§ 30.37(b)).

4. Shipments from one point in the United States to another point in the United States by routes passing through Canada or Mexico (§ 30.37(c)).

5. Shipments from one point in Canada or Mexico to another point in the same country by routes through the United States (§ 30.37(d)).

6. Shipments transported inbond through the United States for export to a third country and exported from another U.S. port or transshipped and exported directly from the port of arrival never having made entry into the United States. If entry for consumption or warehousing in the United States is made, then an EEI is required if the goods are then exported to a third country from the United States (§ 30.37(e)).

7. Exports of technology and software as defined in 15 CFR 772 of the EAR that do not require an export license. However, EEI is required for mass-market software (§ 30.37(f)).

8. Shipments to foreign libraries, government establishments, or similar institutions, as provided in FTR Subpart D § 30.40 (d). (§ 30.37(h)).

9. Shipments as authorized under License Exception GFT for gift parcels and humanitarian donations (EAR 15 CFR 740.12); § 30.37(i)).

10. Diplomatic pouches and their contents (§ 30.37(j)).

11. Human remains and accompanying appropriate receptacles and flowers (§ 30.37(k)).

12. Shipments of interplant correspondence, executed invoices and other documents, and other shipments of company business records from a U.S. firm to its subsidiary or affiliate. This excludes highly technical plans, correspondence, etc. that could be licensed (§ 30.37(l)).

13. Shipments of pets as baggage (§ 30.37(m)).

14. Carrier's stores, not shipped under a bill of lading or an air waybill, supplies and equipment, including usual and reasonable kinds and quantities of bunker fuel, deck engine and steward department stores, provisions and supplies, medicinal and surgical supplies, food stores, slop chest articles, and saloon stores or supplies for use or consumption on board and not intended for unlading in a foreign country. (See Table 5 if shipped under a bill of lading or an air waybill (§ 30.37(n)).

15. Dunnage not shipped under a bill of lading or an air waybill, of usual and reasonable kinds and quantities not intended for unlading in a foreign country (§ 30.37(o)).

16. Shipments of aircraft parts and equipment; food, saloon, slop chest, and related stores; and provisions and supplies for use on aircraft by a U.S. airline. (EAR license exception (AVS) for aircraft and vessels 15 CFR 740.15(c); § 30.37(p)).

17. Baggage and personal effects, accompanied or unaccompanied, of persons leaving the United States including members of crews on vessels and aircraft, when they are not shipped as cargo under a bill of lading or an air waybill and do not require an export license (§ 30.37(q)).

18. Temporary exports, whether shipped or hand carried, (*e.g.*, carnet) that are exported from or returned to the United States in less than one year (12 months) from date of export (§ 30.37(r)).

19. Goods previously imported under Temporary Import Bond for return in the same condition as when imported including: goods for testing, experimentation, or demonstration; goods imported for exhibition; samples and models imported for review or for taking orders; goods for imported for participation in races or contests; and animals imported for breeding or exhibition and imported for use by representatives of foreign government or international organizations or by members of the armed forces of a foreign country. Goods that were imported under bond for processing and re-exportation are not covered by this exemption (§ 30.37(s)).

20. Issued banknotes and securities and coins in circulation exported as evidence of financial claims. The EEI must be filed for unissued bank notes and securities and coins not in circulation (such as bank notes printed in the United States and exported in fulfillment of the printing contract or as part of collections), which should be reported at their commercial or current value (§ 30.37(t)).

21. Documents used in international transactions, documents moving out of the United States to facilitate international transactions including airline tickets, internal revenue stamps, liquor stamps, and advertising literature. Export of such documents in fulfillment of a contract for their production, however, are not exempt and must be reported at the transaction value for their production (§ 30.37(u)).

B. The following types of transactions are outside the scope of the FTR and shall be excluded from EEI filing:

1. Goods shipped under CBP bond through the United States, Puerto Rico, or the U.S. Virgin Islands from one foreign country or area to another where such goods do not enter the consumption channels of the United States.

2. Goods shipped from the U.S. territories of Guam Island, American Samoa, Wake Island, Midway Island, and Northern Mariana Islands to foreign countries or areas, and goods shipped between the U.S. and these territories (§ 30.2(d)(2)).

3. Electronic transmissions and intangible transfers. See FTR, Subpart B, for export control requirements for these types of transactions (§ 30.2(d)(3)).

4. Goods shipped to Guantanamo Bay Naval Base in Cuba from the United States, Puerto Rico, or the U.S. Virgin Islands and from Guantanamo Bay Naval Base to the United States, Puerto Rico, or the U.S. Virgin Islands. (See FTR Subpart D § 30.39 for filing requirements for shipments exported by the U.S. Armed Services.) (§ 30.2(d)(4)).

[1] Exemption from the requirements for reporting complete commodity information is covered in § 30.38; Special exemptions for shipments to the U.S. Armed Services and covered in § 30.39; and Special exemptions for certain shipments to U.S. Government agencies and employees are covered in § 30.40.

Appendix D to Part 30

AES FILING CITATION, EXEMPTION AND EXCLUSION LEGENDS

I. USML Proof of Filing Citation	AES ITN Example: AES X20060101987654.
II. AES Proof of Filing Citation subpart A § 30.7	AES ITN Example: AES X20060101987654.
III. AES Postdeparture Citation-USPPIUSPPI is filing the EEI	AESPOST USPPI EIN mm/dd/yyyy Example: AESPOST 12345678912 01/01/2006.
IV. Postdeparture Citation-Agent	AESPOST USPPI EIN—Filer ID mm/dd/yyyy Example: AESPOST 12345678912—987654321 01/01/2006.
V. AES Downtime Citation-Use only when AES or AES*Direct* is unavailable.	AESDOWN Filer ID mm/dd/yyyy Example: AESDOWN 123456789 01/01/2006.
VI. Standard Exclusions are found in 15 CFR 30, Subpart A, § 30.2(d)(1) through § 30.2(d)(4).	
The following types of transactions shall be excluded from EEI filing:	
(1) Goods Shipped from U.S. territories	NOEEI § 30.2(d)(site corresponding number).
(2) Goods Shipped to or from Guantanamo Bay Naval Base in Cuba and the United States.	
(3) Inbond Shipments through the United States, Puerto Rico, and the U.S. Virgin Islands.	
VII. Exemption for Shipments to Canada	NOEEI § 30.36.
VIII. Exemption for Low-Value Shipments	NOEEI § 30.37(a).
IX. Miscellaneous Exemption Statements are found in 15 CFR 30 Subpart D § 30.37(b) through § 30.37(u).	NOEEI § 30.37 (site corresponding alphabet).
X. Special Exemption for Shipments to the U.S. Armed Forces	NOEEI § 30.39
XI. Special Exemptions for Certain Shipments to U.S. Government Agencies and Employees (Exemption Statements are found in 15 CFR 30 Subpart D § 30.40(a) through § 30.40(d).	NOEEI § 30.40 (site corresponding alphabet).
XII. Split Shipments by Air "Split Shipments" should be referenced as such on the manifest in accordance with provisions contained in § 30.28, "Split Shipments by Air." The notation should be easily identifiable on the manifest.	AES ITN SS Example: AES X20060101987654 SS.
It is preferable to include a reference to a split shipment in the exemption statements cited in the example, the notation SS should be included at the end of the appropriate exemption statement.	
Proof of filing citations by pipeline	NOEEI § 30.8(b).

Appendix E to Part 30—FTSR to FTR Concordance

FTSR	FTSR regulatory topic	FTR	FTR regulatory topic
	Subpart A—General Requirements—USPPI		
30.1	General statement of requirement for Shipper's Export Declarations (SEDs).	30.2	General requirements for filing Electronic Export Information (EEI).
30.1(a)	General requirements for filing SEDs		General requirements for filing EEI.
30.1(b)	General requirements for reporting regarding method of transportation.		NA.
30.1(c)	AES as an alternative to SED reporting		NA.
30.1(d)	Electronic transmissions and intangible transfers	30.2(d)(3)	Exclusions from filing EEI.
30.2	Related export control requirements	30.15	Export control and licensing requirements introduction.
		30.16	EAR requirements for export information on shipments from U.S. Possessions to foreign destinations or areas.
		30.17	Customs and Border Protection Regulations.
30.3	Shipper's Export Declaration forms		NA.
30.4	Preparation and signature of Shipper's Export Declarations (SED).	30.3	Electronic Export Information filer requirements, parties to export transactions, responsibilities of parties to export transactions.
30.4(a)	General requirements (SED)	30.3(a)	General Requirements.
		30.3(b)	Parties to the export transaction.
30.4(b)	Responsibilities of parties in export transactions	30.3(c)	General responsibilities of parties in export transactions.
		30.3(d)	Filer responsibilities.
30.4(c)	Responsibilities of parties in a routed export transactions.	30.3(e)	Responsibilities of parties in a routed export transaction.
30.4(d)	Information on the Shipper's Export Declaration (SED) or Automated Export System (AES) record.	30.3(a)	General requirements.
30.4(e)	Authorizing a forwarding or other agent	30.3(f)	Authorizing an agent.
30.4(f)	Format requirements for SEDs		NA.
30.5	Number and copies of Shipper's Export Declaration required.		NA.

FTSR	FTSR regulatory topic	FTR	FTR regulatory topic
30.6	Requirements as to separate Shipper's Export Declarations.		NA.
30.7	Information required on Shipper's Export Declarations		NA.
30.8	Additional information required on shipper's Export Declaration for In-Transit Goods (ENG Form 7513).		NA.
30.9	Requirements for separation and alignment of items on shipper's Export Declarations.		NA.
30.10	Continuation sheets for Shipper's Export Declaration ...		NA.
30.11	Authority to require production of document	30.10(b)	Authority to require production of documents and retaining electronic data.
30.12	Time and place for presenting the SED, exemption legends or proof of filing citations.	30.4	Electronic export information filing procedures, deadlines, and certification statements.
		30.8	Time and place for presenting proof of filing citations, postdeparture filing citations, AES downtime citations, and exemption legends.
30.15	Procedure for presentation of declarations covering shipments from an interior point.		NA.
30.16	Corrections to Shipper's Export Declarations	30.9	Transmitting and correcting Electronic Export Information.
	Subpart B—General Requirements—Exporting Carriers		
30.20	General statement of requirement for the filing of manifests * * *.	30.45	General statement of requirements for the filing of carrier manifests with proof of filing.
30.20(a)	Carriers transporting merchandise from the United States, Puerto Rico, or U.S. territories to foreign countries.	30.45(a)	Requirements for filing carrier manifest.
30.20(b)	For carriers transporting merchandise from the United States to Puerto Rico.	30.45(a)	Requirements for filing carrier manifest.
30.20(c)	Except as otherwise specifically provided, declarations should not be filed at the place where the shipment originates.	30.45(a)	Requirements for filing carrier manifest.
30.20(d)	For purposes of these regulations, the port of exportation is defined as * * *.	30.1(c)	Definition used with EEI.
30.21	Requirements for the filing of Manifests	30.45	General statement of requirements for the filing of carrier manifests with proof of filing citations for the electronic submission of export information or exemption legends when EEI is not required.
30.21(a)	Vessel	30.45(a)(1)	Vessel.
30.21(b)	Aircraft	30.45(a)(2)	Aircraft.
30.21(c)	Rail Carrier	30.45(a)(3)	Rail Carrier.
30.21(d)	Carriers not required to file manifests	30.45(a)(4)	Carriers not required to file manifests.
30.22(a)	Requirements for the filing of SEDs or AES exemption legends and AES proof of filing citations by departing carriers.	30.8	Time and place for presenting proof of filing citation, exemption, and exclusion legends.
30.22(b)	The exporting carrier shall be responsible for the accuracy of the following items of information.		NA.
30.22(c)	Except as provided in paragraph (d) of this section, when a transportation company finds, prior to the filing of declarations and manifest as provided in paragraph (a) of this section, that due to circumstances beyond the control of the transportation company or to inadvertence, a portion of the merchandise covered by an individual Shipper's Export Declaration has not been exported on the intended carrier.		NA.
30.22(d)	When a shipment by air covered by a single Shipper's Export Declaration is divided by the transportation company and exported in more than one aircraft of the transportation.	30.45(c)	Split shipments by air.
30.22(e)	Exporting carriers are authorized to amend incorrect shipping weights reported on Shipper's Export Declarations.		NA.
30.23	Requirements for the filing of Shipper's Export Declarations by pipeline carriers.	30.46	Requirements for the filing of export information by pipeline carriers.
30.24	Clearance or departure of carriers under bond on incomplete manifest on Shipper's Export Declarations.	30.47	Clearance or departure of carriers under bond on incomplete manifests.
	Subpart C—Special Provisions Applicable Under Particular Circumstances		
30.30	Values for certain types of transactions	30.25	Values for certain types of transactions.
30.31	Identification of certain nonstatistical and other unusual transactions.	30.29	Reporting of repairs and replacements.
30.31(a)	Merchandise exported for repair only, and other temporary exports.	30.29(a)	The return of goods previously imported for repair * * *.

Federal Register / Vol. 73, No. 106 / Monday, June 2, 2008 / Rules and Regulations 31585

FTSR	FTSR regulatory topic	FTR	FTR regulatory topic
30.31(b)	The return of merchandise previously imported for repair only.	30.29(b)	Goods that are covered under warranty and other temporary exports.
30.31(c)	Shipments of material in connection with construction, maintenance, and related work being done on projects for the U.S. Armed Forces.		NA.
30.33	Vessels, planes, cargo vans, and other carriers and containers sold foreign.	30.26	Reporting of vessels, aircraft, cargo vans, and other carriers and containers.
30.34	Return of exported cargo to the United States prior to reaching its final destination.	30.27	Return of exported cargo to the United States prior to reaching its final destination.
30.37	Exceptions from the requirement for reporting complete commodity detail on the Shipper's Export Declaration.	30.38	Exemption from the requirements for reporting complete commodity information.
30.37(a)	Where it can be determined that particular types of U.S. Government shipments, or shipments for government projects, are of such nature that they should not be included in the export statistics.	30.39	Special exemptions for shipments to the U.S. Armed Services. (Note, this section does not specifically address construction materials nor related work being done on projects).
30.37(b)	Special exemptions to specific portions of the requirements of § 30.7 with respect to the reporting of detailed information.		NA.
30.39	Authorization for reporting statistical information other than by means of individual Shipper's Export Declarations filed for each shipment.		NA.
30.40	Single declaration for multiple consignees		NA.
30.41	"Split shipments" by air	30.28	"Split shipments" by air.
	Subpart D—Exemptions From the Requirements for the Filing of Shipper's Export Declarations		
30.50	Procedure for shipments exempt from the requirements for Shipper's Export Declarations.	30.35	Procedure for shipments exempt from filing requirements.
30.51	Government shipments not generally exempt	30.39	Special exemption for shipments to the U.S. Armed Services.
30.52	Special exemptions for shipments to the U.S. Armed Services.	30.39	Special exemptions for shipments to the U.S. Armed Services.
30.53	Special exemptions for certain shipments to U.S. Government agencies and employees.	30.40	Special exemptions for certain shipments to U.S. Government agencies and employees.
30.53(e)	All commodities shipped to and for the exclusive use of the Panama Canal Zone or the Panama Canal Company.		NA.
30.55	Miscellaneous exemptions	30.37	Miscellaneous exemptions.
30.55(a)	Diplomatic pouches and their contents	30.37(i)	Diplomatic pouches and their contents.
30.55(b)	Human remains and accompanying appropriate receptacles and flowers.	30.37(j)	Human remains and accompanying appropriate receptacles and flowers.
30.55(c)	Shipments from one point in the United States to another thereof by routes passing through Mexico.	30.37(c)	Shipments from one point in the United States to another point in the United States by routes passing through Canada or Mexico.
30.55(d)	Shipments from one point in Mexico to another point thereof by routes through the United States.	30.37(d)	Shipments from one point in Canada or Mexico to another point in the same country by routes through the United States.
30.55(e)	Shipments, other than by vessel, or merchandise for which no validated export licenses are required, transported in-bond through the United States, and exported from another U.S. port, or transshipped and exported directly from the port of arrival.	30.37(e)	Shipments, transported in-bond through the United States, and exported from another U.S. port, or transshipped and exported directly from the port of arrival.
30.55(f)	Shipments to foreign libraries, government establishments, or similar institutions, as provided in § 30.53(d).	30.37(g)	Shipments to foreign libraries, government establishments, or similar institutions, as provided in § 30.40(d).
30.55(g)	Shipments of single gift parcels as authorized by the Bureau of Industry and Security under License Exception GFT, see 15 CFR 740.12 of the EAR.	30.37(h)	Shipments authorized by License Exception GFT for gift parcels, humanitarian donations.
30.55(h)	Except as noted in paragraph (h)(2) of this section, exports of commodities where the value of the commodities shipped from one exporter to one consignee on a single exporting carrier, classified under an individual Schedule B number, is $2,500 or less.	30.37(a)	Except as noted in § 30.2(a)(e)(iv), exports of commodities where the value of the commodities shipped USPPI to one consignee on a single exporting carrier, classified under an individual Schedule B or HTSUSA commodity classification code, is $2,500 or less.
30.55(i)	Shipments of interplant correspondence, executed invoices, and other documents and other shipments of company business records from a U.S. firm to its subsidiary or affiliate.	30.37(k)	Shipments of interplant correspondence, executed invoices, and other documents and other shipments of company business records from a U.S. firm to its subsidiary or affiliate.
30.55(j)	Shipments of pets as baggage, accompanied or unaccompanied, of persons leaving the United States, including members of crews on vessels and aircraft.	30.37(l)	Shipments of pets as baggage, accompanied or unaccompanied, of persons leaving the United States, including members of crews on vessels and aircraft.

31586 **Federal Register** / Vol. 73, No. 106 / Monday, June 2, 2008 / Rules and Regulations

FTSR	FTSR regulatory topic	FTR	FTR regulatory topic
30.55(k)	Shipments for use in connection with NASA tracking systems under Office of Export Administration Project License DL–5355–S.		NA.
30.55(l)	Shipments of aircraft parts and equipment, and food, saloon, slop chest, and related stores, provisions, and supplies for use on aircraft by a U.S. airline to its own installations, aircraft, and agent aboard, under Department of Commerce, Office of Export Administration General License, RCS.		NA.
30.55(m)	Shipments for use in connection with NOAA operations under the Office of Export Administration General License G–NOAA.		NA.
30.55(n)	Exports of technology and software as defined in 15 CFR 772 of the EAR that do not require an export license.	30.37(f)	Exports of technology and software as defined in 15 CFR 772 of the EAR that do not require an export license.
30.55(o)	Intangible exports of software and technology, such as downloaded software and technical data, including technology and software that requires an export license and mass market software exported electronically.	30.2(d)(3)	Intangible exports of software and technology, such as downloaded software and technical data, including technology and software that requires an export license and mass market software exported electronically.
30.56	Conditional Exemptions	30.37	Miscellaneous exemptions.
30.56(a)	Baggage and personal effects * * *	30.38	Exemption from the requirements for reporting complete commodity information.
30.56(b)	Tools of trade * * *	30.37(b)	Tools of trade * * *.
30.56(c)	Carriers' stores * * *	30.37(m)	Carriers' stores * * *.
30.56(d)	Dunnage * * *	30.37(n)	Dunnage * * *.
30.57	Information on export declarations for shipments of types of goods covered by § 30.56 not conditionally exempt.		NA.
30.58	Exemption for shipments from the United States to Canada.	30.36	Exemption for shipments destined to Canada.
	Subpart E—Electronic Filing Requirements—Shipper's Export Information		
30.60	General requirements for filing export and manifest data electronically using the Automated Export System (AES).	30.2	General requirements for filing Electronic Export Information.
30.60(a)	Participation		NA.
30.60(b)	Letter of Intent	30.5(a)(1)	Postdeparture filing application.
30.60(c)	General filing and transmission requirements	30.4	NA.
30.60(d)	General responsibilities of exporters, filing agents, and sea carriers—.	30.3	Electronic Export Information filer requirements, parties to export transactions, and responsibilities of parties to export transactions.
30.61	Electronic filing options	30.4	Electronic Export Information filing procedure, deadlines, and certification statement.
30.62	AES Certification, qualifications, and standards	30.5	EEI filing application and certification processes and standards.
30.63	Information required to be reported electronically through AES (data elements).	30.6	Electronic Export Information data elements.
30.64	Transmitting and correcting AES information	30.9	Transmitting and correcting Electronic Export Information.
30.65	Annotating the proper exemption legends or proof of filing citations for shipments transmitted electronically.	30.7	Annotating the bill of lading, air waybill, and other commercial loading documents with the proper proof of filing citations, approved postdeparture filing citations, downtime filing citation, or exemption legends.
30.66	Recordkeeping and requirements	30.5(f)	Support.
30.66	Support, documentation, and recordkeeping requirements.	30.10	Retention of export information and the authority to require production of documents.
	Subpart F—General Requirements—Importers		
30.70	Statistical information required on import entries	30.50 30.51	General requirements for filing import entries. Statistical information required for import entries.
30.80	Imports from Canada	30.54	Special provisions for imports from Canada.
30.81	Imports of merchandise into Guam		NA.
30.82	Identification of U.S. merchandise returned for repair and reexport.	30.53	Import of goods returned for repair.
30.83	Statistical copy of mail and informal entries		NA.
	Subpart H—General Administrative Provisions		
30.90	Confidential information, import entries, and withdrawals.	30.55	Confidentiality information, import entries, and withdrawals.
30.91	Confidential information, Shipper's Export Declarations	30.60	Confidentiality of Electronic Export Information.

Appendix C

FTSR	FTSR regulatory topic	FTR	FTR regulatory topic
30.92	Statistical classification schedules	30.61	Statistical classification schedules.
30.93	Emergency exceptions	30.62	Emergency exceptions.
30.94	Instructions to CBP		NA.
30.95	Penalties for violations		Subpart H.
30.95(a)	Exports (reexports) of rough diamonds	30.70	Violation of the Clean Diamond Trade Act.
30.95(b)	Exports of other than rough diamonds	30.71	False or fraudulent reporting.
30.99	OMB control numbers assigned pursuant to the Paperwork Reduction Act.	30.63	Office of Management and Budget control numbers assigned pursuant to the Paperwork Reduction Act.

Appendix F to Part 30—FTR to FTSR Concordance

FTR	FTR regulatory topic	FTSR	FTSR regulatory topic
	Subpart A—General Requirements		
30.1	Purpose and definitions	NA	NA.
30.2	General requirements for filing Electronic Export Information.	30.1	General statement of requirement for Shipper's Export Declarations.
30.2(a)	Filing Requirements		Filing Requirements.
30.2(b)	General requirements.		NA.
30.2(c)	Certification and filing requirements		NA.
30.2(d)	(d) Exclusions from filing EEI		NA.
30.2(e)	(e) Penalties		NA.
30.3	Electronic Export Information filer requirements, parties to export transactionns, and responsibilities of parties to export transactions.	30.4	Preparation and signature of Shipper's Export Declaration.
30.4	Electronic Export Information filing procedures, deadlines, and certification statements.	30.61	Electronic filing options.
30.4(a)	EEI transmitted predeparture	30.61(a)	EEI transmitted predeparture.
30.4(b)	Filing deadlines for EEI transmitted predeparture		NA.
30.4(c)	EEI transmitted postdeparture	30.61(b)	EEI transmitted post departure.
30.4(d)	Proof of filing citation or exemption legend	30.12(d)	Exports file via AES.
30.5	Electronic Export Information filing application and certification processes and standards.	30.62	AES Certification, qualifications, and standards.
30.5(a)	AES application process	30.60(b)	AES Participant Application.
30.5(b)	Certification process	30.66	Recordkeeping and requirements.
30.5(c)	Postdeparture filing approval process.		
30.5(d)	Electronic Export Information filing standards.		
30.5(e)	Monitoring the filing of Electronic Export Information.		
30.5(f)	Support.		
30.6	Electronic Export Information data elements	30.63	Information required to be reported electronically through AES (data elements).
30.7	Annotating the bill of lading * * *	30.65	Annotating the proper exemption legends or proof of filing citations * * *.
30.8	Time and place for preenting proof of filing citations, postdeparture filing citations, downtime filing citation, or exemption legends.	30.12	Time and place for presenting the SED, exemption legends, or proof of filing citations.
30.9	Transmitting and correcting Electronic Export Information.	30.64	Transmitting and correcting AES information.
		30.16	Corrections to Shipper's Export Declarations.
30.10(a)	Retention of Export information	30.66	Support, documentation and recordkeeping, and documentation requirements.
30.10(b)	Authority to require production of documents	30.11	Authority to require production of documents.
	Subpart B—Export Control and Licensing Requirements		
30.15	Introduction	30.2	Related export control requirements.
30.16	Export Administration Regulations	30.2	Related export control requirements.
30.17	Customs and Border Protection Regulations	30.2	Related export control requirements.
30.18	Department of State Regulations	30.2	Related export control requirements.
30.19	Other Federal agency regulations	30.2	Related export control requirements.
	Subpart C—Special Provisions and Specific-Type Transactions		
30.25	Values for certain types of transactions	30.30	Values for certain types of transactions.
30.26	Reporting of vessels, aircraft, cargo vans, and other carriers and containers.	30.33	Vessels, planes, cargo vans, and other carriers and containers sold foreign.
30.27	Return of exported cargo to the United States prior to reaching its final destination.	30.34	Return of exported cargo to the United States prior to reaching its final destination.
30.28	"Split shipments" by air	30.41	"Split shipments" by air.

31588 **Federal Register** / Vol. 73, No. 106 / Monday, June 2, 2008 / Rules and Regulations

FTR	FTR regulatory topic	FTSR	FTSR regulatory topic
30.29	Reporting of repairs and replacements	30.31	Identification of certain nonstatistical and other unusual transactions.
	Subpart D—Exemptions From the Requirements for the Filing of Electronic Export Information		
30.35	Procedure for shipments exempt from filing requirements.	30.50	Procedure for shipments exempt from the requirements for SEDs.
30.36	Exemption for shipments destined to Canada	30.58	Exemption for shipments from the United states to Canada.
30.37	Miscellaneous exemptions	30.55	Miscellaneous exemptions.
		30.55	Conditional exemptions.
30.37(a)	Except as noted in § 30.2(a)(1)(iv), exports of commodities where the value * * * is $2,500 or less.		Except as noted in paragraph h(2) of this section, exports of commodities where the value * * * is $2,500 or less.
30.37(b)	Tools of trade * * *	30.56(b)	Tools of trade * * *.
30.37(c)	Shipments from one point in the United States to another point in the United States by routes passing through Canada or Mexico	30.55(c)	Shipments from one point in the United States to another thereof by routes passing through Mexico.
		30.58(a)	* * * this exemption also applies to shipments from one point in the United States or Canada to another point thereof * * *.
30.37(d)	Shipments from one point in Canada or Mexico to another point thereof by routes through the United States	30.55(d)	Shipments from one point in Canada or Mexico to another point in the same country by routes through the United States.
		30.58(a)	* * * this exemption also applies to shipments from one point in the United States or Canada to another point thereof * * *.
30.37(e)	Shipments transported inbound through the United States * * *.	30.55(e)	Shipments, other than by vessel, or merchandise for which no validated licenses required, transported inbound through the United States * * *.
30.37(f)	Exports of technology and software as defined in 15 CFR of the EAR that do not require an export license * * *.	30.55(n)	Exports of technology and software as defined in 15 CFR 772 of the EAR that do not require an export license * * *.
30.37(g)	Shipments to foreign libraries, government establishments, or similar institutions, as provided in § 30.40(d).	....	Shipments to foreign libraries, government establishments, or similar institutions, as provided in § 30.53(d).
30.37(h)	Shipments as authorized under License Exception GFT for gift parcels and humanitarian donations.	30.55(g)	Shipments of single gift parcels as authorized by the Bureau of Industry and Security under license exception GFT.
30.37(i)	Diplomatic pouches and their contents	30.55(a)	Diplomatic pouches and their contents.
30.37(j)	Human remains and accompanying appropriate receptacles and flowers.	30.55(b)	Human remains and accompanying appropriate receptacles and flowers.
30.37(k)	Shipments of interplant correspondence, executed invoices and other documents, and other shipments of company business records from a U.S. firm to its subsidiary or affiliate.	30.55(i)	Shipments of interplant correspondence, executed invoices and other documents, and other shipments of company business records from a U.S. firm to its subsidiary or affiliate.
30.37(l)	Shipments of pets as baggage, accompanied or unaccompanied, of persons leaving the United States, including members of crews on vessels and aircraft.	30.55(j)	Shipments of pets as baggage, accompanied or unaccompanied, of persons leaving the United States, including members of crews on vessels and aircraft.
30.37(m)	Carriers' stores * * *	30.56(c)	Carriers' stores * * *.

Appendix C

FTR	FTR regulatory topic	FTSR	FTSR regulatory topic
30.37(n)	Dunnage * * *	30.56(d)	Dunnage * * *.
30.37(o)	Shipments of aircraft parts and equipment; food, saloon, slop chest, and related stores, * * *.	30.55(l)	Shipments of aircraft parts and equipment; food, saloon, slop chest, and related stores, * * *.
30.37(p)	Baggage and personal effects not shipped as cargo under a bill of lading or an air waybill and not requiring an export license * * *.	30.56(a)	Baggage and personal effects not shipped as cargo under a bill of lading or an air waybill and not requiring an export license * * *.
30.37(q)	Temporary exports, whether shipped or hand carried (*e.g.* carnet), which are exported from or returned to the United States in less than one year (21 months) from the date of export	30.31(a)	* * * and other temporary exports.
		30.37(a)(2)	Temporary exports by or to U.S. Government agencies.
30.37(r)	Goods previously imported under a Temporary Import Bond for return in the same condition as when imported * * *.	30.31(b)	* * * and other returns to the foreign shipper of other temporarily imported merchandise.
30.37(s)	Issued bank notes and securities and coins in circulation exported as evidence of financial claims.		NA.
30.37(t)	Documents used in international transactions * * *		NA.
30.38	Exemption from the requirements for reporting complete commodity information.	30.56	Conditional exemptions.
30.38(a)	Usual and reasonable kinds and quantities of wearing apparel, articles of personal adornment, toilet articles, medicinal supplies, food, souvenirs, games, and similar personal effects and their containers.	30.56(a)(1)	Usual and reasonable kinds and quantities of wearing apparel, articles of personal adornment, toilet articles, medicinal supplies, food, souvenirs, games, and similar personal effects and their containers.
30.38(b)	Usual and reasonable kinds and quantities of furniture, household effects, household furnishings, and their containers.	30.56(a)(2)	Usual and reasonable kinds and quantities of furniture, household effects, household furnishings, and their containers.
30.38(c)	Usual and reasonable kinds and quantities of vehicles, such as passenger cars, station wagons, trucks, * * *.	30.56(a)(3)	Usual and reasonable kinds and quantities of vehicles, such as passenger cars, station wagons, trucks, * * *.
30.39	Special exemptions for certain shipments to U.S. Government agencies and employees.	30.53	Special exemptions for certain shipments to U.S. Government agencies and employees
30.40	Special exemptions for certain shipments to U.S. Government agencies and employees.	30.53	Special exemptions for certain shipments to U.S. Government agencies and employees
	Subpart E—General Carrier and Manifest Requirements		
30.45	General statement of requirements for the filing of carrier manifests with proof of filing citations	30.20	General statement of requirements for the filing of manifests * * *.
		30.21	Requirements for the filing of manifests.
		30.22	Requirements for filing of Shipper's Export Declarations by departing carriers.
30.46	Requirements for the filing of export information by pipeline carriers.	30.23	Requirement for the filing of Shipper's Export declarations by pipeline carriers.
30.47	Clearance or departure of carriers under bond on incomplete manifests.	30.24	Clearance or departure of carriers under bond on incomplete manifest * * *.
	Subpart F—Import Requirements		
30.50	General requirements for filing import entries	30.70	Statistical information required on import entries.
30.53	Import of goods returned for repair	30.82	Identification of U.S. merchandise returned for repair and reexport.
30.54	Special provisions for imports from Canada	30.80	Imports from Canada.
30.55	Confidential information, import entries, and withdrawals.	30.90	Confidential information import entries, and withdrawals.
	Subpart G—General Administrative Provisions		
30.60	Confidentiality of Electronic Export Information	30.91	Confidential information, Shipper's Export Declaration.
30.61	Statistical classification schedules	30.92	Statistical classification schedules.

31590 **Federal Register** / Vol. 73, No. 106 / Monday, June 2, 2008 / Rules and Regulations

FTR	FTR regulatory topic	FTSR	FTSR regulatory topic
30.62	Emergency exceptions	30.93	Emergency exceptions.
30.63	Office of Management and Budget control numbers assigned pursuant to the Paperwork Reduction Act.	30.99	OMB control numbers assigned pursuant to the Paperwork Reduction Act.
	Subpart H—Penalties		
30.70	Violation of the Clean Diamond Trade Act	30.95(a)	Penalties for violations for export (reexport) of rough diamonds.
30.71	False or fraudulent reporting on or misuse of the Automated Export System.	30.95(b)	Penalties for violations of exports other than diamonds.
30.71(a)	Criminal penalties.		
30.71(b)	Civil penalties.		
30.72	Civil penalty procedures	....	NA.
30.73	Enforcement	....	NA.
30.73(a)	Department of Commerce.		
30.73(b)	Department of Homeland Security.		
30.74	Voluntary self-disclosure	....	NA.
30.75–30.99	[Reserved].		

Dated: May 20, 2008.

Steve H. Murdock,

Director, Bureau of the Census.

[FR Doc. E8–12133 Filed 5–30–08; 8:45 am]

BILLING CODE 3510–07–P

Appendix D

Informed Compliance: Reasonable Care

What Every Member of the Trade Community Should Know About:

Reasonable Care

(A Checklist for Compliance)

U.S. CUSTOMS and BORDER PROTECTION

AN INFORMED COMPLIANCE PUBLICATION

FEBRUARY 2004

NOTICE:

This publication is intended to provide guidance and information to the trade community. It reflects the position on or interpretation of the applicable laws or regulations by U.S. Customs and Border Protection (CBP) as of the date of publication, which is shown on the front cover. It does not in any way replace or supersede those laws or regulations. Only the latest official version of the laws or regulations is authoritative.

Publication History

First Published January 1998
Revised February 2004

PRINTING NOTE:

This publication was designed for electronic distribution via the CBP website (http://www.cbp.gov) and is being distributed in a variety of formats. It was originally set up in Microsoft Word97®. Pagination and margins in downloaded versions may vary depending upon which word processor or printer you use. If you wish to maintain the original settings, you may wish to download the .pdf version, which can then be printed using the freely available Adobe Acrobat Reader®.

PREFACE

On December 8, 1993, Title VI of the North American Free Trade Agreement Implementation Act (Pub. L. 103-182, 107 Stat. 2057), also known as the Customs Modernization or "Mod" Act, became effective. These provisions amended many sections of the Tariff Act of 1930 and related laws.

Two new concepts that emerge from the Mod Act are "***informed compliance***" and "***shared responsibility***," which are premised on the idea that in order to maximize voluntary compliance with laws and regulations of U.S. Customs and Border Protection, the trade community needs to be clearly and completely informed of its legal obligations. Accordingly, the Mod Act imposes a greater obligation on CBP to provide the public with improved information concerning the trade community's rights and responsibilities under customs regulations and related laws. In addition, both the trade and U.S. Customs and Border Protection share responsibility for carrying out these requirements. For example, under Section 484 of the Tariff Act, as amended (19 U.S.C. 1484), the importer of record is responsible for using reasonable care to enter, classify and determine the value of imported merchandise and to provide any other information necessary to enable U.S. Customs and Border Protection to properly assess duties, collect accurate statistics, and determine whether other applicable legal requirements, if any, have been met. CBP is then responsible for fixing the final classification and value of the merchandise. An importer of record's failure to exercise reasonable care could delay release of the merchandise and, in some cases, could result in the imposition of penalties.

The Office of Regulations and Rulings (ORR) has been given a major role in meeting the informed compliance responsibilities of U.S. Customs and Border Protection. In order to provide information to the public, CBP has issued a series of informed compliance publications, and videos, on new or revised requirements, regulations or procedures, and a variety of classification and valuation issues.

This publication, prepared by the International Trade Compliance Division, ORR, is a Reasonable Care checklist. "Reasonable Care (A Checklist for Compliance)" is part of a series of informed compliance publications advising the public of Customs regulations and procedures. We sincerely hope that this material, together with seminars and increased access to rulings of U.S. Customs and Border Protection, will help the trade community to improve voluntary compliance with customs laws and to understand the relevant administrative processes.

The material in this publication is provided for general information purposes only. Because many complicated factors can be involved in customs issues, an importer may wish to obtain a ruling under Regulations of U.S. Customs and Border Protection, 19 C.F.R. Part 177, or to obtain advice from an expert who specializes in customs matters, for example, a licensed customs broker, attorney or consultant.

Comments and suggestions are welcomed and should be addressed to the Assistant Commissioner at the Office of Regulations and Rulings, U.S. Customs and Border Protection, 1300 Pennsylvania Avenue, NW, (Mint Annex), Washington, D.C. 20229.

Michael T. Schmitz,
Assistant Commissioner
Office of Regulations and Rulings

REASONABLE CARE CHECKLIST

INTRODUCTION

One of the most significant effects of the Customs Modernization Act is the establishment of the clear requirement that parties exercise reasonable care in importing into the United States. Section 484 of the Tariff Act, as amended, requires an importer of record using reasonable care to make entry by filing such information as is necessary to enable U.S. Customs and Border Protection to determine whether the merchandise may be released from Customs custody, and using reasonable care, complete the entry by filing with U.S. Customs and Border Protection the declared value, classification and rate of duty and such other documentation or information as is necessary to enable U.S. Customs and Border Protection to properly assess duties, collect accurate statistics, and determine whether any other applicable requirement of law is met. Despite the seemingly simple connotation of the term reasonable care, this explicit responsibility defies easy explanation. The facts and circumstances surrounding every import transaction differ--from the experience of the importer to the nature of the imported articles. Consequently, neither U.S. Customs and Border Protection nor the importing community can develop a foolproof reasonable care checklist which would cover every import transaction. On the other hand, in keeping with the Modernization Act's theme of informed compliance, U.S. Customs and Border Protection would like to take this opportunity to recommend that the importing community examine the list of questions below. In U.S. Customs and Border Protection's view, the list of questions may prompt or suggest a program, framework or methodology which importers may find useful in avoiding compliance problems and meeting reasonable care responsibilities.

Obviously, the questions below cannot be exhaustive or encyclopedic - ordinarily, every import transaction is different. For the same reason, it cannot be overemphasized that although the following information is provided to promote enhanced compliance with the Customs laws and regulations, it has no legal, binding or precedential effect on U.S. Customs and Border Protection or the importing community. In this regard, U.S. Customs and Border Protection notes that the checklist is not an attempt to create a presumption of negligence, but rather, an attempt to educate, inform and provide guidance to the importing community. Consequently, U.S. Customs and Border Protection believes that the following information may be helpful to the importing community and hopes that this document will facilitate and encourage importers to develop their own unique compliance measurement plans, reliable procedures and reasonable care programs.

As a convenience to the public, the checklist also includes the text of a checklist previously published in the Federal Register for use in certain textile and apparel importations. The full document was published in 62 FR 48340 (September 15, 1997).

As a final reminder, it should be noted that to further assist the importing community, U.S. Customs and Border Protection issues rulings and informed compliance publications on a variety of technical subjects and processes. It is strongly recommended that importers always make sure that they are using the latest versions of these publications.

ASKING AND ANSWERING THE FOLLOWING QUESTIONS MAY BE HELPFUL IN ASSISTING IMPORTERS IN THE EXERCISE OF REASONABLE CARE:

GENERAL QUESTIONS FOR ALL TRANSACTIONS:

1. If you have not retained an expert to assist you in complying with Customs requirements, do you have access to the Customs Regulations (Title 19 of the Code of Federal Regulations), the Harmonized Tariff Schedule of the United States, and the GPO publication Customs Bulletin and Decisions? Do you have access to the Customs Internet Website, Customs Bulletin Board or other research service to permit you to establish reliable procedures and facilitate compliance with Customs laws and regulations?

2. Has a responsible and knowledgeable individual within your organization reviewed the Customs documentation prepared by you or your expert to ensure that it is full, complete and accurate? If that documentation was prepared outside your own organization, do you have a reliable system in place to insure that you receive copies of the information as submitted to U.S. Customs and Border Protection; that it is reviewed for accuracy; and that U.S. Customs and Border Protection is timely apprised of any needed corrections?

3. If you use an expert to assist you in complying with Customs requirements, have you discussed your importations in advance with that person and have you provided that person with full, complete and accurate information about the import transactions?

4. Are identical transactions or merchandise handled differently at different ports or U.S. Customs and Border Protection offices within the same port? If so, have you brought this to the attention of the appropriate U.S. Customs and Border Protection officials?

QUESTIONS ARRANGED BY TOPIC:

Merchandise Description & Tariff Classification

Basic Question: Do you know or have you established a reliable procedure or program to ensure that you know what you ordered, where it was made and what it is made of?

1. Have you provided or established reliable procedures to ensure you provide a complete and accurate description of your merchandise to U.S. Customs and Border Protection in accordance with 19 U.S.C. 1481? (Also, see 19 CFR 141.87 and 19 CFR 141.89 for special merchandise description requirements.)

2. Have you provided or established reliable procedures to ensure you provide a correct tariff classification of your merchandise to U.S. Customs and Border Protection in accordance with 19 U.S.C. 1484?

3. Have you obtained a Customs "ruling" regarding the description of the merchandise or its tariff classification (See 19 CFR Part 177), and if so, have you established reliable procedures to ensure that you have followed the ruling and brought it to U.S. Customs and Border Protection's attention?

4. Where merchandise description or tariff classification information is not immediately available, have you established a reliable procedure for providing that information, and is the procedure being followed?

5. Have you participated in a Customs pre-classification of your merchandise relating to proper merchandise description and classification?

6. Have you consulted the tariff schedules, Customs informed compliance publications, court cases and/or Customs rulings to assist you in describing and classifying the merchandise?

7. Have you consulted with a Customs "expert" (e.g., lawyer, Customs broker, accountant, or Customs consultant) to assist in the description and/or classification of the merchandise?

8. If you are claiming a conditionally free or special tariff classification/provision for your merchandise (e.g., GSP, HTS Item 9802, NAFTA, etc.), How have you verified that the merchandise qualifies for such status? Have you obtained or developed reliable procedures to obtain any required or necessary documentation to support the claim? If making a NAFTA preference claim, do you already have a NAFTA certificate of origin in your possession?

9. Is the nature of your merchandise such that a laboratory analysis or other specialized procedure is suggested to assist in proper description and classification?

10. Have you developed a reliable program or procedure to maintain and produce any required Customs entry documentation and supporting information?

Valuation

Basic Questions: Do you know or have you established reliable procedures to know the price actually paid or payable for your merchandise? Do you know the terms of sale; whether there will be rebates, tie-ins, indirect costs, additional payments; whether assists were provided, commissions or royalties paid? Are amounts actual or estimated? Are you and the supplier related parties?

1. Have you provided or established reliable procedures to provide U.S. Customs and Border Protection with a proper declared value for your merchandise in accordance with 19 U.S.C. 1484 and 19 U.S.C. 1401a?

2. Have you obtained a Customs "ruling" regarding the valuation of the merchandise (See 19 CFR Part 177), and if so, have you established reliable procedures to ensure that you have followed the ruling and brought it to U.S. Customs and Border Protection attention?

3. Have you consulted the Customs valuation laws and regulations, Customs Valuation Encyclopedia, Customs informed compliance publications, court cases and Customs rulings to assist you in valuing merchandise?

4. Have you consulted with a Customs "expert" (e.g., lawyer, accountant, Customs broker, Customs consultant) to assist in the valuation of the merchandise?

5. If you purchased the merchandise from a "related" seller, have you established procedures to ensure that you have reported that fact upon entry and taken measures or established reliable procedures to ensure that value reported to U.S. Customs and Border Protection meets one of the "related party" tests?

6. Have you taken measures or established reliable procedures to ensure that all of the legally required costs or payments associated with the imported merchandise have been reported to U.S. Customs and Border Protection (e.g., assists, all commissions, indirect payments or rebates, royalties, etc.)?

7. If you are declaring a value based on a transaction in which you were/are not the buyer, have you substantiated that the transaction is a bona fide sale at arm's length and that the merchandise was clearly destined to the United States at the time of sale?

8. If you are claiming a conditionally free or special tariff classification/provision for your merchandise (e.g., GSP, HTS Item 9802, NAFTA, etc.), have you established a reliable system or program to ensure that you reported the required value information and obtained any required or necessary documentation to support the claim?

9. Have you established a reliable program or procedure to produce any required entry documentation and supporting information?

Country of Origin/Marking/Quota

Basic Question: Have you taken reliable measures to ascertain the correct country of origin for the imported merchandise?

1. Have you established reliable procedures to ensure that you report the correct country of origin on Customs entry documents?

2. Have you established reliable procedures to verify or ensure that the merchandise is properly marked upon entry with the correct country of origin (if required) in accordance with 19 U.S.C. 1304 and any other applicable special marking requirement (watches, gold, textile labeling, etc)?

3. Have you obtained a Customs "ruling" regarding the proper marking and country of origin of the merchandise (See 19 CFR Part 177), and if so, have you established reliable procedures to

ensure that you followed the ruling and brought it to U.S. Customs and Border Protection's attention?

4. Have you consulted with a Customs "expert" (e.g., lawyer, accountant, Customs broker, Customs consultant) regarding the correct country of origin/proper marking of your merchandise?

5. Have you taken reliable and adequate measures to communicate Customs country of origin marking requirements to your foreign supplier prior to importation of your merchandise?

6. If you are claiming a change in the origin of the merchandise or claiming that the goods are of U.S. origin, have you taken required measures to substantiate your claim (e.g. Do you have U.S. milling certificates or manufacturer's affidavits attesting to the production in the U.S.)?

7. If you are importing textiles or apparel, have you developed reliable procedures to ensure that you have ascertained the correct country of origin in accordance with 19 U.S.C. 3592 (Section 334, Pub. Law 103-465) and assured yourself that no illegal transshipment or false or fraudulent practices were involved?

8.Do you know how your goods are made from raw materials to finished goods, by whom and where?

9. Have you checked with U.S. Customs and Border Protection and developed a reliable procedure or system to ensure that the quota category is correct?

10. Have you checked or developed reliable procedures to check the Status Report on Current Import Quotas (Restraint Levels) issued by U.S. Customs and Border Protection to determine if your goods are subject to a quota category which has part categories?

11. Have you taken reliable measures to ensure that you have obtained the correct visas for your goods if they are subject to visa categories?

12. In the case of textile articles, have you prepared or developed a reliable program to prepare the proper country declaration for each entry, i.e., a single country declaration (if wholly obtained/produced) or a multi-country declaration (if raw materials from one country were produced into goods in a second)?

13. Have you established a reliable maintenance program or procedure to ensure you can produce any required entry documentation and supporting information, including any required certificates of origin?

Intellectual Property Rights

Basic Question: Have you determined or established a reliable procedure to permit you to determine whether your merchandise or its packaging bear or use any trademarks or copyrighted matter or are patented and, if so, that you have a legal right to import those items into, and/or use those items in, the U.S.?

1. If you are importing goods or packaging bearing a trademark registered in the U.S., have you checked or established a reliable procedure to ensure that it is genuine and not restricted from importation under the gray-market or parallel import requirements of U.S. law (see 19 CFR 133.21), or that you have permission from the trademark holder to import such merchandise?

2. If you are importing goods or packaging which consist of, or contain registered copyrighted material, have you checked or established a reliable procedure to ensure that it is authorized and genuine? If you are importing sound recordings of live performances, were the recordings authorized?

3. Have you checked or developed a reliable procedure to see if your merchandise is subject to an International Trade Commission or court ordered exclusion order?

4. Have you established a reliable procedure to ensure that you maintain and can produce any required entry documentation and supporting information?

Miscellaneous Questions

1. Have you taken measures or developed reliable procedures to ensure that your merchandise complies with other agency requirements (e.g., FDA, EPA/DOT, CPSC, FTC, Agriculture, etc.) prior to or upon entry, including the procurement of any necessary licenses or permits?

2. Have you taken measures or developed reliable procedures to check to see if your goods are subject to a Commerce Department dumping or countervailing duty investigation or determination, and if so, have you complied or developed reliable procedures to ensure compliance with Customs reporting requirements upon entry (e.g., 19 CFR 141.61)?

3. Is your merchandise subject to quota/visa requirements, and if so, have you provided or developed a reliable procedure to provide a correct visa for the goods upon entry?

4. Have you taken reliable measures to ensure and verify that you are filing the correct type of Customs entry (e.g., TIB, T&E, consumption entry, mail entry, etc.), as well as ensure that you have the right to make entry under the Customs Regulations?

Additional Questions for Textile and Apparel Importers

Note: Section 333 of the Uruguay Round Implementation Act (19 U.S.C. 1592a) authorizes the Secretary of the Treasury to publish a list of foreign producers, manufacturers, suppliers, sellers, exporters, or other foreign persons who have been found to have violated 19 U.S.C. 1592 by using certain false, fraudulent or counterfeit documentation, labeling, or prohibited transshipment practices in connection with textiles and apparel products. Section 1592a also requires any importer of record entering, introducing, or attempting to introduce into the commerce of the United States textile or apparel products that were either directly or indirectly produced, manufactured, supplied, sold, exported, or transported by such named person to show, to the satisfaction of the Secretary, that such importer has exercised reasonable care to ensure that the textile or apparel products are accompanied by documentation, packaging, and labeling that are accurate as to its origin. Under section 1592a, reliance solely upon information regarding the imported product from a person named on the list does not constitute the exercise of reasonable care. Textile and apparel importers who have some commercial relationship with one or more of the listed parties must exercise a degree of reasonable care in ensuring that the documentation covering the imported merchandise, as well as its packaging and labeling, is accurate as to the country of origin of the merchandise. This degree of reasonable care must rely on more than information supplied by the named party.

In meeting the reasonable care standard when importing textile or apparel products and when dealing with a party named on the list published pursuant to section 592A an importer should consider the following questions in attempting to ensure that the documentation, packaging, and labeling is accurate as to the country of origin of the imported merchandise. The list of questions is not exhaustive but is illustrative.

1. Has the importer had a prior relationship with the named party?

2. Has the importer had any detentions and/or seizures of textile or apparel products that were directly or indirectly produced, supplied, or transported by the named party?

3. Has the importer visited the company's premises and ascertained that the company has the capacity to produce the merchandise?

4. Where a claim of an origin conferring process is made in accordance with 19 CFR 102.21, has the importer ascertained that the named party actually performed the required process?

5. Is the named party operating from the same country as is represented by that party on the documentation, packaging or labeling?

6. Have quotas for the imported merchandise closed or are they nearing closing from the main producer countries for this commodity?

7. What is the history of this country regarding this commodity?

8. Have you asked questions of your supplier regarding the origin of the product?

9. Where the importation is accompanied by a visa, permit, or license, has the importer verified with the supplier or manufacturer that the visa, permit, and/or license is both valid and accurate as to its origin? Has the importer scrutinized the visa, permit or license as to any irregularities that would call its authenticity into question?

Reasonable Care
February 2004

ADDITIONAL INFORMATION

The Internet

The home page of U.S. Customs and Border Protection on the Internet's World Wide Web, provides the trade community with current, relevant information regarding CBP operations and items of special interest. The site posts information -- which includes proposed regulations, news releases, publications and notices, etc. -- that can be searched, read on-line, printed or downloaded to your personal computer. The web site was established as a trade-friendly mechanism to assist the importing and exporting community. The web site also links to the home pages of many other agencies whose importing or exporting regulations that U.S. Customs and Border Protection helps to enforce. The web site also contains a wealth of information of interest to a broader public than the trade community. For instance, on June 20, 2001, CBP launched the "Know Before You Go" publication and traveler awareness campaign designed to help educate international travelers.

The web address of U.S. Customs and Border Protection is http://www.cbp.gov

Customs Regulations

The current edition of *Customs Regulations of the United States* is a loose-leaf, subscription publication available from the Superintendent of Documents, U.S. Government Printing Office, Washington, DC 20402; telephone (202) 512-1800. A bound, 2003 edition of Title 19, *Code of Federal Regulations*, which incorporates all changes to the Regulations as of April 1, 2003, is also available for sale from the same address. All proposed and final regulations are published in the *Federal Register*, which is published daily by the Office of the Federal Register, National Archives and Records Administration, and distributed by the Superintendent of Documents. Information about on-line access to the *Federal Register* may be obtained by calling (202) 512-1530 between 7 a.m. and 5 p.m. Eastern time. These notices are also published in the weekly *Customs Bulletin* described below.

Customs Bulletin

The *Customs Bulletin and Decisions ("Customs Bulletin")* is a weekly publication that contains decisions, rulings, regulatory proposals, notices and other information of interest to the trade community. It also contains decisions issued by the U.S. Court of International Trade, as well as customs-related decisions of the U.S. Court of Appeals for the Federal Circuit. Each year, the Government Printing Office publishes bound volumes of the *Customs Bulletin*. Subscriptions may be purchased from the Superintendent of Documents at the address and phone number listed above.

Reasonable Care
February 2004

Importing Into the United States

This publication provides an overview of the importing process and contains general information about import requirements. The February 2002 edition of *Importing Into the United States* contains much new and revised material brought about pursuant to the Customs Modernization Act ("Mod Act"). The Mod Act has fundamentally altered the relationship between importers and U.S. Customs and Border Protection by shifting to the importer the legal responsibility for declaring the value, classification, and rate of duty applicable to entered merchandise.

The February 2002 edition contains a section entitled "Informed Compliance." A key component of informed compliance is the shared responsibility between U.S. Customs and Border Protection and the import community, wherein CBP communicates its requirements to the importer, and the importer, in turn, uses reasonable care to assure that CBP is provided accurate and timely data pertaining to his or her importation.

Single copies may be obtained from local offices of U.S. Customs and Border Protection, or from the Office of Public Affairs, U.S. Customs and Border Protection, 1300 Pennsylvania Avenue NW, Washington, DC 20229. An on-line version is available at the CBP web site. *Importing Into the United States* is also available for sale, in single copies or bulk orders, from the Superintendent of Documents by calling (202) 512-1800, or by mail from the Superintendent of Documents, Government Printing Office, P.O. Box 371954, Pittsburgh, PA 15250-7054.

Informed Compliance Publications

U.S. Customs and Border Protection has prepared a number of Informed Compliance publications in the "*What Every Member of the Trade Community Should Know About:...*" series. Check the Internet web site http://www.cbp.gov for current publications.

Reasonable Care
February 2004

Value Publications

Customs Valuation under the Trade Agreements Act of 1979 is a 96-page book containing a detailed narrative description of the customs valuation system, the customs valuation title of the Trade Agreements Act (§402 of the Tariff Act of 1930, as amended by the Trade Agreements Act of 1979 (19 U.S.C. §1401a)), the Statement of Administrative Action which was sent to the U.S. Congress in conjunction with the TAA, regulations (19 C.F.R. §§152.000-152.108) implementing the valuation system (a few sections of the regulations have been amended subsequent to the publication of the book) and questions and answers concerning the valuation system. A copy may be obtained from U.S. Customs and Border Protection, Office of Regulations and Rulings, Value Branch, 1300 Pennsylvania Avenue, NW, (Mint Annex), Washington, D.C. 20229.

Customs Valuation Encyclopedia (with updates) is comprised of relevant statutory provisions, CBP Regulations implementing the statute, portions of the Customs Valuation Code, judicial precedent, and administrative rulings involving application of valuation law. A copy may be purchased for a nominal charge from the Superintendent of Documents, Government Printing Office, P.O. Box 371954, Pittsburgh, PA 15250-7054. This publication is also available on the Internet web site of U.S. Customs and Border Protection.

> The information provided in this publication is for general information purposes only. Recognizing that many complicated factors may be involved in customs issues, an importer may wish to obtain a ruling under CBP Regulations, 19 C.F.R. Part 177, or obtain advice from an expert (such as a licensed Customs Broker, attorney or consultant) who specializes in customs matters. Reliance solely on the general information in this pamphlet may not be considered reasonable care.

Additional information may also be obtained from U.S. Customs and Border Protection ports of entry. Please consult your telephone directory for an office near you. The listing will be found under U.S. Government, Department of Homeland Security.

Reasonable Care
February 2004

"Your Comments are Important"

The Small Business and Regulatory Enforcement Ombudsman and 10 regional Fairness Boards were established to receive comments from small businesses about Federal agency enforcement activities and rate each agency's responsiveness to small business. If you wish to comment on the enforcement actions of U.S. Customs and Border Protection, call 1-888-REG-FAIR (1-888-734-3247).

REPORT SMUGGLING 1-800-BE-ALERT OR 1-800-NO-DROGA

Visit our Internet web site: http://www.cbp.gov

Appendix E
Harmonized Tariff Schedule

USITC Publication

HARMONIZED TARIFF SCHEDULE

Of the United States (2009) (Revision 1)

Annotated for Statistical Reporting Purposes

Please see the USITC website at www.usitc.gov or *hts.usitc.gov* for the latest tariff information and revisions to the Harmonized Tariff Schedule

United States International Trade Commission
Washington, D.C. 20436

UNITED STATES INTERNATIONAL TRADE COMMISSION

Search: Advanced
All
Go Home
Site Glossary Site Map

Trade Remedy Investigations
- Antidumping and countervaling duty investigations
- Intellectual property infringement and other unfair acts (section 337 investigations)
- Global and special safeguards

Industry and Economic Analysis
- Ongoing Investigations
- Research & Analysis

Tariff Information Center
- Offical Harmonized Tariff Schedule
- Other Related Information

News Releases

Notices

Archive

Publications

Employment Center

Help/Contact Us

Trade Remedies | Industry & Economic Analysis | Tariff Information Center

> Official Harmonized Tariff Schedule > Other Related Information

TARIFF INFORMATION CENTER

By Chapter, Harmonized Tariff Schedule of the United States

This page contains the chapter-by-chapter listing of the Harmonized Tariff Schedule and general notes. The links below correspond to the various sections in the Table of Contents for the Harmonized Tariff Schedule. Clicking on a link will load the corresponding Adobe .pdf file

(Note: Section notes, if any, are attached to the first chapter of each section. "Page down" to view chapter after selecting.)

COVER

CHANGE RECORD

PREFACE

GENERAL NOTES; GENERAL RULES OF INTERPRETATION; GENERAL STATISTICAL NOTES

Notice to Exporters

SECTION I: LIVE ANIMALS; ANIMAL PRODUCTS

	Section Notes
Chapter 1	Live animals
Chapter 2	Meat and edible meat offal
Chapter 3	Fish and crustaceans, molluscs and other aquatic invertebrates
Chapter 4	Dairy produce; birds eggs; natural honey; edible products of animal origin, not elsewhere specified or included
Chapter 5	Products of animal origin, not elsewhere specified or included

SECTION II: VEGETABLE PRODUCTS

	Section Notes
Chapter 6	Live trees and other plants; bulbs, roots and the like; cut flowers and ornamental foliage
Chapter 7	Edible vegetables and certain roots and tubers
Chapter 8	Edible fruit and nuts; peel of citrus fruit or melons
Chapter 9	Coffee, tea, maté and spices
Chapter 10	Cereals
Chapter 11	Products of the milling industry; malt; starches; inulin; wheat gluten
Chapter 12	Oil seeds and oleaginous fruits; miscellaneous grains, seeds and fruits; industrial or medicinal plants; straw and fodder

HTS TOOLS

HTS Online Search

Current HTSA Edition by Chapter

Current HTSA Edition Full Text [PDF]

HTSA Archive

Changes to HTSA

Simplification of the Harmonized Tariff Schedule of U.S.

Current Tariff Database

HTS Help!

RELATED

Background Support for International Agreements

Commission Reports on Miscellaneous Tariff Bills

FTA Annexes

Rulings on Tariffs, Classifications, or Information on Exports

Chapter 13	Lac; gums, resins and other vegetable saps and extracts
Chapter 14	Vegetable plaiting materials; vegetable products not elsewhere specified or included

SECTION III: ANIMAL OR VEGETABLE FATS AND OILS AND THEIR CLEAVAGE PRODUCTS; PREPARED EDIBLE FATS; ANIMAL OR VEGETABLE WAXES

Chapter 15	Animal or vegetable fats and oils and their cleavage products prepared edible fats; animal or vegetable waxes

SECTION IV: PREPARED FOODSTUFFS; BEVERAGES, SPIRITS, AND VINEGAR; TOBACCO AND MANUFACTURED TOBACCO SUBSTITUTES

	Section Notes
Chapter 16	Preparations of meat, of fish or of crustaceans, molluscs or other aquatic invertebrates
Chapter 17	Sugars and sugar confectionery
Chapter 18	Cocoa and cocoa preparations
Chapter 19	Preparations of cereals, flour, starch or milk; bakers' wares
Chapter 20	Preparations of vegetables, fruit, nuts or other parts of plants
Chapter 21	Miscellaneous edible preparations
Chapter 22	Beverages, spirits and vinegar
Chapter 23	Residues and waste from the food industries; prepared animal feed
Chapter 24	Tobacco and manufactured tobacco substitutes

SECTION V: MINERAL PRODUCTS

Chapter 25	Salt; sulfur; earths and stone; plastering materials, lime and cement
Chapter 26	Ores, slag and ash
Chapter 27	Mineral fuels, mineral oils and products of their distillation; bituminous substances; mineral waxes

SECTION VI: PRODUCTS OF THE CHEMICAL OR ALLIED INDUSTRIES

	Section Notes
Chapter 28	Inorganic chemicals; organic or inorganic compounds of precious metals, of rare-earth metals,of radioactive elements or of isotopes
Chapter 29	Organic chemicals
Chapter 30	Pharmaceutical products
Chapter 31	Fertilizers
Chapter 32	Tanning or dyeing extracts; dyes, pigments, paints, varnishes, putty and mastics
Chapter 33	Essential oils and resinoids; perfumery, cosmetic or toilet preparations
Chapter 34	Soap, organic surface-active agents, washing preparations, lubricating preparations, artificial waxes, prepared waxes, polishing or scouring preparations, candles and similar articles, modeling pastes, "dental waxes" and dental preparations with

	a basis of plaster
Chapter 35	Albuminoidal substances; modified starches; glues; enzymes
Chapter 36	Explosives; pyrotechnic products; matches; pyrophoric alloys; certain combustible preparations
Chapter 37	Photographic or cinematographic goods
Chapter 38	Miscellaneous chemical products

SECTION VII: PLASTICS AND ARTICLES THEREOF RUBBER AND ARTICLES THEREOF

	Section Notes
Chapter 39	Plastics and articles thereof
Chapter 40	Rubber and articles thereof

SECTION VIII: RAW HIDES AND SKINS, LEATHER, FURSKINS AND ARTICLES THEREOF; SADDLERY AND HARNESS; TRAVEL GOODS, HANDBAGS AND SIMILAR CONTAINERS; ARTICLES OF ANIMAL GUT (OTHER THAN SILKWORM GUT)

	Section Notes
Chapter 41	Raw hides and skins (other than furskins) and leather
Chapter 42	Articles of leather; saddlery and harness; travel goods, handbags and similar containers; articles of animal gut (other than silkworm gut)
Chapter 43	Furskins and artificial fur; manufactures thereof

SECTION IX: WOOD AND ARTICLES OF WOOD; WOOD CHARCOAL; CORK AND ARTICLES OF CORK; MANUFACTURERS OF STRAW,OF ESPARTO OR OF OTHER PLAITING MATERIALS; BASKETWARE AND WICKERWORK

Chapter 44	Wood and articles of wood; wood charcoal
Chapter 45	Cork and articles of cork
Chapter 46	Manufactures of straw, of esparto or of other plaiting materials; basketware and wickerwork

SECTION X: PULP OF WOOD OR OF OTHER FIBROUS CELLULOSIC MATERIAL; WASTE AND SCRAP OF PAPER OR PAPERBOARD; PAPER AND PAPERBOARD AND ARTICLES THEREOF

	Section Notes
Chapter 47	Pulp of wood or of other fibrous cellulosic material; waste and scrap of paper or paperboard
Chapter 48	Paper and paperboard; articles of paper pulp, of paper or of paperboard
Chapter 49	Printed books, newspapers, pictures and other products of the printing industry; manuscripts, typescripts and plans

SECTION XI: TEXTILE AND TEXTILE ARTICLES

	Section Notes
Chapter 50	Silk
Chapter 51	Wool, fine or coarse animal hair; horsehair yarn and woven fabric
Chapter 52	Cotton
Chapter 53	Other vegetable textile fibers; paper yarn and woven fabric of paper yarn
Chapter 54	Man-made filaments
Chapter 55	Man-made staple fibers
Chapter 56	Wadding, felt and nonwovens; special yarns, twine, cordage, ropes and cables and articles thereof
Chapter 57	Carpets and other textile floor coverings
Chapter 58	Special woven fabrics; tufted textile fabrics; lace, tapestries; trimmings; embroidery
Chapter 59	Impregnated, coated, covered or laminated textile fabrics; textile articles of a kind suitable for industrial use
Chapter 60	Knitted or crocheted fabrics
Chapter 61	Articles of apparel and clothing accessories, knitted or crocheted
Chapter 62	Articles of apparel and clothing accessories, not knitted or crocheted
Chapter 63	Other made up textile articles; sets; worn clothing and worn textile articles; rags

SECTION XII: FOOTWEAR, HEADGEAR, UMBRELLAS, SUN UMBRELLAS, WALKING STICKS, SEATSTICKS, WHIPS, RIDING-CROPS AND PARTS THEREOF; PREPARED FEATHERS AND ARTICLES MADE THEREWITH; ARTIFICIAL FLOWERS; ARTICLES OF HUMAN HAIR

Chapter 64	Footwear, gaiters and the like; parts of such articles
Chapter 65	Headgear and parts thereof
Chapter 66	Umbrellas, sun umbrellas, walking sticks, seatsticks, whips, riding-crops and parts thereof
Chapter 67	Prepared feathers and down and articles made of feathers or of down; artificial flowers; articles of human hair

SECTION XIII: ARTICLES OF STONE, PLASTER, CEMENT, ASBESTOS, MICA OR SIMILAR MATERIALS; CERAMIC PRODUCTS; GLASS AND GLASSWARE

Chapter 68	Articles of stone, plaster, cement, asbestos, mica or similar materials
Chapter 69	Ceramic products
Chapter 70	Glass and glassware

SECTION XIV: NATURAL OR CULTURED PEARLS, PRECIOUS OR SEMIPRECIOUS STONES, PRECIOUS METALS, METALS CLAD WITH PRECIOUS METAL, AND ARTICLES THEREOF; IMITATION JEWELRY; COIN

Chapter 71	Natural or cultured pearls, precious or semi-precious stones,precious metals, metals clad with precious metal and articles thereof; imitation jewelry; coin

SECTION XV:BASE METALS AND ARTICLES OF BASE METAL

	Section Notes
Chapter 72	Iron and steel
Chapter 73	Articles of iron or steel
Chapter 74	Copper and articles thereof
Chapter 75	Nickel and articles thereof
Chapter 76	Aluminum and articles thereof
Chapter 77	(Reserved for possible future use)
Chapter 78	Lead and articles thereof
Chapter 79	Zinc and articles thereof
Chapter 80	Tin and articles thereof
Chapter 81	Other base metals; cermets; articles thereof
Chapter 82	Tools, implements, cutlery, spoons and forks, of base metal; parts thereof of base metal
Chapter 83	Miscellaneous articles of base metal

SECTION XVI: MACHINERY AND MECHANICAL APPLIANCES; ELECTRICAL EQUIPMENT; PARTS THEREOF; SOUND RECORDERS AND REPRODUCERS, TELEVISION IMAGE AND SOUND RECORDERS AND REPRODUCERS, AND PARTS AND ACCESSORIES OF SUCH ARTICLES

	Section Notes
Chapter 84	Nuclear reactors, boilers, machinery and mechanical appliances; parts thereof
Chapter 85	Electrical machinery and equipment and parts thereof; sound recorders and reproducers, television image and sound recorders and reproducers, and parts and accessories of such articles

SECTION XVII: VEHICLES, AIRCRAFT, VESSELS AND ASSOCIATED TRANSPORT EQUIPMENT

	Section Notes
Chapter 86	Railway or tramway locomotives, rolling-stock and parts thereof; railway or tramway track fixtures and fittings and parts thereof; mechanical (including electro-mechanical) traffic signalling equipment of all kinds
Chapter 87	Vehicles other than railway or tramway rolling stock, and parts and accessories thereof
Chapter 88	Aircraft, spacecraft, and parts thereof
Chapter 89	Ships, boats and floating structures

SECTION XVIII: OPTICAL, PHOTOGRAPHIC, CINEMATOGRAPHIC, MEASURING, CHECKING, PRECISION, MEDICAL OR SURGICAL INSTRUMENTS AND APPARATUS; CLOCKS AND WATCHES; MUSICAL INSTRUMENTS; PARTS AND ACCESSORIES THEREOF

Chapter 90	Optical, photographic, cinematographic, measuring, checking, precision, medical or surgical instruments and apparatus; parts and accessories thereof
Chapter 91	Clocks and watches and parts thereof

Chapter 92 Musical instruments; parts and accessories of such articles

SECTION XIX: ARMS AND AMMUNITION; PARTS AND ACCESSORIES THEREOF

Chapter 93 Arms and ammunition; parts and accessories thereof

SECTION XX: MISCELLANEOUS MANUFACTURED ARTICLES

Chapter 94 Furniture; bedding, mattresses, mattress supports, cushions and similar stuffed furnishings; lamps and lighting fittings, not elsewhere specified or included; illuminated sign illuminated nameplates and the like; prefabricated buildings

Chapter 95 Toys, games and sports requisites; parts and accessories thereof

Chapter 96 Miscellaneous manufactured articles

SECTION XXI: WORKS OF ART, COLLECTORS' PIECES AND ANTIQUES

Chapter 97 Works of art, collectors' pieces and antiques

SECTION XXII: SPECIAL CLASSIFICATION PROVISIONS; TEMPORARY LEGISLATION; TEMPORARY MODIFICATIONS PROCLAIMEDPURSUANT TO TRADE AGREEMENTS LEGISLATION; ADDITIONAL IMPORT RESTRICTIONS PROCLAIMED PURSUANT TO SECTION 22 OF THE AGRICULTURAL ADJUSTMENT ACT, AS AMENDED

Chapter 98 Special classification provisions

Chapter 99 Temporary legislation; temporary modifications proclaimed pursuant to trade agreements legislation; additional import restrictions proclaimed pursuant to section 22 of the Agricultural Adjustment Act, as amended

- CHEMICAL APPENDIX TO THE TARIFF SCHEDULE
- PHARMACEUTICAL APPENDIX TO THE TARIFF SCHEDULE
- INTERMEDIATE CHEMICALS FOR DYES APPENDIX TO THE TARIFF SCHEDULE
- STATISTICAL ANNEXES
    - Annex A - Schedule C, Classification of Country and Territory Designations for U.S. Import Statistics
    - Annex B - International Standard Country Codes
    - Annex C - Schedule D, Customs District and Port Codes
- ALPHABETICAL INDEX

United States International Trade Commission
500 E Street, SW, Washington, DC 20436
Telephone: 202-205-2000

FIRSTGOV

Appendix E

Harmonized Tariff Schedule of the United States (2009) (Rev. 1)

Annotated for Statistical Reporting Purposes

GENERAL RULES OF INTERPRETATION

Classification of goods in the tariff schedule shall be governed by the following principles:

1. The table of contents, alphabetical index, and titles of sections, chapters and sub-chapters are provided for ease of reference only; for legal purposes, classification shall be determined according to the terms of the headings and any relative section or chapter notes and, provided such headings or notes do not otherwise require, according to the following provisions:

2. (a) Any reference in a heading to an article shall be taken to include a reference to that article incomplete or unfinished, provided that, as entered, the incomplete or unfinished article has the essential character of the complete or finished article. It shall also include a reference to that article complete or finished (or falling to be classified as complete or finished by virtue of this rule), entered unassembled or disassembled.

   (b) Any reference in a heading to a material or substance shall be taken to include a reference to mixtures or combinations of that material or substance with other materials or substances. Any reference to goods of a given material or substance shall be taken to include a reference to goods consisting wholly or partly of such material or substance. The classification of goods consisting of more than one material or substance shall be according to the principles of rule 3.

3. When, by application of rule 2(b) or for any other reason, goods are, *prima facie*, classifiable under two or more headings, classification shall be effected as follows:

   (a) The heading which provides the most specific description shall be preferred to headings providing a more general description. However, when two or more headings each refer to part only of the materials or substances contained in mixed or composite goods or to part only of the items in a set put up for retail sale, those headings are to be regarded as equally specific in relation to those goods, even if one of them gives a more complete or precise description of the goods.

   (b) Mixtures, composite goods consisting of different materials or made up of different components, and goods put up in sets for retail sale, which cannot be classified by reference to 3(a), shall be classified as if they consisted of the material or component which gives them their essential character, insofar as this criterion is applicable.

   (c) When goods cannot be classified by reference to 3(a) or 3(b), they shall be classified under the heading which occurs last in numerical order among those which equally merit consideration.

4. Goods which cannot be classified in accordance with the above rules shall be classified under the heading appropriate to the goods to which they are most akin.

5. In addition to the foregoing provisions, the following rules shall apply in respect of the goods referred to therein:

   (a) Camera cases, musical instrument cases, gun cases, drawing instrument cases, necklace cases and similar containers, specially shaped or fitted to contain a specific article or set of articles, suitable for long-term use and entered with the articles for which they are intended, shall be classified with such articles when of a kind normally sold therewith. This rule does not, however, apply to containers which give the whole its essential character;

   (b) Subject to the provisions of rule 5(a) above, packing materials and packing containers entered with the goods therein shall be classified with the goods if they are of a kind normally used for packing such goods. However, this provision is not binding when such packing materials or packing containers are clearly suitable for repetitive use.

6. For legal purposes, the classification of goods in the subheadings of a heading shall be determined according to the terms of those subheadings and any related subheading notes and, *mutatis mutandis*, to the above rules, on the understanding that only subheadings at the same level are comparable. For the purposes of this rule, the relative section, chapter and subchapter notes also apply, unless the context otherwise requires.

ADDITIONAL U.S. RULES OF INTERPRETATION

1. In the absence of special language or context which otherwise requires--

(a) a tariff classification controlled by use (other than actual use) is to be determined in accordance with the use in the United States at, or immediately prior to, the date of importation, of goods of that class or kind to which the imported goods belong, and the controlling use is the principal use;

(b) a tariff classification controlled by the actual use to which the imported goods are put in the United States is satisfied only if such use is intended at the time of importation, the goods are so used and proof thereof is furnished within 3 years after the date the goods are entered;

(c) a provision for parts of an article covers products solely or principally used as a part of such articles but a provision for "parts" or "parts and accessories" shall not prevail over a specific provision for such part or accessory; and

(d) the principles of section XI regarding mixtures of two or more textile materials shall apply to the classification of goods in any provision in which a textile material is named.

[COMPILER'S NOTE: The rules of origin provisions for some United States free trade agreements (other than those for the United States-Australia Free Trade Agreement, the United States-Singapore Free Trade Agreement and the United States-Chile Free Trade Agreement, which do reflect proclaimed rectifications) have NOT been updated to reflect changes to the tariff schedule resulting from Presidential Proclamation 8097, which modified the HTS to reflect World Customs Organization changes to the Harmonized Commodity Description and Coding System and was effective as of Feb. 3, 2007. You will therefore see tariff heading/subheading numbers in the pertinent general notes which do not correspond to numbers in chapters 1 through 97 or to other portions of the same general notes. Contact officials of U.S. Customs and Border Protection in order to ascertain whether affected goods qualify for FTA treatment.]

Harmonized Tariff Schedule of the United States (2009) (Rev. 1)

Annotated for Statistical Reporting Purposes

GN p.6

West Bank/Col. 2/Special symbols

(V) A description of the origin and cost or value of any foreign materials used in the article which have not been substantially transformed in the West Bank, the Gaza Strip or a qualifying industrial zone.

(G) For the purposes of this paragraph, a "qualifying industrial zone" means any area that–

(1) encompasses portions of the territory of Israel and Jordan or Israel and Egypt;

(2) has been designated by local authorities as an enclave where merchandise may enter without payment of duty or excise taxes; and

(3) has been designated by the United States Trade Representative in a notice published in the Federal Register as a qualifying industrial zone.

(b) Rate of Duty Column 2. Notwithstanding any of the foregoing provisions of this note, the rates of duty shown in column 2 shall apply to products, whether imported directly or indirectly, of the following countries and areas pursuant to section 401 of the Tariff Classification Act of 1962, to section 231 or 257(e)(2) of the Trade Expansion Act of 1962, to section 404(a) of the Trade Act of 1974 or to any other applicable section of law, or to action taken by the President thereunder:

Cuba North Korea

(c) Products Eligible for Special Tariff Treatment.

(i) Programs under which special tariff treatment may be provided, and the corresponding symbols for such programs as they are indicated in the "Special" subcolumn, are as follows:

Generalized System of Preferences	A, A* or A+
United States-Australia Free Trade Agreement	AU
Automotive Products Trade Act	B
United States-Bahrain Free Trade Agreement Implementation Act	BH
Agreement on Trade in Civil Aircraft	C
North American Free Trade Agreement:	
Goods of Canada, under the terms of general note 12 to this schedule.	CA
Goods of Mexico, under the terms of general note 12 to this schedule	MX
United States-Chile Free Trade Agreement	CL
African Growth and Opportunity Act	D
Caribbean Basin Economic Recovery Act	E or E*
United States-Israel Free Trade Area	IL
Andean Trade Preference Act or Andean Trade Promotion and Drug Eradication Act	J, J* or J+
United States-Jordan Free Trade Area Implementation Act	JO
Agreement on Trade in Pharmaceutical Products	K
Dominican Republic-Central America-United States Free Trade Agreement Implementation Act	P or P+
Uruguay Round Concessions on Intermediate Chemicals for Dyes	L
United States-Caribbean Basin Trade Partnership Act	R
United States-Morocco Free Trade Agreement Implementation Act	MA
United States-Singapore Free Trade Agreement	SG
United States-Oman Free Trade Agreement Implementation Act	OM
"United States-Peru Trade Promotion Agreement Implementation Act	PE

4. Products of Countries Designated Beneficiary Developing Countries for Purposes of the Generalized System of Preferences (GSP).

(a) The following countries, territories and associations of countries eligible for treatment as one country (pursuant to section 507(2) of the Trade Act of 1974 (19 U.S.C. 2467(2)) are designated beneficiary developing countries for the purposes of the Generalized System of Preferences, provided for in Title V of the Trade Act of 1974, as amended (19 U.S.C. 2461 *et seq.*):

Independent Countries

Afghanistan
Albania
Algeria
Angola
Argentina
Armenia
Azerbaijan
Bangladesh
Belize
Benin
Bhutan
Bolivia
Bosnia and Hercegovina
Botswana
Brazil
Burkina Faso
Burundi
Cambodia
Cameroon
Cape Verde
Central African Republic
Chad
Colombia
Comoros
Congo (Brazzaville)
Congo (Kinshasa)
Côte d'Ivoire
Croatia
Djibouti
Dominica
East Timor
Ecuador
Egypt
Equatorial Guinea
Eritrea
Ethiopia
Fiji
Gabon
Gambia, The
Georgia
Ghana
Grenada
Guinea
Guinea-Bissau
Guyana
Haiti
India
Indonesia
Iraq
Jamaica
Jordan
Kazakhstan
Kenya
Kiribati
Kosovo
Kyrgyzstan
Lebanon
Lesotho
Liberia
Macedonia, Former Yugoslav Republic of
Madagascar
Malawi
Mali
Mauritania
Mauritius
Moldova
Mongolia
Montenegro
Mozambique
Namibia
Nepal
Niger
Nigeria
Pakistan
Panama
Papua New Guinea
Paraguay
Philippines
Russia
Rwanda
St. Kitts and Nevis
Saint Lucia
Saint Vincent and the Grenadines
Samoa
Sao Tomé and Principe
Senegal
Serbia
Seychelles
Sierra Leone
Solomon Islands
Somalia
South Africa
Sri Lanka
Suriname
Swaziland
Tanzania
Thailand
Togo
Tonga
Trinidad and Tobago
Tunisia
Turkey
Tuvalu
Uganda
Ukraine
Uruguay
Uzbekistan
Vanuatu
Venezuela
Republic of Yemen
Zambia
Zimbabwe

Harmonized Tariff Schedule of the United States (2009) (Rev. 1)

Annotated for Statistical Reporting Purposes

GN p.12

GSP

Non-Independent Countries and Territories

Anguilla
British Indian Ocean Territory
Christmas Island (Australia)
Cocos (Keeling) Islands
Cook Islands
Falkland Islands (Islas Malvinas)
Gibraltar
Heard Island and McDonald Islands
Montserrat
Niue
Norfolk Island
Pitcairn Islands
Saint Helena
Tokelau
Turks and Caicos Islands
Virgin Islands, British
Wallis and Futuna
West Bank and Gaza Strip
Western Sahara

Associations of Countries (treated as one country)

Member Countries of the Cartagena Agreement (Andean Group)

Consisting of:

Bolivia
Colombia
Ecuador
Venezuela

Member Countries of the Association of South East Asian Nations (ASEAN)

Currently qualifying:

Cambodia
Indonesia
Philippines
Thailand

Member Countries of the Caribbean Common Market (CARICOM),

Currently qualifying:

Belize
Dominica
Grenada
Guyana
Jamaica
Montserrat
St. Kitts and Nevis
Saint Lucia
Saint Vincent and the Grenadines
Trinidad and Tobago

Member Countries of the West African Economic and Monetary Union (WAEMU)

Consisting of:

Benin
Burkina Faso
Côte d'Ivoire
Guinea-Bissau
Mali
Niger
Senegal
Togo

Member Countries of the Southern Africa Development Community (SADC)

Currently qualifying:

Botswana
Mauritius
Tanzania

Member Countries of the South Asian Association for Regional Cooperation (SAARC)

Currently qualifying:

Bangladesh
Bhutan
India
Nepal
Pakistan
Sri Lanka

Harmonized Tariff Schedule of the United States (2009) (Rev. 1)

Annotated for Statistical Reporting Purposes

XI
62-11

Heading/ Subheading	Stat. Suf-fix	Article Description	Unit of Quantity	Rates of Duty 1 General	Rates of Duty 1 Special	Rates of Duty 2
6202 (con.)		Women's or girls' overcoats, carcoats, capes, cloaks, anoraks (including ski-jackets), windbreakers and similar articles (including padded, sleeveless jackets), other than those of heading 6204 (con.):				
		Overcoats, carcoats, capes, cloaks and similar coats (con.):				
6202.13		Of man-made fibers:				
6202.13.10	00	Containing 15 percent or more by weight of down and waterfowl plumage and of which down comprises 35 percent or more by weight; containing 10 percent or more by weight of down (654)	doz. kg	4.4%	Free (BH,CA, CL,IL,JO,MX,OM, P,PE,SG) 0.8% (MA) 3.9% (AU)	60%
		Other:				
6202.13.30		Containing 36 percent or more by weight of wool or fine animal hair		43.5¢/kg + 19.7%	Free (BH,CA, CL,IL,MX,OM, P,PE,SG) 4.4¢/kg + 2% (JO) 8.7¢/kg + 3.9% (MA) 15.5% (AU)	46.3¢/kg + 58.5%
	10	Women's (435)	doz. kg			
	20	Girls' (435)	doz. kg			
6202.13.40		Other		27.7%	Free (BH,CA, CL,IL,MX,OM, P,PE,SG) 2.8% (JO) 5.5% (MA) 15.5% (AU)	90%
		Raincoats:				
	05	Women's (635)	doz. kg			
	10	Girls' (635)	doz. kg			
		Other:				
	20	Women's (635)	doz. kg			
	30	Girls' (635)	doz. kg			

Appendix F

International Purchase Agreement (Import)

FORM

AGREEMENT made December 6, 1981, between Renoir Industrielles et Cie., of Paris, France, a corporation organized under the laws of France (the "Seller"), and H. A. Pannay, Inc., of 142 Trimble Avenue, St. Louis, Missouri, U.S.A., a Missouri corporation (the "Buyer").

1. *Sale.* The Seller shall sell to the Buyer 100,000 long tons of No. 1 heavy steel melting scrap up to a length of 1.50 meters, not over 40 centimeters in width, and not less than five millimeters in thickness.

2. *Price.* The purchase price is $27.18 per long ton, F.A.S. Vessel Cherbourg. The price is free alongside the vessel designated by the Buyer (the "Buyer's vessel"), at Cherbourg, the port of shipment. Payment for all merchandise shall be made in currency of the United States of America.

3. *Delivery.* The Seller shall deliver the scrap, in the kind and quantity specified in paragraph 1, alongside the Buyer's vessel, within reach of its loading tackle, at the port of shipment. The scrap shall be delivered by the Seller at a minimum rate of 14,000 long tons every 30 days. If this minimum rate of delivery is not maintained by the Seller during any 30-day period, the total quantity stated in paragraph 1 shall be reduced by an amount equal to the difference between the amount actually delivered and the minimum rate of delivery for such 30-day period.

4. *Notice.* The Seller shall give notice to the Buyer by cable of the quantity of scrap available for loading, the price

(Text continued on page 4–1097)

thereof, and the date on which the Seller is ready to commence loading for transportation to the port of shipment. Thereafter, the Buyer shall give adequate notice to the Seller by cable of the date on which it is ready to commence loading upon the Buyer's vessel. The notice shall contain the name, sailing date, loading berth, and date of delivery alongside the Buyer's vessel. Upon the receipt of such notice from the Buyer, the Seller shall prepare and commence loading the scrap for transportation to the port of shipment in sufficient quantities for the Buyer to load at the rate of 700 tons per working day; provided that the Seller shall not be required to have the scrap prepared or loaded for transportation to the port of shipment until after receipt of the letter of credit provided for in paragraph 12, and receipt of notice in writing from the bank, referred to in paragraph 12, that the Buyer has made the deposit of earnest money provided for in paragraph 11.

5. *Insurance.* The Buyer shall obtain and pay for all marine insurance for its own account, provided that all marine insurance obtained by the Buyer shall include, for the protection of the Seller, standard warehouse to warehouse coverage.

6. *Demurrage.* The Seller shall be liable for demurrage charges in excess of one day incurred by the Buyer by reason of the Seller's default. The Buyer shall be liable for demurrage or storage charges in excess of one day incurred by the Seller by reason of the Buyer's failure to load or to have his vessel ready for loading on any stipulated date.

7. *Invoices.* The Seller shall issue provisional invoices and final invoices for every shipment of scrap. The weights as established at the time and place of loading upon the Buyer's vessel shall be used in determining the amounts of the provisional invoices. The Buyer shall forward to the Seller certified weight certificates issued at the time and place of loading upon rail or barge, at the point of importation, for shipment to the Buyer's destination, and the weights as established at such time and place shall be final

in determining the total amounts of the final invoices; provided, that if a shipment is lost after loading upon the Buyer's vessel, the weights as established at the time and place of loading upon the Buyer's vessel shall be final in determining the total amounts of the final invoices.

8. *Inspection.* The Buyer shall have the right to inspect the scrap at the yards of the Seller, or at the place of loading upon the Buyer's vessel. All rejected scrap shall be replaced by scrap meeting the description and specifications stated in paragraph 1. The Buyer, or its agent, shall execute a certificate of inspection and acceptance, at its own cost. Failure of the Buyer to inspect shall constitute a waiver of the right of inspection, and shall be deemed acceptance of the scrap as delivered for loading.

9. *Title.* Title to the scrap shall pass to the Buyer upon delivery alongside the Buyer's vessel, provided the Buyer has established the letter of credit and made the deposit of the earnest money provided for in paragraphs 11 and 12.

10. *Covenant against reexportation.* The Buyer covenants that the scrap will be shipped to and delivered in the United States of America, and that the Buyer will not ship the scrap to, or deliver it in, any other country, and will not reexport the scrap after it is delivered in the United States of America.

11. *Earnest money.* Within ten days after the execution of this agreement, the Buyer shall deposit, at the bank at which the Buyer establishes the letter of credit provided for in paragraph 12, the sum of $40,000, in the form of bank cashier's or certified checks payable to the order of the Seller, for disposition in accordance with the terms of this paragraph. Upon full performance of the conditions of this agreement by the Buyer, the earnest money shall be refunded either by direct payment to the Buyer or by application toward the payment for the last shipment. If the Buyer fails to perform all the conditions of this agreement, the earnest money shall be delivered to the Seller as liqui-

dated damages, and not as a penalty, and this agreement shall thereafter become null and void.

12. *Letter of credit.* Within ten days after receipt of the notice from the Seller provided for in paragraph 4, stating the quantity of scrap available for loading and the price thereof, the Buyer shall establish with a bank in New York, New York, a confirmed, revolving, irrevocable letter of credit in favor of the Seller in the amount stated in the notice, for the term of six months, to cover the first shipment. The amount of the letter of credit shall be replenished, and the term thereof extended, to cover any additional shipments, upon receipt of notice from the Seller stating the quantity of additional scrap available for loading and the price thereof. The letter of credit shall provide that partial shipments against the letter of credit shall be permitted, and shall also provide that payment therefrom shall be made in the amount of 90% of the provisional invoice upon presentation of the following documents: (a) provisional commercial invoice; (b) consular invoice, if required; (c) clean dock or ship's receipt, or received-for-shipment ocean bill of lading, or other transportation receipt; (d) certified weight certificate; (e) Buyer's certificate of inspection and acceptance, but if the Buyer has waived his right of inspection under paragraph 8 the Seller shall so state in the invoices.

13. *Adjustment of payment.* Any difference between the amount of the final invoices, determined as provided in paragraph 7, and the amount paid on the provisional invoices shall be paid against the letter of credit upon presentation of the final invoices.

14. *Cancellation.* In the event that delivery in whole or in part, for a period not exceeding 30 days, shall be prevented by causes beyond the control of the Seller, including but not limited to acts of God, labor troubles, failure of essential means of transportation, or changes in policy with respect to exports or otherwise by the French government, this agreement shall be extended for an additional period equal

to the period of delay. In the event, however, that such nondelivery continues after such extended period, the Buyer or the Seller shall have the right to cancel this agreement to the extent of such nondelivery by written notice, and in such case there shall be no obligation or liability on the part of either party with respect to such undelivered scrap; provided that any such notice from the Buyer shall not apply with respect to any scrap which the Seller has prepared or loaded for transportation to the port of shipment prior to the receipt by the Seller of such notice.

15. *Assignment.* The Buyer shall not assign its rights nor delegate the performance of its duties under this contract without the prior written consent of the Seller.

16. *Export license.* This agreement shall be subject to the issue of an export license to the Buyer by the appropriate agency of the French government.

17. *Modifications.* All modifications of this agreement shall be in writing signed by both parties.

18. *Benefit.* This agreement shall be binding upon and shall inure to the benefit of the parties, their successors, and assigns, subject, however, to the limitation of paragraph 15.

In witness whereof the parties have executed this agreement.

Corporate Seal
Attest:
....
Secretary

Renoir Industrielles et Cie.
by ....
President

Corporate Seal
Attest:
....
Secretary

H. A. Pannay, Inc.
by ....
President

Appendix G

Automated Commercial Environment (ACE)

Print this Page
Close this Window

Printer Friendly Version Of:
http://www.cbp.gov/xp/cgov/newsroom/fact_sheets/trade/ace_factsheets/ace_glance_sheet.xml
Printed:
Wed Apr 29 15:51:29 CDT 2009

ACE At a Glance Fact Sheet

04/16/2009

The Automated Commercial Environment is the commercial trade processing system being developed by U.S. Customs and Border Protection to facilitate trade while strengthening border security.

Integrated Online Access

The ACE Secure Data Portal, essentially a customized Web page, connects CBP, the trade community and participating government agencies by providing a single, centralized, online access point for communications and information related to cargo shipments.

Account Management

- The ACE portal enables users to monitor daily operations and identify compliance issues through access to more than 100 reports.
- ACE portal users can electronically update account data, merge accounts, access multiple accounts via one username, create a new importer identification record (the CBP Form 5106) and ensure the accuracy of all account information.
- The number of ACE account types now includes practically every entity doing business with CBP.
- There are nearly 16,200 ACE portal accounts, including 1,786 importer accounts, 987 broker accounts and 13,418 carrier accounts.

Periodic Payments

- With the ACE account-based system, monthly payment and statement capabilities are available, meaning periodic payment participants have the ability to wait until the 15th working day of the next month to pay for shipments released during the previous calendar month.
- More than $35 billion in duties and fees have been paid through the ACE monthly statement process since the first payment was made in July.

Electronic Truck Manifest

- ACE electronic truck manifest capabilities are now fully operational at the northern and southern border, enabling CBP to pre-screen trucks and shipments to ensure the safety and security of incoming cargo.
- Electronic manifests detailing shipment, conveyance and carrier information are now required when entering the nation's 99 land border ports.
- Truck carriers can self-file e-manifests through the ACE portal or via a CBP-approved electronic data interchange, or they can use third parties, such as brokers or border processing centers.
- E-manifests are currently processed 33 percent faster than paper manifests.
- More than 11 million truck e-manifests have been filed through an electronic data interchange or the ACE Secure Data Portal.

International Trade Data System

- The International Trade Data System is a program that is ensuring inter-agency participation in ACE.
- Through ITDS efforts, ACE will provide a "single window" for collecting and sharing trade data with agencies that are responsible for ensuring the compliance of imported and exported cargo with U.S. laws.
- Agencies with licensing and compliance responsibilities are required to join ITDS by the SAFE Port Act of 2006 and an Office of Management and Budget directive based on the recommendations of the President's Working Group on Import Safety.
- To date, there are 46 Participating Government Agencies in ITDS.
- Nearly 500 end-users from 27 PGAs have access to the ACE portal.

Looking Ahead: Future ACE Capabilities

Deployed in phases, ACE will be expanded to provide cargo processing capabilities across all modes of transportation and will replace existing systems with a single, multi-modal manifest system for land, air, rail and sea cargo. Future releases will result in further automation of entry summary processing and enhanced account management features.

Printer Friendly Version Of:
http://www.cbp.gov/xp/cgov/newsroom/fact_sheets/trade/ace_factsheets/ace_overview/importers_fact_sheet.xml
Printed:
Tue Apr 28 14:44:28 CDT 2009

ACE Overview for Importers Fact Sheet

04/13/2009

U.S. Customs and Border Protection (CBP) invites importers to take part in the many advantages of establishing an ACE portal account. Benefits of an importer ACE portal account include access to numerous reports, improved communications with CBP and a consolidated management approach facilitated by the tracking of import activity in a single, comprehensive, account based view. Additional benefits to importers include:

Periodic Monthly Statement for Duties and Fees

- Transition to an interest-free monthly statement process from a transaction-by-transaction payment process
- Pay for eligible shipments released during a month by the 15th working day of the following month for your account on either a national or a port monthly statement

Compliance, Transactional and Financial Data

- Access over 125 reports on company specific compliance, transactional and financial data
- Schedule large customized bulk data download reports
- Review CBP entry summary data in near real-time
- Run a customized report and save it to the Shared Reports folder for access by other authorized reports users of the account

Account Management

- Create an account based on your company's organizational structure and restrict user access to select account information
- Request a modification of an existing account structure (i.e, merger, acquisition) and obtain historical data, if acquiring a company or part of a company that is also an ACE portal account
- Offer cross account access to other ACE portal accounts (e.g., brokers) while maintaining control over access privileges
- View, sort, and print account lists by name and number; create CBP Form 5106 (Importer ID Input Record) information; and access an expanded number of reference files, including port and country codes and Manufacturer ID
- View related blanket licenses, permits, or certificates posted by participating government agencies on goods routinely imported
- Attach electronic information (e.g., pdf, Word, Excel, etc.), track or respond to CBP on compliance and operational issues via the Business Activity Log
- Respond to a CBP Form 28, 29, and 4647 via the Portal
- Submit blanket declarations via the Portal
- Track changes made to ACE portal account information by user and date
- View and search bond information

Additional Information

For more information on ACE and how to apply, visit the ACE: Modernization Information Systems page or send an e-mail to CBP.CSPO@dhs.gov. (ACE: Modernization Information Systems)

see also:

on cbp.gov:

ACE Overview for Importers Fact Sheet - Printable Version (pdf - 26 KB.)

ACE: Modernization Information Systems

ACE Entry Summary, Accounts and Revenue at a Glance Fact Sheet

08/01/2008

New Automated Commercial Environment (ACE) Entry Summary, Accounts and Revenue (ESAR) features will enable U.S. Customs and Border Protection (CBP) and its trade partners to truly interact electronically. Throughout the upcoming years, these enhanced account capabilities, affecting virtually all CBP cargo processes, will bring a dramatic, comprehensive change in the way CBP conducts business.

The ACE Secure Data Portal, essentially a customized Web page connecting CBP and the trade community, currently provides an account-based structure through which trade community participants can view CBP data. ACE portal account holders currently have access to more than 100 customizable reports that can be used to identify compliance issues and monitor daily operations. With the ACE periodic monthly statement feature, participants have until the 15th working day of the month, following cargo release, to pay duties and fees for imported merchandise.

In September 2007, CBP deployed ESAR capabilities that built upon the account-based features already available in the ACE Secure Data Portal. The enhancements expanded the number of account types, incorporated reference data formerly in the CBP Automated Commercial System (ACS) and integrated account management features, such as electronic access to all account master data and a single sign-on capability to access multiple accounts.

In 2009, CBP will deploy ESAR features that enable carriers to create, maintain and display ocean conveyances in the ACE portal as well as an in-bond authorization file, which will allow the carrier to designate who is authorized to use its bond to move goods in-bond.

Future ESAR capabilities, to be delivered incrementally beginning in mid-2009, will result in integrated and enhanced automated entry summary processing in ACE. This incremental approach will allow trade partners more time for testing to ensure their systems are compatible with ACE and will allow CBP more time to prepare for the decommissioning of its existing ACS entry summary processing modules.

Initial Entry Summary Types: 2009

- In early 2009, CBP will take the first steps toward implementing an updated automated entry summary process when entry summaries for the most common entry types (consumption and informal entries) are filed in ACE.
- A new Census warning process will enable the trade community to electronically override Census warnings via the submission of an override code through the Automated Broker Interface (ABI).
- A new "team review" capability will make entry summary processing more efficient and will provide a case-management approach that electronically traces the review history of the entry summary.
- CBP Forms 28, 29 and 4647, "Request for Information," "Notice of Action" and "Notice to Mark or Redelivery," respectively, will be available electronically via the ACE Secure Data Portal. The trade community will be able to respond to these requests and attach supporting documentation online through ACE portal accounts, automating

a previously paper-based process.
- Scanning technology will be introduced to reduce costs associated with document submission, storage and retrieval for CBP and the trade community.

Remaining Entry Summary Types

- CBP will begin deploying additional capabilities enabling the remaining entry summary types to be processed in ACE.

Enhanced Entry Summary Functionality

- CBP will introduce an electronic entry summary correction process that allows a filer to make post-summary corrections prior to liquidation without having to fax or e-mail a request.
- The ACE subsidiary ledger will be integrated with the CBP general ledger, enabling CBP officials to access the financial status of an entry summary. The flexibility of payment options will be expanded, giving the trade community the option of making secure electronic payments via the Pay.gov website, a Department of the Treasury system. (Pay.gov)
- The current system of refund payments, made on a per-transaction basis, will be consolidated into a weekly distribution.
- Filers of electronic bonds will be able to transmit bonds using ABI, giving filers more control over the issuance and validation of their bonds and providing sureties more visibility into their bond liability.
- The reconciliation notification process will be enhanced to include "flag" notations at the line-item level of the entry summary. Reconciliation procedures will also be expanded to include other entry summary types.
- The drawback process, which is a refund of duty, taxes and certain fees that have been lawfully collected on imported goods that are subsequently exported, will be further automated.
- The process for filing protests will be further modernized and streamlined through ACE.

Future Functionality

An automated ACE Importer Activity Summary Statement will be an option for the filing of statistical and revenue data for multiple releases. With ACE, the process will be automated and summaries will be able to be filed on an aggregate basis.

Upon completion, ACE will be the official trade processing system for more than 350 United States ports and other facilities around the world. The implementation of ESAR capabilities will improve trade processing automation, enhance border security and foster our nation's economic security by facilitating lawful international trade.

see also:

on cbp.gov:

ACE Entry Summary, Accounts and Revenue at a Glance – Printable Version (pdf - 357 KB.)

on the web:

Pay.gov

ACE Periodic Monthly Statement Fact Sheet

01/14/2009

The Automated Commercial Environment enhances account-based processing of duties and fees paid to U.S. Customs and Border Protection. Account-based processing allows CBP to more efficiently focus its efforts on enhanced border security while benefiting the trade community with expedited payment processing. With ACE, duties and fees no longer have to be paid on a transaction-per-transaction basis and companies can more easily track their activities through customized account views and reports that better meet their needs.

The ACE periodic monthly statement feature simplifies the processing of duties and fees for importers and brokers with ACE accounts. ACE periodic monthly statements can streamline accounting and report processing and provide the ability to make periodic payments on an interest-free monthly basis. Account owners mark the entries they wish to be paid on the statement and then submit payments through Automated Clearing House (ACH) processing. ACE account holders have the ability to pay for shipments released during the previous month by the 15th business day of the following month.

How to Participate in Periodic Monthly Statements
Importers can establish their own ACE Secure Data Portal account. The ACE portal is essentially a customized homepage that connects CBP, the trade community and participating government agencies.

Establishing a "non-portal" account allows importers to make payments via a broker with an already established ACE Secure Data Portal account. hat connects CBP, the trade community and participating government agencies.

ACE Periodic Monthly Statement Benefits
ACE is the commercial trade processing system being developed by CBP to enhance border security and expedite legitimate trade. ACE trade community benefits include:

- Payment of duties and fees on a monthly basis;
- Duty payments on the 15th working day of the month, which can result in significant cash flow benefits;
- Online tracking of trade activities through customized account views; and,
- Access to more than 100 customizable reports that can be used to track compliance and monitor daily operations.

To date, more than $32 billion dollars in duties and fees have been paid via the ACE monthly statement process since the first payment was made in July 2004. CBP collects more than 40 percent of all duties and fees via ACE monthly statements, representing more than $1 billion dollars per month. Overall, there are more than 15,500 ACE accounts.

For information on how to establish an ACE account, please visit the ACE: Modernization Information Systems page. (ACE: Modernization Information Systems)

see also:

on cbp.gov:

ACE: Modernization Information Systems

ACE Periodic Monthly Statement - Printable Version
(pdf - 275 KB.)

Topic: How to Participate in Periodic Monthly Statement

Participation in Periodic Monthly Statement Overview

Importers have two options to participate in Periodic Monthly Statement. First, importers can establish their own ACE Portal account and not only participate in Periodic Monthly Statement processing, but also have direct access the ACE portal which includes having an ability to better manage your CBP account and run customizable reports. An alternative for participation is to have the importer participate through their broker, who is an ACE Portal Account, by establishing a Non-Portal Account.

To encourage maximum participation in Periodic Monthly Statement, U.S. Customs and Border Protection (CBP) created non-portal accounts to allow importers who are not seeking the benefits of having an ACE portal account, but wish to participate in Periodic Monthly Statement. (*See* 69 **FR** 5362 on the ACE Federal Register Notices link at www.cbp.gov/modernization).

Entry summaries not eligible for inclusion on a Periodic Monthly Statement include:

- NAFTA Duty Deferral, Entry Type 08;
- Reconciliation, Entry Type 09; and
- Entry summaries with IRS tax class codes.

Entry summaries flagged for reconciliation may be included on a Periodic Monthly Statement if they do not include tax.

The importer must have a continuous bond on file with CBP to participate in Periodic Monthly Statement.

Topic: How to Participate in Periodic Monthly Statement

Participation as a Non-Portal Account

Importers who have their customs duties and fees paid by their broker (a) via their own Automated Clearinghouse (ACH) account or (b) via their broker's ACH account can now participate in Periodic Monthly Statement as non-portal accounts. Brokers would continue to flag entry summaries for a statement and effect payment as they do today. Filers are able to place eligible entry summaries for activated non-portal accounts on a broker or importer statement. A single ACH payer unit number must be used to pay for all eligible entry summaries on a statement.

An importer interested in participating in Periodic Monthly Statement does not have to have an ACE portal account. The importer can apply to participate as a non-portal account through a broker who has an ACE portal account.

Procedures to Apply for Participation

The following diagrams outline the procedures to follow to apply for participation in Periodic Monthly Statement. If the importer is an ACE portal account holder, follow the instructions under "Instructions for Participation as a Current ACE Portal Accounts." If the importer is not an ACE Portal Account holder and would like to participate in Periodic Monthly Statement, the importer can do so via their broker. Instructions are outlined below under" Instructions for Participation as a Non-Portal Account."

Topic: How to Participate in Periodic Monthly Statement

Instructions for Participation

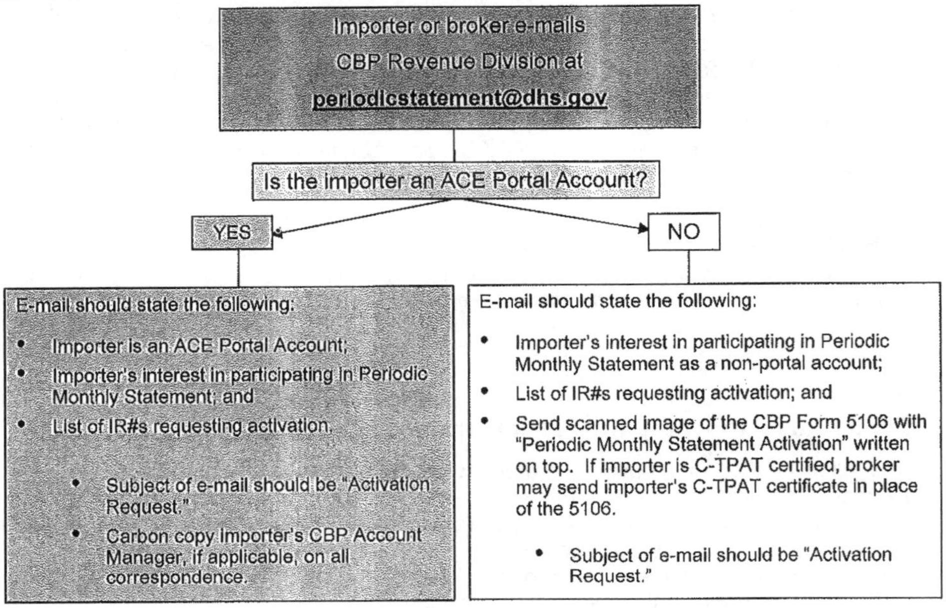

Confirmation from CBP

Importers will only be able to view Periodic Monthly Statements for those Importer of Record (IR) numbers that are part of their Account List, and for which they have been approved for Periodic Monthly Statement. An importer would know that their IR numbers have been activated for Periodic Monthly Statement by one of the following ways:

1. The account may receive an e-mail message from CBP Revenue Division and/or their CBP Account Manager;
2. The account may be notified by their Customhouse Broker if they were the party who submitted the initial Periodic Monthly Statement participation request to CBP; and/or

Topic: How to Participate in Periodic Monthly Statement

3. ACE Portal accounts can run a report AR006 in the ACE Secure Data Portal Reports Tool to determine if the IR number(s) have been activated for Periodic Monthly Statement. If no data appears for the IR number, no entries were flagged or the IR number has not been flagged for Periodic Monthly Statement during the date range specified for that IR number.

If confirmation from CBP is not received within 10 business days, resubmit application.

Additional ACE Resources

Do you need additional assistance with Periodic Monthly Statement? *Please contact your CBP Client Representative or e-mail PMSUsersMailbox@cbp.dhs.gov. If you are a trade caller or if you are calling outside the United States, you may also contact the* ***Technology Support Center*** *at 1-866-530-4172.*

Topic: Periodic Monthly Statement

Periodic Monthly Statement Overview

Periodic Monthly Statement is a feature of the Automated Commercial Environment (ACE) that simplifies the processing of duties and fees and promotes account based processing

Periodic Monthly Statement allows users to consolidate periodic daily statements and make payments on a monthly basis. With the inception of the periodic monthly statement, operations for many filers have changed from a day-by-day payment process to a consolidated account-based periodic monthly statement process. Filers now have three payment options for each entry summary:

1. Single Pay – Users pay per entry
2. Daily Statement – Users consolidate all shipments and pay per day
3. Periodic Monthly Statement – Users combine eligible shipments and pay monthly

To include entry summaries on a periodic monthly statement, they must be covered under a continuous bond and paid via Automated Clearinghouse (ACH) Debit or Credit.

Topic: Periodic Monthly Statement

Periodic Monthly Statement summarizes Periodic Daily Statements into a consolidated statement each month. Periodic Daily Statements contain entry summaries that the filer has scheduled for entry summary filing for a single day and that are due to be paid on the 15th working day of the following month. Entries not eligible for inclusion on a Periodic Monthly Statement include:

- NAFTA Duty Deferral, Entry Type 08;
- Reconciliation Entry Type 09; and
- Entry summaries with IRS tax class codes.

Entry summaries flagged for reconciliation may be included on a Periodic Monthly Statement if they do not include tax.

Periodic Monthly Statement Benefits

Participation in Periodic Monthly Statement offers many benefits to importers and brokers, such as:

- Consolidates individual entry summaries for goods that are either entered or released during the previous month and allows them to be paid as late as the 15th working day of the following month;
- Provides additional flexibility in the management of the working capital required for duty payments as well as potentially significant cash flow advantages;
- Allows importer/filers to pay designated entry summaries for a given month on one statement;
- Streamlines accounting and reporting processes;
- Allows the filer to select either a national or a port statement;
- Allows the broker to pay on behalf of the importer;
- Shifts the payment process from a transaction-by-transaction payment process to an interest-free periodic monthly statement process; and
- Allows users to view the periodic monthly statement as it is being built during the month.

Only the statement filer can view the statement. An importer who uses a broker to prepare their monthly statement can only view entry summaries that are scheduled for periodic payment. The importer will not be able to view the broker's statement.

Topic: Periodic Monthly Statement

Information on the ACE Portal

Within the ACE Secure Data Portal, periodic monthly statement information can be found within the "*Accounts*" tab. Follow the steps below:

1. Select the **Accounts** tab.

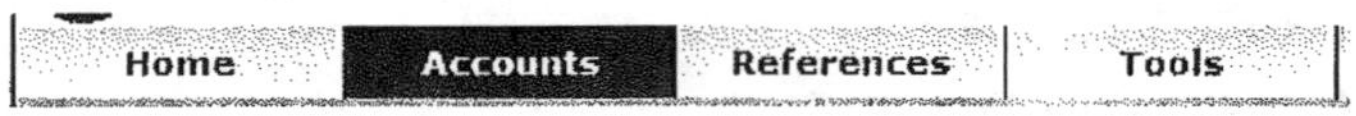

2. Once you are on the "*Accounts*" page, the "*Task Selector*" portlet will appear on the left. Select the **Statements** link.

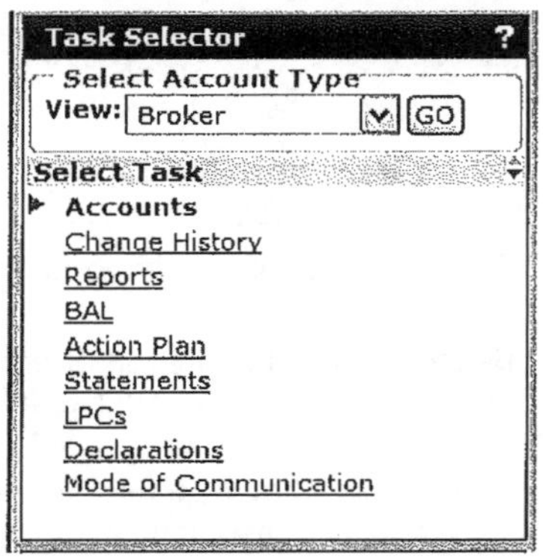

Within this Statements task, there are several portlets.

1. Account Selector
2. Statement Designation (for brokers or self filers)
3. Broker or Importer Summary
4. Periodic Statement Calendar
5. Periodic Statement Quickview

Topic: Periodic Monthly Statement

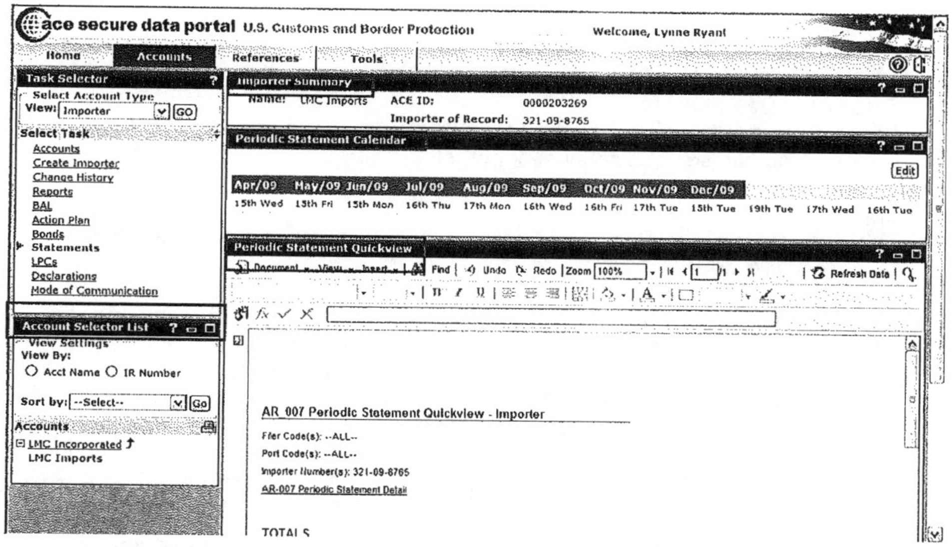

Account Selector List

The "*Account Selector List*" will display all Importer of Record numbers associated with the account.

An importer will know their IR numbers have been activated for Periodic Monthly Statement by one of the following ways:

1. The account may receive an e-mail message from CBP Revenue Division and/or their CBP Account Manager;
2. The account may be notified by their customs broker if they were the party who submitted the initial periodic monthly statement participation request to CBP; and/or
3. The account can run a report AR006 or AR007 in the ACE Secure Data Portal Reports Tool to determine if the IR number(s) have been activated for Periodic Monthly Statement. If no data appears for the IR number, no entry summaries were flagged or the IR number has not been flagged for periodic monthly statement during the date range specified for that IR number.

Topic: Periodic Monthly Statement

Statement Designation
For brokers, a "*Statement Designation*" portlet will appear in the bottom left corner. This is where you can select a national or port statement

Importer or Broker Summary
This portlet displays the name of the entity, ACE ID number and the corresponding IR number or filer code.

Periodic Statement Calendar
Within this portlet, importers can choose a date, between the 1st and 11th working day of each month, for which the preliminary Periodic Monthly Statement will be generated by CBP. The default date is the 11th working day of the month and CBP recommends all parties use this default date. If you wish to change the preliminary Periodic Monthly Statement date, select **Edit** in the Periodic Statement Calendar portlet. Once the "*Edit – Periodic Statement Calendar*" portlet appears, use the drop down arrow for each month and select the date for which you want the statement to be generated.

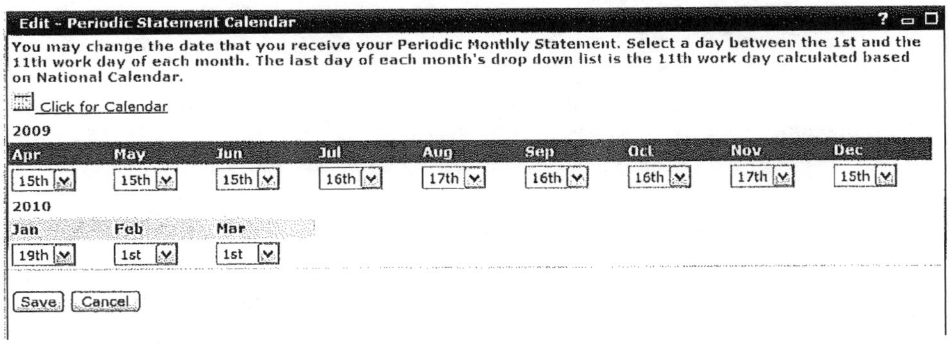

Periodic Statement Quickview
This portlet displays the most current AR007 "Periodic Statement Quickview – Importer or Broker" report where all open entries flagged fro periodic monthly statement are listed.

Monitor Periodic Monthly Statement Entries

Importers who are self filers, will be able to monitor entry summaries flagged for Periodic Monthly Statement.

Topic: Periodic Monthly Statement

1. Within the "*Account Selector List*" portlet, select the company under "*Accounts*" to display the specific IR number of interest.
2. The "*Periodic Statement Quickview*" portlet will show all periodic daily and monthly statements containing open entries.
3. From the "*Statements*" tab, you may select any periodic daily or monthly statement number to view the details.
4. Another option to view all current open entries flagged for periodic monthly statement is to click on the "*Reports*" tab and run AR007B from the Accounts Revenue list of available reports.
5.

IR numbers activated for Periodic Monthly Statement that are not included within the Account List are considered non-portal accounts. Users will not be to view non-portal account statements.

An importer can take advantage of periodic monthly statement through their customs broker if their broker has an ACE Secure Data Portal account.

Brokers can access all entry summaries flagged for periodic monthly statement that are associated with their filer code by following the steps described above.

Periodic Monthly Statement Process

For brokers and self-filers, the procedure for obtaining, viewing, and processing Periodic Monthly Statements can be broken down into 11 steps (four of which are optional and used in situations in which entries are to be removed). The following is a description of each of the 11 steps:

Step 1) **Process entry summaries for periodic daily statement**

- This process may be thought of as the existing daily statement process with no payment due until the 15th working day of the month following entry or release.
- The periodic statement month (new field on record identifier 30) indicates the month for payment. This controls the periodic monthly statement on which the entry summary will be included.
  - ***Please note:*** Entry summary receivables can be viewed on the sub-ledger report (AR006) through the "*Reports*" tab of the ACE Secure Data Portal. Also note that CBP does not edit the accuracy of the statement month. The accuracy and timeliness of the statement date and payment remain the filer's responsibility.

Topic: Periodic Monthly Statement

Step 2) ***Optional*: Remove entries before preliminary periodic daily statement**

- The entry summary payment type indicator can be updated using the Statement Delete or 'HP' application identifier.
  - This allows the method of payment to change from a single payment to a statement payment (daily statement or periodic daily statement) or vice versa.
- If changing the entry summary to appear on a periodic daily statement, the periodic statement month indicates the month for payment. This designation controls the periodic monthly statement in which the entry summary will be included.
- An entry summary change reverses/updates a receivable in the subsidiary ledger for the entry summary.

Step 3) **Produce preliminary periodic daily statement**

- Preliminary periodic daily statements are generated on the predetermined date established by the filer at the time the entry summary was filed.
- Based on the preliminary statement print date indicated on the entry summary transmission, CBP will route the preliminary periodic daily statement (application identifier QR) to the filer through Automated Broker Interface.
- The record layouts for a daily statement and a periodic daily statement are the same.
- The payment type indicator value (record identifier B of the QR application identifier) indicates the statement type:
  - 2 - Broker/Filer Daily Statement
  - 3 - Importer Daily Statement
  - 5 - Combined Importer Daily Statement
  - 6 - Broker/Filer Periodic Daily Statement
  - 7 - Importer Periodic Daily Statement
  - 8 - Importer Combined Periodic Daily Statement
- This step adds the periodic daily statement number to the entry summary receivables in the subsidiary ledger.

Topic: Periodic Monthly Statement

Step 4) ***Optional*: Remove entries before final periodic daily statement**

- The entry summary payment type indicator can be updated using the HP application identifier. This allows for the following:
  - Deletion of an entry from an unpaid preliminary statement (daily statement or periodic daily statement).
  - Payment type indicator and preliminary statement print date (record identifier H) to be changed after the preliminary daily statement is issued.
- If changing the entry summary to appear on a periodic daily statement, the periodic statement month (new field on record identifier H) indicates the month for payment. This allows the user to choose on which periodic monthly statement the entry summary will be included.
- If an entry summary is deleted from a preliminary statement (daily statement or periodic daily statement) it will be included with record identifier Q7 as part of the final daily statement transmission.
- This reverses/updates a receivable in the subsidiary ledger for the entry summary.

Step 5) **Process periodic daily statement Automated ClearingHouse (ACH) Debit authorization and/or entry summary presentation**

- New application identifier (PN) is used for periodic daily statement ACH Debit authorization and/or entry summary presentation.
- For ACH Debit participants this is similar to the existing ACH Debit authorization (application identifier QN) for daily statements.
- For ACH Credit participants, this is new. They will not use the payer unit number field of this transaction. (They will fill this field by hitting the space bar.)
- Like the QN transaction for the existing daily statement, multiple periodic daily statements can be included in a single PN transaction.
- The PN transaction stops the '10 working day' clock for entry summary filing purposes and sets the entry summary filing date. Please remember to present entry summaries and a copy of the periodic daily statement.
- When the PN transaction is processed, the periodic monthly statement number is added to the entry summary receivables in the subsidiary ledger.
- At this time the periodic monthly statement (that this periodic daily statement belongs to) can be viewed through the 'Statements' tab of the ACE Secure Data Portal.

Topic: Periodic Monthly Statement

Step 6) **Produce final periodic daily statement**

- Final periodic daily statements are generated after the periodic daily statement ACH Debit authorization and/or entry summary presentation is processed. This signifies the user's acceptance of the periodic daily statement.
- During the Automated Commercial System (ACS) end-of-day cycle, on the night the PN transaction is processed, CBP will route the final periodic daily statement (application identifier QR) to the filer.

Brokers can establish non-portal accounts for their importers to participate in periodic monthly statement. For further details, please see the Federal Register Notice (FRN), 70 FR 61466, published on October 24, 2005, announcing the establishment of non-portal accounts, as well as any other applicable FRNs, at the following link: www.cbp.gov/modernization.

Importers will not receive a national statement unless they file using their own filer code.

Step 7) ***Optional:*** **Remove entries before preliminary Periodic Monthly Statement**

- An entry summary can be removed from a periodic daily statement after the final periodic daily statement has been generated but prior to payment of the periodic monthly statement.
- An entry summary is removed using the existing HP application identifier.
- When the entry summary is removed after the final periodic daily statement has been generated, the entry summary becomes a 'single pay'. (A 'single pay' is an entry summary that is paid individually by cash or check at the CBP cashier desk. It is not paid by ACH).
- This reverses a receivable in the subsidiary ledger for the entry summary.
- If an entry summary is removed after the final periodic daily statement has been generated, it will be included with record identifier Q7 as part of the preliminary and final periodic monthly statement transmission (application identifier MS).

Please note: *An account is liable for liquidated damages if a 'single pay' is not paid by the 10th working day.*

Topic: Periodic Monthly Statement

Step 8) Produce preliminary periodic monthly statement

- Preliminary periodic monthly statements are generated on the predetermined date established by the trade account owner through the ACE Secure Data Portal.
- Importers designate the preliminary Periodic Monthly Statement print date for importer statements.
- Filers designate preliminary Periodic Monthly Statement print dates for filer statements.
- CBP will route the preliminary Periodic Monthly Statement (new application identifier MS) to the filer on the date selected.
- A date from the 1st through the 11th working day of the month may be selected, but the default date will be the 11th working day of the month, which CBP recommends all parties use.
- The payment type indicator value (record identifier B of the MS application identifier) indicates the statement type:
  - 6 - Broker/Filer Periodic Monthly Statement
  - 7 - Importer Periodic Monthly Statement
  - 8 - Importer Combined Periodic Monthly Statement

Step 9) *Optional*: Remove entries before final Periodic Monthly Statement

- Follows the same process as Step 7.

Filers are able to designate whether their Periodic Monthly Statements are to be consolidated to include all ports (national level) or generated for each port (port level). The port level is the default selection, while the national level statement is for filers only.

Step 10) Process payment using ACH Credit / ACH Debit

- **Using ACH Credit involves the following**:
  - Users must initiate a periodic monthly statement payment with their bank.
  - The receivables created for the entry summaries are marked 'paid' in the sub-ledger.
  - The periodic monthly statement is marked 'paid.'
- **Using ACH Debit involves the following**:

Topic: Periodic Monthly Statement

- On the 15th working day of the month, CBP initiates payment. No action is required by the ACH Debit user.
- The debit authorization(s) processed during the month are sent to the bank for processing.
- The receivable(s) created for the entry summaries are marked 'paid' in the sub-ledger.
- The Periodic Monthly Statement is marked 'paid.'

Step 11) Produce final Periodic Monthly Statement

- Final Periodic Monthly Statements are generated after the payment has been processed.
- After the payment is processed during the ACS end-of-day cycle, the final Periodic Monthly Statement (new application identifier MS) is routed to the filer.
- The payment type indicator value (record identifier B of the MS application identifier) indicates the statement type:
  - 6 – Broker/Filer Periodic Monthly Statement
  - 7 – Importer Periodic Monthly Statement
  - 8 – Importer Combined Periodic Monthly Statement

Participation in Periodic Monthly Statement

Importers have two options to participate in Periodic Monthly Statement.

- Importers can establish their own ACE Portal account and not only participate in Periodic Monthly Statement processing, but also have direct access the ACE portal which includes having an ability to better manage your CBP account and run customizable reports.
- An alternative for participation is to have the importer participate through their broker, who is an ACE Portal Account, by establishing a Non-Portal Account.

To encourage maximum participation in Periodic Monthly Statement, U.S. Customs and Border Protection (CBP) created non-portal accounts for importers not seeking the benefits of having an ACE portal account, but wishing to participate in Periodic Monthly Statement. (*See* 69 **FR** 5362 on the ACE Federal Register Notices link at www.cbp.gov/modernization).

Topic: Periodic Monthly Statement

Entry summaries flagged for reconciliation may be included on a Periodic Monthly Statement if they do not include tax.

The importer must have a continuous bond on file with CBP to participate in Periodic Monthly Statement.

Participation as a Non-Portal Account

Importers who have their customs duties and fees paid by their broker (a) via their own Automated Clearinghouse (ACH) account or (b) via their broker's ACH account can now participate in Periodic Monthly Statement as non-portal accounts. Brokers would continue to flag entry summaries for a statement and effect payment as they do today. Filers are able to place eligible entry summaries for activated non-portal accounts on a broker or importer statement. A single ACH payer unit number must be used to pay for all eligible entry summaries on a statement.

An importer interested in participating in Periodic Monthly Statement does not have to have an ACE portal account. The importer can apply to participate as a non-portal account through a broker who has an ACE portal account.

Procedures to Apply for Participation

The following diagrams outline the procedures to follow to apply for participation in Periodic Monthly Statement. If the importer is an ACE portal account holder, follow the instructions under "Instructions for Participation as a Current ACE Portal Account." If the importer is not an ACE Portal Account holder and would like to participate in Periodic Monthly Statement, the importer can do so via their broker. Instructions are outlined below under "Instructions for Participation as a Non-Portal Account."

Topic: Periodic Monthly Statement

Instructions for Participation

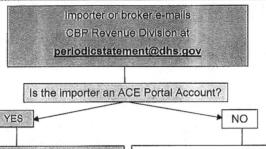

Importer or broker e-mails CBP Revenue Division at periodicstatement@dhs.gov

Is the importer an ACE Portal Account?

YES

E-mail should state the following:

- Importer is an ACE Portal Account;
- Importer's interest in participating in Periodic Monthly Statement; and
- List of IR#s requesting activation.
    - Subject of e-mail should be "Activation Request."
    - Carbon copy Importer's CBP Account Manager, if applicable, on all correspondence.

NO

E-mail should state the following:

- Importer's interest in participating in Periodic Monthly Statement as a non-portal account;
- List of IR#s requesting activation; and
- Send scanned image of the CBP Form 5106 with "Periodic Monthly Statement Activation" written on top. If importer is C-TPAT certified, broker may send importer's C-TPAT certificate in place of the 5106.
    - Subject of e-mail should be "Activation Request."

Confirmation from CBP

Importers will only be able to view Periodic Monthly Statements for those Importer of Record (IR) numbers that are part of their Account List and which have been approved for Periodic Monthly Statement. An importer will know that their IR numbers have been activated for Periodic Monthly Statement by one of the following ways:

1. The account may receive an e-mail message from CBP Revenue Division and/or their CBP Account Manager;
2. The account may be notified by their customs broker if they were the party who submitted the initial Periodic Monthly Statement participation request to CBP; and/or

Topic: Periodic Monthly Statement

3. ACE Portal accounts can run report AR006 in the ACE Secure Data Portal Reports Tool to determine if the IR number(s) have been activated for Periodic Monthly Statement. If no data appears for the IR number, no entries were flagged or the IR number has not been flagged for Periodic Monthly Statement during the date range specified for that IR number.

If confirmation from CBP is not received within 10 business days, resubmit application.

Additional ACE Resources

For additional assistance, take the web-based training (WBT) titled "*Multi-Modal Manifest and ESAR Enhancements.*"

The URL for the ACE Online Training Center and the required user name and password are:

https://nemo.customs.gov/ace_online

User name = user01

Password = 1Password

Multi-Modal Manifest and ESAR Enhancements A2

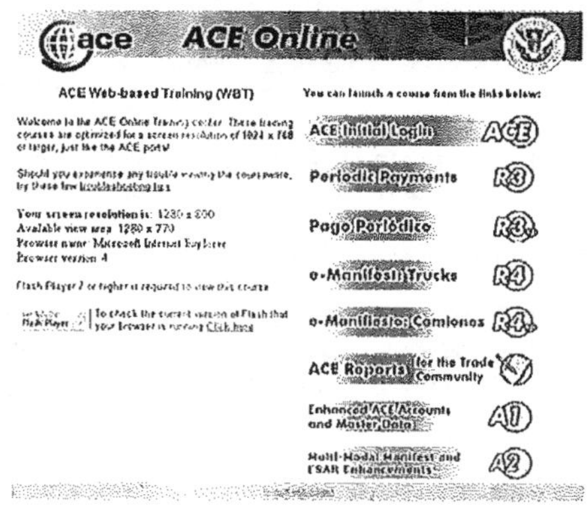

Do you need additional assistance with Periodic Monthly Statement? *Please contact your CBP Client Representative or e-mail PMSUsersMailbox@cbp.dhs.gov. If you are a trade caller or if you are calling outside the United States, you may also contact **Technology Support** at 1-866-530-4172.*

Printer Friendly Version Of:
http://www.cbp.gov/xp/cgov/newsroom/fact_sheets/trade/ace_factsheets/ace_portal_reports.xml
Printed:
Wed Apr 29 15:53:51 CDT 2009

ACE Secure Data Portal Reports Fact Sheet

08/28/2008

The U.S. Customs and Border Protection (CBP) Automated Commercial Environment (ACE) Secure Data Portal provides information with which account holders can identify and evaluate compliance issues and monitor daily operations. ACE allows users to access the reports tool, compile data and perform national trend analysis versus individual transactions-based analysis.

Features of ACE reports

- ACE portal users can access over 100 standard reports on company-specific compliance, transaction and financial data from both ACE and the Automated Commercial System.
- Users can customize and design reports to fit individual business needs with user-friendly features that facilitate the:
    - Sorting, adding or removal of data.
    - Creation of custom charts and graphs.
    - Saving of personalized or uniquely formatted reports as templates so that data can be easily recompiled.
- Users can schedule reports to run automatically, at the date, time and frequency of their choosing.
- Authorized data extracts provide users greater flexibility by allowing them to download large sums of account data and import it into a local reporting system.

Benefits of using ACE reports

Through ACE, users can improve their trade law compliance by running targeted reports to conduct in-house audits, discrepancy reports to identify systemic errors and entry summary reports to provide insight into entries under review by CBP. Access to the ACE reports tool allows users to compile account data and use that data to:

- Identify unauthorized filers.
- Proactively monitor trade compliance and identify discrepancies.
- Check the accuracy of periodic monthly statements.
- Review entry summary data.

Near real-time access to account data

- CBP updates periodic monthly statement data hourly.
- CBP updates the following types of data nightly:
    - Entry and entry summary
    - Enforcement and transaction
    - Performance measures
    - Bond
- CBP updates compliance data monthly.

ACE reports resources

Multiple resources are available via the CBP Web site to assist both experienced and new ACE users.

- ACE Portal Reports Dictionaries, designed for brokers, importers and carriers, serve as reference guides to the most frequently used reports and include each report's corresponding data attributes. (ACE Portal Reports Dictionary)
- Web-Based Training consists of interactive, online courses to familiarize users with the ACE portal. (ACE Training and Reference Guides)
- ACE Reports User Guides contain user-specific instructions on how to use ACE reports. (ACE Reports)

For more information, please visit the CBP Web site.
(ACE: Modernization Information Systems)

Types of Reports:

- **Account management reports** include "quick view" reports as well as aggregate and detail reports on cargo entry, cargo exam, entry summary, entry summary compliance, account profile, bond, broker permits and employees.
- **Account revenue reports** include information on periodic monthly statement totals and the duties and fees owed and paid.
- **Transaction reports** include data on Border Release Advance Screening and Selectivity, carrier activity and compliance as well as in-bond and transaction details.
- **Authorized data extract reports** compile up to one million lines of cargo entry, entry summary, entry summary compliance or account revenue data into a single download.

see also:

on cbp.gov:

ACE Portal Reports Dictionary

ACE Training and Reference Guides

ACE Reports

ACE: Modernization Information Systems

ACE Reports Fact Sheet—Printable Version
(pdf - 444 KB.)

Topic: Running ACE Reports

(For all trade users, except truck carriers)

Appendix

Account Management: Account Profile

Report Number	Report Name	Report Description
AM 5096 Broker	Broker -Account Profile	This report displays all information contained within an account profile by specific account type. Note this report is for brokers and filers.
AM 5096 Trade Carrier	Trade Carrier - Account Profile	This report displays all information contained within an account profile by specific account type.
AM 5096 Importer	Importer – Account Profile	This report displays all information contained within an account profile by specific account type.
AM 5291	Power of Attorney File Listing	For Sureties only, this report displays the current Power of Attorney (POA) on file with CBP.

Account Management: Aggregate Reports, Cargo Entry

Report Number	Report Name	Report Description
	Cargo Entry Reports - Summary	This report displays the entered value and number of entries, by all of the tabs listed below.
Mfr Codes Tab	Summary of Manufacturer (Mfr) Codes by Value	This report displays the entered value and number of entries, cargo lines (number of line items) and discrepancies by manufacturer code during the specified date range. The end user is prompted for the IR number, entry date period, or creation date.
HTS Nbrs Tab	Summary of Harmonized Tariff Schedule (HTS) Numbers by Value	This report displays the total entered value and number of entries, cargo lines, and discrepancies by ten-digit HTS number for the specified date range. The end user is prompted for the IR number, entry date period, or creation date.
Entry Type Codes Tab	Summary of Entry Type Codes by Value	This report displays the total entered value and number of entries, cargo lines, and discrepancies by entry type code for the specified date range. The end user is prompted for the IR number, entry date period, or creation date.
POE Codes Tab	Summary of Port of Entry (POE) Codes by Value	This report displays the total entered value and number of entries, cargo lines, and discrepancies by port of entry code for the specified date range. The end user is prompted for the IR number, entry date period, or creation date.

Topic: Running ACE Reports

(For all trade users, except truck carriers)

Account Management: Aggregate Reports, Cargo Entry (Continued)

Report Number	Report Name	Report Description
COO Codes Tab	Summary of Country of Origin (COO) Codes by Value	This report displays the total entered value and number of entries, cargo lines, and discrepancies by country of origin code for the specified date range. The end user is prompted for the IR number, entry date period, or creation date.
IR Nbrs Tab	Summary of IR Numbers by Value	This report displays a list of IR numbers (related to the importer account) ordered by the total entered value and number of entries, cargo lines, and discrepancies during the specified date range. The end user is prompted for the IR number, entry date period, or creation date.
Consignees Tab	Summary of Consignees by Value	This report displays a list of consignees ordered by the total entered value and number of entries, cargo lines, and discrepancies during the specified date range. The end user is prompted for the IR number, entry date period, or creation date.
IR Nbrs by Date Tab	Summary of IR Numbers by Date and by Value	This report displays a list of IR numbers sorted by date and ordered by the total entered value, number of entries, cargo lines, and discrepancies grouped by month for the specified date range. The end user is prompted for the IR number, entry date period, or creation date.
Consignees by Date Tab	Summary of Consignees by Date by Value	This report displays a list of consignees sorted by date and ordered by the total entered value, number of entries, cargo lines, and discrepancies grouped by month for the specified date range. The end user is prompted for the IR number, entry date period, or creation date.
Filer Codes Tab	Summary of Filer Codes by Value	This report displays a list of filer codes ordered by the total entered value and number of entries, cargo lines, and discrepancies during the specified date range. The end user is prompted for the IR number, entry date period, or creation date.
AM_086	Summary of Entry Type Codes by Number of Cargo Entries	This report displays a list of entry type codes ordered by the total entered value and number of entries, cargo lines, and discrepancies during the specified date range. The end user is prompted for the IR number, entry date period, or creation date.

Topic: Running ACE Reports

(For all trade users, except truck carriers)

Account Management: Aggregate Reports, Cargo Exam

Report Number	Report Name	Report Description
	Cargo Exams Reports - Trade	This report displays the number of entries, line items and discrepancies by all of the tabs listed below.
POE Codes Tab	Summary of Point of Entry (POE) Codes by Number of Cargo Exams	This report displays a list of POE codes ordered by the number of entries, line items, and discrepancies as well as the types of discrepancies found during the specified date range. This report also shows the number of discrepant lines and a count for each type of discrepancy. The end user is prompted with the IR number, filer code, and exam date period.
IR Nbrs Tab	Summary of IR Numbers by Number of Cargo Exams	This report displays a list of IR numbers ordered by the number of entries, line items, and discrepancies found during the specified date range. This report also shows the number of discrepant lines and a count for each type of discrepancy. The end user is prompted with the IR number, filer code, and exam date period.
Filer Codes Tab	Summary of Filer Codes by Number of Cargo Exams	This report displays a list of filer codes ordered by the number of entries, line items, and discrepancies found during the specified date range. This report also shows the number of discrepant lines and a count for each type of discrepancy. The end user is prompted with the IR number, filer code, and exam date period.
HTS Nbrs Tab	Summary of HTS Numbers by Number of Cargo Exams	This report displays a list of HTS numbers ordered by the number of entries, line items, and discrepancies found during the specified date range. This report also shows the number of discrepant lines and a count for each type of discrepancy. The end user is prompted with the IR number, filer code, and exam date period.
Consignees Nbrs Tab	Summary of Consignee Numbers by Number of Cargo Exams	This report displays a list of consignees ordered by the number of entries, line items, and discrepancies found during the specified date range. This report also shows the number of discrepant lines and a count for each type of discrepancy. The end user is prompted with the IR number, filer code, and exam date period.
Entry Type Codes Tab	Summary of Entry Type Codes by Number of Cargo Exams	This report displays a list of entry type codes ordered by the number of entries, line items, and discrepancies found during the specified date range. This report also shows the number of discrepant lines and a count for each type of discrepancy. The end user is prompted with the IR number, filer code, and exam date period.
COO Codes Tab	Summary of Country of Origin (COO) Codes by Number of Cargo Exams	This report displays a list of COO codes ordered by the number of entries, line items, and discrepancies found during the specified date range. This report also shows the number of discrepant lines and a count for each type of discrepancy. The end user is prompted with the IR number, filer code, and exam date period.

Topic: Running ACE Reports

(For all trade users, except truck carriers)

Account Management: Aggregate Reports, Cargo Exam (Continued)

Report Number	Report Name	Report Description
Mfr Codes Tab	Summary of Manufacturer IDs by Number of Cargo Exams	This report displays a list of manufacturer identifications (IDs) ordered by the number of entries, line items, and discrepancies found during the specified date range. This report also shows the number of discrepant lines and a count for each type of discrepancy. The end user is prompted with the IR number, filer code, and exam date period.
Exams by Month Tab	Summary of Number of Cargo Exams by Month	This report displays the number of entries, line items, and discrepancies, as well as the types of discrepancies found by exam month and year. The end user is prompted with the IR number, filer code, and exam date period.

Account Management: Aggregate Reports, Entry Summary

Report Number	Report Name	Report Description
AM_009	Summary of Manufacturer Code by Value	This report displays the entered value, number of entries, cargo lines, and discrepancies by manufacturer code during the specified date range. This report also shows the number of discrepant lines and a count for each type of discrepancy. The end user is prompted with the IR number, filer code, creation date, or entry date period.
AM_010	Summary of HTS Numbers by Value	This report displays the entered value, number of entries, cargo lines, and discrepancies by HTS number during the specified date range. This report also shows the number of discrepant lines and a count for each type of discrepancy. The end user is prompted with the IR number, filer code, creation date, or entry date period.
AM_011	Summary of Entry Type Codes by Value	This report displays the entered value, number of entries, cargo lines, and discrepancies by entry type code during the specified date range. The end user is prompted with the IR number, filer code, creation date, or entry date period.
AM_012	Summary of Port of Entry (POE) Codes by Value	This report displays the entered value, number of entries, cargo lines, and discrepancies by POE code during the specified date range. The end user is prompted with the IR number, filer code, creation date, or entry date period.
AM_013	Summary of COO Codes by Value	This report displays the entered value, number of entries, cargo lines, and discrepancies by COO code during the specified date range. The end user is prompted with the IR number, filer code, creation date, or entry date period.
AM_014	Summary of Country Of Export (COE) Codes by Value	This report displays the entered value, number of entries, cargo lines, and discrepancies by COE code during the specified date range. The end user is prompted with the IR number, filer code, creation date, or entry date period.

Topic: Running ACE Reports

(For all trade users, except truck carriers)

Account Management: Aggregate Reports, Entry Summary (Continued)

Report Number	Report Name	Report Description
AM_015	Summary of IR Numbers by Value	This report displays the entered value, number of entries, cargo lines, and discrepancies by IR number during the specified date range. The end user is prompted with the IR number, filer code, creation date, or entry date period.
AM_016	Summary of Consignee numbers by Value	This report displays the entered value, number of entries, cargo lines, and discrepancies by consignee numbers during the specified date range. The end user is prompted with the IR number, filer code, creation date, or entry date period.
AM_017	Summary of IR Numbers by Date and by Value	This report displays the entered value and number of entries, cargo lines, and discrepancies by IR number during the specified date range. Results are by year/month and entered value. The end user is prompted with the IR number, filer code, creation date, or entry date period.
AM_018	Summary of Consignee Numbers by Date and by Value	This report displays the entered value and number of entries, cargo lines, and discrepancies by consignee number grouped by month during the specified date range. Results are by date and entered value. The end user is prompted with the IR number, filer code, creation date, or entry date period.
AM_019	Summary of Filer Codes by Value	This report displays the entered value and number of entries, cargo lines, and discrepancies by filer code grouped by month during the specified date range. The end user is prompted with the IR number, filer code, creation date, or entry date period.

Account Management: Aggregate Reports, Entry Summary Compliance

Report Number	Report Name	Report Description
	ES Compliance - Trade	This report displays the number of entry summaries reviewed and the discrepant lines by date range for all of the tabs listed below.
POE Codes Tab	Summary of POE Codes by Number of Team Reviews	This report displays a list of POE codes ordered by the number of entries reviewed during the specified date range. This report also shows the number of discrepant lines and a count for each type of discrepancy. The end user is prompted with the IR number, filer code, or review date period.
IR Nbrs Tab	Summary of IR Numbers by Number of Team Reviews	This report displays a list of IR numbers ordered by the number of entries reviewed during the specified date range. This report also shows the number of discrepant lines and a count for each type of discrepancy. The end user is prompted with the IR number, filer code, or review date period.
Filer Codes Tab	Summary of Filer Codes by Number of Team Reviews	This report displays a list of filer codes ordered by the number of entries reviewed during the specified date range. This report also shows the number of discrepant lines and a count for each type of discrepancy. The end user is prompted with the IR number, filer code, or review date period.

Providing the Right Information to the Right People at the Right Time and Place

Topic: Running ACE Reports

(For all trade users, except truck carriers)

Account Management: Aggregate Reports, Entry Summary Compliance (Continued)

Report Number	Report Name	Report Description
HTS Tab	Summary of HTS Numbers by Number of Team Reviews	This report displays a list of HTS numbers ordered by the number of entries reviewed during the specified date range. This report also shows the number of discrepant lines and a count for each type of discrepancy.
Consignee Nbrs Tab	Summary of Consignee Numbers by Number of Team Reviews	This report displays a list of consignees ordered by the number of entries reviewed during the specified date range. This report also shows the number of discrepant lines and a count for each type of discrepancy. The end user is prompted with the IR number, filer code, or review date period.
Entry Type Codes Tab	Summary of Entry Type Codes by Number of Team Reviews	This report displays a list of entry type codes ordered by the number of entries reviewed during the specified date range. This report also shows the number of discrepant lines and a count for each type of discrepancy. The end user is prompted with the IR number, filer code, or review date period.
COO Codes Tab	Summary of COO Codes by Number of Team Reviews	This report displays a list of COO codes ordered by the number of entries reviewed during the specified date range. This report also shows the number of discrepant lines and a count for each type of discrepancy. The end user is prompted with the IR number, filer code, or review date period.
Mfr Codes Tab	Summary of Manufacturer Codes by Number of Team Reviews	This report displays a list of manufacturer code ordered by the number of entries reviewed during the specified date range. This report also shows the number of discrepant lines and a count for each type of discrepancy. The end user is prompted with the IR number, filer code, or review date period.
Team Reviews by Month Tab	Summary of Team Reviews by Month	This report displays a list by year and month of the number of entries reviewed during the specified date range. This report also shows the number of discrepant lines and a count for each type of discrepancy. The end user is prompted with the IR number, filer code, or review date period.

Topic: Running ACE Reports

(For all trade users, except truck carriers)

Account Management: Broker Permits and Employees

Report Number	Report Name	Report Description
AM-5278	Broker Employee List	This report lists the names of people employed by the broker for a given port, providing the number of employees by office code, by port or nationwide. A drill down capability to the employee's address history is provided by selecting the Address History column.
AM-5278.1	Broker Employee Address History	This reports shows the employee address history. We recommend using the frill down capability to view additional addresses for the employee.
AM-5288	Filer Code	This report lists the name and address of all offices for all filer codes. A drill down capability to the Filer Points of Contact report is provided by selecting the Point of Contact field.
AM-5288.1	Filer Points of Contacts	This report displays all points of contact entered by the Filer.

Account Management: Detailed Reports, Cargo Entry

Report Number	Report Name	Report Description
AM_065	Cargo Entry Details Report	This report displays detailed information related to cargo entries, including entered value. The results are sorted by entry date, creation date, entered value, or IR number. Other filter values include: entry number, filer, manufacturer code, HTS, consignee, entry type, mode of transportation, POE, COO, and date range.
AM_069	Cargo Entry Lines by HTS Number	This report displays detailed information related to cargo entries, including entered value, by HTS number for a specified date range. The end user is prompted with the IR number, creation date, or entry date period.
AM_070	Cargo Entry Lines by POE Code	This report displays detailed information related to cargo entries, including entered value, by POE code for a specified date range. The end user is prompted with the IR number, creation date, or entry date period.

Topic: Running ACE Reports

(For all trade users, except truck carriers)

Account Management: Detailed Reports, Cargo Entry (Continued)

Report Number	Report Name	Report Description
AM_071	Cargo Entry Lines by Filer Code	This report displays detailed information related to cargo entries, including entered value, by filer code for a specified date range. The end user is prompted with the IR number, creation date, or entry date period.
AM_072	Cargo Entry Lines by Entry Type Code	This report displays detailed information related to cargo entries, including entered value, by entry type code for a specified date range. The end user is prompted with the IR number, creation date, or entry date period.
AM_073	Cargo Entry Lines by COO Code	This report displays detailed information related to cargo entries, including entered value, by COO code for a specified date range. The end user is prompted with the IR number, creation date, or entry date period.
AM_074	Cargo Entry Lines by Manufacturer Code	This report displays detailed information related to cargo entries, including entered value, by manufacturer code for a specified date range. The end user is prompted with the IR number, creation date, or entry date period.
AM_075	Cargo Entry Lines by Entry Number	This report displays detailed information related to cargo entries, including entered value, by entry number for a specified date range. The end user is prompted with the IR number and entry date period.

Account Management: Detailed Reports, Cargo Exam

	Report Name	Report Description
AM_058	Cargo Exam Details by Date Range	This report displays the number of discrepancies by type related to cargo exams for a specified date range. Results are sorted by exam date, entry and line. The end user is prompted with the IR number, filer code, and exam date period.
AM_059	Cargo Exam Details by Entry Number	This report displays the cargo exam results by type for a specified entry number. Results are sorted by exam date, entry and line. The end user is prompted with the IR number, filer code, and exam date period.
AM_066	Cargo Exam Details	This report displays specifics about cargo exams based on multiple filter values (i.e., entry number, IR number, filer, manufacturer code, HTS, consignee, entry type, mode of transportation, POE, COO, and date range) over a user-specified date range. This report will allow the user to drill down to view details on cargo exam discrepancies.

Topic: Running ACE Reports

(For all trade users, except truck carriers)

Account Management: Detailed Reports, Entry Summary Reports

Report Number	Report Name	Report Description
AM_001	Entry Summary Lines by HTS Number	This report displays a detailed list of entry summary lines ordered by HTS number for a specified date range. The results are sorted by entry date, creation date, HTS number, or IR number.
AM_002	Entry Summary Lines by POE Code	This report displays a detailed list of entry summary lines ordered by POE code for a specified date range. The results are sorted by entry date, creation date, POE code, or IR number.
AM_003	Entry Summary Lines by Filer Code	This report displays a detailed list of entry summary lines ordered by filer code for a chosen date range. The results are sorted by entry date, creation date, filer code, or IR number.
AM_004	Entry Summary Lines by Entry Type Code	This report displays a detailed list of entry summary lines ordered by entry type code for a specified date range. The results are sorted by entry date, creation date, entry type, or IR number.
AM_005	Entry Summary Lines by COO Code	This report displays a detailed list of entry summary lines ordered by COO code for a specified date range. The results are sorted by entry date, creation date, country of origin code, or IR number.
AM_006	Entry Summary Lines by COE Code	This report displays a detailed list of entry summary lines ordered by COE code for a specified date range. The results are sorted by entry date, creation date, COE code, or IR number.
AM_007	Entry Summary Lines by Manufacturer Code	This report displays a detailed list of entry summary lines ordered by manufacturer code for a specified date range. The results are sorted by entry date, creation date, manufacturer code, or IR number.
AM_008	Entry Summary Line Detail	This report displays all the entry summary lines associated with a specific entry number. The results are sorted by entry date, creation date, entry summary number, or entry summary line number.
AM_064	Entry Summary Line by Entry Number	This report displays specific account entry summary information over a user-specified date range for a specific entry summary number. Users can link to reports on entry summary line, tariff, and quantity information.
AM_068	Entry Summary	This report displays specific account entry summary header information over a specified date range for a specific entry summary number. Users can link to reports on entry summary line, tariff, quantity, anti-dumping countervailing duty, and team review information. This report will allow the user to drill down from the entry summary line to either the tariff level or to view information about antidumping / countervailing duties.
AM_087	Filer Summary	This report displays, for a given importer number, a summary of filer information, sorted by port of entry code, by filer code, and by IR number for a specified date range. The user will be prompted for the POE code, filer code, creation date, or entry date period.

ace

Topic: Running ACE Reports

(For all trade users, except truck carriers)

Account Management: Detailed Reports, Entry Summary Compliance

Report Number	Report Name	Report Description
AM_062	Team Review Details by Date Range	This report displays the team review details and discrepancy information for a specified date range. This report is sorted by review date, entry summary number, or entry summary line number.
AM_063	Team Review Details by Entry Number	This report displays the team review details and discrepancy information for a specified entry number. This report is sorted by review date, entry summary number, or entry summary line number.
AM_067	Team Review Details	This report will display specifics about team reviews that occurred over a user-specified date range. Multiple filter values can be used and include entry number, filer, manufacturer code, HTS number, consignee, entry type, mode of transportation, POE, COO, and date range). This report will allow the user to drill down to view details on team review discrepancies.

Account Management: Quick Views, Filer (Fiscal Year)

**Please note, the fiscal year for U.S. Customs and Border Protection (CBP) is October 1st - September 30th.*

Report Number	Report Name	Report Description
N/A	Filer Activity Summary: Number of Entries & Value	This report displays the filer's activity for the current year and past three fiscal years. The activity displayed includes the total number of entries filed, estimated value of the entries, and the associated duties.
N/A	Filer Activity Summary: Top 5 Customers (IR Numbers)	This report displays a list of the five most active IR numbers by number of entries filed for each of the last three years plus current year to month. Users are prompted for the IR number, and filer code.
N/A	Filer Activity Summary: Top 5 Ports	This report displays a list of the top five most actively used ports for each of the last three years plus current year to month. Users are prompted for the IR number, filer code, and HTS numbers.
N/A	Filer Activity Summary: Top 5 HTS Numbers	This report displays a list of the top five most actively used HTS numbers for each of the last three years plus current year to month. Users are prompted for the IR number, and filer code.
N/A	Filer Discrepancy Rate	This report displays exam and discrepancy quantities by fiscal year and compliance type for the current and last 3 fiscal years. Users are prompted for the IR number and filer code.

Account Management: Quick Views, Filer (Calendar Year)

Report Number	Report Name	Report Description

Topic: Running ACE Reports

(For all trade users, except truck carriers)

N/A	Filer Activity Summary: Number of Entries & Value	This report displays the filer's activity for the current year and past three calendar years. The activity displayed includes the total number of entries filed, estimated value of the entries, and the associated duties.
N/A	Filer Activity Summary: Top 5 Customers (IR Numbers)	This report displays a list of the five most active IR numbers by number of entries filed for each of the last three years plus current year to month. Users are prompted for the IR number, and filer code.
N/A	Filer Activity Summary: Top 5 Ports	This report displays a list of the top five most actively used ports for each of the last three years plus current year to month. Users are prompted for the IR number, filer code, and HTS numbers.
N/A	Filer Activity Summary: Top 5 HTS Numbers	This report displays a list of the top five most actively used HTS numbers for each of the last three years plus current year to month. Users are prompted for the IR number, and filer code.
N/A	Filer Discrepancy Rate	This report displays exam and discrepancy quantities by calendar year and compliance type for the current and last 3 calendar years. Users are prompted for the IR number and filer code.

Account Management: Quick Views, Importer (Fiscal Year)
**Please note, the fiscal year for CBP is October 1st - September 30th.*

Report Number	Report Name	Report Description
N/A	Importer Activity Summary: Number of Entries & Value	This report displays the importer's activity for the current year and last three fiscal years. The activity displayed includes the total number of entries filed, estimated value of the entries, and the associated duties.
N/A	Importer Activity Summary: Top 5 Filers	This report displays a list of the five most active filers by number of entries filed for each of the last three years plus current year to month.
N/A	Importer Activity Summary: Top 5 HTS Numbers	This report displays a list of the top five most actively used HTS numbers for each of the last three years plus current year to month.
N/A	Importer Activity Summary: Top 5 Ports	This report displays a list of the top five most actively used ports for each of the last three years plus current year to month.

Account Management: Quick Views, Importer (Fiscal Year) (Continued)
**Please note, the fiscal year for CBP is October 1st - September 30th.*

Report Number	Report Name	Report Description
N/A	Importer Discrepancy Rate	This report displays exam and discrepancy quantities by fiscal year and compliance type. The data will be displayed for the current year and prior three fiscal years. Users are prompted for the IR number and filer code.

Account Management: Quick Views, Importer (Calendar Year)

Report Number	Report Name	Report Description
N/A	Importer Activity Summary: Number of Entries & Value	This report displays the importer's activity for the current year and last three calendar years. The activity displayed includes the total number of entries filed, estimated value of the entries, and the associated duties.
N/A	Importer Activity Summary: Top 5 Filers	This report displays a list of the five most active filers by number of entries filed for each of the last three years plus current year to month.
N/A	Importer Activity Summary: Top 5 HTS Numbers	This report displays a list of the top five most actively used HTS numbers for each of the last three years plus current year to month.
N/A	Importer Activity Summary: Top 5 Ports	This report displays a list of the top five most actively used ports for each of the last three years plus current year to month.
N/A	Importer Discrepancy Rate	This report displays exam and discrepancy quantities by calendar year and compliance type. The data will be displayed for the current year and prior three calendar years. Users are prompted for the IR number and filer code.

Topic: Running ACE Reports

(For all trade users, except truck carriers)

Account Revenue Reports

Report Number	Report Name	Report Description
AR_002	Aged Entry Data	This report displays entries which were created more than 45 days prior but no entry summary or release dates have been defined or no entry summary PN (application identifier) has been received.
AR_006	Sub-ledger Report	This report displays the current account balance and the list of receivable line items, as well as details for each specific line item.
AR_007	Periodic Statement Quick View – Broker	This report displays a Periodic Statement (PS) list and allows the user to drill down to a PS, daily statement, and entry summary details. This is not a hardcopy of the actual statement.
AR_007	Periodic Statement Quick View – Importer	This report displays a PS list and allows the user to drill down to a PS, daily statement, and entry summary details. This is not a hardcopy of the actual statement.

Account Revenue Workflows Reports

Report Number	Report Name	Report Description
AR_007	Periodic Statement Detail	This report displays complete periodic monthly statement, periodic daily statement and entry number data in one report. The AR 007 Periodic Statement Detail report contains both an importer and a broker tab. Users will find entries flagged for an importer statement or importer combined statement on the importer tab. Entries flagged for a broker statement will be displayed on the broker tab.
AR_007A	Periodic Monthly Statement Broker	This report displays all open periodic daily statements by periodic daily statement number for the broker statement. Users can click the blue hyperlink to view the entry summaries included on each individual daily statement.
AR_007A	Periodic Monthly Statement Importer	This report displays all open periodic daily statements by periodic daily statement number for importer statements. Users can click the blue hyperlink to view the entry summaries included on each individual daily statement.
AR_007B	Periodic Daily Statement Broker	This report displays all open entry summaries associated with broker periodic daily statements and periodic monthly statements. Users can click the blue hyperlink to see fees by class code for each entry summary.
AR_ 007B	Periodic Daily Statement Importer	This report displays all open entry summaries associated with an importer periodic daily statements and periodic monthly statement. Users can click the blue hyperlink to see fees by class code for each entry summary.
AR_ 007C	Entry Summary Class Codes Broker	This report displays all fees by class code on each entry summary for each broker periodic daily statement and monthly statement.

Topic: Running ACE Reports

(For all trade users, except truck carriers)

Account Revenue Workflows Reports (Continued)

Report Number	Report Name	Report Description
AR_007C	Entry Summary Class Codes Importer	This report displays all fees by class code on each entry summary for each importer periodic daily statement and monthly statement.
AR_ 007D	Entry Summaries Deleted Broker	This report displays all entry summaries deleted from the periodic daily statements.

Authorized Data Extract Reports

Report Number	Report Name	Report Description
AD_001	Entry Summary Report	This report displays all data included in aggregate and detail entry summary reports.
AD_002	ADD/CVD Case Report	This report displays all ADD/CVD case data.
AD_003	Cargo Entry Report	This report displays all data included in aggregate and detail cargo entry reports.
AD_004	Cargo Exam Result Report	This report displays all data included in aggregate and detail cargo exam reports. Note: This report is currently not available.
AD_ 005	Team Review Report	This report displays all data included in aggregate and detail entry summary compliance reports.
AD_006	Account Revenue - Receivables	This report displays all periodic monthly statement, periodic daily statement and entry number and fee data in one report. It includes all data contained in AR 006 and AR 007 reports.
AD_008	Account Revenue – Aged Entry Report	This report displays all entries which were created more than 45 days prior but no entry summary or release dates have been defined or no entry summary PN (application identifier) has been received.

Transactions: BRASS Report

Report Number	Report Name	Report Description
TR 022	Entry Number Bank Status Report	This report displays information concerning the status of the bank of entry numbers for a specific filer. (FAST and BRASS).

Appendix H
Guidance on Internet Purchases

Print this Page
Close this Window

Printer Friendly Version Of:
http://www.cbp.gov/xp/cgov/trade/basic_trade/internet_purchases.xml
Printed:
Wed Apr 29 16:07:47 CDT 2009

Internet Purchases

Importing into the United States
For detailed information read **Importing into the United States** (Importing into the United States (doc - 1,588 KB.) (pdf - 467 KB.))

Your Responsibility and Liability

The Internet has made it easy to find and purchase items from almost anywhere in the world. However, many people are discovering that getting a foreign-bought item successfully delivered to the United States is much more complicated.

When goods move from any foreign country to the United States, they are being IMPORTED. There are specific rules and regulations that govern the act of importing - and they can be extremely complex and confusing - and costly.

That artisan cheese from Italy may be a snap to find and buy on the Internet, but U.S. Customs and Border Protection could seize your purchase because certain regulations prohibit the importation of dairy products from particular countries without a permit.

Your great auction purchase of gorgeous linen products? Depending upon the country of origin, quota restrictions could hold them up in CBP for a long time. And storage charges in such cases can be expensive.

In other words, "Buyer, Beware." When you buy goods from foreign sources, you become the importer. And it is the importer - in this case, **YOU** - who is responsible for assuring that the goods comply with a variety of both state and federal government import regulations. Importing goods that are unsafe, that fail to meet health code requirements, or that violate quota restrictions could end up costing you quite a bit of money in fines and penalties. At the very least, such goods would be detained, and possibly destroyed, by CBP.

Knowing what is admissible is just part of the story. The other part is knowing how to import. Depending upon what you are importing and its value, the procedures can be very complicated.

It does not matter whether you bought the item from an established business or from an individual selling items in an on-line auction. If merchandise, used or new, is imported into the United States, it must clear CBP and may be subject to the payment of duty as well as to whatever rules and regulations govern the importation of that particular product into the United States.

back to top

Checklist

Keep the following questions in mind before you buy something from a foreign source. The answers will have far-reaching CBP implications (explained below) that could influence your decision to buy.

- Can the goods be legally imported? Are there restrictions on, or special forms required, for your purchase's importation?
- Are you buying the item(s) for your personal use or for commercial purposes?
- Will you be responsible for shipping costs? If so, you should discuss with the seller how your purchase will be shipped. The choices are freight, courier service or international postal service. If you're not careful, transportation and handling costs could far outweigh the cost of your purchase. Sometimes, the seemingly cheaper methods can be more expensive in the long run because they are more susceptible to theft, misdeliveries and logistical problems.
- You should discuss with the seller what the exact delivery arrangements will be. If the seller does not make arrangements for postal or door-to-door delivery, you will either need to hire a customs broker to clear your goods and forward them on to you, or go the port of entry and clear them yourself.
- Can you trust the seller to provide accurate information about the item being shipped in the Customs section of the shipping documents? Giving misleading or inaccurate information about the nature of the item and its value is illegal. And it is the importer - **YOU** - who could face legal action and fines for this violation!

The following is a brief primer on the various factors that can impact the clearance of your goods through CBP. Follow the links for more detailed information.

back to top

U.S. Customs and Border Protection Declarations

All paperwork for sending packages internationally has a section for providing CBP information. A U.S. Customs and Border Protection Declaration is a form obtainable at most foreign post offices. This declaration form should include a full and accurate description of the merchandise, and should be securely attached to the outside of your shipment. Declaration forms vary from country to country, and they don't all ask for the information required by the U.S. Customs and Border Protection. You should ask the seller to provide the following information, whether or not it is asked for on the paperwork.

Seller's name and address. Description of the item(s) in English (a legal requirement). For example, antique silver teapot, silk kimono, 18-karat gold rope necklace. It is very important that this information be detailed and accurate. What is described here will determine the classification number and duty rate that Customs assigns the item when it arrives in the United States. If this information is inaccurate, you could end up paying the wrong duty rate for what you purchased. If it is inaccurate enough to seem deliberately misleading -- keep in mind that CBP does randomly inspect packages -- your goods could be seized and you may be assessed a fine.

Quantity of each type of item being shipped. For example, two watches (14-karat gold, 17 jewel), one leather purse.

Purchase price in U.S. dollars. Provide both the unit price, and if more than one unit was purchased, the total value for all like items. Fudging or miscalculating the price paid for goods is a bad idea. Many sellers offer to misrepresent costs in an effort to save the purchaser from having to pay duty, but this is illegal. Others sellers are wary of package handlers and do not want them to know how valuable something may be, which could result in its theft. The most common legal precaution against theft is to insure the package when sending it. You should discuss insurance options with your seller, keeping in mind that misrepresenting the value of an item on the Customs declaration is illegal.

Weight of the item(s).

Country of origin of the product itself. Be aware that this is not necessarily the country where the item was purchased.

Note: It is important to know that foreign shipments that are not accompanied by a U.S. Customs and Border Protection declaration form and an invoice may be subject to seizure, forfeiture or return to sender.

back to top

Postal Service, Couriers and Freight

There are three ways goods can be sent to you from abroad. In order to avoid costly problems, you and the seller of your goods should agree on which will be used the international postal service, a courier service, or freight carriers.

International Postal Service: Merchandise shipped through the international postal service is forwarded upon its arrival in the United States to one of U.S. Customs and Border Protection International Mail Branches for clearance. If the item is less than $2,000 in value and is not subject to a quota or is not a restricted or prohibited item, a CBP official will usually prepare the paperwork for importing it, assess the proper duty, and release it for delivery. This procedure is generally referred to as a mail entry.

Packages whose declared value is under $200 ($100 if being sent as a gift to someone other than the purchaser) will generally be cleared without any additional paperwork prepared by CBP. However, CBP always reserves the right to require a formal entry for any importation and generally exercises this option if there is something unusual about the importation, or if important documents such as an invoice or bill of sale do not accompany the item.

If any duty is owed, CBP will charge a processing fee for clearing your package. Duty and the processing fee are usually paid at your local post office, where your package is forwarded.

> **Hint:** To speed a package through CBP examination at a port's International Mail Branch, the seller should affix a completed CN 22 or CN 23 (U.S. Customs and Border Protection Declaration Form) to the outside of the package. This form may be obtained at local post offices worldwide.
>
> **Plus:** Pretty economical.
>
> **Pitfalls:** If the item's value is more than $2,000, it may be held at the mail facility until you can arrange for a formal entry. This may require either hiring a customs broker to clear your goods or you may file the paperwork yourself.
>
> Lost packages are hard to find. Since most packages sent through the mail do not have tracking numbers unless they are insured or you've paid to have a tracking number, it can be impossible to trace a "lost" package. If a package is lost a "tracer" should be initiated by the sender of the package.

Courier Shipping: Goods shipped by courier, express, or other commercial service usually are expedited through CBP by a customs broker hired by that commercial service and then delivered seamlessly to your door. Customs brokers are not CBP employees. There are a number of different charges associated with these services, including shipping and handling, the fees charged by the service for clearing the merchandise through CBP, as well as any Customs duty and processing fees that may be owed on your importation.

> **Pluses:** Get seamless delivery. All you have to do is sign for the package when it arrives. In most cases delivery is quick and reliable. When there's a problem, there is a tracking number that can help resolve the matter.
>
> **Pitfalls:** Many people have found the various charges and fees levied to be higher then they expected, and sometimes exceed the cost of their purchase (s).

Buyers often have the misunderstanding that when the purchase price includes shipping and handling, all the costs associated with clearing the package through CBP are covered by the seller. They don't realize that brokers fees and CBP duties may be an additional charge that the buyer is responsible for.

Freight Shipping: Merchandise shipped by freight can arrive in the United States at an air, sea or land port. If your goods are being shipped by freight, you should ask the seller to instruct the freight company to forward them to your doorstep, which may entail the shipper's use of a customs broker to clear your goods. Alternatively, ask that the goods be forwarded to a port of entry near where you live so that you can clear or "enter" them yourself (advisable only if the shipment is under $2000 in value. See Formal Entry below.)

Pluses: Can be economical, particularly, if you're prepared to handle the logistics of clearing the goods through Customs yourself.

Also, the best way to handle large bulky purchases.

Pitfall: If the freight company has not been instructed to forward your goods, they could end up sitting on the dock at the port where they first entered the country. If this is the case....

back to top

Heads-Up

U.S. Customs and Border Protection does not inform importers of the arrival of cargo or freight. When cargo or freight arrives at a U.S. port of entry, it is the responsibility of the shipper or a designated agent to inform the importer of its arrival. However, proper notification does not always happen, particularly, if the shipper has incomplete contact information for you, the importer. Therefore, it is important to find out the scheduled arrival date of your import and follow-up.

If you are not notified that your goods have arrived and you or your broker have not presented the proper paperwork to CBP within 15 days of your goods' arrival, your goods will be transferred to a warehouse, and you will be liable for storage charges. If you have not claimed your goods within six months of their arrival in the USA, they could be sold at auction. (See the Checklist under item #3.)

back to top

Importing Process

Paying Duty: The importer is ultimately responsible for paying any duty owed on an import. Determining duty can be very complicated, and while shipping services will often give an estimate for what the duty rate on an item might be, only CBP can make a final determination about what is owed. You should not be misled into thinking your purchase price includes duty because the seller cannot say with absolute certainty what the duty will be. As a rule, a purchase price that includes shipping and handling does not include duty or any costs associated with clearing the goods through CBP. First time importers are often surprised by bills they receive for duty, U.S. Customs and Border Protection merchandise processing fee, and something referred to as "customs fees," which are actually charges for the services of the broker who cleared your goods through CBP.

How you pay duty depends on how your goods were shipped. If your goods were shipped through the International Postal Service, you will need to pay the mail carrier and/or go to your local post office to pay any duty and processing fees owed when your package arrives at that post office. If your goods were sent by a courier service, that service will either bill you for the duty they paid on your behalf or require payment on delivery.

If your goods were sent by freight, there are two possible scenarios for paying duty.

- If no arrangements were made to forward the goods to your door, you will need to either clear them through CBP yourself, in which case you will pay duty directly to CBP at the port where your goods arrived. Alternatively, you will need to arrange for a broker to clear your goods. If you hire a broker, they will bill you for their services and any duty they paid on your behalf.
- If arrangements were made to forward your goods to you, you will be billed for any duty owed, and for the services of the broker who cleared them through CBP.

Reminder: U.S. Customs and Border Protection holds the importer - YOU - liable for the payment of duty not the seller.

back to top

Personal vs. Commercial Use: Many import regulations only apply to goods imported for commercial - business or resale - purposes. For instance, most goods imported for personal use are not subject to quota. The one exception to this is made-to-measure suits from Hong Kong, which are subject to quota restrictions regardless of the use they are imported for. On the other hand, import restrictions that are based on health, safety and protecting endangered species apply across the board.

Note: *U.S. Customs and Border Protection is authorized to make judgment calls about what qualifies as personal use. Several suits that are identical or a number of very similar handbags will have a hard time passing the credibility test as items for personal use.*

back to top

For Commercial Purposes: Goods imported for commercial purposes must comply with a variety of special requirements, such as marking of country of origin, which vary depending upon the particular commodity. Please see our publication, "Importing Into the United States," for more detailed information. Be particularly aware that an invoice should always accompany commercial shipments.

back to top

Informal Entries: If the value of your purchase(s) is less than $2000 and your goods are being shipped by mail or freight, they may, in most cases, be imported as an informal entry. However, there are exceptions to this. For instance, if the importation is determined to be for commercial purposes, the value limit for filing an informal entry for many textile items is either $250 or $0 - depending on whether or not the item is subject to Quota (see below). Clearing goods through CBP as an informal entry is less arduous a process than clearing them by filing a formal entry. Essentially, when goods are cleared as an informal entry, CBP will prepare the paperwork, including determining the classification number and duty rate for your merchandise.

The duty rate for many items typically bought in an on-line auction is zero, however, CBP may charge a small processing fee for mail imports that do require the payment of duty.

If your goods are sent by a courier or express service, their brokers will usually handle the paperwork, and bill you for their services.

If your goods are being shipped by freight, and you want to clear them through CBP yourself, be sure the shipping company has instructions to deliver them to a port near you. Otherwise, you will need to arrange for someone else to clear the goods for you when they arrive. Your alternative is to ask the seller to make arrangements to have your goods forwarded to your door, in which case you should expect to pay for the services of the customs broker who coordinates this when your goods arrive in the U.S.A.

back to top

Formal Entries: If your goods are valued at more than $2000, or for commercial textile shipments (clothes/materials) regardless of value, you will be required to file a formal entry, which can require extensive paperwork and the filing of a U.S. Customs and Border Protection bond. As mentioned above and for various reasons, CBP may require a formal entry for any importation. CBP, however, rarely exercises this right unless there is a particular concern about the circumstances surrounding an importation.

Because filing a formal entry can be complicated, the U.S. Customs and Border Protection recommends importers consider hiring a customs broker to complete the transaction. Lists of brokers can be found on the port pages of CBP web site.

One of the most difficult things about filing formal entries is accurately identifying the correct classification number of the item being imported. The Harmonized Tariff Schedule of the United States (HTSUS) lists classification numbers for every conceivable item under the Sun. The HTSUS is the size of an unabridged dictionary, and specialists train for months to learn how to correctly classify goods.

The classification number of an item determines many requirements pertaining to that item's importation such as it's duty rate, eligibility for special import programs like the Generalized System of Preferences (GSP) or the North American Free Trade Agreement (NAFTA), and whether or not the item is subject to quota restrictions.

Failure to correctly classify an item can result in fines and/or delays in delivery. You may write to U.S. Customs and Border Protection for a binding ruling, and/or contact an import specialist at your local port for help to identify the proper classification number for your imported item.

back to top

Quota

Many kinds of goods imported for commercial use may be subject to a quota limit. It is the classification number of the article as identified in the Harmonized Tariff Schedule of the United States and the country of origin that determine whether or not an item is subject to quota requirements.

In some cases, the quota is absolute, meaning that once the quota is filled - because the quota has reached its limit for that particular period of time - no additional quantities of that item may be imported until the next open period. Such merchandise must be warehoused or exported. Other quotas are tariff-related, which means that a certain quantity of goods may enter at a low rate of duty, but once that threshold is reached - during a specified period of time - a higher duty rate will be assessed for any additional quantities of that particular imported good. Unlimited quantities of some merchandise subject to tariff-rate quota may, however, enter at over the quota rates.

If you are importing goods for commercial use or resale, it's a good idea to contact your local port of entry for more specific information.

Fill levels for quotas are currently posted on the CBP Electronic Bulletin Board in the file called Quota Threshold Status. Fill levels for textile items can be found in the Quota section of Importing/Exporting.

The Quota program is generally applied only to commercial importations. While the importation of many goods imported under "personal use" quantities are not affected by quota restrictions, there is one exception; made-to-measure suits made in Hong Kong, which are restricted for both personal and commercial use.

back to top

Prohibited Merchandise

Purchasers should also be aware that some products might be considered contraband and cannot be brought into the United States under any circumstances. This includes the obvious, such as narcotics and child pornography, as well as less obvious items such as tainted food products, and other items, a list of which can be found in "Importing Into the United States." Such merchandise can be seized by CBP, and attempts to import it may subject the importer to civil or even criminal sanctions. If you have any question at all about your purchase, you should contact your closest CBP port and get an opinion before you complete the transaction.

back to top

Restricted Merchandise

Many items cannot be imported into the United States unless the importer has the proper permit or license from the appropriate regulatory authority. Some of the most common restricted items include food, plant and dairy products; alcohol and tobacco products; birds, fish or animals and products thereof, goods from embargoed countries, firearms and ammunition, cultural artifacts from certain countries, and copyrighted materials.

The entry of prescription medicines is restricted and subject to the approval of the U.S. Food and Drug Administration (FDA). Depending on the FDA review of the medicine, it may be released to the addressee or seized. There are, however, provisions allowing passengers to hand carry prescription drugs into the United States if they enter through a land border with Canada or Mexico.

back to top

Electronic Transmissions

Information and materials downloaded from the Internet are not subject to duty. This applies to any goods or merchandise that are electronically transmitted to the purchaser, such as CDs, books, or posters. However, the unauthorized downloading of copyrighted items could subject you to prosecution. Downloading child pornography is also a crime. U.S. Customs and Border Protection has the authority to investigate and prosecute persons involved in this and other illegal activities.

Exporting

If you are sending goods to someone outside the United States, you should be aware that most countries have similar regulations governing the importation of goods into their territory. If you are selling goods on a "Payment on Delivery" basis, you might want to contact the Customs authority of the country where the goods are being shipped to make sure they can legally be imported into that country. In addition, some commodities sold for export are subject to enforcement requirements of U.S. Customs and Border Protection and other U.S. government agencies. In particular, cars and goods with potential military applications, including some electronics and software, must be cleared through CBP before they are exported. And if you export goods worth more than $2,500, you will have to follow formal export procedures.

see also:

on cbp.gov:

Locate a Port Of Entry - Air, Land, or Sea

Medication/Drugs

Exporting a Motor Vehicle

Export Licenses

Customs Administrative Enforcement Process: Fines, Penalties, Forfeitures and Liquidated Damages (pdf - 656 KB.)

What are Ruling Letters

Determining Duty Rates

Textile Status Report for Absolute Quotas

publications:

Importing into the United States
(doc - 1,588 KB.) (pdf - 467 KB.)

on the web:

CPSC Issues Policy On Imported Consumer Products

The Harmonized Tariff Schedule of the United States

North American Free Trade Agreement

USDA - Import Program System Information

U.S. Food and Drug Administration - Center for Food Safety and Applied Nutrition

USDA - APHIS Travel Web

U.S. Food and Drug Administration - ORA Import Start Page

Foreign Embassies of Washington, D.C.

World Customs Organization

Appendix I

Regulatory Audit Questionnaires

U. S. Customs and Border Protection
Office of Strategic Trade
Regulatory Audit Division

Internal Control Questionnaire for Focused Assessments

Introduction

In March 2003, the U.S. Customs Service became part of U.S. Customs and Border Protection, which will continue to be referenced as Customs in this document.

The purpose of the Internal Control Questionnaire for Focused Assessments (FAs) is to obtain information about the company's organizational structure and internal controls related to Customs transactions. The questionnaire is designed to give the audit team a general understanding of the company's import operations and internal control structure as well as to inform the audit candidates of the areas on which the assessment may focus. As each company's operations are unique, this questionnaire may have been modified to fit the circumstances of each audit candidate.

Review Scope

When the importer responds to the questionnaire completely and comprehensively, the Pre-Assessment Survey (PAS) team can plan its approach to the Focused Assessment. The results of the questionnaire, interviews with company officials and Customs personnel, survey of company procedures, and limited testing will be used to determine the effectiveness of the company's internal control system. A PAS of the company's importing operations and internal controls will be used to determine whether more extensive testing is necessary. Any additional testing will be done in the Assessment Compliance Testing (ACT) phase of the Focused Assessment.

Answering the questionnaire affords the company the opportunity to evaluate its own internal controls and operations pertaining to Customs activities. The company will also be more prepared for the Focused Assessment.

I. General

A. Provide the name, title, and telephone number of the official(s) preparing information for this questionnaire.

B. Provide the name, title, and telephone number of the person who will be the contact for Customs during the Focused Assessment.

II. Control Environment

A. <u>Organizational Structure, Policy and Procedures, Assignment of Responsibilities</u>

1. Provide a copy of the company's organizational chart and related department descriptions. Include the detail to show the location of the Import Department identified and any structure descriptions that are relevant.

2. Identify the key individuals in each office responsible for Customs compliance (may be included on the organization chart).
3. Provide the names and addresses of any related foreign and/or domestic companies, such as the company's parent, sister, subsidiaries, or joint ventures.
4. If the company has operating policies and procedures manuals for Customs operations, provide a copy of the manuals (preferably in electronic format).
5. If the policies and procedures have the support and approval of management, identify the individuals who approve the procedures.

B. Employee Awareness Training
1. What specialized Customs training is required for key personnel working in the Import Department? If available, provide copies of training logs or other records supporting training.
2. What Customs experience have key personnel involved in Customs-related activities had?
3. Who in other departments is responsible for reporting Customs-related activities to the Import Department?
4. What training is provided to personnel in other departments responsible for reporting Customs-related activities to the Import Department?
5. How does the company obtain current information on Customs requirements?
6. Does the company use the U.S. Customs and Border Protection Web site?
7. Does the company request and disseminate binding rulings?

III. Risk Assessment

A. How does the company identify, analyze, and manage risks related to Customs activities?

B. What risks related to Customs activities has the company identified, and what control mechanisms has it implemented?

IV. Control Procedures

A. Using source records for support, provide a description and/or flowchart of the company's activities, including general ledger account numbers for recording the acquisition of foreign merchandise in the following areas:
- Purchase of foreign merchandise
- Receipt of foreign merchandise
- Recording in inventory
- Payments made to foreign vendor
- Distribution to customers (e.g., drop shipments)
- Export of merchandise (e.g., assists, Chapter 98)

B. For each aspect of value listed below, respond to the following. Where procedures are documented, reference the applicable sections.
1. What internal control procedures are used to assure accurate reporting to Customs?
2. Who is the person assigned responsibility for accurate reporting?
3. What records are maintained?
   - ☐ Basis of Appraisement (19 CFR 152.101)

- ❑ Price Actually Paid or Payable
- ❑ Packing
- ❑ Selling Commissions
- ❑ Assists (e.g., Materials/Component Parts, Tools, Dies, Molds, Merchandise Consumed, Engineering, Development, Art Work, Design Work, Plans)
- ❑ Royalties and License Fees
- ❑ Proceeds of Subsequent Resale
- ❑ Transportation Costs (e.g., International Freight, Foreign inland Freight, Transportation Rebates, Insurance)
- ❑ Retroactive Price Adjustments
- ❑ Price Increases
- ❑ Rebates
- ❑ Allowances
- ❑ Indirect Payments
- ❑ Payment of Seller's Debt by Buyer (e.g., quota)
- ❑ Price Reductions to Buyer to Settle debts (e.g., Reductions for Defective Merchandise)
- ❑ Purchases on Consignment
- ❑ Quota/Visa
- ❑ Currency Exchange Adjustments

C. For each of the following Customs-related activities, respond to the following. Where procedures are documented, reference the applicable sections.
  1. What internal control procedures are used to assure accurate reporting to Customs?
  2. Who is the person assigned responsibility for accurate reporting?
  3. What records are maintained?
     - ❑ Classification
     - ❑ Quantity
     - ❑ Reconciliation
     - ❑ Trade Agreements
       - (1) Generalized System of Preferences (GSP)
       - (2) Caribbean Basin Economic Recovery Act (also known as Caribbean Basin Initiative(and Special Access Provision (SAP)
       - (3) Israel Free Trade
       - (4) Insular Possessions
       - (5) Andean Trade Preference
       - (6) Trade Development Act of 2000
         - i. African Growth and Opportunity Act (AGOA)
         - ii. Caribbean Basin Trade Partnership Act (CBTPA)
     - ❑ Special Duty Provisions
       - (1) 9801.00.10
       - (2) 9802.00.40
       - (3) 9802.00.50
       - (4) 9802.00.60
       - (5) 9802.00.80
       - (6) 9802.00.90
     - ❑ Antidumping/Countervailing Duties

V. Information and Communication

A. Describe the procedures for the Import Department to disseminate relevant Customs information to other departments.

B. Describe the procedures for other departments to communicate with the Import Department on matters affecting imported merchandise.

C. Describe the procedures for the Import Department to participate in major planning processes involving importation activities.

VI. Monitoring

A. What methods of oversight and monitoring does the Import Department management use to ensure compliance with Customs requirements?

B. Provide information and/or reports on the review and evaluation of compliance with Customs requirements by other internal and external entities (e.g., internal audit department, financial statement auditors).

C. What level of management are these self-reviews reported to for action?

VII. Miscellaneous

A. Identify the account numbers in which costs for imported merchandise are recorded.

U.S. Customs and Border Protection
Office of Strategic Trade
Regulatory Audit Division

Electronic Data Processing (EDP) Questionnaire for Focused Assessments

In March 2003, the U.S. Customs Service became part of the U.S. Customs and Border Protection, which will continue to be referenced as Customs in this document.

An important factor in conducting Focused Assessments (FAs) in a timely manner may include obtaining electronic data files needed to facilitate comparisons between the company's data and Customs data, sampling, and transactional testing. Generally, two or more data universes are identified. The first universe consists of a fiscal year's imports. The sampling unit may be entry line items unless a more efficient sampling unit, such as invoice line items or the equivalent, is available from the company. Other universes of financial transactions are used to test for possible unreported dutiable expenses. These universes and sampling items will be determined after the team has an understanding of your system and Customs procedures.

Typically, files useful for the FA program may include, but not be limited to: Customs entry log, purchase orders, vendor master, general ledger (GL), invoice line detail, chart of accounts, foreign purchases journal, AP (Payment History File) or GL expense file for imported merchandise, accounts payable with GL reference, cash disbursements, wire transfers, letters of credit, and inventory records.

Please return a hard copy and a *disk copy* of the completed questionnaire to

U.S. Customs and Border Protection

Regulatory Audit Division

Attention:

[address]

Email:

Phone:

Fax:

1. List the files, or an equivalent of the same information, that are maintained on each of your computer systems, and describe how each system communicates or links with other systems. For each system, identify the contact person responsible for maintaining that system or information. Identify which information is maintained manually. The following format may be used:

Record	System	Link to Other System	Contact Person	Title	Division
Customs entry (CF 7501)					
Special duty provision					
Payment history					
Accounts Payable					
Purchase order					
Invoice line detail					
Inventory and receiving					
Shipping, freight, insurance, and bill of lading					
Vendor codes and addresses					
Finished product specifications					
Country of origin certification					
Imported product					
Cost data					
Letters of credit					
Wire transfers					
Cash disbursement					

2. Provide flowcharts and/or narrative description of the data flow between systems

3. Are your computer systems IBM Compatible? Yes/No

4. What types of electronic media do you use to transport data? [C-Tape, E-Tape, CD-ROM, Zip Cartridge

5. Specify the capacity for your electronic media

6. List data center location(s).

7. Specify the EDP Department contact person and phone number.

Appendix J

List of Export/Import–Related Websites

EXPORT/IMPORT WEB SITES

EXPORTS	
Bureau of Industry and Security	www.bis.doc.gov
-Export Enforcement	
-Licensing	
-Antiboycott Compliance	
-Embargoed Exports	
-Denied Persons List	
-Ag/Med Licensing to Cuba/Syria	
Office of Foreign Assets Control	www.treas.gov/ofac.
-Embargoed Countries	
-Specially Designated Nationals/Terrorist Lists	
Census Bureau	www.census.gov.
-Electronic Export Information	
-Schedule B Numbers	
-Trade Data Statistics	
Automated Export System	www.aesdirect.gov
Defense Trade Controls	www.pmddtc.state.gov.
-United States Munitions List goods	
-Prohibited Destinations	
U.S. Customs Export Enforcement (EXODUS)	www.cbp.gov

IMPORTS	
U.S. Customs and Border Protection	www.cbp.gov
-Informed Compliance Publications	
-Regulations	
-Rulings	
-Traveler Information	
-Drawback	
-Customs Forms	
-Customs Publications	
-Reconciliation	
-C-TPAT	
-ACE	
Office of Foreign Assets Control	www.treas.gov./ofac
-Embargoed imports	
International Trade Administration	www.ita.doc.gov
-Antidumping/Countervailing Duties	
International Trade Commission	www.usitc.gov
-Harmonized Tariff Schedule	
-Antidumping/Countervailing Duties	

OTHER GOVERNMENT AGENCIES	
Consumer Products Safety Administration	www.cpsc.gov

Appendix J

EXPORT/IMPORT WEB SITES

-CPSIA and Certificates of Conformity	
Department of Agriculture	www.usda.gov
-Animal and Plant Health Inspection Service	www.aphis.usda.gov
-Plant Protection and Quarantine	
-Lacey Act	
Department of Commerce	www.doc.gov
Department of Transportation	www.dot.gov
Environmental Protection Agency	www.epa.gov
Federal Maritime Commission	www.fmc.gov
Federal Trade Commission	www.ftc.gov
-Made in America Standards	
Fish and Wildlife Service	www.fws.gov
Food and Drug Administration	www.fda.gov
Foreign Agricultural Service	www.fas.usda.gov
Hazardous Materials	www.hazmat.dot.gov
Office of the United States Trade Representative	www.ustr.gov

OTHER GOVERNMENT RESOURCES	
Agricultural Exporter Assistance	www.fas.usda.gov.
Code of Federal Regulations	http://www.gpoaccess.gov/cfr/index.html.
Congressional Information	http://www.gpoaccess.gov/crecord/index.html.
Federal Register	http://www.gpoaccess.gov/fr/index.html.
NAFTA Facts	http://www.export.gov/fta/nafta/doc_fta_nafta.asp.
National Trade Data Bank and STAT USA	http://www.stat-usa.gov/
Public Laws	http://www.gpoaccess.gov/plaws/index.html.
Small Business Association	http://www.sba.gov/
U.S. Business Advisor	http://www.business.gov/
U.S. Export Assistance Centers	http://www.export.gov/eac/index.asp.

FINANCIAL	
Asian Development Bank	http://www.adb.org/

EXPORT/IMPORT WEB SITES

Export-Import Bank of the United States	http://www.exim.gov/
Inter-American Development Bank	http://www.iadb.org/
International Monetary Fund	http://www.imf.org.
Overseas Private Investment Corporation	http://www.opic.gov/
World Bank	http://www.worldbank.org/

TRADE ASSOCIATIONS	
American Association of Exporters and Importers	http://www.aaei.org/
American Association of Port Authorities	http://www.aapa-ports.org/
Federation of International Trade Associations	http://www.fita.org/
International Chamber of Commerce	http://www.iccwbo.org/
Joint Industry Group	http://www.jig.org
National Association of Foreign Trade Zone Operators	http://www.naftz.org/
International Compliance Professionals Association	http://www.icpainc.org/
National Council on International Trade Development	http://www.ncitd.org/
National Customs Brokers and Forwarders Assocation of America	http://www.ncbfaa.org/
National Industrial Transportation League	http://www.nitl.org/
National Foreign Trade Council	http://www.nftc.org/
Organization of Women in International Trade	http://owit.org
World Chambers of Commerce	http://www.worldchambers.com/
World Trade Centers Association	http://world.wtca.org/portal/site/wtcaonline

FOREIGN CUSTOMS SERVICES AND TARIFFS	
Argentina	http://www.afip.gov.ar/Aduana/
Australia	http://www.customs.gov.au.
Brazil	http://www.receita.fazenda.gov.br/

Appendix J

EXPORT/IMPORT WEB SITES

Canada	http://www.cbsa-asfc.gc.ca/menu-eng.html
Chile	http://www.aduana.cl/prontus_aduana_eng
China	http://english.customs.gov.cn/publish/portal191/
Colombia	http://www.dian.gov.co/
European Union Customs	http://ec.europa.eu/taxation_customs/index_en.htm
France	http://www.douane.gouv.fr/
Germany	http://www.zoll.de/english_version/index.html
Hong Kong	http://www.customs.gov.hk/
Hungary	http://vam.gov.hu/welcomeEn.do
India	http://www.customs.gov.in/cae1-english.htm
Indonesia	http://www.beacukai.go.id/
Ireland	http://www.revenue.ie/en/index.html
Israel	http://ozar.mof.gov.il/customs/eng/mainpage.htm
Japan	http://www.customs.go.jp/english/index.htm
Jordan	http://www.customs.gov.jo/English/about_jordan.shtm
Korea	http://english.customs.go.kr/
Latin American Trade Council	http://www.latco.org/tools.htm
Malaysia	http://www.customs.gov.my/
Mexico	http://www.aduanas.sat.gob.mx/aduana_mexico/2008/home.asp
Netherlands	http://www.douane.nl/organisatie/en/customs/
New Zealand	http://www.customs.govt.nz
Peru	http://www.aduanet.gob.pe/aduanas/version_ingles/aduanetingles.htm
Russia	http://www.customs.ru/en/
Saudi Arabia	http://www.customs.gov.sa/CustomsNew/default_E.aspx
Singapore	http://www.customs.gov.sg/topNav/hom/
Sweden	http://www.tullverket.se/en/
Taiwan	http://eweb.customs.gov.tw/mp.asp?mp=21

EXPORT/IMPORT WEB SITES

Thailand	http://www.customs.go.th/Customs-Eng/indexEng.jsp
United Kingdom	http://www.hmrc.gov.uk/index.htm
World Customs Organization	http://www.wcoomd.org/home.htm
World Trade Organization	www.wto.org

MISCELLANEOUS TRADE/LEGAL INFORMATION	
American National Standards Institute	www.ansi.org
Carnets	www.uscib.org
CIA's World Fact Book	https://www.cia.gov/library/publications/the-world-factbook/
Currency Converter	http://www.xe.com/ucc/
Federal Reserve Board Foreign Exchange Rates	http://www.federalreserve.gov/Releases/H10/Hist/
Foreign Trade Statistics	http://www.census.gov/foreign-trade/statistics/index.html
Incoterms	http://www.iccwbo.org/incoterms/id3045/index.html
International Organization for Standardization	http://www.iso.org/iso/home.htm
International Trademark Association	http://www.inta.org/
Office of International Trade and Ecomonic Analysis	http://www.ita.doc.gov/td/industry/otea/
United Nations	www.un.org

MARKETING	
Commerce Business Daily	http://cbdnet.gpo.gov/
Office of Technology and Electronic Commerce	http://web.ita.doc.gov/ITI/itiHome.nsf/(HotNews)/HotNews
Export.Gov	http://www.export.gov
Online Exporter Services	http://www.buyusa.gov
Trade Opportunities	http://www.commerce.gov/TradeOpportunities/index.htm
U.S. Agency for International Development	http://www.usaid.gov

Appendix K

Steel License Information

Steel License Information

IMPORTADMINISTRATION
STEELIMPORTLICENSE

OMB NO: 0625-0245
Expire: September 30, 2011

☐ Foreign Trade Zone

01) Applicant Company:	**02) Customs Entry Number:**	**03) License Number:**
04) Contact Name:	**05) Address of Applicant:**	
06) Contact Phone:	**07) Contact Fax:**	**08) Contact Email:**
09) Importer Name:	**10) Exporter Name:**	**11) Manufacturer Name:**
12) Country of Origin (Customs Basis):	**13) Country of Exportation:**	**14) Expected Port of Entry:**
15) Expected Date of Export:	**16) Expected Date of Importation:**	**17) Date of Application:**
18) Date License Valid From:	**19) Date License Valid Through:**	

PRODUCT ONE			
20) HTS Number:	**21) Product Description:**		**22) Product Category:**
23) Volume (Quantity):	**24) Unit:**	**25) Customs Value (U.S.$):**	**26) Unit Value ($/mt):**
	Kilograms		
PRODUCT TWO			
27) HTS Number:	**28) Product Description:**		**29) Product Category:**

30) Volume (Quantity):	31) Unit:	32) Customs Value (U.S.$):	33) Unit Value ($/mt):
	Kilograms		
PRODUCT THREE			
34) HTS Number:	35) Product Description:		36) Product Category:
37) Volume (Quantity):	38) Unit:	39) Customs Value (U.S.$):	40) Unit Value ($/mt):
	Kilograms		
PRODUCT FOUR			
41) HTS Number:	42) Product Description:		43) Product Category:
44) Volume (Quantity):	45) Unit:	46) Customs Value (U.S.$):	47) Unit Value ($/mt):
	Kilograms		
PRODUCT FIVE			
48) HTS Number:	49) Product Description:		50) Product Category:
51) Volume (Quantity):	52) Unit:	53) Customs Value (U.S.$):	54) Unit Value ($/mt):
	Kilograms		
PRODUCT SIX			
55) HTS Number:	56) Product Description:		57) Product Category:
58) Volume (Quantity):	59) Unit:	60) Customs Value (U.S.$):	61) Unit Value ($/mt):
	Kilograms		
PRODUCT SEVEN			
62) HTS Number:	63) Product Description:		64) Product Category:

65) Volume (Quantity):	66) Unit:	67) Customs Value (U.S.$):	68) Unit Value ($/mt):
	Kilograms		
PRODUCT EIGHT			
69) HTS Number:	60) Product Description:		71) Product Category:
72) Volume (Quantity):	73) Unit:	74) Customs Value (U.S.$):	75) Unit Value ($/mt):
	Kilograms		
PRODUCT NINE			
76) HTS Number:	77) Product Description:		78) Product Category:
79) Volume (Quantity):	80) Unit:	81) Customs Value (U.S.$):	82) Unit Value ($/mt):
	Kilograms		
PRODUCT TEN			
83) HTS Number:	84) Product Description:		85) Product Category:
86) Volume (Quantity):	87) Unit:	88) Customs Value (U.S.$):	89) Unit Value ($/mt):
	Kilograms		

Before submitting this form to the Department of Commerce, you must check the box below to certify that, as a representative of the manufacturer or importer, the above information is accurate and complete to the best of your knowledge.

☐ I certify that the above information is accurate and complete to the best of my knowledge.

I also understand that certain information on this license regarding volume (or quantity), value and country of origin will be posted on public website aggregated with similar data from other licenses.

Public reporting for this collection of information is estimated to be 10 minutes per response, including the time for reviewing instructions, and completing and reviewing the collection of information. All responses to this collection of information are required, and will be provided confidentially to the extent allowed by law. Notwithstanding any other provision of law, no person is required to respond to nor shall a person be subject to a penalty for failure to comply with a collection of information subject to the requirements of the Paperwork Reduction Act unless that collection of information displays a current valid OMB Control Number. Send comments regarding the burden estimate or any other aspect of this collection of information, including suggestions for reducing this burden, to the Reports Clearance Officer, International Trade Administration, Department of Commerce, Room 4001, 14th and Constitution Avenue, N.W., Washington, D.C. 20230.

The Steel Import Licensing System: Frequently Asked Questions

Updated on 27 February 2009

Contents:

The SIMA System

What does SIMA stand for? SIMA is the Steel Import Monitoring and Analysis (SIMA) system. It is made up of the steel import licensing system and the Steel Import monitor. Both portions can be accessed via http://ia.ita.doc.gov/steel/license.

Why was the Steel Import License created? The purpose of the licensing system is to provide statistical data on steel imports entering the United States seven weeks earlier than would otherwise be available. The licenses allow the Department of Commerce to collect early and accurate statistics. The data collected from the licenses is made available to the public in an aggregated form after enough information has been collected and it has been reviewed within the Department of Commerce.

What do you do with this information? Once a week the data submitted on the steel licenses are compiled, checked and used in the Steel Import Monitoring and Analysis (SIMA) system public monitor. The SIMA system displays a series of aggregate tables and graphs, which show imports of the steel mill products by country and type of steel product. The SIMA system has close to real-time data available for the public to analyze. Import Administration updates the SIMA system website on Tuesday evenings.

Information on Licenses

Who is required to fill out the license? Any business importing steel mill products covered under the licensing program. Importers, importing agents, or brokers may apply for the license. Please ensure that the contact person named on the license is knowledgeable about the license, should we have questions about it.

Do I need a license for each shipment? Yes, a license is required for each customs entry. You may include up to 10 products on one license if the importer, exporter, manufacturer and the country of origin and exportation are all of the same. Shipments with more than ten products need additional import licenses.

May foreign filers apply for a license? Yes, foreign filers may apply for a license as long as they have a valid U.S. street address.

Is there an application fee? No, the application is free of charge.

Which products are covered? Please refer to the Steel Mill Products included under SIMA (http://ia.ita.doc.gov/steel/license/SMP_byHTS-010109.pdf) link on SIMA website for the list of products currently subject to steel import monitoring and analysis (SIMA) system.

Do products entering into a Foreign Trade Zone (FTZ) require a license? Yes, products entering an FTZ will require a license, but they do not need an additional license when leaving the FTZ for consumption in the US market.

Does a license for products entering into an FTZ zone expire? No, the licenses used for products entering into an FTZ do not expire.

Do U.S.-origin goods processed in a foreign country need a license when re-entered into the United States? This is a very complex issue that is dependent upon the good and the extent to which it undergoes further processing. All questions regarding U.S. goods returned and country-of-origin designation should be raised with your local Customs import specialist.

The ruling states that informal entries will not require a license. On what basis is "informal entry" defined? Informal entry as defined by Customs: see 19 CFR 143.21-143.28. The general value limit for informal entries is $2,000, but may be less in certain instances. If you have specific questions, you should contact your local Customs import specialist.

At what point in the importation process must I fill out the license? You must fill out the license prior to completing the Customs import summary documentation (CF-7501); you will need the license number (issued by Commerce) to complete the Customs Entry documentation. The license may be filled out up to 60 days prior to the date of importation. You will need a username prior to applying for the license (also issued by Commerce).

How long is the license valid? The license may be filed up to 60 days prior to the expected date of entry and will be valid for 75 days.

What is the first step for applying for a license? First, you need to create an account at: http://hq-web03.ita.doc.gov/steel/steelLogin.nsf/newaccount?openform.

User Accounts/Profiles

I had a user ID under the old SIMA system. Do I still need to create a new account? Yes. We require new and existing steel license applicants to create an account with the updated licensing system that began March 2, 2009. Please create your account at: http://hq-web03.ita.doc.gov/steel/steelLogin.nsf/newaccount?openform.

U.S. Department of Commerce | International Trade Administration

Do I need a password for my account? Yes. Passwords are required to log on to the system to access your account and to apply for licenses. You will receive a password when you register for a user ID, which you can then change upon logging in. Passwords must be between 6 and 12 characters long and contain lower case characters (a - z), a numeric character (0 - 9), and a special character (! @ # $ & *).

What if I forget my username or password? In case of a forgotten username or password there are helpful links on the left-hand menu of the licensing system homepage (http://hq-web03.ita.doc.gov/steel/steelLogin.nsf). In order to retrieve a lost or forgotten username or password, you will be required to provide basic information associated with the account, as well as the answers to the preselected security questions.

What is my user profile? It is a record of your username, name, and contact information obtained from your registration. It is used to fill out the top portion of each new license for which you apply. Please keep your contact information updated. You may at any time update your profile, by clicking on "Update Profile" after logging into the system.

What is an Employer Identification Number? Your Employer Identification Number (EIN) is also known as the Federal Tax or IRS identification number, and is used to identify a business entity.

What is the alternate email option? If you enter an alternate email address, that address is copied on emails sent to your account. It is not used to access your account. You will use the primary email address to log in to the system.

Why do I have to enter my e-mail address twice in order to sign in to the system? The first entry is designed to see if your user ID is in the system. Once that is confirmed, the second entry will give you access to the system.

Why are there Outstanding Licenses listed on my account home page? "Outstanding Licenses" are any licenses that have been flagged as potentially containing errors. You will receive an email addressing the issue. If you see a "No documents found" message then you don't have any outstanding licenses to address.

Creating a License

How do I apply for a license? Once you have logged in to your account, please select "New License" from the home page menu options. A tutorial (http://ia.ita.doc.gov/steel/license/SIMA-Tutorial-012109.pdf) with step-by-step instructions to guide you through the license application process is available among the menu options at the top of the page. Additional information for filling out the license application is available by clicking on the help button (http://hq-web03.ita.doc.gov/steel/steellicense.nsf/help?OpenForm) located on the license form.

Under which HTS code would my product be classified? For classification questions, please contact the Import Specialist in the port where the steel products will arrive. Please refer to the US Customs & Border Protection's website (http://www.cbp.gov/) for the contact information for a particular port of entry.

Which value should I enter under "Customs Value"? As the instructions indicate, that value is to be the customs entered value (which does not include duties, brokerage fees or freight), not the invoice value.

How exactly is "Manufacturer" defined? Manufacturer refers to the producer of the steel product. The license requires only the name of the manufacturer; no manufacturer identification codes are required. The Customs MID refers to the manufacturer or shipper. You may list multiple manufacturers or leave the field blank if the manufacturer is unknown.

What if I am unsure as to the manufacturer or origin of the steel I would like to import? Filers must provide the country of origin/exporting country information when filling out the license form; however, filers may mark "unknown" in the manufacturer field.

May I fill out one license application for multiple covered products? A single license application may contain multiple products if the importer, exporter, manufacturer and the country of origin and exportation are all of the same; however, if any of the above information differs, separate license applications must be used. Applicants may include no more than 10 products on a license.

My records show a different unit value. Why is the unit value automatically populated? The license application automatically calculates the unit value per metric ton for each product based on the entered volume and customs value. Please check to make sure that values entered are correct, and that the volume entered is in kilograms.

How long do I have to wait to receive my license number? There is no waiting period; the license number will be generated immediately upon submitting the information. Afterwards you will receive an e-mail confirmation with your license number. Should the Department find an error on your license, a SIMA team member will contact you for confirmation and/or correction.

How many digits long is the license number (I need to know to re-program my ABI interface)? In the new system, you will notice that license numbers will be 9 characters long and will include both numbers and letters. An example will be 7N5Rxxxxx.

What do I need to do if I get a blank screen applying for a license or if I do not receive your e-mail confirmation? Please do not click the submit button more than once (this may create duplicates). First, go into the "View/Update License" feature to see whether your license has gone through. If you don't see it on your list of licenses, a SIMA team member will be happy to assist you. You may contact SIMA by phone: (202)482-2105 or by e-mail steel_license@ita.doc.gov.

How do I obtain a Re-Usable Low Value License Number? If you have a shipment in which the portion covered by the steel licensing requirement is less than $250, then you are eligible to use a Low Value License Number for that entry. Please fill out the form (http://ia.ita.doc.gov/steel/license/Low-Value-Steel-License.pdf) to obtain a low-value license number and fax (202-501-1377) or e-mail it to us. If you would like further information on this option, please contact us.

How do I print my license? After creating a license, you will receive a confirmation page with a link to open the license in a printer-friendly format. You may also print out those licenses up to 90 days old located in your license history. Simply click on "Update/View License", select the license you wish to print, and click on the "Printer Friendly" button.

Modifying/Cancelling a License

What if I discover an error after I submit the license? After logging in to your account, an option to correct a license is available on the Welcome page and also among the menu options on the left-hand side. Simply click on the "Update/View License" link to view a list of your past licenses (up to 90 days old). Click on the license you need to update, and then click on the "Correct License" button, to then make changes, and submit changes.

The information on the license should match the information presented on the CF-7501 as closely as possible; this includes the value and volume of the shipment, the expected date of importation, and the customs district of entry. You will receive an email showing the corrected information.

How exactly do I cancel my license? After logging in to your account, an option to cancel a license is available on the Welcome page and also among the menu options on the left-hand side. Simply click on the "Update/View License" link to view a list of your past licenses (up to 90 days old). Click on the license you need to cancel, and then click on the "Cancel License" button to cancel the license. You will receive an email confirming that cancelation.

Templates

What is the template feature? Compliance with the import license program is extremely important and everyone importing covered products must, by law, fill out a license. We would like to make the process as convenient as possible. If you find yourself repeatedly filling out recurring licenses, we will recommend you to use the template feature in our system. Templates allow you to store the importer & exporter names, manufacturer, countries of origin & exportation, expected port of entry, and up to 10 HTS codes.

What happened to the saved templates I used under the old system? Unfortunately as part of the switchover of the system, templates previously created will no longer be available. However, the new templates system makes it easier to remember which templates you use by allowing you to name them. You may enter names specific to products, shipments, clients, or any other way that works for you. You may also update or delete templates from the new system.

How do I use a template after I created and saved it? You will be able to create a license from a created and saved template by clicking on "Access/View Template", and then by clicking on the name of the template you saved. After you click on the template name, you will see a button that says "New License". Once you click on that button, a license application will appear with the saved information populated into the fields. You will then submit the application just as if you were submitting a new one. Instructions may be found on pages 29-31 of the tutorial (http://hq-web03.ita.doc.gov/steel/steelLogin.nsf/Tutorial?OpenForm).

How do I modify a template? Select "Access/View Template" from your account menu options to bring up your template history page and select the template you wish to modify. Next, click on the "Correct" button to make changes, click "Continue" to verify your changes, and then click "Submit."

How do I delete a template? Click on the "Access/View Template" link from your account menu options to bring up your template history. Check the box next to the template you wish to cancel and then click "Delete." If you deleted a template, you may select it and click "Undelete." If you click "Empty Trash Can", those templates will be permanently deleted.

Additional Questions/Contact us

What should I do when contacted about a steel license? If you are contacted by the SIMA team regarding duplicate licenses or possible errors in the license it is critical that you respond immediately so that SIMA keeps its data as up to date as possible. Please respond to any correspondence to indicate if there was a correction or if the license is accurate.

What should I do if I need to fill out a license urgently and there is a problem with the Internet? Please contact us first if you are having trouble accessing our site. In instances where the system has gone down the Department is usually able to get the site running within the same business day, so we ask that you remain patient. However, in emergency situations, you may print out the PDF license application form and fax it to: (202) 501-1377. Please make sure all forms are typed.

Who should we contact with additional questions? The steel licensing team is happy to answer your questions: (202) 482-2105 or by email: steel_license@ita.doc.gov.

Additionally, there are updated instructions available once you log on as a registered user and are prepared to fill out a license. Please refer to the instructions on our website (http://ia.ita.doc.gov/steel/license/forminstructions.html) on how to fill out the form.

Any suggestions? As always the SIMA team is happy to hear from you. Please feel free to e-mail us any comments/suggestions you may have regarding the SIMA license system or monitor. The office is staffed during normal business hours (Monday-Friday, 9am-5pm EST).

SIMA Team Contact Information
Import Administration
Office of Policy
14PthP & Constitution Ave., NW, Suite 2837
Washington, DC 20230
(202) 482-2105
(202) 501-1377
Steel_License@ita.doc.gov
http://ia.ita.doc.gov/steel/license/index.html

U.S. Department of Commerce | International Trade Administration

STEEL MILL PRODUCTS - hts codes that require steel import licenses as of July 1, 2009

HTS Code (2007)	HTS Description	Category	Aggregate Category
7206100000	IRON AND NONALLOY STEEL INGOTS	Ingots and Steel for Castings	Semi-Finished
7206900000	IRON AND NONALLOY STEEL, PRIMARY FORMS NOT INGOTS	Ingots and Steel for Castings	Semi-Finished
7218100000	STAINLESS STEEL INGOTS AND OTHER PRIMARY FORMS	Ingots and Steel for Castings	Semi-Finished
7224100005	INGOTS A OTH PRIM FORMS OF HIGH-NICKEL ALLOY STEEL	Ingots and Steel for Castings	Semi-Finished
7224100075	INGOTS A OTHER PRIMARY FORMS OF OTHER ALLOY STEEL	Ingots and Steel for Castings	Semi-Finished
7207110000	SMFD IOS NA LT.25% CRBN,REC/SQ CS WDTH LT 2X THKNS	Blooms, Billets and Slabs	Semi-Finished
7207120010	SEMI IRON/STL GT .25%CARBON XSECT WDTH GT 4X THK	Blooms, Billets and Slabs	Semi-Finished
7207120050	SEMIFIN IR/STL GT 0.25%CARB CROS-SECT WD GT 4X THK	Blooms, Billets and Slabs	Semi-Finished
7207190030	SEMIFIN IRON/STL GT 0.25% CARBON CIRCULAR XSECT	Blooms, Billets and Slabs	Semi-Finished
7207190090	SEMIFINISHED IRON/NALLOY STL GT 0.25% CARB; NESOI	Blooms, Billets and Slabs	Semi-Finished
7207200025	SEMI IRON/STL GT 0.25% CRB RECT/SQR XSEC GT 4XTHK	Blooms, Billets and Slabs	Semi-Finished
7207200045	SMFD IOS NA .25PCT CRBN AO RCT/SQ CS WDTH 4X TH AO	Blooms, Billets and Slabs	Semi-Finished
7207200075	SMFD IOS NA .25PCT CRBN AO CIRC CRSS-SCTN	Blooms, Billets and Slabs	Semi-Finished
7207200090	SMFD IOS NA .25PCT CRBN AO CRS-SEC NT CIRC REC SQR	Blooms, Billets and Slabs	Semi-Finished
7218910015	STAINLESS STEEL RECT, WDTH LT 4X THICK,LT 232 CM2	Blooms, Billets and Slabs	Semi-Finished
7218910030	STAINLESS STEEL RECT,WDTH LT 4X THICK,GT=232 CM2	Blooms, Billets and Slabs	Semi-Finished
7218910060	STAINLS STEEL RECTANG, WDTH AT LEAST 4X THICKNESS	Blooms, Billets and Slabs	Semi-Finished
7218990015	STAINLESS STL SQUARE X-SECTIONAL AREA LT 232CM2	Blooms, Billets and Slabs	Semi-Finished
7218990030	STAIN STEEL,SQUARE CROSS SEC,CROSS SEC GT=232 CM2	Blooms, Billets and Slabs	Semi-Finished
7218990045	STAINLESS STEEL,CIRC CROSS-SEC, AREA LT 232 CM2	Blooms, Billets and Slabs	Semi-Finished
7218990060	STAINLS STEEL,CIRC CROSS-SEC,AREA GT=232 CM2	Blooms, Billets and Slabs	Semi-Finished
7218990090	SEMIFINISHED PRODUCTS OF STAINLESS STEEL, NESOI	Blooms, Billets and Slabs	Semi-Finished
7224900005	SMFD PRODUCTS OF OTHER HIGH-NICKEL ALLOY STEEL	Blooms, Billets and Slabs	Semi-Finished
7224900045	OTH SMF AL STL, WDTH UN 4X THKNS, RCT/SQ CS	Blooms, Billets and Slabs	Semi-Finished
7224900055	SMFD AL STL NT SS OR TS,REC/SQ,WIDTH 4X THKNS AOV	Blooms, Billets and Slabs	Semi-Finished
7224900065	SMFD ALLOY STEEL, NOT SS OR TOOL, CIRC CS	Blooms, Billets and Slabs	Semi-Finished
7224900075	SMFD AL STL, NOT SS OR TOOL, NOT REC/SQ/CIRC CS	Blooms, Billets and Slabs	Semi-Finished
7213913011	TIRE CORD WIR RODS,<14MM,NOTE 9,SUBCHP 3,CHP 99	Wire Rods	Long Products
7213913015	BAR ROD CHQ STEEL HOT-ROLLD IRR COILS DIAM LT 14MM	Wire Rods	Long Products
7213913020	BAR ROD IRON/STEEL HOT-ROLLD IRR DIA <10MM,STAT NOTE 6	Wire Rods	Long Products
7213913093	BAR ROD IRON/STEEL HOT-ROLLD IRR DIA <10MM,OTH, STAT NOTE 6	Wire Rods	Long Products
7213914500	BARS&RODS IRON/STL; HOT RLD;LT 14MM; GT=0.6% CARB	Wire Rods	Long Products
7213916000	BAR/ROD;IR/NALLOY STL; HOT ROLLED;LT 14MM; NESOI	Wire Rods	Long Products
7213990030	BARS & RODS IRON/NALLOY STL; HOT-ROLLED; 14MM-19MM	Wire Rods	Long Products
7213990090	BARS & RODS IRON/NALLOY STEEL; HOT-ROLLED; NESOI	Wire Rods	Long Products
7221000015	SS BARS/RODS COLIS CIRC CS DIAM LS THN 14MM, OTHER	Wire Rods	Long Products
7221000030	SS BAR HR COIL CIRC CS OD 14MM AOV LS THN 19MM OTH	Wire Rods	Long Products
7216310000	ANGLES,U SECT,IOS NA,HT-RLD/DRWN/EXTRD GT/=80MM HI	Structural Shapes Heavy	Long Products
7216320000	ANGLES,I SECT,IOS NA,HT-RLD/DRWN/EXTRD GT/=80MM HI	Structural Shapes Heavy	Long Products
7216330030	H SEC IR/STL,HI GT=80MM,HT RLD,WT LT=11.3KG/30.5CM	Structural Shapes Heavy	Long Products
7216330060	H SEC IR/STL,HOTR,GT=80 MM HT,(11.3-27.2KG)/30.5CM	Structural Shapes Heavy	Long Products
7216330090	OTH H SECTIONS,IRON/NONALY STEEL,HOT-RL,GT 80MM HT	Structural Shapes Heavy	Long Products
7216400010	ANGLES,L SECTION,IRON/NALY STL HOT-RLD,GT=80MM HI	Structural Shapes Heavy	Long Products
7216400050	T SECTION,IRON OR NONALY STEEL,HOT-RLD GT=80MM HI	Structural Shapes Heavy	Long Products
7216500000	ANGLS,SHPES,& SECS IOS NA HT-RLD/DRWN/EXTRD NESOI	Structural Shapes Heavy	Long Products
7216990010	ANGLES,SHAPS,SECTNS IRON/NONALLOY STEL,DRILD/NTCH	Structural Shapes Heavy	Long Products
7216990090	ANGLES, SHAPES, SECTIONS IRON/NONALLOY STEEL NESOI	Structural Shapes Heavy	Long Products
7222403025	ANGLS SS HR N DRLD/PNCHD/OTHWS ADV MAX CS 80MM AO	Structural Shapes Heavy	Long Products
7222403045	SHPS SECS SS HR NT DLD/PCH/OTHWS ADV MX CS UN 80MM	Structural Shapes Heavy	Long Products
7228703010	U, I, H, T SEC AS NT SS HR NT DR/PN/OADV	Structural Shapes Heavy	Long Products
7228703020	ANGS ALLOY STL NT SS HR NT DR/PN/OAD MX CS 76MM AO	Structural Shapes Heavy	Long Products
7228703041	SHPS SEC O/T ANGS,U,I,H,T AS NT SS HR NT DR/PN/OADV MX CS 76MM AO	Structural Shapes Heavy	Long Products
7301100000	SHEET PILING OF IRON OR STEEL	Steel Piling	Long Products
7208403030	FLT RLD IRN/NALLOY STL N COIL GT=600MM;GT 10MM THK	Plates Cut Lengths	Flat Products
7208403060	FLAT RLD IRON/STL N COIL; GT=600MM; 4.75-10MM THK	Plates Cut Lengths	Flat Products
7208510030	UNVRSL ML PLT,IOS NA,GT/=600MM,HT-RLD,GT 10MM THK	Plates Cut Lengths	Flat Products
7208510045	FLAT RLD HISTRG STL; GT=600MM;GT 10MM THK;NOT COIL	Plates Cut Lengths	Flat Products
7208510060	FLT RLD IRON/STL;N COIL;GT=600MM;GT 10MM THK;NESOI	Plates Cut Lengths	Flat Products
7208520000	FLT RLD IOS NA,NT CLS,GT/=600MM,4.75-10MM THCK	Plates Cut Lengths	Flat Products
7210901000	FLT RLD IOS NA GT/=600MM W,CLAD,NESOI	Plates Cut Lengths	Flat Products
7211130000	FLT RLD HI-STR IOS NA LT 600MM,UNVRSL MILPLT,HT-RL	Plates Cut Lengths	Flat Products
7211140030	FLT RLD HISTRG STEEL;LT 600MM;HOT RLD;GT=4.75MMTHK	Plates Cut Lengths	Flat Products
7211140045	FLT RLD IR/NALLOY STL;LT 600MM;GT=4.75MMTHK;N COIL	Plates Cut Lengths	Flat Products
7219210005	FR HN SS 600MM AO W HR NT CLD OV 10MM THCK	Plates Cut Lengths	Flat Products
7219210020	FLT RLD STNLS STL;HOT RLD;NOT COIL; WID LT 1575MM	Plates Cut Lengths	Flat Products
7219210040	FLT RLD STNLS STL;HOT RLD;NOT COIL; 1575 LT 1880MM	Plates Cut Lengths	Flat Products
7219210060	FLT RLD STNLS STL;HOT RLD;NOT COIL; WID GT 1880MM	Plates Cut Lengths	Flat Products

Appendix K

7219220005	FR H-N SS 600MM AO W HR NT CLD 4.75-NOV 10MM THCK	Plates Cut Lengths	Flat Products
7219220015	FLT RLD STN STL;.5%NI;(1.5%-5%) MOLYBDNM LT 1575MM	Plates Cut Lengths	Flat Products
7219220020	FLAT RLD;STNLS STL;.5%NI;1.5%-5% MOLY;1575-1880MM	Plates Cut Lengths	Flat Products
7219220025	FLT RLD STN STL;.5% NI;(1.5%-5% MOLY);GT 1880MM	Plates Cut Lengths	Flat Products
7219220035	FLAT ROLLED;STAINLESS STEEL;OTHER;WIDTH LT 1575MM	Plates Cut Lengths	Flat Products
7219220040	FLAT ROLL;STAINLESS STEEL;OTHER;WID 1575 LT 1880MM	Plates Cut Lengths	Flat Products
7219220045	FLAT ROLL;STAINLESS STEEL;OTHER;WIDTH GT 1880MM	Plates Cut Lengths	Flat Products
7219220070	FLT RLD;STNLS STL;TH 4.75-10MM;WD LT 1575MM;NESOI	Plates Cut Lengths	Flat Products
7219220075	FLT RLD;STNLS STL;4.75-10MMTHCK;WD 1575-1880;OTH	Plates Cut Lengths	Flat Products
7219220080	FLT RLD;STNLS STL;THK 4.75-10MM;WD GT 1880MM;NESOI	Plates Cut Lengths	Flat Products
7219310050	FR SS 600MM AO W CR 4.75MM AO THCK NT COILD	Plates Cut Lengths	Flat Products
7220110000	FLT-RLD,STNLS STL, LT 600MM, HT-RLD GT/=4.75MM THK	Plates Cut Lengths	Flat Products
7225403005	FR OTH HI-NI AL ST,W 600MM AOV,NCL,OV 4.75MM THICK	Plates Cut Lengths	Flat Products
7225403050	FR OTH AL STL,WTH 600MM AOV,HR,NCL,OV 4.75MM THICK	Plates Cut Lengths	Flat Products
7225506000	FR OTH ALLOY STL 600MM W AO CR 4.75MM AO THCK	Plates Cut Lengths	Flat Products
7226915000	FR OTH ALLOY STL U 600MM W HR 4.75MM AO THCK	Plates Cut Lengths	Flat Products
7208101500	FLT RLD IOS NA CLS,GT/=600MM WD,HT RLD,PKLD,PATRN	Plates In Coils	Flat Products
7208103000	FLT RLD IR/NALLOY STL GT=600MM;HOT ROLL; GT=4.75MM	Plates In Coils	Flat Products
7208253000	FLT RLD HI-STR IOS NA CLS,GT/= 600MM,PKLD,4.75MM T	Plates In Coils	Flat Products
7208256000	FLT RLD IOS NA CLS,GT/=600MM,PKLD,4.75MM THK,NT HI	Plates In Coils	Flat Products
7208360030	FLT RLD HI-STR IOS NA CLS,GT/=600MM,GT 10MM THK	Plates In Coils	Flat Products
7208360060	FLT RLD IOS NA CLS,EX HI-STR,GT/=600MM,GT 10MM TH	Plates In Coils	Flat Products
7208370030	FLT RLD HI-STR IOS NA CLS,GT/=600MM,4.75-10MM THK	Plates In Coils	Flat Products
7208370060	FLAT RLD IOS NA CLS,EX HI-STR,GT/=600MM,4.75-10MM	Plates In Coils	Flat Products
7211140090	FLT RLD IR/STL;COIL;HOT RLD;LT 600MM;GT=4.75MM THK	Plates In Coils	Flat Products
7219110030	FLAT RLD STAINLS STEEL;HOT ROLLED;WIDTH LT 1575MM	Plates In Coils	Flat Products
7219110060	FLAT RLD STAINLESS STEEL;HOT ROLLED;WID GT 1575MM	Plates In Coils	Flat Products
7219120002	FR SS OV 600-1370MM W HR OV 4.75-10MM NA OR NP	Plates In Coils	Flat Products
7219120006	FR H-N SS 600MM AO W HR CL 4.75 NO 10MM TH NESOI	Plates In Coils	Flat Products
7219120021	FLT RLD STN STL;TH EX 4.75MM 10MM WD NOT GT 1575MM	Plates In Coils	Flat Products
7219120026	FLT RLD STN STL;HOT RLD;THK GT 6.8MM;WID GT 1575MM	Plates In Coils	Flat Products
7219120051	FLAT RLD STNLS STEEL;HOT ROLLED;OTH;WID GT 1575MM	Plates In Coils	Flat Products
7219120056	FLAT RLD STNLS STEEL;HOT ROLLED;OTH;WID GT 1575MM	Plates In Coils	Flat Products
7219120066	FRSS CLS OV 600-1370MM W HR OV 4.75-UN 10MM ETC	Plates In Coils	Flat Products
7219120071	FR SS CL OV 600-1370MM W HR OV 4.75-UN 10MM ETC	Plates In Coils	Flat Products
7219120081	FR SS CLS OV 600-1370MM W HR OV 4.75-10MM THK NES	Plates In Coils	Flat Products
7219310010	FR SS 600MM AO CR 4.75MM AO THCK COILS	Plates In Coils	Flat Products
7225303005	FR HI-NI AL ST,WTH 600MM AOV,HR CLS,4.75MM THICKOV	Plates In Coils	Flat Products
7225303050	FR OTH AL STL,WDTH 600MM AOV,HR CLS,4.75MM THCK AO	Plates In Coils	Flat Products
7302101010	TEE RAILS,NEW,IRON/STEEL, NOT HEAT TREAT GT 30KG/M	Rails Standard	Long Products
7302101035	TEE RAILS, NEW, IRON/STEEL,HEAT-TREATED GT 30 KG/M	Rails Standard	Long Products
7302105020	RAILS OF ALLOY STEEL, NEW	Rails Standard	Long Products
7302101015	RAILS,NEW,IRON/STEEL,N HEAT-TREAT GT 30KG/M,NESOI	Rails All Other	Long Products
7302101025	RAILS, NEW, IRON/STEEL, NOT HEAT-TREATED, NESOI	Rails All Other	Long Products
7302101045	RAILS,NEW,IRON/NALLOY STEEL,HEAT TREAT,GT 30KG/MTR	Rails All Other	Long Products
7302101055	RAILS,NEW,IRON/STEEL,HEAT TREATED,LT=30KG/M, NESOI	Rails All Other	Long Products
7302400000	FISH PLATES AND SOLE PLATES OF IRON OR STEEL	Railroad Accessories	Long Products
7302901000	SLEEPERS (CROSS-TIES) OF IRON OR STEEL	Railroad Accessories	Long Products
7213200010	BARS & RODS FREE-CUT STL GT=0.1% LEAD HOT-ROLD IRR	Bars-Hot Rolled	Long Products
7213200080	BAR ROD FREE-CUTTING STL HOT-ROLLD IRR COILS NESOI	Bars-Hot Rolled	Long Products
7213990060	BARS & RODS IRON/NALLOY STEEL; HOT-ROLLED; GT=19MM	Bars-Hot Rolled	Long Products
7214100000	BAR & ROD OF IOS NA,FORGED	Bars-Hot Rolled	Long Products
7214300010	BARS & RODS OF FREE-CUTTNG STEEL GT=0.1% LEAD, ETC	Bars-Hot Rolled	Long Products
7214300080	BARS & ROD FREE-CUTTING STEEL HOT-ROLLED ETC NESOI	Bars-Hot Rolled	Long Products
7214910015	BAR&ROD IOS NA RCTNGLR X-SEC,LT 0.25%CRBN,HT-RL/DR	Bars-Hot Rolled	Long Products
7214910060	BAR&ROD IOS NA,RCTNGLR X-SEC(.25-.6%)CARBN,HT-RL/D	Bars-Hot Rolled	Long Products
7214910090	BAR&ROD IOS NA,RCTNGLR X-SEC,GT/=.6% CARBN,HT-RL/D	Bars-Hot Rolled	Long Products
7214990015	OTHER BARS IRON/STL;ROUNDS;HOT-WKD;LT 0.25%CARBON	Bars-Hot Rolled	Long Products
7214990030	OTHER BARS IRON/STL; ROUNDS; (0.25%-0.6%) CARBON	Bars-Hot Rolled	Long Products
7214990045	OTHER BARS IRON/STL; HOTWRKD; RNDS; GT .6% CARBON	Bars-Hot Rolled	Long Products
7214990060	OTHER BARS IRON/STL HOTWORK;LT 0.25% CARBON;NESOI	Bars-Hot Rolled	Long Products
7214990075	OTH BARS IRON/STL;HOT WRKD;(0.25%-0.6%) CARB;NESOI	Bars-Hot Rolled	Long Products
7214990090	OTHER BARS IRON/STL; HOT WORKD;GT 0.6% CARB; NESOI	Bars-Hot Rolled	Long Products
7215901000	OTH BRS RDS IRON/STL,COATD/PLTD W METL,NOT COLD-FM	Bars-Hot Rolled	Long Products
7221000005	SS BARS/RODS HOT-ROLLED IN COILS OF HIGH NI ALLOY	Bars-Hot Rolled	Long Products
7221000045	SS BARS/RODS HR COILS CIRC CS DIAM 19MM AOV, OTHER	Bars-Hot Rolled	Long Products
7221000075	SS BARS/RODS HR IRREG WOUND COILS, OTHER, OTHER	Bars-Hot Rolled	Long Products
7222110005	BARS&RODS STAINL STL HOT-WKED HI-NI ALLOY STL CIR	Bars-Hot Rolled	Long Products
7222110055	BARS&RODS STAINL STL HOT-WKD CIR, X-SECTION MAX < 152.4MM	Bars-Hot Rolled	Long Products
7222110080	BARS&RODS STAINL STL HOT-WKD CIR, X-SECTION MAX > 152.4MM	Bars-Hot Rolled	Long Products
7222190005	BARS&RODS STAINL STL HOT-WKD HI-NI ALLOY ST NONCIR	Bars-Hot Rolled	Long Products
7222190050	BARS&RODS STAINL STL HOT-WKD NOT CIR X-SECTI NESOI	Bars-Hot Rolled	Long Products
7227200030	BRS A RDS SLCO-MN STL IRRG COILS HOT-ROLLD, WELDING QUAL, STAT NOTE 6	Bars-Hot Rolled	Long Products
7227200080	BRS A RDS SLCO-MN STL IRRG COILS HOT-ROLLD, OTHER	Bars-Hot Rolled	Long Products
7227906005	BARS/RODS OTHER HI-NI AL STL, IRREG COILS, HR	Bars-Hot Rolled	Long Products
7227906010*	BARS/RODS OTH AL STL, IRREG COILS, HOT-ROLLED, OTH	Bars-Hot Rolled	Long Products
7227906020	BARS/RODS OTH AL STL, IRR COILS, HOT-ROLLED, OTH, WELD, <10mm, STAT NOTE 6	Bars-Hot Rolled	Long Products
7227906050	BARS/RODS OTH AL STL, IRREG COILS, HOT-ROLLED, OTH	Bars-Hot Rolled	Long Products

7227906085	BARS/RODS OTH AL STL, IRREG COILS, HOT-ROLLED, OTH, OTH, STAT NOTE 6	Bars-Hot Rolled	Long Products
7228201000	OTH BRS A RDS SILICO-MNGNSE STL NT COLD-FRMD	Bars-Hot Rolled	Long Products
7228308005	OTH BARS/RODS OTH HI-NI AL STL, HOT-WORKED	Bars-Hot Rolled	Long Products
7228308050	OTHER BARS/RODS OF OTHER ALLOY STEEL, HOT-WORKED	Bars-Hot Rolled	Long Products
7228400000	BARS & RODS OF OTHER ALLOY STEEL, FORGED	Bars-Hot Rolled	Long Products
7228606000	OTH BARS A RODS OTH ALLOY STL NT COLD-FMD NESOI	Bars-Hot Rolled	Long Products
7228800000	HOLLOW DRILL BARS AND RODS, ALLOY/NALLOY STL,NESOI	Bars-Hot Rolled	Long Products
7216100010	ANGLES,U SECT,IRON/NON ALY STL,HOTRLD, LT 80MM HGH	Bars-Light Shaped	Long Products
7216100050	ANGLS,I OR H SEC IRN/STL,NALY,HOTRLD LT 80MM HGH	Bars-Light Shaped	Long Products
7216210000	ANGLES,L SECT,IOS NA,HT-RLD/DRWN/EXTRD LT 80MM HI	Bars-Light Shaped	Long Products
7216220000	ANGLES,T SECT,IOS NA,HT-RLD/DRWN/EXTRD LT 80MM HI	Bars-Light Shaped	Long Products
7222403065	ANGLS SS HR NT DRLD/PNCHD/OTHWS ADV MAX CS UN 80MM	Bars-Light Shaped	Long Products
7222403085	SHPS SECS SS HR NT DLD/PCH/OTHWS ADV MX CS UN 80MM	Bars-Light Shaped	Long Products
7228703060	ANGS ALLY STL NT SS HR NT DR/PN/OADV MX CS UN 76MM	Bars-Light Shaped	Long Products
7228703081	SHPS SEC O/T ANGS,U,I,H,T AS NT SS HR NT DR/PN/OADV MX CS UN 76MM	Bars-Light Shaped	Long Products
7213100000	CONCRETE REINFORCING IOS NA BARS&RODS,HT-RLD,CLS	Bars-Reinforcing	Long Products
7214200000	CONCRETE REINFORCING BAR & ROD IOS NA,HT-RLD/DRWN	Bars-Reinforcing	Long Products
7215100010	BAR ROD FREE-CUT STEEL GT=0.1% LEAD COLD-FORM ETC	Bars-Cold Finished	Long Products
7215100080	BAR ROD FREE-CUTTING STEEL COLD-FORMD/FINSHD NESOI	Bars-Cold Finished	Long Products
7215500015	BARS&RODS IOS NA, CLD-FRM/FNSHD,WT LT .25%CRB	Bars-Cold Finished	Long Products
7215500060	BAR&RODS IOS NA,CLD-FRM/FNSHD,WT (.25-6%) CARBON	Bars-Cold Finished	Long Products
7215500090	BAR&RODS IOS NA,CLD-FRM/FNSHD,WT GT/=.6% CRB	Bars-Cold Finished	Long Products
7215903000	OTH BRS RDS IRON/STL,COATD/PLTD W METAL, COLD-FORM	Bars-Cold Finished	Long Products
7215905000	OTHER BARS AND RODS IRON OR NONALLOY STEEL, NESOI	Bars-Cold Finished	Long Products
7222200005	OTH SS BARS/RODS COLD FORM O FINISH, HIGH-NI ALLOY	Bars-Cold Finished	Long Products
7222200045	OTH SS BAR/ROD C-FRM O FIN MAX CS LS THN 18MM, OTH	Bars-Cold Finished	Long Products
7222200080	OTH SS BAR/ROD COLD FORM OR FINISH, MAX CS >18MM AND <152.4MM	Bars-Cold Finished	Long Products
7222200085	OTH SS BAR/ROD COLD FORM OR FINISH, MAX CS >152.4MM	Bars-Cold Finished	Long Products
7222300010	OTH SS BAR/ROD NESOI, MAX CS <152.4MM	Bars-Cold Finished	Long Products
7222300080	OTH SS BAR/ROD NESOI, MAX CS >152.4MM	Bars-Cold Finished	Long Products
7228205000	OTH BRS RDS SILICO-MNGNSE STL COLD-FORMD	Bars-Cold Finished	Long Products
7228505005	OTH BRS RDS HI-NI ALY STL COLD-FORMED O COLD-FNSHD	Bars-Cold Finished	Long Products
7228505050	OTH BRS RDS OTH ALY ST COLD-FRMD OR COLD-FNSHD OTH	Bars-Cold Finished	Long Products
7228608000	OTHER BARS AND RODS OTHER ALLOY STEEL COLD-FORMED	Bars-Cold Finished	Long Products
7224100045	INGOTS AND OTHER PRIMARY FORMS OF TOOL STEEL	Tool Steel	Long Products
7224900015	SMFSHD TOOL STL,REC/SQ CS,WIDTH LS THAN 4X THKNS	Tool Steel	Long Products
7224900025	SMFSHD TOOL STL, REC/SQ CS, WDTH AT LEAST 4X THKNS	Tool Steel	Long Products
7224900035	SMFSHD TOOL STL, NOT RECT/SQUARE CROSS SECTIONS	Tool Steel	Long Products
7225301110	FLAT ROLLED PROD OF HIGH SPEED STEEL,WID => 4.75MM	Tool Steel	Long Products
7225301180	FLAT ROLLED PROD OF TOOL STEEL O/THAN HIGH SPEED STEEL,WID =>4.75MM	Tool Steel	Long Products
7225305110	FLT-RLD PROD,TOOL,W =>600MM,TH <4.75MM,COIL,HIGH-SPEED STL	Tool Steel	Long Products
7225305130	FLT-RLD PROD,TOOL,W =>600MM,TH <4.75MM,COIL,BALL-BEARING ST	Tool Steel	Long Products
7225305160	FLT-RLD PROD,TOOL STEEL,WD =>600MM,TH <4.75MM,IN COIL, OTHE	Tool Steel	Long Products
7225401110	FLT-RLD PROD,TOOL,W =>600MM,TH>=4.75MM,N/COIL,HIGH-SPEED ST	Tool Steel	Long Products
7225401115	FLT-RLD PROD,TOOL,W =>600MM,TH>=4.75MM,N/COIL,BALLBEARNG ST	Tool Steel	Long Products
7225401190	FLT-RLD PROD NOT IN COIL,W =>600MM,TH >4.75MM,TOOL STEEL,OT	Tool Steel	Long Products
7225405110	FLT-RLD PROD,TOOL,W =>600MM,TH <4.75MM,N/COIL,HIGH SPEED ST	Tool Steel	Long Products
7225405130	FLT-RLD PROD,TOOL,W =>600MM,TH <4.75MM,N/COIL,BALLBEARNG ST	Tool Steel	Long Products
7225405160	FLT-RLD PROD,TOOL STEEL,WD =>600MM,TH <4.75MM,NT COIL, OTHE	Tool Steel	Long Products
7225501110	FLAT-ROLLD PRODS,HIGH-SPPED STEEL,WIDTH =>600MM,COLD-ROLLED	Tool Steel	Long Products
7225501130	FLAT-ROLLD PRODS,BALL-BEARNG STEEL,WIDTH =>600MM,COLD-ROLLE	Tool Steel	Long Products
7225501160	OTHER FLAT-ROLLED PRODS OF TOOL STEEL,COLD-ROLLD,WD=>600MM	Tool Steel	Long Products
7226200000	FLAT-ROLLED, HIGH-SPEED STEEL LESS THAN 600MM WIDE	Tool Steel	Long Products
7226910500	FLT-RLLD CHIPPR KNFE STL LSS THN 600 MM WDE,HT RLD	Tool Steel	Long Products
7226911530	FR BLL-BRG STEEL 300-UN 600MM WIDE HOT-ROLLD	Tool Steel	Long Products
7226911560	FR OTH ALLOY STL 300-UN 600MM WD HOT-ROLLD	Tool Steel	Long Products
7226912530	FR BLL-BRG STL UNDR 300MM WD HOT-ROLLD	Tool Steel	Long Products
7226912560	FLT RLLD OTH ALLOY STL UNDR 300MM WD HOT-ROLLD	Tool Steel	Long Products
7226921030	FLAT-ROLLED BALL-BEARING STEEL 300-UN600MM W CR	Tool Steel	Long Products
7226921060	FR OTH TOOL STL 300-UN 600MM W CLD-RLLD	Tool Steel	Long Products
7226923030	FLAT-ROLLED BALL-BEARING STEEL UN 300MM W CR	Tool Steel	Long Products
7226923060	FLAT-ROLLED OTHER TOOL STEEL UN 300MM W CR	Tool Steel	Long Products
7227100000	BARS & RODS, HIGH-SPEED STEEL,IRREG COILS,HOT-ROLL	Tool Steel	Long Products
7227901030	BRS RDS BLL-BRG STL IRG CLS HR N TMD/TTD/PTLY MFTD	Tool Steel	Long Products
7227901060	BRS RDS OTH TS IRRG CLS HR N TMPD/TTD/PTLY MNFRD	Tool Steel	Long Products
7227902030	BRS RDS BLL-BRG STL IRRG COILS HR OTHER	Tool Steel	Long Products
7227902060	BRS RDS OTH TOOL STL IRRG COILS HR OTHER	Tool Steel	Long Products
7228100010	OTHER BARS AND RODS HIGH-SPEED STEEL NT COLD-FORMD	Tool Steel	Long Products
7228100030	OTH BRS RDS HSPD STL CF MAX CS UN 18MM	Tool Steel	Long Products
7228100060	OTH BRS RDS HSPD STL CF MAX CS 18MM AO	Tool Steel	Long Products
7228302000	OTHER BARS AND RODS BALL-BEARING STEEL HOT-WORKED	Tool Steel	Long Products
7228304000	OTH BRS RDS CHPPR KNF STL HOT-WKD NT COLD-FMD	Tool Steel	Long Products
7228306000	OTHER BARS AND RODS OTHER TOOL STEEL HOT-WORKED	Tool Steel	Long Products
7228501010	OTH BRS RDS BLL-BRG STL COLD-FRMD O COLD-FNSHD	Tool Steel	Long Products
7228501020	OTH BRS RDS OTS CF/FN RND/REC CS U18MM G/ML/POL SF	Tool Steel	Long Products
7228501040	OTH BRS RDS OTH TS CF/FN MX CS UN 18MM OTHR	Tool Steel	Long Products
7228501060	OTH BRS RDS OTS CF/FN RND/REC CS 18MM AO G/ML/PL S	Tool Steel	Long Products
7228501080	OTH BRS RDS OTS CF/FN MX CS 18MM AO OTHR	Tool Steel	Long Products
7228601030	OTHER BARS AND RODS BALL-BEARING STEEL NESOI	Tool Steel	Long Products

Appendix K

7228601060	OTHER BARS AND RODS OTHER TOOL STEEL NESOI	Tool Steel	Long Products
7229900500	WIRE OF HIGH-SPEED STEEL	Tool Steel	Long Products
7304390016	TUBE,PIPE,PROF,SMLS,IRN/STL,GALVANIZED,LT=114.3MM	Standard Pipe	Pipe and Tube
7304390020	TUBE,PIPE,PROFIL,SMLS,IRN/STL,NESOI,DIAM LT 38.1MM	Standard Pipe	Pipe and Tube
7304390024	TUBE,SMLS,IR/STL,NESOI,38.1 LT=114.3 WAL LT 6.4MM	Standard Pipe	Pipe and Tube
7304390036	PIPE,SMLS,IRN/STL,OTH, DIAM114.3-190.5WAL LT12.7MM	Standard Pipe	Pipe and Tube
7304390048	PIPES,SMLS,I/S,NESOI,DIAM,190.5-285.8,WAL LT12.7MM	Standard Pipe	Pipe and Tube
7304390062	PIPE,SMLS,I/S,NESOI,DIAM 285.8-406.4,WAL LT 12.7MM	Standard Pipe	Pipe and Tube
7304390076	TUBE,PIPE,SMLS,I/S,NESOI,DIAM GT 406.4,WAL LT 19MM	Standard Pipe	Pipe and Tube
7304390080	TUBE,PIPE,SMLS,I/S,NESOI,DIAM GT 406.4,WAL GT=19MM	Standard Pipe	Pipe and Tube
7304598010	OTH TPS,SMS,ASNSS,CS,NTCL-T,NESOI,OD UN 38.1 MM	Standard Pipe	Pipe and Tube
7304598015	OTH TPS,SMS,ASNSS,CS,NESOI OD38.1NOV114.3MMWL6.4MM	Standard Pipe	Pipe and Tube
7304598030	OTH TPS,SMS,ASNSS,CS NES,ODOV114.3UN190.5,WTUN12.7	Standard Pipe	Pipe and Tube
7304598045	OTH TPS,SMS,ASNSS,CS,NES,OD190.5,NTOV285.8WTUN12.7	Standard Pipe	Pipe and Tube
7304598060	OTH TPS,SMS,ASNSS,CS,NESOI,ODO285.8NOV406.4WTU12.7	Standard Pipe	Pipe and Tube
7304598080	OTH TPS,SMS,ASNSS,CS,NESOI,OD OV 406.4 MM	Standard Pipe	Pipe and Tube
7306305025	OTH TUBES ETC NES WLD CIRC OD NO 114.3, GAL W CPLG	Standard Pipe	Pipe and Tube
7306305028	OTH TUBES ETC WLD CIR GALV WO CPL INTNL CTD OR LND	Standard Pipe	Pipe and Tube
7306305032	OTH PIPES ETC WLD CIR GLV WO CPLG O LNG ETC	Standard Pipe	Pipe and Tube
7306305040	OTH TUBES ETC NES OD NO 114.3MM NGAL IMP W COUPLNG	Standard Pipe	Pipe and Tube
7306305055	OTH TUBES ETC IOS NONAL WLD NO 114.3 OD CCS NGL NS	Standard Pipe	Pipe and Tube
7306305085	PIPES ETC IOS CRC GV WL 1.65MM AO TH OD 114-406MM	Standard Pipe	Pipe and Tube
7306305090	PIPES ETC IR/ST NGL WL THKNS 1.65MM AO OD 114-406	Standard Pipe	Pipe and Tube
7304220030	DRILL PIPE,STAINLESS STEEL,DIAM <=168.3,THICK <=9.5MM SEAMLESS	Oil Country Goods	Pipe and Tube
7304220045	DRILL PIPE,STAINLESS STEEL,DIAM <=168.3,THICK > 9.5MM SEAMLESS	Oil Country Goods	Pipe and Tube
7304220060	DRILL PIPE,STAINLESS STEEL,DIAM >168.3 SEAMLESS	Oil Country Goods	Pipe and Tube
7304233000	DRILL PIPE,IRON OR NON ALLOY STEEL SEAMLESS	Oil Country Goods	Pipe and Tube
7304236030	DRILL PIPE,ALLOY STEEL,DIAM <=168.3,THICK <=9.5MM SEAMLESS	Oil Country Goods	Pipe and Tube
7304236045	DRILL PIPE,ALLOY STEEL,DIAM <=168.3,THICK > 9.5MM SEAMLESS	Oil Country Goods	Pipe and Tube
7304236060	DRILL PIPE,ALLOY STEEL,DIAM >168.3 SEAMLESS	Oil Country Goods	Pipe and Tube
7304243010	CAS,DRLL F/OIL/GAS,STAINLESS STL,THRD/COUPL,OUTD<215.9,WT<12.7 SEAMLESS	Oil Country Goods	Pipe and Tube
7304243020	CAS,DRLL F/OIL/GAS,STAINLESS STL,THRD/COUPL,OUTD<215.9,W>=12.7 SEAMLESS	Oil Country Goods	Pipe and Tube
7304243030	CAS,DRLL,OIL/GAS,STAINLESS STL,THRD/C,OD>=215.9<=285,W<12.7 SEAMLESS	Oil Country Goods	Pipe and Tube
7304243040	CAS,DRLL,OIL/GAS,STAINLESS STL,THRD/C,OD>=215.9<=285,W>12.7 SEAMLESS	Oil Country Goods	Pipe and Tube
7304243050	CAS,DRLL,OIL/GAS,STAINLESS STL,THRD/C,OD>285.8<=406.W<12.7 SEAMLESS	Oil Country Goods	Pipe and Tube
7304243060	CAS,DRLL,OIL/GAS,STAINLESS STL,THRD/C,OD>=285.8<=406.W>=12.7 SEAMLESS	Oil Country Goods	Pipe and Tube
7304243080	CAS,DRLL,OIL/GAS,STAINLESS STL,THRD/C,OUTS DIA >406.4 SEAMLESS	Oil Country Goods	Pipe and Tube
7304244010	STAINLESS STL,N/THRD/CPLD,OUTD<215.9,WT<12.7 SEAMLESS	Oil Country Goods	Pipe and Tube
7304244020	STAINLESS STL,N/THRD/CPLD,OUTD<215.9,WT>=12.7 SEAMLESS	Oil Country Goods	Pipe and Tube
7304244030	STAINLESS STL,N/THRD/CPLD,OUTD>=215.9<=285,WT<12.7 SEAMLESS	Oil Country Goods	Pipe and Tube
7304244040	STAINLESS STL,N/THRD/CPLD,OUTD>=215.9<=285,WT>=12.7 SEAMLESS	Oil Country Goods	Pipe and Tube
7304244050	STAINLESS STL,N/THRD/CPLD,OUTD>285.8<=406,WT<12.7 SEAMLESS	Oil Country Goods	Pipe and Tube
7304244060	STAINLESS STL,N/THRD/CPLD,OUTD>=285.8<=406,WT>=12.7 SEAMLESS	Oil Country Goods	Pipe and Tube
7304244080	STAINLESS STL,N/THRD/CPLD,OUTSIDE DIA>406.4 SEAMLESS	Oil Country Goods	Pipe and Tube
7304246015	OIL WELL TUBING OF STAINLESS STEEL,OUTS D <=114.3,WALL TH <=9.5 SEAMLESS	Oil Country Goods	Pipe and Tube
7304246030	OIL WELL TUBING OF STAINLESS STEEL,OUTS D <=114.3,WALL TH >9.5 SEAMLESS	Oil Country Goods	Pipe and Tube
7304246045	OIL WELL TUBING OF STAINLESS STEEL,OUTS D >114.3<215.9MM SEAMLESS	Oil Country Goods	Pipe and Tube
7304246060	OIL WELL TUBING OF STAINLESS STEEL,OUTS D=>215.9<=406.4MM SEAMLESS	Oil Country Goods	Pipe and Tube
7304246075	OIL WELL TUBING OF STAINLESS STEEL,OUTS D>406.4MM SEAMLESS	Oil Country Goods	Pipe and Tube
7304291010	CASING, SEAMLESS,IRON/STEEL,THREAD,DIAM LT 215.9MM	Oil Country Goods	Pipe and Tube
7304291020	CASING,SEMLES,RN/STL,DIAM LT 215.9MM,WALL GT=12.7	Oil Country Goods	Pipe and Tube
7304291030	CASING,SEMLES,IRON/STELL,THREAD,DIAM 215.9-285.8MM	Oil Country Goods	Pipe and Tube
7304291040	CASING,SEM,IRN/STL,THRD,215.9-285.8,THK GT 12.7MM	Oil Country Goods	Pipe and Tube
7304291050	CASING,SEM,IRN/STL,THRD(285.8-406.4),THK LT 12.7MM	Oil Country Goods	Pipe and Tube
7304291060	CASING,SMLES,IRN/STL,(285.8-406.4)THK GT=12.7MM	Oil Country Goods	Pipe and Tube
7304291080	CASING,SEAMLES,IRON/STEEL,THREAD,DIAM GT 406.4MM	Oil Country Goods	Pipe and Tube
7304292010	CASING,SEM,IRN/STL,NESOI,DIA LT 215.9THK LT 12.7MM	Oil Country Goods	Pipe and Tube
7304292020	CASING,SEM,IRN/STL,NESOI,DIAM LT 215.9,GT=12.7MM	Oil Country Goods	Pipe and Tube
7304292030	CASING,SEMLES,IRN/STL,NESOI,215.9-285.8 LT 12.7MM	Oil Country Goods	Pipe and Tube
7304292040	CASING,SMLES,IRN/STL,NESOI,215.9-285.8 GT=12.7MM	Oil Country Goods	Pipe and Tube
7304292050	CASING,SEMLES,IRN/STL,NESOI,285.8-406.4 LT 12.7MM	Oil Country Goods	Pipe and Tube
7304292060	CASING,SMLES,IRN/STL,NESOI,285.8-406.4 GT=12.7MM	Oil Country Goods	Pipe and Tube
7304292080	CASING, SEMLES, IRON/STEEL, NESOI,DIAM GT 406.4MM	Oil Country Goods	Pipe and Tube
7304293110	CAS,DRLL F/OIL/GAS,ALLOY STL,THRD/COUPL,OUTD<215.9,WT<12.7 SEAMLESS	Oil Country Goods	Pipe and Tube
7304293120	CAS,DRLL F/OIL/GAS,ALLOY STL,THRD/COUPL,OUTD<215.9,W>=12.7 SEAMLESS	Oil Country Goods	Pipe and Tube
7304293130	CAS,DRLL,OIL/GAS,ALLOY STL,THRD/C,OD>=215.9<=285,W<12.7SEAMLESS	Oil Country Goods	Pipe and Tube
7304293140	CAS,DRLL,OIL/GAS,ALLOY STL,THRD/C,OD>=215.9<=285,W>=12.7 SEAMLESS	Oil Country Goods	Pipe and Tube
7304293150	CAS,DRLL,OIL/GAS,ALLOY STL,THRD/C,OD>285.8<=406.W<12.7 SEAMLESS	Oil Country Goods	Pipe and Tube
7304293160	CAS,DRLL,OIL/GAS,ALLOY STL,THRD/C,OD>=285.8<=406.W>=12.7 SEAMLESS	Oil Country Goods	Pipe and Tube
7304293180	CAS,DRLL,OIL/GAS,ALLOY STL,THRD/C,OUTS DIA >406.4 SEAMLESS	Oil Country Goods	Pipe and Tube
7304294110	ALLOY STL,N/THRD/CPLD,OUTD<215.9,WT<12.7 SEAMLESS	Oil Country Goods	Pipe and Tube
7304294120	ALLOY STL,N/THRD/CPLD,OUTD<215.9,WT>=12.7 SEAMLESS	Oil Country Goods	Pipe and Tube
7304294130	ALLY STL,N/THRD/CPLD,OUTD>=215.9<=285,WT<12.7 SEAMLESS	Oil Country Goods	Pipe and Tube
7304294140	ALLY STL,N/THRD/CPLD,OUTD>=215.9<=285,WT>=12.7 SEAMLESS	Oil Country Goods	Pipe and Tube
7304294150	ALLY STL,N/THRD/CPLD,OUTD>285.8<=406,WT<12.7 SEAMLESS	Oil Country Goods	Pipe and Tube
7304294160	ALLY STL,N/THRD/CPLD,OUTD>=285.8<=406,WT>=12.7 SEAMLESS	Oil Country Goods	Pipe and Tube
7304294180	ALLY STL,N/THRD/CPLD,OUTSIDE DIA>406.4 SEAMLESS	Oil Country Goods	Pipe and Tube
7304295015	TUBING,SM,OIL/GAS,IRN/STL,DIAM GT 114.3,LT=9.5MM	Oil Country Goods	Pipe and Tube
7304295030	TUBING,SEM,OIL/GAS,IRN/STL,DIAM GT 114.3,GT 9.5MM	Oil Country Goods	Pipe and Tube
7304295045	TUBING,SEM,OIL/GAS,IRON/STL,DIAM 114.3-215.9MM	Oil Country Goods	Pipe and Tube
7304295060	TUBING,SEMLS,OIL/GAS,IR/STL,DIAM (215.9-406.4MM)	Oil Country Goods	Pipe and Tube

7304295075	TUBING,SEMLS,OIL/GAS,IRON/STEEL,DIAM GT 406.4MM	Oil Country Goods	Pipe and Tube
7304296115	OIL WELL TUBING OF ALLOY STEEL,OUTS D <=114.3,WALL TH <=9.5 SEAMLESS	Oil Country Goods	Pipe and Tube
7304296130	OIL WELL TUBING OF ALLOY STEEL,OUTS D <=114.3,WALL TH >9.5 SEAMLESS	Oil Country Goods	Pipe and Tube
7304296145	OIL WELL TUBING OF ALLOY STEEL,OUTS D >114.3<215.9MM SEAMLESS	Oil Country Goods	Pipe and Tube
7304296160	OIL WELL TUBING OF ALLOY STEEL,OUTS D=>215.9<=406.4MM SEAMLESS	Oil Country Goods	Pipe and Tube
7304296175	OIL WELL TUBING OF ALLOY STEEL,OUTS D>406.4MM SEAMLESS	Oil Country Goods	Pipe and Tube
7305202000	CASING OIL/GAS DRILLNG,I/S,THREAD,GT 406.4MM DI	Oil Country Goods	Pipe and Tube
7305204000	CASING OIL/GAS DRILL IRN/STL,DIAM GT 406.4MM,NESOI	Oil Country Goods	Pipe and Tube
7305206000	CASING OIL/GAS DRILLNG ALLOY STL,THREAD,GT 406.4MM	Oil Country Goods	Pipe and Tube
7305208000	CASING OIL/GAS DRLL ALLOY STL,DIA GT 406.4MM,NESOI	Oil Country Goods	Pipe and Tube
7306213000	OILWELL CASING,STAINLESS STEEL, THREADED OR COUPLED O/THN SEAMLESS	Oil Country Goods	Pipe and Tube
7306214000	OILWELL CASING,STAINLESS STEEL, OTHER O/THN SEAMLESS	Oil Country Goods	Pipe and Tube
7306218010	OILWELL TUBE,STAINLESS STEEL,W/COUPL O/THN SEAMLESS	Oil Country Goods	Pipe and Tube
7306218050	OILWELL TUBING,STAINLESS STEEL, OTHER O/THN SEAMLESS	Oil Country Goods	Pipe and Tube
7306291030	OILWELL CASING,IRON OR NONALLOY STEEL, THREADED OR COUPLED W/CPL O/THN	Oil Country Goods	Pipe and Tube
7306291090	OILWELL TUBING,IRON OR NONALLOY STEEL, THREADED OTHER O/THN SEAMLESS	Oil Country Goods	Pipe and Tube
7306292000	OILWELL CASINGS, IRON/N/ALLOY, NOT THREADED/COUPL O/THN SEAMLESS	Oil Country Goods	Pipe and Tube
7306293100	OILWELL CASINGS, ALLO&, THREADED OR COUPLED O/THN SEAMLESS	Oil Country Goods	Pipe and Tube
7306294100	TUBES,PIPES,OIL CSNG,ALLOY STL,N/THREAD,CPLD O/THN SEAMLESS	Oil Country Goods	Pipe and Tube
7306296010	OILWELL TUBE,IRON/NONALLOY STEEL,WITH COUPLING O/THN SEAMLESS	Oil Country Goods	Pipe and Tube
7306296050	OILWELL TUBE,IRON OR N/ALLOY STEEL,WO/CPLG O/THN SEAMLESS	Oil Country Goods	Pipe and Tube
7306298110	OILWELL TUBE,ALLOY,OTHER,W/COUPL O/THN SEAMLESS	Oil Country Goods	Pipe and Tube
7306298150	OILWELL TUBES,ALLOY,OTHER,W/O COUPLING O/THN SEAMLESS	Oil Country Goods	Pipe and Tube
7304110020	TUBES,PIPES STAINLESS STEEL WITH AN OUTSIDE DIAMETE=<114.3 MM SEAMLESS	Line Pipe	Pipe and Tube
7304110050	TUBE,PIPE STAINLESS STEEL WI OUTSIDE DIAMETR>114.3<=406.4 MM SEAMLESS	Line Pipe	Pipe and Tube
7304110080	TUBES/PIPES OF STAINLESS STEEL W/ OUTSIDE DIAMTER>406.4 MM SEAMLESS	Line Pipe	Pipe and Tube
7304191020	IRON/NONALLOY ST LINE PIPE WITH OUTSIDE DIA NT EXC 114.3 M, SEAMLESS	Line Pipe	Pipe and Tube
7304191030	IRON/NONALLOY ST WITH OUTSI DIA EXC 114.3 MM NT EXC 215.9 M SEAMLESS	Line Pipe	Pipe and Tube
7304191045	IRON/NONALLOY ST,OUTSI DIA>215.9 MM<=406.4 MM,WALL TH<12.7M SEAMLESS	Line Pipe	Pipe and Tube
7304191060	IRON/NONALLOY ST,OUTSI DIA>215.9 MM<=406.4 MM,WALL T>=12.7M SEAMLESS	Line Pipe	Pipe and Tube
7304191080	TUBES,PIPES IRON OR NONALLOY STEEL W/ OUTSIDE DIA>406.4 MM SEAMLESS	Line Pipe	Pipe and Tube
7304195020	TUBES,PIPES ALLOY STEEL WITH AN OUTSIDE DIAMETE=<114.3 MM SEAMLESS	Line Pipe	Pipe and Tube
7304195050	TUBE,PIPE ALLOY STEEL WI OUTSIDE DIAMETR>114.3<=406.4 MM SEAMLESS	Line Pipe	Pipe and Tube
7304195080	TUBES/PIPES OF ALLOY STEEL W/ OUTSIDE DIAMTER>406.4 MM SEAMLESS	Line Pipe	Pipe and Tube
7305111030	OIL LNEPIPE IRON/STL LONGITUDNLY SUBMRGED ARC WELD	Line Pipe	Pipe and Tube
7305111060	LNPIPE IRON/STL LONGT SBMRG ARC WELD,DIAM GT 609.6	Line Pipe	Pipe and Tube
7305115000	LNPIP ALLOY/STL LONGTD SBMERGE ARC WELD,GT 406.4MM	Line Pipe	Pipe and Tube
7305121030	LNPIPE IRON/STL LONGTD WELD,406.4MM-609.6MM DIAM	Line Pipe	Pipe and Tube
7305121060	LINEPIPE IRON/STL LONGITUDNLY WELD,GT 609.6MM DIAM	Line Pipe	Pipe and Tube
7305125000	LINEPIPE ALLOY STL LONGITUD WELD,GT 406.4MM DIAM	Line Pipe	Pipe and Tube
7305191030	LINEPIPE IRON/STL,406.4MM-609.6MM DIAMETER,NESOI	Line Pipe	Pipe and Tube
7305191060	OIL LINEPIPE IRON/STL, EXTNL DIAM GT 609.6MM,NESOI	Line Pipe	Pipe and Tube
7305195000	OIL LINEPIPE ALLOY STL,EXTNL DIAM GT 406.4MM,NESOI	Line Pipe	Pipe and Tube
7306110010	WELDED LINEPIPE OIL/GAS LINE,IRON/N/ALLOY STL,OD NTE 114.3MM STAINLESS	Line Pipe	Pipe and Tube
7306110050	WELDED LINEPIPE OIL/GAS LINE,IRON/N/ALLOY STL,OD >114.3M STAINLESS	Line Pipe	Pipe and Tube
7306191010	LINE PIPES,OIL/GAS LINE,IRON OR NONALLOY STEEL,OD NTE 114.3MM O/THN SEAMLE	Line Pipe	Pipe and Tube
7306191050	LINE PIPES,OIL/GAS LINE, IRON OR NONALLOY, OD OVER 114.3M, O/THN SEAMLESS	Line Pipe	Pipe and Tube
7306195110	LINE PIPES,CLOSED,OIL/GAS LINE,ALLOY STEEL,OD NTE 114.3MM	Line Pipe	Pipe and Tube
7306195150	LINE PIPES,OIL/GAS LINE, ALLOY STEEL, OD OVER 114.3M, O/THN SEAMLESS	Line Pipe	Pipe and Tube
7304313000	HOLLOW BARS,SMLS,NESOI,IRN/STL,CIRCS,COLD-DRWN/ROL	Mechanical Tubing	Pipe and Tube
7304316050	TUBES,PIPE,HOLLO PROFIL,SMLS,IRN/STL,CIR SEC,NESOI	Mechanical Tubing	Pipe and Tube
7304390028	TUBE,PIPE,I/S,NESOI,38.1 LT=114.3WAL6.4 LT=12.7MM	Mechanical Tubing	Pipe and Tube
7304390032	TUBE,PIPE,SMLS,NESOI,38.1 LT=114.3WALGT 12.7MM	Mechanical Tubing	Pipe and Tube
7304390040	PIPE,SMLS,I/S,NESOI,DIAM 114.3-190.5	Mechanical Tubing	Pipe and Tube
7304390044	PIPE,SMLS,IRN/STL,NESOI,DIAM 114.3-190.5WAL GT19MM	Mechanical Tubing	Pipe and Tube
7304390052	PIPE,SMLS,I/S,NESOI,DIAM190.5-285.8,WALL12.7-19MM	Mechanical Tubing	Pipe and Tube
7304390056	PIPE,SMLS,NESOI,DIAM 190.5-285.8,WALL GT=19MM	Mechanical Tubing	Pipe and Tube
7304390068	PIPE,SMLS,I/S,NESOI,DIAM 285.8-406.4WALL12.7-19MM	Mechanical Tubing	Pipe and Tube
7304390072	PIPE,SMLS,IR/STL,NESOI,DIAM 285.8-406.4WAL GT 19MM	Mechanical Tubing	Pipe and Tube
7304511000	TUBES ETC SMLS CIRC ALY NT STNL C-R FR BAL BEARNGS	Mechanical Tubing	Pipe and Tube
7304515060	TUBES ETC SMLS CIRC ALY STL NT SS CR NT FR BLRS ET	Mechanical Tubing	Pipe and Tube
7304591000	TUBES ETC SMLS CIRC ALY NT STLS NT C-R FR BL BRNGS	Mechanical Tubing	Pipe and Tube
7304596000	TUBES ETC SMLS CIRC HT RESIS ST NES NCR NT FR BLRS	Mechanical Tubing	Pipe and Tube
7304598020	OTH TPS,SMS,ASNSS,CS,NES,OD38.1NOV114.3W6.4NOV12.7	Mechanical Tubing	Pipe and Tube
7304598025	OTH TPS,SMS,ASNSS,CS,NESOI,OD38.1 NOV114.3WTOV12.7	Mechanical Tubing	Pipe and Tube
7304598035	OTH TPS,SMS,ASNSS,CS NES,ODOV114.3UN190.5WT12.7U19	Mechanical Tubing	Pipe and Tube
7304598040	OTH TPS,SMS,ASNSS,CS,NESOI,ODO114.3UN190.5WT19O O	Mechanical Tubing	Pipe and Tube
7304598050	OTH TPS,SMS,ASNSS,CS,NES,OD190.5 NOV285.8WT12.7U19	Mechanical Tubing	Pipe and Tube
7304598055	OTH TPS,SMS,ASNSS,CS,NES,OD190.5 NOV285.8 WT19O OV	Mechanical Tubing	Pipe and Tube
7304598065	OTH TPS,SMS,ASNSS,CS,NES,ODOV285.8NOV406.4W12.7U19	Mechanical Tubing	Pipe and Tube
7304598070	OTH TPS,SMS,ASNSS,CS,NES,ODOV285.8NOV406.4,WT19 AO	Mechanical Tubing	Pipe and Tube
7304905000	TUBES ETC SMLS NES NONCIRC CS 4MM THCK OR LS I/NAS	Mechanical Tubing	Pipe and Tube
7304907000	TUBES ETC SMLS NES NONCIRC CS 4MM THCK OR LS ALSTL	Mechanical Tubing	Pipe and Tube
7306301000	OTH TUBES ETC NES CIRC WLD NAS WLS LSTH 1.65MM THK	Mechanical Tubing	Pipe and Tube
7306305015	TUBES ETC WLD CIR NES NAS OV 1.65 THK COLD-DRAWN	Mechanical Tubing	Pipe and Tube
7306305020	OTH TUBES ETC NES WLD CIRCS CLD-RLD WLS 1.65-2.54	Mechanical Tubing	Pipe and Tube
7306305035	TUBE/PIPE HOLLOWS FR REDRWNG WLD CCS IOS NAL NESOI	Mechanical Tubing	Pipe and Tube
7306501000	OTH TUBES ETC NES WLD CIR ALY STL NT ST WLS LT1.65	Mechanical Tubing	Pipe and Tube
7306505030	OTH TUBES ETC NES WLD CIR ALY STL C-WKD NT STNLS	Mechanical Tubing	Pipe and Tube
7306505050	OTH TUBES ETC NES WLD CIR ALY ST NS OD NOV 114.3MM	Mechanical Tubing	Pipe and Tube
7306505070	OTH TUBES ETC NES WLD CIR ALY ST OD 114.3-406.4 MM	Mechanical Tubing	Pipe and Tube

Appendix K

7306615000	TUBES,PIPES,WELDED,SQR/RECT,IOS N/ALLOY,WALL THICK < 4MM	Mechanical Tubing	Pipe and Tube
7306617060	TUBES,PIPES,WELDED,SQR/RECT,ALLOY ST,WALL THICK < 4MM,OTHE	Mechanical Tubing	Pipe and Tube
7306695000	TUBES,PIPES,O/WELDED,NON-CIR,IOS N/ALLOY,WALL THICK < 4MM	Mechanical Tubing	Pipe and Tube
7306697060	TUBES,PIPES,O/WELDED,NON-CIR,ALLOY ST,WALL THICK < 4MM,OTHE	Mechanical Tubing	Pipe and Tube
7304316010	TUBES,PIPE,HOLOW PROFILE,SMLS,NESOI,IRN/STL,BOILER	Pressure Tubing	Pipe and Tube
7304390002	TUBS,PIPE,HOLOW PROFIL,SMLS,IRN/STL,BOIL,LT 38.1MM	Pressure Tubing	Pipe and Tube
7304390004	TUBE,PIPE,PROFIL,SMLS,IRN/STL,BOILER 38.1-190.5MM	Pressure Tubing	Pipe and Tube
7304390006	TUBS,PIPE,PROFIL,SMLS,IRN/STL,BOILR,190.5-285.8MM	Pressure Tubing	Pipe and Tube
7304390008	TUBS,PIPE,PROFIL,SMLS,IRN/STL,BOIL,DIAM GT 285.8MM	Pressure Tubing	Pipe and Tube
7304515015	TUBES ETC SMLS CIRC CS HEAT RESIS ST NES CR FR BLR	Pressure Tubing	Pipe and Tube
7304515045	TUBES ETC SMLS CIRC CS CR FR BOILRS NT HT RESIS ST	Pressure Tubing	Pipe and Tube
7304592030	TUBES ETC SMLS CIRC HT RESIS ST NES NCR FR BOILERS	Pressure Tubing	Pipe and Tube
7304592040	OTH TPS,SMS,ASNSS,CS,FR BLRS,ETC,NT HRS OD38.1MMOL	Pressure Tubing	Pipe and Tube
7304592045	OTH TPS,SMS,ASNSS,CS,FBLRS,ETCNHRSOD38.1NOV114.3MM	Pressure Tubing	Pipe and Tube
7304592055	OYH TPS;SMLS;ASNSS;CS;FBLRS,NHR OD OV114.3NOV190.5	Pressure Tubing	Pipe and Tube
7304592060	OTH TPS;SMS;ASNSS;CS;FBLRS,NHR OD 190.5NOV285.8MM	Pressure Tubing	Pipe and Tube
7304592070	OTH TPS,SMS,ASNSS,CS,FBLRS,NHR OD OV285.8 L406.4MM	Pressure Tubing	Pipe and Tube
7304592080	OTH TPS,SMS,ASNSS,CS,FBLRS,ETC,NHRS OD OV 406.4 MM	Pressure Tubing	Pipe and Tube
7306305010	TUBES ETC WLD CIRC NES NAS OV 1.65 THK FR BOILR ET	Pressure Tubing	Pipe and Tube
7306505010	OTH TUBES ETC NES WLD CIR ALY STL NT SS F BLRS ETC	Pressure Tubing	Pipe and Tube
7304413005	TUBES/ETC SMLS CCS HI-NI SS CLD-RLD EXT DI UN 19MM	Stainless Pipe & Tubing	Pipe and Tube
7304413015	TUBES PPS ETC SMLS CS SS BLRS ETC CR EXT DIA UN 19	Stainless Pipe & Tubing	Pipe and Tube
7304413045	TUBES PPES ETC SMLS CCS SS CR NES EXT DIAM UN 19MM	Stainless Pipe & Tubing	Pipe and Tube
7304416005	TBES/ETC SMLS CCS HI-NI SS CLD-RLD EXT DIA 19MM OM	Stainless Pipe & Tubing	Pipe and Tube
7304416015	TUBES PPS ETC SMLS CCS SS CR BLRS EXT DI 19MM OM	Stainless Pipe & Tubing	Pipe and Tube
7304416045	TUBES PPES ETC SMLS CCS SS CR NES EXT DIAM 19MM OM	Stainless Pipe & Tubing	Pipe and Tube
7304490005	TUBES PIPES ETC SMLS CIRC CS HI-NI SS NOT COLD-RLD	Stainless Pipe & Tubing	Pipe and Tube
7304490015	HOLLOW BRS SS SMLS CIRC CS NOT COLD-DRAWN, NESOI	Stainless Pipe & Tubing	Pipe and Tube
7304490045	TUBES PIPES ETC SS CIRC CS NT HLW BARS FOR BOILERS	Stainless Pipe & Tubing	Pipe and Tube
7304490060	TUBES PIPES ETC SS CIRC CS NT HLW BRS NT FR BOILRS	Stainless Pipe & Tubing	Pipe and Tube
7306401010	OTH SS P/T/HP WD CIRC WL UN 1.65MM OV .5% NCKL ETC	Stainless Pipe & Tubing	Pipe and Tube
7306401015	OTH SS P/T/HP WD CCS WL UN 1.65 OV .5% NCKL NESOI	Stainless Pipe & Tubing	Pipe and Tube
7306401090	OTH TUBES WLD CCS SS WLS LT 1.65MM TH NOV 0.5% NI	Stainless Pipe & Tubing	Pipe and Tube
7306405005	TUBES ETC WLD CIRC CS HI-NI STAINLS STL 1.65MMOM	Stainless Pipe & Tubing	Pipe and Tube
7306405015	TUBES ETC NES WLD CIRC STNLS STL 1.65MMOM FR BOILR	Stainless Pipe & Tubing	Pipe and Tube
7306405040	TUBES WLD CCS SS 1.65MM OM CR OV 0.5 BUT LT 24% NI	Stainless Pipe & Tubing	Pipe and Tube
7306405042	OTH SS P/T/HP CR CRC CS WLL 1.65MM AO UN 15% CHROM	Stainless Pipe & Tubing	Pipe and Tube
7306405044	OTH SS T/P/HP CR CIRC CS WLL 1.65MM AO THCK NESOI	Stainless Pipe & Tubing	Pipe and Tube
7306405062	OTH SS T/P/HP CCS WL 1.65 AO THK OD NOV 114.3 ETC	Stainless Pipe & Tubing	Pipe and Tube
7306405064	TUBES WD CS SS WLS OV1.65 OD NO114.3 0.5 LT 24% NI	Stainless Pipe & Tubing	Pipe and Tube
7306405080	TUBES WD CS SS WLS OV 1.65 OD NO114.3 NOV 0.5% NI	Stainless Pipe & Tubing	Pipe and Tube
7306405085	TUBES WLD CCS SS OD 114.3-406.4MM OV 0.5 LT 24% NI	Stainless Pipe & Tubing	Pipe and Tube
7306405090	TUBES WLD CCS SS OD 114.3-406.4MM NOV 0.5% NICKEL	Stainless Pipe & Tubing	Pipe and Tube
7306617030	TUBES,PIPES,WELDED,SQR/RECT,ALLOY ST,WT < 4MM, STAINLESS S	Stainless Pipe & Tubing	Pipe and Tube
7306697030	TUBES,PIPES,O/WELDED,NON-CIR,ALLOY ST,WT < 4MM, STAINLESS S	Stainless Pipe & Tubing	Pipe and Tube
7304515005	TUBES ETC SMLS CIRC CS HI-NI ALY STL NES CLD-ROLLD	Pipe & Tubing Nonclassified	Pipe and Tube
7305901000	OTH TUBES, PIPES NESOI RIVETED ETC NT WLD IR/NALST	Pipe & Tubing Nonclassified	Pipe and Tube
7305905000	OTH TUBES, PIPES NESOI RIVETED ETC NT WLD AL	Pipe & Tubing Nonclassified	Pipe and Tube
7306901000	OTH TUBES ETC, NESOI, OF IRON OR NONALLOY STEEL	Pipe & Tubing Nonclassified	Pipe and Tube
7306905000	OTH TUBES ETC, NESOI, OF ALLOY STEEL	Pipe & Tubing Nonclassified	Pipe and Tube
7304901000	TUBES ETC SMLS NES NONCIRC CS OV 4MM THCK IR/NALST	Structural Pipe & Tube	Pipe and Tube
7304903000	TUBES ETC SMLS NES NONCIRC CS OV 4MM THCK ALLOY ST	Structural Pipe & Tube	Pipe and Tube
7305312000	TAPERED STL PIPES, TUBES LONG WLD FOR LIGHT POLES	Structural Pipe & Tube	Pipe and Tube
7305314000	TUBES, PIPES NESOI, LONGITUDNLY WELDED IRN/NAL STL	Structural Pipe & Tube	Pipe and Tube
7305316000	TUBES, PIPES NESOI LONGITUD WELDED OF ALLOY STEEL	Structural Pipe & Tube	Pipe and Tube
7306303000	TAPRD PIPES ETC NES WLD CIRC 1.65 AO IOS NA LT PLS	Structural Pipe & Tube	Pipe and Tube
7306503000	TAPERED PIPES, ALY STL EX STNLS OV1.65MM FR LITEPL	Structural Pipe & Tube	Pipe and Tube
7306611000	TUBES,PIPES,WELDED,SQR/RECT,IOS N/ALLOY,WALL THICK => 4MM	Structural Pipe & Tube	Pipe and Tube
7306613000	TUBES,PIPES,WELDED,SQR/RECT,ALLOY,WALL THICK => 4MM	Structural Pipe & Tube	Pipe and Tube
7306691000	TUBES,PIPES,WELDED,OTH NON-CIR,IOS N/ALLOY,WALL THICK => 4MM	Structural Pipe & Tube	Pipe and Tube
7306693000	TUBES,PIPES,WELDED,OTH NON-CIR,ALLOY,WALL THICK => 4MM	Structural Pipe & Tube	Pipe and Tube
7305391000	TUBES, PIPES NESOI, WLD NOT LONGIT, IRN/NAL STL	Pipe for Piling	Pipe and Tube
7305395000	TUBES, PIPES NESOI, WLD NOT LONGITUD, ALLOY ST	Pipe for Piling	Pipe and Tube
7217101000	FLAT WIRE IR/STL NOT PLAT/COTD,LT .25%CA,LT=.25MM	Wire Drawn	Long Products
7217102000	FLAT WIRE,IR/STL NOT PLT LT .25%CARB,(.25-1.25MM)	Wire Drawn	Long Products
7217103000	FLT WIRE,IR/STL NOT PLTD,LT .25%CARB,GT 1.25MM TH	Wire Drawn	Long Products
7217104030	ROUND WIRE,IR/STL,NOT/PLT LT .25%CAR,LT 1.5MM HEAT	Wire Drawn	Long Products
7217104090	ROUND WIRE,IR/STL NOT/PLTD LT.25%CA,LT 1.5MM,NHEAT	Wire Drawn	Long Products
7217105030	ROUND WIRE,IR/STL N PLT LT .25%CAR,GT=1.5MM, HEATD	Wire Drawn	Long Products
7217105090	ROUND WIRE,IR/STL N PLT LT .25%CA GT=1.5MM N HEATD	Wire Drawn	Long Products
7217106000	OTH WIRE,IR/NONALY STEEL NOT PLATD, LT 0.25% CARB	Wire Drawn	Long Products
7217107000	FLAT WIRE IRON/NALY STEEL,NOT PLATED,GT=0.25% CARB	Wire Drawn	Long Products
7217108010	RND WIRE IRON/STEEL,NT PLT (.25-.6% CARBON),HEATED	Wire Drawn	Long Products
7217108020	RND WIRE IRON/STL NT PLT(.25-.6%CARB), NOT HEATED	Wire Drawn	Long Products
7217108025	RND WIRE IRON/STL,N/PLTD,HEAT LT 1MM, GT 0.6%CARB	Wire Drawn	Long Products
7217108030	RND WIRE IRN/STL,N/PLTD,HEAT,(1-1.5MM),GT 0.6%CARB	Wire Drawn	Long Products
7217108045	RND WIRE,IRON/STL,N/PLTD,LT=1.5MM,GT 0.6% CARB,HT	Wire Drawn	Long Products

7217108060	RND WIRE IRON/STL,N/PLTD,LT 1MM,GT .6%CARB,N HEAT	Wire Drawn	Long Products
7217108075	RND WIRE,IR/STL,N/PLTD,(1.0-1.5MM),GT .6%CRB,N/HTD	Wire Drawn	Long Products
7217108090	RND WIRE,IRN/STL,N/PLT,GT=1.5MM DI,GT .6%CRB,N/HT	Wire Drawn	Long Products
7217109000	OTHER WIRE,IRON/NON ALLOY STEEL, NT PLATED, NESOI	Wire Drawn	Long Products
7217201500	FLAT WIRE,IRON/NONALY STL,PLATED OR COATD WTH ZINC	Wire Drawn	Long Products
7217203000	RND WIRE,IRN/STL,PLT W/ZINC,GT=1.5MM,LT 0.25% CARB	Wire Drawn	Long Products
7217204510	ROUND WIRE,IR/STL PLTD W/ZINC,LT 1.0MM,LT .25%CARB	Wire Drawn	Long Products
7217204520	RND WIRE IRON/STL,ZINC PLT,LT 1MM ,(.25-.6%CARBON)	Wire Drawn	Long Products
7217204530	RND WIRE IRON/STL,ZINC PLTD, LT 1.0MM,GT=.6% CARB	Wire Drawn	Long Products
7217204540	RND WI,IR/STL,PLT W/ZI,GT=1.0M,LT 1.5MM,GT .25%CRB	Wire Drawn	Long Products
7217204550	RND WI IR/STL,PLT ZINC,(1-1.5MM),(0.25-0.6%) CARB	Wire Drawn	Long Products
7217204560	RND WIRE,IR/STL,PLT ZINC,(1.0-1.5MM),GT=.6% CARBON	Wire Drawn	Long Products
7217204570	RND WIRE IR/STL ZINC,PLT,GT 1.5MM,(0.25-0.6%) CARB	Wire Drawn	Long Products
7217204580	ROUND WIRE,IR/STL,ZINC PLT,GT=1.5MM DI,GT=.6%CARB	Wire Drawn	Long Products
7217206000	OTH WIRE IR/NALLOY STL,ZINC PLATED,LT 0.25%CARBN	Wire Drawn	Long Products
7217207500	OTH WIRE IRON/NALY STEEL,ZINC PLTD,GT 0.25% CARBN	Wire Drawn	Long Products
7217301530	FLAT WIRE,IR/STL,PLT BASE MTL EX ZIN,GT=.6%CARBON	Wire Drawn	Long Products
7217301560	FLAT WIRE IR/STL,PLT BASE MTL EX ZINC,LT .6% CARB	Wire Drawn	Long Products
7217303000	RND WIRE,IRN/STL PLT BSE MTL,GT=1.5MM,LT.25%CARBON	Wire Drawn	Long Products
7217304504	RND WIRE,IR/STL,PLT BASE MTL,< .20%CAR,ARC WELDING	Wire Drawn	Long Products
7217304511	RND WIRE,IR/STL,PLT BASE MTL,< 1MM,< .25%CARBON	Wire Drawn	Long Products
7217304520	RD WIRE IR/STL,BASE MTL PLT,LT 1MM,(.25-.6%CARBON)	Wire Drawn	Long Products
7217304530	RND WR,IR/STL,PLT BASE MTL EX ZINC,GT 1MM,GT.6%CAR	Wire Drawn	Long Products
7217304541	RD WIRE IR/STL PLT BSE MTL,(1-1.5MM),< .25% CARB	Wire Drawn	Long Products
7217304550	RD WR IR/STL BSE MTL PLT (1.0-1.5MM), (.25-.6CRB)	Wire Drawn	Long Products
7217304560	RND WIRE IRN/STL,PLT BS MTL,(1.0-1.5M),GT .6%CARB	Wire Drawn	Long Products
7217304590	RD WIRE IR/NALY STL,BSE MTL PLTD,GT=1.5MM DIAM	Wire Drawn	Long Products
7217306000	OTH WIRE IR/STL,BASE MTL PLTED EX ZINC,LT .25%CARB	Wire Drawn	Long Products
7217307500	OTH WIRE IR/STL,BSE MTL PLTD EX ZINC,GT=.25% CARB	Wire Drawn	Long Products
7217905030	WIRE IRON/NALY STEEL,PLT/COATD,LT 0.25% CARB,NESOI	Wire Drawn	Long Products
7217905060	WIRE IRON/NALLY STEEL,PLT,(0.25-0.6%CARB),NESOI	Wire Drawn	Long Products
7217905090	WIRE,IRON/NALLOY STEEL,PLTD/CTD,GT=0.6% CARB,NESOI	Wire Drawn	Long Products
7223001015	WIRE STAINLESS STEEL ROUND UNDER 0.25MM DIAMETER	Wire Drawn	Long Products
7223001030	WIRE STAINLESS STEEL ROUND 0.25-UNDER 0.76MM DIAM	Wire Drawn	Long Products
7223001045	WIRE STAINLESS STEEL ROUND 0.76-UNDER 1.52MM DIAM	Wire Drawn	Long Products
7223001060	WIRE STAINLESS STEEL ROUND 1.52-UNDER 5.1MM DIAM	Wire Drawn	Long Products
7223001075	WIRE STAINLESS STEEL ROUND 5.1MM OR MORE DIAMETER	Wire Drawn	Long Products
7223005000	WIRE STAINLESS STEEL FLAT	Wire Drawn	Long Products
7223009000	WIRE STAINLESS STEEL OTHER THAN ROUND OR FLAT	Wire Drawn	Long Products
7229200010	SILICO-MANG WIRE,RND,< 1.6MM,< .20% CAR,PLT COPPER	Wire Drawn	Long Products
7229200015	SILICO-MANG WIRE,RND,< 1.6MM,< .20% CAR,ARC WELD	Wire Drawn	Long Products
7229200090	WIRE OF SILICO-MANGANESE STEEL, NESOI	Wire Drawn	Long Products
7229901000	FLAT WIRE OF OTHER ALLOY STEEL	Wire Drawn	Long Products
7229905006	RND WIRE OTH ALY STL,< 1.6MM, <.20% CAR,COPPER PLT	Wire Drawn	Long Products
7229905008	RND WIRE OTH ALLOY STL,<1.6MM, < .20% CAR, NESOI	Wire Drawn	Long Products
7229905016	ROUND WIRE OTHER ALLOY STEEL DIAMETER UNDER 1.0 MM	Wire Drawn	Long Products
7229905031	RND WIRE OTH ALLOY STL 1.0MM TO UNDR 1.5MM DIAM	Wire Drawn	Long Products
7229905051	ROUND WIRE OTHER ALLOY STEEL DIAMETR 1.5MM OR MORE	Wire Drawn	Long Products
7229909000	OTHER WIRE, NESOI OF OTHER ALLOY STEEL	Wire Drawn	Long Products
7209182510	FLAT RLD IRON/STL;APERATURE MASK CRT;LT .361MM THK	Black Plate	Flat Products
7209182520	FLAT RLD IR/STL;COIL;GT=600MM;< .361MM THK;ANNEALD	Black Plate	Flat Products
7209182580	FLAT RLD IR/STL;COIL;GT=600MM;LT .361MM THK; NESOI	Black Plate	Flat Products
7210110000	FLT RLD IOS NA GT/=600MM W,PLTD/CTD W/TIN,GT/=0.55	Tin Plate	Flat Products
7210120000	FLT RLD IOS NA GT/=600MM,PLTD/CTD TIN,LT 0.5MM THK	Tin Plate	Flat Products
7212100000	FLT RLD IOS NA, LT 600MM, PLTD/CTD W/ TIN	Tin Plate	Flat Products
7210500000	FLT RLD IOS NA GT/=600MM,PLTD/CTD W/CHROM	Tin Free Steel	Flat Products
7208106000	FLT RLD IR/NALLOY STL GT=600MM; HOT ROLL;LT=4.75MM	Sheets Hot Rolled	Flat Products
7208260030	FLT RLD HI-STR IOS NA CLS,GT/=600MM,3-4.75MM THK	Sheets Hot Rolled	Flat Products
7208260060	FLT RLD IOS NA CLS,GT/=600MM,PKLD,3-4.75MMTHCK	Sheets Hot Rolled	Flat Products
7208270030	FLT RLD HI-STR IOS NA CLS,GT/= 600MM,LT 3MM THCK	Sheets Hot Rolled	Flat Products
7208270060	FLAT RLD IOS NA CLS,EX HI-STR,GT/=600MM,LT 3MM THK	Sheets Hot Rolled	Flat Products
7208380015	FLT RLD HI-STR IOS NA CLS,GT/=600MM,3-4.75MM THK	Sheets Hot Rolled	Flat Products
7208380030	FLAT RLD IRON/STL COIL;3-4.75MM THK;UNTRIMMED EDGE	Sheets Hot Rolled	Flat Products
7208380090	FLT RLD IR/NALLOY STL GT=600MM;3-4.75MM THK;NESOI	Sheets Hot Rolled	Flat Products
7208390015	FLT RLD HI-STR IOS NA CLS,GT/=600MM,LT 3MM THCK	Sheets Hot Rolled	Flat Products
7208390030	FLT RLD IRON/STL GT=600MM;LT 3MM THK; UNTRIM EDGE	Sheets Hot Rolled	Flat Products
7208390090	FLT RLD IRN/NALLOY STL GT=600MM;LT 3MM THICK;NESOI	Sheets Hot Rolled	Flat Products
7208406030	FLT RLD IRON/NALLOY STL N COIL GT=600MM;LT 3MM THK	Sheets Hot Rolled	Flat Products
7208406060	FLAT RLD IRON/STL; N COIL;GT=600MM; 3-4.75MM THK	Sheets Hot Rolled	Flat Products
7208530000	FLAT RLD IOS NA,NT CLS,GT/=600MM,3-4.75MM THICK	Sheets Hot Rolled	Flat Products
7208540000	FLT RLD IOS NA, NT CLS, GT/=600MM, LT 3MM THK	Sheets Hot Rolled	Flat Products
7208900000	FLT RLD IOS NA CLS/NT GT/= 600MM,HOT RLD,NESOI	Sheets Hot Rolled	Flat Products
7219130002	FR SS CLS 600MM W HR 3-UN 4.75MM THK ETC	Sheets Hot Rolled	Flat Products
7219130031	FR SS HR CL 3-UN 4.75MM THCK NESOI 1370 MM WD OM	Sheets Hot Rolled	Flat Products
7219130051	FR SS CLS 600-UN 1370 MM W HR 3-UN 4.75MM THK ETC	Sheets Hot Rolled	Flat Products
7219130071	FR SS CLS 600-UN 1370MM W HR 3-UN 4.75MM THK ETC	Sheets Hot Rolled	Flat Products
7219130081	FR SS CLS, OTH, 600-UN 1370 MM W HR NCKL CONTNT N	Sheets Hot Rolled	Flat Products
7219140030	FR SS 1370MM AO W HR CLS UN 3MM THCK	Sheets Hot Rolled	Flat Products
7219140065	HI-NICKEL SS FRLD 600-UN 1370 MM HR CLS UN 3MM THK	Sheets Hot Rolled	Flat Products

7219140090	STNLS STL FR 600-UN 1370MM W HR CLS UN 3MM TH,OTHR	Sheets Hot Rolled	Flat Products
7219230030	FR SS 1370MM AO W HR NT CLD 3-UN 4.75MM THCK	Sheets Hot Rolled	Flat Products
7219230060	FR SS 600 LS THN 1370MM W HR NT CLD 3-UN 4.75MM TK	Sheets Hot Rolled	Flat Products
7219240030	FR SS 1370MM AO W HR NT CLD UNDR 3MM THCK	Sheets Hot Rolled	Flat Products
7219240060	FR SS 600 LS THN 1370MM W HR NT CLD UNDR 3MM TH	Sheets Hot Rolled	Flat Products
7225307000	FR OTH ALLOY STL 600MM W AO HR CLS UN 4.75MM THCK	Sheets Hot Rolled	Flat Products
7225407000	FR OTH ALLOY STL 600MM W AO HR NCL UN 4.75MM THCK	Sheets Hot Rolled	Flat Products
7209150000	FLT RLD IOS NA CLS GT/=600MM W,GT/=3MM THK,CLD-RLD	Sheets Cold Rolled	Flat Products
7209160030	FLAT RLD HI-STRTH IRON/STL;COIL;1-3MM THK;ANNEALED	Sheets Cold Rolled	Flat Products
7209160060	FLAT & COLD RLD HI-STRTH IRON/STL;COIL;1-3MM;NESOI	Sheets Cold Rolled	Flat Products
7209160070	FLT RLD IOS NA GT/=600MM, (1-3MM) THK,CLD-RLD,ANLD	Sheets Cold Rolled	Flat Products
7209160091	FLAT RLD IOS NA CLS GT/=600MM, (1-3MM) THK,CLD-RLD	Sheets Cold Rolled	Flat Products
7209170030	FLT RLD HI-STRTH IRON/STL;COIL;0.5-1MMTHK;ANNEALED	Sheets Cold Rolled	Flat Products
7209170060	FLAT&COLD RLD HI-STRTH IRON/STL;COIL;0.5-1MM;NESOI	Sheets Cold Rolled	Flat Products
7209170070	FLT RLD IOS NA GT/=600MM,(0.5-1MM)THK,CLD-RLD,ANLD	Sheets Cold Rolled	Flat Products
7209170091	FLT RLD IOS NA CLS GT/=600MM,(0.5-1MM) THK,CLD-RLD	Sheets Cold Rolled	Flat Products
7209181530	FLAT RLD HISTRTH IRON/STL;COIL;LT 0.5MMTHK;ANNEAL	Sheets Cold Rolled	Flat Products
7209181560	FLAT RLD IRN/STL; COIL;GT=600MM;LT 0.5MM THK;NESOI	Sheets Cold Rolled	Flat Products
7209186020	FLT RLD IOS NA GT/=600MM,CLD-RLD,ANNEALED,NESOI	Sheets Cold Rolled	Flat Products
7209186090	FLT RLD IOS NA CLS GT/=600MM,CLD-RLD,NESOI	Sheets Cold Rolled	Flat Products
7209250000	FLT RLD IOS NA NT CLS GT/=600MM,GT/=3MM THK,CLD-RL	Sheets Cold Rolled	Flat Products
7209260000	FTD RLD IOS NA NT CLS GT/=600MM,(1-3MM)THK,CLD-RLD	Sheets Cold Rolled	Flat Products
7209270000	FLT RLD IOS NA NT CLS GT/=600MM,0.5-1MMTHK,CLD-RLD	Sheets Cold Rolled	Flat Products
7209280000	FLT RLD IOS NA NT CLS GT/=600MM,LT 0.5MM THK,CLD-R	Sheets Cold Rolled	Flat Products
7209900000	FLT RLD IOS NA CLS/NT GT/=600MM, CLD-RLD, NESOI	Sheets Cold Rolled	Flat Products
7210703000	FLT RLD IRON/STL;PAINTED W/PLSTIC;NT COATD W/METAL	Sheets Cold Rolled	Flat Products
7219320005	HI-NICKEL SS FR 1370MM AO CRLD 3-UN 4.75MM THK CLS	Sheets Cold Rolled	Flat Products
7219320020	FR SS CLS 1370MM AO W CR 3-UN 4.75MM THK OV 0.5% N	Sheets Cold Rolled	Flat Products
7219320025	FR SS CLS 1370MM AO W CR 3-UN 4.75 THK NCKL NESOI	Sheets Cold Rolled	Flat Products
7219320035	HI-NCKL SS FR 600-UN 1370MM CR 3-UN 4.75MM THK CLS	Sheets Cold Rolled	Flat Products
7219320036	FR SS CLS 600-UN 1370MM W CR 3-UN 4.75MM THK, ETC	Sheets Cold Rolled	Flat Products
7219320038	FR SS CLS 600-UN 1370MM W CR 3-UN 4.75MM THCK, ETC	Sheets Cold Rolled	Flat Products
7219320042	OTHR SS FR 600-UN 1370MM CR 3-UN 4.75MM THK COILS	Sheets Cold Rolled	Flat Products
7219320044	FR SS CLS 600-UN 1370MM W CR 3-UN 4.75MM THK,OTHER	Sheets Cold Rolled	Flat Products
7219320045	FR SS 1370MM AO W CR 3-UN 4.75MM THCK NT COILD	Sheets Cold Rolled	Flat Products
7219320060	FR SS 600 LS THN 1370MM W CR 3-UN 4.75MM THCK NCLD	Sheets Cold Rolled	Flat Products
7219330005	HI-NICKEL SS FR 1370 MM AO W CR 1-UN 3MM THK CLS	Sheets Cold Rolled	Flat Products
7219330020	FR SS CLS 1370 AO W CR OV 1-UN 3MM THCK OV 0.5% NK	Sheets Cold Rolled	Flat Products
7219330025	HI-NICKEL SS FR 1370MM AO W CR 1-UN 3MM THCK COILS	Sheets Cold Rolled	Flat Products
7219330035	HI-NICKEL SS FR 600-UN 1370MM CR 1-UN 3MM THK CLS	Sheets Cold Rolled	Flat Products
7219330036	OTH SS 600 COILS,MOLYBDENUM (1.5%-5%)	Sheets Cold Rolled	Flat Products
7219330038	OTHR SS FR 600-UN 1370MM W CR 1-UN 3MM THCK COILS	Sheets Cold Rolled	Flat Products
7219330042	FR SS CLS 600-UN 1370MM W CR OV 1-UN 3MM THK, ETC	Sheets Cold Rolled	Flat Products
7219330044	OTHR SS FR 600-UN 1370MM W CR 1-UN 3MM THCK COILS	Sheets Cold Rolled	Flat Products
7219330045	FR SS 1370MM AO W CR 1-UN 3MM THCK NT COILED	Sheets Cold Rolled	Flat Products
7219330070	FR SS 600-UN 1370 W CR OV 1-UN 3MM TH, NT CLS, NES	Sheets Cold Rolled	Flat Products
7219330080	FR SS 600-UN 1370MM W CR NT CLS 1-UN 3MM THCK NES	Sheets Cold Rolled	Flat Products
7219340005	HI-NICKEL FR SS 600MM AO W CR 0.5-UN 1MM THK COILS	Sheets Cold Rolled	Flat Products
7219340020	FR SS CLS 600MM,THK=0.5-1MM LT .5%NCKL,&(1.5-5%MB)	Sheets Cold Rolled	Flat Products
7219340025	FR SS CLS 600MM THKNS= 0.5-1MM GT 0.5% NCKL,NESO	Sheets Cold Rolled	Flat Products
7219340030	FR SS CLS 600MM AO W CR 0.5-1MM TH UN 15% CHROMIUM	Sheets Cold Rolled	Flat Products
7219340035	FR SS CLS 600MM AO W CR 0.5-1MM THCK, NESOI	Sheets Cold Rolled	Flat Products
7219340050	FR SS 600MM AO W CR 0.5-NOV 1MM THCK NT COILED	Sheets Cold Rolled	Flat Products
7219350005	FR SS 600MM AO W CR UN 0.5MM TH OV 0.5-UN 24% NCKL	Sheets Cold Rolled	Flat Products
7219350015	FR SS 600MM AO W CR UN 0.5MM THK OV 0.5-24% NCKL	Sheets Cold Rolled	Flat Products
7219350030	FR SS 600MM AO W CR UN 0.5MM THCK UN 15% CHROMIUM	Sheets Cold Rolled	Flat Products
7219350035	FR SS CLS 600MM AO W CR UN 0.5MM TH NESOI	Sheets Cold Rolled	Flat Products
7219350050	FR SS 600MM AO W CR LS THN 0.5MM THCK NT COILD	Sheets Cold Rolled	Flat Products
7219900010	HIGH-NICKEL STAINLESS STEELS FR 600M OR MORE NESOI	Sheets Cold Rolled	Flat Products
7219900020	OTH FR SS 600MM AO W OV 0.5% NKL OV 1.5-UN 5% MOLY	Sheets Cold Rolled	Flat Products
7219900025	OTHR FR STNLS STL 600MM AO WIDE, OV 0.5% NCKL NES	Sheets Cold Rolled	Flat Products
7219900060	OTH FR STNLS STL 600MM AO W 0.5% OR LSS NKL, ETC	Sheets Cold Rolled	Flat Products
7219900080	OTHR FR STNLS STL 600MM OR MORE WIDE, NESOI	Sheets Cold Rolled	Flat Products
7225507000	FR HT-RSSTNG STL 600MM W AO CR UN 4.75MM THCK	Sheets Cold Rolled	Flat Products
7225508010	OTH ALLOY STL FR HI-NCKL 600MM AO CR UN 4.75MM THK	Sheets Cold Rolled	Flat Products
7225508015	FR ALLOY S 600MM AO CR UN 4.75MM THK APERTURE MASK	Sheets Cold Rolled	Flat Products
7225508085	FR ALLOY STL NT TOOL 600MM AO CR UN4.75MM THK NESO	Sheets Cold Rolled	Flat Products
7225990010	FR HI-NICKEL ALLOY STL NT STNL STL 600MM W OM NESO	Sheets Cold Rolled	Flat Products
7225990090	FR ALLOY STEEL NT STAINL 600MM OR MORE WIDE NESOI	Sheets Cold Rolled	Flat Products
7210410000	FLT RLD IOS NA GT/=600MM,CRGTD,PLTD/CTD W/ZINC	Sheets & Strip Galv Hot Dipped	Flat Products
7210490030	FLT RLD HI-STR IOS NA GT/=600MM,PLTD/CTD W/ZN,NESO	Sheets & Strip Galv Hot Dipped	Flat Products
7210490091	FTD RLD IOS NA GT=600MM, PLTD/CTD W/ZINC, NESOI, THICK >=0.4mm	Sheets & Strip Galv Hot Dippeded	Flat Products
7210490095	FTD RLD IOS NA GT=600MM, PLTD/CTD W/ZINC, NESOI, THICK <=0.4mm	Sheets & Strip Galv Hot Dippeded	Flat Products
7210706060	FLT RLD IRON/STL;PAINTED PLASTIC;ZINC COATED;NESOI	Sheets & Strip Galv Hot Dipped	Flat Products
7212301030	FLAT RLD IR/STL;PLAT W/ZINC;LT 300MM;LT 51MM COILS	Sheets & Strip Galv Hot Dipped	Flat Products
7212301090	FLT RLD IR/STL;PLD W/ZINC;GT 51MM;CL;GT 0.25MM THK	Sheets & Strip Galv Hot Dipped	Flat Products
7212303000	FLAT ROLL IRON/STL;LT 300MM; PLATED W/ZINC; NESOI	Sheets & Strip Galv Hot Dipped	Flat Products
7212305000	FLAT ROLL IRON/NALLOY STL; PLATED W/ZINC; GT 300MM	Sheets & Strip Galv Hot Dipped	Flat Products
7225920000	FLT-RLD,ALY STL GT/=600MM W,PLT/CT ZINC NT ELCT	Sheets & Strip Galv Hot Dipped	Flat Products
7226990130	FLAT-RLD PROD,ALY STL, FURTH WRKD, PLTED w/ZINC not ELECTROLYTIC. <600 mm wi	Sheets & Strip Galv Hot-Dipped	Flat Products

7210300030	FLT RLD HI-STR NA IOS GT/=600MM, PLTD/CTD W/ZINC	Sheets & Strip Galv Electrolyt	Flat Products
7210300060	FLT RLD IOS NA GT/=600MM,PLTD/CTD W/ZN,EX HI-STR	Sheets & Strip Galv Electrolyt	Flat Products
7210706030	FLT RLD IRON/STL;PNTD W/PLSTIC;ZINC COATD;ELECTRLY	Sheets & Strip Galv Electrolyt	Flat Products
7212200000	FLT RLD IOS NA, LT 600MM,ELCTRLYTC PLTD/CTD W/ZINC	Sheets & Strip Galv Electrolyt	Flat Products
7225910000	FLT-RLD,ALY STL GT/=600MM W,ELCTLC PLT/CT ZN NESOI	Sheets & Strip Galv Electrolyt	Flat Products
7226990110	FLAT-RLD PROD,ALY STL,FURTH WRKD,ELECTROLYTIC. PLTED W/ZINC <600 mm wide	Sheets & Strip Galv Electrolyt	Flat Products
7210200000	FLT RLD IOS NA GT/=600MM,CTD/PLTD W/LEAD,TERNPLT	Sheets & Strip All Other Metalic Coat	Flat Products
7210610000	FLT RLD IOS NA GT/=600MM, PLTD/CTD W/ AL/ZN ALLOYS	Sheets & Strip All Other Metalic Coat	Flat Products
7210690000	FLT RLD IOS NA GT/=600MM,PLTD/CTD W/AL	Sheets & Strip All Other Metalic Coat	Flat Products
7210706090	FLAT RLD IRON/STL;GT=600MM; PAINTED PLASTIC; NESOI	Sheets & Strip All Other Metalic Coat	Flat Products
7210906000	FLT RLD IRON/STL;GT=600MM;ELECTRL COATD W/METAL	Sheets & Strip All Other Metalic Coat	Flat Products
7210909000	FLT RLD IRN/NALLOY STL;GT=600MM;PLATD/COATD; NESOI	Sheets & Strip All Other Metalic Coat	Flat Products
7212500000	FLT RLD IOS NA, LT 600MM, PLATED/COATED, NESOI	Sheets & Strip All Other Metalic Coat	Flat Products
7212600000	FLT-RLD IOS NA, LT 600MM, CLAD, NESOI	Sheets & Strip All Other Metalic Coat	Flat Products
7225110000	FLT-RLD,SILICON ELCTRCL STL,GRAIN ORIENT GT/=600MM	Sheets & Strip-Electrical	Flat Products
7225190000	FLT-RLD,SLCN ELCTRCL STL,NT GRAIN-ORIENT,GT/=600MM	Sheets & Strip-Electrical	Flat Products
7226111000	FR SILICO ELECTRIC STL GRN-ORNTD WDTH 300-600MM W	Sheets & Strip-Electrical	Flat Products
7226119030	FR SILIC ELEC STL GRN-ORN LT 300MM W NOV .25MM THK	Sheets & Strip-Electrical	Flat Products
7226119060	FR SILIC ELECT STL GRN-ORN LT 300MM GT 0.25MM THCK	Sheets & Strip-Electrical	Flat Products
7226191000	FR SILICO ELECTRIC STL NT GRN-ORNTD 300-600MM WIDE	Sheets & Strip-Electrical	Flat Products
7226199000	FR SI ELEC STL NT GRN-ORN LT 300MM W NOV .25MM THK	Sheets & Strip-Electrical	Flat Products
7211191500	FLAT ROLLED; HI-STRENGTH STEEL;HOT ROLL;LT 300MM	Strip-Hot Rolled	Flat Products
7211192000	FLT&HOT RLD IRN/STL;LT 300MM;NOT CLAD;GT 1.25MMTHK	Strip-Hot Rolled	Flat Products
7211193000	FLT&HOT RLD IRN/STL;LT 300MM;NOT CLAD;LT 1.25MMTHK	Strip-Hot Rolled	Flat Products
7211194500	FLAT&HOT ROLLED HI-STRGH STEEL;(300-600MM); NESOI	Strip-Hot Rolled	Flat Products
7211196000	FLAT & HOT RLD IRON/NALLOY STL;(300-600MM);PICKLED	Strip-Hot Rolled	Flat Products
7211197530	FLT&HOT RLD IRON/STL;(300-600MM);COIL;UNTRIM EDGE	Strip-Hot Rolled	Flat Products
7211197560	FLAT&HOT ROLLED IRON/STL;(300-600MM); COIL; NESOL	Strip-Hot Rolled	Flat Products
7211197590	FLAT&HOT RLD IRON/NALLOY STL;(300-600MM);NOT COIL	Strip-Hot Rolled	Flat Products
7220121000	FR SS 300 TO UNDR 600MM W HR UNDR 4.75MM THCK	Strip-Hot Rolled	Flat Products
7220125000	FR SS LS THN 300MM W HR UNDR 4.75MM THCK	Strip-Hot Rolled	Flat Products
7226917000	FR OTH ALLOY STL 300-UN600MM W HR UN 4.75MM THCK	Strip-Hot Rolled	Flat Products
7226918000	FR OTH ALLOY STL UN 300MM W HR UN 4.75MM THCK	Strip-Hot Rolled	Flat Products
7211231500	FLT RLD HI-STR IOS NA LT 300MM,LT 25% CRBN,LT 1.25	Strip-Cold Rolled	Flat Products
7211232000	FLT&CLD RLD IRON/NALLOY STL;LT 300MM;GT 1.25MM THK	Strip-Cold Rolled	Flat Products
7211233000	FLT&COLD RLD IRON/STL;LT 300MM;(0.25MM-1.25MM)THK	Strip-Cold Rolled	Flat Products
7211234500	FLT&CLD RLD IR/STL;LT 300MM;LT 0.25MMTHK;.25% CAR	Strip-Cold Rolled	Flat Products
7211236030	FLAT&COLD RLD IRON/STL;(300MM-600MM);GT 1.25MM THK	Strip-Cold Rolled	Flat Products
7211236060	FLAT&COLD RLD IRON/STL;(300-600MM);0.25-1.25MM THK	Strip-Cold Rolled	Flat Products
7211236075	FLAT RLD IR/STL; APERATURE MASK CRT; LT 0.25MM THK	Strip-Cold Rolled	Flat Products
7211236085	FLT&CLD RLD IR/STL;(300-600MM);GT 0.25MM THK;NESOI	Strip-Cold Rolled	Flat Products
7211292030	FLT&CLD RLD IR/STL; COIL;LT 51MM; GT 0.25MM THICK	Strip-Cold Rolled	Flat Products
7211292090	FLAT&COLD RLD IRON/STL; LT 300MM; NOT COIL; NESOI	Strip-Cold Rolled	Flat Products
7211294500	FLT&CLD RLD IRON/NALLOY STL;LT 300MM; GT 0.25 THK	Strip-Cold Rolled	Flat Products
7211296030	FLT&CLD RLD IRON/STL;(300MM-600MM); GT 1.25MM THK	Strip-Cold Rolled	Flat Products
7211296080	FLAT&COLD RLD IRON/ST;(300MM-600MM); LT=1.25MM THK	Strip-Cold Rolled	Flat Products
7211900000	FLT RLD IOS NA,LT 600MM, NT CLD/PLTD/CTD, NESOI	Strip-Cold Rolled	Flat Products
7212401000	FLT RLD IRON/NALLOY STL; PAINT W/PLASTIC; LT 300MM	Strip-Cold Rolled	Flat Products
7212405000	FLT RLD IRON/STL; (300MM-600MM); PAINTED W/PLASTIC	Strip-Cold Rolled	Flat Products
7220201010	FR SS 300-UN 600MM W CR OV 0.5-UN 24% NKL ETC	Strip-Cold Rolled	Flat Products
7220201015	FR SS 300 TO UNDR 600MM W CR OV 0.5-UN 24% NCK,NES	Strip-Cold Rolled	Flat Products
7220201060	FR SS 300-UN 600MM W CR NCKL NESOI UN 15% CHROMIUM	Strip-Cold Rolled	Flat Products
7220201080	FR STNLESS STL 300-UN 600MM WIDE, COLD-RLD, NESOI	Strip-Cold Rolled	Flat Products
7220206005	FR SS WIDTH LS THN 300MM CR THKNS OV 1.25MM HI-NI	Strip-Cold Rolled	Flat Products
7220206010	FR SS UN 300MM W CR OV 1.25MM TH OV 0.5% NCKL, ETC	Strip-Cold Rolled	Flat Products
7220206015	FR SS UN 300MM W CR OV 1.25MM TH OV 0.5% NKL NESOI	Strip-Cold Rolled	Flat Products
7220206060	FR SS UN 300MM W CR OV 1.25 TH 0.5% OR UN NCKL ETC	Strip-Cold Rolled	Flat Products
7220206080	FR STNLSS STL UN 300MM W CR OV 1.25MM THCK, NESOI	Strip-Cold Rolled	Flat Products
7220207005	FR SS UN 300MM CR THKNS OV .25 NT OV 1.25MM HI-NI	Strip-Cold Rolled	Flat Products
7220207010	FR SS UN 300MM W CR OV 0.25-1.25 TH OV 0.5% NK ETC	Strip-Cold Rolled	Flat Products
7220207015	FR SS UN 300MM W CR OV 0.25-1.25 TH OV 0.5 NKL ETC	Strip-Cold Rolled	Flat Products
7220207060	FR SS UN 300MM W CR OV 0.25-1.25 TH LOW NCKL, ETC	Strip-Cold Rolled	Flat Products
7220207080	FR SS UN 300MM W CR OV 0.25MM-1.25MM THK, NESOI	Strip-Cold Rolled	Flat Products
7220208000	FR SS UN 300MM W CR RZR BLD STL NOV 0.25MM THCK	Strip-Cold Rolled	Flat Products
7220209030	FR SS UN 300MM W CR NOV 0.25 TH, OV.5-UN 24% N NES	Strip-Cold Rolled	Flat Products
7220209060	FR STNLSS STL UN 300MM W CR NOV 0.25MM THCK, NESOI	Strip-Cold Rolled	Flat Products
7220900010	OTH FR STNLSS STL UN 600MM W OV .5-UN 24% NKL, ETC	Strip-Cold Rolled	Flat Products
7220900015	OTH FR SS UN 600MM W OV .5-UN 24% NCKL, NESOI	Strip-Cold Rolled	Flat Products
7220900060	OTH FR SS UN 600MM W NICKL NESOI UN 15% CHROMIUM	Strip-Cold Rolled	Flat Products
7220900080	OTHR FLAT-ROLLD STNLESS STL UNDER 600MM WIDE NESOI	Strip-Cold Rolled	Flat Products
7226925000	FLAT-ROLLED OTHER ALLOY STEEL 300-UN 600MM W CR	Strip-Cold Rolled	Flat Products
7226927005	FR OTH HI-NI AL ST,UN 300M W,CR,NT OV 0.25MM THICK	Strip-Cold Rolled	Flat Products
7226927050	FR OTH AL STL, UN 300M WIDE, CR, THKNS NT OV .25MM	Strip-Cold Rolled	Flat Products
7226928005	FR OTH HI-NI AL ST,UN 300MM WIDE,CR,THKNS OV .25MM	Strip-Cold Rolled	Flat Products
7226928050	FR OTH AL STL,CR,UN 300MM WIDE, OV .25MM THICK	Strip-Cold Rolled	Flat Products
7226990180	FLAT-RLD PROD,ALY STL,FURTH WRKD THAN COLD ROLLED,OTHER <600 mm wide	Strip-Cold Rolled	Flat Products

These HTS codes have been REMOVED from the licensing requirement		(2009 HTS Changes)	
7222110050	BARS&RODS STAINL STL HOT-WKD CIR X-SECTION NESOI	Bars-Hot Rolled	Long Products

7222200075	OTH SS BARS/ROD COLD-FRM O FIN MAX CS 18MM AOV OTH	Bars-Cold Finished	Long Products
7222300000	BARS AND RODS, STAINLESS STEEL, NESOI	Bars-Cold Finished	Long Products

These hts codes have been REMOVED from the licensing requirement (2008 HTS Changes)

7213913092	BAR ROD IRON/STEEL HOT-ROLLD IRR DIA LT 14MM NESOI	Wire Rods	Long Products
7227200000	BRS A RDS SLCO-MN STL IRRG COILS HOT-ROLLD	Bars-Hot Rolled	Long Products
7227906080*	BARS/RODS OTH AL STL, IRREG COILS, HOT-ROLLED, OTH	Bars-Hot Rolled	Long Products

* codes added 1/1/06

These hts codes have been REMOVED from the licensing requirement (2007 HTS Changes)

7210490090	FTD RLD IOS NA GT/=600MM, PLTD/CTD W/ZINC,NESOI	Sheets & Strip Galv Hot Dipped	Flat Products
7226990000	FLAT-ROLLED, OTHER ALLOY STEEL LT 600MM WIDE,NESOI	Strip-Cold Rolled	Flat Products
7226930000	FLT-RLD,ALY STL LT 600MM ELCTRLYTLY PLT W/ZINC	Sheets & Strip Galv Electrolyt	Flat Products
7226940000	FLT-RLD,ALLY STL,LT 600MM,PLTD/CTD W/ZINC NT ELCTR	Sheets & Strip Galv Hot Dipped	Flat Products
7306601000	OTH TUBES ETC NES WLD NONCIRC CS WLS OV4MM IR/NALS	Structural Pipe & Tube	Pipe and Tube
7306603000	OTH TUBES ETC NES WLD NONCIRC CS WLS OV4MM ALLOYST	Structural Pipe & Tube	Pipe and Tube
7306607030	TUBES WELDED WALL LT= 4MM OF STAINLESS STEEL	Stainless Pipe & Tubing	Pipe and Tube
7225200000	FLAT-ROLLED, HIGH-SPEED STEEL GT/=600MM WIDE	Tool Steel	Long Products
7225301000	FR TS NT HSPD 600MM W AO HR CLS 4.75MM THCK AO	Tool Steel	Long Products
7225305030	FR BLL-BRG STL 600MM W AO HR CLS UN 4.75MM THCK	Tool Steel	Long Products
7225305060	FR OTH TOOL STL 600MM W AO HR CLS UN 4.75MM THCK	Tool Steel	Long Products
7225401015	FR BLL-BRG STL 600MM W AO HR NCL 4.75MM THCK AO	Tool Steel	Long Products
7225401090	FR OTH TOOL STL 600MM W AO HR NCL 4.75MM AO THCK	Tool Steel	Long Products
7225405030	FR BL-BRG STL 600MM W AO HR NCL UN 4.75MM THCK	Tool Steel	Long Products
7225405060	FR OTH TOOL STL 600MM W AO HR NCL UN 4.75MM THCK	Tool Steel	Long Products
7225501030	FLAT RLLD BALL BRNG STL 600MM WD AO CLD-RLLD	Tool Steel	Long Products
7225501060	FR TOOL STL NT HSPD NT BL-BRNG 600MM W AO CLD-ROLD	Tool Steel	Long Products
7229100000	WIRE OF HIGH-SPEED STEEL	Tool Steel	Long Products
7304213000	OIL WELL DRILL PIPE, OF IRON OR NONALLOY STEEL	Oil Country Goods	Pipe and Tube
7304216030	DRILL PIPE,SEAM,STL,DIAM LT=168.3MM,THK LT=9.5MM	Oil Country Goods	Pipe and Tube
7304216045	DRILL PIPE,SEAMLS,STL,DIAM LT=168.3MM,THK GT 9.5MM	Oil Country Goods	Pipe and Tube
7304216060	DRILL PIPE, SEAMLESS,OIL/GAS,STEEL,DIAM GT 168.3MM	Oil Country Goods	Pipe and Tube
7304293010	CASING,SEMLES,STL,THR,DIAM LT 215.9,THK LT 12.7MM	Oil Country Goods	Pipe and Tube
7304293020	CASING,SEMLES,STL,THRD,DIAM LT 215.9,THK GT=12.7MM	Oil Country Goods	Pipe and Tube
7304293030	CASING,SEAMLES,STL,THR,215.9-285.8,THK LT 12.7MM	Oil Country Goods	Pipe and Tube
7304293040	CASING,SEMLES,STEEL,THRED,215.9-285.9,GT=12.7MM	Oil Country Goods	Pipe and Tube
7304293050	CASING,SMLES,STEEL,THRD,DIAM 285.8-406.4 LT 12.7MM	Oil Country Goods	Pipe and Tube
7304293060	CASING,SMLES,STL,THRD,DIAM 285.8-406.4 GT=12.7MM	Oil Country Goods	Pipe and Tube
7304293080	CASING,SEMLES,OIL/GAS,STEEL,THREAD,DIAM GT 406.4MM	Oil Country Goods	Pipe and Tube
7304294010	CASING,SEM,STEEL,NESOI,DIAM LT 215.9,THK LT 12.7MM	Oil Country Goods	Pipe and Tube
7304294020	CASING,SEM,STEEL,NESOI,DIAM LT 215.9,THK GT=12.7MM	Oil Country Goods	Pipe and Tube
7304294030	CASING,SEMLES,STL,NESOI,DIM 215.9-285.8,LT 12.7MM	Oil Country Goods	Pipe and Tube
7304294040	CASING,SEMLES,STEEL,NESOI,215.9-285.8,GT=12.7MM	Oil Country Goods	Pipe and Tube
7304294050	CASING,SMLES,STL,NSOI,DIAM 285.8-406.4,LT 12.7MM	Oil Country Goods	Pipe and Tube
7304294060	CASING,SMLES,STL,NESOI,DIAM 285.8-406.4 GT 12.7MM	Oil Country Goods	Pipe and Tube
7304294080	CASING,SEAMLES,OIL/GAS,STEEL,NESOI,DIAM GT 406.4MM	Oil Country Goods	Pipe and Tube
7304296015	TUBING,SEM,OIL/GAS,STL,DIAM LT=114.3,LT=9.5MM	Oil Country Goods	Pipe and Tube
7304296030	TUBING,SEMLS,OIL/GAS,STL,DIAM LT 114.3,TH GT 9.5MM	Oil Country Goods	Pipe and Tube
7304296045	TUBING,SEM,OIL/GAS,STL,DIAM GT 114.3MM LT 215.9MM	Oil Country Goods	Pipe and Tube
7304296060	TUBING,SEM,OIL/GAS,STL,DIAM 215.9MM GT=406.4MM	Oil Country Goods	Pipe and Tube
7304296075	TUBING,SEMLES,OIL/GAS,ALLOY STEEL,DIAM GT 406.4MM	Oil Country Goods	Pipe and Tube
7306201030	OLWL CSNG NESOI IOS NA THDD W CPLG NTSML	Oil Country Goods	Pipe and Tube
7306201090	OLWL CSNG NESOI IOS NA THDD W/O CPLG NTSMLS	Oil Country Goods	Pipe and Tube
7306202000	OIL WELL CASING NSMLS NESOI IOS NA NT THDD OR CPLD	Oil Country Goods	Pipe and Tube
7306203000	OIL WELL CASING NSMLS NESOI AL STL THREAD OR COUPL	Oil Country Goods	Pipe and Tube
7306204000	OILWELL CASING NSMLS NESOI AL ST NT THRD OR COUPLD	Oil Country Goods	Pipe and Tube
7306206010	OILWELL TUBING NSMLS NESOI IR/NAL ST IMP W COUPLNG	Oil Country Goods	Pipe and Tube
7306206050	OILWELL TUBING NSMLS NES IR/NAS NT IMP W COUPLING	Oil Country Goods	Pipe and Tube
7306208010	OILWELL TUBING NSMLS NESOI ALY STL IMP W COUPLING	Oil Country Goods	Pipe and Tube
7306208050	OILWELL TUBING NSMLS NES ALY STL NT IMP W COUPLNG	Oil Country Goods	Pipe and Tube
7304101020	LNEPPE FOR OIL/GAS,IOS NA,SEMLES,DIAM LT/=114.3MM	Line Pipe	Pipe and Tube
7304101030	LINE PIPE,SEMLESS,OIL/GAS,IR/STEEL (114.3-215.9MM)	Line Pipe	Pipe and Tube
7304101045	LINE PIPE,SEAMLESS, IRON/STEEL, DIAM 215.9-406.4MM	Line Pipe	Pipe and Tube
7304101060	SLMS O/G LNP,I/NAL,OD 215.9-406.4MM,WTK 12.7MM AOV	Line Pipe	Pipe and Tube
7304101080	LINEPIPE FOR OIL/GAS, IRN/NAL STL, DIAM OV 406.4MM	Line Pipe	Pipe and Tube
7304105020	LNEPPE FOR OIL/GAS,ALY STL,SEMLES,DIAM LT/=114.3MM	Line Pipe	Pipe and Tube
7304105050	LNEPPE FR OIL/GAS,AL STL,SEMLES,DIAM 114.3-406.4MM	Line Pipe	Pipe and Tube
7304105080	LNEPPE FR OIL/GAS,ALY STL,SEMLES,DIAM GT 406.4MM	Line Pipe	Pipe and Tube
7306101010	LNPIPE FOR OIL/GS PIPLN, NSMLS IR/NAS ODNO 114.3MM	Line Pipe	Pipe and Tube
7306101050	LNPIPE FOR OIL/GS PIPLN, NSMLS IR/NAS ODOV 114.3MM	Line Pipe	Pipe and Tube
7306105010	LNPIPE FOR OIL/GS PIPLN, NSMLS ALST OD NOV 114.3MM	Line Pipe	Pipe and Tube
7306105050	LNPIPE FOR OIL/GS PIPLN, NSMLS AL ST OD OV 114.3MM	Line Pipe	Pipe and Tube
7306605000	OTH TUBES ETC NES WLD NONCIRC WLS LT4MM IR/NAL STL	Mechanical Tubing	Pipe and Tube
7306607060	TUBES WELDES WALL LT=4MM OF ALLOY STEEL	Mechanical Tubing	Pipe and Tube

These hts codes have been REMOVED from the licensing requirement (201 Category)

7216910000	ANGL,SHAPE,SECT IOS NA,CLD-FRMD/FNSHD,FLT-RL,NESOI	Carbon & Alloy Steel Hot-rolled bar
7307915010	FLANGES, IRN/NALY STL NESOI W INSD DIAM LSTH 360MM	Carbon & Alloy Steel Fittings & Flanges
7307915030	FLANGES, ALY STL EXC STNLS NESOI INS DIAM LT 360MM	Carbon & Alloy Steel Fittings & Flanges
7307915050	FLANGES, IRN/NALY STL NESOI W INSD DIAM 360MM ORMR	Carbon & Alloy Steel Fittings & Flanges
7307915070	FLANGES, ALY STL EXC STNLS NESOI INS DIAM 360MM OM	Carbon & Alloy Steel Fittings & Flanges
7307923010	SLEEVES (PIPE COUPLINGS) OF IRON OR NONALLOY STEEL	Carbon & Alloy Steel Fittings & Flanges
7307923030	SLEEVES (PIPE COUPLINGS), ALLOY STEEL EXC STAINLES	Carbon & Alloy Steel Fittings & Flanges

7307929000	THREADED ELBOWS AND BENDS OF IOS (EXC SS CSTIR)	Carbon & Alloy Steel Fittings & Flanges
7307933000	BUTT WELDING FITTINGS IR/NAL STL INS DIAM LT 360MM	Carbon & Alloy Steel Fittings & Flanges
7307936000	BUTT WELDING FITTINGS ALY STL EX STNLS DIM LT 360M	Carbon & Alloy Steel Fittings & Flanges
7307939030	BUTT WELDING FITTINGS IR/NAL STL INS DIAM 360MM OM	Carbon & Alloy Steel Fittings & Flanges
7307939060	BUTT WELDING FITTINGS ALY STL EX STNL DIA 360MM OM	Carbon & Alloy Steel Fittings & Flanges
7307995015	NIPPLES, PIPE AND TUBE I/NAL STEEL MACH, TLD, PROC	Carbon & Alloy Steel Fittings & Flanges
7307995045	OTH TUBE/PIPE FITT NESOI I/NAL STL MACH, TLD, PROC	Carbon & Alloy Steel Fittings & Flanges
7307995060	OTH PIPE FITTINGS NES AL ST EX STNLS MACHND TLD ET	Carbon & Alloy Steel Fittings & Flanges
7216610000	ANGLES,SHAPES,SECT,IOS NA,CLD-FRMD/FNSHD,FLT-RL	Carbon & Alloy Steel Hot-rolled bar
7216690000	ANGLES,SHAPES,SECT,IOS NA,CLD-FRMD/FNSHD,EX FLT-RL	Carbon & Alloy Steel Hot-rolled bar
7216910010	ANGL,SHP,SECT IOS NA,CLD-FRMD/FNSHD FLT-RL,DRILLED	Carbon & Alloy Steel Hot-rolled bar
7216910090	ANGL,SHAPE,SECT IOS NA,CLD-FRMD/FNSHD,FLT-RL,NESOI	Carbon & Alloy Steel Hot-rolled bar
7222406000	ANGS SHPS SECS STAINLESS STEEL, NESOI	Stainless Steel Bar
7228706000	ANGLS SHPS SEC AS NT SS OTH THN HOT-ROLLD	Carbon & Alloy Steel Hot-rolled bar

Glossary of International Trade Terms

Absolute Quota: A fixed limit on the quantity of goods that can be imported into a country during the quota period, usually one year.

Acceptance: A drawee's signed agreement to pay a draft as presented. It must be written on the draft and may consist of the drawee's signature alone. In documentary collections where the exporter (seller) draws a draft on the purchaser, the purchaser does not become legally liable to make payment until he receives the draft and accepts it. Then, at the maturity date of the draft, the drawee should pay. However, if the drawee fails to pay, there is no bank guarantee of payment even if the presentation of the draft was made to the purchaser through banking channels.

Acceptor, Accepter: A drawee who has accepted a draft.

ACE: Automated Commercial Environment—U.S. Customs and Border Protection's new Internet-based commercial trade processing system.

Adjustment Assistance: Financial, training, and re-employment technical assistance to workers and technical assistance to firms and industries to help them cope with difficulties arising from increased import competition. The objective of the assistance is usually to help an industry to become more competitive in the same line of production, or to move into other economic activities. The aid to workers can take the form of training (to qualify the affected individuals for employment in new or expanding industries), relocation allowances (to help them move from areas characterized by high unemployment to areas where employment may be available), or unemployment compensation (while they are searching for new jobs).

Ad Valorem Tariff: A tariff calculated as a percentage of the value of goods; for example, "15 percent ad valorem" means 15 percent of the value. Usually, but not always, the value is the sales price between the exporter (seller) and the importer (buyer).

Advising Bank: A bank located in the exporter's (seller's) country notifying the exporter that the purchaser has opened a letter of credit in favor of the exporter through another (issuing) bank.

Affreightment, Contract of: An agreement by a steamship line to provide cargo space on a vessel at a specified time and for a specified price for an exporter or importer. See "Booking Cargo."

Agent: In a general sense, a person who acts on behalf of another person. This may include selling agents and buying agents. Sales agents are sometimes called sales representatives or manufacturer's representatives. Their role is to perform services for their principal, such as obtaining orders, and they are usually paid a commission for their services.

Air Waybill: A bill of lading for air transportation. Air waybills specify the terms under which the air carrier is agreeing to transport the goods and contain limitations of liability. They are not negotiable.

All Risk Clause: An insurance provision that all loss or damage to goods is insured except that caused by inherent vice (self-caused). This clause affords one of the broadest obtainable protections; however, it excludes war risks and strikes, riots, and civil commotion unless added by special endorsement for an additional premium.

Antidumping Duties: See "Dumping."

Applicant: The person at whose request or for whose account a letter of credit is issued—for example, the purchaser in a sale transaction opening a letter of credit with the purchaser's bank to pay the exporter (seller).

Appraisement: The process of determination by a Customs official of the dutiable value of imported merchandise. This is usually the price paid by the importer for the goods unless Customs believes that the price does not reflect a reasonable value, in which case Customs calculates its own value for the assessment of duties using the methods specified in the customs law.

Arbitrage: The business of making profits by buying and selling currencies that differ in value due to fluctuating exchange rates in world currency markets. Sometimes used to describe the existence of a difference in value from one currency to another and the decision to buy or sell in a particular currency because of the belief that a particular currency is stronger or will strengthen in the future.

Arms Export Control Act: A U.S. law regulating the export (and in some cases import) of defense articles and services listed on the U.S. Munitions List. The International Traffic in Arms Regulations (ITAR) are issued under the law. It is administered by the Department of State, Office of Defense Trade Controls.

Arrival Draft: A modified sight draft that does not require payment until after arrival of the goods at the port of destination. Similar to cash on delivery.

Arrival Notice: A notification by the steamship line, railroad, or over-the-road trucker. It informs the consignee of the arrival of the goods and usually indicates the pickup location and the allowed free time before storage charges begin.

ASEAN: A free trade area established by the Association of Southeast Asian Nations.

Assist: The situation in which an importer, directly or indirectly, is furnishing to a foreign manufacturer raw materials, tools, dies, molds, manufacturing equipment, certain types of research and development know-how or design work, or other things without receiving payment for such items (or receiving payment for less than their full value) in order that the importer can purchase a product manufactured by the foreign manufacturer at a lower price. An assist must be disclosed to the importing country's customs administration and customs duties paid as an addition to the purchase price for the goods.

Assured: The beneficiary of an insurance policy, for example, covering damage or casualty to cargo or goods during transport.

ATA Carnet: An international customs document that may be used in lieu of national customs entry documents and as security for import duties and taxes to cover the temporary admission and transit of goods.

At Sight: A draft drawn by a seller (exporter) for payment for the goods. It must be paid at the time the draft is presented to the buyer (importer) by the seller's agent, such as a freight forwarder or a bank.

Audit: A procedure whereby the customs authorities visit the premises of an importer or exporter and inspect documents and records and interview personnel to determine if importations and/or exportations are being conducted in accordance with applicable law and regulations.

Authority to Pay: Advice from a buyer, addressed through the buyer's bank to the seller, by way of the correspondent of the buyer's bank in the seller's country, authorizing the correspondent bank to pay the seller's drafts for a stipulated amount. The seller has no recourse against cancellation or modification of the Authority to Pay before the drafts are presented, but, once the *drafts drawn on the correspondent bank* are paid by it, the seller is no longer liable as drawer. An Authority to Pay is usually not confirmed by the seller's bank. It is not as safe for a seller as a letter of credit because it is not a promise or guarantee of payment by a bank.

Authority to Purchase: A document similar to an Authority to Pay but differing in that under an Authority to Purchase, the *drafts are drawn directly on the buyer* rather than on the seller's bank. They are purchased by the correspondent bank with or without recourse against the drawer. The Authority to Pay is usually not confirmed by the seller's bank.

Automated Commercial System: The electronic data transmission system used by U.S. Customs and Border Protection, customs brokers, and importers to complete import transactions. It contains various modules such as the Automated Broker Interface, the Automated Manifest System, the Cargo Selectivity System, and the Entry Summary System.

Average: See "General Average" and "Particular Average."

Average Adjuster: When a steamship line transporting goods encounters a condition covered by a general average or a particular average, an independent average adjuster will determine the contribution that each owner of goods being transported on the steamship will have to pay to make the steamship line and the other owners of goods whole.

BAF (Bunker Adjustment Factor): A charge added by ocean carriers to compensate for fluctuating fuel costs.

Bank Draft: A check, drawn by a bank on another bank, customarily used where it is necessary for the customer to provide funds that are payable at a bank in some distant location.

Banker's Acceptance: A time draft where a bank is drawee and acceptor.

Barter: The direct exchange of goods for other goods, without the use of money as a medium of exchange and without the involvement of a third party. For customs purposes, the values still need to be determined and proper duties paid if the exchange involves an importation. See "Countertrade."

Beneficiary: (1) Under a letter of credit, the person who is entitled to receive payment, usually the seller (exporter) of the goods. (2) Under an insurance policy, the assured, or the person who is to receive payment in case of loss of or damage to the goods.

Bill of Exchange: An unconditional order in writing addressed by one person to another, signed by the person issuing it and requiring the addressee to pay a certain sum of money to the order of a specified party at a fixed or determinable future time. In export transactions, it is drawn by the seller (exporter) on the purchaser (importer) or bank specified in a letter of credit or specified by the purchaser. See "Draft."

Bill of Lading (B/L): A document issued by a carrier (railroad, steamship line, or trucking company) that serves as a receipt for the goods to be delivered to a designated person or to her order. The bill of lading describes the conditions under which the goods are accepted by the carrier and details the nature and quantity of the goods, the name of the vessel (if shipped by sea), identifying marks and numbers, destination, etc. The person sending the goods is the "shipper" or "consignor," the company or agent transporting the goods is the "carrier," and the person for whom the goods are destined is the "consignee." Bills of lading may be negotiable or non-negotiable. If they are negotiable, that is, payable to the shipper's order and properly endorsed, title to the goods passes upon delivery of the bill of lading.

Blank Endorsement: The signature, usually on the reverse of a draft (bill of exchange), bill of lading, or insurance certificate, without any qualification, which then becomes payable or consigned to the person to whom the document is delivered.

Bond: A guaranty issued by an insurance or surety company in favor of an importer's government to ensure payment of customs duties in case the importer fails to pay, for example, due to bankruptcy.

Bonded Warehouse: A warehouse in which goods subject to excise taxes or customs duties are temporarily stored without the taxes or duties being assessed. A bond or security is given for the payment of all taxes and duties that may eventually become due. Operations in the warehouse may include assembly, manipulation, or storage, but usually not manufacturing.

Booking Cargo: The reservation of space on a specified vessel for a scheduled sailing, by or on behalf of a shipper. Technically, it may be effected in two ways, either (1) by signing a contract of affreightment, a procedure that applies only to bulk commodities, raw materials, or a large movement of special cargo, such as the transfer of a whole manufacturing plant, or to particular types of goods requiring special stowage, like unboxed cars or trucks; or (2) by informal request (verbal) for general cargo.

Booking Number: A number assigned to a cargo booking by the steamship line, used as an identifying reference on bills and correspondence.

Boycott: A refusal to deal commercially or otherwise with a person, firm, or country.

Buying Commission: A commission paid by a purchaser to an agent or person under the purchaser's control who identifies suppliers, assists with shipments, and provides other services for the purchaser. Under the GATT Valuation Code, amounts separately paid for such services are not dutiable as part of the purchase price of the goods.

Buy National Policy: A price preference, usually by a government purchaser, for purchasing goods produced in the same country as the purchaser's or an absolute prohibition against purchasing foreign goods.

Cabotage: Shipping, navigation, and trading along the coast of a country. In the United States, these services include traffic between any parts of the continental United States, or between Hawaii, Alaska, and Puerto Rico, and are reserved to U.S. flag ships.

CAF (Currency Adjustment Factor): A charge added by ocean carriers to offset currency exchange fluctuations.

CAFTA-DR: The Dominican Republic–Central America–United States Free Trade Agreement allows for preferential duty rates for goods imported that meet the rules of origin from member countries. Member countries include the Dominican Republic, El Salvador, Guatemala, Nicaragua, and Honduras.

Carnet: See "ATA Carnet."

Cash Against Documents (C.A.D.): A method of payment for goods in which documents transferring title—for example, a negotiable bill of lading and a draft—are transferred to the buyer upon payment of cash to an intermediary acting for the seller (usually a bank or freight forwarder).

Cash in Advance (C.I.A.): A method of payment for goods in which the buyer pays the seller in advance of the shipment of the goods. A C.I.A. is usually employed when the goods are built to order, such as specialized machinery.

Cash With Order (C.W.O.): A method of payment for goods in which cash is paid at the time of the order.

Casualty Loss: Damage to goods incurred during transportation, loading, or unloading.

CE Mark: A mark required on certain products imported to the European Community certifying that the product has been tested by an authorized certification agency and meets applicable standards, usually of safety.

Certificate of Conformity: The Consumer Product Safety Commission requires the importer to file a Certificate of Conformity to attest that imported or domestic goods are in compliance with the CPSC laws and regulations.

Certificate of Inspection: A document issued by an inspection company or other person independent of the seller and buyer that has inspected the goods for quality and/or value. It may be required for payment under the terms of the sales agreement or a letter of credit.

Certificate of Insurance: A document containing certain terms of a full-length insurance policy. A one-page document, it is evidence that there is insurance coverage for a shipment. Beneficiaries of open cargo or blanket insurance policies are authorized to issue their own certificates of insurance.

Certificate of Origin: A document in which the exporter certifies the place of origin (manufacture) of the merchandise being exported. Sometimes these certificates must be legalized by the consul of the country of destination, but more often they may be legalized by a commercial organization, such as a chamber of commerce, in the country of manufacture. Such information is needed primarily to comply with tariff laws, which may extend more favorable treatment to products of certain countries. More recently, certain types of certificates of origin, for example, NAFTA Certificates of Origin, require significant analysis of the origin of the raw materials used in production of the product to determine the country of origin.

Certificate of Weight and Measurement: A certificate issued by a company or person independent of the seller and buyer certifying the quantity and dimensions of goods. In some cases, the buyer or buyer's government will allow the seller to make a self-certification.

Charter Party: The contract between the owner of a vessel and a shipper to lease the vessel or a part thereof to transport, usually bulk, goods.

Clean Bill of Lading: One in which the goods are described as having been received in "apparent good order and condition" and without damage. May be required for payment under the sales agreement or letter of credit. See "Foul Bill of Lading."

Collecting Bank: A bank requested by an exporter (seller) to obtain payment from the purchaser. Ordinarily the exporter (seller) will draw a draft on the purchaser and deliver it to the collecting bank with a negotiable bill of lading. The bank will transmit it overseas to its correspondent bank (which is also a collecting bank in the chain). If the draft drawn is a sight draft, the bank will deliver the negotiable bill of lading to the purchaser in return for payment. If it is a time draft, the bank will release the bill of lading, thereby permitting the purchaser to obtain the goods, upon acceptance of the draft by the purchaser. At the time of maturity of the draft, the purchaser will make payment and the collecting banks will remit the proceeds to the exporter (seller). See "Uniform Rules for Collections."

Combined Transport Bill of Lading: See "Through Bill of Lading."

Commercial Invoice: A document prepared by the exporter (seller) describing the goods being sold, the sales price for the goods, and other charges being billed to the purchaser. Because a commercial invoice is commonly required in order to enable the purchaser to clear the goods through customs, it is necessary to include all information required by the purchaser's country. This may include legalization of the commercial invoice by the purchaser's country's embassy or consulate in the exporter's country, certification by a chamber of commerce in the exporter's country, or particular statements, certifications, or information in the invoice.

Commingling: A condition in which goods subject to different rates of customs duty are packed together. This may result in all goods being assessed the highest duty rate applicable to any of the items.

Commission Agent: See "Agent."

Common Carrier: A transportation carrier such as a steamship line, trucking company, or railroad that accepts shipments from the public. Private carriers are those that are under contract for or owned by particular shippers. Common carriers are usually subject to government regulation, including the filing of tariffs (transportation rates) in some countries so that shippers all pay a uniform charge. Laws in some countries permit exceptions to this so that large-volume shippers may obtain discounts in certain circumstances.

Common Market: An agreement between two or more countries to permit importation or exportation of goods between those countries without the payment of customs duties and to permit freedom of travel and employment and freedom of investment. Goods imported from outside the common market will be subject to a common duty rate.

Compound Duty: A tax imposed on imported merchandise based on a percentage of value and also on the net weight or quantity.

Conference Tariff: Two or more steamship lines that have agreed to set the same price for transporting goods in the same ocean lane that they serve. Generally, such agreements are valid if they are properly registered with the government authorities of the countries served.

Confirming Bank: A bank in the exporter's (seller's) country that also adds its own guarantee of payment to a letter of credit issued by the purchaser's bank in the purchaser's country.

Consignment: (1) The shipment or delivery of goods to a person without making a sale. Under consignment arrangements, the consignee will usually have an agreement that when the consignee is able to sell the goods to a purchaser, the consignee will simultaneously purchase the goods from the consignor and make payment. (2) In some international trade documentation—for example, bills of lading—a transportation carrier may not know whether the transportation that it is effecting is pursuant to a sale or not; therefore, the person to whom the goods are to be delivered is referred to as the consignee, and the delivery transaction is loosely referred to as a consignment.

Consular Invoice: A document required by some foreign countries showing information as to the consignor, consignee, value, and description of the shipment. It is usually sold or legalized by the embassy or consulate of the purchaser's country located in the seller's country.

Consulate: An office of a foreign government in the exporter's (seller's) country. The main office is usually the embassy, located in the capital city of the exporter's country, and other offices in different cities in the exporter's country are consulates.

Contract of Affreightment: See "Affreightment, Contract of."

Convention on Contracts for the International Sale of Goods: An international treaty describing the obligations and rights of sellers and buyers in international sales. The Convention automatically applies to international sales where the seller and the buyer are located in countries that are parties to the Convention unless the buyer and the seller have agreed specifically in their sales documentation to exclude applicability of the Convention. The United States and many other countries are parties to the Convention.

Countertrade: A reciprocal trading arrangement. Countertrade transactions include:

A. *Counterpurchase transactions,* which obligate the seller to purchase from the buyer goods and services unrelated to the goods and services sold (usually within a one- to five-year period).
B. *Reverse countertrade contracts,* which require the importer to export goods equivalent in value to a specified percentage of the value of the imported goods—an obligation that can be sold to an exporter in a third country.
C. *Buyback transactions,* which obligate the seller of plant, machinery, or technology to buy from the importer a portion of the resultant production during a five- to twenty-five-year period.
D. *Clearing agreements* between two countries that agree to purchase specific amounts of each other's products over a specified period of time, using a designated "clearing currency" in the transactions.
E. *Switch transactions,* which permit the sale of unpaid balances in a clearing account to a third party, usually at a discount, that may be used for producing goods in the country holding the balance.
F. *Swap transactions,* through which products from different locations are traded to save transportation costs (for example, Soviet oil may be "swapped" for oil from a Latin American producer, so that the Soviet oil is shipped to a country in South Asia, while the Latin American oil is shipped to Cuba).
G. *Barter transactions,* through which two parties directly exchange goods deemed to be of approximately equivalent value without any exchange of money taking place.

Countervailing Duty: Considered a form of unfair competition under the GATT Subsidies Code, an additional duty imposed by the importer's government in order to offset export grants, bounties, or subsidies paid to foreign exporters or manufacturers in certain countries by the governments of those countries for the purpose of promoting export.

CPSIA: Consumer Products Safety Improvement Act, which requires both importers and domestic manufacturers to certify that their products comply with all U.S. consumer products regulations.

C-TPAT: Customs and Trade Partnership Against Terrorism. A voluntary program whereby importers, brokers, carriers, warehouses, consolidators, and exporters enact security measures to protect cargo and containers from the introduction of contraband or terrorist devices.

Customs Broker: A person or firm licensed by an importer's government and engaged in entering and clearing goods through customs. The responsibilities of a broker include preparing the entry form and filing it, advising the importer on duties to be paid, advancing duties and other costs, and arranging for delivery to the importer.

Customs Classification: The particular category in a tariff nomenclature (usually the Harmonized Tariff System) in which a product is classified for tariff purposes, or the procedure for determining the appropriate tariff category in a country's nomenclature used for the classification, coding, and description of internationally traded goods. Classification is necessary in order to determine the duty rate applicable to the imported goods.

Customs Union: An agreement between two or more countries to eliminate tariffs and other import restrictions on each other's goods and establish a common tariff for goods imported from other countries.

Cut-Off Time: The latest time a container may be delivered to a terminal for loading on a departing ship or train.

Date Draft: A draft maturing a stipulated number of days after its date, regardless of the time of its acceptance. Unless otherwise agreed upon in the contract of sale, the date of the draft should not be prior to that of the ocean bill of lading or of the corresponding document on shipments by other means.

DDC (Destination Delivery Charge): A charge added by ocean carriers to compensate for crane lifts off the vessel, drayage of the container within the terminal, and gate fees at the terminal.

***Del Credere* Agent:** One who guarantees payments; a sales agent who, for a certain percentage in addition to her sales commission, will guarantee payment by the purchasers of goods.

Delivery Order: An order addressed to the holder of goods and issued by anyone who has authority to do so, that is, one who has the legal right to order delivery of merchandise. It is not considered a title document like a negotiable bill of lading. It is addressed and forwarded, together with the dock receipt, if any, to the transportation company effecting the transfer from the pickup location to the shipside pier.

Demurrage: Excess time taken for loading or unloading of a vessel that is not caused by the vessel operator but is due to the acts of a charterer or shipper. A charge is made for such delay. See "Lay Days."

Destination Control Statement: Specific words (legend) inserted in a commercial invoice and bill of lading prohibiting diversion of destination for exported goods subject to U.S. export control laws.

Devaluation: An official lowering of the value of a country's currency in relation to other currencies by a direct government decision to reduce gold content or to establish a new ratio to another agreed standard, such as the U.S. dollar. Devaluation tends to reduce domestic demand for imports in a country by raising their prices in terms of the devalued currency and to raise foreign demand for the country's exports by reducing their prices in terms of foreign currencies. Devaluation can therefore help to correct a balance of payments deficit and sometimes provide a short-term basis for economic adjustment of a national economy. See "Revaluation."

Discrepancy: The failure of a beneficiary of a letter of credit to tender to the advising bank the exact documents required by the letter of credit to obtain payment.

Distributor: A person who purchases goods for the purpose of reselling such goods. The distributor is distinguished from an agent because it takes title to the goods, assumes the risk of loss or damage to the goods, and is compensated by marking up the goods on resale.

Dock Receipt: A receipt given for a shipment received or delivered at a steamship pier. A dock receipt is usually a form supplied by the steamship line and prepared by the shipper or its freight forwarder. When delivery of a shipment is completed, the dock receipt is surrendered to the vessel operator or his agent and serves as the basis for preparation of the ocean bill of lading.

Documentary Bill: A draft (bill of exchange) accompanied by other documents required by the buyer for payment, for example, the bill of lading and inspection certificate.

Documents Against Acceptance (D/A): Instructions given by an exporter to a bank or freight forwarder that the documents (usually a negotiable bill of lading) attached to a draft for collection are deliverable to the drawee (importer/purchaser) only against her acceptance of the draft. The actual payment will be made by the purchaser at some agreed-upon time or date specified in the draft after acceptance. See "Uniform Rules for Collections."

Documents Against Payment (D/P): A type of payment for goods in which the documents transferring title to the goods (negotiable bill of lading) are not given to the purchaser until he has paid the value of a draft drawn on him. Collection may be made through a bank, a freight forwarder, or some other agent. See "Uniform Rules for Collections."

Draft: A negotiable instrument wherein a drawer orders a drawee to pay a fixed amount of money (with or without interest or other charges) described in the draft, payable on demand or at a definite time. It must be payable "to order" or bearer, and it must not contain any other instructions, conditions, or orders except an order to pay money. A draft is commonly drawn by an exporter (seller) on the purchaser (drawee) and delivered to a collecting bank or freight forwarder for presentation to the purchaser. See "Bill of Exchange."

Drawback: Import duties or taxes refunded by a government, in whole or in part, when the imported goods are re-exported or used in the manufacture of exported goods.

Drawee: A person (usually the purchaser of goods) ordered in a draft to make payment.

Drawer: A person who makes, creates, or issues a draft and instructs a drawee to make payment to the drawer or another person ("pay to the order of").

Drayage: A charge for delivery of goods or pickup of goods from docks or other port terminals.

Dumping: Under the GATT Antidumping Code (to which the United States is a party), the export sale of a commodity at "less than normal value," usually considered to be a price lower than that at which it is sold within the exporting country or to third countries. Dumping is generally recognized as an unfair trade practice that can disrupt markets and injure producers of competitive products in the importing country. Article VI of GATT permits the imposition of special antidumping duties against "dumped" goods equal to the difference between their export price and their normal value in the exporting country.

Dunnage: Packing material consisting mainly of rough pine board used as flooring for the ship's hold before loading is begun.

Duty: The tax imposed by a customs authority on imported merchandise.

Embargo: A prohibition upon exports or imports, with respect to either specific products or specific countries. Historically, embargoes have been ordered most frequently in time of war, but they may also be applied for political, economic, or sanitary purposes. Embargoes imposed against an individual country by the United Nations—or a group of nations—in an effort to influence that country's conduct or its policies are sometimes called "sanctions."

Embassy: The chief diplomatic office of a foreign government in the exporter's country, usually located at the capital city of the exporter's country.

Entry: The formal process by which goods are imported into a country, consisting of the filing of documents with the importing country's customs service and the payment of customs duties. Various types of entries are used in different circumstances, such as consumption entries, warehouse entries, immediate transportation entries, and transportation and exportation entries.

Escape Clause: A provision in a bilateral or multilateral trade agreement permitting a signatory nation to suspend tariff or other duty reductions when imports threaten serious harm to the producers of competitive domestic goods. Such agreements as the North American Free Trade Agreement contain such "safeguard" provisions to help firms and workers that are adversely affected by a relatively sudden surge of imports adjust to the rising level of import competition.

European Union: A monetary and political union entered into in 1992 in Maastricht, Netherlands, by twelve European countries; twenty-seven countries are now members.

Examination: The process by which the customs authorities of an importing country inspect the goods identified in the customs entry documents and confirm whether the goods are the same as those described in the documents and whether the goods are eligible for entry.

Exchange Controls: Government regulations rationing foreign currencies, bank drafts, and other instruments for settling international financial obligations by countries seeking to ameliorate acute balance of payments difficulties. When such measures are imposed, importers must apply for prior authorization from the government to obtain the foreign currency required to bring in designated amounts and types of goods. Since such measures have the effect of restricting imports, they are considered non-tariff barriers to trade.

Exchange Rate Risk: The possibility that an exporter (seller) will receive less value (for example, fewer U.S. dollars) than it is expecting in a sales transaction. This arises because exchange rates are generally floating rates, and if the exporter (seller) agrees to accept payment in the purchaser's currency (for example, yen) and the value of the yen vis-à-vis the U.S. dollar fluctuates between the time of price quotation and the date of payment, the exporter (seller) may receive more or less in U.S. dollars than it anticipated at the time that it quoted its price and accepted the purchase order. Sellers and purchasers may agree to share the exchange rate risk in their sales agreement.

Exchange Rates: The price at which banks or other currency traders are willing to buy or sell various currencies that a buyer may need in order to make payment.

For example, if a contract for sale is in U.S. dollars, a purchaser in a foreign country will need to purchase U.S. dollars from a bank or currency trader in order to make proper payment. Usually, the exchange rate floats or fluctuates based on supply and demand, but it may also be fixed by government regulation.

Export License: A permit required to engage in the export of certain commodities to certain destinations. In the United States, such controls are usually determined by the Department of Commerce, Bureau of Export Administration; the Department of State, Office of Defense Trade Controls; or Department of Treasury, Office of Foreign Assets Control. Controls are imposed to implement U.S. foreign policy, ensure U.S. national security, prevent proliferation, or protect against short supply.

Export Quotas: Specific restriction or ceilings imposed by an exporting country on the value or volume of certain exports, designed to protect domestic consumers from temporary shortages of the goods, to bolster their prices in world markets, or to reduce injury to producers in importing countries. Some international commodity agreements explicitly indicate when producers should apply such restraints. Export quotas are also often applied in orderly marketing agreements and voluntary restraint agreements, and to promote domestic processing of raw materials in countries that produce them.

Export Trading Company: A corporation or other business unit organized and operated principally for the purpose of exporting goods and services, or for providing export-related services to other companies. The Export Trading Company Act of 1982 exempts authorized trading companies from certain provisions of the U.S. antitrust laws and authorizes banks to own and operate trading companies.

Factoring: A procedure whereby an exporter (seller) that is selling on open account or time drafts may sell its accounts receivable or drafts to a factoring company, which will make immediate payment of the face value of the accounts receivable less some discount amount to the seller and will then collect the amounts owed from the purchasers at the due date for payment.

FEU (Forty-foot Equivalent Unit): A measurement of container capacity.

Fixed Exchange Rate: The establishment of a price at which two currencies can be purchased or sold, set either by government regulation or in a sales agreement between a seller and a buyer. In such cases, there is no exchange rate risk because there is no exchange rate fluctuation between the date of price quotation and the date of payment.

Floating Exchange Rate: A condition where the governments issuing two different currencies do not legally regulate the price at which either currency can be bought or sold. See "Exchange Rate Risk."

Force Majeure: The title of a standard clause often found in contracts for the sale of goods or transportation exempting the parties from liability for non-fulfillment of their obligations by reason of certain acts beyond their control, such as natural disasters or war.

Foreign Assembler's Declaration: Under U.S. Harmonized Tariff Section 9802.00.80, an importer may pay reduced customs duties when importing a product that has been assembled abroad from U.S.-origin components. The foreign assembler must provide a declaration that is endorsed by the importer certifying that the assembly operation meets the regulatory requirements. If Customs agrees, the U.S. importer pays duty only on the foreign-origin materials, labor, and value added after deducting the U.S.-origin materials exported for assembly.

Foreign Corrupt Practices Act: A U.S. law prohibiting the payment of anything of value to a foreign government employee in order to obtain or retain business. The law also prohibits the maintenance of "slush funds" for such payments.

Foreign Sales Corporation (FSC): A company incorporated in Guam, the U.S. Virgin Islands, the Commonwealth of the Northern Mariana Islands, American Samoa, or any foreign country that has a satisfactory exchange-of-information agreement with the United States and is utilized in an export transaction. Use of an FSC in export sales transactions permits a U.S. exporter to exempt a portion of its export profits from U.S. income taxation.

Foreign Trade Zone: An area where goods may be received, stored, manipulated, and manufactured without entering a country's customs jurisdiction and hence without payment of duty. Outside the United States, it is usually called a "free trade zone."

Forward Exchange: A market offering various currencies for sale where the sales price of a currency is quoted and sold based on delivery of the currency to the purchaser at some date in the future, for example, the due date when the purchaser must make payment of a time draft. Purchasing currency in forward contracts is one method of eliminating exchange rate risk.

Foul Bill of Lading: A bill of lading issued by a carrier bearing a notation that the outward containers or the goods have been damaged. A foul bill of lading may not be acceptable for payment under a letter of credit.

Free In and Out (F.I.O.): The cost of loading and unloading of a vessel that is borne by the charterer.

Free of Capture and Seizure (F.C.&S.): An insurance clause providing that a loss is not insured if it is due to capture, seizure, confiscation, and like actions, whether legal or not, or from such acts as piracy, civil war, rebellion, and civil strife.

Free of Particular Average (F.P.A.): The phrase means that the insurance company will not cover partial losses resulting from perils of the sea except when caused by stranding, sinking, burning, or collision. American conditions (F.P.A.A.C.): Partial loss is not insured unless it is caused by the vessel's being sunk, stranded, burned, on fire, or in collision. English conditions (F.P.A.E.C.): Partial loss is not insured unless it is a result of the vessel's being sunk, stranded, burned, on fire, or in collision.

Free Out (F.O.): The cost of unloading a vessel that is borne by the charterer.

Free Port: An ocean port and its adjacent area where imported goods may be temporarily stored and sometimes repackaged; manipulated; or, under the laws of some countries, further processed or manufactured without payment of customs duties until the merchandise is sold in the country or the time period for exportation expires.

Free Trade: A theoretical concept that assumes that international trade is unhampered by government measures such as tariffs or non-tariff barriers. The objective of trade liberalization is to achieve "freer trade" rather than "free trade," it being generally recognized among trade policy officials that some restrictions on trade are likely to remain.

Free Trade Area: An arrangement between two or more countries for free trade among themselves while each nation maintains its own independent tariffs toward nonmember nations.

Free Trade Zone: See "Foreign Trade Zone."

Freight All Kinds (FAK): The general transportation rate for a shipment of multiple types of merchandise.

Freight Collect: The shipment of goods by an exporter (seller) where the purchaser has agreed to pay the transportation costs and the transportation carrier has agreed to transport the goods on the condition that the goods will not be released unless the purchaser makes payment for the transportation charges.

Freight Forwarder: A person who dispatches shipments via common carriers, books or otherwise arranges space for those shipments on behalf of shippers, and processes the documentation or performs related activities incident to those shipments.

Freight Prepaid: An agreement between the seller and a buyer that the seller will pay for the transportation charges before delivery to the transportation carrier.

Full Set: Generally used in reference to bills of lading. Where a steamship line undertakes to transport goods, it issues a sole original or full set (generally three copies, which are all originals) of the bill of lading. Where the bill of lading is negotiable, the steamship line is authorized to make delivery as soon as any person presents one original bill of lading at the destination.

GATT: The General Agreement on Tariffs and Trade. This is an international treaty that has now been superseded by the World Trade Organization. A number of agreements negotiated under GATT continue in force, such as the Valuation Code, the Antidumping Code, and the Subsidies Code. See "World Trade Organization."

General Average: A deliberate loss of or damage to goods in the face of a peril, such as dumping overboard, which sacrifice is made for the preservation of the vessel and other goods. The cost of the loss is shared by the owners of the saved goods.

Generalized System of Preferences (GSP): The United Nations program adopted by the United States and many other countries and designed to benefit less developed countries by extending duty-free treatment to imports from such countries. Sometimes certain countries or products are "graduated" and are no longer eligible to receive GSP benefits.

General Order: Merchandise for which proper customs entry has not been made within five working days after arrival is sent to a general order warehouse. All costs of storage are at the expense of the importer.

Gray Market Goods: Products that have been manufactured and sold by the inventor or duly authorized licensee that are being resold by purchasers into geographical areas not intended or authorized by the original seller. Depending upon the laws of the countries involved, gray marketing may be illegal, encouraged, or regulated. Sometimes economic incentives for gray marketing occur as a result of a manufacturer selling the products to different trade channels at different prices or due to fluctuating exchange rates.

Harmonized Tariff System (Codes): The system adopted by most of the commercial countries of the world in 1989, classifying products manufactured and sold in world commerce according to an agreed-upon numerical system. Common international classifications facilitate balance of trade statistics collection, customs classification, and country of origin determination.

In Bond: The transportation or storage of goods in a condition or location that is exempt under the customs laws from the payment of customs duties for the time period that is allowed by law for transportation or storage. Transportation or storage in bond may be effected by transportation carriers or warehouses that have posted a bond with the customs authorities guaranteeing payment of all customs duties in the event that the goods are improperly released without the payment of customs duties by the owner of the goods.

Inchmaree Clause: A provision in an ocean casualty insurance policy covering the assured against damage to the owner's goods as a result of negligence or mismanagement by the captain or the crew in navigation of the ship or damage due to latent defects in the ship.

Incoterms: A set of sales and delivery terms issued by the International Chamber of Commerce and widely used in international trade. These terms, such as "ex-works," "CIF," and "delivered duty paid," set out in detail the responsibilities and rights of the seller and purchaser in an international sale transaction. See also "Convention on Contracts for the International Sale of Goods" and "Uniform Commercial Code."

Indent Merchant: One who assembles a number of orders from merchants in his locality, such orders being placed with foreign manufacturers by the indent merchant for his own account. He assumes the full credit risk and obtains his commission from those for whom he orders.

Insurable Interest: The legal interest that a person must have in goods in order to be covered by insurance. For example, in an international sale under the Incoterm "ex-works," delivery and risk of loss for damage to the goods passes to the purchaser when the goods are loaded on and leave the seller's factory or warehouse. If the seller has already been paid for the goods at that time, the seller no longer has any legal interest in ownership or payment and cannot receive payment under any insurance coverage that the seller may have, such as a blanket insurance policy covering all sales.

Intellectual Property: Ownership conferring the right to possess, use, or dispose of products created by human ingenuity, including patents, trademarks, and copyrights. These rights are protected when properly registered, but registration in one country does not create rights in another country.

Invisible Trade: Items such as freight, insurance, and financial services that are included in a country's balance of payments accounts (in the "current" account), even though they are not recorded as physically visible exports and imports.

Invoice: See "Commercial Invoice" and "Consular Invoice."

Irrevocable Credit: A letter of credit issued by the purchaser's bank in favor of the seller that cannot be revoked without the consent of the seller (who is the beneficiary of the letter of credit). Under the Uniform Customs and Practice for Documentary Credits (No. 500), all letters of credit are irrevocable unless specifically stated otherwise on their face. This protects the seller against the risk of non-payment due to revocation after release of the goods to the buyer or the buyer's agent.

ISO 9000: A series of quality control standards promulgated by the International Standards Organization.

ITAR: See "Arms Export Control Act."

Jettison: The act of throwing the goods off a steamship into the ocean to lighten the ship in time of peril. It may occur as a way to save a sinking ship or through illegal or improper action by steamship employees. Certain jettisons are covered by insurance or general average, but others are not.

Lacey Act: The Lacey Act was originally enacted in 1900 to protect wildlife, fish, and plants. Recent amendments to the act were enacted to prohibit illegal logging and require importers to file a certification on the source of any plant products or products with plant components.

Lay Days: The dates between which a chartered vessel is to be available in a port for loading of cargo.

LCL: Less than a full container load.

Legalization: A procedure whereby an embassy or consular employee of the purchaser's country located in the exporter's (seller's) country signs or stamps an export document, for example, a commercial invoice, in order to enable the goods to be admitted upon arrival at the purchaser's country.

Letter of Credit (L/C): A formal letter issued by a bank that authorizes the drawing of drafts on the bank up to a fixed limit and under terms specified in the letter. Through the issuance of such letters, a bank guarantees payment on behalf of its customers (purchasers of goods) and thereby facilitates the transaction of business between parties who may not be otherwise acquainted with each other. The letter of credit may be sent directly by the issuing bank or its customer to the beneficiary (sellers of goods), or the terms of the credit may be transmitted through a correspondent bank. In the latter event, the correspondent may add its guarantee (confirmation) to that of the issuing bank, depending on the arrangements made between the seller and the purchaser. Letters of credit may be revocable or irrevocable depending on whether the issuing bank reserves the right to cancel the credit prior to its expiration date.

Letter of Indemnity/Guaranty: (1) A document issued by a shipper to a steamship line instructing the steamship line to issue a clean bill of lading even though the goods are damaged, and agreeing to hold the steamship line harmless from any claims. (2) An agreement by a beneficiary of a letter of credit to hold a bank harmless for making payment to the beneficiary, even though there are some discrepancies between the documents required by the letter of credit and those presented by the beneficiary. (3) An agreement by an exporter and/or importer to hold a steamship line harmless from any claims that may arise as a result of the steamship line's releasing goods where a negotiable bill of lading covering the goods has been lost or destroyed.

Lighterage: The cost for conveying the goods by lighters or barges between ships and shore and vice versa, including the loading into and discharging out of lighters.

Liner Service: Regularly scheduled departures of steamships to specific destinations (trade lanes).

Liquidation: A U.S. Customs term of art describing the official final determination by the customs authorities of the classification and value of the imported merchandise. For example, any importer, by posting a customs bond, may obtain immediate delivery of merchandise by classifying the imported product and paying customs duties at that time. The importer's classification and value, however, are not binding on U.S. Customs and Border Protection, and within an additional period of time, for example, three to six months, Customs will make its own analysis of the goods and determine whether or not it agrees with the classification, value, and duties paid.

Long Ton: 2,240 pounds.

LTL: A shipment of less than a full truckload.

Manifest: A listing of the cargo being transported by the transportation carrier.

Marine Extension Clause: A provision in an ocean casualty insurance policy extending the ordinary coverage to include time periods where goods have been received for shipment but not yet loaded on a steamship and have been loaded off the steamship but not yet delivered to the buyer, and periods where the ship deviates from its intended course or the goods are transshipped.

Marine Insurance: Insurance that will compensate the owner of goods transported overseas in the event of loss or damage. Some "marine" insurance policies also cover air shipments.

Marine Surveyor: A company or individual that assesses the extent of damage to cargo incurred during ocean transportation. Such survey reports are necessary in order for insurance companies to make payment to the beneficiary of the insurance policy.

Marking Laws: Laws requiring articles of foreign origin and/or their containers imported into a country to be marked in a specified manner that would indicate to the purchaser the country of origin of the article.

Mate's Receipt: Commonly used in Europe, a document similar to a dock receipt. A mate's receipt is issued by an employee of a steamship line, usually at the wharf or pier where the goods are received from the transportation carrier delivering the goods to the port. It evidences that delivery was made by the ground carrier. The steamship line will prepare the bill of lading based on the information in the mate's receipt.

Maturity: The date on which a time draft must be paid.

Measurement Ton: An alternative way of calculating the transportation charge for articles that may be unusually bulky or light. The steamship line ordinarily will charge the higher of the actual weight or a calculated or constructed weight based upon the dimensions of the goods being transported.

MERCOSUR: A common market established by Argentina, Brazil, Paraguay, and Uruguay.

Metric Ton: 2,200 pounds.

Minimum Freight: The minimum amount that a transportation carrier will charge for transportation. Because such minimum charges exist, freight consolidators provide the service of aggregating small shipments so that lower freight rates can be obtained, which are then partially passed back to the shippers.

Most Favored Nation: An agreement in a treaty or in a sales contract whereby one party promises to give to the other party benefits at least equal to the benefits that party has extended to any other country or customer.

NAFTA: North American Free Trade Agreement, a trade agreement between the United States, Canada, and Mexico allowing for preferential duty rates on imports that meet the criteria.

Negotiable Instrument: A document containing an unconditional promise or order to pay a fixed amount of money with or without interest or other charges described in the promise or order if it is payable to bearer or order at the time it is issued, is payable on demand or at a definite time, and does not state any other undertaking or instructions in addition to the payment of money. Examples of negotiable instruments include checks and drafts.

Negotiation: A transfer of possession of a negotiable instrument, whether voluntary or involuntary, for value received by a person to another person, who thereby becomes its holder.

Non-Negotiable: A document that is incapable of transferring legal ownership or rights to possession of the goods by transfer or endorsement of the document, for example, a railroad, sea, or air waybill.

Non-Tariff Barriers: Obstacles to selling or importing activities other than the customs duties assessed on imported goods, for example, inspections that delay importation, foreign exchange controls that make payment difficult, foreign language labeling regulations, buy national policies, product standards, and quotas.

Non-Vessel-Operating Common Carrier (NVOCC): A cargo consolidator of small shipments in ocean trade, generally soliciting business and arranging for or performing containerization functions at the port. The NVOCC is recognized by the Federal Maritime Commission as a common carrier that does not own or operate steamships, but that publishes tariffs after having filed them with the Commission and becomes the shipper of the goods.

Notify Party: The person listed on a bill of lading or other document that the transportation carrier is supposed to notify upon arrival. A notify party may be the purchaser of the goods, a foreign freight forwarder or customs broker, or a bank or other party, depending upon the terms of the sales agreement and the agreement relating to payment for the goods.

On Board Notation, On Board Endorsement: A legend, stamp, or handwritten statement on the face of a bill of lading issued by a steamship line certifying that the goods have actually been loaded on the ship. Often letters of credit will specify that the goods must be on board before the expiration date of the letter of credit in order for the exporter (seller) to receive payment under the letter of credit. See "Received Bill of Lading."

Open Account (O/A): A sale payable when specified, that is, R/M: return mail; E.O.M: end of month; 30 days: thirty days from date of invoice; 2/10/60: 2 percent discount for payment in ten days, net if paid sixty days from date of invoice. Unlike a letter of credit, there is no security or bank guaranty of payment.

Order Bill of Lading: Usually, "To Order" bills of lading are made to the order of the shipper and endorsed in blank, thereby giving the holder of the bill of lading title to the goods being shipped. They may also be to the order of the consignee or the bank financing the transaction. Order bills of lading are negotiable (whereas straight bills of lading are not).

Orderly Marketing Agreements (OMAs): International agreements negotiated between two or more governments in which the trading partners agree to restrain the growth of trade in specified "sensitive" products, usually through the imposition of export or import quotas. Orderly marketing agreements are intended to ensure that future trade increases will not disrupt, threaten, or impair competitive industries or their workers in importing countries.

OSD: A notation on a carrier receipt or bill of lading signifying "Over, Short, or Damaged."

Packing List: A document describing the contents of a shipment. It includes more detail than is contained in a commercial invoice but does not contain prices or values. It is used for insurance claims as well as by the foreign customs authorities when examining goods to verify proper customs entry.

Particular Average (P.A.): A partial loss or damage to cargo that solely affects "particular" interests. These damages or partial losses are not shared by other interests but are excepted in the ocean carrier's bill of lading. Therefore, unless negligence is involved, claims under particular average cannot be directed against the steamship line.

Passport: An official document issued by a country authorizing one of its citizens or legal residents to leave the country and to be readmitted to the country upon return. See "Visa."

Performance Bond: A guarantee issued by an insurance company, surety company, or other person acceptable to the beneficiary guaranteeing that the applicant (for example, a seller of goods) will manufacture and deliver the goods to the purchaser in accordance with the specifications and delivery schedule.

Perils of the Seas: Conditions covered by marine insurance, including heavy weather, stranding, collision, lightning, and seawater damage.

Permanent Establishment: An office, warehouse, or place of business in a foreign country that may cause its owner or lessor to be subject to income taxes in that country. Under the common international tax treaties negotiated between countries of the world, profits made by a seller are not taxable in the buyer's country unless the seller also has a permanent establishment in the buyer's country that has played some part in arranging the sale transaction.

Pickup Order: A document used when city or suburban export cargo has to be delivered to a dock, or for pickup of goods from storage places.

Power of Attorney: A legal document wherein a person authorizes another person to act on the first person's behalf. It may be issued to an attorney-at-law or to any person and authorizes that person to act as an agent for the issuer of the power of attorney for general or limited purposes.

Preshipment Inspections: A procedure whereby a buyer, through an independent agent such as an inspection company, will examine the goods being purchased prior to exportation by the foreign seller. These examinations may be for quality alone or, in some cases where the buyer's government requires it, the inspection company may require information on the value of the goods.

Product Liability: The responsibility of a manufacturer and, in some cases, a seller for defects in goods that cause injury to a purchaser, user, or consumer of the goods or cause damage to the purchaser's business.

Pro Forma Invoice: An abbreviated invoice sent at the beginning of a sale transaction, usually to enable the buyer to obtain an import permit or a foreign exchange permit or both. The pro forma invoice gives a close approximation of the weights and values of a shipment that is to be made.

Provisional Insurance: Temporary insurance issued by an agent of an insurance company covering a temporary time period until the actual insurance application can be reviewed by the insurance company and the insurance policy issued.

Quota: A limitation or restriction on the quantity or duty rate payable on imported goods. See "Absolute Quota" and "Tariff Rate Quota."

Received Bill of Lading: A document issued by a steamship company acknowledging that it has received delivery of goods to be transported at some later time, usually on the first available steamship going to the destination specified by the shipper. Since the goods are not yet loaded on board, there is no guarantee that the goods will be shipped in the near future, and, therefore, such bills of lading are generally not acceptable if presented by a seller for payment under a letter of credit that is about to expire.

Recourse: The right to claim a refund for amounts paid to a payee. For example, a factoring company may purchase accounts receivable from an exporter (seller), pay the exporter a discounted amount, and collect the accounts receivable as they become due from the purchasers of the goods. If the purchase of the accounts receivable by the factor is with recourse, if any of the purchasers fails to pay, the factor has the option of pursuing the purchaser or claiming a refund for that amount from the exporter (seller) from whom the accounts receivable were purchased.

Remittance: A payment, usually from one collecting bank to another, for example, under a documentary collection. However, a remittance may also include payments directly by the purchaser to the seller.

Revaluation: A government action whereby its currency is valued upward in relationship to another currency. See "Devaluation."

Revocable Credit: A letter of credit issued by a bank that is subject to revocation by the applicant (purchaser of the goods) at any time. Under the new Uniform Customs and Practice for Documentary Credits, No. 500, letters of credit are irrevocable unless expressly stated to be revocable.

Revolving Credit: An agreement by a bank issuing a letter of credit with the applicant (purchaser of goods) that as soon as the purchaser makes payment for a particular shipment or amount of goods to the seller, the bank will automatically issue a new letter of credit covering the next shipment or the amount agreed upon between the applicant and the bank.

Royalty: An amount paid by a licensee to acquire certain rights, for example, a lump sum or an ongoing amount to manufacture or sell goods in accordance with the licensed patent, trademark, copyright, or trade secrets. In some situations, royalties paid by the purchaser of goods to the seller of goods must be included in the dutiable value of the goods.

Sales Agreement or Contract: The agreement, oral or written, between the exporter (seller) and the importer (purchaser) describing the terms and conditions upon which the seller and purchaser will execute the sale and describing the rights and responsibilities of each party.

Schedule B: A classification system based on the Harmonized Tariff System applicable to U.S. exports.

Section 301 (of the Trade Act of 1974): A provision of U.S. law that enables the president to withdraw duty reductions or restrict imports from countries that discriminate against U.S. exports, subsidize their own exports to the United States, or engage in other unjustifiable or unreasonable practices that burden or discriminate against U.S. trade.

Selling Commission: Money or compensation paid by the seller of goods to the seller's agent for services performed by that agent, such as identifying prospective purchasers and assisting with export of the goods. If the amount of the selling commission is charged to the purchaser of the goods, it will usually become subject to customs duties in the country of importation.

Service Contract: A contract between an ocean carrier and a shipper or a shippers' association, in which the shipper commits to a minimum quantity of freight for transport within a fixed period of time and the carrier discounts its usual transportation charges and guarantees levels of service, such as assured space and transit time.

Shippers' Association: A group of exporters who negotiate with transportation carriers for lower freight rates by committing their aggregate volume of cargo.

Shipper's Export Declaration: A form required by the Treasury Department for shipments over $2,500 ($500 for mail shipments) to all countries except Canada. It is completed by a shipper or its freight forwarder showing the value, weight, consignee, designation, Schedule B number, etc., for the export shipment.

Shipper's Letter of Instructions: A document issued by an exporter or importer instructing the freight forwarder to effect transportation and exportation in accordance with the terms specified in the letter of instructions.

Shipping Conference: Steamship lines establishing regularly scheduled service and common transportation rates in the same trade lanes.

Shipping Permit: Sometimes called delivery permit, a document issued by the traffic department of an ocean carrier after the booking of cargo has been made. It directs the receiving clerk at the pier at which the vessel will load to receive from a named party (exporter or forwarder) on a specified day or time the goods for loading and ocean shipment measurement.

Ship's Manifest: A document containing a list of the shipments making up the cargo of a vessel.

Short Ton: 2,000 pounds.

Sight Draft (S/D): Similar to cash on delivery, a draft so drawn by the seller as to be payable on presentation to the drawee (importer) or within a brief period thereafter known as days of grace. Also referred to as a demand draft, a sight draft is used when the seller wishes to retain control of the shipment until payment.

Single Administrative Document: The document now used throughout the European Union to effect exports and customs clearance among member nations and external countries.

SL&C (Shipper's Load and Count): Shipments loaded and sealed by the shipper and not checked or verified by the carrier.

Special Endorsement: A direction by the payee of a draft specifying the name of an alternative payee to whom the drawee is authorized to make payment after delivery of the draft to the alternative payee.

Specific Duty: A tax imposed on imported merchandise without regard to value. It is usually based on the net weight or number of pieces.

Spot Exchange: The exchange rate that exists between two currencies for immediate purchase and sale.

Stale Bill of Lading: A bill of lading that has not been presented under a letter of credit to the issuing or confirming bank within a reasonable time (usually twenty-one days) after its date, thus precluding its arrival at the port of discharge by the time the vessel carrying the shipment has arrived.

Standby Credit: A letter of credit issued by a bank that is payable upon a simple certification by the beneficiary of the letter of credit that a particular condition or duty has not been performed by the applicant for the letter of credit. For example, an exporter (seller) may have to apply for and obtain a standby letter of credit issued in favor of the purchaser when the purchaser is a foreign government to guarantee that the exporter (seller) will perform the sales agreement and deliver the goods in accordance with the delivery schedule. This is to be distinguished from a documentary letter of credit, where the purchaser is the applicant and payment is made by the bank issuing the letter of credit upon presentation to the bank of certain specified documents, such as bills of lading, insurance certificates, inspection certificates, and weight certificates.

Stevedoring: A charge, generally so much per ton, agreed upon between the ocean carrier and a stevedoring, or terminal, operator covering the allocation of men (longshoremen), gear, and all other equipment for working the cargo into or out of the vessel, under the supervision and control of the ship's master.

Stowage: The placing of cargo into a vessel.

Straight Bill of Lading: A bill of lading in which the goods are consigned directly to a named consignee and not to the seller's or buyer's "order." Delivery can be made only to the named person; such a bill of lading is non-negotiable.

Strikes, Riots and Civil Commotions (S.R.&C.C.): A term referring to an insurance clause excluding insurance for loss caused by labor disturbances, riots, and civil commotions or any person engaged in such actions.

Stripping: Unloading (devanning) a container.

Stuffing: Loading a container.

Subrogation: The right that one person, usually an insurance or surety company, has after payment to the beneficiary of the insurance policy, for example, for damage to goods, to pursue any third party against whom the beneficiary would have had a claim, such as the person causing the damage to the goods.

Sue & Labor Clause: A provision in a marine insurance policy obligating the assured to do those things necessary after a loss to prevent further loss and to cooperate with, and act in the best interests of, the insurer.

Surveyor: A company or individual that assesses the extent of damages to cargo incurred during ocean transportation. Such survey reports are necessary in order for insurance companies to make payment to the beneficiary of the insurance policy.

Tariff: A duty (or tax) levied upon goods transported from one customs area to another. Tariffs raise the prices of imported goods, thus making them less competitive within the market of the importing country.

Tariff Rate Quota: An increase in the tariff duty rate imposed upon goods imported to a country after the quantity of the goods imported within the quota period reaches a certain pre-established level.

Tax Haven: A country that imposes a low or no income tax on business transactions conducted by its nationals.

Tender: A solicitation or request for quotations or bids issued by a prospective purchaser, usually a government entity, to select the supplier or seller for a procurement or project.

Tenor: The term fixed for the payment of a draft.

TEU (Twenty-Foot Equivalent Unit): A measurement of container capacity.

Theft, Pilferage &/or Non-Delivery: A type of risk that may be covered under a transportation insurance policy either within the terms of the main coverage or by special endorsement and payment of the corresponding premium.

Through Bill of Lading: Also called a combined transport bill of lading or intermodal bill of lading, a document issued by the transportation carrier that thereby agrees to effect delivery to the required destination by utilizing various means of transportation, such as truck, railroad, and/or steamship line.

Time Draft: A draft maturing at a certain fixed time after presentation or acceptance. This may be a given number of days after sight (acceptance) or a given number of days after the date of the draft.

TL: A truckload shipment.

Total Loss: A situation in which damaged goods covered by an insurance policy are adjudged to have no commercial value and their full value will be paid under the insurance policy.

Trademark: A brand name, word, or symbol placed on a product to distinguish that product from other similar types of products. The right to sell products under a trademark is regulated by the laws and regulations applicable in each country of sale.

Tramp: A steamship or steamship line that does not adhere to a shipping conference and, therefore, is free to charge whatever transportation rates and to sail in any ocean lane it desires.

Transferable Credit: A letter of credit in which the applicant (purchaser of goods) has authorized the beneficiary of the letter of credit (exporting seller of the goods) to transfer its right to payment to a third party, for example, the manufacturer of the goods being sold by the exporter to the purchaser.

Transfer Pricing: Sales of goods between sellers and buyers that are affiliated, for example, by common stock ownership. In such cases, the price may be artificially increased or decreased to vary from the price charged in an arms-length transaction. As a result, income tax and customs authorities may readjust the price.

Trust Receipt: A document signed by a buyer, based on which a bank holding title to goods releases possession of the goods to the buyer for the purpose of sale. The buyer obligates himself to maintain the identity of the goods or the proceeds thereof distinct from the rest of his assets and to hold them subject to repossession by the bank. Trust receipts are used extensively in the Far East, where it is customary to sell on terms of sixty or ninety days, documents against acceptance. The collecting bank permits buyers of good standing to obtain the goods, under a trust receipt contract, before the maturity date of the draft. In some countries, warrants serve the same purpose.

Unconfirmed Credit: A letter of credit issued by the applicant's (purchaser of goods') bank, usually in the purchaser's own country. See also "Confirming Bank."

Uniform Commercial Code: A series of laws applicable in the United States governing commercial transactions, such as sales, leasing, negotiable instruments, bank collections, warehousing, bills of lading, investment securities, and security interests. See also "Convention on Contracts for the International Sale of Goods" and "Incoterms."

Uniform Customs and Practice for Documentary Credits (UCP): A set of international rules and standards agreed upon and applied by many banks in the issuance of letters of credit. The most recent edition (No. 600) went into effect on January 1, 2007.

Uniform Rules for Collections (URC): A set of international rules and standards agreed upon and applied by many banks when acting as a collecting bank in a documentary collection. The most recent edition (No. 522), published by the International Chamber of Commerce, went into effect on January 1, 1996. See "Collecting Bank."

Unitization: The consolidation of a quantity of individual items into one large shipping unit for easier handling.

Usance: The time period during which credit is being extended and during which the purchaser of goods or borrower of monies must pay interest.

Valuation: The appraisal of the value of imported goods by customs officials for the purpose of determining the amount of ad valorem duty payable in the importing country. The GATT Customs Valuation Code obligates governments that are party to it to use the "transaction value" of imported goods—usually the price actually paid or payable for the goods—as the principal basis for valuing the goods for customs purposes.

Value-Added Tax (VAT): An indirect tax on consumption that is levied at each discrete point in the chain of production and distribution, from the raw material stage to final consumption. Each processor or merchant pays a tax proportional to the amount by which she increases the value or marks up the goods she purchases for resale.

Visa: (1) A stamp put into a traveler's passport by officials of an embassy or consulate authorizing a traveler to enter a foreign country. (2) The document issued by an exporting country allowing the export of products subject to an export quota that is in effect in the exporting country.

Voluntary Restraint Agreements (VRAs): Informal arrangements through which exporters voluntarily restrain certain exports, usually through export quotas, to avoid economic dislocation in an importing country and to avert the possible imposition of mandatory import restrictions.

Warehouse Receipt: A receipt given by a warehouseman for goods received by him for storage. A warehouse receipt in which it is stated that the commodities referred to therein will be delivered to the depositor or to any other specified person or company is a negotiable warehouse receipt. Endorsement and delivery of a negotiable warehouse receipt serves to transfer ownership of the property covered by the receipt.

Warehouse to Warehouse Clause: A provision in a transportation insurance policy extending coverage from the time of transport from the seller's place of business to the purchaser's place of business.

War Risk Insurance: Separate insurance coverage for loss of goods that results from any act of war. This insurance is necessary during peacetime because of objects, such as floating mines, left over from previous wars.

Wharfage: A charge assessed by a pier or dock owner against freight moving over the pier or dock or against carriers using the pier or dock.

With Average (W.A.): An insurance coverage broader than F.P.A. and representing protection for partial damage caused by the perils of the sea. Additional named perils, such as theft, pilferage, non-delivery, and freshwater damage, can be added to a W.A. clause. Generally, however, damage must be caused by seawater. A minimum percentage of damage may be required before payment is made.

World Trade Organization (WTO): The World Trade Organization consists of 123 signatory countries. The Uruguay Round of negotiations resulted in the formation of the WTO and in numerous agreements relating to the reduction of tariffs and non-tariff barriers to trade. The WTO supersedes GATT, but a number of agreements reached under GATT, such as the Valuation Code, the Antidumping Code, the Subsidies Code, and the Agreement on Government Procurement, continue in revised form under the WTO.

York Antwerp Rules of General Average: An international treaty prescribing the conditions and rules under which damage to a steamship or to goods will be shared by the other owners of goods on the steamship.

Index

(Page numbers in *Italics* refer to figures)

Index

Index

Index

Index

Index

Index